THE MISSISSIPPI PUBLIC JUNIOR COLLEGE STORY

THE MISSISSIPPI PUBLIC JUNIOR COLLEGE STORY

The First Fifty Years
1922–1972

James B. Young and James M. Ewing

PUBLISHED FOR THE
MISSISSIPPI JUNIOR COLLEGE ASSOCIATION
BY THE UNIVERSITY PRESS OF MISSISSIPPI
JACKSON 1978

Copyright © 1978 by the
University Press of Mississippi
Manufactured in the United States of America

Library of Congress Cataloging in Publication Data
Young, James Bonnard, 1902–
     The Mississippi public junior college story.

     Bibliography: p.
     Includes index.
          1.   Community colleges—Mississippi—History.
I.   Ewing, James M., joint author.   II.   Title.
LB2328.Y68   378.1′543′09762   76–56228
ISBN 0–87805–031–0

To the thousands of students
who walked through the open door.

Contents

List of Photographs

Acknowledgments

I express for myself and for the family of the late James M. Ewing sincere gratitude to all persons who were interested and helpful in the completion of this story. It is not possible to list all the people who were helpful in the writing of this book. To the many friends, named and not named, who gave suggestions and offered inspiration and encouragement, a debt of gratitude is felt. I want, by this list, to thank specifically some who have facilitated the actual preparation of the material for printing.

Mrs. Patti Young, my wife, Ellisville, Mississippi, for her assistance, understanding, and encouragement through a long period of time.

Mrs. Beverly Langford, my daughter, Atlanta, Georgia, for her encouragement and help in reading and rewriting materials.

Mrs. James M. Ewing, Clinton, Mississippi, wife of James M. Ewing (deceased), for her continued interest and helpfulness.

Dr. R. A. McLemore, Clinton, Mississippi, President Emeritus of Mississippi College and retired director of Mississippi Department of Archives and History.

Dr. E. R. Jobe, Jackson, Mississippi, retired executive director, Board of Institutions of Higher Learning.

Dr. Garvin H. Johnston, Jackson, Mississippi, Mississippi State Superintendent of Education.

Mr. R. W. Griffith, Jackson, Mississippi, Assistant State Superintendent of Education.

Dr. Ralph Brand, Ellisville, Mississippi, Director of Guidance, Jones County Junior College, and his staff.

Mr. M. P. Carter, Ellisville, Mississippi, Director of Technical Education, Jones County Junior College, and his staff.

Mr. R. P. Webb, Sr., Ellisville, Mississippi, retired faculty member, Jones County Junior College.

Mr. Luther Hill, Ellisville, Mississippi, retired faculty member, Jones County Junior College.

Mrs. Theresa Blackledge, Ellisville, Mississippi, Librarian, Jones County Junior College Memorial Library, and her staff.

Mrs. Pat Cooley, Ellisville, Mississippi, Assistant Librarian, Jones County Junior College Memorial Library.

Miss Ada Kelly, Ellisville, Mississippi, former associate editor of *American Education*, U. S. Office of Education, Washington, D. C.

Mrs. Nan M. Sibley, Jackson, Mississippi, Associate Registrar, Mississippi College, Clinton, Mississippi.

Mrs. Winnie Dilmore, Clinton, Mississippi, secretary to the Superintendent of the Baptist Children's Village, Jackson, Mississippi.

Mrs. Virginia Jones, Ellisville, Mississippi, secretary in dean's office, Jones County Junior College.

Mrs. Charles Laseter, Ellisville, Mississippi, office secretary.

Presidents of each of the Mississippi Public Junior Colleges and their staffs.

The State Division of Junior Colleges, Mississippi State Department of Education, Jackson, Mississippi:
Mr. George Moody, Director
Mr. Ray Busby, Supervisor Student Activities
Office Staff

Dr. Terrell Tisdale, President of Jones County Junior College, Ellisville, Mississippi, for special assistance relating to office space and equipment.

Preface

In 1922 a legislative act authorized the first extension of a high school curriculum to offer college level courses. The first junior college session opened in the fall of 1922, making 1972 the Golden Anniversary Year of public junior college education in Mississippi. As the junior college system approached this important date, the Mississippi Junior College Association, made up of the presidents of the institutions, the Mississippi Junior College Inter-Alumni Association, the Mississippi Junior College Commission, the Mississippi State Board of Education, and many individuals throughout the state unanimously agreed that the story of these institutions should be recorded; and they selected James M. Ewing and James B. Young to undertake the project.

James M. Ewing, who retired as President Emeritus of Delta State College after serving as its president for fifteen years and whose tenure at Copiah-Lincoln Junior College and Agricultural High School spanned the years 1922–1956, served as president of Copiah-Lincoln Junior College for twenty-four years. Although Dr. Ewing's untimely death on September 4, 1973, prevented his seeing this work to its completion, his contribution is of great significance. His great interest in and appreciation of the Mississippi state system of public junior colleges caused him to present to the Mississippi Junior College Association the importance of recording a story of the first fifty years of the development of this first state system.

James B. Young began his association with Jones County Junior College and Agricultural High School in 1930. He was elected president of Jones County Junior College in 1940 and served in that capacity until 1970. He is now President Emeritus of that institution.

Mississippi was the first state to establish a system of public junior colleges, and these schools have made an unparalleled contribution to the state. In these first fifty years the junior colleges have continued to move forward through the great depression, World War II, and two additional conflicts of extended duration. A major contribution to this success has been the dedicated service by the many men and women of the administrations, faculties, and staffs who were willing to work at low salaries because of inadequate financial support which the junior colleges received during the greater part of the first fifty years. This dedication was inspired by the fact that these public junior colleges were providing an opportunity for many young people to attend college who would not otherwise have been able to pursue their education beyond high school. Fortunately, the public junior colleges in Mississippi are now well equipped and are receiving support that will enable them more efficiently to meet the needs of both young people and adults during the next fifty years.

This volume is intended not only as a narrative but also as a source for further study of the history of the Mississippi public junior colleges. Section one is a short account of the establishment and growth of the system. Each of the three following sections is relatively self-contained and therefore by necessity and intent to some extent repetitive in introducing and presenting the original documents that provided the sources for the story in section one. Section two elaborates the human aspect of the story with short biographies of some of the major figures influential in the development of the system and with accounts of the histories of each junior college as provided by the colleges themselves. Section three gives detailed accounts of the several diverse bodies that had major roles in the guidance and control of the junior colleges. The section opens with a discussion of the agricultural high schools and closes with a special collection of personal statements from a selected group of graduates. Section four reproduces copies of the pertinent legislation and lists the responsible supervisors and trustees.

It is our hope that this story will cause all who read it to see the public junior colleges as truly remarkable institutions and to feel a deep appreciation for all those who, from the beginning, believed in this program of education and whose faith and determination could not be shaken throughout all the years.

J. B. Y.
Ellisville, 1976

Foreword

Mississippi was among the first of the states to establish public junior colleges and the first state to organize a statewide system of junior colleges. Within the framework of the first legislative act, originally adopted in 1922, the growth of the junior college educational service to the people of Mississippi has been continuous, stable, and practical. Financial support of the program from local as well as state sources was meager in the early years when measured in dollars but substantial when computed as the percentage of per capita income. After World War II, support improved rapidly as the per capita income increased.

One important factor in this growth was the able and dedicated leadership of the young men who served as the early presidents of these institutions. A tabulation of the tenure of a group of sixteen presidents, who continued their services or began serving during the second and third decade, shows that at the time they retired they had served a total of more than three hundred years. Another important factor in this growth was the dedication and pride of the junior college faculties. In spite of low salaries, the teachers were service oriented and were proud to be a part of the system. They saw that they were providing educational opportunities of college grade to hundreds of worthy Mississippians who otherwise would have been denied the benefits of a college education. Today, every resident of Mississippi is within commuting distance of a junior college. The list is long of state and national leaders who received their first college experience in a junior college and who were inspired and encouraged by this experience.

Perhaps in no other state, where incomes were so low and needs so great, has institutionalized education contributed more than through the junior colleges of Mississippi. It was their easily seen achievements that brought a sense of mission to those who were directly joined in the junior college movement. This sense of mission persists even though most of the early leaders are deceased.

Several years ago, these early leaders commissioned two of their number of write this remarkable record: James M. Ewing, for thirty-four years at Copiah-Lincoln Junior College, as president for nineteen years, and James B. Young, forty years at Jones County Junior College and as president for thirty years. However, because of the death of Dr. Ewing in 1973, it has been left for James B. Young to complete this task.

President Emeritus James B. Young and James M. Ewing have made outstanding contributions to the recorded history of education in Mississippi. For this, they have the gratitude of all those in education everywhere and especially of their fellow Mississippians.

J. D. Williams
Chancellor Emeritus
The University of Mississippi

THE MISSISSIPPI PUBLIC JUNIOR COLLEGE STORY

THE FIVE DECADES

FIRST DECADE

The Beginning Years
1922–1932

The Mississippi public junior college story began in 1922 with passage of the first permissive legislation. This first law was Senate Bill No. 251, introduced by Dr. Julius Christian Zeller, Senator from Yazoo County of the Nineteenth Senatorial District.[1]* The story in this volume terminates in September 1972— on the Golden Anniversary.

Two of the state's fifty-odd agricultural high schools took advantage of Senate Bill 251 and extended their curriculums to "include the studies of the freshman . . . year . . . of college work" (p. 271). Pearl River County Agricultural High School in Poplarville and Hinds County Agricultural High School in Raymond each offered college courses with the opening of the 1922–1923 session. Pearl River, which had offered college work to twelve students during the 1921–1922 session without state authority, enrolled thirteen students, and Hinds enrolled thirty students during the first official year of Mississippi public junior college history.[2] No other agricultural high school for the next three years extended its curriculum to include college work. In 1925–1926 two additional schools offered college work: Holmes County Agricultural High School in Goodman and Harrison-Stone Agricultural High School in Perkinston. In 1926–1927 Sunflower County Agricultural High School in Moorhead extended the curriculum. In 1927 three new junior colleges opened—Kemper County Agricultural High School at Scooba, Jones County Agricultural High School at Ellisville, and Tate County Agricultural

High School at Senatobia. Two agricultural high schools began college work in 1928: Copiah-Lincoln at Wesson and Newton County at Decatur. In 1929 Pike County at Summit brought the total to eleven, where it remained for eighteen years. These institutions thus constituted the junior college program of the beginning years. The eleven are sometimes referred to as the "original" junior colleges.

During the regular session of the legislature in 1928, Senator Zeller introduced Senate Bill No. 131, eventually signed by Gov. Theodore G. Bilbo. This legislation, much more comprehensive than the law of 1922, set up a commission to control this new group of "borning" institutions "known as the Commission of Junior Colleges."[3]

Prior to the law of 1928, work of the freshman and sophomore years of college was financed entirely by the regular funds for the operation of the agricultural high school offering college courses.[4] House Bill 263 appropriated $475,000 for agricultural high schools and included in the same paragraph, "There is hereby appropriated the additional sum of eighty-five thousand dollars ($85,000) for agricultural high school-junior colleges."[5]

In addition to the legislators in the beginning years, many individuals and official groups, aided by favorable conditions and situations, had a part in the establishment of public junior colleges in Mississippi. The situation now seems comparable to the casting and setting of a play for a gigantic production. Students

---

*Notes appear at end of chapter.

desirous of further education, with an intense interest in learning, were to be the most important members of the cast. Good teachers played star roles. The agricultural high school superintendents were the directors, and the boards of trustees were the producers who selected the directors and furnished the properties. The boards of supervisors provided the primary funds for operation. The legislators wrote the ground rules and, after six years, made a small financial investment in the production. The state board of education served as judges. The Commission of Junior Colleges approved, or disapproved, production sites. The Junior College Accrediting Commission, a creation of the Mississippi Association of Colleges, without legal status, was delegated the responsibility of evaluation by the Statutory Commission of Junior Colleges.

One must understand the rural background of Mississippians to appreciate fully the cast and setting of the new drama about to open in Mississippi. The law of 1922 provided for the trustees of a separate school district containing a municipality with a population of 10,000 or more to "extend the curriculum . . . to include the studies of the freshman or sophomore years or both, of college work."[6] This provision applied to only a few cities and school districts in 1922, but until 1972 only Meridian Junior College had been organized by a municipality, effective for the session of 1937–1938.

According to the U. S. Census, the population of the state in 1922 was 86.6 percent rural and 13.4 percent urban. The same census report showed 70.9 percent living on farms. When the comprehensive junior college law was enacted in 1928, the rural-urban relationship, according to the U. S. Census, had changed by only 3.5 percentage points to 83.1 percent rural and 16.9 percent urban, with 62.7 percent living on farms.

When the original agricultural high school law was passed in 1908 and amended in 1910,[7] the state had practically no high schools for rural children. Most of the rural schools had one teacher and were operated from four to six months. By 1924, fifty-one county agricultural high schools had been organized and then had an enrollment of 7,249. Of this number, 1,438 graduated. State Superintendent of Public Education W. F. Bond, who gave these figures, emphasized in his biennial report of 1924–1925 to the legislature, "It is safe to say that, at least 1,000 of these [1,400] would never have finished high school had it not been for the agricultural high school."

When the first junior college law was enacted in 1922, the drama was ready to be staged. The superintendents of the eleven junior colleges in the 1920s had seen a limited number of their high school graduates enter college. They had seen an even larger number fully qualified but unable to go on for lack of funds. The agricultural high school graduates since 1908 had been leaders in the establishment of consolidated schools. The graduates of these new high schools joined the hundreds from the fifty agricultural high schools and the students graduating from the large number of schools in the separate districts in being ready but financially unable to enter college. Many agricultural high school superintendents saw a tragic waste of human resources.

The directors of this drama-in-the-making, the agricultural high school superintendents, knew that a limited number of high schools throughout the nation had begun to add college work to their curriculums. Also, a limited number of private and church-related two-year institutions were being called junior colleges. The 15,000 students enrolled in these institutions throughout the nation, according to the American Association of Community and Junior College Offices, attested to the young people's desire to do college work when they could afford to. The number throughout the United States was extremely small, but a new door was being opened in the nation. Why not in Mississippi?

These educational leaders discussed possibilities of providing at least two years of college education for potentially thousands of students from the state's low income families. Undoubtedly the planning was not prompted entirely by unselfish motives. With a program of superconsolidation developing, the traditional boarding agricultural high school had to change its program and its direction or else furnish the facilities for a local consolidated school. This deduction is to some degree substantiated by at least two pieces of evidence.

First, in his biennial report to the Mississippi legislature for the years 1923–1924 and 1924–1925, Superintendent W. F. Bond included a section on agricultural high schools, in which he made these prophetic observations about their future:

1. Some will become Smith-Hughes consolidated schools.
2. Several will become junior colleges.
3. Many will continue for years as agricultural high schools with special emphasis on the eleventh and twelfth

grades, cooperating with consolidated schools accredited for only two years of work.

Second, the author of the first two junior college bills in the state senate, Dr. Zeller, had served as superintendent of Bolivar County Agricultural High School and had seen the school close because consolidated schools were serving the entire county. Though no one had publicly suggested as much, it stands to reason that Dr. Zeller, a financially independent professional educator who had come under the influence of President Harper of the University of Chicago, had visualized a network of two-year public colleges, organized at locations where faculty and facilities were soon to be deactivated as boarding high schools. His motivation must surely have been his desire to open doors to young people of low income families and not personal aggrandizement. He had no inclination to head such an institution, and he was financially able to send his own children to any prestigious university of their choosing.

The two possible incentives take nothing from the altruistic foresight of the agricultural high school superintendents to provide higher education at a low cost to Mississippi youth. They could visualize an abundance of students; dormitories where students could be provided room and board for ten dollars or less per month; a farm and a dairy for teaching practical agriculture while also supplying dining rooms with vegetables, meat, milk and butter; and an opportunity for students to earn a part, or all, of the low cost by working on the farm, in the dining halls, or in the dormitories. Moreover, teachers of a generally high caliber staffed the faculties; the administrative organization was there; leading citizens served as trustees; supervisors were accustomed to making countywide tax levies; top level state leadership was assured in the person of Superintendent W. F. Bond; and of important consequence, senior colleges and the single university (University of Mississippi) were willing to accept transfer credit, if courses were taught by competent faculty members.

With all of the necessary elements, the drama was ready for staging. To be sure, not every agricultural high school superintendent had the vision or the courage to go into a production that was not only innovative in Mississippi but also in the stage of infancy throughout the nation. The oldest public junior college in the United States, the one at Joliet, Illinois, had not yet reached a legal majority in age.[8] Not every

agricultural high school superintendent, faculty, and board of trustees properly evaluated the stringent requirements for extending the curriculum, and several made the mistake of attempting an operation that could not survive. But there was a surprisingly small number of failures, and these operations started prior to the 1928 comprehensive law. Only two institutions to receive state funds were not eventually approved as permanent junior colleges. Disbursement records show that Leake County and Simpson County received a portion of the first appropriation in 1928 for the academic year of 1927–1928. Possibly one other agricultural high school offered some college courses in the mid-1920s but was never officially recognized. Leake County continued to operate until it joined East Central of Decatur. Simpson County ceased to operate after the 1928–1929 session and joined Copiah-Lincoln in 1934.

The production was underway. The directors were outstanding men in Mississippi education, dedicated to providing an opportunity for the rural youth of the state and for graduates of the municipal schools of their districts. Listed below in chronological order are the names of the first presidents and the year when each junior college opened:

Since *Pearl River* Agricultural High School at Poplarville offered courses of college transfer credit during the 1921–1922 session, it must be considered the oldest public junior college in Mississippi.[9] The first superintendent (*president* did not come into vogue until after the 1928 law was passed) was James Huff, who was succeeded in 1926 by S. L. Stringer.

Hinds Junior College at Raymond extended its curriculum in 1922, soon after the first junior college law was passed by the legislature.[10] The first president was R. E. L. Sutherland, who took a leave of absence in 1928. During his leave, G. J. Cain served as acting president and was made president when Mr. Sutherland assumed the office of president of Mississippi State College for Women.

Harrison-Stone Agricultural High School at Perkinston offered college courses in 1925–1926. The first president was J. Lee Denson, succeeded by Cooper J. Darby in 1929.

Holmes Junior College at Goodman also offered college work during the session 1925–1926. M. E. Morehead, the first president, organized the college department and was followed in 1928 by Major C. McDaniel.

Sunflower Agricultural High School at Moorhead

extended its curriculum to offer college work during the 1926–1927 session. The first executive head was J. S. Vandiver.

Kemper County Agricultural High School at Scooba, J. D. Wallace, President; *Jones County* of Ellisville, M. P. Bush, President; and *Tate County* at Senatobia, Porter Berry, President, each added college work for the first time during the 1927–1928 session.

Copiah-Lincoln Agricultural High School at Wesson, Russel Ellzey, President, and *Newton County* Agricultural High School at Decatur, R. C. Pugh, President, each extended the curriculum to include college work in 1928–1929.

Pike County Agricultural High School at Summit added college work in 1929–1930, with J. M. Kenna, President.

(See chapter entitled "Organizers and Builders" for elaboration on the leadership and personal attributes of each of these men.)

GEOGRAPHICAL DISTRIBUTION

Of the eleven original junior colleges, four—Sunflower (now Mississippi Delta Junior College), Holmes, Kemper County (now East Mississippi Junior College), and Tate County (now Northwest Mississippi Junior College)—are located in North Mississippi. Prior to the 1928 law, any agricultural high school could extend its curriculum since no commission of junior colleges controlled these institutions. Whether this orderly geographical distribution was coincidental or providential, three of Mississippi's public senior colleges and the University of Mississippi were in North Mississippi, and only State Teacher's College (now the University of Southern Mississippi) and Alcorn A. & M. at Lorman, at that time for members of the Negro race only, were located in South Mississippi.

Even though a divine providence may have guided in the limited number and the geographical distribution, this same providence undoubtedly had a hand in placing the right man at the right place at the right time. Had a weaker school administrator happened to be superintendent of the agricultural high school in any of the eleven junior colleges established in the early years, the institution would never have developed.

JUNIOR COLLEGE COMMISSION

By the end of the first decade, the beginning years, concern developed lest the number of junior colleges should mushroom and thus weaken the base by spreading too thin the financial support and the number of available students. But an effective safeguard was provided by the comprehensive law of 1928 (General Laws, pp. 398–401—see section four). The Commission of Junior Colleges, as specified in this law, was to consist of the Chancellor of the University of Mississippi, the President of the Agricultural and Mechanical College (Mississippi State University), and the President of the Mississippi State College for Women; the heads of three public junior colleges; with the state superintendent of public education as chairman. A study of the minutes of the Junior College Commission shows no conflict between the senior institution heads and the junior college heads. Had controversial situations developed, the elected state superintendent of education would have held the balance of power.

As evidence of apprehension concerning the possibility of such mushrooming, a member of the Junior College Commission, S. L. Stringer, President of Pearl River Junior College, wrote an article in 1930 entitled "Junior College Birth Control in Mississippi."[11] Several points of the article are pertinent here. In 1930 "birth control" was simply not used in polite society. The title of the article therefore attracted attention, and the article was widely quoted throughout the United States. More important was the content setting forth the powers vested in this legal Junior College Commission as well as the quasilegal Junior College Accrediting Commission to whom the legal group delegated all the responsibility for academic accreditation.

But a proliferation of public junior colleges was prevented by the Commission's adoption of a set of proposed zones at its fourth meeting on February 7, 1928.[12] The zoning system was based on a number of criteria, including but not limited to:

1. High school enrollment and number of annual graduates in district.
2. Evaluation of taxable property in zone, with a minimum of $20,000 valuation.
3. Local attitude toward junior college including tax levy of up to three mills in sufficient amount to support college work.

4. Reasonably adequate physical plant.

5. Reduction of teaching load below high school level.

6. Ability and willingness to pay annual teachers salaries of $200. to $300. above high school level.[13]

During the ensuing half-century each of the original zones set up by the Commission had been developed, with one partial exception—Simpson County, where the curriculum had been extended to include freshman college work. This agricultural high school-junior college shared in the state appropriation made in 1928 for the academic session 1927–1928.[14] The school could not meet the minimum requirements, and each of the temporarily designated counties soon joined other districts to support a stable ongoing junior college.

Furthermore, no Mississippi public junior college approved by the Junior College Commission as a permanent junior college has ever ceased to operate. On the contrary, each has prospered by fully developing in enrollment, physical plant, accreditation, and both district and state financial support.

In zoning the state, the Commission never intended that a specific county could not, if local interest dictated, be transferred to a different zone. By 1972, according to the Office of Director of Junior Colleges, eighty-one of the eighty-two counties of the state had levied a local advalorem tax for support of the junior college in its district. The exception was Wilkinson County located in the extreme southwest corner of the state. Some half dozen counties have been transferred from their original zones to some other district, each time after deliberate consideration and final approval of the Junior College Commission.

Obviously, the early fear of proliferation and the need for "birth control" has not developed. During the beginning years the executive heads of the senior institutions who served on the Junior College Commission proved to be cooperative, unselfish, and far-sighted in helping to shape a state system which has stood the test of half a century. The same can be said of the three representatives of the junior colleges, as well as the four different chairmen.

Most of the early members of this accrediting commission were either classicists or scientists. Professor M. Latimer of Mississippi College, a Greek and Latin scholar, served for a number of years as chairman. Professor G. L. Harrell of Millsaps College was a physicist and served as secretary. Miss Lena Vaughn of Mississippi State College for Women was also a physicist and a valuable member, as was Professor Fritz Waddell of what was then A. & M. College, an English teacher. Dr. O. A. Shaw of the University of Mississippi was the only early member of the accrediting group who might be classed as an educationist. Each member of this quasilegal commission rendered yeoman service in providing sympathetic, yet firm, supervision and advice to the new institutions in meeting the academic requirements for the transfer of credits to four-year colleges and universities.

STUDENTS

No evidence in the available records indicates that the agricultural high school-junior college superintendents feared a shortage of students when a new college program was initiated. The freshman enrollment for the beginning year of every institution was fewer than one hundred, and the Information Forms show that the number ranges from thirteen at Pearl River in 1922–1923 to ninety-one at Copiah-Lincoln in 1928–1929. One reason for this optimistic attitude regarding enrollment was that each institution also operated an accredited agricultural high school of substantial size. In practically every instance the best qualified agricultural high school teachers were simply assigned one or more sections of college work in their respective fields. This shift of teaching personnel may have weakened the high school programs.

Another reason the first superintendents (presidents) did not fear a dearth of students was, in fact, the indomitable spirits of these men. They knew the importance of education, and they shared a philosophical dream that at least two years of college work could be made available to any young person with a desire and reasonable ability, regardless of a rural background and a low family income. Bringing this dream to fruition seems to have been a part of the basic philosophy of practically every junior college president throughout the half-century involved in this story. Those with lesser faith and lower ideals have been short-lived in their positions.

The optimism of the early leaders has proven to be well-founded. With few exceptions, the total junior college enrollment has increased each year. The purpose of the Mississippi junior college through the years has been to meet the needs of students and to keep an open door for all high school graduates. With such a policy in operation, very few, if any, normal, determined, sincere students with a willingness to work and cooperate, have been denied admission and full opportunity. If a financial hurdle has existed, it has usually been surmounted by a job opportunity, bus transportation, scholarships, or loans.

The scope of this history does not include a survey of the thousands of junior college graduates who have made from moderate to great success in their chosen fields of labor. Many have remained in their home communities to become leaders in churches, to promote educational opportunities, and to participate actively in government. Their greatest contribution has been in rearing families of decent citizens. Others have transferred with full acceptance of credits to senior colleges and universities in the state and throughout the nation. Among this group are outstanding clergymen, doctors, lawyers, teachers, statesmen, scientists, farmers, businessmen, and persons of every other conceivable occupation. (In section three of this volume are testimonials from a very few of the early graduates and junior college teachers of the beginning years.) During this period, the junior college students came almost entirely from families whose financial condition made an education in senior institutions impossible. At the Golden Anniversary period, the enrollees in junior colleges represented a cross section of families from all walks of life and from both low and high income groups.

BUILDINGS – LAND – EQUIPMENT

In some cases an agricultural high school superintendent and his board of trustees would decide in late spring to extend the curriculum, announce the decision even as late as July, and open a junior college in September. In retrospect such action would seem impossible. But most of the agricultural high schools had at least fair academic buildings and livable dormitories for that day. The law required each agricultural high school to have a farm, a dairy, a garden, and other facilities in land, animals, and equipment. Of the eleven colleges established during the first decade of this record, practically all have remaining at least one or more of the agricultural high school buildings on campus when the junior college was established.

Not every agricultural high school superintendent was willing to offer college work unless the people were willing to issue bonds and construct more mod-

ern and more nearly adequate buildings. To facilitate the issuance of such bonds, House Bill 412 was passed during the regular session of 1928. The legislation was introduced and followed to approval on April 4, 1928, by Rep. Lewis Bufkin of Auburn, Lincoln County. It provided in essence that when ten percent of the qualified electors signed a petition requesting an election for a prospective bond issue for buildings or repair, the county supervisors must hold such an election. If such an election carried, the supervisors were required to issue bonds for the trustees of an agricultural high school or an agricultural high school – junior college to construct or repair buildings.

In most cases buildings and equipment were of minimum standards; however, they were to accommodate students who, in many cases, had spent twelve years in rural schools of lesser caliber. The electric lights and the steam heat in the dormitories were decidedly above the living standard of most students. The defects in buildings were largely overcome by the challenging teachers, by the student's desire to learn, and by the indomitable school spirit and loyalty generated largely through the dynamic personality and leadership of the superintendent.

The laws of 1922 and 1928 each set the same minimum standards for library books and laboratory equipment: "The library in a junior college attempting to do freshman work shall have not less than one thousand well selected volumes . . . and if attempting both freshman and sophomore work it shall not have less than one thousand and five hundred volumes." A minimum standard was also set for laboratory equipment, although the type of equipment is defined only to "have an aggregate value of not less than two thousand dollars."[15] These standards seem low fifty years later, but they were minimum quantitative criteria which the accrediting agency and the legal commission might use in evaluation of a new institution. Few of the first eleven junior colleges met the library requirements. The average number of books for the first year of operation at each junior college was approximately 1,100 volumes, and the average value of laboratory equipment as reported on the Information Forms by the eleven institutions was $2,700.

FACULTY

Probably no group of people was ever more dedicated to educating the individual student than the first-decade teachers. From the very beginning their students were able to transfer to recognized colleges and universities and make passing or superior grades. An unpublished study by Dr. W. H. Sumrall (once Dean of the Graduate School, University of Southern Mississippi) indicated that there was no appreciable difference between the grades made during the junior and senior years by students who had been enrolled in the senior institutions for their freshman and sophomore years and those transferring from the junior colleges. This record of success is directly attributable to the caliber of junior college teachers.

The early laws were not silent on the matter of the training of teachers who should offer college work. Both the 1922 law and the 1928 law stated:

The minimum scholastic requirements of all teachers or instructors in the junior college shall be graduation, either from the University of Mississippi, the Agricultural and Mechanical College, the Mississippi State College for Women, or any college of equal grade, provided the teachers giving instruction in subjects for which sophomore credit is given shall have had in addition to said graduation, post-graduate work in a university or college of recognized standing amounting to at least one year.[16]

So far as can be ascertained, this was the only time in Mississippi's history that the specific academic qualifications of college teachers were prescribed by law—which remained in effect until the general junior college laws were completely revised in 1950.[17] As an indication that some of the eight colleges organized under the 1922 laws were having difficulty meeting the full academic requirements, Senate Bill 131, Chapter 303 added to the law of 1928:

Provided, however, that in junior colleges now established the above requirements shall apply to at least one-third of the teachers and instructors in the scholastic year of 1928–1929, two-thirds in 1929–1930, and to all such teachers and instructors for the scholastic year of 1930–1931 (p. 82).

The Information Forms from the eleven institutions in operation at the end of the first decade indicate a total of eighty-eight persons were teaching college courses during the first year each offered college work. The number teaching only college subjects was seventeen—or twenty percent; the cumulative full-time equivalent college faculty for the first year of each was forty-seven; the total number of teachers with a master's degree was fourteen—or sixteen percent.

This data, on first glimpse, might indicate that the students in a beginning junior college suffered from inferior teaching. Although there is no objective data to the contrary, most any early student and administrator would vehemently deny such an allegation (see section three, "Testimonies"). These early teachers were the "cream of the crop" in the agricultural high schools which had expanded their curriculums.

The permissive law of 1922 and the more formal law of 1928 each had inserted under minimum standards the following statement: "The work of the junior college must be on a collegiate and not a high school basis."[18] This statement in itself served as a challenge to every participant in the drama—superintendents, faculty, trustees, and, most important, students, most of whom expected to transfer their credits to a senior institution in pursuit of a baccalaureate degree. Unfortunately, there is no objective data on the number of teachers with the master's degree by the second and third years of each college's operation. But most beginning teachers who did not hold a master's degree attended summer school fulltime until they earned the master's. The axiom, "the test of the pudding is in the eating," is certainly confirmed by the fact that the transfer students proved themselves capable of passing in the various higher institutions they attended.

FINANCIAL SUPPORT

The first agricultural high school law passed in 1908 provided that the board of supervisors of the county "shall have the power to levy a tax not to exceed two mills per year" for the support of such countywide high schools.[19] The two-mill authority remained in effect for a number of years until it was raised to the present three mills. The three-mill authority remains in effect for all junior colleges, except for the Gulf Coast Junior College District, which in 1968 was given legislative authority to levy a tax of a minimum of four mills for maintenance and operation.[20]

This pattern for local support which originated in the beginning years is now the salvation of the Mississippi junior college system. As previously stated, eighty-one of the eighty-two counties in the state now levy a tax for support of their district junior college. This financial support at the local level has provided more than money. When a county levies a tax for support of an institution, additional benefits result, such as loyalty, interest in activities, legislative support, and enrollment increases.

In addition to a local tax levy, there was also a pattern of support from legislative appropriations. As mentioned, an appropriation of $475,000 was made for agricultural high schools in 1928, when the first $85,000 was appropriated for junior colleges.[21]

The authors of the bill to provide this first junior college appropriation were Representatives Byrd of Lucedale, L. Q. C. Williams of Newton, and J. B. Snider of Senatobia. The vote was: yea 109, nay 1; absent and not voting 30.[22] An interesting story about this first appropriation bill that committed the state of Mississippi to assist in the financing of an entirely new phase of education is told by the late Knox M. Broom:

Soon after the public junior college law was passed (in 1928) someone dared to suggest that if the state could be induced to make a small appropriation for the support of these schools that this would encourage local support. A committee approached Governor Theodore G. Bilbo, who was known as a "School Governor," concerning the advisability of asking for an appropriation. The governor inquired as to the amount the committee had in mind, and someone modestly suggested twenty or thirty thousand dollars. Like a flash the governor said, "I am opposed to that." The committee was dumbfounded to hear him say he was opposed to any school measure which had for its purpose greater educational opportunities for the masses. However, after a slight pause, he said, "Ask for one hundred thousand dollars and I will send a special message recommending it."[23]

The general and legislative popularity of the new colleges had grown by 1930, to the extent that the appropriation was doubled, to $170,000, and the agricultural high school amount remained at $475,000.[24] From this very modest amount, the appropriation had increased to the nearly unbelievable sum of $12,800,000 for the academic year 1973–74.[25] Since the original appropriation of 1928 was for a biennium, the equivalent figure for a current two-year period would be $25,600,000. In addition to this general support fund for 1973–1974 a sizable amount for support of the vocational-technical programs and capital improvements was appropriated. These economic facts indicate the acceptance of the public junior college over a fifty-year period.

COMPETITIVE ACTIVITIES

The story of the beginning years would not be complete without a brief statement about the various activities of the early colleges. A tradition of competition promoted a lively spirit in the agricultural high schools from which the first eleven junior colleges emerged. Agricultural high school students had competed with those of the separate districts and with the consolidated schools of their geographical areas. A general attitude of superiority among the "city schools" served as an incentive to stimulate agricultural high school students to win, not only in athletics but also in the literary examinations and the platform events conducted by the Mississippi High School Literary and Athletic Association. In most cases it was not difficult to develop a spirit of school loyalty among the students who entered junior college during the beginning years. According to a statement in a taped interview by a member of the National Football Hall of Fame, E. W. "Goat" Hale, Pearl River fielded the first football team, coached by "Goat" himself. During the session of 1922–1923, Pearl River played one of two out-of-state high schools, freshman college teams, and two games with Clark Memorial, a church supported junior college at Newton, Mississippi. The Pearl River College trophy case displays a mounted football trophy, properly inscribed "Junior College Champions–1925." This appears to be the first championship claimed by any junior college.

By 1928–1929, seven or eight schools had football teams, as well as boys' and girls' basketball teams. In 1928–1929 competitive examinations were given in thirty-seven subjects. "Platform events" included some ten contests ranging from male and female vocal solos to debate and little theater. A joint system for the evaluation of winners was formulated, based largely on the system in vogue under the High School Literary and Athletic Association. A record of the cumulative points scored by each college was kept by the supervisor of junior colleges in the state department of education. Some years the winner of the "big loving cup" was determined by the one-mile relay, the last track event in the culminating junior college field meet. Trophies and/or medals were awarded to all winning teams or individuals, but the "grand slam" prize was the "big cup." This trophy might be kept permanently if won for three consecutive years by one junior college. While this entire activity may seem elementary in 1972, it was in the beginning years a very valuable tool to build school spirit and develop loyalty.

JUNIOR COLLEGE SUPERVISOR

By 1928 a designated official in the state department of education had as his chief responsibility supervision of the work of some fifty agricultural high schools and the junior colleges then in operation. The title of this official was Supervisor of Agricultural High Schools and Junior Colleges. This title was used by the legislature in making appropriations for administrative expenses of the department of education through the regular session of 1946, when the appropriating bill for salaries included, "Supervisor of Agricultural High Schools and Junior Colleges—$8,000.00."[26] The bill also specified that this amount and other expenses of his office be paid out of appropriations made to the agricultural high schools and junior colleges. The stipulated salary was for the biennium 1946–1948. The 1948 appropriation specified, "Supervisor of Junior Colleges, salary . . . $10,400.00."[27] Thus, 1948 was a transition year when the legislature recognized the supervisor's office as primarily for junior colleges, with his responsibility to the remaining independent agricultural high schools as incidental.

The supervisor has always served a most important function in the Mississippi public junior college program. He immediately became Secretary of the Commission of Junior Colleges,[28] and the arbitrator when differences arose within the activities program. The latter function became so important that before the end of the first decade Russell Ellzey, President of Copiah-Lincoln Junior College, called him the "commissioner" and indicated he should have powers and functions similar to those of Commissioner Landis of organized baseball.[29] The "handle" stuck and was used for some forty years. Then the title of the position was changed, by the 1968 legislature, to Director of Junior Colleges, in an act which also defined in some detail the functions and duties of the director.[30]

The first supervisor of agricultural high schools was Claude Bennett. The Junior College Commission held its first meeting on May 10, 1928, just two calendar weeks after its creation on April 26, 1928, and "Claude Bennett, state supervisor of A. H. S., was made secretary."[31] Mr. Bennett was later named president of the State Teachers College, now the University of Southern Mississippi, and was succeeded by Knox M. Broom. The first official record of Mr. Broom in his new position shows in the minutes of the third meeting. "On motion of Mr. Vandiver, seconded by Mr. Denson, Knox M. Broom was made secretary of the Commission, succeeding Claude Bennett."[32] The precedent of the first Commission, in having the

Supervisor, now director of Junior Colleges, serve as secretary has been followed since the first meeting.

In his duty as arbiter in points of eligibility, the supervisor has made many far-reaching decisions. Such decisions have always been subject to appeal to the Executive Committee and finally to the entire Junior College Association. It is a compliment to the eight men who have served as supervisor and director (and one acting supervisor) that few decisions have been appealed. In the vast majority of cases, the decisions have been sustained. The names of the only two supervisors to serve during the beginning years have already been mentioned—Claude Bennett and Knox M. Broom. These men and their successors have had multitudinous duties and responsibilities to perform, and each has served, in turn, with dignity, honor, sincerity, and integrity.

As far back as 1920 the senior colleges had organized the Mississippi Association of Colleges. One of their first projects was to set up a committee to be responsible for college accreditation. At the first meeting on May 10, 1928, of the (legalized) Junior College Commission, Dr. B. M. Walker of A. & M. and J. S. Vandiver of Sunflower Junior College successfully moved "that the present junior college accrediting commission of the senior colleges be accepted as the standardizing agency as far as quality of work is concerned, and that said Junior College Accrediting Commission make an annual report to the commission created by law the same to be accepted as far as quality of work is concerned in disbursing state aid."[33] This motion represents the thinking of the men who constituted the Commission. It relieved college and university heads, as well as the state superintendent of education, from tedious problems, but more important it recognized academic accreditation as a professional rather than a legal responsibility.

Some claim that passage of Senate Bill 131, as approved on April 26, 1928,[34] marked the creation of a "system of junior colleges" in Mississippi, by setting up a commission to govern the new institutions. Others would say that the "system" was created, not by legislative action, per se, but by the Junior College Commission at its fourth meeting, on February 7, 1929, by passage of a "motion by Denson, seconded by Stringer, that zones and standards proposed by the secretary Knox M. Broom, be accepted by the Commission and recommend that they be strictly adhered to in the future." [35] The legislature, which stated "All junior colleges seeking to qualify under this act shall be under the control of a state commission, known as the commission of junior colleges" [36] delegated authority, and the commission created the system. Under the legislative creation hypothesis, the date would be April 26, 1928; under the commission created hypothesis, the date would be February 7, 1929.

Under either hypothesis, Mississippi can claim without question the first state system of junior colleges in the nation. Dr. Jesse Parker Bogue, longtime Executive Secretary of the American Association of Junior Colleges says:

Mississippi is the only state which has a real system of junior colleges. Texas approaches Mississippi in this respect. Illinois is now passing a law to provide for 97 public junior colleges with proper distribution on a state-wide plan. While California has the largest number of junior colleges of any state, they have been described as a collection, not a system.

Mississippi, therefore, has set a pattern for other states. The wisdom of a state-wide system may be seen in the location of colleges so that they may be accessible to young people and adults in all sections of the state. A tax base also can be created to produce ample funds without excessive tax rates, supplemented by state funds. It is commonly agreed that there should be a state equalization fund whereby the colleges in less favored financial districts may have as good facilities and personnel as those in the more well-to-do districts.

A state-wide system of junior colleges can provide for the allocation of certain specialized curricula to meet state as well as local needs. The demand for personnel in some occupations can be met by one or two colleges. Equipment costs can be saved by this plan, and when the needs of the state are considered as a whole, a wider variety of curricula can be offered. One college might train dental assistants, another floriculture, another forestry, and still another laboratory technicians.

The Mississippi state system then is the logical approach to the proper distribution of colleges, an ample tax base with a reasonable tax rate, an equalization provision to insure the relative progress of all colleges, and the acceptance of responsibility among the colleges by common agreement for specialized curricula. [37]

Dr. C. C. Colvert, Professor Emeritus and Consultant in Junior College Education, University of Texas, says, "I often quote to people the fact that Mississippi was the first state in the Union to set up a state-wide junior college system whereby each county interested was assigned to a junior college district." [38]

Answers to a questionnaire sent by Dr. Garvin H. Johnston, State Superintendent of Education of Mississippi, dated May 8, 1973, to the fifty chief state school officers, were received and tabulated, with each of the fifty states responding. The results are shown in the following letter from Dr. Johnston:

A recent survey of the fifty states made by J. B. Young, a former president of Jones County Junior College, Ellisville, Mississippi, revealed that data received from each of the fifty states indicated that Mississippi, in 1928, was the first state to legally provide a state system of public junior colleges.

Mississippi's state system of public junior colleges, initiated more than 50 years ago, is composed of 16 junior colleges and operates on 25 campuses throughout the state. These centrally located campuses provide low-cost college education within commuting distance of virtually all Mississippians. Students may pursue either the first two years of the regular academic work required for a four-year college degree or enroll in one of the many vocational and technical programs that are available. Also taking advantage of training opportunities offered by junior colleges are businesses and industries which enroll their employees in the various schools. Night classes are offered for adults who desire to upgrade job skills or learn new skills.

The state and the local junior college districts share the financial responsibility for the operation, maintenance, and expansion of these institutions. This unique plan of local-state partnership has been very successful. Local control and administration are retained, while broad, general supervision is provided by the state. The state exercises control only in those areas which are required for the general welfare and interest of all the junior colleges and all the people of the state. The local people through their local trustees have full authority to operate their local junior college as the type of school which most effectively meets the needs of their district. [39]

Mississippians are extremely proud of their state system of public junior colleges. The legal structure set up by the legislature in Senate Bill 131, Laws of 1928, to control such institutions was titled, "Commission of Junior Colleges." [40] This title remained, legally, until the general rewriting of the laws in 1950, when the present title "Junior College Commission" was used for the first time in the law. [41] Actually, the Commission was often called the Legalized Commission for several decades to distinguish it from the professional Junior College Accrediting Commission, which predated the legal body.

Before the curtain closes on the beginning years, something must be said of difficulties encountered by the new institutions, as well as outstanding achievements as yet unmentioned.

As pointed out, the first state appropriation for junior colleges was requested as a kind of "foot-in-the-door" process. The $85,000 appropriated for the first two years amounted to $42,500 each year to be divided equally among ten colleges.[42] The law provided that one-half "shall be distributed on the basis of average daily attendance of junior college students for the current sessions."[43] This method of distribution was fine for the first year of a biennium, since one-half became immediately available and the remainder within four to six weeks when the total average daily attendance could be completed. During the second year of a biennium, the one-half distributed equally could be disbursed soon after school opened—the fiscal year was October 1 to September 30—but the other half could not be distributed until after the close of all schools in the late spring.

Reference has been made to the disbursement of the 1928–1930 appropriation. The following table reveals how the $42,500 for 1927–1928 was distributed:

high schools attempting one or more years of college work. Before the next disbursement is sent out a very strict check will be made as to the requirements of Senate Bill 131."[45]

The 1930 legislative appropriation of $179,000 for the 1930–1932 biennium was introduced in the House of Representatives by the Hon. John Lumpkin of Pearl River County.[46] This one hundred percent increase resulted in a great boost to junior college morale. On the other hand, the appropriation represented a very sharp decrease in state funds per student. While the total enrollment in 1928 was 487 (A.D.A. 439), by 1930 this figure had reached 1248 students, or a 156.3 percent increase. This decrease in state support per student had little effect on the total operation of the colleges.

Major support for the new junior colleges came from local tax funds, and many had added counties to their districts, due largely to the official zoning system established in 1929.[47] Moreover, county property

Disbursements by State Board of Education
Jackson, Mississippi, July 26, 1928
To Agricultural High School-Junior Colleges
For Sessions of 1927–1928

A.H.S.-Junior College	General A.D.A.*	Amount Distributed Equally	Amount Based on A.D.A.	Total
Harrison-Stone-Jackson	75	$ 2,125.00	$ 3,630.00	$ 5,755.00
Hinds	104	2,125.00	5,034.10	7,159.10
Holmes	17	2,125.00	822.80	2,947.80
Jones	24	2,125.00	1,162.00	3,287.00
Kemper	18	2,125.00	871.20	2,996.20
Leake	20	2,125.00	968.50	3,093.50
Pearl River	92	2,125.00	4,453.30	6,528.30
Simpson	21	2,125.00	1,016.90	3,141.90
Sunflower	48	2,125.00	2,323.20	4,448.20
Tate	20	2,125.00	968.00	3,093.00
Total	439	$21,250.00	$21,250.00	$42,500.00

* Average Daily Attendance
(Signed) W. F. Bond, Chairman, Junior College Commission and President, State Board of Education[44]

With each distribution sheet was a letter of transmittal signed by W. F. Bond, State Superintendent of Education. By virtue of his office he was, and so signed the letter, Chairman of the Junior College Commission and President of the State Board of Education. The final paragraph of Superintendent Bond's letter stated: "We felt that for the first year the disbursement would be made to all ten of the agricultural

valuations had increased, and a number of junior college districts had raised their millage for regular support and operation. The full impact of the Great Depression had not really hit Mississippi by the time the legislation was approved on May 17, 1930. In addition, Gov. Theodore G. Bilbo was completing the second regular session of the legislature during his second four-year term and was by common knowledge not too much concerned with a balanced budget. He felt that the economy would soon return to normal.

The succeeding regular session of the legislature was in 1932. By this time everyone knew that "the bottom had dropped out" and that the state could not meet its obligations. By the laws of 1930 and 1932 the state appropriation for junior colleges was reduced from $170,000 to $115,000. This 32.35 percent loss of state funds would not have been too severe had not local tax income gone down, delinquent taxes hit a new high, and in some cases the county millage reduced. With the economic hardships, all the junior college leaders adjusted their expenses to match income and in comparison considered themselves somewhat fortunate. Their 32.35 percent loss of state appropriation seemed reasonable when compared to a 41.45 percent decrease for the state supported institutions of higher learning, and an 18.3 percent decrease in appropriation for the common (public) schools.

Most junior colleges had reduced salaries for the 1931–1932 session. There were further salary reductions for 1932–1933. Excellent teachers felt a loss in salary from $150 per month to $115 per month. New faculty members were employed at much lower salaries.[48] This was a sad situation but one that existed throughout the nation. It is doubtful that the caliber of instruction suffered a great deal, and it may well have been strengthened. According to one college president, teachers in most any area of specialization with a master's or even a doctor's degree were seeking jobs and could be employed for room and board and any amount that could be paid.

While the beginning years ended on a low financial note, the spirit of the new institutions was on the rise. The low cost of attendance and the general public acceptance combined to bring greatly increased enrollments. By 1932, the number of students in the eleven public junior colleges had increased to 2,761. Since the first state funds were made available, the total enrollment had increased on an average of more than 400 students per year.[49] Three colleges had received full accreditation by the Southern Association of Colleges and Secondary Schools.[50] Seven of the remaining colleges had been fully accredited by the Junior College Accrediting Commission (according to the Information Forms).

And the Forms indicate that four of the eleven schools had experienced changes in administrative

heads. G. J. Cain had succeeded R. E. L. Sutherland in 1929 as president of Hinds; Major C. McDaniel replaced M. E. Morehead at Holmes in 1928; S. L. Stringer succeeded Jim Huff at Pearl River in 1926; and C. J. Darby replaced Lee Denson at Harrison-Stone-Jackson in 1929.

There has never been any attempt to standardize the curriculums offered by the Mississippi junior colleges. While the 1922 law set forth specific requirements for teachers, no mention was made of courses to be offered. There was a legal requirement of "at least fifteen units of high school work [the requirement for high school graduation of that day] as defined by the State Accrediting Commission," and a most significant requirement by the law was in Section 2, paragraph 3: "The work of the junior college must be organized on collegiate and not on a high school basis."[51] The 1928 law was more specific regarding curriculum and stated in the second paragraph:

These courses shall consist of agriculture, including horticulture, dairying, animal husbandry and commercial gardening; domestic science and household arts; commercial branches, including banking, accountancy and transportation; and the mechanical arts, such as carpentry, masonry, painting, shop work in iron and wood and repairing and constructing of moor vehicles. Wherever it is practicable, instruction shall also be given in teacher training, music, and public speaking. Insofar as possible the junior colleges shall offer a complete course of instruction so that their graduates may immediately thereafter enter professional schools if they so elect.[52]

Institutions never deliberately violated this law. The simple fact was that the money, manpower, knowhow, and facilities were not available for vocational aspects of the law. The early organizers had made a faithful attempt to accomplish the vocational training in their agricultural high schools and had largely failed. Dr. E. R. Jobe in his doctoral dissertation suggested three reasons for the decline of agricultural high schools: first, the people expected too much; second, consolidation; and third, the policy of the vocational education department in the state department of education.[53]

The superintendents knew they could not succeed in the diverse vocational curriculum. Consequently, they never attempted it and avoided failure. They had no doubt that students could be provided two years of regular collegiate education, transfer to senior institutions, and make acceptable records. They were convinced that good transfer records would gain for the new colleges academic respectability and acceptance by local officials and the legislature. This prognostication proved imminently correct. It is doubtful that even one percent of the students, faculty, trustees, or other officials ever knew that the legally mandatory vocational curriculum was a part of the law. But the vocational aspect of the law was not irretrievably lost. Later chapters in this volume will point out that when "need, money, and men" met, diverse courses and programs were set up for almost every conceivable type of vocational as well as technical education.

The curricular offerings of all Mississippi public junior colleges during the beginning years were such as would be accepted by the accrediting agencies that had no background for vocational accreditation and also be transferable to senior institutions. The predominant programs were in the broad area of the arts and sciences, with requisite elementary courses available for those who desired to pursue baccalaureate degrees in agriculture, home economics, and business. One notable exception was for students who planned to teach in elementary schools. During the 1920s, fewer than one-half the elementary teachers in Mississippi had as much as two years of college preparation; therefore, the early junior colleges included in their curriculum from six to twelve semester hours in education courses, which qualified a graduate for a "sophomore license," good for two years.[54] The junior colleges made a great contribution during the beginning years in the training of elementary teachers.

Other acts passed by the legislature during the beginning years included:

(1) "An act to authorize the board of trustees of any agricultural high school and junior college . . . to borrow money for the use and benefit . . . and providing how same may be used."[55] Due to the method of collecting and disbursing tax funds, most local and state funds were not available until the second semester of an academic year. This legislation made it possible for a junior college to borrow funds for operating the first semester on a cash basis.

(2) Another act provided that "a junior college maintained by two or more counties may borrow not more than $25,000.00 for completing unfinished buildings, making additions to or repairing . . . furnishing or equipping . . . or for paying teachers and other operating expenses of said school, during the fall months."[56] The board of trustees could borrow under

this act at an interest not to exceed six percent, without securing approval of the board of supervisors.

(3) An important act was passed by the Extraordinary Session of 1929, which validated all bonds, notes, certificates of indebtedness, loan warrants or other obligations of any agricultural high school or agricultural high school-junior college.[57]

(4) The Regular Session of 1930 passed an act that a county with two judicial districts might borrow up to $35,000 for buildings and repair, provided the junior college "has been designated by the Junior College Commission as a permanent junior college."[58] The act was introduced by Wiley B. Shows, of Ovett, Jones County, and would apply only to Jones and Hinds County Junior Colleges.

(5) Similar legislation, introduced by John Stennis and J. H. Daws of DeKalb, Kemper County, authorized a junior college supported by a tax levy from three or more counties to borrow $50,000, provided the levy was "for a permanent junior college."[59] This legislation seems to have been designed specifically for East Mississippi Junior College, Scooba.

Except for the state appropriation, no legislation dealing specifically with junior colleges was enacted during the 1932 Regular Session of the legislature.

The beginning years ended with a state system of public junior colleges well established. Some mistakes had been made, for the leaders had no landmarks by which to plot their course. Eleven institutions had been firmly established with at least one in every geographical area of the state, except Northeast Mississippi. Provision had been made and methods well established to prevent any proliferation of junior colleges. Virtually no vocational courses were offered, but colleges and universities of the state and throughout the nation were accepting transfer credit without question. Each of the eleven schools was accredited by the Mississippi Junior College Accrediting Commission. Four of the oldest were accredited by the Southern Association of Colleges and Secondary (sic) Schools. The four included: Hinds Junior College of Raymond, accredited in 1928; Pearl River Junior College of Poplarville, and Harrison-Stone-Jackson Junior College of Perkinston (now Mississippi Gulf Coast Junior College), in 1929, and Sunflower Junior College of Moorhead (now Mississippi Delta Junior College), in 1930.[60]

In 1922, forty-three students were enrolled in two

junior colleges. In 1932, 2,761 were enrolled in the eleven schools. State support, which began in 1928, was small, but junior colleges had a permanent place in the legislative budget. The unique organization of junior colleges in Mississippi provided a legal Junior College Commission for control from the state level and individual boards of trustees for all functional operation at the local level.[61]

The end of the first decade found the eleven new institutions in the throes of the Great Depression. Funds were short, salaries were low, and capital improvements were out of the question. On the other hand, enrollments were moving up, general acceptance was established, and, most of all, an indomitable spirit of forward movement inspired the presidents, the faculties, the students and the entire junior college families. The first chapter of the Mississippi public junior college story had been well done, and Mississippians would be proud of the rest of the story.

NOTES TO "THE BEGINNING YEARS"

1. General Laws of Mississippi, 1922, Senate Bill 251, p. 270.
2. Information supplied by Dean Seale of Pearl River Junior College and Miss Mildred Herrin of Hinds Junior College.
3. Laws of 1928, Regular Session, Senate Bill 131, Chapter 303, pp. 81–83.
4. Laws of 1922, Senate Bill 251, Chapter 204, pp. 270–272.
5. Laws of 1928, Senate Bill 131, Chapter 303, p. 231.
6. Laws of 1922, Senate Bill 251, Chapter 204, p. 271.
7. Laws of 1908, Senate Bill 302, p. 19, and Laws of 1910, Senate Bill 4, p. 10.
8. Leonard Koos, The Junior College Movement (Greenwood Press: Westport, Conn., 1970), p. 4.
9. Names and dates from an Information Form, furnished the authors by each 1972 junior college president (hereafter cited as Information Form).
10. Laws of 1922, Senate Bill No. 251, pp. 270–272, approved March 24, 1922.
11. The Junior College Journal, I, No. 1 (October 1930), pp. 12–14.
12. Junior College Commission Minutes; State Department of Education, Junior College Division Office, February 7, 1929, p. 9.
13. Department of Education Bulletin Number 58, by Knox M. Broom, issued by W. F. Bond, State Superintendent of Education.
14. Laws of Mississippi, 1928, House Bill 263, Chapter 173, p. 231, and Disbursement Records of State Board of Education, July 26, 1928.
15. Laws of 1922, Senate Bill 251, and Laws of 1928, Senate Bill 131, p. 400 (5) (6).
16. General Laws of 1922, p. 270, and General Laws of 1928, pp. 399–400.
17. Ibid., Chapter 369, House Bill 541, pp. 421–428.
18. General Laws of 1922, Chapter 204, Senate Bill 251; 1928, Senate Bill 131, p. 400 (3).
19. Laws of 1908, Chapter 102, Senate Bill 302, p. 79.
20. Laws of 1968, Chapter 390, House Bill 509, p. 607.
21. Laws of 1928, Chapter 173, House Bill 253, p. 231.
22. House Journal, 1928.
23. History of Mississippi Public Junior Colleges, 1928–1953, pp. 12–13. Published through the State Department of Education, approved May 18, 1954.
24. Laws of 1930, Chapter 205, House Bill 682, p. 408.
25. Laws of 1973.
26. Laws of 1946, Chapter 6, House Bill 1094, p. 14.
27. Laws of 1948, Chapter 31, House Bill 1090, p. 33.
28. Junior College Commission Minutes, May 10, 1928, Book One, Director's Office.
29. Validated by conference with Russell Ellzey, June 27, 1973.
30. Laws of 1968, Chapter 388, Senate Bill 1832, pp. 603–607.
31. Junior College Commission Minutes, May 10, 1928, Book One, Director's Office.
32. Ibid., October 20, 1928.
33. Ibid., May 10, 1928.
34. Laws of 1928, Chapter 303, Senate Bill 131, pp. 398–401.
35. Junior College Commission Minutes, Fourth Meeting, February 7, 1929, Book One, Director's Office.
36. Laws of 1928, Senate Bill 131, p. 401.
37. "The Mississippi State System of Junior Colleges," The Educational Advance (April 1947), 38, No. 7, p. 27.
38. Letter from C. C. Colvert to J. M. Ewing, March 9, 1972.
39. Letter of May 8, 1973.
40. Laws of 1928, Chapter 303, Senate Bill 131, pp. 398–401.
41. General Laws of 1950, Chapter 369, House Bill 541, pp. 421–428.
42. Laws of 1928, Chapter 173, House Bill 263, p. 231.
43. Ibid., Section 2.
44. Disbursement form from files of Holmes Junior College, copy in author's file.
45. Letter from files of Holmes Junior College, copy in author's file.
46. Laws of 1930, Chapter 205, House Bill 682, p. 408; also, House Journal.
47. State Department of Education Bulletin Number 58.
48. Budget reports for 1931 and 1932, Copiah-Lincoln Junior College.
49. Broom, History, Table 4, p. 35.
50. Southern Association Quarterly, 1932, initial accreditation reaffirmed Southern Association proceedings, December 1968, pp. 60–61.
51. Laws of 1922, Chapter 204, Senate Bill 251, p. 271.
52. Laws of 1928, Chapter 303, Senate Bill 131, p. 398.
53. E. R. Jobe, "Curriculum Development in Mississippi Public White High Schools," (Ph.D. dissertation, George Peabody College for Teachers, 1950), pp. 83–84.
54. Junior College Catalogues on file in office of Director of Junior Colleges.
55. Laws of Extraordinary Session, 1928, Chapter 42, House Bill 122, p. 65.
56. Laws of Extraordinary Session, 1929, Chapter 13, House Bill 43, pp. 10–11.
57. Ibid., Chapter 14, House Bill 42, p. 11.
58. Laws of 1930, Chapter 65, House Bill 754, p. 113.
59. Ibid., Chapter 78, House Bill 636, p. 135.
60. Southern Association Proceedings, December 11, 1972.
61. Laws of 1928, pp. 398–401.

The Years of Struggle
1932-1942

The second decade of the Mississippi public junior college story began with the 1932-1933 school session. Enrollment in each junior college increased each year and reached a total of 4,074 students during the 1939-1940 session of the second decade.[1] This steady increase indicated an acceptance of this new program of higher education by both high school graduates and their parents. The quality of the academic programs had been established. The presidents were confident that these educational institutions would be supported by the counties in each district and by the state of Mississippi. Many of the counties in the junior college districts were already levying local taxes for the support of agricultural high schools. Therefore, the tax levying authorities felt a responsibility for supporting the college program. Twenty-six counties had levied a direct tax for junior colleges during the first decade. This number increased to forty-one counties by the close of this second decade.

A major concern at the beginning of the second decade was for additional buildings and equipment, but funds to meet these needs were not available because of the Great Depression. However, this tragedy did not weaken the courage and spirit of the junior college presidents, faculties, students, and officials. A less determined group might have weakened. The presidents at the beginning of this decade were men who were listed as the founders and builders; however, with only one exception, each

junior college had to select a new administrative head. The majority of these new presidents gave many years to the junior college program. The presidents at the beginning of the second decade were:

Russell Ellzey	Copiah-Lincoln	1928-1932
S. L. Stringer	Pearl River	1926-1932
J. S. Vandiver	Sunflower	1926-1935
P. W. Berry	Northwest	1926-1935
M. P. Bush	Jones County	1927-1940
J. D. Wallace	East Mississippi	1927-1939
M. C. McDaniels	Holmes	1928-1940
R. C. Pugh	East Central	1928-1934
Cooper J. Darby	Perkinston	1929-1941
J. M. Kenna	Southwest	1929-1947
G. J. Cain	Hinds	1929-1938

Two new presidents were part of the leadership at the beginning of this period. At Copiah-Lincoln, J. M. Ewing succeeded Russell Ellzey, who had been elected to the United States Congress. Mr. Ewing had participated in the establishment of the junior college and had been a part of the program from the very beginning. J. F. Stuart also moved from a member of the faculty to the presidency of Pearl River Junior College, succeeding S. L. Stringer. The new presidents were:

J. M. Ewing	Copiah-Lincoln	1932-1956
J. F. Stuart	Pearl River	1932-1936
A. B. Nicholson	Pearl River	1936-1937
R. E. L. Sutherland	Pearl River	1937-1942
G. M. McLendon	Hinds	1938-1965

Albert L. May	Perkinston	1941–1953
Ras M. Branch	Holmes	1940–1949
Paul M. West	Sunflower	1935–1944
J. M. Tubb	East Mississippi	1939–1946
J. B. Young	Jones County	1940–1970
R. C. Pugh	Northwest	1934–1952
L. O. Todd	East Central	1934–1952

The first new junior college to be added to the original eleven multicounty junior colleges was organized in 1937. The new institution was the Meridian Municipal Junior College, established in a junior college district coterminous with the Meridian Separate School District. This was the only municipal junior college district established within the state during this fifty-year period. Harris Junior College for Negroes was approved within this district at a later date. The organizer of this new junior college was H. M. Ivy (1937–1953), Superintendent of the Meridian Public School System, Meridian, Mississippi. Dr. Ivy had been State High School Supervisor in the state department of education under State Superintendent Bond, when Sen. J. C. Zeller introduced the legislation during the regular session of 1928, establishing a state system of junior colleges in Mississippi. A statement from Dr. Ivy, which is on tape, certifies that he was requested by Senator Zeller to prepare the law to be introduced authorizing the establishment of the system.

The presidents and boards of trustees of public junior colleges in Mississippi felt from the beginning that they were a part of a state system of junior colleges. Through a self-established organization known in the beginning as the Mississippi Junior College Literary and Athletic Association, the presidents began regular meetings together and through this organization gave direction to the state program of junior colleges in Mississippi.

The earliest recorded minutes, now on file in the office of the State Junior College Division, are dated July 1, 1932, Kirby P. Walker, Supervisor. This date was the beginning of the second decade. The minutes during this decade record the names of four supervisors serving during this period. These were:

Kirby P. Walker, July 1, 1932–June 30, 1933
R. L. Anderson, July 1, 1933–June 1, 1935
J. A. Travis, First Meeting with the Association, June 13, 1935
Knox Broom, First Meeting listed in minutes of the Association, January 23, 1936 (Mr. Broom had previously served during the first decade as Supervisor, 1928–1932.)

If minutes of meetings of the presidents held during the beginning years of the first decade were recorded, they are not on file with the state office, and no institution has located any minutes for this period. The only printed records are the copies of the printed handbook of the organization of the Literary and Athletic Association and rules and regulations of the competitive literary and athletic activities (see "Competitive Athletics—The Spirit Builder," section three).

This handbook gave evidence of fulfillment and accomplishment and was an expression of confidence in the development of these institutions. Ten out of eleven of these junior colleges that were a part of the public junior college movement during this decade became active members of the American Association of Junior Colleges and provided leadership on a national basis.

The presidents of the public junior colleges in Mississippi realized the importance of the quality of the academic program. One measure of the quality of the academic program was through studies of the achievement of the students transferring to senior colleges, and the comparison of their achievement with that of the four-year students of the senior college, using records of the junior and senior years of the junior college transfers and those of the junior and senior years of the four-year students. A meaningful study, made by W. H. Sumrall of Mississippi College, showed that the junior college students were equal in achievement with the four-year students.

The matter of regional accreditation was urgent to these new developing institutions. Regional accreditation had been recognized as an acceptable criterion for the quality of the academic program in educational institutions. The transfer of junior college credit hours to senior colleges or universities was not questioned by the schools that were approved by the regional accrediting association, the Southern Association of Colleges and Schools. Students graduating from accredited high schools during this decade were very well informed regarding the earning of college credits from an institution with full regional accreditation. This made the securing of regional accreditation a matter of high priority to the presidents of the Mississippi public junior colleges.[2]

Twelve junior colleges were in operation during the decade 1932–1942. At the end of this period, nine of the twelve were fully accredited by the regional association. The presidents of Mississippi's public junior colleges were also participating in the activities of the association.

Four of the state's junior colleges had received accreditation during the first decade. They were Hinds Junior College (1928), Pearl River Junior College (1929), Perkinston Junior College (1929), and Mississippi Delta Junior College (1930). The public junior colleges in Mississippi receiving regional accreditation during this difficult second decade were Holmes Junior College (1934), Copiah-Lincoln Junior College (1936), East Central Junior College (1939), Jones County Junior College (1940), and Meridian Junior College (1942).[3]

At the close of the second decade, nine of the twelve operating public junior colleges in Mississippi had received full regional accreditation, and this accomplishment represents the purpose and philosophy of the junior college leaders to establish and develop a collegiate academic program meeting the standards of other junior college programs in the southern region and over the nation, while also meeting the standards of the lower division collegiate work in the senior colleges and universities.

The minutes for this period record the control and direction given to the state junior college competitive athletic program. The actions taken by the junior college presidents became the rules and regulations for all competitive athletic programs. These actions covered many areas, such as eligibility of participants, regulations covering all tournaments and statewide meetings, memberships in regional and national organizations, athletic insurance, a philosophy governing junior college athletics, and out-of-state athletics.

The title of the organization, Literary and Athletic Association, was significant. During the early decades, the junior colleges in Mississippi entered into statewide competition in academic areas which included statewide examinations in the subjects taught: debating, dramatic performances, little theater, competition in an area designated as platform events, including male quartets, male vocal solo, female vocal solo, piano solos and duets, choral groups, and statewide band contests.

The presidents of the Mississippi public junior colleges became increasingly aware, during the second decade, of the efforts the junior colleges of the nation were making to meet the total educational needs of youth and adults beyond the high school level. The popular phrase in reference to this training was "terminal education," the type of educational program which includes both general education and occupational training in various skills.

As early as 1936 the leaders of the public junior colleges realized that curriculum revisions were necessary and that courses referred to as terminal courses must be added. These courses were designed to provide job opportunity training for students who did not desire college transfer and preprofessional courses. The general idea was that at the end of two years each student would be qualified for employment in a variety of areas, including industry, business and commerce, agriculture, and many trades.

The basic laws authorized Mississippi public junior colleges to provide training in specific fields, just as definitely as it provided for academic transfer, preprofessional and general education programs. The 1928 general law for the organization and operation of Mississippi public junior colleges includes the following:

Section 308. That junior colleges consisting of the work of the freshman and sophomore years shall be organized for the purpose of providing such courses as will make the studies of the agricultural high schools and the junior colleges a connected and correlated whole or complete unit of educational work. These courses shall consist of agriculture, including horticulture, dairying, animal husbandry and commercial gardening; domestic science and household arts; commercial branches, including banking, accountancy and transportation; and the mechanical arts, such as carpentry, masonry, painting, shop work in iron and wood, and repairing and constructing of motor vehicles. Wherever it is practical, instruction shall also be given in teacher training, music and public speaking. Insofar as possible, the junior colleges shall offer a complete course of instruction so that their graduates may immediately thereafter enter professional schools if they so elect.[4]

The title for this decade is "The Years of Struggle." These words are most fitting for this decade; yet, in the face of struggle, the door was opened for the development of a comprehensive program designed to meet, as nearly as possible, the total educational needs of youth and adults in each junior college district. Some very important steps were taken during the latter part of this period.

The first reference in the recorded minutes of the Mississippi Junior College Association for terminal education was dated 1936.[5] During this same year an application was filed with the General Education Board of New York for a grant to finance studies of such programs. An amount of $75,000 was obtained. A short time later a committee from the Mississippi Junior College Association was appointed to consider the advisability of a seminar or laboratory school for Mississippi junior college administrators and faculty members. In 1939 a two-day planning conference was held at Mississippi State College with Dr. John Napier, Auburn, California, as counsellor. This conference approved a laboratory school or workshop. In the summer of 1940 some thirty Mississippi junior college teachers participated for six weeks in this workshop at Peabody College. During the session 1940–1941, several of the traditional subjects were taught on an experimental basis emphasizing the terminal point of view. During the session the teachers had two general meetings with the state supervisor of junior colleges as adviser.

The Mississippi Peabody Workshop of 1941 instituted the Terminal Education Workshop, of which the Mississippi group was an integral part, although they held their identity as a working unit. This group published an "Improvement of Instruction" bulletin.

The American Association of Junior Colleges contributed to the national interest in terminal education by arranging with the General Education Board of New York City for the financing of a special study on terminal education. This study was inaugurated on January 21, 1940.

The Mississippi Junior College Association presented to the Mississippi Vocational Education Board a proposal for regional centers for technical and vocational training. The established junior college districts met the needs for these centers. A committee of the Mississippi Junior College Association, members of the State Vocational Board, and the State Supervisor of Junior Colleges met with the National Legislative Committee of the American Vocational Association regarding legislation that would permit a more liberal application of the Federal Vocational Act regarding regional centers for vocational-technical programs.

Contained in the Biennial Report of 1937–1939, Recommendations of the State Superintendent of Public Instruction to the Legislature of Mississippi is information affirming the early interest that the public junior colleges of Mississippi were exemplifying in meeting the vocational needs of its students:

A study covering a five-year period comparing junior college transfers with junior and seniors in senior colleges failed to show any significant difference between them and the university and senior college students who did their freshman and sophomore work in their own institutions. While the junior colleges are proud of this showing, they regard preparatory courses as only one of their four-fold functions. Those who enter junior college and, as a matter of fact, 60 percent of those who enter senior college, will never get a standard degree. Therefore, the junior colleges attempt to teach their students how to live and how to make a living in terms of conditions in their communities with special emphasis placed on making worthy citizens. The public junior colleges have also made some progress toward the development of technical courses for those who never go beyond the junior college level. One of our major objectives for next year is the development of a junior college seminar for the training of junior college teachers for the specific task of teaching on junior college level, giving special attention to the specific techniques characteristic of that level.[6]

The following junior colleges were listed in this report: Copiah-Lincoln, Harrison-Stone-Jackson, Hinds, Holmes, Jones, East Mississippi, Meridian, East Central, Pearl River, Southwest, Sunflower, and Northwest.

Furthermore, the Biennial Report of the State Superintendent of Public Education for 1941–1942 and 1942–1943 states that the legislature appropriated $60,000 with which to initiate a program to upgrade and expand vocational training. Sixty thousand dollars was a very meager sum with which to begin the development of such an ambitious program, but it did represent an endorsement by the legislature and stimulated the administration of these institutions in their study of the possibilities of such an expanded program of services to the people of the area they served. As a result of this humble beginning, these institutions expanded, within twelve months, and built twenty-six shop buildings with more than 65,000 square feet of floor space valued at $80,515. Included in the building program were twenty-three CCC camp buildings valued at $13,138. These institutions increased their equipment values in the expansion of their general shop program by approximately $267,233. Three-fourths of this equipment was secured through the National Youth Administration and the federal defense program, with the remainder coming from state money and local budgets. Approximately $16,000 was invested in farm shop programs, much of this in connection with the food production program to meet labor shortages. About $25,000 was invested in expanded technical laboratories to meet adequately the demands for wartime training programs. The inventoried values of the upgraded and expanded vocational programs during the year in Mississippi public junior colleges was $357,749.

In addition to the training facilities provided for the regular enrollment for the session 1942–1943, the Mississippi public junior colleges, through their upgraded and expanded vocational training, defense courses, and food production courses, provided training facilities and served 8,863 persons. Numerous pieces of farm machinery were repaired through adult programs.

A major contribution was also being made to the industrial development of Mississippi. The Mississippi public junior colleges have met the needs of many groups at various levels. The basic program at college grade was organized for students beyond the high school who qualified for college entrance, and the program provided college credit toward junior college graduation. This program included a designated amount of technical and vocational training and a designated number of courses in the general or specific academic areas.

Job opportunity vocational trade training is also available below college grade for students and adults not qualified for college entrance—short-term or two-year programs, some on campus and some off campus. But all are designed to meet specific needs for self-employment or for employment in industry.

The Great Depression forced the legislature of 1932 to reduce the state appropriation of 1930 from $170,000 to $115,000. The members of the state legislature recognized the grave possible result of their action in reducing the state's support for the new colleges. The following action indicated their apprehension in an act passed and approved on May 18, 1932:

To authorize boards of trustees of agricultural high schools and of junior colleges to lease buildings and equipment for a private school and lease land for agricultural purposes where no funds were available for running schools.[7]

No evidence indicates that any junior college established and approved by the commission at the time this act was passed gave any thought to closing its doors. They have continued operation throughout this fifty-year period. The years ahead brought increases in both state and local support.

The junior college presidents soon realized the supporting counties would hesitate to increase tax levies and that it would be very difficult to get the boards of supervisors of any supporting counties to levy a tax for enlargement and improvement. New sources of support would be necessary.

The 1932 fall enrollment in the eleven public junior colleges increased by some four hundred students while the senior institutions experienced a substantial decrease. The low cost of attending junior college was a factor in the increase in enrollment; but even with the low cost, most Mississippians were unable to meet the cost of college expenses.

The beginning of the second decade was a national election year with Franklin Delano Roosevelt challenging incumbent Herbert Hoover in the summer and fall of 1932. Since the "good times" proclaimed by President Hoover as being "just around the corner" had not materialized, the American people were ready for a change and so voted in November. President Roosevelt came from a family of immense independent wealth and few dreamed that he would initiate a program of great social and economic reforms. A public works program was recommended by the president and passed by the Congress to meet the needs of thousands who were hungry and millions who were out of jobs.

The Civil Works Administration, commonly called the CWA, was the first such program in which Mississippi public junior colleges shared (according to the supervisors of Lincoln County). The congressman from one junior college district was home for the 1933 congressional vacation and advised the local college president to "Work up a project." "As soon as the Congress re-convenes," he said, "there will be a big public works program and the government will put up practically all of the money; just be certain the project is largely for labor as employment will be the major objective." The situation was typical. A number of the state's junior colleges profited substantially by the Civil Works Administration, while the unemployed were given jobs. Common labor was paid $0.75 per hour, semiskilled $1.25, and skilled workers even higher. This great boom for local communities enabled thousands of parents to keep their children in school, from first grade through university.

This first program was originated and established under the leadership of Harry Hopkins, who accompanied President Roosevelt to Washington in 1933 as Federal Emergency Relief Administrator. This program was closed by President Roosevelt within the year, but a number of other relief programs were established on a more permanent basis.

President Roosevelt initiated a program known as the Public Works Administration, or PWA. This agency was established by the Congress under Title II of the N.I.R.A., the National Industrial Recovery Act, on June 16, 1933. This program was authorized to make loans and grants-in-aid to states, municipalities, and other public bodies. The public junior colleges were eligible to participate in various ways. Grants from this program would enable the junior colleges to construct new buildings and to remodel and equip existing buildings. The established programs were operating in the buildings constructed for the agricultural high schools; and since the buildings were often used jointly by the existing agricultural high school and the junior college, expansion of the physical plant was urgent. However, no state appropriations for enlargement and improvement were available to the junior colleges during this decade.

The following act was passed at the extraordinary session of the Mississippi legislature in 1935, authorizing the trustees of an agricultural high school, a junior college, or an agricultural junior college to borrow money for building purposes which would be matched by a PWA free grant:

An ACT to authorize and impower the board of trustees of any agricultural high school-junior college or "agricultural junior college" which has been designated as a permanent junior college, with the assent and approval of the boards of supervisors of the county or counties owning such institutions, to borrow not exceeding $200,000; prescribing the purpose of said loan, and the method of repayment of the same.[8]

The provisions of this act included "constructing, erecting, repairing, remodeling and equipping all buildings belonging to or connected with such an institution."

There were several interesting items in this legislation:

1. The term "agricultural junior college" was used. So far as is known, this was the first and only time this terminology was used.

2. The terms "to borrow a sum of money" and "such loan or loans shall be evidenced by negotiable notes signed by the president and secretary of the board of trustees," the unusual items being "loan or loans" and "negotiable notes" and signed by the "trustees" rather than "bond issue," and signed by the board of supervisors.

3. No election to pass on the loan by submitting to

the people was required; thus the use of the terms above. The loans could be executed and signed by the president of the board of trustees.

4. The maximum rate of interest permitted was four percent while the state was still in the throes of the depression of the thirties.

5. The act required the board(s) of supervisors to levy the necessary tax to pay the principal and interest on the loan.

6. Section 8 of the act provided: "That no money shall be borrowed under authority of this act unless the United States of America, or some agency thereof, shall have first obligated itself to make a grant or otherwise aid in the construction of the proposed improvement for which such loan shall be made."

7. While the act was approved on December 3, 1935, its terms of authority expired on December 3, 1936. Thus, the junior colleges had to secure trustees' and supervisors' approval, secure the federal grant, and make the loan at four percent, all within this short period.

8. Of course the federal agency was the Public Works Administration (PWA—not the WPA). Yet a large number of the eleven eligible junior colleges availed themselves of this law in a short time. Some junior colleges were never able to get approval of the trustees and/or supervisors.

9. It is significant that a delegation of junior college presidents called on the late Sen. Theodore G. Bilbo at his home and office at Poplarville and secured his assistance.

10. The terms of the PWA were forty-five percent free grant by the U. S. Government and fifty-five percent by the institution.

Several items of special significance may be noted regarding the $50,000 appropriated by the 1935 extraordinary session of the Mississippi legislature.

(a) Drastic reductions had been made in the junior college appropriation of 1932.

(b) The appropriation of $50,000 was for the session 1935–1936 only and therefore equivalent to a $100,000 biennial increase, thus bringing the junior college appropriation to the highest level in its short history since the first appropriation of $85,000 in 1928. This level was short-lived.

The PWA program was designated in the original act to last two years, but the Congress prolonged its operation and transferred it in 1943 to the Office of the Federal Works Administration for liquidation. The program continued to operate for a period of several years. The public junior colleges in Mississippi were greatly benefitted by grants from this program.

An agency of the United States Government created in 1935 by executive order of President Roosevelt was the Works Progress Administration, renamed in 1939 the Works Projects Administration and placed under the Federal Works Agency. The Works Projects Administration was known as the WPA. Harry Hopkins was named head of this agency at its beginning in 1935. This program provided useful public work for needy unemployed persons.

Many of the projects provided services beneficial to the public junior colleges. The art projects produced paintings, drawings, sculpture, and murals in buildings. Writers prepared a number of notable guide books. The theater projects helped develop striking dramatic techniques. Many kinds of musical groups gave performances. Adult education classes were conducted in many of the junior colleges. These projects were the beginning of a comprehensive program in the junior college, the strengthening of the community aspect of the program which has continued to grow and develop.

The WPA supervised from 1935 to 1939 a program known as the National Youth Administration, which was transferred to the Federal Security Agency from 1939 to 1942. At that time it became a part of the program of the War Manpower Commission, exclusively concerned with training youth for war industry. The work was abolished by the Congress in 1944.

The NYA program was beneficial to the public junior colleges in that a part of the program was to create suitable public relief projects in connection with colleges and schools that would create part time employment for needy students enrolled in colleges. The recorded minutes of the regular meeting on April 5, 1937, of the Junior College Literary and Athletic Association, composed of the presidents of each public junior college, met with the Director of the National Youth Administration in Mississippi and agreed to cooperate in a proposed NYA program on the campus of each junior college. This meeting resulted in a large number of beneficial projects being approved and established; and in some cases needed buildings were constructed, many were repaired, and much campus improvement resulted.

Another very important result of the NYA program in Mississippi as related to the public junior colleges was the transfer of equipment for technical and vocational programs. When the National Youth Administration was transferred, in 1942, to the War Manpower Commission, and became exclusively concerned with training youth for war industry, the War Manpower Commission established a large number of training centers over the state and equipped the centers with excellent machinery and tools for training purposes. This training equipment was largely for woodworking, metal, and machinist training. When this program was abolished in 1944, this excellent equipment was declared surplus, and the public junior colleges were eligible to request the transfer of this equipment to individual junior colleges.

The two organizations which contributed to the growth and development of the junior colleges were the Junior College-Senior College Conference and the Southern Association of Junior Colleges. Under the sponsorship of G. D. Humphrey, President of Mississippi State College, now Mississippi State University, a pioneering movement was begun in 1934 for the purpose of bringing about a closer relationship between the eleven public junior colleges and the state supported senior colleges of Mississippi. President Humphrey in October 1934 invited the presidents and other administrative officers of the public junior colleges to a conference on the campus of Mississippi State College for "A better understanding of the common problems affecting the junior colleges and State College, with particular emphasis on curriculum problems affecting junior college students who desire to complete work for a degree."[9] The organization has met annually since this first meeting.

Representatives of the junior colleges of the southern area met in the Atlanta-Biltmore Hotel, Atlanta, Georgia, on April 9, 1940, at 6:30 P.M., with President C. C. Colvert presiding. The group voted unanimously to establish a permanent organization. Also by unanimous vote the organization would be the Southern Association of Junior Colleges.[10] Dr. J. L. Robb, President of Tennessee Wesleyan College of Athens, Tennessee, was elected president, and Mr. Curtis Bishop of Averett College in Danville, Virginia, was elected secretary.

Eight of the eleven public junior colleges in Mississippi were charter members of the Southern Association of Junior Colleges. All Mississippi public junior colleges are now active members of the Association. Administrative personnel from the Mississippi public junior colleges have been active in the work and have provided leadership in many areas. Five Mississippi public junior college presidents have served as presidents of the Association.

The second decade began with an enrollment of 2,761 students. The total enrollment reached the high point of 4,074 during the 1939–1940 session, an increase of 600 students over the 1938–1939 session. Enrollment had been increasing each year. A real note of encouragement is found not only in the increase in enrollment but also in the increase in financial support. At the beginning of this second decade, twenty-six counties were levying a local tax for the support of public junior colleges. This number had increased to forty-one counties by the close of the period. Some of the supporting counties had also increased the tax levy. The increase in direct state appropriation was most helpful. During the first decade the state appropriated a total of $255,000. During this second decade the total increased to $799,750.

Despite the disappointments, the frustrations, and the uncertainties, the leaders retained a great faith in the need and importance of this new educational venture. As this period came to a close, the calamities of World War II were upon this nation. The United States declared war on Japan on December 8, 1941, and Germany and Italy declared war on the United States on December 11, 1941. This tragic condition created the certainty that the years of struggle had not ended and that the years ahead would be difficult.

NOTES TO "THE YEARS OF STRUGGLE"

1. Knox M. Broom, *History of Mississippi Public Junior Colleges*, Table 4, p. 35.
2. Broom, Table 4, p. 35.
3. Proceedings, Seventy-Third Annual Meeting, Southern Association of Colleges and Schools, Atlanta, Georgia, December 2, 1968, p. 60.
4. General Laws of 1928, Senate Bill 131, Chapter 303, p. 31.
5. Minutes in the office of Division of Junior Colleges, July 15, 1936, State Department of Education.
6. Biennial Report of 1937–1939 on file in office of State Superintendent of Education, State Department of Education, Jackson, Mississippi, p. 47.
7. Laws of 1932, House Bill 870, Chapter 166, p. 465.
8. Laws of 1935, Extraordinary Session, Chapter 48, House Bill 67, p. 182.
9. G. D. Humphrey, "Mississippi State Alumnus," State College, Mississippi, January 1935, Vol. 10, No. 1, p. 1.
10. Minutes of the meeting of the Southern Association of Junior Colleges, Atlanta-Biltmore Hotel, Atlanta, Georgia, April 9, 1940.

The War Years and Returning Veterans
1942–1952

When the third decade began the majority of the public junior college presidents had experienced the difficulties of the Great Depression and the recovery years. Any expectations of less difficult years ahead in the growth and development of the public junior college disappeared at the end of the second decade.

On the morning of December 8, 1941, the student bodies and faculties met for assembly and heard the President of the United States inform the nation that because of the Japanese attack on Pearl Harbor war had been declared. Three days later, on December 11, the message came that Germany and Italy had declared war on the United States. The emphasis and direction of the junior college program immediately changed. The total involvement of the United States caused a sharp decrease in enrollment. Records in the state division of junior colleges show that the enrollment in the public junior colleges, which had reached a high of 4,074 students prior to the beginning of the war years, fell to a low of 1,375 students for the year 1943–1944. At the same time the schools were experiencing the great decrease in student enrollment, many were faced with the problem of strong faculty members becoming involved in the war efforts.

Leaders of the public junior colleges were again, in a short number of years in the life of these new institutions, faced with many difficulties. Long-range plans for growth and development had to be postponed.

This frustration and disappointment had appeared before and had been met with courage and determination. The colleges were faced with the twofold problem of maintaining a program of excellence for those who were in attendance and cooperating in every way possible with the war effort.

The determination of the junior college presidents to cooperate fully in the nation's effort to meet the demands of a total war is expressed in the following statements and recommendations in the minutes of a regular meeting of the Mississippi Junior College Association on June 15, 1942:

In the present supreme crisis we pledge to the President of the United States, Commander-in-Chief of our Nation, to the Governor of Mississippi, and to the military authorities the total strength of our junior colleges—our faculties, our students, our administrative organizations, and our physical facilities.

Our instructors are organized for action. They offer their united power for decisive military victory, and for the ultimate and even more difficult task of establishing a just and long-lasting peace.

All the needs to win a total war cannot be actually defined now. Nor can total present and future resources of trained manpower be fully appraised. New areas of need of potential service will develop as the months pass. We pledge our unstinted effort to meet these needs as they arise.

For the immediate and more effective prosecution of our varied tasks in the service of our nation and state, the Mississippi Junior College Association proposes the following resolutions and makes the following recommendations:

The State Supervisor of Junior Colleges to be named as acting agent for collecting all possible information regarding the basic requirements of the various military services and production industries and clear through his office such information to all member schools as (1) a means of encouraging and stabilizing those in pre-selective service training courses, and (2) to counteract commercialized agencies which are charging exorbitant fees and demoralizing our youth through high pressure advertising.

The following areas were identified as significant in this effort. The guidance program should be more effective to include a thorough knowledge and understanding of basic, technical, and semi-technical skills required by the various phases of the army, navy, air corps, and war production industries with special emphasis on food production and home defense.

Unanimous approval was given to fulltime year-round utilization of the junior college facilities for the educational development and productive employment of our students in full co-operation with the needs of our nation at war with special emphasis on each individual rendering most effective service to his country.

In order to encourage students who are called to service to complete for credit subjects in courses at the time of his call, we recommend special arrangements to enable each such student to use the interim before his time to report to meet the maximum requirements of such courses.

Expanded course offerings were recommended in a number of areas in order to meet requirements of the armed forces, civil service commission, and wartime production industries. A number of courses should be adjusted, expanded, and intensified to meet wartime needs. These include:

1. Commercial departments, special typists, company clerks, etc.
2. Mechanized shops—including auto, radio, aircraft, etc.
3. Woodwork shops—including building trades, etc.
4. Regular and special courses in nutrition, gardening, military Spanish, navigation, mathematics, etc.
5. Special training in the basic sciences, which include chemistry, physics, economics, mathematics, etc.
6. Special courses relating to war industries, such as, personnel and production management.

The junior colleges sponsored civilian morale and defense efforts, both on the campus and throughout the communities served by these institutions, through such organizations and activities as:

1. Public and student forums.
2. Fire prevention and control.
3. Patriotic programs, including music.
4. Red Cross activities, including First Aid, knitting, etc.
5. Photography.
6. Promotion of the sale of defense bonds and stamps.
7. Conservation of paper, metals, and other essentials.
8. Promotion and dissemination of pertinent war news —by means of addresses, bulletin boards, radio, etc.

In order that the junior colleges may contribute most to the physical development of their students and the morale of their students and communities during the war period, we recommend that a committee be appointed to study the adjustments necessary in our inter-collegiate activities program under wartime economics and report back to the Association recommendations together with suggestions for expanding intramural activities programs.

Realizing that religious and spiritual values and ideals are among America's greatest assets, we recommend emphasis on spiritual values. The junior colleges can help meet this need by placing greater emphasis on such training among its students which is available in organizations such as YWCA, YMCA, Training Unions, Leagues, and other young people's church organizations, and that members of the faculty be urged to take a definite stand in the promotion of these activities, and that greater effort be made to extend this work throughout the community and the area served by each junior college.

The Mississippi Junior College Association approved the appointment of a committee to cooperate in developing desirable articulation in academic calendars of the junior and senior colleges to facilitate acceleration of total educational progress. Also the Mississippi junior colleges extended their full facilities and cooperation to the degree granting institutions in the offering of technical courses for which only degree granting institutions were held to be eligible under the defense program, yet where these courses might be offered by ineligible institutions with adequate facilities for same.

The presidents who were providing the leadership for the public junior colleges at the beginning of this third decade, 1942–1952, were:

J. M. Tubb	East Mississippi	1939–1946
R. D. McLendon	Pearl River	1942–1953
R. C. Pugh	Northwest	1936–1952
P. M. West	Sunflower	1935–1944
J. B. Young	Jones County	1940–1970
Ras M. Branch	Holmes	1940–1949
A. L. May	Perkinston	1941–1953
George McLendon	Hinds	1938–1965
H. M. Ivy	Meridian	1937–1953
L. O. Todd	East Central	1934–1953
J. M. Ewing	Copiah-Lincoln	1932–1956
J. M. Kenna	Southwest	1929–1947

The new multicounty junior colleges that were established in the already approved districts in Northeast Mississippi were:

R. O. Stringer	Northeast	1948–1952
Phillip Sheffield	Itawamba	1948–1960
B. F. McLaurin	Coahoma	1949–1966

Changes made during the decade were:

W. B. Horton	Sunflower	1944–1966
C. W. Lorance	Holmes	1949–1955
H. D. Pickens	Southwest	1947–1948
C. H. Snell	Southwest	1948–1951
C. C. Moore	Southwest	1951–1952
Willie Smith (acting)	Copiah-Lincoln	1943–1945
Cruce Stark	East Mississippi	1945–1953

The supervision of the public junior colleges, in the state department of education, at the beginning of this decade was a continuation of the leadership of Knox M. Broom, who began serving in 1936 and served until 1944, at which time he was appointed field representative for the U. S. Office of Education. J. C. Windham was appointed to serve as supervisor. B. L. Hill was appointed in 1946 and served until 1968.

There was much evidence on each campus that our nation was at war and that the colleges must convert their program into training for the armed forces. A visit to the junior college campuses during these days reflected the effort to meet the many needs. One would see young men in flight training under the Civilian Aeronautics Administration war training service of the navy, army, and marines. It was a new experience for the campus to attend ceremonies presenting wings to cadets. The United States Army, Navy, and Marine Enlisted Reserve Corps involved most of the young men on the campuses, and recruiting and examinations for reclassification were a part of the program. The reality of the reserve program had its impact on both students and faculty, as groups of reservists were ordered to active duty, yet these conditions were met with deliberate calm. New courses, including technical programs, ground courses in aviation, special physical education programs, and military related subjects were offered to contribute to the local war effort. Military drill and discipline were added to the activities on the campus, and many student and faculty committees were created to deal with patriotism, sale of war bonds and stamps, drills and air raid practices, military attitudes, preinduction vocational training, and community programs. In addition, military service was performed by the young women from the student bodies as they enlisted in the WAVEs and WACs.

The events occurring on the opposite side of the

earth became increasingly real as those back home read the headlines in daily and student newspapers of acts of heroism and achievements of former students. The news headlines also brought sadness to many as former students were listed as missing in action.

RETURNING VETERANS

Perhaps at no time in this century have American schools been called upon to make such far-reaching adjustments as during the forties. The nation moved from the Great Depression to total war, then from the end of war to the great influx of returning veterans. The colleges felt immediately a new responsibility for providing programs designed to meet the adjustment needs of these veterans. These new demands came with very short notice. Realizing that many of these returning veterans required family housing and that the colleges must provide it, the junior colleges, within a few months, expanded their dormitory facilities, and temporary facilities were grouped about on the campuses. These facilities, made available through the Federal Public Housing Act, became small villages on the campuses and attracted much attention from the regular students. The housing units were transferred from armed service installations, and, in some cases, the quality of the buildings made them acceptable to convert into permanent housing. An example of this type of facility was the navy steel barracks slated for overseas shipment located at Gulfport, Mississippi. The junior colleges found that they had been assigned 102 of these buildings. Each two-story building contained about 13,260 square feet of floor space. An interesting part of this story was the shock that came to the governor of the state and the Board of Institutions of Higher Learning for the universities and colleges when they realized that all these buildings belonged to the public junior colleges. Because the junior colleges could not use all these buildings, they were able to execute favorable negotiations with the senior colleges and at the same time receive all the buildings they needed.

The need for the junior colleges averaged about three buildings per campus. The Junior College Association agreed to assign the buildings to the State Building Commission under an agreement that the Commission would move the needed buildings to each junior college campus and would allocate the sum of $62,000 to each junior college to help erect the buildings. This allocation met the immediate financial need for constructing good buildings on the campuses and opened the door for state appropriations for building construction at the junior colleges.

These buildings and many other war surplus buildings erected on the junior college campuses met an urgent need in providing space for technical and vocational programs that were being rapidly developed to meet the training needs of returning veterans. With space available, the junior colleges were able to secure much valuable equipment needed for various programs.

The Mississippi public junior college leaders had given priority in the early development of the Mississippi state system to the establishment of a quality program in the academic, preprofessional, and general education fields. However, they were concerned that the basic law authorized the public junior colleges to provide vocational and technical training in specific fields, and they felt that a definite need existed. The junior college presidents and faculty members undertook early to participate in laboratory workshops and special studies regarding vocational and technical training. These workshops determined how to provide the necessary shop facilities and adequate equipment to meet these training needs. The presidents realized early in their study and planning that these programs required a capital outlay beyond the amount that could be supplied by the local area. Therefore, they turned to the state and other sources for financial support. The regular session of the Mississippi legislature of 1942 appropriated $60,000 for the vocational and technical programs in the public junior colleges. The federal government released on loan to the public junior colleges the first major items of equipment through the liquidation of the National Youth Administration. The leaders in the junior colleges were aware at this point that industry was expanding rapidly in the state, that this expansion would increase the demand for trained employees, and that an increase in demand for training services would coincide with the return of veterans to civilian life. When these veterans were discharged from service at the end of World War II, they immediately began taking advantage of the education and training provided under the G. I. Bill. The academic course offerings were expanded, and specific trade and occupational training programs were established in each of the junior colleges. Evidence of the progress made in

meeting these training needs is shown in the *History of the Mississippi Public Junior Colleges* by Knox M. Broom (Table Six, p. 37). This table shows that the fourteen public junior colleges were offering thirty-eight different types of vocational-technical programs in a total of 104 units on these campuses. The number of different types of courses offered on each campus ranged from four to fifteen. The Mississippi state system and various units in individual junior colleges received commendation for their part in providing training for veterans. The Chief of the Vocational Rehabilitation and Education Division of the Veterans Administration Center, Jackson, Mississippi, appreciated the part Mississippi public junior colleges had in training the 134,991 individual veterans in Mississippi who pursued education or training after their discharge from service in World War II:

The Mississippi Public Junior Colleges met a challenge not only for providing instruction in the academic courses during the first two years of college, but made definite provisions for and met the needs for training veterans in the trade and occupational fields. The long range planning which provided for the allocation of training functions in the several junior colleges gives evidence of good planning, better utilization of instructional personnel, and economy of funds for plant and teaching facilities—a program probably unprecedented in scope and variety of training services, and is an example of their flexibility in meeting the educational and training needs of the citizenship of the state.[1]

These programs were the foundation of the expanded vocational and technical education programs offered in Mississippi public junior colleges. At the end of this fifty-year period, the sixteen public junior colleges were offering sixty-one different types of programs in 306 units of the sixteen campuses. The number of units taught on the individual campuses ranged from nine to forty, with an average of nineteen units to the campus. For the year closing this decade these units had a total enrollment of 13,625. These vocational-technical units are a vital part of the total comprehensive junior college program established on a district basis which constitutes the Mississippi state system of public junior colleges.

As this decade closed with the 1951–1952 session the junior colleges had provided vocational and technical training for 11,992 students,[2] a large percent of which were veterans. The record also shows that thirty-eight different technical and vocational programs were being operated in providing this training.[3]

FINANCIAL SUPPORT

Because a prime objective of the public junior college was to offer programs at a minimum cost to the student, the major part of the financial support of such a college has been from the local tax levies and the direct state appropriation. Students enrolling from counties levying a local tax paid minimum fees and no tuition charge. Students from counties in each junior college district not levying a tax for support of the colleges were charged a small tuition fee in addition to small fees charged to all students. The local tax levy from the counties in a district was the responsibility of the county supervisors who were the tax levying authority. Many conditions—local, state, and national—influenced their decisions, which were not mandatory. However, year by year, additional counties added the local tax levy in support of the junior college in their district.

The third decade, which began with forty-one counties supporting the junior colleges with a local tax levy, ended with support from fifty-four counties. Each of the counties was providing funds for general support, and a number of the counties were levying a tax for enlargement and improvement. This increased support by the counties indicated the confidence of community leaders and the status of the public junior colleges in the estimation of the people in the local districts. Further evidence of support is that by 1972 eighty-one of the eighty-two counties in Mississippi were levying a local tax for general support of the junior college, and the majority of the counties were also levying a local tax for enlargement and improvement. The local tax levy grew in importance as the tax base increased in each county.

STATE APPROPRIATIONS

The state appropriations from 1942 to 1952 were also encouraging. The increase in the appropriation during the war years was small: 1942—$240,000; 1944—$240,000; 1946—$300,000. However, at an extraordinary session during the 1946 biennium an additional appropriation of $175,000 for 1947 was allocated, which permitted the colleges to operate that year on the equivalent of a biennium appropriation of $650,000, a substantial increase.

The 1952 biennial appropriation was increased to $1,850,000, after the state appropriation reached the one million mark in the 1948 regular session. State appropriation for the support of public junior colleges has been increased at each successive legislative session. In 1970 the Mississippi state legislature began meeting annually. The present annual appropriation is equivalent to a biennial appropriation of twenty million dollars.

Two major changes occurred during the period 1942–1952. The Mississippi state legislature made its first appropriation designated for vocational-technical education in the junior colleges. The 1952 legislative session appropriated $450,000 for this purpose.

The legislative body considered the urgent needs to provide funds for building. The returning veterans and the increase in the number of high school graduates entering college showed the critical need for buildings and equipment. The colleges had moved many of the war surplus buildings to the campuses. Although these buildings were used for housing, classrooms, shops, and other purposes, they were temporary and were not meeting the needs adequately. The public junior college leaders made a request at the 1950 session for direct state appropriation for building. This request received support, and an appropriation of $750,000 was made and designated for buildings. The amount was doubled at the 1952 session to $1,500,000. This state support for buildings and equipment began a period of growth and development in plant expansion that enabled the junior colleges to make significant curriculum changes and to establish a comprehensive program to meet the total educational and training needs for each district. Realizing that the years ahead would be a period of rapid growth, the junior colleges at this point began a series of long-range planning. The visions of future growth became a reality in a short period of time.

Evidence of the growing influence of the junior colleges was manifested in an editorial by a leading newspaper editor, Frederick Sullens, in the *Jackson Daily News*, January 23, 1944.

Our Junior Colleges

Mississippi has no educational need greater than that of giving more adequate recognition to our junior colleges.

When the history of higher education in America is written, the amazing growth of the junior college movement will be looked upon as one of the most significant academic developments of the present century. Concentrated in the early years on the West Coast, but rapidly spreading through the Middle West to the South and East, the two-year college has now become a vital part of the total educational scene. Mississippi was foremost among Southern states in adoption of the junior college system. At the start of the war, this country could boast of nearly 600 such institutions, enrolling 200,000 students, and they were the first to co-ordinate their work with the war program. Somehow, the two-year college program has met a popular need among the student body of America. Various reasons are advanced for this new trend. Many high school graduates cannot afford to go to college for four years, others are academically unsuited for the type of studies offered. Still others are anxious to learn a trade or vocation in the quickest possible time. There is no type of educational work in Mississippi today of more merit than that of the junior colleges. They need, and should have, more liberal appropriations. More efficient work will quickly follow and justify the enlarged budgets.

Specifically, the chief reason why junior colleges in Mississippi should be given the $400,000 budget they have asked for is the part they are destined to play in rehabilitation work among discharged soldiers.

The line of war casualties, back from combat zones and now forming at our government hospitals, will continue to lengthen until victory is ours. For many of these the chance to earn a livelihood depends upon rehabilitation training. A grateful nation has already set up its plans for rehabilitating both. Our state has always been generous with her veterans and her physically handicapped—she will not overlook opportunities for them this time. Eighty percent of the occupations shown by the frequency of rehabilitation clients fall in the general fields of training which the junior colleges could provide.

President Roosevelt in a recent message declared that the program of rehabilitation for our discharged soldiers should be of the widest possible variety. The junior colleges of the nation must build a program of wide range, limited only by their means to meet the individual interests of the students and the needs of the state. This program should continue, they believe, to emphasize those moral and intellectual values needed for good citizenship and to offer education for vocational purposes in agriculture, business, teacher education, home economics, music, and professional courses, and should expand the work in industrial fields (shop work) started under an appropriation at the 1942 session of the legislature.

The administration of training programs to meet the need of various fields of deficiency deserves a prominent place in the program. With some additional equipment the junior colleges, because of their boarding facilities, location, and present equipment could be made to fit admirably into rehabilitation programs. No one junior college would presume to offer training in all specific fields, but by distributing these departments among the junior colleges, facilities could be provided within the state for a majority of the rehabilitation cases. In the past altogether too much of this type training had to be done outside the state.

Many returning veterans will want a specific course that can be completed within a year or less, but in addition will want general education. Certainly they should have available to them somewhere this opportunity. The junior colleges would like to help meet this need.

Many of the returning veterans and defense workers will not have completed high school and will, as many did in 1919, want to continue their education. They will not want to go back to the social situation of the regular high school. They will be nervous, several years above the high school age, and mature. It is logical that the junior colleges with their high school departments, varied courses, and dormitories would be the place for many of these men and women.

The 1942 legislature appropriated to the junior colleges $60,000.00 for the purchase of equipment. For every dollar spent from this appropriation, they secured from other sources approximately $5.00—exclusive of buildings. Here is the record:

Nat'l. Youth Administration (equipment)	$180,000.00
CCC Camps (buildings)	13,138.06
Federal Defense Funds (equipment)	16,809.00
State Appropriation (equipment)	60,000.00
School Budgets	87,801.95
(buildings $67,377.47, equipment $20,424.48)	
Total, expansion, equipment, and buildings	$357,749.01

The attitude of the people toward the junior colleges has been strengthened by the adjustments made in an effort to serve more adequately the respective areas under wartime conditions. The facilities of these institutions are open to their people twelve months in the year. 1,663 regular students were enrolled in the 1943 summer session; 3,110 high school students and 2,266 college students in the regular session 1942–43; or a grand total of 7,039 regular students served the past year. In addition to the training facilities provided for the regular enrollment, these institutions through an expanded training program provided training facilities for 8,863 other persons distributed as follows: general shop program 2,497; defense course 2,529; food production 3,479; and miscellaneous 358; making a grand total of 15,902 persons served the past year.

To the everlasting credit of all the heads of our junior colleges let it be said that they have never tried to exaggerate their needs when presenting budgets to the legislature. They have been frank, sincere, truthful, and all they are now saying to the 1944 lawmaking body is entitled to the fullest credence. It is a program wholly devoid of any semblance of non-essential spending. If granted, every dollar will be put to practical use.

NEW JUNIOR COLLEGES

It is significant that two multicounty junior colleges were established in two proposed zones during this decade. These junior colleges were opened in 1948 and were the upward extension of two county agricultural high schools, Itawamba County A.H.S. and Prentiss County A.H.S. These were the only multicounty junior colleges for white students added to the original eleven established during the beginning years. A decision in 1941 had been made to establish two junior colleges in Northeast Mississippi. The war caused the delay until 1948. The first public junior college for black students was established at Coahoma County A.H.S. in 1949. Two agricultural high schools for blacks were earlier established in Mississippi. Coahoma County in 1924 became the first county in Mississippi to provide an agricultural high school for Negroes under the "separate but equal" doctrine of education. The junior college curriculum was added in 1949. The second agricultural high school to be established for Negroes in Mississippi was at Utica, Mississippi, in 1946. The junior college curriculum was added, beginning with the 1954–1955 school session. Both junior colleges have continued operation to the present time. A third junior college for blacks was established in the Municipal Separate School District of Meridian, but operated as such for only a few years.

The establishment of Itawamba Junior College and Northeast Junior College placed a multicounty junior college in two proposed zones or districts which did not have a junior college. These institutions completed the statewide system as proposed.

REVISION OF STATE LAW

The junior college presidents expressed concern as to the adequacy of the basic law of 1928 in meeting the needs of the state system of junior colleges. The minutes of the December meeting of 1948 of the Junior College Literary and Athletic Association show that a recommendation to rewrite the basic law was presented to the association and was approved. A committee was appointed to implement the recommendation and secure the services of Knox Huff, an attorney in Forest, Mississippi, who had served as a member of the board of trustees of East Central Junior College for twenty-two years, to provide the legal services. The initial law was written at a time when an agricultural high school program was operated on the same campus and in the same building with the junior college program. The junior college presidents considered in their recommendation to rewrite the basic law that the work of the agricultural high schools was no longer connected or correlated with the junior college programs. The following revised law was introduced in the House on February 14, 1950, and signed into law on March 31, 1950:

An Act to establish junior colleges in the State of Mississippi, and to declare their purpose and function; and to provide for the personnel of the junior college commission, and to define their powers and duties; and to authorize the levy of taxes for the support and enlargement of junior colleges, and to provide for the the distribution of revenue thereby derived; and to validate existing junior college districts; and to provide for the operation, management, maintenance, enlargement, and improvement of junior colleges; and for other purposes.[4]

The official title of these institutions during the early years was "Agricultural High School and Junior College." The names were changed to "Junior College" only. This change was important. One of the benefits was that the supervisors of the supporting counties were designating the local tax levy for junior college support, and they wanted to know that it was not being used to support an agricultural high school.

Section eleven of the Public Junior College Law, State of Mississippi, as passed in 1950, reads as follows:

Taxes for the support, enlargement and improvement of junior colleges shall be levied annually against all of the property of each county and of each municipal separate school district, including added territory, which has established or may hereafter establish, or which has joined or may hereafter join, in the establishment or support of a junior college; but in no case shall such levy exceed three mills for support and three mills for enlargement and improvement for each junior college within the district of which the county or municipal separate school district may be a component.

The levy for support for any year in any given county or separate school district is that presently prevailing therein unless a change is recommended to the tax levying authorities by the board of trustees or by a vote of the people ascertained in an election called for that purpose by the tax levying authorities subsequent to the petition therefor signed by twenty per cent (20%) of the qualified electors.[5]

This statute identified the taxing authority of each county for the support, enlargement and improvement of junior colleges. This law also provided for the stability of the local tax levy. It included several other items that contributed much to the growth and development of the junior colleges. The duties of the president of a junior college were defined and his authority strengthened. This action set the president in a strong professional role.

The responsibilities and authority of the Junior College Commission, as established under the law of 1928, were strengthened under the 1950 statute. This statute also changed the method of designating trustees and their terms of office. The authority to appoint trustees was placed in the hands of the supervisors, with the county school board serving in advisory capacity. The law maintained the policy of having the county superintendent serve as an ex-officio member of the board. The importance and authority of the local board of trustees in each junior college district has been recognized through the years and has never been challenged effectively. The ex-officio status of the county superintendent has been questioned and discussed by the presidents at meetings of the Literary and Athletic Association. However, no recommendations have been approved by the association regarding this matter. This statute expanded the role of the Junior College Commission and strengthened its authority. (The work of this commission will be discussed in a separate chapter.) This statute has been referred to by junior college administrators as "a very monumental set of laws," which had been adopted without a dissenting vote.

With the passage of the Comprehensive Junior College Law of 1950, the junior colleges had, to a large degree, separated the college program from the agricultural high schools, and the plans for the future of the junior colleges included removing the high school program from the campuses. The small direct state appropriation for agricultural high schools, which was made at the regular legislative session of 1952, was the last designated appropriation for agricultural high schools. The small number of separate agricultural high schools that were operating after 1952 received state support from the State Minimum Education Program and also received funds for transportation.[6] This change was beneficial to the junior college support from the state level and also from the local district. The tax levying authorities from the junior college districts had come to believe that some of the county support for junior colleges was being used to support the agricultural high school on the same campus.

Significant legislation was passed during the decade. The public junior colleges began the 1942–1943 session, which was the first session of the third decade, with a state appropriation for an upgraded and expanded vocational or trade type of program of education in line with the war effort.[7] The amount of this appropriation was $60,000. This was called "Landmark" junior college legislation because it was the first time an appropriation was made specifically for upgraded vocational or trade programs. The legislature has made a biennial appropriation for technical and upgraded vocational education at each regular session since the 1942 biennium. The amount for the 1968 biennium and the 1970 biennium was $2,000,000 each.

In addition to the state appropriation for the support of technical and vocational education in the junior colleges, a "first" appropriation for buildings was made at the regular 1950 biennial session of the legislature. This initial $750,000 appropriation from the state for buildings was also land-mark legislation. Funds for buildings have been appropriated by the Mississippi legislature at each biennium since 1950 with the exception of the 1954 legislative session.

The opportunity to secure war surplus buildings and equipment had opened the door for expansion in many areas. The junior colleges for the first time were able to establish programs in technical and vocational areas.

Enrollments were increasing rapidly. State and local support was moving upward, and this support indicated to the leadership of the public junior colleges that these institutions represented a very important phase of higher education in Mississippi.

Knox M. Broom, Field Representative for the U. S. Office of Education, and formerly State Supervisor of Public Junior Colleges in Mississippi for twelve years, stated in a published article that "The Mississippi State System of public junior colleges has received approbation from educational leaders of many other states in our nation. The reason for this is that the Mississippi system stands at the top among the junior college systems of the country."[8]

Dr. Jesse P. Bogue, Executive Secretary of the American Association of Junior Colleges, stated in a published article in April 1947, that "Mississippi is the only state which has a real system of junior colleges and that this state system has set a pattern for other states. The Mississippi state system is the logical approach to the proper distribution of colleges, an ample tax base with a reasonable tax rate, an equalization provision to insure the relative progress of all colleges, and the acceptance of responsibility among the colleges by common agreement for specialized curricula."[9]

In the article entitled "Mississippi Public Junior Colleges," Knox M. Broom further states:

It did not just happen that the Mississippi system ranks among the best, but rather this favorable position is the result of (a) a basic philosophy of educational service to the low and average income groups, which underlies the state system of public junior colleges; (b) a very definite preconceived plan for the location and development of these institutions; and (c) the whole-hearted co-operation of other educational enterprises in the growth and development of the system. Mississippians probably have given neither the recognition nor the publicity to the unique features of our junior college program which the system deserves.

A little more than three decades ago the boys and girls of the low income group in the rural areas of our state found their first opportunity for high school education in our county agricultural high schools. As a result of an aroused high school consciousness in the rural districts and improved transportation facilities, the consolidated high school movement took form. By the middle of the twenties the need for high school boarding facilities had been met by consolidated high schools in most of the counties. Then followed the persistent demand for educational opportunities extending through the first two years of college, at low cost, nearer home, and under closer supervision, for the greatly increased number of relatively immature high school graduates. A number of the county agricultural high schools began to experiment with one or two years of college work—such experiments were without legal authority.

By 1928 there were four agricultural high schools offering some college work, and thirty-five other communities were manifesting keen interest. Public demand for upgraded educational opportunities was obvious; and if the movement was to be controlled, definite and immediate action was imperative.

In 1928 the Regular Session of the Mississippi Legislature enacted a law authorizing the establishment of public junior colleges and provided for two phases of training: (a) college preparatory, and (b) terminal and trade type courses. The act listed a number of the vocational-technical type courses and further provided for a Junior College Commission with authority to locate and approve institutions under the act.

Mississippi tried to profit by the experiences of other states in the development of her public junior college program. After a careful analysis of the statutes of all states legalizing public junior colleges and a detailed interpretation of the standards found in the published statements of national, regional, and state standardizing agencies, a criterion for the establishment and control of this new educational unit was worked out and approved by the Junior College Legalized Commission dealing with such items as need, cost, source of revenue, timeliness, and apparent prospects. The state was zoned into twelve possible zones meeting these minimum requirements.

The validity of the criterion for the "birth control" of these institutions is emphasized by the fact that the 1946 Regular Session of the State Legislature approved the location of a public junior college in the last zone provided for, and is further emphasized by the fact that each institution located and developed has conformed to the original zones.

The Junior College Commission approved the zones established under the criterion for the location and development of junior colleges and delegated to the Junior College Accrediting Commission of the Mississippi Association of Colleges the function of passing on the quality of work.

The junior colleges have had in the development of their program not only the co-operation of the University and other senior college officials on the Legalized and Accrediting Commissions, but also the co-operation and counsel of executive heads, deans, and registrars in regularly scheduled junior and senior college conferences where details concerning the articulation of courses were mutually agreed to.

We have always insisted that the Mississippi public junior college was authorized to meet a need not otherwise provided for, that our high school graduates were usually too young to adjust themselves properly to the freedom of a university campus, that in most cases for two more years these students should have closer supervision and more direct personal contact between teachers and students, and that for many of our boys and girls the junior college would be their "finishing school."

In 1938 the Mississippi junior colleges organized and held a number of seminar and laboratory schools with the idea of achieving the purposes for which these institutions were authorized in a more satisfactory manner and in keeping with the needs of those served. This organized program expanded into National Junior College Work Shops, but was interrupted by the war.

Emphasis upon war production training tended to accelerate the vocational-technical phases of the junior college program, and soon it was found desirable in order to avoid unnecessary duplications to allocate training functions to the several institutions based upon labor market demands in the area served. Upon the return of the veterans, the Mississippi public junior colleges, with their varied training programs, were found to be peculiarly suited to that type of training provided for under the terms of the G. I. Bill. This is evidenced by the fact that more than 3,300 veterans have enrolled to date. To care for this increased enrollment and to offer courses suited to the varied needs of the students, additional buildings and equipment were necessary.

Visit the campus of any one of these junior colleges, and you will be amazed at the rapid expansion in physical plants and the wide variety of training opportunities in the vocational-technical fields.[10]

Many of the veterans enrolled in the junior colleges elected to take refresher courses without credit and necessary foundation subjects in high school along with college work. Others chose to forfeit their right to take the General Educational Development test for college entrance and chose to complete all requirements for graduation in the high school department of a junior college. Many began or continued plans for professional careers; some chose terminal courses in general and vocational education; and many combined vocational and liberal arts study, training for a vocation while becoming educated for breadth of knowledge and interest.

It has been said that Harvard College was founded as a vocational school, training men as ministers, preparing them to do something and do it in an intelligent way—to make a living and to live. This is certainly the definite function of the junior college.

Perhaps the most lasting benefits the veterans received from their junior college experiences were those in the field of personal counseling and guidance. Though understaffed, the junior colleges, through psychological and aptitude tests, and family relations clinics, offered specific solutions to vital individual problems. Comparatively small enrollments made it possible for each faculty member to be a personal counselor. There were many G. I.'s enrolled in college who could not concentrate, who were still uneasy, who found adjustment to college extremely difficult; there were those who were struggling against emotional disturbances, marital upsets, financial worries, devastating feelings of inadequacy and inferiority. These found the humanized counseling of instructors of inestimable value in salvaging courage for intelligently coping with problems concerning their jobs, their homes, and other responsibilities. Many of the junior college instructors were themselves G. I.'s who knew first hand the veterans' problems and talked in their own language. It was in this area of guidance and counseling that the junior colleges strengthened themselves to go forward in service to veterans, as well as to all others who were seeking admission at their doors.[11]

The decade ended with a 1950–1952 biennium appropriation of $2,050,000, the largest state appropria-tion in the history of public junior colleges in Mississippi. The appropriation increased the designated amount for technical and vocational education to $250,000 and designated $750,000 for buildings, which was the first direct state appropriation for buildings.

The number of counties levying taxes for support at the beginning of this period was forty-one, and this number had increased to fifty-four at the close of the decade, with increases in millage and in the assessed valuation of the counties giving greater support.

The prospects for the future were very encouraging as the Mississippi public junior colleges were strong and moving forward. The enrollment, which had decreased to a low of 1,375 students during the 1943–1944 session, when the nation was involved in a total war, closed this decade with the 1951–1952 session enrollment at 7,047.

NOTES FOR "THE WAR YEARS AND RETURNING VETERANS"

1. Knox M. Broom, *History of Mississippi Public Junior Colleges*, Table 6, p. 37.
2. Broom, Table 7, p. 38.
3. Broom, Table 6, p. 37.
4. Laws of 1950, House Bill No. 541, Chapter 369, p. 421.
5. Ibid.
6. Laws of 1954, House Bill 295, Chapter 268, p. 305.
7. Laws of 1942, House Bill 622, Chapter 18, p. 28.
8. Knox M. Broom, "Mississippi Public Junior Colleges," *Mississippi Educational Advance*, 38, No. 7, p. 26.
9. Jesse P. Bogue, "The Mississippi State System of Junior Colleges," *Mississippi Educational Advance*, 38, No. 7, p. 27.
10. Broom, "Mississippi Public Junior Colleges," *Mississippi Educational Advance*, 38, No. 7, p. 26.
11. Ibid., pp. 30–31.

The Maturing Years
1952–1962

The natural growth that had been taking place in educational institutions led to the realization that the junior colleges were at this point maturing into fully developed two-year college programs. The leaders of the public junior colleges in Mississippi saw that the people of the state were making some fundamental decisions regarding the necessity of the public junior colleges and their part in meeting the increased demand for higher education on both a state and a national basis. The Mississippi junior colleges had established themselves as leaders in higher education on the state and regional levels and were participating in all areas of development of the junior college movement on a national basis.

Of the twelve junior colleges in existence in 1942, ten were fully accredited by the Southern Association of Colleges and Schools by the end of the third decade. During the fourth decade the remaining two were accredited, and the two additional multicounty district junior colleges which were established in 1948 also received regional accreditation.[1] Two junior colleges for black students were in operation during the period of 1952–1962. Coahoma Junior College, which was organized in 1949, and Utica Junior College, which began operation in 1954, did not receive regional accreditation during this period.

The leadership of the Mississippi public junior colleges became active in the organization of the American Association of Junior Colleges, and the Missis-

sippi Junior Colleges furnished leadership during the early years of its operation. The records of the activities of this association through the years will include, year by year, the names of many Mississippi junior college presidents and other administrative officials in places of leadership, and one Mississippi junior college president, J. M. Ewing of Copiah-Lincoln Junior College, who served as the national president of the association. All the existing sixteen public junior colleges had become active members of the American Association of Junior Colleges.[2]

The development of the Mississippi public junior colleges during the past decade was in part due to certain purposes and objectives which evolved through the years and which the leaders considered basic to this growth. These men recognized the social worth of individuals who differed in interest, aptitude, and types of intelligence and accepted the evidence that a lack of money is a most important reason that many able young people do not go to college or receive any training beyond the high school. Former students have declared that the junior colleges provided the only opportunity to continue their education and that low cost was a very important factor. Accessibility is a contributing force in the growth of Mississippi junior colleges. A junior college is within commuting distance of the great majority of high school graduates. Evidence of the value of this system is that today approximately seven out of the ten high school graduates in Mississippi who enter college began their college work in a junior college. Locating Mississippi junior colleges within driving distance makes it possible for many to attend college who would otherwise be denied this privilege, which would consequently deny their society the benefit of more competent service.

The Mississippi public junior colleges have maintained an open door policy for admission. This has meant that any high school graduate who wanted an opportunity to try college level work would be given the privilege of enrolling. Also, there must be available a wide range of programs to meet various needs, and the board, administration, and faculty are responsible for developing programs to meet these needs. A factor in creating the flexibility needed in constantly changing programs is that the control of the Mississippi junior colleges is in the hands of a local board of trustees drawn from the district served by each junior college. The local board of trustees of each junior college district is a contributing force in determining the most effective programs to meet the needs of all students.

In addition to the acceptance of character building as an essential part of a college program is the recognition that the heart of the junior college program is good teaching. Its attainment depends on the individuals who teach, because good teaching cannot be organized, rationalized, delegated or processed. The junior colleges have been willing and eager to experiment and not fear to fail. The words of Arnold Toynbee, "A voyage, not a harbor," express the attitude of the leaders in the public junior colleges in their growth and development.

The leadership of the Mississippi public junior colleges approached this decade with the determination that the goal of the junior colleges was the development of an institution oriented to the distinctive community needs and the needs of the students to be served.

The fourth decade began with the following presidents:

R. D. McLendon	Pearl River	1942–1953
R. C. Pugh	Northwest	1936–1953
A. L. May	Perkinston (now Gulf Coast)	1941–1953
H. M. Ivy	Meridian	1937–1953
C. W. Lorance	Holmes	1949–1955
Cruce Stark	East Mississippi	1945–1953
J. M. Ewing	Copiah-Lincoln	1932–1956

Ben N. Jones	Northeast	1952–1956
W. B. Horton	Delta	1944–1966
H. T. Huddleston	Southwest	1952–1972
B. F. McLaurin	Coahoma	1949–1966
G. M. McLendon	Hinds	1938–1965
Phillip Sheffield	Itawamba	1948–1960
J. B. Young	Jones County	1940–1970
L. O. Todd	East Central	1934–1953

At the end of the first year six new presidents were elected, and by the end of the fourth year in this decade three more changes were made. More than half of the junior colleges were under new leadership. The following changes were made during this decade:

R. D. McLendon	Northwest	1953–1972
L. O. Todd	Meridian	1953–1971
Arno Vinson	East Central	1953–1962
J. J. Hayden	Perkinston	1953—
G. H. Johnson	Pearl River	1953–1967
R. A. Harbour	East Mississippi	1953–1970
J. D. Boyd	Utica	1954–1957
Walter Washington	Utica	1957–1969
W. B. Hinton	Northeast	1956–1960
Earl F. Hargett	Northeast	1960–1961
E. A. Knight	Northeast	1961–1965
Frank Branch	Holmes	1955—
J. S. Crubaugh	Itawamba	1960—
F. M. Fortenberry	Copiah-Lincoln	1956–1968

At the close of the third decade and during the early years of the fourth decade, some favorable state legislation was passed. In the early years of the junior college system many members of the state lawmaking bodies had taken the position that this phase of higher education in Mississippi was largely the responsibility of the local districts. For this reason the state contribution had been small. This position was influenced partly by the fact that the state was, in most cases, supporting an agricultural high school and a junior college on the same campus. The closing of the majority of the separate agricultural high schools and the developing interest in a program of reorganization in grades one through twelve changed the focus of attention. The junior colleges assumed a place as a very necessary part of Mississippi's program of higher education.

The table below shows the amount of money appropriated by the state of Mississippi for support and in later years for enlargement and improvement. These appropriations are for each of the five decades, beginning in 1922 and ending in 1972.

| First Decade | 1922–1932 | $ 25,000.00 |
| Second Decade | 1932–1942 | 799,750.00 |

Third Decade	1942–1952	4,595,000.00
Fourth Decade	1952–1962	21,972,684.00
Fifth Decade	1962–1972	75,166,389.00[3]

The Mississippi public junior colleges had completed an evaluation criteria study at the end of the third decade—a study somewhat new on the college level. The evaluation criteria evolved through a cooperative study of secondary school standards by the six regional accrediting agencies. It provided one of the most effective means for the in-service training of teachers, the improvement of instructional programs, the strengthening of techniques for public relations with other educational institutions and the public in general, and the evaluating of a system's strengths and weaknesses.

The most important benefit to the institution during this period came from the self-study made by the faculty members and the administration, rather than from the findings of the visiting committee of thirty-one members, including consultants from various types of institutions with a specialist in each of the subject fields. The visiting committee spent three days on the campus checking the institution against the report submitted by the staff and identifying strengths and weaknesses. Its findings were helpful to development. Some of the benefits accruing to the institution might be summarized as follows:

1. A clearer understanding of the school's philosophy and objectives.
2. Needed plant facilities, new departments, and community services.
3. A better understanding between faculty and administration and of the community and its educational needs.
4. An awareness of common problems leading to statewide studies of testing programs, state norms, and dropouts.

TECHNICAL PROGRAMS

More evidence of expansion in the development of the technical program came at the beginning of this period. A special junior college planning committee on vocational and technical education met at Hinds Junior College in May 1952, gave an encouraging report, and recommended that an expanded program of terminal training be provided in regional centers where a wide range of vocational and technical courses might be offered, such as auto mechanics, building trades, sheet metal work, machine shop and welding, nursing, medical and dental secretarial training and cosmetology.

Information was presented to the state legislative bodies in 1952 emphasizing the importance of technical training for career jobs and the great need for coordinating this program with industrial training needs to encourage industry to locate in Mississippi. The materials revealed that no program for technical training would be of worth unless high school graduates and their parents were impressed enough with the importance of this type of training for students to enroll. The leaders of the junior colleges believed that a very important step to take in this direction was to encourage the state and the district to provide money for adequate buildings and equipment. An oft-repeated statement was that *the facilities for job opportunity programs must be moved from the back lot to the front campus*, and that up-to-date training equipment must be used if the student was trained to be useful to industry as well as to be qualified for a career.

The Mississippi legislative bodies at the biennial session in 1962 accepted the challenge to provide adequate buildings and equipment in each junior college district for the purpose of making available training opportunities to meet the needs of both students and industry. This attempt has continued since that date.

Mrs. Emily Duncan Mathis in her doctoral dissertation, "An Historical Study of Curricular Changes in Selected Public Junior Colleges in Mississippi," states that the largest number of changes occurred in technical and vocational education. In addition to developments in vocational and technical training much development was taking place in the medically related areas and allied health fields and nursing.

NEGRO JUNIOR COLLEGES

During this period, the leaders of the Mississippi junior colleges decided that the state had a definite responsibility for establishing Negro junior colleges. An education study committee for the state of Mississippi, as authorized by the Mississippi legislature at the 1960 regular session, included a committee on junior colleges.[4] This group functioned as "the Junior College Advisory Group Seven." The group operated under the leadership of Eddie Khayat, Chairman, a businessman and public official, and C. C. Colvert from the University of Texas as consultant. The other ten members included two Mississippi junior college presidents, two junior college board members, two representatives from a university and college, a minister, a secondary school superintendent of a municipal high school, and two representatives of industry.

The report on junior colleges, dated August 31, 1961, included a recommendation that Negro junior colleges should be established in the already existing junior college districts when sufficient high school graduates are available to provide enrollment for a junior college. The Mississippi Junior College Association at its regular meeting on April 19, 1961,[5] considered the proposed recommendation of the legislative study committee regarding Negro education, which was presented to the junior college presidents at this meeting by the consultant, Dr. Colvert. The presidents agreed to study recommendations for establishing Negro junior colleges and to present completed proposals to the Mississippi Junior College Commission with the suggestion that a request be made to the Mississippi legislature to provide the funds necessary to establish and operate such centers to meet the needs of Negro junior college education.

Recommendations of the Junior College Association Regarding Negro Junior Colleges

Considering recent developments and facts now available regarding the Negro enrollments and number of high school graduates, it is now urgent that serious study be given to the establishment of junior college centers for Negroes in Mississippi. In the light of these facts, the Junior College Association requests the Mississippi Junior College Commission to consider the following recommendations, and thereby requests the Legislature to provide funds necessary to establish and operate these centers to meet the needs of Negro junior college education.

1. The trend in the junior colleges on the state and national level is toward providing academic facilities within commuting distance, therefore reducing the necessity for providing on-campus housing. We recommend that we operate on the principle of establishing centers approximately 40 to 60 miles within commuting distance.

2. The Junior College Association does not recommend the addition of the 13th and 14th grades to any existing high school. We feel that our responsibility in meeting the needs for Negro junior college education would require the provision of separate college facilities.

3. On the basis of population and number of high school graduates, we believe the state should be divided into several districts for Negro junior colleges, and that one or more attendance centers should be located in each district. The

data provided by the Legislative Study Committee, as shown on the attached mat, indicates a need for approximately seven such districts.

We suggest that the Junior College Commission provide necessary leadership in determining the location of the attendance centers within the districts which may be established.

4. Recommendations pertaining to the location of centers:
District 1. A center should be located in the extreme southern part of this district (on the coast). Another center should be located in the northern part of the district.
District 2 & 3. Harris Junior College now serves District 2. We recommend that another center be located near the center of District 2 and District 3.
District 4. This district is served now by Coahoma Junior College at Clarksdale. We recommend that an additional center be located near the eastern boundary of District 4 and the western boundary of District 3.
District 5. This district will require a center located in the area of Humphreys County.
District 6. District 6 is now being served by Utica Junior College, and considering the number of senior colleges located in this area, we feel the needs are being met at the present.
District 7. We recommend that a center be located in the area of Adams, Franklin, and Jefferson Counties to serve this district.

5. In making a study to determine the exact location of these centers, we recommend that careful consideration be given to factors such as population centers, assessed valuation, transportation and proximity to existing junior and senior colleges for Negroes. It is recommended that the attendance centers be located near the presently existing junior colleges so that in the event of future developments which might complicate matters the solution might be reached more easily.

6. The junior colleges now operating in the state are jointly financed by the state and local districts. We believe that the plan of jointly financing the presently organized junior colleges from state and local funds is wise and should be continued, but that the junior colleges proposed in the above recommendations should be financed entirely by the state.[6]

The state Junior College Commission did not recommend the establishing of the proposed Negro junior college districts. The Association's proposal became a part of much discussion and consideration given to Negro education which was being influenced by federal legislation and decisions.

The Mississippi Junior College Commission at its regular meeting, on January 31, 1963, considered recommendations that had been prepared and approved by the Mississippi Junior College Association at an earlier date regarding the establishment of Negro junior college districts for the location of Negro junior colleges in Mississippi.

The final report of the Legislative Education Study Committee, State of Mississippi, from Advisory Group Seven, dealing with the junior colleges of Mississippi, recommended the establishing of Negro junior colleges.

A delegation of educators appeared before the Junior College Commission in the interest of Negro junior colleges in the recommended Southeastern District composed of seventeen counties. The presentation was based on a survey which showed that there were 2899 Negro high school graduates in this district during a five-year period.

The Junior College Commission accepted the report from the Mississippi Junior College Association with a motion that Chairman J. M. Tubb appoint a committee from the Commission to analyze the information presented and secure legal advice from the attorney general's office. The Commission also suggested that the Committee prepare information relating to transportation, proximity of existing colleges, population centers, and other factors such as administration, finance, and legal aspects.

The Commission, after further study of the proposals and recommendations from the Mississippi Association of Colleges, did not recommend the establishing of additional Negro junior colleges in Mississippi.

MINIMUM EDUCATION PROGRAM

Legislation affecting all grades from one through twelve was passed at the extraordinary session of 1953. This legislation included the "Re-organization Act," which reconstituted all school districts in Mississippi. It created the "Education Finance Commission," which provided state aid for school construction, and the "Minimum Education Program."[7]

The majority of the agricultural high schools had closed prior to the beginning of the fourth decade. However, four separate agricultural high schools were still in operation, and several were operated in connection with the junior colleges. The financing of all of these high schools was transferred to the "Minimum Foundation Program." This action was beneficial to the junior college program. It, more clearly than ever, identified the public junior colleges as institutions of higher learning, and it removed completely the confusion that had resulted from two

appropriations being made to the same institution— one for the agricultural high school and one for the junior college. This change caused the administration and board of trustees to remove the words "agricultural high school" from the name of the institution. The name became "junior college" only.

The last special appropriation for agricultural high schools in Mississippi was made at the 1952 regular session when House Bill 787 appropriated $250,000 for agricultural high schools for July 1, 1952–June 30, 1954.[8]

A Legislative Recess Education Committee was created by the legislature at the regular session in 1952. The purpose of this committee was to make recommendations regarding the reorganization of all education grades from one through twelve. This resulted in Gov. Hugh White calling the Extraordinary Session of 1953 to consider the report of this committee. The report resulted in the passage of legislation generally known as the Re-organization Act, House Bill 3, Chapter 12, Section 1, 1953. The reorganization included the minimum education program, Senate Bill 1205, Chapter 14, page 45. It also included the creation of "The Education Finance Commission" for state aid in school construction. This legislation constituted great advance for public education in Mississippi.

The interest and influence of three organizations aided in the passage of this legislation which resulted in a great advance for public education in Mississippi. The three were the Mississippi Citizens Council on Education, the Legal Education Advisory Committee, and the Mississippi Chamber of Commerce. Their interest and influence stimulated citizens in Mississippi to become more alert to the need of a quality educational program in all areas. This aid has been very beneficial to the junior colleges, whose major objective is to see that no high school graduate in the district is denied the opportunity to try college work.

NURSING EDUCATION

Nursing education became a vital part of the public junior college program in Mississippi during this decade. Some phases of nursing education had entered the Mississippi public junior colleges at the beginning of the decade. The junior colleges were offering a prenursing curriculum which allowed nursing students enrolled in hospital nursing programs to enroll in certain transfer courses needed for nursing students. Many junior or community colleges in Mississippi and over the nation became involved in some way in nursing education. The American Association of Junior Colleges became active in helping junior and community colleges deal with the developing programs. As stated above, the early involvement of the nation's public junior colleges in nursing education dealt with students who were enrolled in programs under the control of hospitals. However, within a short time a new nursing program developed which was education centered, and this program was controlled by the junior college. Known as the Associate Degree Program in Nursing, it became a part of the American System of Nursing Education in 1952. This program requires two years to complete, in some cases two academic years and in others two calendar years. A student at the completion of these two years is qualified to take the State Board Test for licensure and also qualified for graduation from the junior college with an A. A. Degree.

Also, at the beginning of this decade the first Practical Nursing Program began at one of Mississippi's public junior colleges. Continued since its establishment, the program has become a vital part of the total effort in technical-vocational training in the junior colleges. This beginning in the area of nursing opened the door for training in a number of allied health areas in the public junior colleges.

This special program was expensive, and the majority of the public junior colleges in the state were delayed in adding programs in nursing education. The American Association of Junior and Community Colleges encouraged the establishing and financing of a research project dealing with nursing education. This project involved pilot programs over the nation, and an advisory committee was named on a nationwide basis to work with this research project to determine whether education qualifying students as registered nurses could be established and conducted effectively as a part of junior and community college education. One of Mississippi's junior college presidents, J. B. Young, representing the Southern Region, was appointed to serve on this advisory committee. The work of the committee was under the leadership of a staff at Columbia University, and the meetings were held there. This committee had the results of the seven pilot programs, and the conclusions of this committee's study have influenced the establishment of nurses' training in junior colleges on a national

basis. Mississippi's public junior colleges have kept pace in this program. In 1957 the first Associate Degree Program was established in a Mississippi public junior college.

As the fifty-year period closed, eight public junior colleges were operating Associate Degree Programs, and two other programs were being operated in junior college districts by senior institutions. Two additional programs were opened on public junior college campuses in 1972. There were 594 students enrolled in Associate Degree Programs under the direction of sixty-four faculty members.[9] In addition to the associate degree programs mentioned, four bachelor of science programs are operating in the universities and colleges of Mississippi and two master's programs. The public junior colleges are conducting health occupation programs through the State Division of Vocational-technical Education in many areas, including twenty-seven licensed practical nursing programs.

An act was passed by the Mississippi legislature in 1964 supporting nursing training as the responsibility of educational institutions, both in the junior colleges and in the senior institutions.[10]

BUS TRANSPORTATION

Information received from the high schools in the various districts showed that bus transportation would make it possible for a large number of students to attend junior college who were being denied this opportunity. The first system began operating from Wayne County on the morning of December 3, 1953.[11] The bus traveled twenty-seven miles one way, and twelve students rode it on the first trip. The acceptance of bus transportation by the students was evidence of need to expand transportation for junior college students in the district. In November 1971 a report from the sixteen junior colleges showed that fifteen of the sixteen public junior colleges were operating one or more buses within the district. The total number in operation was one hundred and eleven. The greatest number from any one district was seventeen. This system of transportation has increased the percentage of students attending college. In this category Mississippi now ranks near the top among the southern states.

Bus transportation unified the district. In the early years of the development of a junior college some felt the college belonged more to the county in which it was located than to the other supporting counties in the district. Bus transportation brought about a feeling of "our junior college," not "their junior college." The following editorial, taken from a weekly newspaper of a supporting county of one of Mississippi's public junior colleges, causes one to feel that bus transportation opened the door for many high school graduates to go beyond high school:

Truly An Asset

This week's editorial page cartoon shows a bus load of college youths headed for a junior college in Mississippi.

It means that high school graduates can live at home and achieve academic credits for the first two years of college in a fully accredited institution, or if they so desire, take special courses, including technical and vocational educational training.

Students are required to pay no tuition. The cost, excluding lab fees, books, and certain miscellaneous items, is only $168. per year for those who ride the bus.

This is quite a contrast to about $3,000 which many parents find is the yearly cost in sending their children to a standard four-year college where they must pay for room and board in addition to heavy tuition and general higher costs in all categories.

This may come as news to many of our readers, but students are happy to be able to participate in a first-class academic offering at modest prices which, in many cases, would have been denied them were it not for the junior college.

In talking to authorities there we have come to the conclusion that no one who really wants to attend college and is willing to work is denied entrance. Even jobs and scholarships are available. This means that financial conditions can no longer determine whether a youth can go to college, at least for the first two years.

Space is too limited to go into the various fields of endeavor on the campuses of Mississippi public junior colleges. Needless to say, they certainly have the facilities and staff to do a good job in their area of higher education.

Students who must consider money as a factor in getting an education after high school and don't want to sacrifice quality in making a selection of institutions have no reason not to continue in their pursuit of learning in a junior college.[12]

In addition to the bus transportation, the improved economic conditions enabled some families to provide students with automobiles for commuting.

GIRLS' BASKETBALL

Action was taken at the regular meeting, February 1955, by the Mississippi Junior College Association to eliminate girls' basketball,[13] and the 1954–1955 school session was the last year in which girls' basketball was operated on a competitive basis. Although

the decision to eliminate girls' basketball did not receive unanimous support from the presidents, it was the judgment of the majority to eliminate it. The interest in the sport continued at some of the institutions, and interschool games were played among some of the junior and senior colleges.

At the regular 1962 legislative session a "senate concurrent resolution" was introduced, declaring the value of girls' basketball for athletic, spiritual, and leadership purposes and recommending that a program of girls' basketball be organized. Copies of the resolutions were sent to the state superintendent of education and to all presidents of junior and senior colleges receiving state support. The consideration of the value of the sport resulted in the reinstallation of girls' basketball on a competitive basis by the Mississippi Junior College Association for the 1973–1974 session.[14]

Knox Broom's history of Mississippi's state system of public junior colleges, 1928–1953 was completed in 1953. This history, which records the growth and development of the public junior colleges that constitute the state system, identifies the purposes of these institutions as a part of the total program of higher education in Mississippi and records some of the contributions they made to meet the educational needs of many young people. This history showed that the annual enrollment for academic transfer courses in the fourteen public junior colleges had reached 5,162 students. It also showed that the technical-vocational programs, which began with the 1946–1947 session, had included thirty-eight different types of units and represented one hundred and four programs offered in the fourteen junior colleges. The total number of students served in these programs from the 1946–1947 session through the 1952–1953 session was 13,919.[15]

The end of the fourth decade saw evidence of the maturity of the public junior colleges in Mississippi, and the state expressed its interest and confidence by increasing support. County support was increasing in the districts by additional tax levies for general support, and the supervisors were levying local taxes for enlargement and improvement of physical facilities. The total amount appropriated for the biennium beginning in 1952 was $3,800,000. This included funds for regular support, vocational-technical programs and buildings.

The state appropriation at the regular session of

1962 amounted to $6,943,000. The legislature, at the end of this fourth decade, had the benefit of two reports of an education study committee of the junior colleges in Mississippi. This study was authorized by legislative acts. These reports considered the needs and purposes of the public junior colleges in Mississippi and made recommendations for increased financial support. The first report was completed and presented to the legislative study committee under the date of August 31, 1961. This first report made recommendations regarding state and local funds for the operation of the junior colleges and for capital needs, a formula with emphasis on distribution of available funds and salaries, fiscal responsibility for the boards of trustees, a separate division of junior colleges in the state department of education, each junior college district to be given legal status, the establishing of centers and branches within districts, and the establishing of Negro junior colleges.

A second (unpublished) study by William P. McLure, consultant from the University of Illinois, was presented to the legislative study committee under the date of November 7, 1961. This second study gave special attention to implications of occupational trends for education in junior colleges, the organization and financing of the junior colleges, and the educational task for the future. The majority of the proposals made in these two reports were implemented and contributed to the rapid growth and development of the junior colleges.

NOTES TO "THE MATURING YEARS"

---

1. Proceedings of the Seventy-Third Annual Meeting of Southern Association of Colleges and Schools, Atlanta, Georgia, December 2, 1968.
2. Membership Directory, American Association of Junior and Community Colleges.
3. Records, Division of Junior Colleges, State Department of Education.
4. Senate Concurrent Resolution 1960, Regular Session, Mississippi Legislature.
5. Final Report filed with the office of the Board of Institutions of Higher Learning.
6. Minutes, Mississippi Junior College Association, December 13, 1962, Division of Junior Colleges.
7. Senate Bill 1205, Chapter 14, p. 45, Extraordinary Session, 1953.
8. House Bill 787, Chapter 34, p. 39, Approved April 9, 1952.
9. Information supplied by Annie M. Tucker, Associate Director of Nursing Education, Institutions of Higher Learning.
10. House Bill 797, Chapter 437, p. 647.
11. Records on file in Registrar's Office, Jones County Junior College.
12. *Wayne County News*, Waynesboro, Mississippi, November 4, 1971.
13. Mississippi Junior College Association, Minutes of Meeting, February 8, 1955.
14. Senate Concurrent Resolution, No. 163, 1962, Chapter 705, p. 1204, adopted Senate, May 18; House, May 25, 1962.
15. Knox M. Broom, *History of Mississippi Public Junior Colleges, 1928–1953*, Table 4, p. 35.

Years of Growth and Vision
1962–1972

The beginning of the fifth decade was a point of much thoughtful observation. The leaders of the junior colleges had cause to look in two directions—forward and backward. Much had been accomplished during the four decades since the beginning, and the future promised many developments that would greatly strengthen the junior college programs.

A look backward at the Mississippi state system of public junior colleges at the close of this first fifty years indicates that the developments that have taken place during these years enable the junior colleges to fill a necessary and important place in providing college training for many youths and adults. These junior colleges are providing an answer to Mississippi's problem of increased college enrollment and the mounting cost of a college education. The courses offered in the public junior colleges are the same courses taken by freshmen and sophomores at a senior college or university in the preprofessional and liberal arts areas, and these courses meet the transfer requirements. The credits earned at the junior colleges are accepted, without question, at the senior college or university.

A comprehensive program is well established, with the junior colleges accepting the responsibility for technical training and for many short-term courses. These programs are designed, and are available, to meet the industrial training needs of the state.

Evening classes are providing many opportunities for continuing education. Training in nursing and allied health fields is available. Special emphasis is being given to the handicapped. Many needs of the districts are being met with these short-term programs.

These years have proven the wisdom of the early legislation, which established the Mississippi state system of junior colleges, and zoned the state, thereby recommending the location of a public junior college in every section of the state and within commuting distance of all high school graduates.[1] This plan was strengthened with passage of House Bill No. 215,[2] which was an act to establish junior college districts as individual and separate juristic entities and bodies politic and corporate. This legislation created thirteen multicounty district junior colleges, including all the eighty-two counties in Mississippi, approved three additional junior colleges within these districts, and authorized any junior college district to operate additional attendance centers within the district. This legislation has strengthened the Mississippi state system of junior colleges and has increased the interest in county financial support. Eighty-one of the eighty-two counties are at present levying a tax for support, and a large number are providing additional tax support for enlargement and improvement. This local support is voluntary from seventy-seven of the eighty-one counties. The four-county Gulf Coast District approved special legislation assigning fiscal responsibility to the local board of trustees to determine the local tax levy needed.

The accessibility of the public junior colleges and attendance centers at additional campuses in the established districts has led to an increase in percentage of enrollment of qualified students. The records show that more than fifty percent of the high school graduates in Mississippi who enter college began their college training at a junior college.

During the early years the leaders, in organizing and building the public junior colleges, saw this new phase of college education as necessary and important to the young people of Mississippi, and they believed that certain official groups were essential if the needs of the youth were to be met and if these institutions were to grow. That these groups have continued to function throughout these fifty years has proven their great worth. The local board of trustees is an example, and its importance to each district and each institution has increased. Also, annual meetings of the Mississippi Junior-Senior College Conference, which have been held continuously since 1934, have helped develop an understanding of common problems and objectives and have helped solve most of the serious problems. The efforts of these conferences have resulted in the growth of a fine spirit of cooperation and friendliness among the public and private institutions of higher learning.

The determination of all who are responsible for the administration of each public junior college to provide college training at the lowest possible cost is firmly established as essential to opening the door for many high school graduates and college-age youth who would be denied college training because of mounting college costs.

Those responsible for the administration of the junior colleges must recognize that junior colleges are well defined institutions and that economy and simplicity are required in this phase of college education. The effort to provide substantial savings to the taxpayers and to the students should hold a high priority in the administration of the public junior college in Mississippi.

The decision was made at the beginning that the financial support for the junior colleges should be jointly shared by the state and the districts. The state leaders were aware that higher education was the responsibility of the state. The tax levying authorities

in the local district were convinced that the location of any institution of higher learning, within a local district, would enable a much larger percentage of high school graduates to continue their education beyond the high school. There was also something of an unwritten agreement between junior college administrators and the local tax levying authorities that these colleges would be available to all students without tuition cost, and this condition prevailed during this fifty-year period. The high cost of college education continues to deny many superior young persons the opportunity to continue their education beyond the high school.

Many benefits accrue to persons who attend junior colleges. The experiences over the years emphasize the importance to many students of two more years to mature under the guidance and leadership of their parents and as members of their churches and other community groups. The opportunities of the student to exercise his leadership in social situations, athletics, fine arts areas, and general campus activities contribute much to the maturity of the junior college student. These opportunities for development are available because the beginning student is not completely dominated by upperclassmen in junior colleges. The Mississippi public junior colleges have emphasized, through the years, the importance of promoting a closer relationship between student and faculty members and the awareness that junior college faculty members and administrators must provide a type of leadership that will relate to the total development of each individual student. The junior colleges will continue to justify their support if their efforts are centered on raising the general level in educational, cultural, economic, and spiritual development.

It is very satisfying to observe that the junior colleges are receiving sufficient financial support from both local and state sources to enable them to provide buildings and equipment necessary to operate a quality educational program to meet the needs of the area. This general support has improved and is providing the instruction needed to insure a program of excellence.

The sixteen presidents of the junior colleges at the beginning of this decade, with the exception of two presidents, were men with years of experience as the chief administrators of a Mississippi public junior college, having served a total of 189 years. By the end of

1972 the presidents who began this decade increased the total number of years served to a total of 296 years. They were well informed about the accomplishment of the first decades, and they were able to see the decade before them as years of growth, with the capabilities for greater service in all areas. They were assured that the Mississippi public junior colleges were an indispensable part of higher education in the state's total education program. Since many of these presidents had experienced many years without adequate funds for salaries, buildings or equipment, they found it a satisfying experience to remove war surplus buildings and replace them with beautiful permanent buildings which were air conditioned, well lighted, and attractive, and which met high standards of quality construction. They were also able to discard much obsolete equipment and secure adequate instructional equipment and supplies.

The presidents who began this decade were:

G. M. McLendon	Hinds	1938–1965
W. B. Horton	Mississippi Delta	1944–1966
B. F. McLaurin	Coahoma	1949–1966
H. T. Huddleston	Southwest	1952–1972
G. H. Johnson	Pearl River	1953–1967
F. M. Fortenberry	Copiah-Lincoln	1956–1968
Walter Washington	Utica	1957–1969
J. S. Crubaugh	Itawamba	1960–1972
J. B. Young	Jones County	1940–1970
R. A. Harbour	East Mississippi	1956–1970
L. O. Todd	Meridian (formerly with East Central)	1953–1971 1934–1953
J. J. Hayden	Mississippi Gulf Coast	1953—
Frank Branch	Holmes	1955—
E. A. Knight	Northeast	1961–1965
R. D. McLendon	Northwest (formerly with Pearl River)	1953— 1942–1953
W. Arno Vincent	East Central	1953–1962

Changes that came about during this decade were:

Robert Mayo	Hinds	1965—
J. T. Hall	Mississippi Delta	1966—
James E. Miller	Coahoma	1966—
Martin R. White	Pearl River	1967—
Douglas M. Montgomery	East Central	1962–1966
Charles V. Wright	East Central	1966—
B. B. Thames	Copiah-Lincoln	1968—
Louis J. Stokes	Utica	1969—
W. C. Benjamin	Itawamba	1972—
Arthur H. Kinnard	Utica (acting)	1972—
Terrell Tisdale	Jones County	1970—

Earl Stennis	East Mississippi	1970–1972
William Reeves	East Mississippi	1972—
Horace Holmes	Southwest	1972—
William Scaggs	Meridian	1971—
Harold T. White	Northeast	1965—
Joe Childers	Northeast (acting)	1972—

A new junior college law, which the leaders considered a milestone, was passed during the regular Mississippi legislative session of 1964 and approved on June 11, 1964. House Bill 215, which replaces much of the comprehensive junior college laws of 1950 is: "*An Act* to establish junior college districts as individual and separate juristic entities and bodies politic and corporate; to more clearly define the role of junior colleges and the financial support thereof in this state; to repeal Sections 6475–04, 6475–07 and 6476–01 Mississippi Code of 1942, and for related purposes." [3]

A legislative House Bill, No. 597, which was approved on May 10, 1962, established a junior college district comprised of four counties: Harrison, Stone, George, and Jackson. This district was named "Mississippi Gulf Coast Junior College, District of Mississippi, and constituted a legal political governmental subdivision and a body corporate." [4]

The twelve districts designated in House Bill No. 215, 1964 legislative session and the above-mentioned Gulf Coast District served all of the eighty-two counties in the state of Mississippi. [5] At the close of this decade in 1972, eighty-one of the eighty-two counties had levied a tax to support the junior college of its district.

Three public junior colleges remain which are not set up as legal districts. They are: Meridian Junior College, provided for under Section Fifteen of the Act as territory of a municipal separate school district; Coahoma Junior College, by Board of Supervisors provided for under Section Sixteen of the Act with counties overlapping; and Utica Junior College, which continues in the Hinds District with one or more counties supporting it.

Specific additions in this law include:

(a) The transfer of all property at existing campuses belonging to counties or agricultural high schools to the boards of trustees of the enumerated junior college districts.

(b) The establishing of attendance centers on campuses, within a junior college district legalized—subject to the approval of the State Junior College Commission.

(c) The continuance of the tax levy that had been established in any county for support or for capital improvement secured.

An act was passed in the general legislative session of 1964, effective with ad valorem taxes assessed as of January 1, 1966. Referred to as "the 307 law," it provided that counties withhold an amount of state ad valorem tax collected up to two mills provided the said county shall levy one-half mill. The purpose for which the said tax may be withheld and expended must be a purpose or purposes within the economic, industrial, or educational fields, and which will be substantially beneficial to areas of the state beyond a county, and that the benefits will be statewide or to a large portion of the state.[6]

The public junior colleges qualified under this act, which gave great impetus to plans for new and renovated buildings and for purchase of much needed equipment. This law created an inequality in funds available for some of the junior college districts in the state. An earlier law authorizing the withholding of state ad valorem revenue to noneducational areas created the opportunity for a number of counties in various sections of the state to legally withhold taxes. The taxes withheld were assigned to various state areas of development. These included such projects as: The Tombigbee Valley Authority, the Cotton Research at Delta Branch, Mississippi Experiment Station, the Pat Harrison Waterway, the Pearl River Water Basin, the Delta Port Authority, and the Port Authority Gulf Coast. Some junior college districts were not eligible for any withholding. During the 1973 regular legislative session the inequality was corrected to some degree with the passage of House Bill No. 1402, which allowed each junior college district in Mississippi to benefit by this withholding law. This was another step in giving junior colleges the opportunity to develop buildings and provide equipment necessary for a comprehensive program of high quality.

This source of revenue was increased in 1967 when a legislative act authorized boards of trustees of the public junior colleges to borrow money for a period of fifteen years and to repay from general funds derived from an ad valorem tax or other sources.[7] A junior college could borrow money or issue bonds on a fifteen year basis and repay from the revenue derived from the 307 Act.

The junior colleges immediately began a long range

building program which represented growth and vision for the future. The state appropriation for buildings during this fifth decade, 1962 to 1972, was slightly above $28,000,000 and contributed much to the growth of the junior colleges.

Funds for capital improvements in the public junior colleges came from two other sources:

(1) *County Taxes*—"As with county support for operations, each county is empowered to levy up to three mills of county-wide tax for the enlargement and improvement of the junior college in their district. At the end of this decade forty-three (43) counties levied total levies of 54.20, or an average of 1.26 mill per county for this purpose."[8]

(2) *Federal Support*—A real thrust toward developing comprehensive vocational and technical programs came with the passage of the Federal Vocational Act, Public Law 88–210, 1964.[9] This act provided funds for construction of area technical and vocational schools in post-secondary schools. The act was strengthened by amendments.[10]

Federal grants for amounts up to approximately forty percent of the cost of instructional facilities were obtained by most junior colleges in the middle and late 1960s. There has been little federal support for this purpose since 1970.

Federal funds for vocational education facilities have been made available through the Division of Vocational Education, State Department of Education and, when available, provide approximately fifty percent of the cost of a facility for vocational-technical education.

Expenditures are made from plant funds for construction of new facilities; renovations, remodeling and additions to existing facilities; acquisition of furnishings and equipment; improvements in sites and grounds, including walkways, streets, curbs, drainage, lighting, landscape planting, utility system, and acquisition of land.[11] This decade of growth received the benefits of favorable legislation in a number of areas.

A significant act was passed during the regular session of 1964 which stimulated technical and vocational training programs. Known as the Mississippi Junior College Vocational and Technical Training Act of 1964, the purpose of this act was "to authorize the use of state funds to be supplemented at least equally by local funds for the purpose of stimulating technical and vocational training programs within the public junior college system; to provide procedure and requirements necessary to obtain such funds; and for related purposes."[12]

This legislative enactment was proposed by a resolution setting forth the need for the training of a skilled and semiskilled labor force for economic development. The funds appropriated for accomplishing the purpose of this act were placed with the state building commission. The importance and concern related to this legislation is identified with the steps to be taken in making application for funds.

The act provided that the board of trustees of a junior college district make an application to the State Junior College Commission, from there to the State Building Commission, thence to the State Agricultural and Industrial Board to determine if a need existed in the junior college district. If the need did exist a "certificate of necessity" was issued and the application returned to the State Junior College Commission for final approval. These steps proved to be of value. These agencies, in studying the facts regarding the existing needs in the districts for technical and vocational programs, became enthusiastic in their support of this development and were of great help with future legislation.

As a result of these two acts and a major increase in vocational-technical education funds at both state and federal levels, the state's junior college districts, from January 1, 1964, to June 30, 1973, constructed and equipped twenty-five area vocational-technical training centers in Mississippi. As of 1972 the state of Mississippi had appropriated $4,387,000 for this purpose. These acts, with the help of the local district, enabled the public junior colleges to take a very basic step necessary to encourage high school graduates to enroll in technical and vocational job opportunity programs. This step was to construct buildings for technical and vocational classes equal in quality and location to other academic facilities. This included adequate instructional equipment and supplies and qualified instructors. Technical and vocational programs were established and organized as college credit courses. These programs for high school graduates were developed to meet the standards for regional accreditation.

Mississippi's industrialists, industrial developers in the state, recognize that one of the biggest drawing cards for persuading "Blue Chip" industrialists to locate new plants—or to expand existing plants—in

Mississippi has been the interest and desire of all public junior college officials to supply trained workers for industrial employment. Industrialists in Mississippi today have found that trained vocational-technical workers are very much interested in giving a full day's work for a day's pay. Many industrialists in Mississippi have commended the state's public junior college vocational training programs.

In developing the twenty-five area vocational and technical centers the various colleges have spent more than $32,000,000 on construction of buildings and equipment needed in teaching the various occupations that have been included in their vocational curriculums.

The junior colleges have recognized that "start-up training" for new and expanding industry is one of their most important objectives. They have therefore pledged complete cooperation with the State Department of Education, Vocational Division, in using their equipment and resources to provide new and expanding industry with trained labor so they can begin their operations in any given area of the state with an adequate supply of well trained labor. Each vocational-technical training center is fully equipped with modern machinery and equipment available for pre-employment training.

Information obtained from Mr. Troy Majure, Director of Division of Vocational Education, State Department of Education, showed that over five hundred and eighty regular vocational and technical education instructors who were teaching in the junior colleges were reimbursed on their salaries by the vocational division of the state department of education. For the year ending June 30, 1973, 10,867 "in school" students and 25,335 adults were enrolled in a wide offering of vocational and technical education occupations. Over seven thousand of these adults were enrolled in "start-up" training for new and expanding industries.

Mississippi should be proud of the progress that vocational and technical education has made through the junior college system, which covers the entire state. Training people for both new and existing occupations is contributing immeasurably to the economy of our state.

A typical statement from a president of one of the companies that received "start-up" training is: "Mississippi has one of the finest vocational-technical education systems in the United States; programs are

47

tailored for each industry and many can be conducted at the owner's plant." [13]

A junior college president says, "We feel that 'start-up' training is one of our most important objectives. Each of us needs to recognize that new industry is a tremendous asset to the State of Mississippi and perhaps more importantly to local school districts; they will be taxpayers and supporters of our junior colleges. We are glad to give this item top priority in planning, implementation, and public relations." [14]

THE DIVISION OF JUNIOR COLLEGES

The junior college presidents, through the Mississippi Junior College Association, began during this decade to consider the importance of securing legislation that would create a division of junior colleges in the state department of education. During the years of development of the Mississippi junior college system, the organization had been a part of the Division of Instruction of the State Department of Education; however, the junior college system had been very loosely connected with the Division of Instruction and had found little occasion to relate its work to it. The presidents felt that this system of higher education should be related to the state department of education with the status of a division. The recommendations of the presidents had the full support of the state superintendent of education.

During the regular legislative session of 1968, an act was passed, "To establish a Division of Junior Colleges within the State Department of Education; to provide for a division director to be appointed by the State Superintendent of Education; to define more clearly the functions of the division and the existing junior college commission; to amend Section 6245–08, Mississippi Code of 1942, recompiled, as amended, to define duties of the director of the Division of Junior Colleges; and for related purposes." [15]

The division has increased the service to the junior colleges from the central office. The act, under section two, identifies the principal functions of the division through its director and personnel. The growth and development of the division in providing these services as recommended has made distinct contributions to the state system of junior colleges.

NEGRO JUNIOR COLLEGE DISTRICTS

The Mississippi Junior College Commission, at its regular meeting on January 31, 1963, considered rec-

ommendations that had been prepared and approved by the Mississippi Junior College Association at an earlier date regarding the establishment of Negro junior college districts for the location of Negro junior colleges in Mississippi. The final report to the Legislative Education Study Committee, State of Mississippi, from Advisory Group Seven, dealing with the junior colleges of Mississippi, recommended the establishment of Negro junior colleges. A delegation of educators appeared before the Junior College Commission in the interest of Negro junior colleges in the recommended Southeastern District composed of seventeen counties.

The presentation was based on a survey which showed that there were 2,899 Negro high school graduates in this district during a five year period.

The Junior College Commission accepted the report from the Mississippi Junior College Association with a motion that Chairman J. M. Tubb appoint a committee from the commission to analyze the information presented and secure legal advice from the attorney general's office. The commission also suggested that the committee prepare information relating to transportation, proximity of existing colleges, population centers, and other factors such as administration, finance, and legal aspects.

This committee, after further study of the proposals and recommendation from the Mississippi Association of Colleges, did not recommend the establishing of additional Negro junior colleges in Mississippi.

MISSISSIPPI JUNIOR COLLEGE INTER-ALUMNI ASSOCIATION

The presidents of the public junior colleges were aware that after forty years of operation some of the state's leaders in every area of activity were graduates of a public junior college. The vast majority of the alumni of the public junior colleges were young men and women who felt that they might have been denied the opportunity for formal education beyond high school had the junior college not existed. Most of the institutions had an active alumni organization, and a deep feeling of loyalty existed among the alumni. The feeling of loyalty and interest was displayed at the annual meetings. The number of alumni filling places of leadership on the state level had included over the years a governor, a lieutenant governor, a secretary of state, an attorney general, and other statewide leaders, as well as many state representatives and senators; also a great number of professional people, leaders in the economic and industrial areas, and many individual citizens. This alumni group supported many opportunities for growth and development. A look at the alumni caused the presidents, through the Mississippi Junior College Association, to feel the need of a statewide organization.

At the meeting on August 24, 1964 a proposal was made to the Mississippi Junior College Association by John Monroe of Lucedale, an alumnus of Pearl River Junior College, to organize the Mississippi Junior College Inter-Alumni Association.[16] This proposal was formally approved and the organization established at a meeting in December 1964.

The first annual meeting of the association was held on the campus of Pearl River Junior College on July 15, 1965.[17] A proposal was made and approved at this meeting to incorporate the Mississippi Junior College Inter-Alumni Association as a nonprofit corporation. This was accomplished, and the charter of incorporation was signed by Gov. Paul B. Johnson on July 11, 1966. The charter states:

The non-profit corporation is for the purpose of assisting junior colleges in the State of Mississippi by assisting where needed in formulating policy, proposing and working with the legislators as to statutes to assist junior colleges in an orderly upgrading program, to better fill the need for this type of institution; to assist in general in the growth and function of junior colleges in Mississippi and to unite statewide those interested in assisting in this area of education.[18]

The Inter-Alumni Association has developed slowly. One of its great services has been to strengthen the local district alumni organizations. The presidents of the junior colleges appreciate the work of the alumni who contribute to the development of this statewide organization and feel that it will add strength to the state system of junior colleges.

RECOGNITIONS AND TRIBUTES

This story began with the statement that many individuals, official groups, conditions and situations had a part in the unfolding and advancement of this new phase of higher education. Those having a part were students eager to further their academic or vocational education, good teachers, superintendents, the directors, local boards of trustees, supervisors, legislators, the state board of education, the Junior College Commission, and the accrediting commissions. Each group mentioned in the beginning has contributed in many ways during this period of time.

THE STUDENT

This fifty-year story, as it has unfolded and developed, has revealed the great need for the junior college phase of higher education. The need relates directly to the many students who, by increasing numbers, have found the door open for college training.

The graduating seniors of agricultural high schools were the first to hear announcements made at some of these schools that if they wanted to go to college they could return and get college courses at the agricultural high school. Many rural students and others had hardly considered that college training would be available to them. The testimonies of these students as they were able to move into all areas of professional life and to choose a career in all areas of activity are very gratifying.

It would require many volumes to tell the story of the accomplishments and contributions of students in all walks of life who would have been denied the opportunity to choose their life's work had the public junior colleges not been available.

The following statement was published in *The Mississippi Educational Advance* in the issue of April 1947.

Many of the distinguished members of the various professions in this country are people who had their preparation in Mississippi junior colleges. Included in the number are doctors, dentists, engineers, musicians, painters, teachers, ministers of the gospel, lawyers, etc. A larger number of the former students are in the businesses, large and small, of the country, are operating farms, keeping house, are working as technicians and nurses in laboratories and hospitals, are carrying on the skilled trades that they were prepared for in junior colleges, and doing other useful work. Former junior college students by the thousands are effective citizens in the vocational and social life of the state because of the time spent in the junior colleges.[19]

It is very gratifying to quote from an article in *The Clarion-Ledger*, dated Wednesday, January 2, 1974, which stated from a report filed by the Southern Association of Colleges and Schools in Atlanta, Georgia, that in the ten-state southern region Mississippi had a larger percentage than other states of its black college-age population enrolled in college and that Mississippi leads the South in white college-age population enrolled in college. The Mississippi state system of public junior colleges has as its purpose for the future to increase this number.[20]

The number of students enrolled in the public junior colleges of Mississippi for the 1922–1923 session was forty-three students.[21] The record in the central office of the State Division of Junior Colleges shows that the cumulative enrollment for the 1971–1972 session, which closed the first fifty years, was 60,869.[22] The record of the students and their contributions justify in every way the courage, the determination, and the sacrifices of the men and women who gave so much to secure the opportunity for young people to attend college.

BOARDS OF TRUSTEES

The local board of trustees from the junior college district was the chief authority for each junior college. Each junior college in Mississippi is a multicounty district junior college, with the exception of one municipal public junior college, which was established in accordance with the basic law establishing the Mississippi state system of junior colleges. Each of the multicounty districts of junior colleges came into existence as the extension of the curriculum of an agricultural high school. This local board of trustees was referred to in the beginning of this story as "the producers who selected the directors and furnished the facilities." The board of trustees of each agricultural high school that extended its curriculum became the official board of the beginning agricultural high school and junior college. In accordance with the laws governing the Mississippi junior college system, new members were added to the board from each county in the junior college district that levied a tax for the support of the junior college. Some characteristics of the local board have not changed during the fifty years. Each supporting county has representation on the board of trustees. The county superintendent of education in each county is an ex-officio member during his term of office, which is four years, and the county in which the junior college is located is represented by six members. All members other than the county superintendent are by appointment.

Some changes have taken place. The term of office for those appointed remained at four years until passage of the junior college law of 1950, House Bill No. 541. This law set the length of the term at five years

and staggered the terms by making the first appointments on a 5-4-3-2-1 basis. This law also provided for all trustee appointments to be the responsibility of the boards of supervisors of each county. Prior to this law the county school board was responsible for appointment of two members of the board from a county having six members. This law also added the statement "*by and with consent of the county school board.*" This requirement was later removed by statute.[23]

The local board of trustees in each junior college district has added great strength to junior colleges. Their worth to the Mississippi state system has not been questioned. The need for a local board and the responsibilities assigned it has never been challenged during the fifty-year period. (The name of each board member from each institution is listed in Section Four.) Their contribution to this phase of higher education in Mississippi is appreciable, and they have the acclaim and support of those who have been a part of the development of the junior colleges. They richly deserve the honor that has been bestowed upon them.

BOARDS OF SUPERVISORS

During the first six years in the life of the junior college the work was financed by the regular funds for the operation of the agricultural high schools offering college work. These funds were provided by a local tax from the counties supporting an agricultural high school and from district state appropriation. The policy of both state and local support has remained through the years.

The boards of supervisors were authorized, *at their discretion*, to levy an annual tax for the support of the junior colleges. While the local tax support provided by the boards of supervisors is voluntary and at their discretion, the supervisors have supported the colleges and have been as generous as their total responsibility to the counties would permit. Evidence of their effort to be helpful in the progress of the colleges in providing a program meeting high standards is shown by the fact that eighty-one of the eighty-two counties in the state are, at the close of this fifty years, supporting a public junior college.

The fact that support from the county was on a voluntary basis meant that progress in this support would be gradual. At the end of the first decade, twenty-six counties provided a tax levy for support.

At the end of the second decade, the number increased to forty-one counties. Continued progress brought the number to fifty-four counties. The end of the fourth decade showed sixty-seven counties, and at the end of the fifty-year period, eighty-one counties were giving their support to the state system of public junior colleges. The junior colleges operated financially under the agricultural high school law in the beginning, except for the permissive legislation of 1922. However, in 1924, the law was passed authorizing the boards of supervisors to levy a tax not to exceed three mills for building, repair, and equipment. Since this time the boards of supervisors have had the authority to levy three mills for support and maintenance and three mills for building and equipment.

The boards of supervisors have had a responsibility in the appointment of the trustees since the beginning of these institutions. The authority given to the boards of supervisors at the beginning was to elect three members of the six trustees from a county. This policy continued until passage of the junior college law of 1950. This law provided that each trustee appointment be made by the board of supervisors by and with the consent of the county school board.[24] A final change was made by statute at the regular session of 1964 when the phrase "*by and with the consent of the county school board*" was removed and the supervisors were assigned the responsibility for all trustee appointments.[25]

The supervisors have been influenced by the commitment to the theory that the tax support from the county would make it possible for any high school graduate who wanted to go to college to have the opportunity. Their commitment was strengthened when the supervisors gave support to bus transportation for college students at no additional cost to the student. Progress of the junior colleges and the vast expansion in buildings and equipment would not have been possible without the support given by the boards of supervisors. It is in keeping with our appreciation for the contributions that have come to the institution because of the interest and support of the supervisors that personal testimonies of gratitude and praise have been given to them for the things they have provided. (The names of the men who have served these institutions as members of the boards of supervisors are listed in Section Four of this book.)

THE TEACHERS

This story in the beginning recognized that the teachers played star roles. The majority of the first teachers in junior colleges were teaching in the agricultural high schools. They were devoted to the purposes and objectives of these schools that had opened the door for many rural youths in the state to secure a high school education.

They were referred to in the beginning as "good teachers." This title was appropriate. The philosophy of these "good teachers" was that they were teaching individuals. They had deep concern for the intellectual and cultural development of the student. They understood the need for improvement in their capacity for understanding, discernment and sound judgment. Yet, the teachers felt a deep sense of obligation to help each individual develop his sense of social responsibility, his concern for right conduct, and the importance of being morally excellent as well as academically efficient. The teachers were sensitive to the spiritual nature of each student and felt a responsibility to contribute to his spiritual growth by example and guidance. They encouraged the student to recognize the importance of the church and the Holy Scripture. It was evident that teachers were selected not only on the basis of their academic training but also on the basis of a deep concern for right habits and Christian attitudes.

The dedication of these teachers to the public junior colleges was tested many times. The salaries remained at a low level during the greater part of this fifty-year period, and funds were not available to employ extra persons to direct the extra-curricular activities of the students on the campus, in the dormitories, and through a seven-day-week program. These duties were normal in addition to a teaching load. There are many examples of teachers assuming responsibilities that in later years, when loads were reduced, became the work of three persons. Many words of praise have been spoken by those who spent their junior college years under "good teachers." The teachers were worthy of the acclaim and commendation that they received.

Today there is a whole generation of able faculty members who are not well acquainted with extremely low salaries, inadequate facilities and equipment, long hours, and heavy loads. They are acquainted only with the times when affluence prevails. This condition should have an influence on the spirit and qualities of life that make for good teaching.

The concern for the future will be that the image of junior colleges as institutions that place emphasis on "good teaching" will not in any way diminish. This is of great importance to the future of the public junior college. "May the spirit not grow thin."

THE PRESIDENTS

As the first fifty years come to a close and the conditions and situations that have been a part of those years are observed, obviously no group has played a greater role than the presidents. Each of the original eleven district junior colleges has continued and expanded. Four other district junior colleges and one municipal college have been added. Sixty-six junior college presidents served the now existing sixteen junior colleges during the fifty-year period. (The list of the presidents is included in section four.)

The tenure of these who gave leadership to the colleges is impressive. The records show that these colleges had six hundred and thirty-seven years of operation. This would indicate an average of nine plus years for each of the sixty-six presidents. Three presidents served thirty or more years, four others twenty or more years, and eight sixteen or more years. These continuous years of service contributed much to the stability and growth and helped overcome the serious effects of the depression and the wars. Without the faith and vision of this leadership, and without an indomitable spirit, courage and determination, some of these institutions might not have survived.

THE COMMISSION

The Junior College Commission and the state board of education represent two legal bodies that have had major responsibilities in determining the characteristics and functioning of the Mississippi state system of public junior colleges.

Since the first comprehensive junior college laws of 1928, as rewritten in 1950, the Junior College Commission has been composed of the state superintendent of education, chairman; the chancellor of the University of Mississippi; the president of Mississippi State University; the president of Mississippi's university for women, and three junior college presidents selected by the Mississippi Junior College Association. House Bill 428, Chapter 352, p. 610, approved on

May 26, 1962, made two significant changes in the commission. Section two of House Bill 428 added three members, to be appointed by the governor with the advice and consent of the senate, one from each of the three supreme court districts for a six-year term with one to be appointed every two years. The qualifications of membership, as defined in the statute, require that members shall be of demonstrated industrial leadership and that they shall give emphasis to technical and vocational education. The commission has contributed much to the expansion of the technical and vocational training through leadership in coordinating the needs of industry in Mississippi with the work of the junior colleges in providing training to meet industry's needs.

The leadership in the public junior colleges feels that these changes have added strength to the commission. The relationship between the commission and the Mississippi Junior College Association, a body without legal status made up of the presidents of the public junior colleges, has been one of complete cooperation and coordination. The commission has encouraged the acceptance of the recommendations of the presidents for major changes. The commission has maintained the stability of the districts; and in its authority to fix the territorial boundaries, it has controlled the establishing of new junior colleges. The influence of the commission has been very effective in controlling the number of junior colleges established. The Mississippi state system of junior colleges, the first to be established in the nation, has grown strong because of the help of many individuals and groups. The stability and strength of public junior colleges is clearly shown through the programs and activities of the institutions now operating as a part of the state system. The eleven junior colleges established and approved by the Junior College Commission at the beginning of the state system have continued through the years, and have developed into strong district institutions with fully developed comprehensive programs. The state system, at the close of this fifty-year period, includes thirteen multicounty district junior colleges involving the eighty-two counties in Mississippi and receiving tax support from eighty-one of the counties. House Bill No. 215, passed during the regular legislative session of 1964, established junior college districts as individual and separate juristic entities and bodies politic and corporate. In addition to the thirteen district junior colleges mentioned is one municipal junior college and two junior colleges for blacks. Establishment of nine additional campuses within these districts makes a total of twenty-five campuses in operation at the end of the fifty years.

The leaders of the public junior colleges felt that the thirteen multicounty district junior colleges, with new campuses to be added within districts to meet specific needs, would provide opportunities for all college-age youths in the state. A major contributor to the common purpose of building this strong system of junior colleges has been the Junior College Commission.

THE STATE BOARD OF EDUCATION

The initial legislative act, Senate Bill No. 251, Laws of Mississippi, Regular Session of the Mississippi Legislature, approved March 24, 1922, permitting the addition of work of junior college grade to municipal separate district high schools and to an agricultural high school, stated in section four of the act, "That the state board of education shall be responsibile for the enforcement of the provisions of the act."[26] This provision identified the state board of education as an official group with responsibility relating to the growth and development of this new phase of higher education in Mississippi.

The state board of education is a constitutional body written into the constitution of the state of Mississippi, adopted November 1, 1890, Section 203, Article Eight. This section states, "There shall be a board of education consisting of the secretary of state, the attorney-general, and the superintendent of public education for the management and investment of the school funds according to law, and for the performance of such other duties as may be prescribed."[27]

The establishing of the State Commission of Junior Colleges, under the junior college law of 1928, state of Mississippi, and other legislation expanding the duties and responsibility of the State Junior College Commission, has limited the activities of the state board of education to the disbursement of appropriations for junior colleges. The junior college law, passed at the regular legislative session of 1950, states in section two regarding the junior college commission, that a responsibility of the commission is "to certify annually to the state board of education or other organization, board, agency or administration designated by law to disburse appropriations for junior colleges."[28] This constitutional body has

functioned in this capacity from the beginning of the establishment of the public junior college and has made distinct contributions as an official body to the development of the state system of public junior colleges.

In addition to the services to the state system of public junior colleges through this official body, a much greater service has been given on an individual basis by the three public officials who are the members of the state board. Each of these men, through their offices, as state superintendent of education, secretary of state, and attorney-general, in a personal way through the years, has provided leadership and services that have influenced legislation and created public approval and encouraged support for this important phase of higher education. Their services could not be replaced.

THE LAWMAKERS

The Mississippi legislature observed these college programs being developed on the campuses of some of the existing agricultural high schools. During the first six years they did not consider a designated appropriation for the junior colleges. They watched the presidents struggle to operate the programs out of the agricultural high school appropriation. With the opening of the 1928 legislative session, legislators were aware that ten junior colleges opened the 1928–1929 school session with eighty-eight students enrolled and that student enrollment was increasing rapidly year by year. The acceptance of this new phase of higher education in Mississippi was very favorable from both students and parents. The legislative bodies made the decision that a more comprehensive law was needed to expand the 1922 and the 1924 acts. Thus, the 1928 basic and more comprehensive law was passed.[29] And at the same time, $85,000 was appropriated for the junior colleges.[30] This was the beginning of direct state support for the public junior colleges in Mississippi.

The legislative bodies have kept pace with the growth and development of these institutions. They accepted what was happening to many young people graduating from high school and wanting to go to college and that the junior colleges were opening the door to many. The results achieved year by year have been sufficient to encourage state support in an increasing amount year by year. The legislature accepted with this initial appropriation the idea that the cost of operating public junior college education was a joint responsibility of both the state and the college district.

It is very satisfying to members of the house and senate to know that in some of the junior college districts seven out of ten of the high school graduates who enroll in a college program began their college work in a junior college. The Mississippi legislature expressed its interest in strengthening the public junior colleges through education study committees and consultive services provided by the state to determine future needs. Special emphasis was given in these studies to determine the financial needs of the institutions. This legislative interest encouraged state agencies and organizations to assist in studies and planning for development. Some of the agencies and organizations included in this group are the Mississippi Agricultural and Industrial Board, the Mississippi Manufacturers Association, the Mississippi Regional Development Districts, the Mississippi Economic Council, and the industrial development departments of various organizations.

Many members of the Mississippi house and senate have an understanding of the contributions that the public junior colleges are making to Mississippi's program of higher education, and they are aware that this phase of education provides the only opportunity many young people will have for education beyond the high school. When the tremendous progress that has been made in Mississippi during the given decades included in this story is recorded, it will show that because of the interest and support given to the public junior colleges these institutions have played a vital part in this progress.

Some concluding statements taken from a doctoral dissertation based on curricular changes in Mississippi public junior colleges by Emily Duncan Mathis, dated December 1971, are significant at the close of this first fifty years.

The Mississippi public junior colleges are now becoming more concerned with the increasing number of older adults who are returning to school on a part time basis. The regular expansion of occupational programs reflects its efforts to serve the community in a more meaningful capacity. Greater efforts are being made to provide curricula that will accommodate business and industry of the community, as well as private citizens.

The clientele of the junior college is varied; therefore, the programs which serve them must also be varied. Because most junior colleges operate on the "open door" policy, the need for remedial programs is great. Many of those enrolled deliberately choose a type of institution which assumes, as one of its major objectives, the education of the under-achiever. Others who have been out of school for several years choose to attend a junior college because they feel that the individualized approach to learning which characterizes these institutions will lessen the trauma of the re-entry process into a world of books and papers and "midnight oil." Some who plan to transfer to a four year college later, choose to attend a junior college for a year or two because it is less expensive and often more conveniently located. Also, free transportation is provided daily for students residing in the geographical area which the college serves. Others attend the junior college because it provides training in vocational and technical areas which are not to be found in four year colleges. And still others attend simply to improve skills, to broaden cultural experiences, or to pursue a craft or hobby. Whatever their reason for being there, such a varied clientele present a never-ending challenge to those who endeavor to meet the needs.

The success with which those needs are being met is, in part, a reflection of the far-sightedness of the junior college pioneers in Mississippi. Their tedious efforts to expand a new type of educational institution based on a solid foundation were not in vain, for what began as a foster child of the four-year college has now gained an identity of its own in the field of higher education, not only in Mississippi but around the world.

Its educational leadership is far-reaching. In addition to instructional duties the junior colleges assume, as a part of their responsibility to the communities they serve, the presentation of workshops, forums, plays, concerts, and lecture series. The quality of junior college personnel is constantly being upgraded, often at the expense of a particular junior college or the federal government under provisions of an educational act. Both administrators and faculty are utilized in consulting capacities by local schools, and often they are asked to speak at social, civic, or church functions. Their physical plants are also utilized often by both the local community and the school system.

The junior colleges of Mississippi also assume a leadership role in social and civic developments. Their activities are carefully planned to provide a variety of social experiences for young men and women whose backgrounds are largely rural and unsophisticated. Clubs and organizations are encouraged to promote programs of a civic nature and, thus, to be of service to the community. When desegregation in the public schools of Mississippi was ordered by the courts, the junior colleges were receptive to the change, and despite objections of some individuals, exerted a positive influence on the community. Very few unpleasant incidents related to desegregation have been reported in Mississippi's junior colleges.

Although the junior colleges in Mississippi seem to be somewhat slower to change than those in some other parts of the country, the changes which have occurred have been, for the most part, sound ones, and there is good reason to believe that this will continue to be true. Unfortunately, many of the changes in curriculum which have been desirable have also been impossible until recently because of limited funds. Federal monies have altered that situation considerably in the last few years, and vast expansions have become evident. Many new buildings which are the pride of administrators, have been constructed; and much new equipment, which is the panacea of faculty, has been added, thus making possible the addition and expansion of programs. Because great changes in the vocational-technical areas began occurring in the mid-fifties when the government started putting large sums of money into the programs, it can hardly be denied that the federal government has been a factor in curriculum changes.[31]

The materials provided by each junior college on information forms mailed to each junior college president provide comparative materials showing the growth and development in many areas.

The development of the physical plant at each institution is a remarkable story. This represents continuous effort from the local district and from state appropriations. The colleges have received substantial assistance from federal sources. Each of the junior colleges, with one exception, began operation in the buildings used by an existing agricultural high school, and for a period of time it was very difficult to secure funds to expand these inadequate facilities. However, step by step, these needs were met.

A tabulation of the plant values as these sixteen junior colleges began the operation of the college was approximately $2,786,000. The value of the original eleven was $1,833,000. The value of the one municipal and four agricultural high school plants which were added at later years during the fifty-year period, was $953,000. The established value of these plants at the end of fifty years is $94,493,782. Other figures that give evidence of growth relate to a number of areas. One or two individual buildings on the campus of a single junior college today represents a greater investment than the total value of all the plants on the agricultural high school campuses where the junior colleges began.

The estimated value, at the beginning years, of library books, laboratory and instructional equipment, including projection equipment for visual instruction and vocational shops for the agricultural departments, was reported at a total of approximately $135,000.[32] The value, as reported for 1972 at the end of the fifty-year period, assigned to the areas mentioned which relate to instruction is $21,000,000.[33]

These comparative figures show the remarkable progress that the Mississippi state system of public junior colleges has made in providing adequate equipment for instruction.

The number of students enrolled in the eleven institutions operating at the end of the first decade was 2,283. The number enrolled in the sixteen public junior colleges and nine branch campuses in the various districts had increased to 60,869 students at the end of the fifty-year period.[34]

The record of growth in every area of activity relating to the Mississippi state system of public junior colleges tells a part of the fifty-year story. The major contribution is not found in the objective as related to buildings and equipment, the number of students and faculty members, and other conditions which we will record in statements to follow. The real story is found year by year in the contributions made by young men and women who were encouraged and inspired as students in the junior colleges and received training and experiences that caused these students to continue their efforts toward acquiring greater capabilities in their chosen fields.

The factors in the growth and development, which are recorded as we close this fifty-year period, are a tribute to the efforts, the fixed purposes, the resolute spirit and visions of the many individuals who were a part of a determined effort to see that young men and young women were not denied an opportunity to attend college.

NOTES TO "YEARS OF GROWTH AND VISION"

1. Laws of 1928, Senate Bill 131, Chapter 303, p. 231.
2. Laws of 1964, House Bill 215, Chapter 398, pp. 577–583.
3. Ibid.
4. Laws of 1962, House Bill 597, Chapter 381, pp. 657–665.
5. Laws of 1964, House Bill 215, Chapter 398, Section 17, p. 583.
6. General Laws, Regular Session 1964, House Bill 308, Chapter 276, pp. 370–374.
7. Laws of 1966, Regular Session, Senate Bill 1967, Chapter 416, pp. 766–767.
8. Reports filed with the Division of Junior Colleges, State Department of Education.
9. Public Law 88–210, 88 Congress, H. R. 4955, Dec. 18, 1963, Voc-Ed. Act 1963.
10. Public Law 90–576, 90 Congress, H. R. 18366, October 16, 1968, Voc-Ed. Amendment 1968.
11. Laws of 1964, Regular Legislative Session 1964, Senate Bill 1587, Chapter 401, pp. 584–587.

12. Ibid.

13. Information obtained by letter from Mr. Troy Majure, Director of Division of Vocational Education, State Department of Education.

14. Ibid.

15. Laws of 1968, Senate Bill 1832, Chapter 388, p. 603, June 10, 1968.

16. Minutes of the Mississippi Junior College Association. August 24, 1964, State Division of Junior Colleges.

17. Minutes of the First Inter-Alumni Association Meeting, July 15, 1965, filed in Book of Minutes with President of the Association.

18. Ibid.

19. Knox M. Broom, "Junior College Students: Why, What, Who, and Where," *The Mississippi Educational Advance*, Vol. 38, No. 7, p. 29.

20. *The Clarion-Ledger*, January 2, 1947.

21. *History of Mississippi's Public Junior Colleges, 1928–1953*, Table 4.

22. Enrollment Reports filed in office of Division of Junior Colleges, State Department of Education.

23. Laws of 1964, Senate Bill 1846, Chapter 402, pp. 587–588.

24. General Laws of 1950, House Bill 541, Chapter 369, pp. 421–428.

25. Laws of 1964, Regular Session 1964, Senate Bill 1846, Chapter 402, pp. 587–588.

26. Laws of 1922, Regular Session, Senate Bill 251, Chapter 204, pp. 270–272.

27. The Constitution of the State of Mississippi, 1890, Mississippi Code, 1930, Volume 1.

28. Laws of 1950, Regular Session, House Bill 541, Chapter 369, pp. 421–428.

29. Laws of 1928, Regular Session, Senate Bill 131, Chapter 303, pp. 398–401.

30. Ibid., p. 231.

31. Emily Duncan Mathis, "An Historical Study of Curricular Changes in Selected Public Junior Colleges in Mississippi," (Ph.D. dissertation, University of Tennessee, 1971), pp. 94–96.

32. Information Blanks received from each Junior College President.

33. Ibid.

34. Enrollment Report supplied by the Central Office of the State Division of Junior Colleges, State Department of Education.

THE INDIVIDUAL INSTITUTIONS

Organizers and Builders

The presidents of the Mississippi public junior colleges, as members of the Mississippi Junior College Association, under the leadership of Knox M. Broom, expressed an interest in paying tribute to sixteen beginning junior college presidents who were identified as the "organizers and builders" of Mississippi's public junior colleges. These men organized and developed the eleven original multicounty junior colleges and the one municipal junior college located in the Meridian separate school district.

Fifteen of these men were superintendents of an agricultural high school prior to assuming the responsibility as head of a public junior college. One was superintendent of the Meridian separate school district. Reflection on the influences responsible for the eleven agricultural high schools to establish a public junior college suggests that the superintendents deserve much credit.

Testimonies from educational leaders, students, and trustees during these early years identify these sixteen men as leaders and organizers and forward-looking, dynamic individuals. The leadership of some of these men is unquestionable as we recall the contributions made in other areas of public service. One became the state superintendent of education in Mississippi, another was elected to the Congress of the United States, one was a state senator, and others made contributions to various fields of public service. One became president of a senior college in the state, and one, who was in the state department of education

prior to becoming a junior college president, wrote the early laws authorizing the establishing of junior colleges.

I quote some statements copied from tape recordings regarding these men:

"He was quite a leader, a dynamic individual and very persuasive."

"One of the most remarkable men I have known in Mississippi and one of the most capable leaders."

"An excellent planner and one that might be called an organizer."

"From the point of view of finances, this man was one of the best managers in the schools of Mississippi."

"One of the outstanding developers of Mississippi's education, contributed much toward the passage of needed legislation, a man of good judgment, and never failed to do more than his share of the work."

"A man to whom education was his life, and one who gave great attention to details."

A general statement was, "If you are interested in information on Mississippi education, this is the man to talk to."

A look at these eleven agricultural high schools that originally added junior college work identifies them as among the strongest agricultural high schools in the state. The dormitories and administration buildings were of brick construction, and each institution owned a large tract of land. The amount owned by each institution ranged from 200 to 900 acres. The eleven institutions own, as of this date, 5,500 acres. These leaders were aware that a most important factor in the success of a junior college was multicounty support based on assessed valuations and an adequate number of high school graduates within the adjoining counties.

Each of the sixteen public junior colleges in Mississippi, as previously stated, began on an existing agricultural high school campus, with the exception of the Meridian Municipal Public Junior College, which was organized in accordance with the original law in the Meridian Separate School District. Even though the original law provided for municipalities with a population of 10,000 or more to establish a public junior college, this was the only city to implement this phase of the law.

No additional junior colleges were added to the Mississippi state system until the middle of the third decade. Four additional agricultural high schools established junior colleges during the latter part of the third decade and the beginning of the fourth. Two were established for white students and two for black students. Two of these opened at the beginning of the 1948–1949 school session, one at the beginning of the 1949–1950 school session, and the other with the 1954–1955 school session.

The pages to follow will include photographs and biographical sketches of the sixteen men who were identified by the membership of the Mississippi Junior College Association as the "organizers and builders" of the Mississippi public junior colleges.

JAMES ANDREW HUFF

James Andrew Huff was born in Jasper County, Mississippi, on July 22, 1868. He was the son of Philip and Frances (Duckworth) Huff and was the youngest of a family of nine children, which consisted of four boys and five girls. His father was a native of Georgia and his mother a native of South Carolina. The father was a prosperous farmer and was the son of William Huff, a native of Virginia.

James Huff received his early education in a private school and afterward completed a course in the high school at Sylvarena, Smith County, Mississippi, known as Sylvarena Academy, which was a tuition supported school established by William Harris Hardy in 1856. This school served Sylvarena until 1907 when a public school was established. The academy became a high school in 1886. His college training, which qualified him for the teaching profession, was at Mississippi A. & M. College, the University of Mississippi, and the University of Illinois.

After finishing his undergraduate degree, he took a six-year correspondence course in education.

His first teaching appointment was as an assistant at Sylvarena Academy. From 1892 until 1896, James Huff served as county superintendent of education of Smith County at a salary of $18 per month. From 1896 until 1898, he was principal of the Raleigh High School in Raleigh, Mississippi. In 1898, he was made superintendent of schools in Forest, Mississippi, and remained in that position until 1912. From 1903 until 1916, Mr. Huff was engaged in institute and normal work under the state department of education. In 1912, he accepted a position as superintendent of the Harrison-Stone County Agricultural High School at Perkinston, Mississippi, and remained until 1917.

JAMES ANDREW HUFF

In 1917, James A. Huff went to Pearl River County Agricultural High School as superintendent. While there he was instrumental in helping to organize Pearl River Junior College, and served as its first president from 1922 until 1926. He was well suited for the job at the agricultural high school and junior college, as he possessed executive force, a comprehensive understanding of educational affairs, and was very successful in the vocation he had chosen.

On September 16, 1891, James Andrew Huff was married to Miss Julia May McCurdy, a daughter of Captain and Mrs. William McCurdy of Claiborne, Jasper County, Mississippi. Captain McCurdy had served as an officer in the Confederate Army during the Civil War. Five children were born to Mr. and Mrs. Huff: James Hatton, Lillian May, Howard Payne, John Charles, and Virginia McCurdy. Mrs. Julia McCurdy Huff died in June 1927. In March 1929, James Huff married Emma Lucille Paige of Covington, Louisiana. One daughter, Jimmie Lucille, was born to this union.

During World War I, Mr. Huff acted as food dispenser of Pearl River County and also sold Liberty Bonds. He also found time for civic affairs and served as both mayor and alderman at Forest and as alderman at Poplarville. Mr. Huff took a deep interest in politics and was an influential figure in the ranks of the Democratic party.

Mr. Huff was an active member of the Baptist Church and devoted much time to church work, serving as a deacon and as a teacher in the Sunday School. He was an active member of the Poplarville Chamber of Commerce and the Parent-Teacher Association. He was a Royal Arch Mason and while living in Forest served as Master of the Lodge and High Priest of the chapter. He was also a member of the Woodmen of the World and the Knights of Pythias. He served for a period of time as superintendent of Pearl River County Hospital.

James Andrew Huff died on June 24, 1931, but he has long been remembered for his work as an educator, which was of great value to his county and state, and his life was an inspiring example of good citizenship to all who knew him.

ROBERT EDWARD LEE SUTHERLAND

Robert Edward Lee Sutherland was born at Booneville, Prentiss County, Mississippi, on May 1, 1878. His parents were Dr. W. W. and Annie Naomi (Nelson) Sutherland.

He was reared and received his early education in Prentiss County and was graduated from Booneville High School. He received his higher education at Peabody College in Nashville, Tennessee, where he received a Normal Degree in 1905, a Bachelor of Science in 1929, and a Master of Arts in 1930.

R. E. L. Sutherland was married to Ollie Wallace on October 16, 1910. Three daughters were born to this union—(Bolivar Lee) Mrs. Kenneth B. Hait of Lafayette, Louisiana, an assistant professor of English at USL; Miriam, teacher of history in Baldwyn High School, Baldwyn, Mississippi; and (Annette) Mrs. James Boutwell, in public relations, Raleigh, North Carolina.

Mr. Sutherland was actively engaged as an educator in Mississippi for over fifty years. Beginning as a teacher of a one-room school, he taught at Pisgah High School 1905–1906 and Wheeler High School 1906–1908. He served two terms as Prentiss County Superintendent of Education, 1908–1916, after which he was superintendent of Alcorn County Agricultural High School at Kossuth, 1917–1919. During this time he served a four-year term as a member of the Mississippi legislature, 1918–1922, and served as chairman of its education committee.

In 1917, Mr. Sutherland moved to Raymond, Mississippi, after his appointment to the faculty of the Smith-Hughes High School, later known as Hinds Agricultural High School. Under his guidance the school became Hinds Junior College, one of the first junior colleges in the state, and, in 1926, was the first to gain accreditation by the Southern Association. For the next thirteen years, Mr. Sutherland was a dedicated leader of the junior college movement in Mississippi.

In 1930, Mr. Sutherland left Raymond and went to Columbus, where he was president of Mississippi State College for Women from 1930 to 1932. At this time he also served as a member of the board of trustees for Mississippi State Teachers College in Hattiesburg. In 1932 he went to Wheeler High School where he served as superintendent until 1934. From 1934 to 1937, he was a district supervisor of adult education in Tupelo, Mississippi.

Mr. Sutherland was again involved in junior college work when he was elected president of Pearl River Junior College at Poplarville, Mississippi, where he served from 1937 to 1942, when he retired. Later, however, he returned to Prentiss County where he served his third term as Superintendent of Education of Prentiss County, 1948–1952. In 1952 R. E. L. Sutherland again retired. He was honored at this time in a special ceremony by the state department of

ROBERT EDWARD LEE SUTHERLAND

JEFFERSON LEE DENSON

education for his fifty years as an educator. He remained in his native county until his death in 1961.

Mr. Sutherland was a member of the National Education Association, the Mississippi Education Association, and Kappa Delta Pi. He was listed in *Who's Who of America* in 1936 and in *Leaders in Education* in 1941.

JEFFERSON LEE DENSON

Jefferson Lee Denson was born at Lake Como, Mississippi, in 1889, the son of Ernest Absalom Denson and Janie Thigpen Denson. The family later moved to Olah, Mississippi, where his father then taught school. His father finished medical school and practiced in Gitano, Mississippi, from 1897 until 1900. They moved to Soso in 1900 where Lee lived on a farm as a country doctor's son.

In 1908 Lee Denson entered Clarke Memorial College at Newton, Mississippi, and received his B.S. degree from State Teachers College in 1912. He did

graduate work at the University of Colorado. In the meantime, his family—parents, two brothers, and three sisters—moved to Bay Springs in 1910 and to Agricola in 1912.

At this time Agricola had a one-room school, which operated only five months each year. When Lee got home after finishing college, he personally scouted around and found enough pupils for two teachers. Miss Zona Dean, a local girl, taught through the sixth grade in the old school house, and Lee taught the seventh, eighth, and ninth grades in the church building nearby. While teaching under this arrangement for two years, he created enough interest in the community to build a larger school. So, in 1914, by personally supervising the carpentry work himself and wielding the hammer and saw, by September he had a new school building with six classrooms and an auditorium. However, Lee was interested in a larger school, so he moved to Rocky Creek as principal and teacher during 1914–1915.

In 1915–1916 he moved to College Hill where he

taught and coached in Lafayette County Agricultural High School. Mr. M. P. Bush, a friend whom Lee had known at Clarke Memorial College, was head of this school. This friendship and professional association led to what later became a factor in the junior college development in Mississippi.

In the fall of 1916, Lee Denson went to Lucedale High School, where he was teacher and principal from 1916 until 1922. In 1922 he became head of the Wilkerson County Agricultural High School at Woodville, Mississippi, where he remained for two years (1922–1924).

In 1924 he went to Perkinston, Mississippi, as superintendent of Harrison-Stone-Jackson Agricultural High School. Through his efforts the junior college division was added to the high school in 1925, and in 1926 Perkinston became the Harrison-Stone-Jackson Agricultural High School and Junior College. As president (1925–1929), he initiated a building program that resulted in the construction of two dormitories, an administration building with classrooms and auditorium, a gymnasium (the first in this area of the state) and a president's home. These programs were apparently financed by the board's signing bank notes for six-month periods and repaying them from whatever revenues remained as a balance at the end of the year.

Mr. Denson was described as a progressive educator, with a vision for the future of the school that most people did not understand. He had abundant energy and enthusiasm and spent a great part of his time recruiting students and faculty. Students apparently held him in high esteem even though he was a strong disciplinarian.

In 1929 Lee Denson left the teaching profession to go into the life insurance business. He was very successful in the insurance business until his death in 1954. He died of a heart attack while on a fishing trip on the Pascagoula River.

While teaching at Agricola, Mississippi, Lee Denson married Mamie Ward. They were the parents of two sons and three daughters: Curtis Lee, who is an electrical engineer with Mississippi Power Company in New Orleans, Louisiana; Charles, who is with American National Insurance in Galveston, Texas; Jane Covington, who teaches at Noxapater, Mississippi; Corinne King, who lives in Hurley, Mississippi, and teaches in Mobile, Alabama; and Rose Nell Kander, who lives in Alamo, California.

MARVIN EUGENE MOREHEAD

Marvin Eugene Morehead was born in Panola County, Mississippi, on June 23, 1875, the son of the Rev. H. C. and Eliza (Fowler) Morehead, both natives of Mississippi. The father was a Methodist minister, who began preaching at the age of nineteen and devoted the active years of his life to service as a minister of his church. He died at the age of seventy and had served as a presiding elder for about sixteen years. His wife died when thirty-five years of age. Mr. Morehead's paternal ancestors were Scotch-Irish, and his paternal grandfather came from North Carolina. His maternal grandfather came from Scotland. Besides Marvin Eugene, the following children were born to his parents: Stella, Mabel, Gertrude, Lucille, Nina, Ernest, and Perry.

Marvin Eugene Morehead attended Grenada College and later Southern University at Greensboro, Alabama, receiving from the latter institution the degree of A. B. and graduating with the class of 1894.

Mr. Morehead began his life work as principal and teacher at the Carrville High School in Carrville, Mississippi, 1895–1902. He then became principal of the high school in Lumberton, Mississippi, where he remained for ten years, 1902–1912. Mr. Morehead then organized Panola County Agricultural High School at Courtland, of which he became superintendent, and remained for twelve years, 1912–1923. In June 1923, he became superintendent of Holmes County Agricultural High School at Goodman, Mississippi, and served in this position until 1925. In 1925 Marvin Eugene Morehead was instrumental in organizing Holmes County Junior College and served as president of Holmes County Agricultural High School and Junior College from 1925 until 1928.

Mr. Morehead then went to the state department of education where he served as assistant state superintendent of education from 1928 to 1936. He then became assistant county superintendent of education in Hinds County and remained in this position from 1936 to 1953. While there he served under three elected county superintendents—T. H. Naylor, C. H. Snell, and Robert Mayo. Mr. T. H. Naylor and Mr. C. H. Snell resigned prior to completing an elected term, and M. E. Morehead was acting county superintendent in each case until an election could be called. During the years he served as Assistant County Superintendent of Education of Hinds County, he

61

MARVIN EUGENE MOREHEAD

made a distinct contribution to the control and use of sixteenth section land.

Mr. Morehead was an active member of the Methodist Episcopal Church, South, belonging to its board of stewards and serving as superintendent of the Sunday School and as teacher. He was affiliated with the Masonic Order, the Knights of Pythias, and the Woodmen of the World. He also belonged to Alpha Tau Omega of Southern University. He was a member of the Mississippi Education Association, the National Education Association, the State Textbook Commission for eight years, and the "Committee of Five" appointed to arrange a course of study for Mississippi agricultural high schools. He served as president of the department of high schools in the Mississippi Education Commission and served for four years as a member of the committee on agricultural high school legislation.

Mr. Morehead owned and operated a farm consisting of nine hundred acres two miles from the town of Courtland, in Panola County, where he had a valuable pecan grove, raised livestock, and carried on diversified and progressive farming.

On February 6, 1898, Marvin Eugene Morehead was married to Miss Blanche Pou, daughter of Dr. J. G. Pou of Courtland, Mississippi. They were the parents of five children: Mildred, Virgil P., Helen Elise, Marion, and Marvin.

Marvin Eugene Morehead died in December 1953. His entire active life was devoted to the profession of teaching and serving as assistant state superintendent of education and assistant county superintendent of education. At one time, he possessed the distinction of having served longer as an agricultural high school superintendent than any other man in Mississippi.

JOSEPH SLOAN VANDIVER

Joseph Sloan Vandiver was born on February 1, 1879, in Toccoa, Stephens County, Georgia, the son of George Albert Calloway and Julia Ann (Ledbetter) Vandiver. He was the middle child of five in his family, with one brother and one sister older, and one of each younger. In 1881, the family moved to a farm near the town of Baldwyn, and the village of Wheeler, Prentiss County, in Northeast Mississippi.

Sloan Vandiver started school at Old Asbury School, located in the Asbury Methodist Church, in rural Prentiss County in 1884, when he was five years old. Thirteen years later, when a boy of eighteen, he began his public school teaching career at the same old school, in the same old church, while he himself still had not completed high school. The school year was four months—two in midwinter, and two in summer, after the cotton had been "laid by" and before September picking demanded the hands of school children. In his first teaching job, he earned no less than $22.25 a month and no more than $27.25 per month, the variation depending on the size of enrollment.

Along with teaching, he completed his own high school training, graduating from Baldwyn High School in 1898 or 1899. He mixed teaching and school attendance for many years, as others of his time did; and for more than three decades he attended, in summers and as he could, teacher normal training institutes and colleges, starting about 1900 at the famous Iuka Normal Institute.

When J. Sloan Vandiver finished high school, he left Asbury to teach in what was, at that time, still a one-teacher school in Rienzi, Alcorn County, Missis-

JOSEPH SLOAN VANDIVER

sippi. In 1903, he moved to Nettleton, Mississippi, on the line between Lee and Monroe Counties, to be principal and teacher in the elementary through high school, in his first multiteacher school.

In Nettleton, he boarded in a home in Monroe County. Directly across the street, in Lee County, lived a high school student, Laura Blanche Feemster, whom he met, wooed, and married in December 1904, a year after she had finished high school. Mrs. Vandiver taught school with her husband for a number of years and contributed much to his success.

In the fall of 1908, the Vandivers moved to Ackerman, Mississippi, where Mr. Vandiver was the superintendent of the schools. They remained in Ackerman until about 1914. Sloan Vandiver then moved to head the schools of the larger town of New Albany, Mississippi. An enthusiastic reorganization of the school system in that town, following the accomplishments of Ackerman, brought wide recognition to Mr. Vandiver, which led to his selection in 1916 by the General Educational Board, an educational

philanthropic foundation with headquarters in New York City, as director of its program to establish in Pearl River County, Mississippi, a model school program on a countywide basis to serve as an example of a system designed to meet the needs of a highly rural and economically handicapped southern county.

In September 1918, after having set up this model program, Mr. Vandiver moved to Moorhead as superintendent of Sunflower County Agricultural High School, which later expanded into a junior college under his presidency. He remained at the head of Sunflower County Agricultural High School and Junior College for eighteen years, and had a tremendous influence in the educational life of Mississippi through his great work there.

During the years at Moorhead, Mr. and Mrs. Vandiver became the parents of two children—a son, Joseph S. Vandiver, Jr., and a daughter, Margaret Feemster Vandiver.

During his teaching years, J. Sloan Vandiver kept studying. He attended summer sessions at the University of Mississippi, Mississippi State, University of Chicago, and the University of Alabama and received his B. A. degree from Mississippi College in 1929 or 1930. Southwestern University in Memphis, Tennessee, conferred upon him the honorary degree of Doctor of Education in 1947, a title he bore with great dignity and honor, and which was perhaps his most cherished honor.

The political aspect of establishing public junior college education in the relatively resistant Mississippi Delta, plus the grass-roots concern which arose from these continuing recruitment visits, contributed to Sloan Vandiver's decision to seek state office. In 1936, he became the holder of the highest elective office in public education in Mississippi—state superintendent of education—a position he held until July 15, 1945. These nine years were most fruitful in the educational progress of Mississippi. He exerted a great influence in the educational affairs of the state. His philosophy of education was sound, his honesty was unquestioned, and his educational leadership bore the marks of statesmanship. His energy, interest, and ability were all centered upon the promotion and development of a great program of education.

In 1945, after serving for one year of a third term, Mr. Vandiver resigned as state superintendent of education to accept the presidency of Chamberlain-Hunt Academy, at Port Gibson, Mississippi, a private boys' school owned by the Presbyterian Church. The institution was at a low ebb at the time J. S. Vandiver took over as president, and great progress was accomplished at Chamberlain-Hunt Academy under his guidance. He remained in this position until his death on February 28, 1950.

Mr. Vandiver was active in the Mississippi Education Association, which he served as the forty-first president, and was also active in the Mississippi Junior College Association and the National Education Association. He enjoyed his membership in the various civic clubs of the towns in which he lived, having had membership in most of them, and belonged to the Rotary, Kiwanis, and Lions Club. He was a Knight of Pythias and a member of the Masonic Lodge. He was a very active and devoted member of the Presbyterian Church, where he taught a men's Bible class and was an elder, having been made an elder in the church at the early age of twenty-eight.

Joseph Sloan Vandiver's first, last, and continuous desire was to improve the educational program of Mississippi to provide maximum opportunities for "all the boys and girls in Mississippi." To this end he concentrated his thoughts, his efforts, and the active years of his life.

PORTER WALKER BERRY

Throughout his life Porter Walker Berry was a student and a worker, and the record of his career is a story of continuous progress that took him at length to a position of prominence in educational circles of Northern Mississippi as superintendent of the Tate County Agricultural High School. He was born on January 28, 1877, in Baldwyn, Mississippi; and his parents, J. S. and Margaret Henrietta (Walker) Berry, were also natives of this state. He was a descendant of the Berrys who founded Blue Mountain College for Women.

A liberal education prepared Porter Walker Berry for his vocation. He was first a pupil in the public schools of Baldwyn and next attended Blue Mountain College. He afterward entered Mississippi College, from which he won the B. S. degree in 1901; and during the summer terms of 1902 and 1903 he was also a student at that institution, which awarded him the M. A. degree. He had worked his way through college doing odd jobs, waiting tables and working in the school office. In 1907 and 1908 he attended the sum-

PORTER WALKER BERRY

mer school of the University of Chicago and also completed a correspondence course in the winter of 1908.

Mr. Berry began his professional career in 1901 as principal of the Hickory Public School, with which he was connected for two years, and then became superintendent of the public schools of Ackerman, filling that position for three years. For some time he was a member of the faculty of Mississippi College, having charge of the preparatory department for a year, and for six years was assistant professor of mathematics and instructor in physics. He left that instituion to assume the duties of superintendent of the Madison County Agricultural High School, which for eight years had the benefit of his services, and in 1921 went to Senatobia as superintendent of the Tate County Agricultural High School. It was established in 1915 and is situated on the Jefferson Davis Highway, a half mile north of Senatobia and thirty-seven miles from Memphis, Tennessee. The property comprised eighty acres of land, on which four substantial buildings were erected.

Professor Berry introduced many improvements in the management of the school, and under his expert direction it reached a high standard of excellence, ranking with the best in the state. He has been called the Father of Northwest Junior College.

He was an educator of broad experience and was local director of the Mississippi Normal College for three years, director of the Tri-County Normal at Camden, Mississippi, instructor in normal work in Holmes and Tallahatchie Counties and director of the Tate County Normal School in the summer of 1923. He was a practical agriculturist and owned a productive, well-improved farm, which used modern, scientific methods and progressive ideas.

At Ackerman, Mississippi, on July 18, 1906, Porter Berry married Miss Margaret Lucas, a daughter of John and Margaret Lucas of French Camp, Mississippi. To this union was born one child, Charles Torbert Berry.

Mr. Berry was a zealous member of the Baptist Church, where he served as a deacon and taught in the Sunday School. At one time, for several years, he was manager of the Madison County Fair, also acting as one of the directors of the Madison County Chamber of Commerce. During World War I he was district manager for all of the drives in operation at that time. He was a member of the state and national education associations. He was also connected with the Knights of Pythias.

The consensus of public opinion names Professor Berry with the most progressive educators of Mississippi in his time, and his life was devoted to good citizenship.

His death came on Friday, October 4, 1935.

MILLARD PERRY BUSH

As time records the history of Jones County Agricultural High School and Junior College it will retain the memory of a giant figure of a man whose able hands guided it through many years. The man was Millard Perry Bush, who officially headed the school from 1923 until 1940, and made his presence felt on the college level throughout the South.

Millard Perry Bush was born in Laurel, Mississippi, on June 25, 1871, of Scotch ancestry, and represents one of the pioneer families of the locality. His parents were Jefferson J. and Susan (Mathews) Bush, the

MILLARD PERRY BUSH

former born in Georgia and died in December 1913. The father was an honored veteran of the Civil War, in which he served for four years as a member of the English Mississippi Regiment, and in times of peace followed agricultural pursuits. He was a son of Harrison Bush, a native of Georgia, who came to Jones County, Mississippi, in 1844.

Mr. Bush attended the rural schools of his native county and the Laurel High School, afterward matriculating in the Mississippi State Normal College, Houston, Mississippi, from which he was graduated in June 1897, receiving the B. S. degree. At State Normal in Houston he roomed with the late and beloved Judge Joe Pack. He taught for three years in the Eucutta High School and for a similar period was an instructor in the Lockhart Male and Female Institute at Lockhart, Lauderdale County, Mississippi. For a year he was a teacher in Handsboro High School and then accepted a position in the Laurel High School, with which he was connected for five years. He next became identified with the Clarke Memorial College at Newton, where he remained for four years, acting first as professor of mathemetics and later as president of that institution. While he was there the state department of education began the task of striving for agricultural high schools in Mississippi. Under the banner of the state department the young educator was sent to Lafayette County where he sold the idea of the school. He accepted the job of superintendent, built the school at College Hill, and remained there from 1912 until 1922.

In July, 1923, M. P. Bush went to the Jones County Agricultural High School as superintendent. The progress of the school and the immense program it offered to students of the eight-county area it serves is a matter of record. Mr. Bush was resourceful in meeting the various problems that arose in connection with its conduct and thoroughly understood the needs of the pupils, while he also had the necessary executive force. He kept in touch with the most advanced educational thought of the day, and under his progressive regime the standard of scholarship was raised and better equipment and facilities secured for the institution.

M. P. Bush served in the Mississippi state senate from 1936 to 1940. His purpose in seeking to serve in the state senate was to promote legislation needed to improve the state's educational system. He had great interest (as president of Jones County Junior College) in the public junior colleges and all phases of higher education. Yet his public statements were that the greatest educational need at the time he was serving was to improve the common schools in the state. His major effort was for better salaries to upgrade the educational level of teachers. He worked diligently for free textbooks for all elementary and secondary students. This legislation was passed during the 1940 legislative session.

At Enterprise, Mississippi, on June 28, 1899, Mr. Bush was married to Miss Eugenia Mundell. He met her when they were both teaching at Eucutta Normal College. At that time he was head of the school, and his bride was teaching music. Mrs. Bush, born and reared at Enterprise, was the daughter of W. W. and Annie (West) Mundell. W. W. Mundell was the engineer who surveyed the G. M. & O. Railroad from Meridian to Mobile and later saw to the maintenance of that line from Tennessee to Mobile. Mr. and Mrs. Bush reared three sons, Millard Mundell, Eugene

Austin, and W. D. The eldest son, Millard Mundell Bush, is no longer living. The two other sons, Dr. Eugene Bush and W. D. Bush, both live in Laurel.

W. D. Bush, youngest of the trio of Bush sons, who makes his home on Euclid Avenue in Laurel, near the site of his father's birthplace, says that when they moved to Ellisville the family lived upstairs in the girls' dormitory, later moving downstairs and living there until the new house of the president was completed.

Mr. and Mrs. Bush left Ellisville in 1940 and went to Columbia where Mr. Bush headed the training school. They remained in Columbia until 1946 when they returned to Jones County and lived out their lives in the home of their son, Dr. Eugene Bush of Laurel.

Mr. Bush was affiliated with the Baptist Church. He belonged to the Lodge, chapter and council in Masonry and was identified with the Independent Order of Odd Fellows, the Knights of Pythias, and the Woodmen of the World. He was a charter member of the Ellisville Rotary Club and served as its second president. He was a member of the Mississippi Education Association and served as vice president during 1936–1937, and as president during the fifty-third year, 1937–1938. He was also a member of the National Education Association Advisory Committee.

M. P. Bush earned the right to classification with Mississippi's leading educators, and his life's record is the story of one whose talents were used for the benefit of his state and the improvement of its system of public schools.

Students who attended school at Jones County Agricultural High School and Jones County Junior College during those years when Mr. M. P. Bush served as administrator of its affairs will never forget him. Standing on the corner of the stage in the mornings for assembly he would make his announcements, introduce the program and, when all was concluded, stand erect, draw his fingers slowly across his nose, and pointing to the rear of the auditorium pronounce the words "junior high, pass out." That was Millard Perry Bush, who served as a teacher in the common schools of the state for a total of fifty-six years, a personality which will forever color the history of Jones County Junior College at Ellisville, Mississippi.

JAMES DAVID WALLACE

James David Wallace was born on February 14, 1868 in Carroll County, Mississippi, near the town of

JAMES DAVID WALLACE

Coila. He was the eldest son of the eight children born to Asa Thomas Wallace, farmer and cavalry captain in the Confederate Army, and Helen Mariah Beck Wallace.

In 1873 at the age of five, James Wallace entered the free schools of the county and attended a few months each year until he was twenty-one. The course of study consisted of the elementary subjects and most high school branches as offered today. Upon completion of the common free school requirements, he was granted a teaching license and taught in two one-teacher schools before entering Lexington Normal College in Lexington, Holmes County, Mississippi.

In September 1890, accompanied by his younger brother, J. T. Wallace, J. D. Wallace began three years work at Lexington Normal College. The faculty, under Professor L. T. Dickey, had been trained in northern universities and were far in advance of teachers in other southern colleges at that time. The course of study was comprehensive and divided into classical, scientific, business and teacher preparatory

subject matter. The last group included grammar, rhetoric, mathematics, history, geography, government, physiology, philosophy, educational theory, and school business. He graduated in 1893, having earned a B. A. and a B. S. degree.

In 1896 J. D. Wallace began work at the University of Mississippi, spending summers in residence and taking correspondence courses during the regular teaching terms. He was allowed fifty points earned at Lexington College out of seventy required for a bachelor's degree at the University. He was granted a B. A. degree in 1902 and M. A. degree in 1910. He spent the summer term of 1916 at the University of Chicago taking courses in philosophy. During the summer of 1931 he attended the University of North Carolina and completed a course in college administration.

In November 1897 James David Wallace was married to Miss Mattie Lee Rogers. Four children were born to this union. They were: James David Wallace, Jr., W. Edward Wallace, Mrs. Ruth Wallace Baxter, and Mrs. Marian Wallace Alexander.

In January 1889 James David Wallace began a teaching career that lasted fifty years, from one-teacher schools in Carroll County to superintendency of high school systems throughout the state, and retired from the presidency of a state junior college in July 1949. His first teaching work was at Old Salem in Carroll County. He also taught in other county schools during the summer months while attending Lexington College. After completing college at Lexington, beginning in 1894, he taught for the next four years with his brother J. T. Wallace at Louisville, Braxton, and Brooksville.

Beginning in 1898, J. D. Wallace served as superintendent of various school systems in the state, including Gloster, Summit, Fayette, Woodville, Ackerman, and Union. From 1921 to 1923 he was vice president of Clarke College in Newton. In July 1923 he was elected superintendent of Kemper County Agricultural High School at Scooba. In 1928 J. D. Wallace was instrumental in helping to develop Kemper County Agricultural High School into East Mississippi Junior College.

During the sixteen years, from 1923 to 1939, that J. D. Wallace served as superintendent of the agricultural high school at Scooba and as president of the junior college, many noticeable improvements were made. New buildings were added and old ones replaced, new furniture was installed, walkways were added and the school property was fenced. Complete scholastic and financial records were established, all debts were paid, and a substantial capital surplus was created. The faculty was increased from seven to twenty-four, high school pupils increased from sixty-seven to one hundred and sixty-seven, and the college enrollment to two hundred students. The high school system was raised to All Southern rating and the college department to approval by the State and National Associations of Junior Colleges.

In 1940 James David Wallace retired from the work he loved so well. He spent his retirement years in Clinton, Mississippi, until his death on June 29, 1949.

He had been a valued and respected leader in the communities in which he lived, a man of integrity who practiced high moral and ethical principles. He was a dedicated member of the Baptist Church where he served as a deacon, and was a Mason. J. D. Wallace was a Christian example and an inspiration to his family, friends, pupils, and those who worked with him. He was a member of various civic and educational organizations through the years. He served as president of the Bank of Clinton and as a member of the board of directors of the Deposit Guaranty Bank in Jackson.

The yearbook of East Mississippi Junior College, "The Lion," was dedicated to the outgoing president, James David Wallace, in 1939, and said of him, "Whatever this institution may become, it would never have existed as a junior college, had it not been for the untiring efforts and unconquerable will of President Wallace."

LAWRENCE RUSSELL ELLZEY

Lawrence Russell Ellzey was born on a farm near Wesson, Copiah County, Mississippi, on March 20, 1891. He was one of four children born to W. Jud and Alice (McPherson) Ellzey. His mother died when he was only seven years old. His father then took Russell and his three sisters and moved to another farm three miles west of Wesson where Russell was reared. His father was later married to Lizie Dupree.

Russell's early education was obtained in the rural schools in Copiah and Lincoln Counties. He first attended a one-teacher school, Ellzey Line School, then his father sent him and his oldest sister for three years to a three-teacher school by the name of Grange Hall. Next, he attended Mt. Zion High School where

LAWRENCE RUSSELL ELLZEY

he graduated. He then attended Mississippi College at Clinton, Mississippi, and was graduated with an A. B. degree in 1912.

Russell Ellzey's first teaching experience was at Auburn High School, a rural high school in Lincoln County, where he taught for three years, 1912–1915. He was then named assistant to the superintendent of the newly established Copiah-Lincoln Agricultural High School at Wesson, Mississippi, his home town. While there he was in charge of the dormitories, he served as coach of all athletics, and he also taught mathematics and Latin, from 1915 to 1917.

Soon after the close of these two years spent at Copiah-Lincoln Agricultural High School, Russell Ellzey enlisted in the army and served in World War I for eighteen months in this country and in France, from 1917 until 1919. After his discharge from the army, he was elected as county superintendent of education in Lincoln County, where he served for two and one-half years, 1920–1922, until he was asked to become superintendent of Copiah-Lincoln Agricultural High School in Wesson. While he was serving in this capacity, it seemed necessary for Copiah-Lincoln to add two college years to the course of study. This was done in 1928, and Russell Ellzey became the first president of Copiah-Lincoln Junior College. He remained in this position until 1932 when he resigned to enter politics. He was elected as representative of what was then the Seventh Judicial District of Congress. As a member of Congress for about three years, he actively supported legislation favorable to public schools. He introduced a bill for $90,000,000 for public schools and was coauthor of the George-Ellzey Vocational Act. He was also very much interested both in promoting appropriations for the National Park at Vicksburg, Mississippi and in all farm legislation.

In 1935, Russell Ellzey became a life insurance agent with Lamar Life Insurance Company in Jackson, Mississippi and remained with this firm until his retirement.

Russell Ellzey was married to Mrs. Edwina Hagaman of Jackson, Mississippi. He is the father of one son, Dr. Clyde Lawrence Ellzey of New Orleans, Louisiana.

He is a member of the Presbyterian Church, the Jackson Touchdown Club, the American Legion, and the Central Mississippi Rose Society.

ROSCOE CONKLING PUGH

Roscoe Conkling Pugh was born on January 22, 1884, in Jasper County, Mississippi, five miles west of Paulding, on a farm which was also the birthplace of his father, J. S. Pugh. His grandfather, William W. Pugh, was a native of Alabama and was of English ancestry. His mother, Mary (Graham) Pugh, was born near Mossville, Mississippi, and her father was William Graham. Roscoe was one of twelve children.

He attended the free schools of his native county and worked hard for his education. He assisted his father in the cultivation of the home farm, early gaining a practical knowledge of agricultural pursuits. He was a pupil in the Rose Hill High School and in 1907 graduated from the Mississippi Conference Training School at Montrose, Mississippi. He next enrolled as a student in Millsaps College and in June 1910 received his A. B. degree. He later earned his M. A. degree from the University of Mississippi and did further graduate study at George Peabody College, Nashville, Tennessee.

ROSCOE CONKLING PUGH

Roscoe Pugh immediately began his teaching career upon graduation from college in 1910, for in September of that year he became a teacher in the high school at Montrose, remaining there for six sessions. In 1916 he went to Decatur as superintendent of the Newton County Agricultural High School, of which he had charge for six years. His able work won for him much favorable attention and led to his selection for the position of superintendent of the Newton Public School in 1922. In 1924 he accepted the position of superintendent of Scott County Agricultural High School at Harperville, Mississippi, where he remained until 1926. He then went to Newton County Agricultural High School at Decatur where he served as superintendent. While serving in this position he played a major role in the organization of East Central Junior College at Decatur and was president of that institution from its founding in 1928 until 1934.

In 1936 Roscoe Pugh assumed the presidency of Northwest Junior College at Senatobia, Mississippi, and continued in that position until his retirement in

1953. He always discharged his duties with characteristic efficiency and thoroughness and exerted his influence to improve school facilities and equipment, holding to the highest standards of service in his professional activities.

In Montrose, Mississippi, on July 20, 1916, Mr. Pugh was married to Miss Eva Alice Alexander, a native of that place and a daughter of C. W. and Alice (Bayless) Alexander. Mrs. Pugh's father's ancestors came from Mecklenburg County, North Carolina, and some of them may have signed the Mecklenburg Declaration of Independence. Mr. and Mrs. Pugh were the parents of three daughters: Mary Charles, who died at the age of fifteen months; Carolyn Pugh Brown, now of Chevy Chase, Maryland; and Mildred Pugh Matthews of Jackson, Mississippi.

Mr. Pugh was identified with the Masonic fraternity, and both Mr. and Mrs. Pugh were members of the Order of the Eastern Star. He was a Noble of Hamasa Temple of the Mystic Shrine at Meridian, Mississippi. He was a member of the Rotary Club and worked in various community activities. Roscoe Pugh was a lifelong member of the Methodist Church in which he served for many years as a member of the administrative board and as an adult Sunday School teacher.

Roscoe Conkling Pugh died in Jackson, Mississippi, in October 1953. His many and varied activities in the educational field for forty-three years brought him a wide acquaintance, and the worth of his work is uniformly acknowledged.

JAMES MURRAY KENNA

James Murray Kenna was born on a farm about four miles west of Summit, Mississippi, in Pike County, on February 11, 1883, the son of W. B. and Sarah (Wilson) Kenna, both natives of Mississippi. His paternal grandfather, James Kenna, was a native of Ireland and came to America with his parents when seven years old. The family located in New York state and lived there some years, and the son, James, received his education there. Later the family moved to the Carolinas and still later to Mississippi, where James applied his talents to the vocation of teacher in Pike and adjoining counties. He died in 1849 when about forty years old. The maternal grandfather, John Wilson, was a native of South Carolina, who moved to Mississippi while a boy. The maternal ancestors came originally from England. James Murray Kenna

JAMES MURRAY KENNA

was one of eight children born to his parents. He had six brothers and one sister.

Mr. Kenna obtained his early education in the rural schools of Pike and Amite Counties. His first six years in school were spent in Pine Grove School, a small rural school near his home, but in the adjoining county of Amite. The junior high school years were spent in Kenna School in Pike County. He then went to Clinton, Mississippi, where he attended prep school and college, receiving his bachelor's degree from Mississippi College in 1907. Prior to his graduation he had taught three years in Wiggins, Mississippi, and upon completion of the degree he accepted a position in the schools of Hattiesburg, Mississippi, where he taught for two years, from 1907 until 1909. From there he went to Ellisville, Mississippi, where he was principal of the city schools for three years, 1909–1912.

In the fall of 1913 he went to Mississippi State College as a teaching fellow in mathematics. He received the master of arts degree from this institution in 1915. After receiving this degree he was principal of

Montgomery County Agricultural High School. While serving in this capacity he felt that he must return to Pike County and do something for the youth at home. He returned to Summit in June 1918, and opened Pike County Agricultural High School in September.

Prior to 1918 no rural high schools existed in Southwest Mississippi. Feeling that the farm youth deserved a chance, Mr. Kenna was instrumental in persuading the board of supervisors of Pike County to purchase what was then known as Godbold's Mineral Wells. Pike County Agricultural High School was organized and, with seven teachers and sixty-three students, began its first session in September 1918.

Mr. Kenna was a dynamic force in promoting the growth of the school from its beginning in 1918. But his chief interest was not in building an elaborate plant; it was in developing the character of young men and women, and his sterling worth impressed itself upon all those who had come and gone during the many years he served in the school.

During the ten years of the history of Pike County Agricultural High School, more than four hundred boys and girls were graduated from the school. In the meantime, Mr. Kenna sensed that the school could serve in a greater capacity as a junior college. The trustees were partially convinced, and in 1928 freshman college work was added as a three-year experiment to see if such an institution was needed in the county and to determine if work at college level could be done effectively there. The response of the youth of the section was such as to show the need, and the fact that students who did college work at Southwest maintained themselves with credit in the various senior colleges that they attended proved that work at the college level could be done. In 1931 sophomore work was added. Since that time many young men and women have attended Southwest Mississippi Junior College, many of whom could not have gone to college had it not been for the vision and the undaunted leadership of James M. Kenna, who served for twenty-nine years as its leader. He took pride in calling Southwest a "poor boy's school," and when boys or girls, regardless of means, wanted to go to school, he always found a way to finance them. At the time of his retirement in 1947 the school was the only junior college in Mississippi which was debt-free.

While teaching in Hattiesburg, Mississippi, James M. Kenna met Miss Bessie Hammack, whom he mar-

ried on December 30, 1909. To this union was born one son, Murray Wilson Kenna, and one daughter, Elise (Mrs. Oliver) Clark.

Mr. Kenna was a devoted member of the Baptist Church; he was a deacon and served as a Sunday School teacher for many years. Fraternally he was affiliated with the Order of Eastern Star, the Masons and the Shrine, and was a Noble of Wahabi Temple, Jackson, Mississippi, Ancient Arabic Order of the Nobles of the Mystic Shrine. He was also a member of the W. O. W. During his long and intensively active Christian lifetime, Mr. Kenna was a member of literally scores of other organizations designed to improve his community, state, or nation in one or another of many worthy ways.

James Murray Kenna passed away on Friday afternoon, November 13, 1953, after having been in failing health for several years. He will be remembered through the years as one of the most capable and beloved of our state educators.

HORACE MACAULAY IVY

Horace Macaulay Ivy was born on January 19, 1884, in Sedalia, Missouri, the son of Henry McPherson and Cynthia Melvine Emmeline (Smith) Ivy, the former born in Wayne County, Missouri, on February 16, 1858, of Scotch-Irish ancestry, and the latter in Bollinger County, Missouri, on April 19, 1863, of English and Dutch ancestry.

H. M. Ivy obtained his early education in the public schools of Cape Girardeau, finishing the eighth grade work in 1896, after which he attended the Missouri Normal School for four years. In 1903 and 1904 he took his A. B. and A. M. degrees from Central College of Missouri and in the fall of the latter year entered the University of Missouri at Columbia, where he remained until 1905. In the summer of 1906 he attended the University of Chicago for special work and in 1919–1920 and 1922 attended the Peabody College for Teachers at Nashville, Tennessee, where he received his Ph. D. degree. During the periods of completing his education Dr. Ivy also taught in the rural schools of Washington County, Alabama, and, at various times, was a teacher, principal of the high school and superintendent of schools in Yazoo City, Mississippi. He was principal of the schools in Flora and superintendent of the schools in Canton, both in Mississippi, later being in the state department of education at Jackson. In 1923 Dr. Ivy was appointed superinten-

HORACE MACAULAY IVY

dent of schools of Meridian, Mississippi, a position he held for thirty years, until 1953. From 1920 to 1923 he was state supervisor of secondary schools and also a member of the state board of vocational education. His military record consists of serving with the Missouri National Guard.

On June 5, 1907, in Fayette, Missouri, Dr. Ivy was united in marriage to Miss Beryl Dean Smith, who was born on September 16, 1883, in Glasgow, Missouri, daughter of Thomas Berry and Emma Marvin (Newland) Smith. Dr. and Mrs. Ivy are the parents of four children; Horace Macaulay (Mack) Jr., Henry Berry, Philip Byrd, and Beryl.

Dr. Ivy is associated with the fraternal orders of the Masons and the Knights of Pythias and is a member of the Rotary Club. His college fraternity is the Phi Delta Kappa. His church association is the United Methodist Church, and his membership is in the Central United Methodist Church of Meridian.

Dr. Ivy has been a member of the Mississippi Education Association for sixty-seven years, outdistancing all other members in number of years as he also has in the magnitude and variety of his service. The editor of the *Mississippi Educational Advance* stated that Dr. Ivy was "our greatest educational leader. He was, without doubt, our and maybe the South's most illustrious educator. His force was felt in every area of education."

Horace M. Ivy was the first football coach at Yazoo City, Mississippi, in 1905; first high school supervisor, in 1919; drafted the bill that first authorized the junior college development in Mississippi, in 1922; the first superintendent to earn the Ph. D. degree, in 1923, an honor he held alone for twenty years. He was a member of the first constitutionally organized board of trustees of institutions of higher learning, holding that position twelve years, and was president for two years. He served on the Millsaps College board for a like period. He is a permanent member of the Peabody College Board of Trustees. He was the first superintendent to be president of the Southern Association of Colleges and Schools.

Dr. Ivy was Mississippi Education Association president in 1926. He early realized the importance of action in the political arena long before MEA developed its present action program. He almost alone dealt with legislative leaders and governors. He was persuasive. He was never awed by the men who held power, and they respected his intelligence and wisdom. He was always a leader and never backed down from a fight. He, along with W. N. Taylor and Fred Young, were most responsible for the first teachers' retirement program, instituted in 1944.

Dr. Ivy realized that Mississippi must have general federal aid to finance the kind of education the state needed. As chairman of the National Education Association Legislative Committee, he persuaded the late Sen. Robert Taft, Senate Majority Leader and great conservative from Ohio, to introduce and fight to pass a general aid bill for education without federal control.

More than forty years ago, Dr. Ivy took under his wing a number of young administrators and introduced them into legislative activities in Jackson and Washington. Many who later became leaders received their training from him. He was the first to see the value in involving classroom teachers in political action.

72

As superintendent of Meridian Schools from 1923 to 1953, he was highly innovative. His own early education was in Latin, Greek and science. He implemented a program suited to the diversity of talents and needs of his students and the community. His efforts resulted in Meridian Junior College having a far-ranging program of vocational and adult education. He initiated the first special education program.

He set up an exemplary program in physical education, as well as music and art, for all pupils. Local athletic teams won top honors. He was a cofounder of the Mississippi High School Activities Association and the Big Eight Conference. He developed and maintained a fine school plant. The first Negro high school accredited by the Southern Association was Harris High School in Meridian in 1946.

People who know Dr. Ivy well would say that their most indelible impression of him was his devotion to Mrs. Ivy, who died in 1969.

It is a widely acknowledged fact that the most important work to which a man can direct his energies is that of teaching, whether it be from the pulpit, from the lecture platform, or from the classroom, and it is to this last work that Dr. H. M. Ivy has so ably devoted his time, energies, and thought.

SIMEON LAFAYETTE STRINGER

Simeon Lafayette Stringer was born on October 22, 1879, at Bay Springs, Mississippi. He was the son of Joseph C. and Fannie (Flanagan) Stringer, both of whose families originally came to Mississippi from South Carolina.

He received all of his early education in the public school system of his native community, though the high school department at that time was known as Lake Como Academy. The high school diploma was awarded him in 1896. He then entered Southern Normal University, located at Huntingdon, Tennessee, from which institution he received both the L. I. and the B. S. degrees in 1899. Shortly after leaving Huntingdon, he enrolled as a student in Western Kentucky State Normal College where he was granted the B. A. degree in 1902. He later spent a full year (1928–1929) at the University of Mississippi as a graduate student, and at the close of the session he received the M. A. degree.

After returning to Mississippi in 1902, Mr. Stringer began his teaching career at Macedonia, Perry County, Mississippi, where he taught during 1902–

SIMEON LAFAYETTE STRINGER

1903. From there he went to the Petal Consolidated School to serve as superintendent during 1903–1904, and to Bay Springs Consolidated School as superintendent in 1904–1905. In 1905, Mr. Stringer accepted a position at the Louin Separate School District as superintendent and remained until 1911. He then went to the Richton Schools as superintendent from 1911 to 1919, and to the Webb-Swan Lake Consolidated School during 1919–1920. The years 1920 to 1926 were spent at Picayune City Schools. He went to Pearl River County Junior College at Poplarville, Mississippi, in 1926, and was instrumental in building the junior college there. He served as president of the institution from 1926 to 1932. Mr. Stringer's next position was at Clark Memorial Junior College at Newton, Mississippi, where he served as president from 1932 to 1935. In 1935, he organized Crosby Special Consolidated Schools and, with the title of "commissioner," directed the school from 1935 to 1941.

In the summers, while carrying on regular school

work Mr. Stringer served for thirteen years in the capacity of extension representative of Mississippi Southern College.

In 1908, Simeon Lafayette Stringer was married to Shellie Estelle McNair of Brandon, Mississippi, who was from a prominent family of that section of the state and who contributed much to the successful career of her husband. They had no children.

All of Mr. Stringer's long and successful teaching experience was within his native state of Mississippi. His leadership in areas of education on the local, state, and national level was a testimony to his deep concern and interest in improvement of all areas of education in Mississippi. He served as one of the early presidents of the Mississippi Junior College Athletic and Literary Associations and was active for many years in the growth and development of the Mississippi Education Association, having served on the board of directors, on committees, and as president of the MEA in 1940. He was active in all legislation for improvement in education and for increased appropriations for financing the educational program. He served as a member of the state board of examiners for a number of years. Mr. Stringer also held membership in the National Education Association (life member).

He was very active and interested in civic and community organizations and contributed much to his church, his community, and to his fellowman. He spent long years of service as a deacon and Sunday School teacher in the Baptist Church. His civic interest was expressed through thirty-eight years as a Rotarian and many years of activity as a Woodman of the World and a Mason. He was also a member of the Knights Templar and Phi Kappa Alpha.

S. L. Stringer was known as a Christian gentleman of courageous strength, striving for a richer and fuller understanding of God and man.

GEORGE JUDSON CAIN

George Judson Cain was born on August 22, 1891, near Learned, Hinds County, Mississippi, the son of J. C. and Rebecca (Vanamen) Cain. He had one brother and four sisters. He attended the elementary public schools in Learned and obtained his high school education at Chamberlain-Hunt Academy at Port Gibson, Mississippi, where he graduated with highest honors. His first college work was done at the University of Mississippi in 1913 and later at Missis-

GEORGE JUDSON CAIN

sippi State University. He also attended Peabody College, Nashville, Tennessee, from which institution he was awarded the bachelor of science degree in 1923 and the master of arts degree in 1927.

George Judson Cain was married to Miss Nina Osborn on August 28, 1917, and they were the parents of one son, George J. Cain, Jr.

Mr. Cain began his teaching career in the public schools of his home county, Hinds, where he served as a principal for four years, from 1914 to 1918. In 1918 when the nation was involved in World War I, he served in the armed service for one year, 1918 to 1919.

Jud Cain's next move was to Hinds County Agricultural High School where he served as an instructor of mathematics from 1919 to 1922. He then went to Hinds Junior College as dean and served in that capacity from 1922 to 1928. He served as acting president of the college while President Sutherland was away from 1928 to 1930. He then served as president of the college from 1930 to 1938.

In July 1938, President Cain resigned his position at

Hinds Junior College and joined the Mississippi State Department of Education as Director of the Division of Administration and Finance, a position he held for the next twenty years.

In 1960–1961, at the request of a legislative committee, Mr. Cain served as the chief resource person for the legislative committee in making an exhaustive study of the state's school system. His duties included the supplying of information needed, the outlining of procedures, forming committees, editing manuscripts, and finally printing the findings and recommendations of the study. This work was completed in about one and one-half years.

In 1964 the legislature enacted a law whereby the state, through the Educational Finance Commission, would aid in the payment of tuition for students attending private schools. The Educational Finance Commission employed Mr. Cain to administer the provisions of this law and to supervise the program. He was in this position for five years, after which time the law was repealed.

In May 1969, Mr. Cain joined the Council School Foundation in Jackson, Mississippi, as superintendent of schools. This is a private school established in 1964 which has acquired an enrollment of about five thousand students. Mr. Cain moved from superintendent to executive director in January 1972, in which position he is still employed.

During his long service in the educational field in Mississippi, George J. Cain has held membership and responsible positions in many of the organizations. He served a three-year term on the Southern Association of Colleges and Schools where he represented the Mississippi junior colleges. He served as president of the Mississippi College Association, the Mississippi Junior College Association, and the Southern States School Finance Directors. He was selected as the Mississippi representative to the White House Conference on Education and was chairman of the Southern States Work Conference Committee on State School Finance Systems. Mr. Cain was a key figure in working with the legislature in devising and implementing the state's school reorganization plan of 1953 and served as consultant to the Education Committee in the Mississippi House of Representatives. He has served as chairman of the Accrediting Commission of the Mississippi Private School Association.

Mr. Cain has been very active in local civic and community organizations and is a member of the

COOPER J. DARBY

Kiwanis Club, the Citizens Councils of America, and the Salvation Army Board. He holds membership in the Phi Delta Kappa, an educational service fraternity. He has been an active member of the Presbyterian Church and serves as an elder in that church.

COOPER J. DARBY

Cooper J. Darby was born on January 24, 1896, on the family homestead in what was then the north-central rural area of Harrison County, Mississippi. When Stone County was formed in 1916 his original homesite became a part of that county. Cooper Darby was the oldest of four sons and one daughter born to Henry Clark Darby and Martha Ann (Johnston) Darby. The little daughter died when ten months of age.

The old homesite is some two miles west of Perryville, an early sawmill village and a flag-stop on the railroad, the first segment of which Mr. Darby's father helped construct. The birthplace is about four miles south of Perkinston, the site where Perkinston Junior

75

College, now Mississippi Gulf Coast Junior College, is located. In his boyhood this country youngster never indulged the fantastic dream that one day he would become the president of a junior college in his native county. In those early years he nourished what was then to him the more captivating thought of becoming a railroad locomotive engineer.

Mr. Darby received his elementary and some high school education in the rural schools of Harrison County, Mississippi. Most rural schools were then small, isolated, one-teacher centers. Few rural teachers then had professional training, and many had less than a high school education.

Henry Clark Darby, the father, died when Cooper Darby was only twelve years of age. A few years prior to his death, the father experienced severe losses in a business venture. As a consequence, Cooper, the oldest son, was forced to drop out of school for two years to help support the family.

This youngster refused to surrender his ambition. He resumed his schooling with the help and steady encouragement of his resolute mother. Between sessions, and after school hours, he and his younger brothers worked at whatever they could find to do. Graduation at the local public school was a pleasing plateau, but not the summit. The steep college hill was yet to be surmounted.

Cooper Darby earned his college education by alternately attending college and teaching or finding other employment. He did his undergraduate study at the Mississippi Normal College (later the State Teachers College, and now the University of Southern Mississippi) at Hattiesburg, Peabody College at Nashville, and Tulane University. In 1921 he received the Normal College diploma, and in 1928 the State Teachers College conferred the B. S. degree upon this more mature young man. He then did three full summers of graduate study at the University of Alabama.

Upon completing the tenth grade, the most advanced studies offered in the local three-teacher school, Cooper Darby immediately attended a six-weeks summer term at the Mississippi Normal College. In the fall of that year (1914) at the age of eighteen, he began his twenty-three years in the field of education. In summary, this experience included: five years as principal of schools, six years as county superintendent of education in Harrison County, and twelve years (September 1929 to August 1941) as president of Perkinston Junior College. He had served

as a trustee of this institution for six years prior to his presidency. He resigned his position at the junior college, after having been elected chancery clerk in Harrison County.

During the Darby administration the curriculum at Perkinston Junior College was reorganized, several terminal vocational courses were added, and the junior college was admitted to membership in the Southern Association of Secondary Schools and Colleges. Under Darby's guidance the existing campus buildings had major repairs, several new buildings were constructed, and the heating, water, and sewer systems were rebuilt and extensions added thereto. The institution experienced a rapid growth in student enrollment.

Mr. Darby's tenure as chancery clerk extended over a span of more than thirty years. He gained the reputation of being an ardent worker, a strong advocate of integrity, and a man ready to speak his mind about county government.

Professional honors which came to Cooper Darby include: membership in Phi Delta Kappa, president of the Association of County Superintendents of Education in Mississippi, president of the Mississippi Junior College Association, and president of the Mississippi Education Association. He is a life member of the National Education Association.

During all his busy years, Mr. Darby was active in the Baptist Church, serving some forty years as a Sunday School teacher and intermittently as a deacon.

Upon voluntary retirement from public office, Cooper Darby said in an interview, "Of all my endeavors through the years, I count my labors at Perkinston Junior College among the most rewarding experiences of my life."

As might be expected, this man, active for many years in the contemporary developments of his era, had no intention of fading into a nonentity; inaction is repugnant to his nature. Personal and business matters have claimed his attention since he left public office, but he has tentative plans to do some writing about his experience in education and county government.

MAJOR CYRUS McDANIEL

Major Cyrus McDaniel was born on October 13, 1895, at Sandersville, Jones County, Mississippi. He was reared at Sandersville, the son of Amos and

MAJOR CYRUS McDANIEL

Sallie E. (Alday) McDaniel, and had four brothers and four sisters.

His early education was obtained in the Sandersville schools, and he was graduated from Sandersville High School. Upon completion of high school, and deciding on a teaching career, he entered Mississippi Normal College, now the University of Southern Mississippi, at Hattiesburg, Mississippi, where he completed the diploma course (equivalent of two years of college), and was granted a professional license to teach, valid for life, in 1915. His first teaching experience began in 1915 at Ozark School, a three-teacher school in Itawamba County, where he remained until 1916. He then taught a year at Spring Hill School in Jones County.

In 1917, Major McDaniel entered the United States Navy in World War I and served as a signal quartermaster for two years on the U.S.S. *Nevada*, one of the largest battleships which operated from the southern coasts of England and Ireland. The ship was engaged in escort duty for army troop ships and later with the Grand Fleet in the North Sea off the coast of Scotland.

Upon his return from navy duty, Mr. McDaniel was elected as principal of Ovett High School in Jones County, where he remained until 1920. At the close of the school year, he decided to enter Mississippi College, Clinton, Mississippi, to complete his college degree. He received his B.A. degree with "special distinction" in 1921, then his M. A. degree in 1931. Further study toward a Ph. D. was done for three summers at the University of North Carolina, one summer at the University of Mississippi, and a special course at Columbia University in New York City.

In September 1921, Mr. McDaniel began work as a teacher of mathematics at Pearl River Agricultural High School and Junior College, Poplarville, Mississippi. In addition to serving as principal of the high school division, he helped organize the course of study for the first year of college work, including mathematics, English, history and education. He remained at Poplarville until 1923, at which time he became vice president and professor at Clark Memorial College, Newton, Mississippi. After serving four years at this institution, he accepted a teaching position in education and history at Mississippi College, Clinton, Mississippi, which gave him an opportunity for pursuit of graduate courses, and where he remained until 1928.

In the spring of 1928, Mr. McDaniel was elected president of Holmes County Agricultural High School and Junior College at Goodman, Mississippi. The 1928–1929 session was the first year for the full two-year college courses to be offered and approved. Mr. McDaniel served this junior college for twelve years and was successful in seeing material growth, as well as enlargement of the student body and full recognition by accrediting associations. When he left this position the board of trustees of the college, in its regular meeting on June 14, 1940, passed a resolution designating the administration building, including the auditorium, as McDaniel Hall.

In 1940–1941, Mr. McDaniel served as superintendent of Kosciusko City Schools. He then accepted a position with the state department of education as state supervisor of adult education, financed by the federal government, for a period of two years, 1941–1943. In May 1943, with World War II underway, he accepted a position with the army and navy YMCA, serving as director of USO operations in Grenada,

Mississippi. After the close of World War II there was no immediate demand for Mr. McDaniel to reenter the field of education, and a position as vocational advisor with the Veterans Administration was accepted, which gave him the opportunity to continue to help servicemen in selecting vocations for which they could receive training. In May 1952, he made a transfer to security investigations of the Civil Service Commission, in which position he remained until his retirement in October 1965. Since his retirement the commission has continued to use him as state supervisor in voter registration programs.

Major McDaniel was married to Anise Pickering, also of Jones County, Mississippi, on September 1, 1922. They are the parents of six children, Anise (Mrs. John Brock of Moss Point, Mississippi); Annette (Mrs. Oscar Robinson of Los Angeles, California); Major, Jr. (a Baptist missionary in Korea); Sarah Frances (Mrs. Carmen Davis of Tennessee); Jane (Mrs. Jane Wade of Bay St. Louis, Mississippi); and Jack (living in Jackson, Mississippi). In September 1972, Mr. and Mrs. McDaniel celebrated their fiftieth wedding anniversary. Traveling has been the hobby of the McDaniel family and is of great interest to them. They have traveled extensively throughout the United States and have also made numerous trips to foreign countries.

During the twenty-five years in educational work in Mississippi, eighteen of which were spent in junior colleges, Major McDaniel held membership and took an active part in county, state, and national educational associations. He is a very faithful and devoted member of the Baptist Church, having served as Sunday School teacher and deacon for more than forty years. He is a former Rotarian with nine years of perfect attendance with the club at Durant, Mississippi. He is a member and past club president of the Clinton Kiwanis Club and served for one year as lieutenant governor for the district. He is a member of the American Legion, the Masonic Lodge, and the Men's Garden Club of Clinton.

The four presidents who established public junior colleges in Mississippi after 1948 were: Phillip A. Sheffield, Itawamba Junior College, Fulton, Mississippi; Roscoe O. Stringer, Northeast Mississippi Junior College, Booneville, Mississippi; Benjamin F. McLaurin, Coahoma Junior College, Clarksdale,

Mississippi; and John D. Boyd, Utica Junior College, Utica, Mississippi.

PHILIP ALFRED SHEFFIELD

Philip Alfred Sheffield was born in Dorsey, Mississippi, a small rural town in Itawamba County, in 1909, the son of Robert Sidney and Leona (Gregory) Sheffield. He was one of a family of nine children and had three brothers and five sisters. He received his elementary education in the Itawamba County schools, graduating from Itawamba Agricultural High School in 1928. He received his B. S. degree from Mississippi State University (formerly Mississippi Agricultural and Mechanical College) in 1932, after which he taught mathematics and coached at Itawamba Agricultural High School until 1937. For two years he was principal of the Amory Elementary School, returning to Fulton as coach from 1939 until 1941.

Philip Sheffield entered the United States Army as a reserve officer in 1941 and served for four years during World War II in the Pacific Theater of Operations, and later as an instructor at the University of Maine.

Following his discharge from the army, Mr. Sheffield returned to Itawamba Agricultural High School in 1945 as superintendent. In 1948 he was instrumental in expanding the school's curriculum to include junior college work. Upon the formal organization of Itawamba Junior College, he was elected president of the institution. Under his leadership the institution had grown into a more than two million dollar school plant. He served with distinction in the capacity as president until his death on September 29, 1960. He was only fifty-one years old at the time of his death.

Philip Sheffield was married to Miss Mildred Moore. Two children were born to this union, Phil and Jane.

In his life devoted to service to others, Philip Sheffield received many honors. Among them were presidencies of the Mississippi Junior College Association and of the Mississippi College Association. He was a member of the Mississippi College Accrediting Commission, Mississippi Veterans Certifying Board and the Tombigbee Inland Waterway Authority. He served as president of the Northeast Mississippi Schoolmaster's Club.

He was honored by the *Itawamba County Times* by

PHILIP ALFRED SHEFFIELD

being named Itawamba County's "Good Citizen" in 1949.

Philip Sheffield was an active member of the Fulton Lions Club. He was once commander of the Itawamba American Legion Post No. 51, and was once district commander of the American Legion. He was a member of the Veterans of Foreign Wars.

Mr. Sheffield served in many capacities in local service organizations, among which were county chairman of the American Red Cross, district fund raising chairman of the Red Cross, and fund raising chairman of the March of Dimes for several years.

He was very active in Boy Scout work. He served as president of the Yocona Area Council, and had been awarded the Silver Beaver as a token of his outstanding contribution in many phases of scouting, including the chairmanship of the council's camping and activities committee.

A deacon of the First Baptist Church in Fulton, he

was also teacher of the Men's Bible Class of that church.

Both a York Rite and a Scottish Rite Mason, he was also a Shriner, a member of the Hamasa Temple of Meridian.

ROSCOE ODAS STRINGER

Roscoe Odas Stringer was born in Moselle, Jones County, Mississippi, on August 19, 1899. He was the second eldest of twelve children born to James Shepard and Annie Virginia Shows Stringer. According to the International Ancestry Guild, London, England, "The Stringer families originated in England in the 12th Century. The first record of the name was Walter Stringere, a landowner noted in 1194 A.D. in the country of Wiltshire." Roscoe Stringer is a descendant of Col. John Stringer, who was born in England about 1590, and came to the new world in 1621 and settled in the colony of Jamestown, Virginia.

His early education was received in the Jones County schools. He graduated from Jones County Agricultural High School, Ellisville, Mississippi, in 1921, and received his B.A. degree from Mississippi College, Clinton, Mississippi, in 1924, and a M.Á. degree in school administration from Louisiana State University, Baton Rouge, Louisiana, in 1940. Further study was done toward a doctorate at the University of Missouri, Columbia, Missouri.

In high school Roscoe Stringer lived in the dormitory and worked to defray his school expenses by milking cows for the school dairy, firing boilers, working on the school farm, and doing many miscellaneous chores. At Mississippi College he paid all of his expenses with a football scholarship, waiting on tables, carrying the mail, and performing various other jobs. During the summer months he sold cookware in Alabama.

Roscoe Stringer was married to the former Iva Flora Lovitt of Moselle, Mississippi, who was also a school teacher, having taught in high schools and junior college for more than thirty years. To this union was born one daughter, Lavona, who is Mrs. Overton Currie of Atlanta, Georgia, and the mother of five children.

Mr. Stringer served for forty years in the educational field in Mississippi, his initial job being that of teaching and coaching at Flora, Mississippi, 1924–1925. From Flora, he went to Sumrall, Mississippi, for

ROSCOE ODAS STRINGER

twenty-two years, serving as principal and coach for two years and as superintendent for twenty years, 1925–1946. In the summers of 1942, 1943 and 1944 and the spring of 1947, he taught mathematics at Mississippi Southern College (now University of Southern Mississippi) at Hattiesburg, Mississippi. In 1947 Roscoe Stringer went to North Mississippi as superintendent of the Booneville Special Consolidated Schools, Booneville, Mississippi, for one year. While there he visualized the need for a junior college; and starting with red clay hills and a few enthusiastic supporters from five counties in the northeastern corner of the state, Roscoe Odas Stringer organized and opened the Northeast Mississippi Junior College, Prentiss County, Booneville, Mississippi, in September 1948. He served as its first president and held this position for four years. During this time, the college enrollment grew to be one of the largest in the state of Mississippi.

The *Jackson Clarion-Ledger*, June 18, 1950, stated, "President Stringer, a friendly man himself, says 'The

school was established on three major premises: truth, friendship, and character, and I am certain that the school is living according to this prospectus.' "

After teaching at Petal, Mississippi, 1952–1953, Mr. Stringer served nine years as superintendent of the J. Z. George School at North Carrollton, 1953–1962. While serving in this capacity he built what is considered one of the most modern school plants in a rural community in the state of Mississippi. His last teaching position was in his native county of Jones as principal of Myrick School, 1963–1964.

After retiring as a school executive, he was employed by the United States Government as Executive Director of Forrest-Stone Area Equal Opportunity, Inc., and was holding this position at the time of his death on May 8, 1970.

Mr. Stringer held many honorable positions in his lifetime, among them serving as president of Mississippi School Administrators, Department of Superintendence of the Mississippi Education Association, the Booneville Rotary Club, Sumrall Lions Club, Carroll County Lions Club, Carroll County Teachers' Association, and the North Carrollton Chamber of Commerce. He was also instrumental in organizing the South Mississippi Livestock Association in 1940 and served as president from 1940 to 1945.

Mr. Stringer is listed in *Who's Who in American Education* for 1951–1952; *Who's Who in American Universities and Colleges* in 1952; *Personalities of the South* in 1967; *Community Leaders of America*, 1969–1970, 1970–1971; *Creative and Successful Personalities* in 1972; *International Men of Achievement* in 1974; and *Dictionary of International Biography* in 1975. He served as a colonel on the staff of Gov. Paul B. Johnson, Jr., 1964–1968.

Mr. Stringer was a devoted member of the Baptist Church where he served as a deacon and Sunday School teacher, and he was a Mason.

Roscoe Stringer's philosophy to all youth whose lives he touched was: "So live, work, and study that the world will be a little better off by your having lived in it."

BENJAMIN FRANKLIN McLAURIN

Benjamin Franklin McLaurin was born on July 21, 1910, at Mount Olive, Covington County, Mississippi. His parents were the Reverend Bert and Jessie Ruth McLaurin. He attended the public schools in the area. He later attended Alcorn A. & M. College from 1931

BENJAMIN FRANKLIN McLAURIN

to 1935 and received a B. S. degree. He then attended Tuskegee Institute from 1948 to 1949 and received an M. S. degree. He did further study at New York University.

Benjamin Franklin McLaurin was married to Sezzie Mae Wheatley. Two children were born to this union: Benjamin Franklin McLaurin, Jr., and Johnnie William McLaurin.

Mr. McLaurin was the vocational agriculture teacher at Coahoma County Agricultural High School from 1935 to 1940. He then served as supervisor with the Farmer's Home Administration from 1940 to 1942 and after that as supervisor of "live-at-home production" with King and Anderson Company from 1942 to 1944. He spent a year as classroom teacher of agronomy and farm manager at St. Augustine, Florida College from 1944 to 1945. From 1946 to 1949 he served as principal of Coahoma County Agricultural High School, and aided the Coahoma County School Board in establishing Coahoma Junior College in 1949. He served as president of Coahoma Junior College from 1949 to 1966, and has served as the administrative assistant since 1966.

B. F. McLaurin has been active in many and various civic, religious, and educational organizations. He has been a leader in the Boy Scouts of America and the National Association for the Advancement of Colored People. He is a member of the Vocational Agricultural Association, Omega Psi Phi, the Mississippi and National Teachers Associations, the American Teachers Association and the Coahoma County Teachers Association. He is an active member of the Friendship A. M. E. Church where he served as chairman of the trustee board. He is a member of the Prince Hall Free and Accepted Masons, the Independent Benevolent Protective Order of Elks, the Chamber of Commerce, and the Alcorn College Alumni Club of which he has served as president.

Mr. McLaurin is the author of a publication entitled "The Effect of Mechanization on Farming in Coahoma County, Mississippi."

A tribute to his many years of dedicated service and leadership was given him on "McLaurin Day in Coahoma County." He was also selected as the Alcornite of the Year in 1965.

JOHN DEWEY BOYD

John Dewey Boyd was born at Doloroso, Wilkinson County, Mississippi, on September 3, 1899, the son of John and Elizabeth (Fry) Boyd. Early efforts to get an education were difficult as there was not a high school in the county. After marrying, farming, working in log camps, and building roads, and being out of school for nine years, he was finally able to return to school and to finish his college education. In 1931, he received his B. S. degree from Alcorn A. & M. College and was awarded his M. S. degree in 1949 at the University of Illinois. He also did special work at Harvard University in 1959.

John Boyd's first professional job was that of principal and agriculture teacher at Moorhead, Mississippi, from 1931 to 1936. He then went to Lampton Vocational High School in Marion County where he served in the same capacity from 1936 until 1947. He served as an instructor of agronomy at Alcorn College from 1947 to 1951 and then went to the Utica Institute as superintendent from 1951 through 1954.

Dr. Boyd organized the Utica Institute into a junior college and became the first president of Utica Junior College in 1954. When he accepted the position at

JOHN DEWEY BOYD

Utica, he felt that the school had great possibilities. It would serve all of Hinds County, it had ample land for expansion, and ample and expanding financial sup-

port, and one of the finest boards of trustees to be found any place. The year before Mr. Boyd became superintendent, the school had approximately two hundred students, and all had to be transported. The school had three army surplus buses for their transportation. As they went about the business of getting the school ready for opening in September 1951, to the surprise of everyone, the enrollment had doubled. They had to buy more buses and hire more teachers. This rapid growth in enrollment continued throughout the years while Mr. Boyd was there. With full cooperation of the board of trustees and the county superintendent of education, they were able to complete a building program in 1954. That year the school was fully accredited as a high school and was permitted to organize as a junior college. The enrollment had passed the nine hundred mark while they were enrolling only high school students. Of the faculty Dr. Boyd assembled at Utica, one is president of Alcorn College, one is vice president, one dean of students, one director of public relations; and several hold other positions. The now acting president of Utica Junior College was also recruited by Dr. Boyd.

John Dewey Boyd was married to Miss Cleopatra Carter in 1921. To this union one child, a daughter, Katye, was born in 1921. Katye died in 1971. The Boyds have two grandchildren, Halbert Dockins and Mrs. Johnetta Dockins Flemings.

During Dr. Boyd's professional life, he was active in many organizations. He served as president of the county, district, and Mississippi State Teachers Associations.

The Supervisors of Public Junior Colleges

The first reference to the establishing of junior colleges in Mississippi is found in an act of the Mississippi Legislature, Senate Bill 251, approved on March 24, 1922, authorizing the boards of trustees of agricultural high schools and separate school districts with a population of not less than 10,000 to establish a junior college. Because of the relationship of these junior colleges to the high schools in Mississippi, this legislation identified them as a part of public education even though this original legislation stated that the work must be on a collegiate basis. All the junior colleges established during the first fifteen years were established on the campuses and in the facilities of agricultural high schools.

The state authority for these institutions became, in the beginning, the responsibility of the state superintendent of education. The large number of agricultural high schools in Mississippi, as a responsibility of the state department of public education, were related to a person in the state department known as the supervisor of agricultural high schools. At the beginning of the development of the junior colleges his title was supervisor of agricultural high schools and junior colleges. Later, with the closing of the agricultural high schools, the title became supervisor of public junior colleges. With the passage of Senate Bill No. 1832 at the regular session of the Mississippi legislature in 1968, a division of junior colleges within the state department of education was established and authorized the state superintendent of education to appoint a director of the division; therefore, the title of *director* was established.

Nine men have served in the capacity of supervisor and later director during the fifty-year period. The services of two of these supervisors cover a large part of this period. Knox Broom, serving at two different periods, was the supervisor for twelve years, and B. L. Hill served for twenty-two years. Each of these men made significant contributions to the growth and development of the Mississippi state system of public junior colleges.

The pages to follow include photographs and biographical sketches of the nine men who gave leadership in the capacity as supervisor or director.

CLAUDE BENNETT

Claude Bennett was born on February 14, 1879, at Silver Creek, Mississippi. His parents were Drury Burton Bennett and Elizabeth (Burkett) Bennett. He was one of five children.

He attended Mississippi College for three years, then went to Trinity College (Duke University) where he received his A. B. degree in 1912. He received his M. A. degree from Peabody College.

Mr. Bennett served as principal of various country schools in Lincoln County and was Lincoln County Superintendent of Education from 1908 until 1912. In 1912 he went to Hattiesburg High School as principal, where he remained for one year. In 1913 he went to Moss Point High School as superintendent for two

CLAUDE BENNETT

years. In 1915 he returned to Hattiesburg as vice president of Mississippi Woman's College until 1917. He spent three years, 1920–1923, as superintendent of schools in Biloxi, Mississippi. In 1923 he became the first supervisor of agricultural high schools and junior colleges in the Mississippi state department of education and served in this capacity until 1928. He served as president of State Teachers College (University of Southern Mississippi) at Hattiesburg from 1928 to 1933. He then accepted a position with the treasury department, Bureau of Internal Revenue, as chief of field division from 1933 to 1945.

Claude Bennett was married to Grace McVey of Highland, Ohio, on September 3, 1914. They were the parents of three daughters, Margaret Nan, Grace McVey, and Mary Ellen. Mrs. Grace Bennett was deceased on August 20, 1940. On May 1, 1943, Mr. Bennett was married to Mary Bentley Gavin of Stafford Springs, Mississippi, who was the mother of three daughters and one son.

He was a member of Sigma Chi fraternity, Phi Delta Kappa, the Rotary Club, and the Masons. He was an active member of the Baptist Church, having taught Sunday School in the various churches in which he was a member.

He was coauthor of a book entitled *Mississippi History* which he and Dr. Charles S. Sydnor wrote in 1929.

Claude Bennett was deceased on March 25, 1970.

KNOX McLEOD BROOM

Knox McLeod Broom was born at Daisy, Mississippi, a rural community in George County, on January 13, 1889. He was the fifth child in a family of nine children of five boys and four girls. His parents, William Wesley Broom and Sarah Jane (Moore) Broom, were of Scotch-Irish descent. His father was a descendant of Jacob Broom of the Northeastern Colonies. His mother was from the Scotch-Irish strain of Moores and Fairleys along the eastern coast of the Carolinas. William Broom was a successful business man, dealing in timber. He was also a local Methodist preacher, and he and Mrs. Broom provided a Christian home where Bible reading and family prayer were the daily custom. Another chief concern of the parents was the educational opportunities for their children.

Knox Broom attended the rural public schools in the area where he lived and was graduated from Wiggins High School in 1908. He attended Millsaps College and received a B. A. degree in June 1915. He was awarded a master's degree from the University of Chicago in 1928.

On September 1, 1915, after completing his college work at Millsaps, Knox Broom accepted a teaching position at Bendale High School, where he remained until May of 1916. In 1916 he moved to Ellisville, Mississippi and taught in the Ellisville High School until January 1918.

On April 23, 1918, at Lucedale, Mississippi, Knox Broom enlisted in the A. E. F. The nation was involved in World War I, and he served overseas for a year before being discharged at Camp Dix, New Jersey, in September 1919.

Upon returning to civilian life, he went to Brandon High School and taught there until June 1923. He then went to Taylorsville High School from September 1923 to February 1924. At this time he moved to

KNOX McLEOD BROOM

Yazoo City, Mississippi, where he accepted the position of superintendent of the Yazoo County Agricultural High School and remained until June 1925. He was called from this position to serve as assistant state superintendent of education, under Dr. W. F. Bond. The position was made available when his brother, Jim Broom, was named to organize Delta State College in 1925, as its first president.

In 1927–1928, Knox Broom took a leave of absence from his work to go to the University of Chicago to earn his master's degree. He then returned to Mississippi where he served as supervisor of agricultural high schools and junior colleges from 1928 until 1932. He resigned this position in 1933 and became assistant state manager of the Home Owner's Loan Corporation, where he remained until 1936. At this time he returned to the state department of education again to serve as supervisor of agricultural high schools and junior colleges. He remained in this position until 1944 when he resigned to became chief of the training

division of the War Manpower Commission and served in this capacity from 1944 to 1946. In 1947 Mr. Broom did special work with the junior college office for three months. In 1949, he went to Copiah-Lincoln Junior College Guidance Center from January until March. He then went to Hinds Junior College as counselor and remained from 1949 until 1954, when he retired.

Knox M. Broom was married to Audra Parkhurst in 1920. Two daughters were born to this union, Audra June and Peggy Joyce. In 1934, Mr. Broom was married to Mrs. Karen Curtis, who was the mother of two sons, L. B. and Tom. Knox M. Broom, Jr. was born to this union. Mr. Broom was a family man devoted to his wife and children. He was justifiably proud of each of his children, as well as every member of the larger Broom family because the Broom blood ran thick with him.

Mr. Broom held many honorable positions in his lifetime. He took an active part in the educational associations and held many positions of leadership in the state and national organizations. He was far ahead of his time in ideas and ideals. His was the master mind in writing the junior college laws setting up the first real state system of junior colleges in the nation. Most of these bills passed in the 1920s are the controlling statutes of today. The early laws dealing with vocational-technical education are as modern as if they had been written today—a tribute to the vision of Knox Broom and his colleagues. He challenged his junior college coworkers to provide educational opportunity beyond the high school for every Mississippian, through what he was pleased to call the "peoples' college."

Knox Broom was also active in many civic organizations and clubs. He especially enjoyed his association in his later years with the Walter Scott Coffee-Break Club in Jackson. He was a member of the Mississippi Society of the National Society of the Sons of the American Revolution.

Mr. Broom was a devoted member of the Methodist Church, a charter member of Van Winkle Methodist Church and a member of the church's official board.

Knox Broom was familiar with the writings of the great philosophers and historians and was himself a great philosopher and Bible scholar. He knew, by personal relationship, the master teacher of two thousand years ago whose principles and teachings served as the rule and guide for his life. His life was dedicated to the cause of improved opportunities and service to others. He often quoted the following lines:

> I have not felt the quickened pulse
> Great symphonies can bring;
> But I have stood in loneliness
> And heard a mother sing.
>
> I have not known many great of earth;
> Nor shared their cup of wine,
> But I have walked a narrow road,
> With a child's hand in mine.

KIRBY PIPKIN WALKER

Kirby Pipkin Walker was born in Dunn, North Carolina, on June 9, 1901, the son of Thomas Jefferson Walker and Bess Davis (Pipkin) Walker. He had one brother, Thomas Jefferson, and two sisters, Bess and Lucille.

He was educated in the Hattiesburg Public Schools of Hattiesburg, Mississippi. He attended college at Southwestern College, Clarksville, Tennessee, where he received his A. B. degree in 1922. He received the M. A. degree from the University of Chicago in 1934, and received the Doctor of Education degree from Southwestern of Memphis in 1953. Mr. Walker did further study at George Peabody College for Teachers in Nashville, the University of Southern Mississippi in Hattiesburg, and the University of Mississippi in Oxford.

Mr. Walker began his teaching career at Forrest County Agricultural High School, Brooklyn, Mississippi, where he served as teacher and superintendent from 1925 until 1932. He then went to the Mississippi State Department of Education where he served as state supervisor of agricultural high schools and junior colleges, 1932–1933, and as state director of the emergency education programs, 1933–1934. Mr. Walker accepted the position as superintendent of the Jackson City Schools in 1935 and remained in this position until 1969. Since 1969, he has been Superintendent Emeritus of the Jackson Public Schools.

Kirby P. Walker was married to Miss Frances Settle of Clarksville, Tennessee. One son, Dr. Kirby P. Walker, Jr. of Jackson, was born to this union.

Dr. Walker is an active member of the Presbyterian Church, the Jackson Rotary Club, the Jackson Touchdown Club, and various other civic organizations.

Dr. Walker has been elected to many positions of

KIRBY PIPKIN WALKER

educational leadership on the local, state, and national levels. His leadership in educational and civic organizations on the state level relates to the Mississippi Educational Association, state department of education, Mississippi Congress of Parents and Teachers, Mississippi Authority for Educational Television, and other organizations. He has served as chairman of the Merit System Council, the Mississippi State Board of Health, the Mississippi Commission on Hospital Care, the Mississippi Interarency Commission on Mental Illness and Mental Retardation, the Mississippi Medicaid Commission, the Mississippi Division of Comprehensive Health Planning, and the Mississippi Division of Law Enforcement Assistance. He is a director of the Southern Educators Life Insurance Company of Atlanta, Georgia.

His regional leadership resulted in his election as president of the Southern Association of Colleges and

Schools, and his services to the activities of this association have extended through many years.

Dr. Walker has been chosen as an outstanding leader to represent Mississippi in various areas on the national level. Some of these areas include the state advisory committee to the U. S. Cabinet Committee on Education, and the council of advisers to the U. S. Commissioner of Education. He has served, and continues to serve, as consultant and lecturer on college campuses and to community service organizations.

Dr. Walker has been the recipient of numerous citations and awards in recognition of his distinguished services, among them being the Distinguished Service Award of the American Association of School Administrators in 1970, and the School Administrator of the Year in 1955 presented by the Mississippi Association of School Administrators. He will long be remembered for his capable and dedicated leadership to the cause of education over the state and nation and for his outstanding and charismatic personality.

ROBERT LEE ANDERSON

Robert Lee Anderson was born on February 10, 1891, at Dumas, Mississippi, in Tippah County. He attended a rural school there and later attended school at Chalybeate in Tippah County. He was a graduate of Mississippi College.

Robert "Bob" Anderson taught school until he entered the army in World War I. He went to Purvis in 1919 and was grammar school principal for four years, and then served as superintendent of the Lamar County Agricultural High School.

He was state supervisor of agricultural high schools and junior colleges and director of the finance department of the state board of education from July 1933 to July 1935. In 1936 he was named State Director of Adult Education under the WPA, and in 1942 was appointed to the War Production Board.

He returned to Purvis and made his home there while operating an appliance business in Hattiesburg from 1947 until his retirement in 1959. He had been on the Purvis School Board since 1948 and served as chairman for many years.

Mr. Anderson was a Baptist and for many years taught a young men's Sunday School, which carries his name today. He financially helped many boys and girls continue their college education.

After retirement he, with his wife, spent much

ROBERT LEE ANDERSON

of their time fishing on the Mississippi Gulf Coast. R. L. Anderson died on October 7, 1962.

JOHN ALNA TRAVIS

John Alna Travis was born on August 13, 1893, in Heidelberg, Jasper County, Mississippi. He was one of seven boys born to Green and Ida (Leggitt) Travis. His father was in the mercantile business in Heidelberg.

J. A. Travis attended the local public schools in his community and was a graduate of Clarke College at Newton and Mississippi College at Clinton. He received a master's degree from Peabody College and did graudate study at Duke University and the University of Chicago. His thesis was written on Negro education in Mississippi.

Mr. Travis served as superintendent of the schools at Chunky from 1918 to 1919; Duck Hill, 1919–1921; Eupora Agricultural High School, 1921–1923; Web-

JOHN ALNA TRAVIS

Mr. Travis was an active member of the Baptist Church where he served as a deacon and taught a Sunday School class for thirty years. He was a life member of the Mississippi Education Association, Retired Teachers Association, and the National Education Association, having won the NEA's Distinguished Service Award for field service. He was also a member of the Red Red Rose school administrators organization. He was a member of Phi Delta Kappa and the American Legion, and was a 33rd Degree Mason.

Death came to Mr. Travis on December 31, 1969, as he watched a bowl game at his home in Jackson on New Year's Eve.

J. A. Travis' tenure at the Mississippi Association headquarters was versatile and varied. He kept up to date on educational developments; was an ever-ready and splendid speaker; educational researcher; legislative contact-research-liaison man; advisor for future teachers—and knew by name almost every school official in the state.

Despite his versatility, it was his human qualities that made his coworkers and friends love and respect him. He had learned the secret of tranquility; was never rushed or hurried. He was always smiling and always cheerful.

One of the state's best loved and most capable educators, J. A. Travis left behind the philosophy that, "There is no boy or girl, within our reach, who—with guidance and understanding,—cannot become a useful, contributing member of society."

JOHN CALHOUN WINDHAM

John Calhoun Windham was born on November 16, 1875, near Sonora, Mississippi, Chickasaw County, the son of a Civil War soldier, Elias Jefferson and Louisiana (Wofford) Windham. His father's family came to Mississippi from Alabama and his mother's from South Carolina. John Calhoun Windham was one of eight children born to this family.

John Windham was educated, as a child, under the guidance of his mother, "Lee" Wofford, whose family established Wofford College in Spartanburg, South Carolina, and he attended the public schools in his local community during his early years. He received his high school diploma from Houston High School, and taught school at Coldwater, Mississippi, for one year, 1903–1904, before entering the University of

ster County Agricultural High School, 1924–1930; and Franklin County Agricultural High School, 1930–1935. He was appointed business manager at Blue Mountain College and served one year, 1923–1924, then served as assistant president at Mississippi College for one year. He served as supervisor of agricultural high schools and junior colleges with the state department of education in 1935–1936. He continued in other capacities for a total of eleven years, and gave fifteen years of dedicated service to the Mississippi Education Association as assistant executive secretary.

John Alna Travis was married to Miss Nell Kelley of Bunkie, Louisiana, on August 13, 1918, at Stafford Springs, Mississippi, immediately after returning from service in World War I. They were the parents of two sons, Jack A. and Kelley, and had four grandchildren.

JOHN CALHOUN WINDHAM

Mississippi in 1904, where he was awarded the B. A. degree.

Mr. Windham again took up his teaching career immediately after graduation from college and served as principal of the Eupora Schools, 1906–1907, and then as superintendent of Coffeeville Schools, 1907–1908. He then served as superintendent of the school system at Canton, Mississippi, 1908–1912. At this time, he resigned to accept a larger and more responsible position as superintendent of the Tupelo Public Schools, Tupelo, Mississippi, where he remained until 1919. Mr. Windham accepted a position as superintendent of Cleveland Consolidated School in 1919 and remained there until 1932. While at Cleveland he had the distinction of directing for thirteen years what was believed to be, at that time, the largest consolidated school in the world. After leaving Cleveland in 1932, Mr. Windham accepted the superintendency of the consolidated schools at Hickory, Missis-

sippi, which he soon developed into one of the largest schools of this type in the state. He resigned this position, however, in 1937, to become superintendent of Forrest County Agricultural High School, which is the only school of that type remaining in the state. Under the wise and practical administration of Superintendent Windham, this school made much progress and made a definite contribution to education in that section of the state.

In 1944, Mr. Windham was asked to serve with the state department of education as supervisor of agricultural high schools and junior colleges to fill a vacancy that had occurred during the war conditions. He remained in this position until 1946 when he went to what was known as the Polio Clinic to serve a short time until the clinic was abolished. Mr. Windham then went to Black Hawk School in Leflore County where he was superintendent and taught for a year or two. At this time, he retired briefly until he was asked to go to Walnut Grove School System as superintendent. While here he helped to reorganize this institution and worked it back to the A-Grade status. Failing health prevented Mr. Windham from completing his term at Walnut Grove, and he went into retirement at Kosciusko. He later moved to Tutwiler, Mississippi.

On November 5, 1903, John Calhoun Windham was married to Miss Mary Westmoreland Evans of Vaiden, Mississippi, a lady of great refinement and strong character who represented one of the prominent and influential families of Carroll County. Three children blessed this marriage—J. C. Windham, Jr.; Mary; and John E.

Mr. Windham was active in the education associations, having been a member of the Mississippi Education Association and the National Education Association. He served as the forty-sixth president of the Mississippi Education Association in 1928, and he served as a member of the state textbook commission several times over the years. Mr. Windham made studies through visits over the United States regarding free textbooks and was influential in helping get free textbooks for the school children of Mississippi. He also was one of the pioneers in the use of school buses in the state.

Mr. Windham was an active member of the Methodist Church. He was active in scouting, he was a Mason and a Knight of Pythias, and he was a member of the Woodmen of the World.

Mr. Windham, like many other outstanding educators of the state of Mississippi, spent his entire teaching career in his native state. He was regarded as one of the most practical and sane school superintendents in the state, and few men have ever made a greater contribution to the cause of education in this respect than did John Calhoun Windham.

BENJAMIN LEON HILL

Benjamin Leon Hill was born and reared in Jones County at Soso, Mississippi. His parents were William David Clinton and Lula Evelyn Powell Hill. He attended Jones County Agricultural High School and earned a B. S. degree in science and mathematics at Mississippi Southern College. For eight years he was principal and coach in Mississippi high schools. In summer sessions he achieved a master of science degree in chemistry and school administration at the University of Alabama. For two years he was head of the chemistry department at Copiah-Lincoln Junior College, also serving as a ground school instructor of meteorology in the evenings, under the Civil Aeronautics Authority. Then he returned to Mississippi Southern College as teacher of science and as acting principal of the demonstration school.

That term was curtailed by the urgent call from the U. S. Navy for all qualified instructors in meteorology and navigation. After an orientation period in Chicago he taught at Lambert Field, St. Louis, Missouri until commissioned Lieutenant, Senior Grade, U. S. Naval Reserve, on January 21, 1943. Further navy duty in Hollywood, Florida and at the Pensacola Naval Air Station involved staff work, navigation in PBY Squadron 8-B and administration. He had been acting head of the air navigation ground school at St. Louis; and after two years as student control officer at Naval Auxiliary Air Station, Bronson Field, Pensacola, he was promoted to lieutenant commander and had charge of the ground school there. He holds permanent rank as Lieutenant Commander, USNR.

For a while, after the war, he served as an educationist for the Civil Aeronautics Authority with headquarters in Atlanta. In June of 1946 he returned to Mississippi to accept the appointment as supervisor of agricultural high schools and junior colleges in the state department of education and served in this capacity for twenty-two years. For that office the job description was probably unique. In addition to coordination, public relations, budgeting, reporting to the

BENJAMIN LEON HILL

legislature on needs and progress—items which one might expect as duties of the supervisor—he was executive secretary of the Junior College Accrediting Commission, secretary of the Junior College Commission, executive secretary of the Junior College Association and a member of the governor's committee for approving training schools for veterans. Also, by law, he served as a member of the five-person College Accrediting Commission set up to determine which institutions might grant degrees.

Mississippi junior colleges were meeting some needs of youth that no other institutions were meeting. Wise geographical spacing made attendance convenient for everyone. Expense to the student was kept low. There were twelve junior colleges, and seven agricultural high schools not connected with junior colleges, at the beginning of Mr. Hill's tenure. Four more junior colleges were established within the ensuing years. Enrollment increased very rapidly as service men and women returned to school under the

Veteran's Education Bill. Vocational-technical programs set up under an allocation-of-functions plan made many, many kinds of training available at reasonable cost and without much duplication. Academic preparation earned the respect of scholars everywhere, for graduates of junior colleges did very, very well. The counterbalance of (1) statewide support of and cooperation among the member institutions of the system and (2) the support and control of each college under a local board of trustees had national acclaim in the educational profession.

Mrs. Hill was the former Catherine Bible of Brandon, Mississippi. Both of their daughters graduated from Hinds Junior College and from the University of Mississippi. The elder, Dr. Belinda Hill Adams, graduated from the school of business administration at the University of North Carolina at Chapel Hill and works for NASA Research Center. The younger, Lu Hill Harding, earned a degree in hospital administration at Medical College of Virginia and is a personnel director for Mississippi Baptist Hospital.

At Brandon Mr. Hill is a former member of the town board, a member and deacon of the First Baptist Church, and a member and former district governor of Lions International. Now that he has retired he has time for recreational reading and touring. He enjoyed visiting Fiji, New Zealand, Australia and Hawaii. Next to Mississippi his favorite place is Yorktown, Virginia, not only for the historic sites there but also because that is the home of his young granddaughter. He pampers a small herd of beef cattle and roams his fields and ponds. Wherever he is, his greatest pride is in the Mississippi junior colleges.

FRANCIS MARION FORTENBERRY

Francis Marion Fortenberry was born on August 29, 1913, at Polkville, Smith County, Mississippi, the son of Walter James and Felle (Barfield) Fortenberry.

He completed his public school work in Clinton, graduating from high school there. He then went to Hinds Junior College, and later received his bachelor's degree from Mississippi College. He obtained his master's degree from the University of Mississippi.

Mr. Fortenberry began his employment at Copiah-Lincoln Junior College in the summer of 1939 as assistant football coach, assistant dean of men, and teacher, where he remained until 1942.

FRANCIS MARION FORTENBERRY

He served his country by joining the United States Navy in 1942 in active duty and by serving during World War II as an instructor in the United States Air Force, 1942–1944.

Mr. Fortenberry returned to Copiah-Lincoln Junior College in 1945 as athletic director and head football coach. He was later named dean of men. In 1950, he was named as administrative assistant to the president and served in that capacity until 1956, when he was elevated to president, a position he held until 1968. During this long tenure of service at Copiah-Lincoln Junior College at Wesson, Mississippi, fifteen years serving as teacher, coach and athletic director, and dean, and then twelve years as its president, Francis M. Fortenberry helped hundreds and thousands of young men and women achieve their educational ambitions.

In 1968, Mr. Fortenberry assumed a position with the state department of education in Jackson, Mississippi, as supervisor and director of the state division

91

of junior colleges. He served in this capacity until his untimely death on August 31, 1970, two days before his fifty-seventh birthday.

Francis Marion Fortenberry was married to Miss Nona Gillis of Ackerman, Mississippi, who is also a teacher. They made their home in Clinton, Missis-

merce, member and president of the Wesson Lions Club, a member of the Brookhaven Kiwanis Club, and a member of the Mississippi Economic Council.

Mr. Fortenberry was an active member of the Baptist Church, where he served as Sunday School teacher, deacon, and chairman of the deacons.

MILLARD RAY BUSBY

GEORGE VAUGHT MOODY

sippi, after he became supervisor and director of the division of junior colleges.

Mr. Fortenberry was affiliated with many professional and academic organizations, including the Mississippi Education Association, the National Education Association, the Southern Association of Colleges and Schools, and Phi Delta Kappa. He served as president of the Mississippi Junior College Association and as secretary-treasurer of the Mississippi Association of Colleges. He was a colonel on the staff of Gov. J. P. Coleman and also a colonel on Gov. John Bell Williams' staff.

His leadership was reflected also in his civic activities. He was a member of the Chamber of Com-

F. M. Fortenberry's death closed a career most useful and fruitful in the educational affairs of Mississippi.

MILLARD RAY BUSBY

Millard Ray Busby joined the staff of the Division of Junior Colleges, State Department of Education in 1969, as supervisor of student activities. He served as acting director of the Division of Junior Colleges from the time of F. M. Fortenberry's stroke in May 1970 until October 1970. Mr. Busby's dedication during this interim period enabled the Division to continue its responsibilities, including completion of the 1970 annual report, the 1972 budget request, and the 1970 fall semester enrollment report and audit. Mr. Busby had served for years at Copiah-Lincoln Junior College as teacher and in student services.

GEORGE VAUGHT MOODY

George Vaught Moody was born on August 12, 1931, the only child of William Osborne and Kathryn Vaught Moody in Tylertown, Walthall County, Mississippi. He attended public schools in Tylertown (1937–1940), Pascagoula (1941–1945) and Poplarville (1945–1949), graduating from Pearl River Agricultural High School in 1949.

George Moody attended Pearl River Junior College from 1949 to 1951. He then attended Mississippi State College (now Mississippi State University) where he received the bachelor of science degree in agriculture with a major in animal husbandry. To complete requirements for teaching mathematics, Mr. Moody attended the University of Southern Mississippi from 1955 to 1957, receiving the master of arts in school administration and supervision. He later returned to Mississippi State University during the summers of 1959, 1960, and 1961, and completed work for a master's degree in mathematics. He continued his pursuit of higher educational preparation from 1954 to 1973 at the University of Southern Mississippi and received the doctorate of education.

George Moody taught mathematics, education, and psychology at Pearl River Agricultural High School and Junior College from 1956 to 1965. From 1965 to 1970, he served in administrative capacities at Pearl River Junior College, including purchasing agent, business manager, director of federal affairs and of student financial aid programs. In November 1970, Mr. Moody became Director, Division of Junior Colleges, State Department of Education.

George Moody is married to the former Mary Lynn Graves of Jackson, and they reside in Clinton, Mississippi. He has two sons, George Vaught, Jr., born in 1959, and Phillip Todd, born in 1962, by a previous marriage.

Mr. Moody served with the United States Army Military Intelligence for two years. He is an active member of the Baptist Church where he serves in church music and education. He is active in community affairs and is a member of the Jaycees and the Rotary Club. He is active in various professional organizations, including Phi Delta Kappa, Mississippi Education Association, Mississippi Association of School Administrators, Red Red Rose, Mississippi Association of Colleges, Mississippi Junior College Association, American Association of Community or Junior Colleges, and the National Council of State Directors of Community or Junior Colleges.

The Mississippi State System of Public Junior Colleges

Some feel that passage of Senate Bill 131, as approved on April 26, 1928, marked the creation of a Mississippi state system of public junior colleges by setting up a commission to govern the new institutions. Others would say that the system was created, not by legislative action, per se, but by the Junior College Commission at its fourth meeting, on February 7, 1929, by passage of a "motion by Denson, seconded by Stringer, that *zones* and *standards* proposed by the secretary, Knox M. Broom, be accepted by the Commission and recommended that they be strictly adhered to in the future." It would seem safe to say that the legislature which stated, "All junior colleges seeking to qualify under this act shall be under the control of a state commission, known as the Commission of Junior Colleges" delegated authority, and the commission created the system. Under the legislative-created hypothesis the date would be April 26, 1928; while under the commission-created hypothesis, the date would be February 7, 1929. Under either thesis, Mississippi can claim, without question, the first state system of junior colleges in the nation.

Dr. Jesse P. Bogue, Executive Secretary of the American Association of Junior Colleges, stated that "Mississippi is the only state which has a real system of junior colleges and this state system has set a pattern for other states. The Mississippi state system is the logical approach to the proper distribution of colleges, an ample tax base with a reasonable tax rate, an equalization provision to insure the relative prog-

ress of all colleges, and the acceptance of responsibility among the colleges by common agreement for specialized curricula."

Dr. C. C. Colvert, Professor Emeritus and Consultant in Junior College Education, University of Texas, says, "I often quote to people the fact that Mississippi was the first state in the Union to set up a state-wide junior college system whereby each county interested was assigned to a junior college district."

Also, the results of a questionnaire sent by Dr. Garvin H. Johnston, State Superintendent of Education of Mississippi, dated May 8, 1973, to the fifty chief state school officers, to which each of the fifty states responded, are included in the following letter: "A recent survey of the fifty states, requested by J. B. Young, a former President of Jones Junior College, Ellisville, Mississippi, and J. M. Ewing, a former President of Copiah-Lincoln Junior College, revealed that data received from each of the fifty states indicated that Mississippi, in 1928, was the first state to legally provide a state system of public junior colleges.

"Mississippi's state system of public junior colleges, which was established in 1928, is composed of 16 junior colleges and operates on 25 campuses throughout the state. These centrally located campuses provide low-cost collegiate education within commuting distance of virtually all Mississippians. Students may pursue either the first two years of the regular academic work required for a four-year college degree or enroll in one of the many vocational and technical programs that are available. Also taking advantage of training opportunities offered by junior colleges are businesses and industries which enroll their employees in the various schools. Night classes are offered for adults who desire to upgrade job skills or learn new skills.

"The state and the local junior college districts share the financial responsibility for the operation, maintenance, and expansion of these institutions. This unique plan of local-state partnership has been very successful. Local control and administration are retained, while broad, general supervision is provided by the state. The state exercises control only in those areas which are required for the general welfare and interest of all the junior colleges and all the people of the state. The local people through their local trustees have full authority to operate their local junior college as the type of school which most effectively meets the needs of their district."

Knox M. Broom, Field Representative for the U. S. Office of Education, and formerly State Supervisor of Public Junior Colleges in Mississippi for twelve years, stated that "The Mississippi state system of public junior colleges has received approbation from educational leaders of many other states in our nation. The reason for this is that the Mississippi system stands at the top among the junior college systems of the country. It did not just happen that the Mississippi system ranks among the best, but rather this favorable position is the result of (a) a basic philosophy of educational service to the low and average income groups, which underlies the state system of public junior colleges; (b) a very definite preconceived plan for the location and development of these institutions; and (c) the wholehearted cooperation of other educational enterprises in the growth and development of the system. Mississippians probably have given neither the recognition nor the publicity to the unique features of our junior college program which the system deserves.

"A little more than three decades ago the boys and girls of the low income group in the rural areas of our state found their first opportunity for high school education in our county agricultural high schools. As a result of an aroused high school consciousness in the rural districts and improved transportation facilities, the consolidated high school movement took form. By the middle of the twenties the need for high school boarding facilities had been met by consolidated high schools in most of the counties. Then followed the persistent demand for educational opportunities extending through the first two years of college, at low cost, nearer home, and under closer supervision, for the greatly increased number of relatively immature high school graduates. A number of the county agricultural high schools began to experiment with one or two years of college work—such experiments were without legal authority."

A first step taken by the Commission of Junior Colleges was the acceptance of proposed zones and standards. The following quotation of the law was included in a *History of Mississippi Public Junior Colleges; a State System of Public Junior Colleges*, by Knox M. Broom, State Supervisor of Junior Colleges, published in 1953:

The zones herein proposed and to which the Accrediting and Legalized Junior College Commission have given their approval have been based upon assessed valuations of 1927 and enrollment for the session 1927–1928, as given by official reports to state departments. Transportation facilities, trade relations and proximity to senior colleges have been considered in the placing of each county in the proposed zone. In the future it may be advisable to make changes in order to meet conditions which may arise, but for the immediate present the following proposed zones represent the Commissions' best judgment for a working basis and they recommend that they be adhered to in the organization and development of a safe system of public junior colleges. However, it should not be interpreted that any county will be barred from any of the benefits to which it may be entitled by electing to support a junior college in another zone.

It was evident immediately that in placing a junior college in each of the proposed zones, and with the accessibility of the senior colleges and universities to students in certain areas of the state, an institution of higher learning would be within commuting distance of a large majority of high school graduates in Mississippi and also would be available to youths and adults who desired training in job opportunity programs that could be developed. The percentage of high school graduates who began their college work in a public junior college is a tribute to those who planned and proposed placing the counties in a junior college zone. Each county in the state, with the exception of five counties, in which a university or senior college was located, and four other counties because of proximity to a senior college, was placed in one of the thirteen zones. The concentration of institutions of higher learning in the counties in Northeast Misssissippi and the fact that a group of counties in this area did not establish an agricultural high school delayed the establishment of a junior college in two proposed zones in this section of the state until 1948.

A tabulation of the counties designated in each proposed zone in 1928 and the counties assigned to each junior college district or zone under House Bill No. 215, Chapter 398, Laws of 1964, shows few basic changes. The original zoning recommended thirteen zones. The 1964 law recommended thirteen districts or zones and included each of the eighty-two counties in the state in a zone. The majority of the counties in the state remained in their original zones. A tabulation of the counties included originally in each proposed zone and those assigned under House Bill 215, 1964, appears immediately below.

The establishing of public junior colleges in Mississippi as a part of an approved state system has shown, by the growth and development of each institution, and by the stability of these junior colleges, at the close of the first fifty years, that the Mississippi state system is sound.

Each of the eleven fully established, and state accredited, junior colleges operating during the beginning years has continued to the present time, and the five colleges established at later dates have continued. These institutions have expanded in all areas. They were basically academic in the beginning, but, through expansion, now operate very comprehensive programs.

The leadership of the public junior colleges in Mississippi has regarded them as a well-defined, clear-cut phase of higher education meeting distinctive needs of college-age youth which could not be met by other institutions of higher learning. The Mississippi public junior colleges are much alike in many characteristics; yet, they are observably different in their efforts to meet the needs of the district to be served.

The acceptance of the junior colleges as a distinct phase of higher education and the influence and leadership of the local boards of trustees have resulted in each junior college remaining through the years as a two-year college. No Mississippi public junior college has requested approval for a four-year status. The chapters to follow will present the story of each of the sixteen public junior colleges.

MISSISSIPPI STATE SYSTEM OF PUBLIC JUNIOR COLLEGES

Original Zones Proposed and Approved by the Commission of Junior Colleges, 1928	Proposed Revision of Zones Accepted and Established by Statute, House Bill No. 215, Laws of 1964, now existing.
Pearl River Junior College District: Counties included: Pearl River, Marion, Hancock, Lamar	Pearl River Junior College District: Counties included: Pearl River, Marion, Hancock, Lamar, Forrest, Jefferson Davis
Hinds Junior College District: Counties Included: Hinds, Rankin, Warren, Madison, Yazoo	Hinds Junior College District: Counties included: Hinds, Rankin, Warren, Claiborne
Harrison, Stone, Jackson Junior College District: Counties included: Harrison, Stone, Jackson, George	Gulf Coast Junior College District: Counties included: Harrison, Stone, Jackson, George
Holmes Junior College District: Counties included: Holmes, Attala, Carroll, Montgomery	Holmes Junior College District: Counties included: Attala, Carroll, Choctaw, Grenada, Holmes, Madison, Montgomery, Webster, Yazoo
Sunflower Junior College District: Counties included: Sunflower, Leflore, Humphreys, Bolivar, Coahoma, Issaquena, Sharkey, Tallahatchie, Washington	Mississippi Delta Junior College District: Counties included; Bolivar, Coahoma, Humphreys, Issaquena, Leflore, Sharkey, Sunflower, Washington

MISSISSIPPI STATE SYSTEM OF PUBLIC JUNIOR COLLEGES

Original Zones Proposed and Approved
by the Commission of Junior Colleges,
1928

Proposed Revision of Zones Accepted
and Established by Statute, House Bill
No. 215, Laws of 1964, now existing.

Jones County Junior College District:
  Counties included: Jones, Covington, Jasper,
  Wayne, Perry, Greene, Clarke

Jones County Junior College District:
  Counties included: Clarke, Covington, Greene,
  Jasper, Jones, Perry, Smith, Wayne

Kemper County Junior College District:
  Counties included: Lauderdale, Kemper, Noxubee

East Mississippi Junior College District:
  Counties included: Clay, Kemper, Lauderdale,
  Lowndes, Noxubee, Oktibbeha

Tate County Junior College District:
  Counties included: Tate, Quitman, Tunica, DeSoto,
  Panola, Marshall

Northwest Junior College District:
  Counties included: Benton, Calhoun, DeSoto,
  Lafayette, Marshall, Panola, Quitman,
  Tallahatchie, Tate, Tunica, Yalobusha

Copiah-Lincoln Junior College District:
  Counties included: Copiah, Lincoln, Claiborne,
  Jefferson, Franklin, Lawrence, Adams

Copiah-Lincoln Junior College District:
  Counties included: Adams, Copiah, Franklin,
  Jefferson, Lawrence, Lincoln, Simpson

Newton County Junior College District:
  Counties included: Scott, Newton, Leake,
  Neshoba, Winston

East Central Junior College District:
  Counties included: Leake, Neshoba, Newton,
  Scott, Winston

Pike County Junior College District:
  Counties included: Pike, Walthall, Amite,
  Wilkinson

Southwest Junior College District:
  Counties included: Amite, Pike, Walthall,
  Wilkinson

(A junior college was not organized in the beginning.)

Northeast Junior College District:
  Counties included: Prentiss, Union, Alcorn,
  Tippah, Tishomingo

(A junior college was not organized in the beginning.)

Itawamba Junior College District:
  Counties included: Itawamba, Chickasaw, Lee,
  Monroe, Pontotoc

Simpson County Junior College District:
  Counties included: Simpson, Jefferson Davis,
  Smith, Lawrence, Rankin (This district began a
  junior college program for three years but did not
  receive state approval; therefore, it closed, and the
  counties began supporting other junior colleges.)

The original zoning system included seventy-three
counties in the approved districts. Nine counties in
the state were not assigned to a junior college district.
A university or senior college was located in five of
the counties not zoned. These were:
Forrest County—State Teachers College at
Hattiesburg.

The thirteen existing zones making up the Mississippi
State System of Public Junior Colleges, and including
each of the eighty-two counties in Mississippi, now
operates sixteen designated junior colleges and nine
additional campuses.

98

Oktibbeha County—State A. & M. College at Starkville.

Lowndes County—Mississippi State College for Women at Columbus.

Grenada County—Grenada College at Grenada.

Lafayette County—University of Mississippi at Oxford.

Choctaw, Webster, Clay, and Yalobusha Counties were omitted due to proximity to senior colleges.

The three junior colleges operating within other designated districts are:

Meridian Municipal Junior College operated in the City of Meridian, located in Lauderdale County, which is in the East Mississippi Junior College District.

Coahoma Junior College, a junior college established for black students at Coahoma Agricultural High School in Clarksdale, receives local support from four counties in the Mississippi Delta Junior College District.

Utica Junior College, established at Utica Agricultural High School and located in the Copiah-Lincoln Junior College District, for black students, receives local support from counties in two junior college districts—Copiah-Lincoln District and Hinds District. These counties are: Hinds, Copiah, Rankin, and Warren.

Other junior college districts operating additional campuses include:

Gulf Coast District:
Jefferson Davis Campus—Gulfport
Jackson County Campus—Gautier George County Center—Lucedale
East Mississippi District:
Golden Triangle Center—Mayhew
Itawamba District:
Tupelo Center—Tupelo
Pearl River District:
Hancock Center—Bay St. Louis
Hattiesburg Center—Hattiesburg
Copiah-Lincoln District:
Natchez Center—Natchez
Hinds District:
Jackson Branch—Jackson

The Individual Story
of Each Junior College

The stories of each institution were presented by the presidents. The list to follow identifies the president of each junior college who provided the story of the institution:

Pearl River	Marvin R. White
Hinds	Robert M. Mayo
Mississippi Gulf Coast	J. J. Hayden, Jr.
Holmes	Frank B. Branch
Mississippi Delta	J. T. Hall
Northwest Mississippi	R. D. McLendon
Jones County	T. Terrell Tisdale
East Mississippi	William E. Reeves
Copiah-Lincoln	Billy B. Thames
East Central	Charles V. Wright
Southwest Mississippi	Horace C. Holmes
Meridian	William F. Scaggs
Itawamba	W. O. Benjamin
Northeast Mississippi	Harold T. White
Coahoma	James E. Miller
Utica	J. Louis Stokes

PEARL RIVER
JUNIOR COLLEGE STORY

The county school board of Pearl River County met in the county superintendent's office on July 6, 1908 to consider the location of an agricultural high school for Pearl River County. Two trustees, Theodore G. Bilbo, who was later to become governor of the state and a United States Senator, and E. B. Ferris, were elected for the proposed school.

A committee was organized to act in behalf of "cer-tain citizens" of Poplarville for the purpose of contributing a sum of $2,245 and ninety acres of land to the proposed school, provided it was located in Poplarville. On July 30, 1908 five members of the county school board met to approve the location of the Pearl River County Agricultural High School in Poplarville. Mr. M. G. Blackwell and Mr. M. D. Tate, representing the citizens of McNeil, Mississippi, made an effort to have the board rescind its former action. If the move had been successful it would have reopened the matter of location and given other localities another opportunity to bid for the school. A "spirited" discussion of the many features of the case followed. After the law governing the matter had been thoroughly examined and argued, the board voted to ratify the action of locating the school in Poplarville. At this time trustees were ordered to place in the hands of the chairman, Mr. Leopold Locke, a certificate stating that the funds donated had been paid according to the proposition as made. As soon as this was done a site was selected, and the trustees began to make the necessary preparations for opening the school. Although Mr. Blackwell and Mr. Tate made a strong fight in behalf of their town, they pledged themselves to abide by the actions of the board and lend their support to the new school.

On July 7, 1909, almost a year later, a reported three thousand people were present to witness the cornerstone laying for the new agricultural high school building and to enjoy the barbecue on the campus of

PEARL RIVER JUNIOR COLLEGE

GUIDED BY THESE
PRESIDENTS

James Andrew Huff
1921–1926

Simeon Lafayette Stringer
1926–1932

Joseph Forrest Stuart
1932–1936

Arthur Benjamin Nicholson
1936–1937

Robert Edward Lee Sutherland
1937–1942

Reese Dermont McLendon
1942–1953

Garvin Howell Johnston
1953–1967

Marvin Ross White
1967–

the Poplarville High School which had been in existence for some time. Early in the morning the crowd began to gather from all directions, and hundreds were reported to be coming in on the regularly scheduled train. A procession was formed on Main Street, headed by a brass band. It marched out to the site of the new school building where the cornerstone ceremonies were held by the principal speaker, J. C. Hardy, President of Mississippi A. & M. College at Starkville. This episode marked the beginning of a new epoch in education for Pearl River County. The speaker paid a glowing tribute to the citizens of the county. He congratulated them upon being among the very first to take advantage of the new law which allowed county agricultural high schools to be created.

A single building served all purposes when operations first began. The first floor of the building consisted of classrooms, dining rooms, and other facilities. The second floor of the building contained sixteen rooms for girls and two rooms for female teachers. The third floor had sixteen rooms for boys and one for Professor J. B. Anthony.

By special permission of the trustees, arrangements could be made with a limited number of boys and girls to act as janitors of the classrooms in payment of their tuition. Arrangements were made to have all the washing of clothes for the dormitory done on the grounds. A charge of fifty cents per month was levied for laundering, with an additional charge of fifty cents for ironing. Female students were given an opportunity to wash and iron in return for their tuition. The boys were taught farming while the girls were taught cooking, sewing, and other aspects of housework. All dormitory students who stayed over the weekend were required to attend a church of their choice.

The first session of Pearl River County Agricultural High School began on Wednesday, September 1, 1909. Seven or eight hundred people, mainly citizens of the county, attended the opening exercises. The principal speaker was Professor J. N. Power, State Superintendent of Education. Following the official ceremonies, forty-two students were enrolled, nineteen of whom lived in the dormitory. In three days the enrollment increased from forty-two to sixty-one students, and by the Christmas holidays eighty-three students were enrolled. The beginning faculty was as follows: Professor T. M. Kelly, principal and teacher of mathematics and history; Professor J. B. Anthony

of Kosciusko, science and agriculture; Miss Clara Stokes of Gloster, languages; Miss Genevieve Jacobs of Gloster, expression; and Miss Callie Newton of Georgia, music.

On June 15, 1910 the trustees of Pearl River County A. H. S. met in Theodore G. Bilbo's office to discuss erection of a brick school building and auditorium annex. The action on the proposition was deferred until proper legal papers could be drawn up. On June 23, 1910 the trustees met to ratify the contract drawn by Senator Bilbo between the trustees and the contractor. This building stood until 1968 as Jacobs Hall. During the next ten years, an administration building, a girls' dormitory, and a combined dining room and boys' dormitory were added.

Seventy-one students graduated from the agricultural high school on May 16, 1920, the largest number in the history of the school. On September 28, 1920 the board of trustees authorized the addition of freshman college work beginning with the 1921–1922 session. Thus, the school was the first in the state to offer college credit.

August 23, 1922 ended the thirteenth year for the school. The same year the enrollment reached 250, with representatives from twenty-five counties.

The school buildings in 1922 consisted of a three-story brick girls' dormitory, with thirty-two rooms on the second and third floors, and the superintendent's home, reception room and hospital on the first floor. Attached to the girls' dormitory were the home science laboratories, and sewing and music rooms described as a "model of beauty, convenience and comfort." The boys' dormitory was one of the most beautiful as well as most serviceable buildings of its kind in the state. The new combination of dining hall and dormitory had a large airy dining room which seated 350 people while the second floor had sixteen bedrooms. The administration building was well-arranged and well-equipped. It contained ten classrooms, a large auditorium, offices, lecture room and science laboratory. Construction on a superintendent's home began in 1923. All these buildings were equipped with electric lights, steam heat, artesian water, and sewerage system. The school owned its own light and water plant.

Board in the dormitory was furnished at actual cost and had never exceeded $12 per month. The rooms were furnished with heat, lights, study tables, chairs, dressers, bedsteads, mattresses, springs, and closets which were all free to the students. Students who were willing to do "honest" work could earn enough money to pay a large part if not all of their expenses.

At the beginning of the 1923–1924 school year the school could boast of having eighteen faculty and staff and one administrator. At the board of trustees meeting in February 1926, Mr. S. L. Stringer was elected superintendent of the school to replace Mr. J. A. Huff, who had served since 1917.

On May 6, 1926 the school joined the Junior College Athletic Association, and on May 13 the agricultural high school was recognized as a junior college by the state and academic credit was to be accepted by all senior colleges in the state. On September 7, 1926 Pearl River Junior College had its formal opening ceremony in a new auditorium with a seating capacity of one thousand at a total cost of $65,000. S. L. Stringer was superintendent of the high school and president of the junior college. The first summer school in connection with Pearl River Junior College opened on May 27, 1929 with over eighty-two students and teachers present.

The board of trustees met in a regular session on February 2, 1932. The most important business taken up at this session was the appointment of Joseph Forrest Stuart as president of the college for the 1932–1933 school session. During the next meeting of the board, President Stuart's contract was extended to three years. Under his administration the official name of the school, adopted by the board of trustees, was changed to Pearl River County Agricultural High School and Junior College, although the school had been going by this name for several years.

In 1933 the board of trustees began its effort to secure financial support from Lamar and Jefferson Davis Counties. These counties began their support in 1935.

During the June meeting in 1933 the major buildings on the campus were named. They were Moody Hall, Batson Hall, Huff Hall, White Hall, Jacobs Hall, and Crosby Hall.

On July 1, 1935 the Pearl River Junior College authorities made application to the war department for the establishment of a junior R.O.T.C. unit. The application was approved, and on August 19, 1934 the first R.O.T.C. unit was formed.

Mr. A. B. Nicholson was unanimously elected president of the college on May 4, 1936, and the next year on July 8, Professor R. E. L. Sutherland was elected president of the college to fill the vacancy caused by the resignation of Mr. Nicholson.

On April 2, 1940 the board of trustees ordered eight full scholarships, including fees, board and tuition, be given for athletics and that fourteen additional athletes be given full board and fees during the first three months of the school session. They were to be allowed the privilege of either paying the balance or working for the school until the account was settled. On June 2, 1942 the first basketball scholarships were awarded by order of the trustees.

On July 1, 1942 Mr. R. D. McLendon was elected president of the college. At this time because of World War II the college was to face about three years of a small, mostly female enrollment.

On June 6, 1944 the trustees agreed to name the various buildings on the campus as follows:

High School Girls' Dormitory	Batson Hall
High School Boys's Dormitory	Huff Hall
College Girls' Dormitory	Hugh L. White Hall
College Boys' Dormitory	Pearl River Hall
Administration Building	Moody Hall
Dining Hall and Dormitory	Crosby Hall

At the beginning of the school year in 1946 the college had a faculty and administration of twenty-three, the largest number in the school's history. At this time veterans of the war were making their presence felt on campuses throughout the country, and Pearl River Junior College was no exception. On August 21 the school was authorized to offer training to veterans under the G. I. Bill of Rights.

On February 18, 1946 President R. D. McLendon recommended that an apartment building for veterans be constructed. The building was to become Bilbo Hall. At the same board of trustees meeting the government donated prefabricated material to the school for a science building, and on May 13, 1947 the school authorized President R. D. McLendon to have the building brick-veneered. On February 23, 1948 the board of trustees introduced a resolution to erect a new gymnasium, to repair and refurnish the building being used as a gymnasium and to convert the gymnasium into an auditorium. A dwelling house for the college agriculture teacher and farm manager was built in 1952. Money for the construction was to come from the sale of timber grown on school property.

The idea of transporting students to Pearl River rather than building more dormitories was accepted on an experimental basis in January 1951 when the board of trustees approved the purchase of two school buses. If the experiment should prove successful the board was to approve purchase of two more buses at a later date.

The first air conditioned offices on campus were the result of a donation by Mr. Sidney Tonner. Four years later, in 1955, he donated an air conditioning system to the library.

In 1953 Garvin H. Johnston was appointed president of the college by the board of trustees. The college continued to make great progress under his leadership.

The junior college severed its direct relations with the high school in the spring of 1960. In the fall of that year the eleventh and twelfth grades were taught in a new senior high school building. At this time they came under the supervision of the superintendent of the Poplarville City School System.

The 1960s were the "building" years at P.R.C. as 1961 saw the completion of a new men's dormitory, Lamar Hall. In 1963 the student center was completed. 1965 and 1966 saw the construcion of a science building, a vocational-technical complex and an athletic field and football stadium. In 1967 bids were approved for an academic building and a library, and plans were accepted for expanding the student center and altering the cafeteria. Ten faculty housing units were begun in 1968, and Jacobs Hall was demolished to provide space for the new administration building which was constructed in 1969. In this year also the cafeteria was air conditioned.

A director for a new associate degree curriculum in nursing was hired in 1964, and the fall semester of 1965 witnessed the enrollment of the first students to attempt a two-year registered nurse program.

In August 1967, President Garvin Johnston was nominated as the Democratic party's candidate for the office of state superintendent of education. Since no opposition of consequence was expected in the general election, the board of trustees authorized Mr. Johnston to send a press release to all the newspapers in the junior college district stating that applications for the job of president of the college would be accepted until September 27, 1967. On October 12, 1967 Mr. Marvin R. White was elected president of Pearl River Junior College to succeed Mr. Johnston. Mr. White, who was dean of the college at the time, officially took office on January 15, 1968.

The administration, the faculty and the clientele looked at the facelifting on the campus with pride until one dreadful night in August 1969, when hurricane Camille wrought such destruction that all six counties within the junior college district were declared disaster areas. Monies earmarked for building were immediately transferred to the hurricane repair fund. Repairs allowed the fall semester to begin on schedule.

In September 1969 a contract was accepted for the construction of the Pearl River Junior College Vocational-Technical Center in Forrest County. Later the same year funds were made available for the renovation of Jeff Davis and Moody Halls. The latter became a fine arts building with an annex for choir and band rehearsal. In March 1972 a bid was accepted for the construction of a vocational-technical center in Hancock County.

After receiving insurance money compensating for the destruction of hurricane Camille, the college let a contract to demolish what was left of Batson Hall, a girls' dormitory which was completely destroyed in the hurricane. In April 1970 bids were accepted for a modern girls' dormitory to be built on the same site as Batson Hall but to be named Marion Hall.

With the beginning of the fall semester of 1971 all classrooms were air conditioned, and the total September enrollment reached 1,336.

Pearl River Junior College has a tradition for competitiveness. Listed below are some of the honors won by the alumni since the formation of the Mississippi Junior College Athletic Association in 1926.

Football
Junior College State Champions 1926
Mississippi Junior College Champions 1928
Mississippi Junior College Champions 1929
Tung Bowl 1946
Mississippi Junior College Champions 1949
Won Mississippi Memorial Bowl Game 1949
Mississippi Junior College Co-Champions 1952
Mississippi Junior College Co-Champions 1953
Hospitality Bowl 1956—State Championship
Hospitality Bowl Champions 1958
Hospitality Bowl Champions 1959—State Championship
Hospitality Bowl Champions 1960—State Championship
Mississippi Junior College Champions 1961—Number one in the Nation
Mississippi Junior College Champions 1963
Mississippi Junior College Champions 1969
Mississippi Junior College Champions 1970

Basketball

Junior College State Champions 1927

Mississippi Junior College Champions 1929
Mississippi Junior College Champions 1935
Mississippi Junior College Champions 1945
State Champions 1947
Mississippi Junior College Champions 1958
Mississippi Junior College Champions 1965

Tennis

Boys' Tennis Champions 1932
Boys' Tennis Champions 1933

Boxing

Champions 1938 Boxers

Debate

Debate 1932
Junior College Affirmative Team 1948–49
1951 Debaters—State Champions
1954 Debaters—State Champions
Mississippi 1954 Forensics Sweepstake Award
South Sweepstakes 1957—South
1971 First Place Honors

Press

Mississippi Junior College Press Association Annual Award
1947–48
Mississippi Junior College Press Association Annual Award
1950–51
Mississippi Junior College Press Association Annual Award
1951–52
Third Place Mississippi Junior College Press Association
Award 1971–72

Baseball

State Junior College Championship 1929

At the end of the first fifty years the college offers a wide range of subjects in three regular attendance centers, and courses are offered at night in three counties within the district. The future looks bright for Pearl River Junior College. The school's philosophy states its devoted effort to serve its clientele to the advantage of all.

HINDS
JUNIOR COLLEGE STORY

Hinds Junior College has two histories—that of a high school and that of a college. The main grounds now occupied by Hinds were trodden by students for the first time in 1917 when the old home site of J. R. Eggleston, captain of the Confederate ironclad *Mer-*

rimac, became the campus of a county agricultural high school.

The idea was conceived even earlier, when an act of the Mississippi legislature of 1908 provided for the establishment of county schools of agriculture. After this act passed, a movement was started immediately for the establishment of such a school for the boys and girls of Hinds County. From time to time, various ideas on the location and scope of the school were proposed, but it was not until May 31, 1916 that the task of building an agricultural high school for the county was undertaken with the determination to provide a school as good as the best in the land.

Attractive bids for the location of the school were presented by the enterprising citizens of Clinton, Edwards, Utica, and Raymond. After considerable deliberation, the county school board selected Raymond for the site of the new institution. In addition to accepting Raymond's bid, Hinds County issued bonds in the sum of $75,000 to erect and equip the four brick buildings and the principal's home.

The school was founded for the express purpose of providing educational opportunities at low cost to students willing to work. It was part of a statewide agricultural high school program and primarily for rural students.

W. N. Taylor was elected the first superintendent. The campus that first year consisted of the administration building, later known as the old science building, two dormitories, Shangri-La and main. Later came a power plant, one barn, and seventy-four acres of land—all valued at $86,663.69.

The original board of trustees consisted of H. V. Watkins, Jackson, president during his tenure of office from 1918 until his death in 1944; C. S. Shann, Raymond, 1918–1923; F. M. Coleman, Jackson, secretary by virtue of his position as county superintendent of education (1918–1936); D. C. Simmons, Utica (1918–1936); and D. W. Graham, Bolton (1918–1936).

The school had an enrollment of 118 students who were taught by a staff of eight faculty members. During the first year of its existence, the school was admitted membership in the Southern Association of Secondary Schools.

In the beginning, all boys were required to take a course in agriculture, covering four years, and a two-year course in manual training. The girls took a required course in home economics, covering four years. Theoretical instruction was supplemented by

HINDS JUNIOR COLLEGE

GUIDED BY THESE
PRESIDENTS

Robert Edward Lee Sutherland
1922–1930

George Judson Cain
1930–1938

George Minor McLendon
1938–1965

Robert Murrah Mayo
1965–

abundant practical work in the kitchen, dining room, and on the farm.

Some basic academic courses were included in the curriculum, using textbooks which the state commission adopted for use in all agricultural schools in the state. But the main purpose of the school was to produce educated farmers and housewives and to stimulate agricultural activities on the county farms through an extension service. The institution acted as a clearing house of useful information to the farmers of the county. A mailing list of the farmers was kept so all useful but recently acquired information along agricultural lines could be properly disseminated.

The school served as the "poor man's college." Before the organization of the agricultural high school, it was impossible for most farm boys and girls to obtain an education because of costs. Hinds gave them a chance to work their way through an education, always maintaining that "no student was turned away if he or she were willing to work."

Military training was introduced in the first year, and all boys were required to take the training. A competent instructor was engaged, and all boys were furnished military khaki uniforms.

Since the school was coeducational, certain restrictions were imposed on the boys and girls. They were not separated entirely. They took their meals together and recited together in the same classrooms. At frequent intervals, on Saturday evenings or Sunday afternoons, the boys went to the girls' dormitory for an hour or two together.

Mr. Taylor resigned in the spring of 1918 because of illness in his family. R. E. L. Sutherland, agriculture instructor, was made acting superintendent for the remainder of that session and was then elected superintendent.

The first year of college work was added to the curriculum during the 1922–1923 academic year, and the ninth grade of high school was discontinued. The first freshman class had thirty members.

Just four years later, the county decided it would do well to add the second year of college work to the curriculum, and in 1926 Hinds Junior College was officially born. That year a new administration building was constructed at a cost of $100,000. The same building stands today but is now called the Auditorium Building.

The fall of 1926 saw the enrollment pass the four hundred mark, with seventy-four of the number registered as college students. The college department "grew up" in 1928, when the school was admitted to membership in the Southern Association of Colleges and Secondary Schools.

Mr. Sutherland resigned to accept a position as president of Mississippi College for Women, and G. J. Cain, principal, became president in 1930. Two faculty houses were constructed at this time. By 1933, Hinds had grown so much that the enrollment had passed the 550 mark. The year 1936 marked the beginning of Hinds' dominance in state competition, as the college won the championships in literary, athletic, and debate competition. The school continued to grow, and by 1937 a well-equipped gymnasium and a second dormitory for boys were erected.

Mr. Cain resigned in 1938 to accept a position with the Mississippi State Department of Education, and G. M. McLendon became president of an institution of 528 students. The next twenty-seven years have become known as "The McLendon Era."

During his first term as president, McLendon had the campus driveways paved, a lighted football field added, additional shops constructed, and the civilian pilot training program approved. The meat curing and cold storage plant was also constructed that year as part of a post-depression project, giving the college the first of three outside agencies owned by the county but transferred to the college for administration. The fall of 1940 found over seven hundred students at Hinds. More recreational facilities were added, and a motion picture machine for visual education was purchased. State championships in athletic, dramatic, and literary events came to the campus each year with each activity receiving the full backing of the president.

In 1946 McLendon was named president of the Mississippi Association of Colleges. During the same period the Hinds Band marched down Capitol Street in Jackson in honor of returned war hero Jonathan Wainwright. A new girls' dormitory was completed, and a veteran's housing project was opened.

By the end of 1950 the college had added a new science building, music hall, band hall, eastside dormitory, and westside dormitory; a housing project with thirty-eight apartments and trailers; recreational facilities at Raymond Lake; two buildings for training in the vocational trades; the John Bell Williams Airport and hangar, classrooms, and office space; 165 acres of land to the school farm with barns and housing; a poultry production unit; the football stadium and athletic practice field; and four houses for faculty and staff.

In instructional offerings, the school had added the entire vocational training program and the program of remedial training for those deficient in the basic educational skills. The year 1956 marked another expansion program. Scheduled first were a new science building, a girls' physical education building, a men's dormitory, a women's dorm, and the expansion of the gymnasium. Also planned were a new library building, a fine arts building, and a massive training center for vocational-technical trades.

The high school division was moved out of the college in 1958. In January of 1962 an ultramodern library containing 20,000 volumes was completed, as well as a science annex and eight new faculty houses. Construction of a technical education building had already been started, and the English and speech departments were moved into remodeled quarters.

During this decade the first building of the "Futurama" planned by McLendon was completed with the opening of a new vocational-technical center. A committee was appointed to study both immediate and future expansion of Hinds' facilities. By January of 1965 the committee, directed by vice president Robert M. Mayo, found the need for one million dollars in new facilities.

In 1965 George M. McLendon reached the mandatory retirement age of 70. The college library was named and dedicated in his honor on May 9.

Dr. Mayo, after serving five years as vice president, was elevated to the presidency in July of 1965. This marked the beginning of one of the most prosperous years in the history of the college, in terms of growth in enrollment, physical additions, and curriculum.

A building boom unparalleled in the history of the college began in the summer of 1965. Three buildings, including the student union, addition to the vocational-technical center, and an agriculture technology building, were constructed. Before the year was out, a new men's dormitory was off the drawing board. By the middle of the fiscal year, four buildings were in construction at the same time. An additional 36.3 acres of property were purchased adjoining the campus.

As the forty-eighth session began, enrollment for the first semester leaped to a twenty-eight percent increase over the previous year with 2,076 students.

Before the year was out, 3,142 students had enrolled in academic, vocational, technical, manpower development and training, health occupation, and night classes. The vocational-technical program progressed, with 1,087 students engaged in training for work in industry and business. Hinds had gained a name for itself in the industrial world.

In 1966 westside dormitory had been renovated, and several changes had been made in the cafeteria. The student union building opened its doors for the first time, and Greaves dormitory was near completion.

In 1967, Dr. Mayo announced plans for a $750,000 fine arts building. The new structure would provide 39,000 square feet of space and house all music, art, language, and speech classes. The president announced that thirty acres of land adjacent to Hawkins Field Industrial Park in Jackson had been bought for a facility for training people in vocational-technical programs.

The Eagle Basketball team under Coach Troy Ricks won the South Crown and continued at the state finals to win the first State Junior College Championship title for the college in basketball.

As the doors opened for the fiftieth session, enrollment in the academic areas increased by 101 students. Total enrollment for Hinds was 2,363. As part of the fiftieth anniversary of the college, homecoming activities involved two former presidents, G. J. Cain and G. M. McLendon. Mississippi's governor-elect, John Bell Williams of Raymond, was selected as "Alumnus of the Year."

During the spring of 1968 Hinds lost its best longtime friend in the death of Frank M. Greaves, president of the board of trustees. For more than thirty-five years he had served on the board and held the position of president for more than twenty. Even at the age of eighty-five he traveled with the Hi-Steppers across the United States.

During the spring of 1968 the college newspaper, *The Hindsonian*, earned the "All American" rating from Associated Collegiate Press. This is the highest award a collegiate newspaper can receive. In one weekend in April three Hinds organizations triumphed in contests at their respective conventions. *The Hindsonian* won the "General Excellence" award at the Mississippi Junior College Press Association conference; the Circle K Club won four awards at their tri-state convention; and the distribution and marketing technology students won three top awards at the first state junior college convention of their organization.

The Hinds Alumni Association received its charter granted by the secretary of state's office. Irl Dean Rhodes of Brandon served as president of the association.

Plans were announced for a five-story women's dormitory to be added to the campus at a cost of $800,000. The dorm would house 257 women and was scheduled for completion in 1969. The educational media laboratory had produced its own video tape production in 1969. Entitled "Psychological Measurements," the production was prepared by Mike Rabalais, psychology instructor, and Ewing Gaby, director of the laboratory.

The debate team won the state championship for the fifth straight year, and Hinds was host to the State Choral Festival.

R. E. Woolley, president of the board of trustees, and Dr. Noel McKey, president of the Hinds County Board of Supervisors, broke ground for the new five-story women's dormitory.

In April, two members of the alumni and one of the college administration were named to appear in the 1969 edition of *Outstanding Young Men of America.* These were Hinds County Rep. Robert Ferguson of Raymond; Irl Dean Rhodes, Chancery Clerk of Rankin County; and HJC Public Relations Director, J. Ralph Sowell, Jr.

Bids were awarded in April of 1969 for the Jackson Branch of Hinds Junior College to be located off Delta Drive. The one-story concrete and steel structure would have 72,000 square feet of space and would cost over $1,000,000.

As the fall 1970–1971 session began, the doors of the Jackson Branch were opened. The branch has been called "The garden spot of Vocational-Technical Education in the South." The new facility offers vocational preparatory training during the day and supplemental training at night.

As school work began, the Hinds Media Center helped students through various methods of learning experiences. One phase was the dial access system which allowed audio and video tapes to be listened to or viewed as study aids for students and instructional aids for classes at various locations on the campus. Overhead transparency production facilities allowed the faculty to bring in their ideas as a rough sketch or a picture and leave with a transparency. Art and graphics work was also done for those who needed assistance. Another aid was the audio-visual classroom which accommodates a class of from thirty to forty students.

A. F. Summer, Hinds alumnus and attorney general for the state of Mississippi, was named the college's "Alumnus of the Year" during homecoming activities.

April brought about the destruction of one of the college's three original buildings. Shangri-La, a men's dormitory built in 1917, was torn down to make room for a new classroom building. At one period, the building was a coed dormitory.

The new 28,000 square-foot classroom building was begun and would cost $463,621. The structure would house thirteen classrooms, thirty-eight faculty offices, a seminar room and a conference room. Mathematics, engineering, graphics, data processing, and computer science would be housed in the building.

Congressman Charles Griffin was named "Alumnus of the Year" at the annual homecoming celebration. Ann Lasater and Nell Ann Pickett, members of the English faculty, completed their second publication, *Handbook for Student Writing*, published by Canfield Press of San Francisco, California. Thomas Hal Phillips, a 1941 graduate, was awarded the National Phi Theta Kappa Alumnus of the Year Award at the national convention in Rochester, Minnesota.

The Hinds Art Gallery was dedicated in honor of Mississippi artist Mrs. Marie Hull on May 14. Serving as cochairman of the ceremonies were Mrs. Robert M. Mayo and Bob Dunaway, chairman of the art department.

By September of 1972, Hinds had a faculty of 284 instructors and administrative employees, twenty-five clerical employees, and forty-four service employees. The physical plant included eight buildings for student housing, forty-four buildings for faculty housing, and twenty-nine buildings which are administrative, classroom, and auxiliary structures. The college and property value was set at $9,093,013.85.

During September, Dr. Mayo announced that the Hinds Airframe and Powerplant Mechanics Program had been certified by the Federal Aviation Administration. At that time, the Hinds program was the only one in the state certified by the FAA.

Plans were announced during September for the construction of an annex to the science building at a cost of $663,000. The annex would be built on the site of the old music building.

During the fall, the faculty and administration began organizing to conduct the self-study program, as recommended by the Southern Association of Colleges and Schools. The study would take eighteen months to complete.

In October, Fred Brooks, Jr., a Hinds faculty member for sixteen years, was notified that his biography would appear in the *Dictionary of International Biography*, volume X. Brooks has served as chairman of the speech department, speech instructor, and debate team coach at Hinds.

During January, David Durham, chairman of the division of mathematics and science, constructed a gas laser for use in the engineering physics course at Hinds. This was the third laser Dr. Durham had built. He had constructed one at Auburn University and one during graduate school at the University of Tennessee.

Enrollment for the regular session, including all programs, reached 7,108 for the 1972–1973 year. The enrollment for the 1972 summer session numbered 903, making a grand total for the year of 8,011.

As the fall semester opened on the 1973–1974 school year, much of the work on the self-study had been completed, and the report was printed. The visiting committee would visit the campus on November 12–14 to make their evaluation.

During homecoming activities, the John Bell Williams Room of the McLendon Library was dedicated to the former Mississippi governor. A. F. Summer, Attorney General of the state of Mississippi, and former Congressman Charles Griffin made dedicatory remarks. At the annual alumni banquet Thomas Hal Phillips, an internationally known writer, was named the HJC Alumnus of the Year.

Work was steadily progressing on the science annex, with a completion date of spring semester in sight.

Hinds had earned the position as the pacesetter for Mississippi junior colleges and upheld this title with an enrollment of 4,957 for the fall semester. According to Joel McNinch, director of admissions and records at Hinds, this figure put Hinds as the fourth largest college in the state.

The goal to make education available and accessible to students took another stride forward when Dr. Mayo announced that plans had been approved

for the construction of a million dollar vocational-education complex for Vicksburg. The complex, which would be built on land made available by the Warren County School Board, would be located on Highway 27 near the county junior high school under construction across from Warren Central. Work was set to begin in early 1974 with completion hoped for by spring semester of the 1974–1975 year.

Changing times, a changing economy, changes in lifestyles and social patterns will continue to result in changes on and challenges to the campuses of the college district. As we move into the last quarter of the twentieth century, we look back with a sense of pride on the role Hinds has played in the economic and population growth of this district and in the educational role it has played in the lives of thousands of youths and adults. We look to the future with expectancy that an even greater role will be our lot in the years ahead.

MISSISSIPPI GULF COAST JUNIOR COLLEGE STORY

During the past sixty years the Mississippi Gulf Coast Junior College has undergone three major phases in its development. From 1911 to 1925 it was an agricultural high school supported through the cooperative efforts of Harrison, Stone, and Jackson Counties. From 1925 to 1962 both high school classes and college courses at the freshman and sophomore levels were offered. Also during this period, in 1941, George County joined Harrison, Stone, and Jackson Counties in support of the institution. The third phase was inaugurated in 1962 when the high school was discontinued, and a master plan for a multicampus junior college system was established.

In the summer of 1911 the Harrison County School Board established the Harrison County Agricultural High School, which marked the beginning of the present institution. To induce the board to locate the school at Perkinston, C. C. Swetman, Walt Davis, Rev. R. N. Davis, W. W. Farnsworth, Van O'Neal, T. T. Garner, E. Garner, Dantzler Lumber Company, and a number of other citizens donated 656 acres of land and $626. Their efforts were successful; the institution began operation in 1912 with Mr. J. A. Huff as principal. Later, in 1916 Stone County was formed

MISSISSIPPI GULF COAST JUNIOR COLLEGE

GUIDED BY THESE
PRESIDENTS

Jefferson Lee Denson
1925–1929

Cooper J. Darby
1929–1941

Albert Louis May
1941–1953

Julius John Hayden, Jr.
1953–

from the northern part of Harrison County, and the school continued under their dual support.

The second phase of Mississippi Gulf Coast Junior College was initiated during the 1925–1926 session under the leadership of Superintendent J. L. Denson. With five well-qualified instructors—E. B. Colmer, agriculture; W. H. Wood, history; Frances Bailey, mathematics; C. O. Hinton, science; and Bernice McMullan, English—and twenty-five students—the college division opened. In 1926 Jackson County added its financial support, and the institution became Harrison-Stone-Jackson County Agricultural High School and Junior College. That year thirty-nine students enrolled, and the following spring Hersel McDaniel of Eastabuchie, Mississippi, became the first graduate of the college and the only member of the 1927 graduating class. Also in 1927 the junior college department was accredited by the state junior college accrediting commission.

Since agriculture was the economic backbone of Mississippi during the 1920s, the supporting counties—Harrison, Stone, and Jackson—endorsed a curriculum centered around agriculture. In addition to agriculture, the curriculum included English, history, Latin, French, Spanish, mathematics, science, and piano; and in 1929, the first pine tree nursery in the state was established at Perkinston. Various extracurricular activities were promoted on campus during the early days. In addition to football, basketball, and baseball, the Wilsonian Club and the Densonian Club were organized for the purpose of encouraging reading and self-expression among the students; and the Hi-Y Club and the Girls Reserve Club were organized to help promote the moral and spiritual development of the students.

During the first part of the second phase under J. L. Denson's administration, additional buildings were constructed: a science annex, a boys' dormitory, a girls' dormitory, a gymnasium—known as the "Pride of the South"—a power plant, a superintendent's home, and an administration building that was later Denson Hall.

During the second phase, under the Darby administration, the college received accreditation from the Southern Association of Colleges and Schools. Cooper J. Darby, assuming the responsibilities as superintendent in 1929, is credited with revising and enlarging the curriculum so that the college would qualify for accreditation. The first year of Mr. Darby's

superintendency was also the first year of the Great Depression which brought difficulties for the college, notably a decrease in enrollment. Fortunately, in the following year enrollment almost doubled and in subsequent years continued to increase. Even with the increasing enrollments, money was scarce. However, because of the superintendent's careful management not only were the employees paid during the depression years but the college also was able to meet other operational costs and pay off an $80,000 construction debt.

It was during the Darby administration that the bookstore began operation, and the college received one of ninety-two Carnegie Library Grants awarded in the United States. The Alumni Association was organized in 1929 through efforts of Dr. C. O. Hinton, science instructor. Noll P. Davis served as its first president. Construction projects included the erection of a girls' dormitory, the installation of a modern water and heating system, and the building of a house for the head of the agriculture department, bringing the value of the college plant in 1941 to $392,747.83.

Succeeding C. J. Darby in 1941 was A. L. May, who served until his death in the summer of 1953. President May was instrumental in gaining the support of George County in 1941, rounding out the four-county district now supporting the college. When George County added its support, the name of the school was changed to Perkinston Junior College, and the title *superintendent* was then changed to *president*.

World War II brought about a change in the junior college programs. Agriculture was on the decline, and more technical programs were needed. On February 11, 1942, the board of trustees passed a resolution to begin vocational training courses in cooperation with the Mississippi State Vocational Board. The first vocational classes, auto mechanics and radio repair, were taught in the old laundry building, long since demolished. Within a short time, nineteen different courses were available for the returning veterans.

After a short decline during World War II, enrollment rose to 423 by the end of the May administration. Many construction projects were begun. The college purchased four barracks buildings for classrooms, dormitories and a cafeteria-music-biology building, with funds saved through good management. The athletic field and stadium, named May Stadium in 1949, were built by a $100,000 county bond issue. The vocational building, named for E. B. Colmer, a pasteurizing plant, and a swimming pool were also built during this time with capital appropriations, the first to be received by the junior colleges from the state.

At the end of World War II a movement to purchase a chapel for a war memorial was started by W. G. Gregory, mathematics instructor and sponsor of the YMCA and Christian Council. The project was completed through the joint efforts of the college and the alumni. Later the building was renovated and named Gregory Chapel.

In 1953, at the age of 33, J. J. Hayden, Jr., was promoted from dean of men to president of Perkinston Junior College, the youngest chief administrator in the history of the school. When he assumed the post, the college enrollment was 513, and the college plant was valued at $1,123,000.

President Hayden's first public statement outlined for the college a philosophy which differs little from what it is today: low cost education, training for employment, preparation for higher education, and service to the community. Dr. Hayden was quick to propose the formation of a board of trustees building committee to guide college expansion programs. Outside expert advice was sought to determine what new facilities were needed to enable the college to keep pace with the times. Consequently, in 1955, an $885,000 building program was initiated under Dr. Hayden's leadership. Other programs have followed at regular intervals since that time.

The building programs initiated in the late 1950s at Perkinston had a strong influence on building programs being started at other junior colleges in the state. The late 1950s and early 1960s became known as a building period in the junior colleges.

Although the third phase of Mississippi Gulf Coast Junior College was inaugurated in 1962, events, actions, and planning that led up to it took place as early as 1945. The need to take higher learning to the coastal area was realized, and the establishment of a college there was proposed annually from 1945 to 1960. To help meet this demand for education, Perkinston began offering evening extension courses in the cities of the coast, with a Jackson County endeavor at Gautier popularly called "Longhorn College" because the building where classes were taught was formerly a saloon. Classes were also offered in Ocean Springs, Gulfport, and Pascagoula. But even this expansion was not sufficient to meet the educational needs of the coastal area. Nor did a plan to establish a branch of Perkinston Junior College on the coast seem feasible.

Later, a consultant from the University of Texas, Dr. C. C. Colvert, working with the college board, the boards of supervisors, and other groups on the coast, formed a plan to create a legal district of the four supporting counties and to build centers in both Gulfport and Gautier. Attorney Joel Blass and Mr. L. A. Krohn were instrumental in writing a bill that would serve as the foundation for the college district. The bill was passed in the legislature and signed into law by Gov. Ross Barnett on May 10, 1962. With the signing of this bill, Perkinston Junior College became the Mississippi Gulf Coast Junior College District. Hence, backed by a strong, cooperative board of trustees, Dr. Hayden was instrumental in gaining the passage of legislation that established the four supporting counties of Harrison, Stone, Jackson, and George as a legal entity which would provide fiscal independence, to a degree, in that the college board of trustees was authorized to set the local budget up to established maximum limits. The bill also provided that branch campuses would be opened. On the fiftieth anniversary of its founding, the high school was discontinued.

The completion of the two coast campuses in 1965 made Gulf Coast the first junior college in the state, and one of the first in the nation, to operate a branch system. The first year enrollments were 411 on the Jackson County Campus; 669 on the Jefferson Davis Campus; and 603 on the Perkinston Campus, for a total of 1683.

Each of the three campuses offers a full college transfer program and some vocational-technical courses. However, each offers specialized programs to meet the needs of the particular area it serves. Jackson County Campus, consisting of 138 acres of wooded terrain, is located on U.S. Highway 90 at Gautier, approximately five miles west of Pascagoula. To serve the highly industrialized Moss Point-Pascagoula area, Jackson County Campus offers courses in electronic technology, electrical technology, in-plant welding, pipe-fitting, sheet metal, and other courses for Ingalls Shipbuilding Corporation. In addition to the courses for industry, the campus offers medical technology courses such as X-ray and nursing.

The 120-acre Jefferson Davis Campus, consisting of sixteen structures laid out to form landscaped courts between them, is located about one and three-quarter miles north of U.S. Highway 90, midway between Gulfport and Biloxi. Since the campus is located in a comparatively high population area and one involved in many activities, including tourism, technical programs such as hotel-motel-restaurant operation, law enforcement, distribution and marketing, and registered nursing are among the courses offered. To serve the needs of an ever-growing urban area, building trades courses are offered such as air conditioning and refrigeration, carpentry, electricity, metal trades, mortar trades, and plumbing as well as many health occupations courses such as dental assisting, licensed practical nursing, surgical technology, and ward clerk.

Perkinston Campus, the only campus with boarding facilities, has five dormitories for men and two for women, with a total capacity of 530 students. All intercollegiate athletic teams are located at Perkinston because it provides boarding facilities for the athletes. The music department directs a large marching band and a large choir. Perkinston is the only campus that offers fulltime programs in home economics, ornamental horticulture, offset printing, and letterpress printing.

After the establishment of the two coast campuses, the administration remained attentive to the future needs of industry and business. The Manpower Training Project on the Harrison County Seaway was developed to work with industry brought into the county by the Harrison County Development Commission. This effort was given a special rating by the federal officials as a Skills Center, the only one so designated in the state. The George County Center was completed in 1972 to offer vocational programs to county residents and to prepare them for employment in this developing area. With the opening in 1972 of the George County Occupational Training Center at Lucedale, Dr. Hayden's philosophy of "taking education to the people" was fulfilled. Now a Gulf Coast facility is within easy reach of citizens of the college district of Harrison, Stone, Jackson, and George Counties.

While expanding physical facilities to meet a projected increase in enrollments, Dr. Hayden has concerned himself with the educational developments of the college. A staunch supporter of vocational-technical education, he has encouraged the development of these programs until today more than fifty

programs are offered at the three campuses and at the George County Center. During the past few years changes in curriculum have occurred, and new teaching methods have been developed and added to the Gulf Coast programs. Remedial courses in mathematics, English, and reading have been included in the curriculum to help those students deficient in these areas. The poorly prepared student can make up learning deficiencies and then proceed to the regular college transfer or vocational-technical programs.

An innovation to assist students is the installation of a dial access retrieval system on the Perkinston Campus, a closed circuit television system on the Jackson County Campus, and the beginnings of a learning resources center on each of the campuses. These centers are being developed by the purchase of various types of audio-visual equipment and materials that have been selected for various faculty who include these as an integral part of their instruction.

One of the newest concepts in trying to carry out the original philosophy of the junior college "to take the student where he is as he enters college and develop him as far as possible during his two years" is the development of special written instructional programs. A number of courses based on these individualized instructional packets are being offered today.

Gulf Coast Junior College has come a long way from its nine courses in 1925 to the numerous courses offered in many areas today. The curriculum includes academic courses that prepare students for transfer programs and a wide range of career programs, courses in vocational and technical training, courses in adult and continuing education, and courses for on-the-job training. There are also noncredit, "special interest," and adult courses, which may be taken for enjoyment, for learning new skills, or for updating old ones. The general purpose of the school then was to develop the intellectual resources of the people and point the way to economic livelihood. Today the same principle prevails—to prepare students for professions, or to enable them to pursue courses of study leading to employment in vocational and technical fields.

In addition to a strong educational program, Mississippi Gulf Coast Junior College has always supported worthwhile extracurricular activities. There are student government organizations on all campuses to maintain clear lines of communication between the administration and the student body. They also plan and sponsor many activities. Also there are newspapers, annuals, literary magazines, dramatic productions, musicals, and club activities on the several campuses. One club that has been especially outstanding through the years is the Phi Theta Kappa. This club has produced five national presidents: Howard Pollock, Len Blackwell, Karl Mertz, Gary Roberts, and Bill Gordon.

Track, tennis, debate, little theater, and music have produced many state winners. Girls' basketball has been resumed, and the Gulf Coast team has won a National Invitational Championship under the guidance of Sue Ross. State championships in boys' basketball date all the way back to 1928, and in more recent years Bob Weathers has coached four championship teams (1964, 1966, 1969, 1970). Gulf Coast's baseball teams have won the state championship almost every year since baseball was revived by Kenneth Farris. Also the teams have entered several regional playoffs. The state football championships came in 1928, 1942, 1948, 1966, 1967, 1971 and 1974.

The 1971 team also won a national championship under the direction of George Sekul.

Building programs under Dr. Hayden's administration (a great portion coming during the third phase) will total $19,192,592 from 1953 to 1978, the end of the current building program.

The entire third historical phase of Mississippi Gulf Coast Junior College has occurred under Dr. Hayden's administration. Although the sixties were the "Golden Age" of higher education generally in the United States, the phenomenal growth of Mississippi Gulf Coast Junior College is largely due to Dr. Hayden's foresight, patience, and leadership. Recognized nationally as a leader of wisdom and devotion to junior college education, he has exhibited creative and responsible leadership during his entire administration. Doubtless, the complex, multicampus college could never have materialized without Dr. Hayden's patient and tireless leadership during those very trying days of organization. He has been able to keep in touch with the many facets of the college through careful organization of advisory councils and committees. In spite of his heavy schedule he always seems to have time to devote to the personal triumphs, problems, and grievances of other administrators, faculty, and students.

Under the leadership of Dr. Hayden, the college has been described as a "happy" college where the faculty "cares" for the students and their needs. Although Gulf Coast has had a phenomenal growth, its basic philosophy has not changed but enlarged to meet the needs of the student.

From its inauspicious beginning as the Harrison County Agricultural High School in 1911, it has become a nationally recognized institution. Its original student enrollment of sixty-two fulltime students has increased to over three thousand; the total number of different people receiving instruction from the college in 1974–1975 was 23,363. Its seven fulltime employees in 1912 have grown to 368 fulltime and ninety-three parttime employees. The 1912 curriculum embraced only half a dozen courses. The 1972 curriculum embraces such a diverse array of academic and technical subjects that the process of numbering and scheduling courses constitutes a problem in itself.

Although the Mississippi Gulf Coast Junior College as it exists today—a multipurpose, multicampus complex—is significantly different from the agricultural high school established in 1911, it retains the basic purpose for which its institutional ancestor was founded.

HOLMES
JUNIOR COLLEGE STORY

The story of Holmes Junior College, Goodman, Mississippi, dates back to 1909, when plans were made for the establishment of Holmes County Agricultural High School, the doors of which were opened to students of Holmes County in September 1911.

There was much deliberation over where the school was to be located, but the matter was settled when Mr. J. M. Kimbrough, Holmes County Superintendent of Education, and the Board of Education of Holmes County—composed of Mr. G. H. Love, Mr. R. L. Smith, Mr. J. D. Weeks, Mr. J. U. Sheehy, and Mr. Ira Jones, received the following letter:

> September 19, 1910
> To the Honorable Superintendent of Education and Board of Education of Holmes County, Mississippi.
> We, the citizens of Goodman and vicinity, desire to make the following proposition for the location of Holmes County Agricultural High School at Goodman, Mississippi, To-wit:

Marvin Eugene Morehead
1925–1928

Major Cyrus McDaniel
1928–1940

Frank Benjamin Branch
1955–

Ras Marshall Branch
1940–1949

Clarence Wilburn Lorance
1949–1955

The school building now owned by the town of Goodman and the one (or larger) acre lot on which the building is located all valued at $ 8,000.00

             40 acres of land   1,200.00

                   Cash   2,000.00

                        $11,200.00

Also free water from our artesian well.

Signed,

C. F. Nelson and Son

W. R. Ellis

Guaranteed by:

W. L. Simmons

President Bank of Goodman

This proposition was accepted, and the board of trustees bought between January 30, 1911, and February 16, 1911, three parcels of land amounting to approximately forty-two acres on the west side of Goodman for location of Holmes County Agricultural High School. Thirty-seven and one-half acres were bought from Mr. J. M. Tate for $800; the amounts paid for the lesser plots are not recorded.

On June 1, 1911, Mr. James W. Sargent was elected principal of the school, and by September the board of trustees had two dormitories (one for girls and one for boys) built and ready for school to begin. The girls' dormitory also housed the dining room and kitchen and quarters for the principal. Classes were conducted in the Goodman School Building. Grounds were landscaped, fifty fruit trees were set out, and garden plots for teaching of agriculture and supplying the dormitory tables were begun. Swine and cows were bought. The usual high school subjects of the time were taught.

Mr. G. H. Love was elected to serve as superintendent, beginning August 1, 1913, at a salary of $1,300 for twelve months, and Mrs. Love was elected matron at a salary of $400. Mrs. Love had the additional duties of planning and supervising the preparation of meals for the boarding students.

Enrollment increased, and in the fall of 1914 Mr. Wirt A. Williams was elected as principal under Mr. Love.

In the fall of 1915, the superintendent and the board of trustees realized that increasing enrollment would necessitate more classroom space than the Goodman School Building afforded and began plans for a building for classes nearer the dormitories.

At the close of the 1918–1919 session, Mr. G. H. Love resigned to run for the position of Holmes County Superintendent of Education, and Mr. Wirt A. Williams was elected as Superintendent of Holmes County Agricultural High School, his term beginning on August 1, 1919.

When Mr. Williams became superintendent, he and the faculty began to formulate rules and regulations to govern all facets of student and teacher behavior and establish procedures of an administrative nature. Since the students were high school students, most had never been from under strict parental control.

Some of the regulations were as follows:

Boys shall be allowed to go to town only on Tuesdays after school hours and on Saturday afternoons.

Girls may go to town with a chaperon on Monday and Friday afternoons after school. Only thirty minutes after arriving in town will be allowed for shopping on Monday and Friday afternoons.

No student shall be excused from Sunday School or from morning preaching service without a legitimate excuse.

Girls who go to church on Sunday nights shall be required to go in a body chaperoned by one teacher. They shall not be allowed to go in separate crowds chaperoned by different teachers. The teacher chaperoning is to be in the lead going to church and in the rear returning.

Teachers must inspect all rooms before going to breakfast and must be in stated places to supervise students who shall march in line to classes. Teachers have been assigned places in the buildings and shall impose discipline in the classrooms, on the campus, and elsewhere as occasions may demand.

The bugle for evening study hour shall be blown at 6:30 P.M. Study hour shall close at 9:00 P.M. No student shall be allowed to go to another student's room during this time; nor shall any student be allowed in the buildings at any time during recess periods or the noon hour.

Teachers may be absent from the campus only one week-end each six weeks to visit families and friends, and then only when scheduled duties will permit.

By 1922, the state legislature made it legal for agricultural high schools to add two years of college work (one year at a time) if facilities, faculty, and course offerings met the standards required by the state department of education. In June of that year the board of trustees instructed Mr. Williams to get all information available from the senior colleges in the state concerning curriculum and academic requirements for faculty, and from the state department of education all other necessary data for the adding of one year of college work. This he did, and the next year they went about fulfilling as many requirements as possible.

In April 1923, Mr. Williams tendered his resignation to the board, effective July 1, 1923, to take a position in the Leland, Mississippi, schools. He was then made head of the history department at Delta Teachers' College at Cleveland, Mississippi, a position he occupied until his death.

Mr. M. E. Morehead was elected to succeed Mr. Williams on July 1, 1923, and served until May 31, 1928. Plans continued for the addition of college work. In May 1925, the board unanimously voted to drop ninth grade high school work effective at the 1925–1926 session (if so approved), and to add the first year of college work.

In 1925, the first year of college work was offered. The institution under the guidance of Mr. M. E. Morehead had a faculty of nine, only two of whom had master's degrees; a student body of one hundred and ten boarding students; a plant of three main buildings—the administration building, the girls' dormitory, and the boys' dormitory; adequate laboratories for agriculture, home science, and general sciences; a well equipped commercial department; and a small one-room library of limited but appropriate books and periodicals. The cost of board and room was $12.50 per month. Two literary societies flourished. All work at college was done by students who were paid twelve and one-half cents per hour. The college was accredited by the Mississippi Association of Colleges in 1926. It became a member of the Mississippi Junior College Literary and Athletic Association in 1928.

The 1925–1926 Bulletin of Holmes County Agricultural High School and Junior College and the minutes of the board of trustees list the faculty as follows: Mr. M. E. Morehead, Superintendent; Mr. L. C. Graves, mathematics; Mr. E. W. Waught, Jr., history; Mr. S. J. Robinson, Jr., agriculture and science; Miss Madge Spiva, English; Miss Louise McGinty, modern languages; Miss Ethel Marley, home economics; Miss Emily Overton, commercial work; Mrs. T. J. Donald, music; and Mrs. M. E. Morehead, matron.

The high school curriculum offered ten required units and twenty-one elective units from which students could choose at least six more, totaling the

sixteen units required for graduation. The college work offered this first year included six hours of English, five hours of mathematics, six hours of history; six hours of French or Spanish; two hours of economics; two hours of sociology; six hours of home economics; three hours of stenography and typing; and three hours of bookkeeping and wholesale accountancy.

The letter which follows is self-explanatory:

State of Mississippi
Department of Education
Jackson, Miss.

June 4, 1925.

Supt. M. E. Morehead,
Goodman, Miss.

My dear Sir:

After having met with your Board of Trustees and discussed the proposed Junior College work in the Holmes County Agricultural High School at Goodman, Mississippi, after having gone into the plan of organization with you fully, we wish to say we heartily endorse your movement and approve your plans for the work. The State Department of Education hereby approves your school for full credits of the Freshman College work for the session of 1925–26, the work to be done according to the requirements of the Commission of the State Association of Mississippi Colleges and the Laws of the State governing same.

Yours sincerely,
W. F. Bond, State Supt. Education,

Claude Bennett,
Secretary, State Accrediting Commission.

Three main buildings—the administration building, the girls' dormitory, and the boys' dormitory—were brick buildings equipped with the modern conveniences of steam heat, electric lights, running water, and screening. The equipment in all departments was modern and adequate.

The farm furnished an effective laboratory for the teaching of agriculture as well as providing vegetables at all times of the year, feed crops, and grazing; a herd of registered Jersey cattle (begun in 1921 with the purchase of four Jersey cows for $900) furnished milk for the school and with a modern dairy barn enabled students to have practical work in dairying; the poultry department, with a flock of White Leghorns of the Ferris strain, furnished eggs and meat for the dormitory as well as providing a laboratory for teaching poultry production; a two-acre orchard furnished fruit for eating and canning, in addition to supplying work in horticulture; and extension services in terracing land, locating ditches, testing seeds and milk, pruning and spraying orchards, vaccinating and inoculating animals were offered free to the farmers except for the transportation of those from the college who did the work.

All the work of the school and farm was done by the students. Besides the practical work in agriculture required by the state, students might work extra time, for which they were paid at the rate of twelve and one-half cents per hour. Several regular jobs were open to boys and girls who wished to earn part of their expenses. The cost of board was $12.50 per month.

The school had teams in all major sports, and students were required to conform to all requirements of the State Literary and Athletic Association of which it was a member.

On January 27, 1927, Mr. Morehead reported to the board of trustees that twenty students were enrolled in college work; that 151 students were enrolled from Holmes, Carroll, and Grenada Counties; and that one hundred students were taking commercial classes. Twenty-seven of the 151 students were residents of Goodman. At this time Mr. Morehead also produced transcripts of work done by the members of the 1925–1926 Holmes freshman college class who had transferred to Mississippi Agricultural and Mechanical College and to the University of Mississippi. These transcripts showed that every student who had transferred was doing very creditable work at those senior colleges. With the apparent success of the first year college program in mind, Mr. Morehead was instructed by the board to proceed with plans for adding the second year of junior college work.

In order to have classroom space for the sophomore classes, it was deemed necessary to make an addition to the administration building. The Holmes County Board of Supervisors was invited to meet with the board of trustees on May 12, 1927, and encouraged the board to pursue their plans.

With the approval of Mr. Claude Bennett, representing the State High School and College Department, the board of trustees awarded the bid for the addition to the administration building. And permission was granted by the board of trustees for Mr. Morehead to make preparation for the second year of college work in the fall of 1927.

The faculty for the 1927–1928 session was upgraded to include three instructors with M. A. degrees and three who were doing graduate work in their teaching fields. Enrollment increased.

On May 9, 1928, Mr. Claude Bennett from the state department visited the school, and after the inspection the board of trustees ordered that the school prepare to offer the second year of college work during the session of 1928–1929.

On May 24, 1928, Dr. H. G. Harrell from Millsaps College, and Professor M. Latimer from Mississippi College—members of the Mississippi Junior College Accrediting Commission—visited the campus as guests of the board of trustees. They inspected the buildings and premises and made the following recommendations:

1. More equipment for science, library, and office.
2. New roofs on all buildings.
3. Steam heat in boys' dormitory.
4. The construction of a gymnasium.
5. Cooperation of other counties in support of the school.

In the spring of 1928, Mr. Morehead resigned to take another position. The board of trustees made a careful search for a man who they thought could meet the many challenges facing the superintendent of a budding institution. They found such a man in Mr. M. C. McDaniel and elected him to succeed Mr. Morehead, on June 1, 1928. When Mr. McDaniel succeeded Mr. Morehead as superintendent he faced many difficulties; the country was entering its worst depression; the physical plant needed repair and expansion; the faculty had to be upgraded; a new building was needed immediately; and the second year of college work was to be offered.

In November 1928, the board of trustees voted to allot $4,000 for the materials to build a gymnasium. The boys and faculty men gave their labor, and by mid-winter a gymnasium was in use.

During the first school year under Mr. McDaniel's leadership, the first school newspaper was published under the name of *The Growl*. It was so named because the Holmes athletic teams had decided to be called the Holmes Bulldogs. In the same year, the first Holmes annual was published under the name of *The Cornerstone*. Because of the great economic depression of the early 1930s, publication was discontinued from 1932–1937. In 1941, the name of the annual was changed to *Horizons*.

121

In September 1929, the Carroll County Board of Supervisors voted to aid in the support of the junior college with the assessment of a quarter of a mill on the assessed valuation of Carroll County. In October 1929, a bond issue of $125,000 from Holmes County enabled the superintendent and the board of trustees to proceed with plans for a building and improvement program which would meet requirements set up by the Junior College Accrediting Commission for a standard two-year college. The buildings and improvements included in this effort were:

1. New dormitory for boys to be located east of the administration building.
2. Auditorium annex to west side of the administration building.
3. Agriculture cottage to be west of the auditorium annex.
4. Present boys' dormitory to be remodeled into dining hall and teachers' quarters.
5. Home science cottage.
6. Renovation of present girls' dormitory.
7. Superintendent's home.
8. Proper equipment for those facilities.

In 1929–1930 the library (located on the second floor of the administration building) grew to 2,300 volumes. A band was organized under the leadership of Professor Leonard, the band director from Millsaps College. The literary societies, organized when Mr. Morehead was superintendent, flourished. The first Glee Club was organized by Miss Mabel Gewin (later Mrs. J. O. Harris).

Teachers and students were not allowed to visit home or elsewhere oftener than once every six weeks. Student labor was raised from twelve and one-half cents to fifteen cents per hour. Attendance at Sunday School and morning church services was compulsory.

The college curriculum was expanded to offer forty-six semester hours of required work and seventy semester hours of elective work from which to complete the sixty-four hours required for graduation. Fifty-four hours of work other than commercial, music, expression, and physical education were required for a diploma.

All requirements of the educational authorities of the state and senior colleges were being met so that full credit was given for Holmes Junior College work in every college in the state.

From 1930 to 1950 the Holmes County Federation of Women's Clubs offered one whole or two half scholarships to worthy girls, preferably from rural sections of Holmes County. Applicants were judged on the basis of character and scholarship and were chosen by Holmes County Federated Clubs.

In July 1930, the board of trustees authorized the digging of a deep well for the school, a project which had been advocated for several years by Dr. A. M. Phillips, a board member. Dr. Phillips was ordered to select the site of the well. In 1933, the trustees ordered a permanent marker erected to show the site of the well, which was officially named the A. M. Phillips Well. This well is still in operation today.

The bids for the buildings, renovations, and improvements were let in August 1930. The work was to proceed at all haste. These plans for building and improvements would meet all the requirements set up by the Junior College Accrediting Commission except that of a home for the president. In order to fulfill that requirement, on September 19, 1930, the board of trustees voted to buy the W. L. Ellis property adjacent to the college grounds for the sum of $4,000 cash, upon which was a residence which with repair and improvement has served as a home for the president since that time.

On February 23, 1931, the board of trustees inspected all work included in the building program and found it to be satisfactory and done as to contract. The work was accepted and the contractors paid in full. These additions and facilities put Holmes Junior College on a par with the other junior college plants in the state.

In the 1932–1933 session, Holmes Junior College awarded four kinds of diplomas; the regular diploma which allowed a student to transfer sixty-four semester hours of college work to a senior college; the Music Diploma, the Expression Diploma, and the Commercial Diploma, all of which required sixty-four hours of work for graduation, all transferable.

The high school had achieved accreditation from the Mississippi State Department of Education in 1920. In 1925, the college was authorized by the Mississippi State Department of Education to offer the first year of college work. In 1926 Holmes Junior College became a member of the Mississippi Association of Colleges; in 1928, it acquired membership in the Mississippi Junior College Literary and Athletic Association. The high school department was accredited by and admitted to membership in the Southern Association of Colleges and Schools in 1930, and four years later, in 1934, the college was admitted as a full-fledged member of the Southern Association of Colleges and Schools and became a member of the American Association of Junior Colleges.

In 1933, the board of trustees voted that henceforth the head of Holmes Agricultural High School and Junior College should have the title of *president* instead of *superintendent*. In 1936, with $15,000 from the Works Progress Administration, a new football field and track were made, complete with lights and seats and enclosed with an eight-foot chain link fence. On October 16, 1936, Mr. W. R. Ellis, President of the Board of Trustees of Holmes Agricultural High School and Junior College, presided at ceremonies dedicating the new athletic facility. Miss Dorothy McBee, secretary of the board, was appointed to dedicate the field as Ras M. Branch Field in honor of the coach.

In April 1939, the board of trustees voted to allow dances on the campus of Holmes Junior College. Regulations regarding the dances were as follows: Dances may be held twice a month during the regular session (excluding summer school). The dances shall be held under supervision of a person designated by the president of the college, who shall have at least two chaperons in attendance at each dance. In the absence of other recreational activities available to students in the community, this move was heralded with much enthusiasm by the student body and the faculty as well.

In 1939, bricks from the old Goodman ice house were bought to veneer the front of a newly-built band hall, which was placed behind the auditorium in a landscaped amphitheatre. Many programs of varying kinds were given in the spring, summer, and early fall on the outdoor stage of the band hall, with the audience seated in folding chairs on the floor of the amphitheatre and with overflow crowds seated on the ground of the sloping sides. Trellises of beautiful wisteria shaded the walks from the roadway down to the dual entrances to the band hall.

By the spring of 1940, under the leadership of President M. C. McDaniel, the faculty and staff numbered twenty-seven persons. The second year of college work had been offered since the fall of 1928. A building program provided a new boys' dormitory, the addition of the auditorium to the west side of the administration building, the agriculture building, renovation of the old boys' dormitory into a dining hall and quarters for teachers, the home economics

cottage, renovation of the girls' dormitory, and the brick-veneered gymnasium with hardwood floor. A home for the president had been bought and improved, and a fine football field put the Holmes Junior College plant on an equal with any other junior college campus in the state. The valuation of the school had increased from $100,000 to $300,000.

Enrollment had increased remarkably: there were eighty high school students; 168 college students; 128 sophomore students, and five special students. The summer school enrollment had risen to ninety-three students.

The curriculum was expanded from two years of general college work to seven special interest groups: Group I, for those expecting to continue for a B. A. or B. S. in the professional work of law, medicine, engineering, pharmacy, ministry, and dentistry; Group II, Agriculture; Group III, Home Economics; Group IV, Business and Commerce; Group V, Music; Group VI, Expression and Dramatics; and Group VII, Elementary Teaching.

The library had grown from the 1,301 books and periodicals in 1928 to over 4,000 volumes in 1940. Located on the second floor of the administration building, the library consisted of one main reading room and a small paper and periodical room, both of which were well lighted, heated, and ventilated. The library also subscribed yearly to between fifty-five and sixty newspapers and magazines.

A well-rounded program of activities complemented the academic program: athletics; the band; the glee club; debating, dramatics, and international relations clubs; religious organizations; and the two school publications—*The Growl*, the college newspaper, and *The Cornerstone*, the annual, all afforded areas of enrichment for students.

In the spring of 1940, Mr. McDaniel resigned. On June 14, 1940, the board of trustees resolved that as a token of appreciation to Mr. McDaniel for his outstanding services in behalf of Holmes Junior College the building known as the administration building, including the auditorium, be designated as the McDaniel Building. Mr. M. C. McDaniel had performed outstanding services not only in the development of Holmes Junior College but also in the development of the Mississippi junior college system. He is deemed one of the "pioneers" of the state junior college system.

Of the faculty members employed by Mr. M. C.

McDaniel, the following dedicated teachers served at Holmes Junior College until their retirement: R. W. Almond, Mr. and Mrs. G. J. Everett, Mr. and Mrs. Billie Montague, Miss Lottie Peebles, and Miss Jessie Van Osdel. One other faculty member, Mr. Stanley F. Allen, employed in 1937, was business manager until his death in 1973. Frank B. Branch, employed in 1936, is the only faculty member of this era still employed at Holmes Junior College.

In selecting the next president of Holmes Junior College, the board of trustees turned to a young man who had come to the college as teacher of science and coach of athletics in 1929 after receiving the B. A. degree from Mississippi College. Ras M. Branch had an outstanding record as a student and as an athlete. Faithful in the performance of his teaching duties, loyal in the support of all school activities, successful as athletic director, his accomplishments developed his capacity for leadership to the extent that in July 1940, Mr. Branch was elected by the trustees to the presidency of Holmes Junior College. Believing in Holmes Junior College and its future, President Branch worked tirelessly during his tenure of office to enlarge the physical plant and to improve and expand the curriculum to meet the growing needs.

The college was still trying to pull out of the depression years, and schools everywhere were being urged to serve the unemployed youths in whatever manner possible. President Branch took advantage of every federal program for which the college could qualify to provide training for the unemployed young men. Courses in woodwork and auto mechanics were initiated under the National Youth Administration; and many young men availed themselves of these opportunities.

In May 1941, the trustees bought the old Goodman Grammar School Building and the grounds connected with it for $3,500. The building was renovated into a dormitory to house fifty male students. At the same time, an annex to the girls' dormitory providing space for fifty girls was built at the cost of $8,000. In August 1941, the college bought 102.83 acres of land adjoining school property from Mr. and Mrs. J. C. McCrory.

In February 1942, the Southern Association of Colleges and Schools and the Mississippi Commission for Accreditation made concurrent evaluations of Holmes Agricultural High School and Junior College. Both found the facilities to be in excellent condition.

The years of World War II brought many changes in all schools as administrators sought to provide training beneficial to the war effort. Intensified academic and vocational courses were offered. National defense programs included mechanical drawing, general shop, physics, photography, Red Cross, and commercial courses. The summer sessions offered many additional academic and vocational courses to meet the needs of the greatly increasing number of students. To help in the war effort, the high school and junior college students put on a drive on the campus in 1943, which resulted in the sale of $8,600 in War Savings Stamps and War Savings Bonds.

In 1943, the trustees voted to provide a building behind the girls' dormitory to house a canning plant which had been acquired through the state vocational department. Cans were furnished at cost, and thousands of cans of food were processed each day. People from all the communities and schools in Holmes County came to avail themselves of this service. It proved to be a money-saver for the school also, for much produce grown in the school gardens was canned for use in the boarding department.

In 1944, new vocational training programs were initiated for veterans: cabinet making; refrigeration; radio repair; expanded commercial courses; house wiring; and elementary electricity.

Enrollments continued to increase, and all dormitories were filled, with four students to the room. The new annex to the girls' dormitory and the old grammar school renovated to accommodate fifty additional male students, did not give, in addition to pre-existing facilities, enough room to house all the student body. Some students rented rooms in Goodman and in neighboring towns.

A much needed facility, a laundry, was installed on the campus in 1945. It was obtained from the National Youth Administration Shop in Tupelo, Mississippi, the only cost to the college being that of transportation and installation. Later the school bought second-hand a small dry cleaning plant to be run in conjunction with the laundry, to serve only college and high school personnel.

In April 1946, the college obtained two wartime prefabricated naval barracks buildings from the government at no cost. The state provided $20,000 toward the construction of each building. The trustees voted to provide funds for equipping them. The larger of the buildings was converted into a dormitory, which doubled the existing space for boys; the other was made into apartments for married couples.

During the 1946–1947 session, the enrollment was 474 college students and 84 high school students. Board was $26.50 per month. The total cost per year for county (Holmes and Carroll) college students was $262; the cost for out-of-county (Mississippi) college students was $307.

In 1947, the old bleachers at the football field were removed and replaced by concrete ones; the two barracks buildings were brick-veneered and improved to make attractive permanent buildings; a large brick-veneered block building was erected below the tennis courts to house high school classes; and a manual arts building was erected south of the new boys' dormitory.

Until 1948, books had been stored in the business office and sold or rented therefrom. However, the greater enrollment necessitated more room for books than existed in the business office. The basement of the dining hall building was converted into an efficient bookstore and canteen.

The library increased to seven thousand volumes. The curriculum offered 109 separate courses in the fields of general college, preprofessional, agriculture, home economics, business and commerce, music, expression, dramatics, and teaching. The pre-engineering course and the one-year concentrated business course were new courses offered.

The plant was valued at $750,000. Holmes County, with cooperation of Carroll County and with appropriations by the state legislature, provided the financial support of the college. As from the beginning, a broader financial base was badly needed.

In May 1948, President Branch suffered a severe heart attack; and on January 14, 1949, he resigned as president of Holmes Junior College. Holmes Junior College had made great strides in his eleven years as coach and his eight and one-half years as its president. On February 1, 1949, the board of trustees elected Mr. Clarence W. Lorance as president of Holmes Junior College. He had been at Holmes for ten years and had served as teacher of mathematics, dean of men, and principal of the high school. Through the years he had demonstrated his ability as an excellent administrator and as a fine school man. Mr. Lorance faced the same challenges and problems which had plagued his predecessors—the maintenance of existing facilities, growth in faculty, low salaries, and need for other facilities.

In 1950, Holmes Junior College received $50,000 from the Mississippi legislature under Senate Bill No. 305 for improving, building, or repairing buildings belonging to the college. The work, begun in July and completed in November 1950, included the following:

1. The central part of the second floor of the administration building was remodeled to give the library more than three times its original space, with new ceiling, floor, and adequate lighting installed.
2. The married veterans building was completely renovated: the first floor was converted into facilities for the music department, including a small auditorium for choral practice and small recitals, four practice rooms, a voice studio, a piano studio, a large lecture room, and an office; the second floor was remodeled to house the science department which included large chemistry, biology, and physics laboratories with storage rooms for each and two large lecture rooms.
3. The old grammar school building was converted into six faculty apartments, relieving the acute problem of faculty housing.
4. A new grade A dairy barn was built to permit the handling of milk for use in the school dining room and for a laboratory for teaching that phase of dairying.
5. An addition to the home economics building was constructed, which allowed the complete renovation of the foods laboratory into a modern attractive facility.
6. General repairs, internal and external painting of some of the older buildings, replacing gutters, re-roofing two buildings, building essential walks, and a garage for the college bus were other improvements made under this program.

In September 1950, the board of trustees requested the board of supervisors of Holmes County to issue and sell bonds in the sum of $100,000 to build and equip a new gymnasium. This was done, and by December 1951, the building was complete.

In 1952, the Mississippi legislature under Senate Bill 212 allocated to Holmes Junior College $100,000 to be used for building and repairs. The bookstore had outgrown the one-room student center under the cafeteria long before, and the board of trustees and Mr. Lorance decided that a student center was the next building needed. It was built from this money on the site of the old gymnasium. It included in addition to the bookstore, the canteen, a recreation hall, a lobby and equipment. This allocation also allowed the complete renovation of the cafeteria kitchen, the replacement of the ranges and ovens, and the repair and painting of the water tank. Other smaller repairs were made.

In July 1955, the student center was totally destroyed by fire. So useful was this facility that the board of trustees immediately asked the board of supervisors of Holmes County to issue and sell bonds in the sum of $50,000 to rebuild the student center at Holmes Junior College. The new building was larger than the first, for it contained a post office facility and offices for several campus organizations in addition to the bookstore, the canteen, and a larger recreational hall and lobby.

In late November 1955, another and greater tragedy befell the school. President C. W. Lorance suffered a severe heart attack and died on November 29, in the midst of a very useful and productive life. In appreciation for his conscientious, faithful service to the school, the board of trustees named the new building Lorance Center. It was so dedicated in April 1956, upon its completion. Mr. Lorance's tenure, like that of each president before him, was marked with the steady struggle for better things for Holmes Junior College.

On December 9, 1955, the board of trustees elected Frank B. Branch as president. With the exception of two years when he was superintendent of schools at Ackerman, Mississippi, he had been a member of the Holmes Junior College faculty since 1936, having served in many capacities as teacher of college history, assistant football coach, head football coach, athletic director, girls' basketball coach, boys' basketball coach, track coach, baseball coach, dean of men, and high school principal.

Having served under the three preceding presidents, the new president was aware that he faced the same serious problems as the foregoing men: much needed repair and improvements on the campus; inadequate facilities; low faculty salaries; and a college in debt through no fault in mismanagement of school finances. There was simply not enough tax base to continue operating the school on the support from Holmes and Carroll Counties alone.

Designed originally to meet the educational needs of Holmes County students, the college had long been providing educational advantages for students from surrounding counties. Carroll County had joined in the support of the school in 1929, but the number of students from that county and others around Holmes

County made an increased tax base absolutely necessary to the continued operation of the institution.

From 1956 to 1964, the administration, the board of trustees, interested alumni and friends of the college made an unceasing effort to acquaint the people of the counties of the area with the needs of Holmes Junior College and its students and to solicit their help in financial support for the college in the following order: Attala County, 1956; Montgomery County, 1958; Grenada County, 1959; Choctaw County, 1959; Madison County, 1961; Webster County, 1963; and Yazoo County, 1964. These counties, along with Holmes and Carroll Counties, participate in the support of the institution and comprise the Holmes Junior College District.

In 1956 and 1958, the Mississippi legislature appropriated funds to be used for building, repair, and renovation in the junior colleges. Holmes Junior College received allocations of $100,000 in 1956 and $100,000 in 1958. The board of trustees decided that repairs and renovations of facilities were of first priority. Hence, an extensive renovation and repair program was initiated in 1956 and was completed in 1960, most of the work being done during the summers of those years.

All the old buildings—administration building, Grenada Hall, Webster Hall, Choctaw Hall, Madison Hall, Science and Music Hall, Industrial Arts Building, Agriculture Building, Home Economics Building, and White House received extensive repairs and renovations. Part of the Agriculture Building was converted into a cosmetology classroom and laboratory. The football field was turtle-backed, new lights installed, and the track and press box improved. A new baseball field and practice football field were made from the hills and gullies west of Branch Stadium, and new tennis courts were built.

After completion of the most necessary repairs to the old buildings and with yearly enrollments increasing rapidly, the board of trustees and President Branch began long-range planning for new facilities. More land was needed, and the board instructed the president to buy as he could what properties were available and suitable for that purpose. During the years, the college was able to obtain at different intervals approximately 128 acres of land for the college, which has allowed space for expansion. However, massive land leveling was necessary for the sites of all new facilities.

During the term of Gov. Paul B. Johnson, Jr.,

House Bill 307, later amended by House Bill 1402, had great impact on the building programs of a large number of the junior colleges, especially Holmes Junior College. House Bill 307, Laws of 1964, allowed a county, with the approval of its board of supervisors and the state budget commission, to withhold for projects benefitting not only the said county but also the surrounding counties up to two of the four mills of the state ad valorum tax, provided the board of supervisors added one-quarter mill local tax for each mill withheld. House Bill 1402 authorized the withholding of up to three mills of the state ad valorum tax with the same provision.

All the nine counties except Yazoo participated in the bond issues of the Holmes Junior College District based on House Bills 307 and 1402. As it had already obligated its state ad valorum taxes to other projects, Yazoo County levied a one-mill tax for a building project at Holmes Junior College from which the District borrowed $380,000 to build Yazoo Hall. In addition Attala County levied a one-mill tax on which $190,000 was borrowed for enlargement and improvement, and Madison County levied a one-mill tax on which $140,000 was borrowed for the same reason. Through the Higher Education Facilities Act, Holmes Junior College obtained $280,241 which was used on the Business and Science-Mathematics Buildings.

With these local and federal monies and the allocations at various times from the state of Mississippi, Holmes Junior College has been able to develop a physical plant valued at approximately $3,000,000 which affords its students and the area which it serves some of the best facilities in the state.

The administration and the board of trustees followed their long-range plan to increase the facilities by constructing the following new buildings:

1961–McMorrough Library
1962–Motel Dormitory for boys
1963–Carroll Cafeteria
1965–Montgomery Fine Arts Building
1966–Vocational-Technical Center
1967–Business Building
1967–Lorance Student Center
1968–Yazoo Hall, dormitory for girls
1970–Addition to auto mechanics shop in Vocational-
   Technical Center
1971–Science-Mathematics Building
1971–Madison Hall
1972–Attala Hall for boys

Other buildings included in the long-range plans to be constructed in the future are as follows:

Frank B. Branch Coliseum
Annex to Vocational-Technical Center
New brick home for President
New library
Athletic field house
Garage for college buses and vehicles
Maintenance warehouse and shop

Since 1960, one frame house and two frame duplexes, one brick duplex and nineteen brick single-family houses were built for faculty. Additions and renovations since 1961 include:

1. New deep well.
2. New lighted tennis courts.
3. Sign and marker at north entrance to campus.
4. Complete renovation of administration building: first floor into administrative offices; second floor into classrooms; both floors air conditioned.
5. Complete renovation of Webster and Grenada Halls: old cafeteria space on first floor of Webster converted into rooms and lobby; new roof on Grenada; aluminum windows, wall paneling, carpets, and air conditioning installed in all rooms in both buildings.
6. Complete renovation of Goodman Grammar School Building in 1967 into up-to-date air conditioned dormitory for boys (named Choctaw Hall).
7. Renovation of Moody House into two apartments for faculty.
8. Conversion of old student center into social science building.
9. New roofs on gymnasium and president's home.
10. Renovation of old science building: first floor converted into recreation hall; second floor made into classrooms for allied health services.
11. Motel dormitory air conditioned and home economics building carpeted.
12. All the buildings erected prior to 1956 were completely refurnished. The new buildings have the most modern of furnishings and equipment. New seats and curtains were installed in the auditorium.
13. Old shop building brick-veneered.
14. Repair of concrete part of stadium; installation of new bleacher seats; enlargements of press box; and other stadium repairs.
15. Blacktop overlay put on all parking areas and streets on campus.
16. Sewer system made adequate for all buildings.
17. Demolition of White House and Choctaw Hall, both being beyond repair.

The provision of an adequate physical plant is only one of the responsibilities of the board of trustees and the president. Increasing enrollments (from 255 college students in 1956 to 2457 on and off campus in

1972) made it necessary to supply an ever increasing number of instructors and a larger staff to provide the services needed. It was a very difficult problem to employ properly qualified instructors, as most secondary teachers of the time could command and get salaries higher than most junior colleges could pay. Each year after 1956, the administration, with the unanimous approval of the board of trustees, raised the salaries of the faculty as much as the budget could bear. They hoped to be able to pay salaries commensurate with the training and experience of the members of the faculty.

In 1956, Holmes Junior College and Agricultural High School had an administrative staff of seven, all of whom taught parttime except the president and the dean of women, twenty-three instructors, and twelve staff members, totaling forty-two persons. This number has increased to fifteen administrators; thirty-eight academic instructors; eighteen vocational-technical instructors; and twenty-five noninstructional staff members, totaling ninety-six persons. In addition, there are off campus one vocational director and twenty-four vocational teachers. Approximately 121 persons are required for the running of the college.

The greatest concern of the administration and president is that of providing courses of study to meet the needs of the people of the area. In 1956, the academic curricula offered at Holmes Junior College were: agriculture; liberal arts; music (piano, voice and instrumental); courses leading to B. S. degree in mathematics and the various sciences; pre-law; pre-engineering; pre-medical, pre-dental, and technician; nursing: business and commerce; secretarial; business education; elementary education; industrial education; physical education; home economics; and two nine-month business courses. The only vocational courses were auto mechanics, radio, and television and FM.

The academic offerings have grown from seventeen to thirty curricula, with 157 subjects being taught. The new curricula added were: forestry; chemistry; biological science; pre-pharmacy; pre-veterinary; pre-engineering technology; physical therapy; architecture; computer science; criminal justice; social work; journalism; and art education. The Army ROTC program was added, and ETV courses were made available.

Holmes Junior College had offered some vocational courses every year since 1925. However, as Mississippi began to change from a purely agricultural state, with the coming of industry, new fields of endeavor opened up; and new areas of study and training had to be supplied to meet the needs of the young people and the adults of the community. In 1959, the college offered the vocational courses of cosmetology, AM and FM radio, and television. In 1961, a course in drafting technology was initiated. In 1966, the vocational-technical center was completed, with additions in 1970 and 1975. Since 1966 the vocational program has offered auto mechanics, cosmetology, electronic servicing, machine shop, practical nurse education, refrigeration and air conditioning, and welding. In 1966, the technical program included secretarial training, drafting and design technology (formerly drafting technology), building and construction technology, and in 1967 data processing, when the business building was completed. The vocational-technical and the business building have combined floor space of 79,381 square feet, and the replacement value of the two buildings is estimated to be $2,381,430. The acquisition value of equipment in these two buildings was $746,095, and the cost of the equipment has more than doubled, making its present value $1,492,190.

In addition to on-campus programs, Holmes Junior College operates a center in Grenada in cooperation with the University of Mississippi, which offers at night any of the freshman and sophomore level classes for which there is sufficient demand; the MDTA Center at Kosciusko; Licensed Practical Nurse programs in Kosciusko, Winona, Canton, Grenada, and Yazoo City; Nurse Aide courses in Yazoo City, Lexington, and Grenada; Emergency Medical Technician courses in Winona, Kilmichael, Canton, Kosciusko, and Grenada. Classes for industry are offered on campus or off campus, and vocational and academic courses are offered on campus if there is sufficient demand.

Students at Holmes Junior College have, in addition to mental and manual development, fine opportunities for moral and cultural enrichment. Qualities of leadership and of civic responsibility are evidenced in all campus activities. The Choir (Concert Choir, Coachmen, Quartette, and Sextette), the Band (Marching Band, Jazz Band, Concert Band, Color Guard, Flag Corps and Rifle Corps), *Horizons* (the yearbook), *The Growl* (college newspaper), the Student Government Association, the Women's Judicial Council, the Collegiate Civitan Club, the Dramatics Club, Phi Theta Kappa, Phi Beta Lambda, the Debating Club, the Lottie Peebles Home Economics Club, the Cosmetology Club, the Chess Club, the Christian Council, Baptist Student Union, Wesley Foundation, the Newman Club, the Vocational-Industrial Clubs of America, and the various activities of the athletic department, one or another, offer opportunities for personal involvement and development to every student on the campus.

Holmes Junior College has from its beginning had an outstanding record of athletic achievement. In no athletic conference is competition more keen, nor the athletic fans more avid and loyal. During the time the Branch brothers, Ras and Frank, coached at Holmes, the Illinois Central Railroad ran special trains to Wesson for students and fans when Holmes played Copiah-Lincoln there and likewise from Wesson to Goodman when Copiah-Lincoln played at Holmes. The treks to and fro of the pink elephant when Hinds and Holmes were arch rivals, and the parading of the big plantation bell when Holmes and Mississippi Delta played, engendered school spirit so intense that the procedures had to be stopped.

Records for a few of the Holmes athletic teams are not on file at the college, but from the yearbooks, from the files of *The Growl*, the school newspaper, and from trophies in the trophy case, the following résumé of Holmes athletic accomplishments is recorded:

Football
Holmes teams have won three state championships and one co-championship in 1935–1936, 1936–1937, and 1945–1946, and were co-champions in 1950–1951. Five teams have won second place in the state: 1919–1930, 1930–1931, 1933–1934, 1937–1938, and 1939–1940. Twice teams have placed third in the state, in 1940–1941, and 1959–1960.

Holmes football teams have played in five bowl games. In 1945, after a tie with Hinds Junior College (6–6) in regular season, Coach Frank Branch's co-champions and Hinds were invited to participate in the Lions Bowl Game in Laurel, Mississippi, the first junior college bowl game to be played in the United States. They played in the Toy and Doll Bowl game in Hattiesburg in 1946 and in the Lions Bowl Game in Laurel in 1950. They also played in the Memorial Bowl Game in Jackson and in the Gulf Bowl in Corpus Christi, Texas.

Boys' Basketball
Holmes teams have won five championships, placed second in state four times, and third in state twice.

Girls' Basketball
Girls' teams have won two state championships, and six times they have been second in the state.

Baseball
Holmes has won six state championships.

Track
In track, Holmes has won three state championships and placed second five times; third, three times; and fourth, twice.

Tennis
Holmes has won five state championships in tennis.

The long tenure of many board members is an important contributing factor in the growth and development of Mississippi public junior colleges. This is illustrated in a story regarding a trustee of Holmes Junior College, Mr. G. H. McMorrough, an eminent lawyer, banker, and citizen who worked diligently for the betterment of the county and state, and resigned as a trustee at the age of ninety-seven. One of his prime interests was the development and growth of Holmes Junior College. For fifty-eight years, first as attorney for the board of trustees and then as president of the board, Mr. McMorrough proved himself a man of wisdom, foresight, and dedication to the progress of Holmes Junior College.

Holmes Junior College has grown and developed into the fine institution it now is not only because of the vision, wisdom and diligence of the board of trustees and its five presidents, but also because of the constancy and stability of a dedicated faculty and staff.

Since 1956, the following faculty and staff have retired after serving the college for fifteen or more years, most with long years of service to the college as indicated:

NAME	YEARS SERVED	TOTAL
Mrs. Billie Montague	1931–1956	25
Miss Jessie Van Osdel	1928–1958	30
Mr. Billie Montague	1930–1958	28
Mr. G. J. Everett	1931–1958	27
Mrs. G. J. Everett	1931–1958	27
Mr. B. A. McBride	1943–1959	16
Miss Lottie Peebles	1929–1959	30
Mrs. Martha Tye McKie	1940–1965	25
Mrs. Allein Douglas	1948–1965	17
Dr. H. M. Terry	1942–1965	23
Mr. R. W. Almond	1931–1968	37
Mrs. Alva S. Jacob	1950–1969	19
Mrs. Pattie E. Lorance	1945–1969	24
Mr. C. F. Moore	1947–1970	23
Mrs. Mabel N. Dorsett	1957–1972	15

Mrs. B. A. McBride	1952–1972	20
Mr. Hilary O. Thomas	1946–1972	26
Mrs. Frank B. Branch	1941–1943	29
	1945–1972	

Others who served the college for fifteen years or more whose dedicated services were cut short by death were:

Mrs. Bernice Rodgers	1938–1953	15
Mr. Stanley F. Allen	1937–1972	35
Mr. Ernest W. Wilson	1941–1942	27
	1946–1972	

Under the leadership of President Frank B. Branch many changes have been brought about at Holmes Junior College. The district now encompasses a nine-county area and has adequate financial support. It has a fine, well-equipped physical plant and land for future expansion. It has a group of competent administrators and a dedicated, well-prepared faculty and staff. Its offerings, academic and vocational-technical, are meeting the needs of the area. Enrollments are increasing as more and more fine young people take advantage of the great opportunities at Holmes Junior College. Holmes Junior College has come into its own.

This is not only the story of a school but also the story of the thinking of men, who have, in their separate ways, met the challenges of the times and contributed greatly in meeting the educational needs of a growing institution and the area which it serves.

These men—the presidents, the trustees, the county boards of supervisors, and in later years the senators and representatives in our state legislature—have been men of vision and integrity, with deep concern for educational progress. To them, Holmes Junior College owes its existence; to them, present students, past students, and students who come in the future, owe gratitude for providing the high quality of academic and vocational-technical training existent here.

Great credit for the excellent instructional, moral, cultural, and social development of students must also go to the dedicated faculty members who, along with the administrators, sought to guide the young people who have come to Holmes Junior College in growing into responsible, useful citizens.

The accomplishments of the first fifty years will enable Holmes Junior College more adequately to meet the needs of its students in the future.

MISSISSIPPI DELTA JUNIOR COLLEGE STORY

Mississippi Delta Junior College, originally Sunflower Junior College, was founded in connection with Sunflower Agricultural High School in 1926, and the first freshman class of twenty-six was enrolled in September of 1926.

The college was fully accredited as a two-year junior college in 1928 by the accrediting commission of the senior colleges of Mississippi. It was admitted to full membership in the Southern Association of Colleges and Schools in December 1930, and it is now a member of the American Association of Community and Junior Colleges.

In its first year, the college was supported only by Sunflower County. It gained the support of Humphreys County in 1928 and that of Leflore County in 1930. Washington and Sharkey Counties became supporting counties in 1961. In 1962, Bolivar, Issaquena, and Coahoma Counties agreed to levy millage for support of the college. The Delta area made up of these eight counties was stipulated as one of the original districts in which a junior college should be located under the Mississippi department of education plan, but it was not until 1964 (House Bill 215, June 11, 1964) that the Mississippi legislature declared it to be a legalized district. The high school and the college were separated in 1965.

At the beginning of the 1960–1961 session, the name of the college was changed from Sunflower Junior College to Mississippi Delta Junior College to make the name more representative of the area the college serves.

Mississippi Delta Junior College is located at Moorhead, Mississippi, near the geographical center of the Mississippi Delta. Moreover, Moorhead was a thriving railroad town in the 1920s and 30s, which made it more accessible to students who had to travel from rural areas of North Mississippi where roads were extremely hazardous most of the year. Consequently, when the agricultural high school was founded in 1911, planners selected Moorhead as an ideal location.

J. S. Vandiver, a graduate of Iuka Institute and Mississippi College, headed the thriving Sunflower Agricultural High School and College from 1918 to 1935. Vandiver and the Sunflower Agricultural High School Board of Trustees were part of a group of

GUIDED BY THESE
PRESIDENTS

Joseph Sloan Vandiver
1926–1935

Paul M. West
1935–1944

William Boyd Horton
1944–1966

James Terry Hall
1966–

131

Mississippi educators who early recognized the revolutionary significance of the American junior college movement because they saw that it offered an answer to the local need for low-cost, educational opportunities at the post-secondary level, similar to those which were being offered in the agricultural high schools. Vandiver, and others working with Claude Bennett and Knox Broom at the state level, actively sought the extension of the Sunflower Agricultural High School program to the college level.

As Mr. Vandiver explained it in a special brochure for parents prepared in 1926:

> We are glad to announce that all arrangements have been made and all conditions met for the opening of the freshman class in college work, September 6. In Hinds and Pearl River Counties, their Agricultural High Schools have maintained freshman college classes for several years. They are pleased with the results. The college work has added but little to the running expense of the high schools, for the head of each department teaches four high school classes. It has cost the college students but little more than the cost of the high school students. The work done in these schools has stood the test in the colleges of the state.

Mississippi Delta Junior College is governed by a board of trustees appointed by the boards of supervisors of each of its supporting counties. Presently, the college board is composed of all the county superintendents of education and other citizens who represent a cross-section of the community in the region. There are twenty members on the board.

The college's financial support comes from three sources: local millage levied by the supervisors, lump sum yearly allotment from the state, and special federal grants. There is also a small student matriculation fee. When the college became a legalized district, the board of trustees gained the authority to request what the tax levy for support and outlay from the counties would be, within legal maximum limitations.

A system of free bus transportation for commuting students was begun in 1953.

The original five buildings on the Moorhead campus have been replaced by more than twenty, valued at eight and one-half million dollars.

The college also operates a manpower training center and a vocational center in Greenville. College classes are also taught at Clarksdale, Cleveland, Indianola, and Greenwood.

Of the original five buildings, four had been constructed for the Sunflower Agricultural High School.

The fifth, the first college building, was an administration building which cost approximately $52,000. The two-story brick building housed science, home economics, and commerce classrooms, a large auditorium, and administrative offices. The first college physical plant was valued at $300,000.

The college library holdings of 1926 included two thousand books. Mr. Vandiver also established an art gallery in the library.

The philosophy of "quality education at low cost" became a basic tenet with the establishment of the school. "If you have a willing heart and a working body, and really want an education, do not let the lack of money keep you away. We have helped others; we will help you," Mr. Vandiver advised students in a letter enclosed with the first college catalog.

Tuition for a boarding student at Sunflower Junior College in 1926, during the regular term, was $146. Summer school attendance cost $37.50—$25.00 for board and $12.50 for tuition.

In 1975 matriculation fees for a regular semester are $100, summer tuition is $45 per three-week term, and costs are still very nominal for contemporary times.

The 1926 board minutes show, however, that even with fees fixed at very low figures, many students had to be granted special extensions for fee payment. The minutes also record Mr. Vandiver's vigorous efforts to gain individual scholarship aid for needy students. The college operated a farm and a cooperative cafeteria to help with boarding expenses of students.

Close personal supervision of college finances was exercised by Mr. Vandiver. College board budgets of the 1926–1927 session contain comments on the increase of yearly cost of floor polish oil by $25, praise for income from stud fees for the use of the college bull, and a lament for the loss of the college mule which had dropped dead at the plow. Even with such close scrutiny, the college still struggled financially and borrowed money frequently during its first ten years.

Establishment of the college's reputation for quality education was even more vigorously sought by Mr. Vandiver and the college board, as an examination of the required course of study, disciplinary methods, and faculty qualifications indicate.

A student enrolling in Sunflower Junior College in 1928 could elect to follow either an academic or a vocational course of study. If he chose the academic curriculum, he was required to take six hours of English, six hours of history, six hours of foreign language (Latin, Spanish, or French), or six hours of either mathematics or chemistry.

A student electing to follow a vocational curriculum was required to schedule history and English, six hours of either mathematics, language, or science, and six to twelve additional hours to be chosen from commerce, agriculture, home economics, music, Bible, or expression.

To qualify for graduation, a student had to earn sixty hours of college work and at least four hours of extracurricular activities. These activities were physical education, band, glee club, and literary society. Daily chapel attendance was also required.

Since most of the students boarded at the school, class cutting was not tolerated. If a student was too ill to attend class, he was quarantined to the infirmary, and he made up missed class time in study sessions on Saturday.

All students were allowed to go home three times during the session. The college catalog "homegoing" policy was that if a student was "doing right and making good records," he was allowed to select three special times for visits home.

Students could elect to take expression, music, or band, but they were required to attend the lyceum and Chautauqua series which the town and the college sponsored jointly.

Every student belonged to a literary society. These competitive societies, known as the "Wilsons" and the "Lees," were carried over to the junior college from the high school. The societies competed in athletics, debate, oral interpretation, vocal and instrumental music, and essay writing. Weekly programs in debating were held the first thing every Monday morning (to ward off "blue Monday" as Mr. Vandiver's note explains). Rally Day was the climax of the year's activities for the two groups. Local winners were sent to state-level competition among junior colleges. Sunflower Junior College won the state debating championship three years in a row, beginning in 1927. The college was well known for its state championship teams in girls' and boys' basketball.

Mr. Vandiver's disciplinary methods have contributed in large measure to his almost legendary local reputation as a schoolmaster. "An important requirement for entrance is that the applicant be of good

moral character. This institution must be kept free from immoral and vicious characters. Any pupil, therefore, who refuses to comply with the regulations is considered a demoralizing element and will be suspended," said Mr. Vandiver in his college catalog.

Every student was required to spend one hour each day in supervised outdoor exercise. Girls could play tennis, volleyball, basketball, and do calisthenics. Football, tennis, volleyball, and track were for boys.

The best description of Vandiver's disciplinary philosophy is expressed in his own terms:

Self-government, self-control is the object of true discipline. To get students to do right, because it is right, and not from fear of being caught, is stressed. A reason for every regulation is given to students. While we are strict in discipline and insist on regularity and system, yet we endeavor to be fair and firm. We find that the taking of privileges of students is generally for better conduct and better work. We have but little difficulty in maintaining the very finest spirit of order and conduct. "Do right and study hard." "Pretty is as pretty does." "Remember there are others." These are a few of our leading mottoes.

And he continues, "Smoking is injurious to boys. We encourage boys to refrain from smoking. However, we permit those that have the habit firmly fixed to smoke only in their rooms."

Student behavior was monitored at all times. Students were assigned places in the dining hall, and a faculty member sat at the head of each table. Faculty members lived in the dormitories, and they served as chaperons when students were marched to church each Sunday. Students were permitted to visit in local homes, provided they were chaperoned.

One female graduate says that she still recalls, with some sensation of trembling, Mr. Vandiver's admonition to "unlock" when she dared to hold hands with her fiancé as they strolled across campus. Other alumni recall their experiences with "stuck time," a disciplinary measure which required a certain number of hours of daily labor rooting out tree stumps on the college farm.

Mr. Vandiver was totally dedicated, however, to making school a pleasant, constructive experience for students. He encouraged the home economics class to sponsor socials, and he purchased a Vitaphone for student amusement in 1934, when depression woes were being experienced at the college as elsewhere.

The college newspaper, *The Sunflower Petals*, and

the college yearbook, *The Retrospect*, were started during the Vandiver administration.

Since Mr. Vandiver's term extended into the depression, he was the first president to deal with federal aid programs. Students were given financial aid through the CWA, and buildings were improved through the PWA. Under the CWA Student Loan Bill, the college was given a quota of thirty-two students who were paid thirty cents an hour for work on special projects.

Mr. Vandiver's instructional staff was almost as closely supervised as were his students. The eighteen instructors who were teaching college-level work in 1926 were paid an average of $125 per month. They were furnished room and board. In return, they taught five classes, served as regular chaperons on weekends, supervised the dormitories and study halls, and directed extracurricular activities. All faculty members who anticipated pay raises understood that they were to attend summer school every summer until they had attained the master's degree in their area of specialization. The basis of the contract signed by each of these teachers was as follows:

1. I promise to get up on time.
2. To try to be regular at meals.
3. To be on duty at crucial times.
4. Never to be away without reporting to the president.
5. To check my department and be ready with suggestions.
6. To be friendly with all teachers and not chummy with just a few.
7. To be willing to take room in dormitory assigned by president at first of school and be willing to change rooms when asked by him to do so.
8. To try to meet my classes promptly and not leave them.
9. To try to create school spirit and interest by competitive contest rather than to destroy by selective method.
10. Never to criticize any teacher or president in the presence of students or teachers. Be ethical at all times.
11. To watch details of administration.
12. To try to grade as uniformly as possible with the standards of this school.
13. To be a member of M.E.A. and to attend the meetings of the county teachers association and pay dues.
14. To do any duty assigned by the president.
15. To take one journal or magazine especially pertaining to my work.

In short, to give 100 percent service to the school; to be willing to help in every way and to pledge without reservation my greatest loyalty to this system and to this school and to each member of the faculty. If at any time I do not abide by this agreement, I shall be glad for the president to call my attention to same. . . . I sign this gladly and willingly.

Substitute teachers were paid one dollar per class in the Vandiver era.

The college operated a dairy and a farm. Besides producing the foodstuffs used in the cafeteria, the farm income was $1,500 in 1926. To meet the school budget of $35,360 that year, SJC received $4,125 from the state, $635 from the Vocational Board, $2,500 from tuition, and $26,610 from Sunflower County.

In the first years of the college, its recruitment area was all of North Mississippi. Students rosters show numerous "hill" as well as "delta" hometowns such as Columbus, Baldwyn, Tupelo, and Water Valley. Currently, the college recruitment area is confined to its eight supporting counties.

Mr. Vandiver resigned in 1935 after he had been elected state superintendent of education. By his last year, Mr. Vandiver had built college enrollment to 318.

Paul West was named to succeed Vandiver. Mr. West, who had been academic dean and language instructor under Mr. Vandiver, served as president until 1944. A highly articulate scholar, Mr. West earned a bachelor's degree at Delta State Teachers College and a master's degree at George Peabody College. During his tenure as president, Mr. West spent several summers at John Hopkins University working on a doctorate. Mr. West's beginning salary as president was $3,600. Mr. West continued most of Mr. Vandiver's policies concerning curriculum and discipline. By 1940, students were being allowed to shop in downtown Moorhead under faculty supervision.

Mr. West and his board replaced the antiquated high school building, built two additional dormitories, added numerous farm buildings, and constructed an athletic building and a stadium. They fought lenghty battles with the town and the utility companies over water and electric bills.

Carl Everett, academic dean and science instructor, added a museum of natural history in 1939.

When the United States entered the Second World War in December of 1941, the action had an immediate impact on Sunflower Junior College, as it did on every other college in the United States. Male enrollment dropped to almost zero when the eighteen-year-old draft was instituted. The curriculum was altered by the introduction of courses designed to train people to help with the war effort. SJC established a flying school and built an airport for the training area. Forty students were enrolled in this program during its first year of operation in 1942. The college offered, under the National Defense Program, courses in gasoline engines and machinery, electricity, and engineering drafting. The C.P.T. (Civilian Pilot Training Program) brought enough government personnel and money to the campus to keep the dormitories open and the cafeteria solvent. Several male faculty members were drafted; others quit to take positions in defense plants. One female member volunteered for the WAVEs. Even Mr. West himself took a leave of absence to serve in the army administrative personnel division. Carl Everett served as temporary president until Mr. West's return the next year. The school was put on a semi-military basis in the fall of 1942 with regular drill and military supervision for boys. Football and all other forms of intercollegiate athletics were dropped in 1942.

As Mr. West had predicted in 1941, the college's philosophy and its whole way of life had been changed by 1944. The college's disciplinary code had become outmoded, its finances had been seriously affected, and its enrollment was being affected, not only by the draft but also by newly acquired affluence of Delta citizens who were beginning to find the senior college curricula in agriculture and home economics more modern, sophisticated, and appealing for their children.

Ill health forced Mr. West to resign in 1944, and he was succeeded by Mr. W. B. Horton, a junior college educator who was serving as dean of men at Hinds Junior College at the time of his election to the presidency of Sunflower Junior College. Mr. Horton had also gained junior college administrative experience at Copiah-Lincoln Junior College. He held a bachelor's degree from Mississippi College and a master's degree from the University of Colorado.

Mr. Horton's first efforts at the college were directed toward strengthening its financial standing in the community and diversifying the college curriculum, to reflect the area's changing socio-economic pattern. Mr. Horton raised tuition, took advantage of army surplus equipment sales, and changed the college farm operation to a cattle operation as he sought to balance college books. By the time of his death in 1966, the college was on a good financial basis.

Veterans returned to campus, beginning in 1945. Mr. Horton supervised the establishment of veterans trade training courses. He encouraged the organiza-tion of a National Guard unit, which was begun in 1945 with an enrollment of forty-five. Trailers were moved in to provide housing for married veterans.

Many of the old disciplinary restrictions were removed by the late 1940s. Intercollegiate competition was restored, but extracurricular activities were made available on a voluntary basis, primarily. All students were required to earn two activities credits in order to graduate.

The commuter generation of students had come to campus by the late 40s. To attract more of these students, Mr. Horton set up a system of free bus transportation from all areas of the Delta.

The first technical program leading to a terminal degree after two years of specialized study was added to the college program in 1952. It was called building construction technology. A similar degree in electronics technology was added in 1959. The college administration undertook the first of several surveys of the vocational needs of the Delta in 1952.

The financial lot of teachers improved after the war. Salaries for SJC teachers in 1950 doubled those of 1941. Their teaching loads were not lightened much, however, since they were still either working parttime in administration or in a supervisory capacity for student activities. Mr. Horton did take notice of their request for a sick-leave policy and a salary schedule.

Standardized entrance tests for achievement and intelligence became part of the admission requirement in 1950.

Although the college enrollment remained low in the 1950s, a revival of community interest and respect for the junior college on both the local and the national levels brought SJC's enrollment up by 1960.

The faculty formed its own association in December of 1965.

The federal work-study program for students, still in progress at the school, was begun in January of 1966.

An extremely hardworking, conservative, traditional Christian gentleman educator, Mr. Horton had, by the time of his death, strengthened the college's ethical and financial reputation in the Delta community. Mr. Herman Thigpin, who had been academic dean during most of Mr. Horton's administration, assumed the presidency in August of 1966, following Mr. Horton's untimely death. He served until September 15, 1966, when the board named Mr. J. T. Hall to succeed Mr. Horton.

The first alumnus of SJC to serve as its president, Dr. Hall earned his baccalaureate degree from the University of Southern Mississippi and his master's and doctorate at the University of Mississippi.

An aggressive young administrator, Dr. Hall set out to modernize the physical plant, improve the professional credentials of the faculty, modernize the administrative organization, and adapt the program of educational training offered by the college to meet the needs of all members of the Delta community more adequately.

Utilizing special federal grants, state appropriations, and local financial assets of the college, Dr. Hall has in the first ten years of office directed the additions of a science center, a fine arts center, a vocational-technical complex, a multiuse coliseum, three residence halls, an administration building, a student union, a library-media center, and administrative faculty housing. All the buildings, materials, and equipment have been designed and constructed to be permanent excellent educational use facilities. Every major area of learning offered by the college is now adequately housed and equipped.

By instituting a policy of subsidized summer school attendance and by granting two series of major leaves of absence, Dr. Hall has stimulated faculty professional growth. Faculty salaries have been dramatically improved. For the first time in the history of the school, most faculty members are completely free of extracurricular responsibilities. The faculty has been encouraged to examine new national trends in teaching techniques through participating in regional consortiums and workshops.

Dr. Hall hired the first fulltime professional student counselors for the school in 1967. He has revamped administrative procedures so that modern computer record keeping and accounting could be accomplished. Five major administrative officers devote fulltime to overseeing the college's operation and development.

Dr. Hall has established rapport with community leaders, and he has used their expert knowledge in making additions to the college program. Thus far, eight technical and eight vocational programs have been established. He has made the college more responsive to special educational needs of older adults. The college now has classes located in many major Delta communities so that adults can work full shifts and still attend school. He has established a full night vocational program.

As have many other junior college administrators nationally, Dr. Hall has recognized the role of the junior college as that of an "open door" institution which should offer learning opportunities to all educable persons. Consequently, in addition to the associate of arts degree which symbolizes the completion of two years of university-parallel study, the college offers the associate of applied science degree in technical terminal programs, and vocational certification in manual skills. Students receiving associate degrees are required to complete at least sixty academic hours with a quality point average of 2.0.

Today's Mississippi Delta Junior College students fall into three distinct categories: older adults studying in attendance centers not located on the main campus in Moorhead, young adults commuting to Moorhead daily, and campus students. The young commuters form the majority group.

Consequently, the college program of extracurricular activities has become totally voluntary. Campus students are counseled to participate, and opportunities are made available to them through band, chorus, folksinging groups, student union programs, and intramural and intercollegiate athletic programs. The college newspaper (now called *The Delta Herald*) and *The Retrospect* are still published. A third student publication, a literary magazine called *At Pen Point*, was begun in 1969.

Disciplinary techniques have been modernized. A dean of students now serves as ombudsman between students and administration. All students are expected to conform to the ordinary rules of polite society; to be truthful; to respect the rights of others; and to have regard for the preservation of public and private property. Many of the details of student discipline are handled by the students themselves through the student government-appointed judicial council. Faculty chaperonage for social events is almost a thing of the past. Residence hall regulations have been liberalized. Class attendance is still checked, but a student must miss twenty percent of the course work before his grade is affected. Campus automobile parking has replaced campus "sparking" as the major disciplinary problem.

Campus students live in motel-type, air conditioned residence halls. They take their meals in a cafeteria supervised by a commercial catering service which offers at least two choices of all dishes served. They study in a million dollar library which houses 23,000 books, numerous periodicals, and a complete audio-visual resources center. In 1975 enrollment was about 2,700.

Mississippi Delta Junior College was founded to serve the educational needs of the majority of its citizens. The democratic foundations and its continuing adaptation to modern educational philosophy make it one of the most viable institutions of higher learning in the state.

NORTHWEST MISSISSIPPI JUNIOR COLLEGE STORY

The administration building of Northwest Mississippi Junior College is not only the landmark of the college but is also symbolic of the metamorphosis undergone by the college since its establishment in the fall of 1926. Actually predating the college by eleven years, the structure is one of the three original buildings of Tate County Agricultural High School formed in 1915.

It was described as "a handsome brick academic building" in the 1916–1917 catalog and, with the two "splendid brick dormitories," was "commodious, modern, and well-adapted to the purposes for which they are built . . . all three of the buildings, forming a crescent, [to] make the . . . School a very inviting place." The concrete threshold of the white-columned building is conspicuously worn from the feet of the thousands of students, faculty and staff, patrons, and visitors who have passed into and out of the structure through fifty-seven years of use.

When the first year of college education was introduced in the fall of 1926, the administration building was unchanged, but its classroom scheduling was expanded to accommodate the additions of new curricula. The high school faculty took on the duties of teaching the thirty-two freshmen who enrolled.

Apparently the institution of college classes was sponsored by the administration of the college and interested citizens with encouragement from the state department of education. The first official record of the junior college, found in the 1926 minutes of the Tate County Board of Supervisors, was a negative one. A resolution adopted on July 13, 1926, reads:

It appeared to the Board that the ½ mill levy will not be sufficient to meet the Sinking Fund obligations for the Agricultural High School for the year 1926 and 1927. It was the purpose of the Board to raise the assessment ½ mill for the purpose of meeting the obligation and not for the purpose of establishing a junior college.[1]

Publicity concerning the opening of a summer normal on May 28, 1928, with about 250 teachers anticipated to attend, indicates that the momentum toward the junior college's being an official fact had been growing. The newspaper states:

With the establishment of a junior college here and the strengthening of the faculty to comply with such standards it is hoped that the normal will become a permanent institution for Senatobia. With the development of the junior college it is easily possible that 500 or more teachers will come here each summer.[2]

The board of supervisors in the session of June 4, 1928 authorized the issuance of a loan warrant not to exceed $10,000 "For the purpose of making additions to the Agricultural High School Building to promote the building of a junior college," the loan to be repaid by a special tax levy. The authorization reads, "Whereas it appearing that it is the desire of a number of citizens to have a junior college in Tate County and in order to provide for said Junior College it will be necessary to borrow money to make additional buildings. . . ."[3]

The action of the board was rescinded at the July meeting and a new order issued authorizing the board of trustees to execute a loan of $10,000 on the school property under the authority conferred in chapter 566 of the 1920 Laws of Mississippi. Thus the special tax levy was avoided. An additional part of the order stated that the rate of taxation for the school was to remain the same during the term of office of the board.[4]

Porter Walker Berry, who had been superintendent of Tate County Agricultural High School since 1921, was instrumental in organizing the junior college. Professor Berry, as he was called, became the first president of the college and was active in getting the necessary support for the venture. Beyond his duties as superintendent and president, the administrator taught college mathematics. His wife, Mrs. Margaret Berry, was noted as a musician and taught music and education.

An editorial in the *Tate County Democrat* following

GUIDED BY THESE
PRESIDENTS

Porter Walker Berry
1926–1936

Roscoe Conklin Pugh
1936–1953

Reese Dermont McLendon
1953–1972

Professor Berry's death on October 9, 1935, tells of his dedication to the college.

Porter Berry was a doer—a person who accomplished much for the educational advancement of Tate County and one who never boasted of his own personal accomplishments, rather preferring to give the credit to his co-workers and the students who attended Northwest.

It was Prof. Berry who provided the spark which ignited the movement to move Tate County Agricultural High School "up a notch" to the junior college class.

It was Prof. Berry who fought hard, day and night, to maintain the standard of curriculum at "Rangertown."

The support of Quitman County was gained at a meeting in Senatobia on June 27, 1928, called to order by Mr. Berry. Six counties were represented by about sixty outstanding citizens at the endorsement meeting. The Quitman County delegation pledged to vote one-half mill for the support of a "permanent institution."[5] Besides Tate and Quitman Counties, Panola, DeSoto, Tunica, and Tallahatchie Counties were represented. Each of the four delegations endorsed the idea of the junior college but did not pledge monetary aid.

The Hon. Claude Bennett, state supervisor of agricultural high schools, had written a letter to Professor Berry, stating in part:

It might be of interest to you to know that the Junior College Commission created by act of Legislature at its 1928 session, has the stamp of its approval upon the logical place for a junior college in Northwest Mississippi. A glance at the map of our State will show that Tate County is in the center of a group of counties that can well afford to maintain a junior college. If the people of your section do not avail themselves of this opportunity to establish in their midst a junior college I feel sure they will regret it in after years. Only a limited number of these schools are going to be established in the State and if Tate County neglects this opportunity some other county in the section of Mississippi is going to grasp the opportunity to provide for its people college facilities.[6]

The fully sanctioned two-year junior college opened on September 4, 1928, with fifty-nine students. It was variously referred to in print as Tate Junior College, Tate-Quitman Junior College, Quitman-Tate Junior College, North West Mississippi Junior College, and finally Northwest Mississippi Junior College. The new institution was accredited by the Mississippi Junior College Accrediting Association.

Reasons for the "movement" given in the catalogue were:

1. To provide for the County's high school graduates who were not financially able to meet the expenses of a regular college course;
2. To take care of younger students who really need more personal supervision than the average college can offer;
3. To provide vocational training for those who cannot take four-year college courses;
4. To bring higher education closer to the people.[7]

The Tate County Board of Supervisors in February 1929 authorized a loan not to exceed $10,000 under the provision of House Bill No. 122 of a special session of the Mississippi legislature, proceeds to be used for building or improvements at the college at the discretion of the board of trustees. In addition one-half mill was to be set aside as a building fund in 1929, 1930, and 1931 for support of the school. The half-mill was, however, to pay off the loan.[8] The town of Senatobia also provided $10,000.

The "new Board of Trustees" of the Quitman-Tate Junior College, headed by W. W. May of Arkabutla as president and W. T. Covington, "prominent Delta planter and widely known legislator," as vice president, inspected the college property at the organization meeting in April 1929. The board's appraisal of the physical plant and farm fixed the value at nearly $100,000. The conclusion was that, with the additional funds ($20,000) from the county and from Senatobia, "the recognition by the State of this system of secondary education assures the permanency of the institution and that it will eventually serve a splendid purpose."[9]

Among the members of the board was Mrs. Henrietta (Walter Sledge) Taylor of Sledge, one of the representatives of Quitman County, who served continuously thereafter and was the only charter member of the board serving in 1972. Another woman of renown in the early days of Northwest was "Aunt" Lizzie McGhee, who served as matron in the girls' dormitory and as dietitian from the establishment of the high school until her death in 1936.

In early 1929 a gymnasium was completed at the college, and later in the same year a science-commerce building was erected. For the first time classes were held outside the administration building, which continued to house both high school and college classes as well as the auditorium, the library, and the office of the president. The new classroom building permitted an expansion of curricula in business, science, and home economics.

The depression had its effect on Northwest, causing among other things a reduction of the school year to eight and a half months beginning in 1931. Students were permitted to pay board and other expenses by bringing garden and farm products for use in the dining hall. In May 1935 the federal government gave financial aid to the college in order that it could continue for the full nine-months session. According to the May 2, 1935 issue of the *Tate County Democrat*, "This . . . proves the fact that Northwest is getting back to normal and is offering standard college hours."

By 1934 Panola and Tallahatchie Counties were contributing funds to the college.

The first Northwest Alumni Association, proposing to foster growth of the college, was organized at the 1934–1935 annual homecoming.[10]

Despite President Berry's deploring the fact that "appropriations were not what they used to be," he was working in 1935 on several projects to be submitted to the Works Progress Administration for improvement of the physical plant.[11] An expansion of the college curricula was also anticipated. His death in October prevented his seeing his projects realized.

S. R. Deen, who had come to Northwest in 1921 as assistant superintendent of the high school and had been named vice president when the school became a college, was elevated to the acting presidency for the remainder of the 1935–1936 session. Mr. Deen continued to serve as head of the vocational agriculture and science departments during and after his administration as president.

Roscoe C. Pugh was elected president in the summer of 1936. Yalobusha County was providing financial support, and enrollment had increased to 132 students. The outlook for the junior college was expressed in the 1936–1937 catalog as "very bright."

For the past seven years [sic] the management has planned and worked for the promotion of the Junior College. We feel sure of the success of the movement. We are greatly encouraged by the fact that the last legislature made increased provision for state support of these new institutions. We are also encouraged by the fact that at least five counties of Northwest Mississippi have joined in the support of this institution. The town of Senatobia has become fully enthusiastic as to the benefit of the Junior College. The people are ready to back the college movement both morally and financially.

The library contained 2,500 volumes. To that number it was expected to add about $300 worth each year.[12] Athletic programs, literary societies, religious activities, a band, and "social life" all had a share in college life. Concerning social life the catalog stated "There is nothing which tends so effectively to give grace, dignity, ease, poise and polish as does the association of the sexes if under the proper chaperonage."[13]

The first major change in the administration building came in 1938, when with Tate County and the federal administration of public works providing $120,000, it was remodeled and an annex built on the rear. The annex provided four additional classrooms. One of the main floor classrooms was converted to a business office with vault and a president's office. The upstairs auditorium was utilized as a study hall as well as for assemblies.

Included in the same public works project was the construction of a second boys' dormitory, later named Yalobusha Hall; the remodeling of the original boys' dormitory, later named Quitman Hall; construction of a new wing on the girls' dormitory, later named Tate Hall, with some remodeling of the original building; and the construction of a heating plant and chimney. Enrollment increased to 153 students. The greatest gain in students, however, came in 1939 with 248 registered. DeSoto and Tippah Counties added millage for the support of Northwest in 1940.

Notations in the 1940–1941 catalog, identified as President Pugh's handwriting, indicate that the president's salary was $3000 per year. Most instructors received $90 or $100 per month, but some salaries were as low as $50 per month. Agriculture teachers, presumed to be employed on a twelve-month basis, were the highest paid employees among the faculty. The fifteen-member faculty included both high school and junior college teachers. Only two held master's degrees.

World War II ravaged the enrollment of students at Northwest. The full impact of the war came in the 1943–1944 session, when only sixty-four students, most of them female, were registered. In the preceding year a new accelerated program had been instituted. Young men were advised "in their own interest, as well as in the interest of the country" to take advantage of the program under which a student could complete requirements for graduation with two summer sessions and one regular session or one summer session and one and a half regular sessions.[14] The accelerated program was continued in the post-war years because of demand, especially by veterans.

Even before the close of the war, enrollment was on the upswing. Two hundred and sixty students, a large percentage of them veterans, registered for the 1946–1947 session. Since the establishment of the junior college the curricula had been expanded from liberal arts, agriculture, and home economics to three major curricula including liberal arts, science, general agriculture, home economics, business, all transfer curricula; and "the general education course," designed to be terminal. For veterans, special training courses in automobile mechanics, refrigerator repair, radio repair, general agriculture, and animal husbandry were offered beginning in the fall of 1946.[15]

Twenty trailer housing units were set up in what came to be known as Trailer, or Vet, Village for married veterans and their families. Buildings were purchased from the federal government as surplus property when Camp McCain, Grenada, was razed. From the surplus property a men's dormitory and an apartment building were erected and brick-veneered by the college maintenance department with the aid of day labor and opened for the second semester 1946–1947. Other surplus properties were a cafeteria and classroom building valued at $55,000 and a bus maintenance shop.

The impact of the enrollment of veterans was felt fully in the 1947–1948 school year. Of 263 students registered in the first semester, 120 were veterans. For the following year *The Ranger Rocket*, student newspaper, notes in the October 4, 1948 issue that enrollment figures showed 234 enrolled in the "college department" and "in addition to these, the veteran on-the-job training department at the shop shows an enrollment of 72 veteran students taking training there." For the first year, 1948, Benton County became a part of the Northwest tax-supporting district.

The former having burned, a new gymnasium was opened in 1948, complete with a heated swimming pool on the lower floor. A stage at one end of the main floor made possible the use of the structure as an auditorium. The auditorium on the top floor of the administration building was converted to a study hall for the high school.

With the establishment of Northeast Junior College in Booneville, Tippah County withdrew its tax support from Northwest in 1949 to join the district closer home. 1949 was also the last year when state teachers' licenses were granted for sixty semester hours of proper credit at Northwest. Another first was the opening of Northwest's first "Rec Hall" with a party on March 7, 1949. The center for recreation was in the old dining hall area on the lower floor of the girls' dormitory. It was fruit basket-turnover for the recreation hall, however, for in latter 1949 the dining hall was moved back to the girls' dormitory after the dormitory had undergone extensive remodeling. Renovations also included those in the boys' dormitory. It was not until 1951 that the Rec Hall was back in business, this time in the former cafeteria of the government surplus building.

The advent of the Korean War decreased enrollment. In the fall semester of 1951–1952 registration showed 252 academic students and 72 in veteran shop classes. A drop of about thirty-five percent in enrollment of academic students was noted for the second semester because of the numbers of male students who had joined the armed forces or had withdrawn expecting to be called.[16] A new draft ruling by the defense department, permitting a student to finish the school year, however, eased the situation somewhat so that enrollment for 1952–1953 had again showed an increase, with 285 academic students. Veteran registration also increased again with Korean War veterans receiving benefits of $110 to $160 per month.

The year 1952–1953 was to be Mr. Pugh's last one as president, for his resignation was effective June 30, 1953.

Tunica joined the Northwest District in 1952, making eight counties contributing tax millage to the college. The Mississippi legislature appropriated $100,000 for each of the state junior colleges for repair and construction of buildings. A committee of the board of trustees was appointed to work with Mr. Pugh to decide the most urgent needs for the campus.[17] As a result a new president's home and a library were constructed.

The antebellum home which was located on the property originally obtained for Tate County Agricultural High School and which had served as the president's home since the establishment of the school was removed after completion of the new home. On the site a library, costing about $77,000, was erected. The library, since named in honor of Mr. Pugh, was accepted by the board on July 24, 1953, after his departure from Northwest. Another project was a new lighted and fenced football field used for the first time in the fall of 1953.

An innovation for the fall term 1952 was the establishment of a bus route providing free transportation to and from the college daily for commuting students. The route originated in Charleston and proceeded on Highway 51 to pick up students at all towns north to the college.

The first move toward seeking membership in the Southern Association of Colleges and Schools also came during Mr. Pugh's last year of administration. The report of the representative of the accrediting organization, among other analyses, commended the financing of the college, saying, "It is evident that a splendid job of financing administration has been accomplished. Clearly a great deal has been accomplished with limited resources. The . . . counties which make up the taxing district are definitely receiving a bargain in educational facilities and their continued support is well-merited." [18]

Other areas of commendation were the curricula, faculty, conditions of faculty service, beautifully landscaped site, and some of the buildings. The faculty and staff were found "alert, active and interested in the institutional welfare of development." Inadequacies were noted in the library holdings and equipment, administrative and general offices, classroom furnishings and equipment, and the student recreation and services center.

The announcement of President Pugh's resignation in the local newspaper stated that "During Mr. Pugh's tenure at Northwest, the school plant has grown from four buildings to 19, which is presently valued at one and a half million dollars. . . . Mr. Pugh has always been active in church and civic affairs of Tate County . . . and identified with all progressive movements. . . ." [19]

The president's wife, who had served as business manager during his administration, also resigned.

It has been said that one of the president's greatest accomplishments was "keeping the school together during the depression years." A man of dry humor often compared to Will Rogers, he was well-liked by students, faculty, and townspeople.

Reese D. McLendon, formerly president of Pearl River Junior College, was unanimously elected president of Northwest by the board of trustees as of July 1, 1953. His first day in his new office was the day that the new library was accepted by the board of trustees.

During his first year a sixteen-member faculty taught the 295 college students enrolled in fifteen major courses of study. One of the first improvements under Mr. McLendon's administration was opening a new recreation center in what had served as storage space in the basement of the administration building.

Northwest was also accredited by the Southern Association of Colleges and Schools in December 1953. President McLendon said that although the library did not meet standards and the science laboratory could boast only one microscope, invoices could be shown to the accrediting committee proving that sufficient numbers of books and microscopes had been ordered for the college to qualify for accreditation.

Building on the firm foundation of the administration of former presidents, President McLendon with the board of trustees formulated long-range plans for the development of the institution, and years of phenomenal growth began in 1954. Lafayette County became a tax supporter of Northwest.

On recommendation of the Tate County members of the board of trustees, the full board voted on June 23, 1954 to discontinue the high school department at Northwest. The action came after the Mississippi legislature failed to appropriate funds for the support of agricultural high schools. Funds were appropriated, however, for vocational technical training. [20] Some of the citizens, particularly of Tate County, felt that the discontinuance of the high school sounded the death knell of the institution; however, it actually heralded the birth of the greater college to come.

An expansion of the academic curriculum to include courses in elementary art, Bible, journalism, family relations, and medical technology presaged the broadening of the offerings in the years to come. A vocational and technical division of the college opened with special terminal courses in animal husbandry, furniture manufacturing and cabinet making, and a nine-month intensified course in secretarial training. Night courses in auto mechanics, which had been offered for the past eighteen months, and in cabinet making were approved by the Mississippi Veterans Approving Board for training of veterans. The first Ranger Band was fielded.

Growth of enrollment was indicated in 1955 with the purchase of three buses to transport commuting students without cost. Enrollment rose to 309.

Two land purchases in 1956 gave impetus to growth

of the college. Fifteen acres of land adjoining the campus were bought to take care of future needs for space. A 147-acre farm west of Senatobia, to be used by the agriculture department for instructional purposes, gave the college the first off-campus acreage and supplemented the ninety-acre farm which adjoined the five acres that had always been known as the campus proper. After the additional land was available and over a period of years the farm per se was gradually moved to the country as needs for space on campus grew.

The barn gave way to a new auditorium completed in 1957. Surveys made at the time indicated that by 1985 enrollment might approach six hundred. The $107,301 structure, therefore, had a seating capacity of six hundred to provide for long-range needs. The prediction was incorrect, however, for in only three years the enrollment went over the six hundred mark.

Drafting technology, auto technology, and the vocational course in cosmetology, offered first in 1957–1958, became the nucleus of the ever-expanding vocational-technical department of Northwest. Twenty coeds of the total enrollment of 373 were in the first cosmetology class.

The theme of homecoming 1959 was "Northwest on the March," and facts substantiated the boast. Enrollment had jumped by almost twenty-five percent over that of the previous year. Some out-of-state applicants for admission had to be turned away for lack of space. Students were particularly impressed with the enlarged and improved recreation center, which included a grill and snack bar.

In a meeting of supervisors of the nine-country Northwest District in November 1959, President McLendon itemized accomplishments which had been realized from the $500,000 building program started two years earlier, all on a pay-as-you-go basis. He cited the recently constructed cafeteria and field house, additional rooms in the girls' dormitory, new faculty homes, a modernized heating system and farm buildings.[21]

A tradition for Northwest, continued in successive years, began with the 1959–1960 school year. Broadening the cultural and esthetic offerings of the college for both students and the public, the first all-campus musical, *The Boy Friend*, was presented.

From his new office in a recently constructed small wing next to the improved business office in the administration building, the president in May 1960 announced that a recent appropriation of $150,000 by the state legislature would be used to build a science building and a fine arts building. As he was to say many times in the following twelve years, Mr. McLendon stated that the additions would "round out" the facilities so that Northwest "will have instructional facilities second to none."[22] The M. L. Burks Science Building and the fine arts building were completed in 1961. The science building was named for the late M. L. Burks, who had been chairman of the science department for twenty-five years and dean for several years. The second wing of the girls' dormitory was also added. This too was the year when Marshall County began its support of the college.

The first structure of the technical-vocational complex, Technical Education Building No. 1, was dedicated at homecoming in fall 1962. A companion building, Technical Education Building No. 2, was completed the next year. The first building housed facilities for drafting and design, and the newer courses in electronics and civil technology; the second, cosmetology, automotive technology, and mechanical technology.

With the educational needs of students adequate for the time, the administration turned in 1964 to additional facilities for physical needs of the growing student body. Mobile housing units in two-bedroom and a bath suites, each unit to house four male students, rolled onto the campus and were permanently installed as an emergency measure. An addition enlarged the cafeteria, and construction of a coed dormitory was underway. Calhoun County added tax support for Northwest in 1965, completing the Northwest District, which was permanently defined by an act of the Mississippi legislature.

It was well that housing had been added, for in 1965 enrollment passed the one thousand mark with 1058 students, giving a thirty-five percent increase over the previous year. Bobo Hall, completed for the fall semester 1965, houses eighty coeds in two-bedroom and a bath suites. The burgeoning demand for additional courses in vocational and technical education was satisfied with the construction of Technical Education Building No. 3. The dormitory and classroom-shop building were dedicated in homecoming festivities which celebrated the fiftieth anniversary of the parent institution, Tate County Agricultural High School. Honored at the celebration was Mrs. Estelle Bobo, beloved dean of women for twenty-five years, who had retired and for whom the dormitory was named.

A landmark decision with long-range effect on Northwest was reached by the board of trustees, which in 1965 signed the Compliance Act of 1964. Blacks were admitted to Northwest beginning in the fall of 1965.

With new buildings already under construction, in November 1965 the foresighted and progressive board of trustees launched another expansion program which, when completed, was thought to provide facilities for an enrollment capacity of 2000 to 2500. Being constructed were the A. P. Fatherree Agriculture Technology Building, so named to honor the state director of vocational-technical education of the Mississippi State Department of Education; and the Berry Building, business-technical center. Gainey Hall, men's residence hall, was begun in spring 1966. Mississippi Gov. Paul Johnson dedicated the structures named for former presidents at the 1966 homecoming. Major courses had increased to forty-three, including thirteen technical and vocational courses, to take care of the demand of the 1,137 students registered. The physical plant was valued at approximately $3,000,000 with an additional some $400,000 in equipment.

In step with the growing college, once again in the summer of 1966 the administration building had undergone changes. Three classrooms on the main floor were converted into suites of offices for administrative personnel. The carpeted, paneled offices lent prestige and were in keeping with the president's motto, "Only the best for Northwest." The business department, formerly housed on the upper floor, had moved to the Berry Building, and the enlarged English department occupied the vacated classrooms.

Northwest continued to march forward to a fast cadence. The demand for married student housing necessitated the purchase of compact mobile apartments to serve as low-rent units, all ready for occupancy for the fall term of 1967. The rapidly increasing enrollment also demanded more instructional space. An addition to the M. L. Burks Science Building as well as an annex and a second story for the fine arts building were constructed.

From fall 1964 to fall 1967 enrollment at the junior college had increased more than sixty percent. In 1964–1965, when Northwest was seeking renewal of accreditation, a self-study by the college departments had included fifty-four recommendations of attainment to be reached. Recommendations also were made in late 1965 by a visiting committee of experts representing the Southern Association of Colleges and Schools. It was reported in the follow-up study in the first semester of 1967 that all requirements of the visiting committee had been met.[23] Northwest was prepared to accept new challenges, and the building program continued to gather momentum.

The college's largest residence halls, one for men and one for women, were occupied in September 1968. Taylor Hall, housing 198 women students, was dedicated with a reception honoring Mrs. Henrietta S. Taylor, who was serving her forty-first consecutive year on the board of trustees. Quitman Hall, for three hundred males, replaced the old Quitman Hall, one of the original buildings of Tate County Agricultural High School. The old building, which was razed, had been in use continuously for fifty-three years, and an estimated four thousand male students had lived in it. DeSoto Apartments, four buildings with four apartments each for faculty, were also occupied. Other construction included an art building and an addition more than doubling the size of the R. C. Pugh Library. Construction was progressing on a union building.

Wilson Edmondson of Crowder, vice president of the board of trustees and chairman of the building committee, commented in late 1968, "We just now are reaching the goals which we had envisioned when President McLendon first came to Northwest in 1953. We now have the essential buildings. We have the best physical plant and facilities in the State, and probably better than that of several adjoining states. We have to give all the credit to Mr. McLendon."[24]

Deserving credit for the well-groomed, attractive campus was the president's wife, Mrs. Corinne H. McLendon, who was in charge of landscaping from the time she and President McLendon had arrived at Northwest. Her interior decoration and beautiful flower arrangements in all the buildings on campus caused comment by visitors as well as the population of the college.

McLendon Center, the union and physical education building, was completed in late spring 1969 and named by the board of trustees. A variety of events heralded the opening of the structure, largest union building in square footage in the state, in late May. In the center were the cafeteria, student offices, meeting rooms, recreation rooms, a spacious lobby, a swimming pool, and the physical education and home economics departments. It was on October 25, 1969 that the building was formally dedicated at homecoming in ceremonies honoring President McLendon.

It has been said that:

The union building . . . represents a peak in President McLendon's career here. The rapid growth in enrollment and enormous expansion of facilities has taken place during his tenure, and the college continues to grow. Much of the success of Northwest since 1953 may be attributed to President McLendon's foresight and interest in continued progress. The Board would like for the union building to stand as a tribute to a dedicated administrator.[25]

Two plots of farm land adjoining the Northwest farm were purchased and farm facilities constructed, also in 1969. The expanding agriculture department utilized the land and facilities as well as an addition for laboratory work constructed on the Fatherree Building.

Again "rounding out" facilities, the college opened the humanities building for the second semester of 1970. The structure, incorporating modern concepts in teaching, contained not only conventional classrooms but also a language laboratory, a reading laboratory, and two large lecture rooms equipped with capabilities for a variety of audio-visual aids. The design also paved the way for the use of communications in closed circuit television, radio, and graphics.

Extensive renovations and remodeling of the administration building, along with the building's next door neighbors, Tate Hall, the original girls' dormitory, and Yalobusha Hall, were accomplished in summer 1970 to bring the historic structure up to date. The last two classrooms on the main floor were removed and the rooms remodeled to give the business office new and larger quarters. The entire upper floor became the offices and supporting facilities for the student personnel department, which had been distributed over the campus. Offices, halls, and other rooms were carpeted and paneled. Students crossed the threshold of the building only for various personal business rather than for classes.

WNJC-FM radio station, Mississippi's first public broadcasting station, went on the air in January 1971, with facilities in the humanities building transmitting to most of the 6004-square mile Northwest District. Benton Apartments, to house twenty-four married student families, were occupied in the fall term 1971, and additional farm facilities and an addition to Tech-

nical Education Building No. 2 were constructed. Fifty-eight acres of land adjacent to the campus were purchased in 1972 to permit further building expansion and to provide needed recreational facilities. A multipurpose building for indoor sports and to seat large numbers of people was on the drawing board, and a classroom building was projected.

Looking to the potential both of Northwest and of the communities served by the college, a new community services department was established in 1972. The primary objective of the new department was to offer educational opportunities of whatever nature and wherever needed for the citizens of the district. One of the first services was offering adult basic education courses on the campus and throughout the district. More than five hundred persons enrolled in the first semester. The offering of off-campus credit and noncredit courses was expanded.

Northwest had been cooperating with industry since 1953, when the college had training programs on the campus for employees of the Wm. Carter Company, which had a new plant under construction in Senatobia. In later years prospective employees of Chromcraft, Inc., another new plant for Senatobia, had also been trained at Northwest. In-plant courses had been taught in other factories in the district through the years. The community services department was designed to extend the services in cooperation with area industry.

Northwest Mississippi Junior College, by the close of the 1971–1972 school year, had facilities and land valued at approximately $10,000,000. The fifty-two major courses offered included twenty-seven academic degree programs, thirteen two-year technical courses, and six vocational courses. Among the additions to the curricula were several in allied health professions courses, radio and television broadcasting, licensed practical nursing, law enforcement, human services, and a broadening of the curricula that had been offered through the years. A registered nursing degree program was to be introduced the following year.

A waning interest in agriculture and agricultural occupations was revitalized at Northwest over a period of years by the expanded degree and technical programs. The former one-member department had grown to have five fulltime faculty members. On the farm were units for cattle, swine, horse, and chicken production. An arena had become a center for livestock shows, rodeos, and other events of community as well as college interest. The livestock judging team had made notable records in state and national competition for a number of years through 1972.

With the widespread district, Northwest encouraged students to live on campus as a part of the "live and learn" philosophy that encompassed participation in the extra-curricular activities as well as in classroom requirements. The full program of activities included intercollegiate and intramural sports, cultural and esthetic events such as drama, art, and music, entertainment, government, and a variety of organizations to suit the interests of all students.

Noted speakers and performers in a variety of professional fields, and politicians, musicians, and entertainers added to both the cultural and the pure entertainment phases of college life. Students learned from and enjoyed the chorus, band, debate team, speech tournaments, publications, and competition in other academic and vocational contests both locally and in the state. A Dozen plus Three, student song and dance group organized in 1969, became famous in the Midsouth for lively concerts. *The Ranger Rocket*, the only weekly student newspaper in the state, won state and national honors for five consecutive years. Members of Phi Beta Lambda, business fraternity, were singularly successful also in state and national competition.

Northwest fielded competitive teams in intercollegiate sports although not as consistent winners. There were times when moments of glory came to the Rangers, first as a member of the Mississippi Valley Conference and later of the Mississippi Junior College Athletic Association. The Rangers were champions in baseball for five consecutive years, 1946–1950, and again were North Division champions in 1972. Three football championships came in 1941, 1960, and 1965. As a result of the 1965 football championship, the Rangers played in the annual Shrine Bowl game in Shreveport, Louisiana, facing another Rangers team, this one of Kilgore, Texas. In basketball the Rangers shared the North Division crown in 1968 and won their first state championship in 1972. Many Northwest athletes have attained individual honors.

The cooperation and funds from the eleven supporting counties and the state, and in recent years the heavy financial support of the federal government, have all contributed to the growth and the success of Northwest Mississippi Junior College to take a place of distinction among Mississippi junior colleges. The nominal cost and the open-door policy of admission brought into the college the advantaged and the disadvantaged youths of the district for training so they might be productive members of society. The college is justly proud of the many former students who have been acknowledged successful in professional, business, and educational fields. An average of sixty-five percent of the high school graduates who entered college entered Northwest for a number of years through 1972. The extensive financial aids program, including both local and federal aids, for students, growing each year, added up to seven hundred students in a year.

Like the administration building, the college has changed, expanded, and grown with the times. Past achievements, worn with time, nevertheless still splendid, are the threshold for a greater, more challenging tomorrow. In 1972, plans were under way for further building; educational opportunities and investments; cultural, social, and economic development; facilities to provide for additional services; an understanding and sound relationship among the citizens of the Northwest District, the state of Mississippi, and the nation.

Notes for "Northwest Mississippi Junior College Story"

1. Minutes, Board of Supervisors, Tate County, Book 1, p. 465.
2. *Tate County Democrat*, May 17, 1928, p. 1.
3. Minutes, Book 2, p. 40.
4. Minutes, Book 2, p. 43.
5. *Tate County Democrat*, June 28, 1928, p. 1.
6. *Tate County Democrat*, July 12, 1928, p. 1.
7. North West Mississippi Junior College Catalogue, 1934–1935, p. 19.
8. Minutes, Book 2, p. 91.
9. *Tate County Democrat*, April 25, 1929, p. 1.
10. *Tate County Democrat*, April 18, 1934, p. 4.
11. *Tate County Democrat*, Sept. 1, 1935, Section 1, p. 4.
12. Catalogue, 1936–1937, p. 9.
13. Ibid, pp. 9, 10.
14. Catalogue, 1942–1943, p. 32.
15. Catalogue, 1946–1947, p. 12.
16. *The Ranger Rocket*, Jan. 25, 1951, p. 1.
17. *Tate County Democrat*, May 8, 1952, p. 1.
18. *Tate County Democrat*, Nov. 27, 1952, pp. 1, 10.
19. *Tate County Democrat*, June 11, 1953, p. 1.
20. *Tate County Democrat*, June 24, 1954, p. 1.
21. *The Ranger Rocket*, Nov. 18, 1959, p. 1.
22. *The Ranger Rocket*, May 18, 1960, p. 1.
23. *The Ranger Rocket*, Sept. 19, 1967.
24. *The Ranger Rocket*, Dec. 4, 1968, p. 1.
25. *The Ranger Rocket*, Dec. 13, 1967, p. 1.

JONES COUNTY
JUNIOR COLLEGE STORY

The beginning of a junior college on the campus of an agricultural high school is an individual story, and Jones County Junior College is no exception. Although its doors opened in September 1927, the first recorded information available on its establishment was in 1924, indicating that considerable discussion had been underway at least as early as 1923, one year after the permissive law was passed.

The driving force behind the establishment of the school was Professor M. B. Bush, the superintendent of the agricultural high school who became the junior college's first president. A great part of Mr. Bush's life was devoted to working with the agricultural high school and junior college programs in Mississippi. He established Lafayette County Agricultural High School in Oxford, Mississippi, in 1914, remaining there until 1923, when be became superintendent of Jones County Agricultural High School. During his tenure at this institution, the enrollment was among the largest in the state, and he was immediately and enthusiastically receptive to the discussion of the junior college program.

The students of the agricultural high school demonstrated an active interest in the projected junior college, as evidenced by an editorial written by the editor of the school's monthly magazine, *The Radionian* (May 1924). This editorial was in support of a proposed bond issue to be considered by the voters of Jones County in June.

Will the great number of boys and girls in Jones and the surrounding counties get to go to college? This question will be answered in the near future by the tax payers of the county. It is for them to say whether they will pay the price for an educated posterity. Many young people in this county will never get college training unless there are provisions made for them to get it in their own county. This fact should make everyone give the proposition a careful consideration.

If there is a need for the school, the next and all important matter is whether the establishment of a junior college is within the reach of the county with its present and prospective resources. Truly the expense of establishing and maintaining the proposed college will be no small matter. But with a county as rich and progressive as ours, with great prospects for unprecedented agricultural development, surely we can make such an institution a reality.

In addition, the board of supervisors expressed their interest in a junior college program in Jones County at their regular meeting in May 1924, when they authorized the issuance of bonds in the amount of $100,000 to contribute to the plant development for the purpose of establishing a junior college. The law giving the board of supervisors permission to authorize the issuance of bonds in the amount of $100,000 made the action valid; however, the law contained a provision that if twenty percent of the voters in the county should file a signed petition, then it would be necessary for the board of supervisors to call an election and give the people an opportunity to vote whether or not they wanted to issue bonds in this amount. Immediately following the action of the board, petitions were drawn up and circulated; and within a few days the board of supervisors was presented with eight petitions signed by 3,200 voters in Jones County. This number represented more than twenty percent of the eligible voters in the county, making it mandatory for the board to order an election on the bond issue, and an election was held on June 5. *The Laurel Daily Leader*, Laurel, Mississippi, recorded on Tuesday, June 10, 1924, these headlines: "Voting Today Over The County," "Junior College is the issue in county-wide election on Tuesday," which was June 10, 1924. The same paper recorded on June 11, 1924, the following statement: "College bond issue is lost by big margin," and the record shows that it was defeated by a large majority.

Although the result of the election was a major disappointment to the proponents of a junior college in Jones County, they did not abandon their goal. Mr. Bush continued to prepare the facilities and faculty of the agricultural high school for the establishment of a junior college.

The accrediting commission required that faculty members at the junior college should have a master's degree or be in the process of earning one, and Mr. Bush was aware of this requirement as he sought a person to assist him in continuing the effort to establish a junior college. He was fortunate in finding a man who had completed his master's degree and whose wife would complete hers in the summer of 1927. Dr. R. A. McLemore, now President Emeritus of Mississippi College, had completed his M. A. at Peabody College when he came to Jones County Agricultural High School as teacher and assistant to Mr. M. P. Bush. Dr. McLemore, at the request of Mr. Bush, organized a curriculum for the beginning junior college based largely upon the catalog of the George Peabody College for Teachers. The program included

GUIDED BY THESE
PRESIDENTS

Millard Perry Bush
1927–1940

James Bonnard Young
1940–1970

Thomas Terrell Tisdale
1970–

148

the numbering system of Peabody College and the establishment of the quarter system. Consequently, Jones County Junior College was the only Mississippi junior college with a program on the quarter system and continues on this system today.

On July 14, 1927, the board of trustees of the Jones County Agricultural High School met and officially accepted the plans which Mr. Bush and Dr. McLemore had set forth. The board members present at this historic meeting were J. T. Taylor, President; B. L. Moss; C. J. Grantham; George M. Smith, and W. N. Jones. These were men with great educational foresight to see the need for a higher local education program and to set the goals such as the Jones County Agricultural High School Board did on July 14, 1927, in adopting the following resolution:

Whereas social and economic circumstances and conditions in Jones County, Mississippi, and adjacent territory are not unlike those existing in other sections of our State and Nation, where new responsibilities in home and community life cannot be adequately met unless the young men and women are amply provided with educational, cultural, and religious facilities and influences to better enable them to keep step with an advancing civilization, and

Whereas it is the firm belief and conviction of those charged with the responsibility for a greater usefulness of Jones County Agricultural High School as an educational and cultural influence, that such usefulness would be greatly enhanced by making suitable provision for teaching, and by teaching the first two years of standard college work at this institution, for the following reasons and purpose:

1. To foster the democratization of higher education through enabling many students who, because of expenses involved, would not be able to otherwise obtain higher education.

2. To enable students to benefit through the prolongation of home influence.

3. To foster a continuation of broad general education by offering such subjects as will contribute to the civic and liberal education of those in the surrounding territory of Jones County Junior College who are qualified to take advantage thereof.

4. To provide higher education on a more economical level to boys and girls in this territory.

5. To provide certain terminal general educational and vocational courses for students who do not plan to transfer to institutions of higher education.

6. To provide for the students in Jones County Junior College an excellent program of student activities in order that by their participation therein they will experience an ever-increasing ability to master their own problems in school and out of school, and be of aid to others endeavoring to measure up to the responsibilities of citizenship.

7. To provide two years of college training acceptable to institutions of higher education for students who plan to transfer to these institutions and continue their work.

Now therefore, premises considered, be it

Resolved, that during the session of 1927/1928 a full and complete curriculum equivalent to acceptable, standard, first year college work be taught in this institution, and thereafter the college curricula of this institution shall comprise full and complete first and second year standard college subjects.

Be it further resolved that the title of this institution be and the same is hereafter to be known as Jones County Agricultural High School and Junior College.

This official action of the board of trustees, along with the establishment of the curriculum and the assembly of the faculty, prepared the new institution to receive students for the 1927–1928 school session. In September 1927, twenty-six students, all personally recruited by Mr. Bush and Dr. McLemore, became the first class of Jones County Junior College. Faculty for this fine group in addition to Mr. McLemore were: Mrs. McLemore, Miss Betty Ridgeway, Mr. W. J. Moody, and Miss Willie Ruth McDaniel.

An editorial entitled "Our College Students" in the October 1927 issue of *The Radionian* is a worthy tribute to the first enrolled college students at Jones County Junior College.

They are here, twenty-six of them, and what a splendid group they are. They move quietly among us with a dignity that is pleasing. They molest us (the high school students) not. They have work, it seems, sufficient to keep them busy and they seemingly have tackled the tasks of the freshman college year with courage and determination to win.

We, the high school students, welcome this splendid group of young men and women who have come for college work. We have talked about, and hoped for, a junior college for a long time. This our first class is making our dream a realization. With their high ideals, and their splendid standards of scholarship, we feel that this our first class is laying a foundation for one of the best junior colleges in the state. And so to them, we say wholeheartedly, we are glad that you have come.

This first class was so well satisfied with the work available to them that they joined in recruiting the second class. The next year sixty students were enrolled in the junior college.

During the second year Mr. Bush inaugurated a program of transportation for the junior college students whereby they could travel with the high school students by bus. He was able to persuade the legislature to provide supporting funds for the county to make this type of transportation possible, and enrollment began to increase rapidly.

Mrs. M. P. Bush, wife of President Bush, expressed a special interest in courses being added to the curriculum in the fine arts area. She was aware in the beginning that a majority of the students in college came from rural areas and that families in many rural homes did not provide opportunities for development in music, art, public speaking, dramatics, and choral fields. The administration was urged to provide training in these areas.

In the early years, trained persons were employed as members of the faculty for fulltime teaching in these fields. Even though faculty and students began with limited space and minimum equipment, yet they established the foundation for a strong department. As the first fifty years of public junior college development came to a close, Jones County Junior College could point with pride to a one million dollar fine arts facility, adequately equipped for all programs in the fine arts field. Sixty-seven numbered courses are offered on a quarter basis and involve a faculty of ten fulltime persons.

The division of the state into public junior college districts began in 1928 with the organization of the Mississippi state system of junior colleges. The Jones County Junior College district included seven counties in the beginning: Jones, Covington, Jasper, Wayne, Clarke, Greene, and Perry. Smith County was added a short time later. In the original zoning, Smith was included in a Simpson County district, which was the only district that did not develop.

The order in which the counties in the district levied taxes for the support of the college was: Jones—1927; Covington—1930; Jasper—1932; Smith—1933; Perry—1934; Greene—1934; Wayne—1937; and Clarke—1949. Within a short time, the majority of these counties were levying the amount for support permitted by law.

In May 1929, the first college graduation was held at Jones County Junior College. Eleven students received Associate of Arts Certificates. The second graduation, held in 1930, awarded certificates to thirty-three graduates. Jones County Junior College's enrollment increased so rapidly that by 1933 Jones was the leader in enrollment among all the Mississippi junior colleges and continued in this position for the next twenty-five years.

The physical plant of the agricultural high school, which the junior college used initially, consisted of six buildings, a home science cottage, and two teacher houses. The brick buildings included an administration building, a boys' dormitory, a girls' dormitory, a gymnasium, an agricultural and farm barn, and a vocational training center. An extensive annex was added to the administration building during the summer of 1927, which included the library and an auditorium with a seating capacity of 850. When this auditorium, the largest in any agricultural high school in Mississippi was completed, there was considerable skepticism as to whether Jones County Agricultural High School and Junior College would ever have 850 persons. The auditorium soon became inadequate. The new classroom area added to the administration building was a three-story construction including six classrooms on the first floor, four classrooms and two large laboratories on the second floor, and four classrooms and a study hall-library on the third floor. The library-study hall included a balcony booth at one end, constructed in a fireproof room for visual education, with the purpose of visual instruction and movie entertainment for resident students. Jones County Junior College pioneered the prepared program in visual instruction for Mississippi's junior colleges. In addition, the library and laboratory space included in this expansion enabled the beginning junior college to meet the standards of the College Accrediting Commission.

Immediately following the passage of permissive legislation of 1922 the College Accrediting Commission began establishing standards for junior colleges. The Commission required each library to have at least 1,500 books available at the time the junior colleges presented a request for accreditation. It also required that specific laboratory space with equipment be provided. The senior class of 1927 at JCAHS proposed that year to raise the necessary funds to purchase enough library books to meet the required number of 1,500. As an incentive to the students in their endeavor, the board of supervisors in Jones County passed a resolution that they would match each dollar that the students raised by public subscription. The records show that these students, with the help of the supervisors, provided sufficient funds to enable the library of JCAHS to meet the requirements of the Accrediting Commission. When the college began, the library contained approximately 1,510 volumes. A former member of this class stated that the agricultural high school dismissed the senior class, enabling them to go all over the county and other counties to sell tags for one dollar each to raise sufficient money to buy the needed books.

In 1930 a building was constructed which provided housing for the first two years of high school and classroom and laboratory space for the college home economics classes. The classrooms for the upper two years of high school and the two years of college were located in the administration building.

The next building to be constructed on the junior college campus was the president's house, built on the site of the home economics cottage. Built in 1933, in the height of the depression, under the Civil Works Administration, the 3274-square-foot house was constructed in twelve days. The contractor, Mr. J. D. Simmons, had all of the skilled labor that was needed because of high unemployment, and at times more than one hundred men were working on the residence.

Included in an overall project at the time the president's house was constructed in 1934 was a football field with lights, seating, and track, which was identified as a stadium. This stadium, with maintenance and repairs through the years, is still serving as the junior college stadium and is known as the Bush-Young Stadium.

Three other buildings were completed on the campus during the decade of the 1930s. These buildings were a band hall (1932), a vocational building (1937), and a classroom-shop building for the vocational agriculture and manual training departments (1938).

Jones County Junior College missed an opportunity to construct some buildings on its campus in 1935–1936. The Federal Emergency Administration of Public Work made available, by way of a grant to the public junior colleges in Mississippi, assistance in the amount of forty-five percent of the cost of a building project to aid in financing, constructing and equipping school buildings. The Federal Emergency Administration approved in November of 1936 a grant to Jones County Junior College in the amount not to exceed $118,636. The board of trustees approved the project in the amount of $181,818. This amount was to be used in the following manner: one academic building—$50,000; one girls' dormitory—$60,000; one service building—$20,000; one auditorium—$40,000; and some land adjoining the campus—$11,818. The

cost of this project required the approval of the board of supervisors. Approval was not granted, and the action was very disappointing to the administration and the board of trustees of the college, since most of the junior colleges in the state took advantage of this opportunity to construct new college buildings. Jones, with its large enrollment, which passed the 1,500 mark prior to the beginning of World War II, was forced to operate for a number of years without adequate facilities. Jones County Junior College decided to do something on its own.

The girls' dormitory included in this project which failed was urgently needed. The one main campus dormitory was overflowing, even though three or four girls were in each room. The college was concerned about students being denied the opportunity to attend junior college because of the lack of housing.

The largest house in Ellisville, located near the college on the main street from the college to town, became available for rent. This house would provide dormitory facilities for approximately twenty-five girls. Mr. and Mrs. W. C. Thomas agreed to operate it as a dormitory, and it immediately became known as "The Thomas House." This house met many needs until funds were available to construct a girls' dormitory.

As a result of failure to receive funds for new buildings as planned, the administration of Jones County Junior College decided to seek approval to establish a project in brickmaking. With brick available, ways could be found to construct some permanent buildings. An approved project under the National Youth Administration provided the labor for making brick. The Laurel Brick and Tile Company, operated by Mr. Ben Snider in Laurel, was not operating at this time, and an agreement was made between Mr. Bush and Mr. Snider to use this plant. Also, Mr. Earl Snider agreed to supervise the making of the brick. A factor in the arrangement was that the vocational-agriculture teacher, Mr. A. C. Smith, had land not too far from Laurel, and he agreed to allow the wood for burning the brick to be secured from his land in exchange for enough brick to build a new home. According to Mr. Earl Snider, who supervised the project, the college made approximately a million and a half bricks. Today, you can point to a number of buildings on the campus—dormitories, shop buildings, the gymnasium, and additions to other buildings—which were constructed because of these bricks. It was an interesting sight to see more than a million bricks stacked on the campus in large piles, some six feet high and forty to sixty feet long. These bricks were not used up for twelve to fifteen years.

The construction of the vocational building in 1937 is an illustration of an effort to meet specific student needs and provided some innovative leadership in the Mississippi public junior college system. The use of this vocational building was moving in a new direction to meet the needs of students who were being denied the opportunity to enter college because of the lack of funds. To solve the formidable problem, the college secured federal assistance in constructing a vocational building for the purpose of establishing a manufacturing unit on the campus of Jones County Junior College.

A hosiery manufacturer of Coopersburg, Pennsylvania, was contacted regarding equipping the building with full-fashioned hosiery machinery to be operated by the junior college. The program was educationally oriented. The contract stated that, "The junior college shall have complete and exclusive authority in the management, control, and operation of the program, and in the determination of its policies." The owner of the machinery agreed to take the hosiery produced by the students and market these on the open market and pay all costs of the operation.

The students employed in the operation were assigned on a work-study basis, a half load of work and a half load in college courses. College credit was also allowed for the technical training received and was acceptable for graduation and transfer. Many students were able to graduate from junior college with the aid of this work-study program. It also provided job opportunity training. A large number continued in the hosiery manufacturing business as a profession.

In 1940, the year that Jones County Junior College was admitted to full membership in the Southern Association of Colleges and Schools, Mr. M. P. Bush resigned to become director of the Industrial Training School in Columbia, Mississippi. He was succeeded by J. B. Young, a graduate of the University of Mississippi and Columbia University, who had been serving as vice president of the college. Mr. Young was aware, as he accepted the leadership of Jones County Agricultural High School and Junior College, that he was faced with challenges that should be met im-

mediately. He was also aware that even though some of the difficulties relating to the depression of the 1930s had been overcome, the threat of a world war was facing the nation. This became a reality when World War II was declared in December 1941.

The high school and college enrollment had passed the 1,500 mark, and the college was still without sufficient funds for urgently needed buildings. President Young was faced with the challenge of operating the institution during the serious drop in enrollment caused by the Second World War. However, the institution geared itself to contribute its part to the war effort. A small air field was built to the west of the campus, and a naval flight training program was established. A large number of students were trained here, and technical courses relating to the war were offered, enabling students who were later drafted to contribute more to their country when they were called into service.

A post-war surge of students found the junior college without sufficient funds for new buildings. A welcome opportunity came, however, when surplus buildings from CCC camps were moved to the campus, supported by federal funds to move and construct them. Over 142,000 square feet of surplus buildings provided housing, shop space, cafeteria space, and classrooms for the burgeoning student body. Housing for married students was provided with house trailers and barracks, which were moved from army camps. Four steel navy barracks were received, which the junior college used to construct a women's dormitory, a men's dormitory, and a large housing and shop building, both of which are still in use at the end of the fifty-year period.

In 1950, the state legislature decided that the state of Mississippi should provide funds for buildings on the junior college campuses, and since that point Jones County Junior College has added several million dollars worth of buildings. In 1954, a gymnasium was constructed, the first permanent construction since the 1930s.

A small permanent brick building, which was known as the "student center," was constructed in 1960–1961. The beginning of a student center for Jones County Junior College is an interesting story. During the 1930s, students requested a place that would serve sandwiches, hamburgers, and drinks. With the moving of a CCC camp from Jasper

County, some barracks buildings were available, which were twenty feet wide and one hundred-twenty feet long. One of these buildings was erected on the campus to be used as a student center. A contest was held for naming the new building, and the name "Snack-Shack" was chosen. Regardless of the appearance of the building, there were heartaches when the "Snack-Shack" gave way to the first brick student center in 1960–1961. Other buildings constructed included the library, the science building, the technical building (which has been expanded), an agriculture-technology building, a fine arts building, and a cafeteria-student center building. The college has continued to add other needed buildings as the second fifty-year period has begun.

Facilities on the campus of Jones County Junior College easily indicate the rapid expansion that has taken place. The expansion and growth that have taken place through curricula changes and the development relating to administration and faculty have been the central force in bringing about the growth and development of Jones County Junior College during the first fifty years.

When the college opened in 1927, courses in science, education, English, modern language, history, and mathematics were offered. A view of the catalog for 1971–1972 shows approximately fifty-eight categories of curricula distributed in thirty academic areas and in twenty-eight vocational and technical areas. Within the categories are approximately five hundred numbered courses offered on the quarter basis. The changes that took place in curricula offering during the first three decades related largely to academic courses. The additions that came about during those years were influenced by requirements in the transferring of credit to a senior college. Some of the early curricula changes in the junior college development included the areas of agriculture, home economics, art, music, and business education.

Additions to the academic curriculum have also taken place in administrative services and faculty. However, these changes have not occurred rapidly. Original administrative officers of the college were president, dean, and registrar. In 1937, a fulltime business manager was employed by the college. During that same year, a fulltime music teacher was employed with a fixed salary of $120 a month, paid out of tuition. A registered nurse was also employed to take care of the campus medical needs, and a night watchman was employed for security purposes. Bible was offered as an optional course for the first time, and a fulltime guidance director was employed.

The period 1945–1953 was one of significant development in the area of technical and vocational education. The administration of the junior colleges in Mississippi had always felt that technical and vocational training was definitely a responsibility of the junior colleges in their districts. The problem of lack of funds was at least partially solved by the development of the veterans program under the G. I. Bill, which provided both surplus property and money for purchase of additional equipment. The earliest equipment that became available to the junior colleges in Mississippi came through the closing of the shops operated in various sections in Mississippi under the National Youth Administration Program. Jones County Junior College was assigned wood shop and machine shop equipment that was located at Ackerman, Mississippi. At the end of the period 1945–1953, during which time the Veteran's Program was operating, Jones County Junior College was operating fifteen vocational-technical programs and had served more than 2,500 students, the largest number of students served in the area of vocational-technical training by any public junior college in Mississippi at that time. At the end of the 1971–1972 session, Jones Junior College was offering work in twenty-three programs of technical and vocational nature. The emphasis given to technical and vocational training stimulated all areas of activities in the district and on the state level to continue the development of technical and vocational areas in the public junior colleges on the district level and to enable the junior colleges to establish a comprehensive program, including all areas of service relating to the needs of the district. The comprehensive program now includes the transfer programs, a program of general education, technical courses, vocational courses, programs in human services such as police science, health services, hospital services, communications, and adult education. All these programs were geared to serve the community and industrial needs of the district and of the state.

Jones County Junior College early developed an interest in a program in nursing education. In 1952, the first LPN nursing program in the Mississippi junior college system was established on the Jones County Junior College campus. At a later date, Jones established its Associate Degree in Nursing, leading to the R. N. degree.

Jones Junior College is the only junior college in Mississippi to establish and continue operating a program in horology, jewelry repair and engraving, and was the only school to establish a program in photolithography. A continuing increase in financial support from its vocational and technical programs by the state of Mississippi and the local district has provided Jones with adequate facilities for these programs. Jones County Junior College was the first institution of college grade to receive funds which were provided for a program of training in law enforcement.

To many other areas of growth and development Jones County Junior College can point with pride. An activity which has brought credit to the institution is that of the Alumni Association, which in 1961–1962 began a program of selecting each year an honor alumnus and placing a tribute and a picture of that individual in the Memorial Library. This has pointed out some distinguished individuals who are graduates of this institution and whose contribution, not only in their profession, but over and beyond their profession, has been outstanding.

The October 1, 1946 issue of *Look* gave national recognition to Jones County Junior College by listing it on the national honor roll of America's one hundred best schools among junior colleges and state universities. Only three junior colleges in the South won a place in this poll. This recognition was significant to the administration, faculty, and students of Jones County Junior College.

The student enrollment at Jones County Junior College has been significant as related to the Mississippi state system of junior colleges. In the 1933–1934 session, which was the seventh year of the operation of Jones County Junior College, the student count from the state department of education showed that Jones County Junior College led all the junior colleges in enrollment. Jones County Junior College continued this leadership through the next twenty-five years, and the record also shows that at the end of the first fifty years of public junior college operation in Mississippi Jones County Junior College had served more fulltime, on-campus students than any other public junior college in the state.

Prior to the entrance of this nation in World War II,

Jones Junior College, during the sessions 1939–1940 and 1940–1941, had passed the seven hundred mark in college enrollment. The impact of World War II had reduced enrollment for the 1943–1944 session to 160 students.

Following the close of the War, and the passage of Public Law 16, Seventy-Eighth Congress, G. I. Bill 346, an upsurge in enrollment began, and for the 1947–1948 session Jones set a new mark for junior college enrollment, the first time enrollment above one thousand was reached by a public junior college in Mississippi.

The large enrollment of veterans, on a tuition basis, provided funds for the college to establish and equip special training programs, which gave Jones County Junior College the first real breakthrough in technical and vocational fields. Job opportunity programs stimulated a special interest from state leaders and from industrial leaders in giving financial support to these programs, and was also the beginning of comprehensive programs, including the technical-vocational programs.

The veteran enrollment at the college for a period of seven years, 1946–1947 through 1952–1953, showed a total of 2967. Another decrease in enrollment came with the advent of the Korean War. However, this was for a short period of time.

Jones Junior College has been proud of the achievement of the institution in all areas of athletic competition. Jones County Junior College has won state championships in all areas of competitive athletics. These include football, basketball, track, tennis, and literary activities. In the school session of 1940–1941 Jones made a clean sweep of state championships and won state championship in all activities operated on the state level that year. Two special achievements in football competition brought honors to the school. Jones is one of two of the public junior colleges in Mississippi to have had an invitation to play in the Little Rose Bowl in Pasadena, California. Jones won the state championship in 1955 and was invited to play in the Little Rose Bowl in Pasadena, playing Compton Junior College of Compton, California.

The band, cheerleaders, and choral groups were referred to many times as the "spirit builders" in the eight-county junior college district. When the football team was invited to participate in the Junior College Rose Bowl game, interest was expressed immediately that the 120-person college band and cheerleaders should be included in the trip, even though it was a long way from Ellisville to Pasadena, California. A young men's quartet that had contributed much to the spirit of the college expressed their interest in making the trip, even to the extent of paying their own way. These groups, with their fine interest, stimulated persons in the junior college district in seeking ways to support the trip. In a short time, the Laurel Lions Club, individuals, and the supervisors in the supporting counties in the district made available adequate funds to pay the expenses of these groups. Some funds were received from an alumnus in California.

Again in 1969, the football team won the National Junior College Championship. This was an achievement appreciated a great deal by all related to the college. At the end of the school session 1971–1972, which was the end of the first fifty years of public junior colleges operating in Mississippi, in football competition Jones Junior College had won more games from each junior college than any of the other schools. Jones County Junior College had also scored the most points over each school.

Jones County Junior College has always realized that an athletic program is of great importance and contributes much to the growth and development of it. Athletics also provide many opportunities for young men and young women to secure jobs in the various fields of physical education. The record of junior college coaches, who are within the junior college district of Jones Junior College, gives evidence to the importance of this job opportunity program.

Jones Junior College has consistently maintained an open-door policy whereby no high school graduate in the district who wanted to go to college would be denied that opportunity; therefore, it has been a firm commitment on the part of the college that any boy or girl who had graduated from high school and who wanted to enter college would be admitted to Jones County Junior College, regardless of the student's financial status, meaning that the college made a way for a student to earn or receive necessary help. Seven out of ten high school graduates in the Jones Junior College District, who entered college anywhere in the state or out, first entered Jones Junior College.

Contributing to the increased opportunity for the high school student to attend junior college was the availability of bus transportation with no cost to the student. When the junior college opened, a large number of high school buses were transporting students to the agricultural high school. Arrangements were made in the beginning for college students to ride these high school buses, and this was very helpful.

As soon as other counties in the district provided tax support for the college program, an interest and need developed for bus transportation from other counties in the district. A lack of financial support of this transportation without charging the student a fee delayed serving other counties. However, in 1953 a bus was provided for Wayne County, which was the first for college students in supporting counties in the district. Within a short time, each of the eight counties was providing bus transportation for college students with no cost to the students.

Jones County Junior College has realized that a major objective of the institution was to provide college education at low cost. To achieve this goal Jones Junior College had, through the years, to be a self-sufficient institution and to carry on activities which would lower the cost of the college education to the students in the district. For many years Jones Junior College was active in truck farming and gardening on the campus. This activity not only provided food but also provided students labor opportunities. A canning unit was established which provided a great part of the canned foods necessary for operation of the dining room.

Toward the end of this first fifty years in the operation of public junior colleges in Mississippi, Jones operated its own dining room and later a cafeteria. In addition to the canned food provided for the dining room, a dairy operating on the campus furnished the milk necessary for the cafeteria. All the pork used by the cafeteria was raised and butchered on the campus of the college. Also, for a period of time, Jones Junior College grew its own beef.

A college laundry operated and was included in the board, even though board was low cost. For the greater part of this fifty-year period, because of county support, Jones did not charge a room rent. A room was free to all boarding students. The amount charged students within the district for the first year of the college operation was $14 per month, which included room and board, in addition to a matriculation fee of $7 for the year. At the end of this first fifty years, Jones County Junior College students were paying $40 per month for board and laundry and $30 per quarter for room fee.

The junior college has been proud of the student publication known as the *Radionian*. This publication has continued since the beginning of the junior college and has made a very fine contribution to the growth and development of the school. This paper has received an award from the State Junior College Division for its achievement. Another student activity, the Phi Theta Kappa, has been outstanding. These students have received national recognition for the work they have done.

Jones Junior College had the first fulltime director in religious denominations on the campus. This work has continued and has made a great contribution to the growth and development of the college. We pay tribute to the leadership of the directors in various religious organizations who have worked on the campus.

State recognition has been received in areas of agricultural achievement. Jones County Junior College began immediately after its organization a program of agriculture, and this work has received recognition, particularly in the area of livestock. Also, the vocational program in horology, jewelry repair and engraving, has received a national award, and especially for contribution to training for the handicapped. This unit has had the largest percentage of students entering employment in the field of that training of any other program of job opportunity in Mississippi. Distributive education received national recognition in 1972, and automotive was awarded some first places on the state level.

On July 1, 1970, President J. B. Young, who had served Jones County Junior College for a period of forty years—thirty years of this period as president of the college—resigned, and Mr. Terrell Tisdale was elected the third president of the college. Mr. Tisdale had been a member of the faculty of Jones County Junior College since 1961 and had served as administrative assistant to the president since 1966. Mr. Tisdale's experience and understanding of the total college program enabled him to continue needed development in facilities and in the comprehensive program. Increased funds from the state and district levels, as well as federal funds, have made possible rapid expansion in facilities and equipment. There is assurance that Jones County Junior College, as it closes its services to the district at the end of the first fifty years, has prepared for the future and that programs and facilities are available to meet the needs of students and adults in this district.

The changing conditions through the years in all areas of living have challenged the administration, faculty, and students of Jones County Junior College, and all have worked together to meet these changes. College officials and citizens of the district feel much satisfaction and encouragement as Jones County Junior College moves into the last quarter of the twentieth century, which is the beginning years of the second fifty-year period of Mississippi's state system of public junior colleges. Jones County Junior College, which opened in 1927, operated for forty-five years during the first half century of the public junior college movement in Mississippi.

The events, conditions, and circumstances that have been recorded in this story, regarding the growth and development of the institution in the Jones County Junior College district, are related to many persons in various categories. The efforts, concern, and dedication of those who are responsible for the contributions and services rendered to individuals, communities, and to the district are worthy of recognition.

Statements written as this story closes are for the purpose of paying tribute to those who have had a vital part in the life of the institution.

A tabulation of the number of on-campus students enrolled for the first forty-five years of the operation of the school, at the close of the 1971–1972 school session, was above 50,000. Their contribution speaks for the worth of this institution.

We look with pride at the accomplishments of the alumni of Jones County Junior College and are aware that many of these would have found the door closed to any formal education beyond the high school had their needs not been met by a college within the district, which was accessible and provided quality education at low cost.

A review of the testimonials given through the years by students of Jones County Junior College speaks clearly to all that the dedicated and trained men and women who have been listed on the faculty roster have, through their teaching and influence, made available to students high quality education that has resulted in the development of young men and women in all areas of living with the dominant purpose of the development of character. Students have been challenged, inspired, and directed by these faculty members. A review of the list of four hundred and seventy-three faculty and administrative personnel through the years includes a list of more than thirty persons who gave from twenty years to more than forty years of service. To all persons who have served the junior college through these years, we express appreciation. At the close of the 1971–1972 school session, Jones County Junior College had a faculty of one hundred twenty-four instructors and administrative personnel, twenty-four clerical personnel, and sixty-four service personnel.

One hundred and thirteen citizens of the Jones County Junior College district served as members of the board of trustees for the district. Some of these were selected to serve as presidents of the board during these years. The list includes J. T. Taylor, George Evans, D. R. Sanders, Fred Bynum, Ellis Cooper, Bernard Powell, Thomas Harris, and D. O. Thoms.

A long list of one hundred eighty-four county officials served as members of the board of supervisors from the eight-county district. These have been responsible for the district financial support. The records show that the effort in tax support, according to ability of the district to provide, has been equal to and above that of other districts in Mississippi.

Many other elected officials, including county officers, members of the state legislative bodies, and citizens too numerous to mention, have contributed to the development of Jones County Junior College.

The increased funds for support and for facilities which are available as the institution plans for the future will bring new challenges to all who are giving leadership to the program. It gives assurance that the total needs of the Jones County Junior College district will be more adequately met in future years.

The value of buildings, academic, residential and service, and equipment of the college is inventoried at approximately seven million dollars.

For many years the foreword in the college catalog of Jones County Junior College has closed with these words:

It is the hope of this institution that those who enter its halls, whether their interests lie in the field of general education, pre-professional training, technical-terminal field, or business, may improve in knowledge, efficiency and character, and that when they leave they will feel that this institu-

tion has made a contribution to each of them during the time that they were a part of this program, and that in turn it will make a contribution to their future.

It is the hope for the future that this junior college will produce men and women with trained intelligence and strength of character that will enable them to assume heavy responsibilities as they meet the changing conditions in the world in which we live.

EAST MISSISSIPPI
JUNIOR COLLEGE STORY

The school known as East Mississippi Junior College was established in 1912 as Kemper County Agricultural High School. The 1924 catalog of the Kemper County Agricultural High School described the facilities as consisting of seven buildings—administration building, boys' dormitory, girls' dormitory, home economics building, and shop. A new dining hall and a superintendent's house were announced in this catalog.

In 1922 a bill passed by the Mississippi legislature authorized agricultural high schools to add one or two years of junior college to their curricula. Many requests were made to the board of trustees of the Kemper County Agricultural High School to add the college-level courses; and after a petition signed by thirty-seven Kemper County students was submitted to this board, they approved the addition of one year of college course work in September 1927. The school became known as the Kemper County Agricultural High School-Junior College. J. D. Wallace, who had served as superintendent of the agricultural high school for several years, was administrator of the new junior college.

A new administration building was constructed and occupied in the 1927–1928 session. The former administration building had been destroyed by fire. The new facility was described as being "a handsome brick structure built in the form of a T. . . . It is up to date in design and is a credit to the school and the county." The building was later used only for academic instruction, until 1974, when it was declared obsolete and was demolished.

On May 17, 1928, the State Junior College Commission visited the campus of the Kemper County Agricultural High School-Junior College and "after a

GUIDED BY THESE
PRESIDENTS

James David Wallace
1927–1940

Jack McWhirter Tubb
1940–1945

Cruce Stark
1945–1953

R. Algene Harbour
1953–1970

Earl A. Stennis
1970–

thorough inspection of everything connected with our school, they expressed satisfaction with our location, appreciation of our buildings and grounds, and gave their approvel to our Junior College work." Twenty students were enrolled in college-level courses.

The second year of college-level work was offered in 1929. The school was given full approval by both the Senior College Accrediting Committee and the State Junior College Committee. "The Senior College Committee stated that it had given us the highest scholastic rank it had ever granted a Junior College for its first year's work," according to the 1929–1930 catalog.

Noxubee County elected to join in the support of the college in 1932, and the name was changed to the Kemper County Agricultural High School and Kemper-Noxubee Junior College.

Enrollment during the 1929–1930 session of the junior college was ninety-six students. The Associate of Agriculture diploma was authorized for men, and an Associate of Arts diploma was awarded to women graduates.

The 1929 state legislature doubled its appropriation for the college, and Lauderdale County was added to the tax supporting district. A Scooba Separate School District was formed for elementary through junior high school students, and the name of the institution was changed to East Mississippi Junior College. The new junior college included the eleventh and twelfth grades of high school and the freshman and sophomore college classes.

Construction began on a new dormitory for women, and a new gymnasium was completed during the 1930–1931 session.

The purposes of East Mississippi Junior College were probably originally drawn up by its first president, J. D. Wallace, although no evidence except the writing style of the president exists as proof.

In 1931, the aims of East Mississippi Junior College were listed as:

1. To place, at small cost, the advantages of a standard high school and junior college within the reach of every country boy and girl.
2. To prepare students not only for college, but to give them training along vocational and industrial lines.
3. To cooperate with the A & M College, the County Farm Agent, and the County Home Economics Agent in carrying valuable assistance to the farm and the farm home.
4. To uplift rural life, to lessen drudgery, to increase comfort, to make the home more attractive, to lead in the

development of an attractive, satisfying, and enduring rural civilization.

The buildings, equipment, and lands belonging to the school were valued at $300,000 in 1931, and enrollment had increased to 155 students.

Reflecting the economic condition of the country, the 1933–1934 catalog said, "As we have done during the previous sessions, in order to assist our patrons in paying matriculation fees and in purchasing books, we will continue to purchase from them, as far as we can use them, the following items: Corn, peas, potatoes, molasses, peanuts, canned goods (gallon size), pork, beef, sausage, butter, eggs, fresh fruits, vegetables, etc." Thus was established East Mississippi Junior College's policy of aiding those students who, for economic reasons, find a college education difficult to attain. This policy continues to the present.

Enrollment at East Mississippi Junior College, in spite of an unsettled economy, began an upward swing: 185 students were enrolled in 1932, 189 in 1933; and by 1936, 190 students were attending the school. The school won approval of the American Association of Junior Colleges, the band was organized, and an orchestra, glee club, drama club, religious organizations, and other societies were formed during this period. Student activities fees were charged for the first time during the 1937–1938 school year so a first-class yearbook and a school paper could be financed.

In 1936 the aims of the school were further expanded, dropping some of the practical aspects of the previous declaration of aims and emphasizing qualities of character development. The down-to-earth statements of purpose were:

1. To furnish, at the lowest possible cost, the advantages of a standard junior college and
2. To discover to the student his talents and capacities and guide [him] in the choice of a vocation.

This purpose remained unchanged for more than a decade.

J. M. Tubb assumed the presidency of East Mississippi Junior College in 1939 and remained until he was elected to the office of State Superintendent of Education in 1945.

The war years virtually halted construction on the campus as students and faculty members dedicated themselves to winning the war in various ways. The 1942–1943 catalog announced that a new vocational defense shop was being erected and that $4,600 worth of new equipment was added to the existing stock to give training "in line with defense work recommended by the Federal Government."

The purposes listed in the catalog of 1943–1944 reflected a change in attitude. At this time the college recognized its responsibility to the adult population of the community:

It is the purpose of East Mississippi Junior College:

1. To provide a curriculum of two years of instruction in the fundamentals of arts and sciences.

2. To offer courses to meet the needs of students preparing for specialized civilian and military service.

3. To aid the youth in discovering his talents and capacities; in career planning, placements, and follow-up choice vocation. Special guidance is given students anticipating government services.

4. To promote the development of personality and leadership through wholesome social experiences, by closer parental influence, and by cooperating with, and participating in the various educational contests.

5. To prepare students to render the best service possible, to develop habits of adjustment in a changing democratic society and encourage cheerfulness and a hopeful outlook on life.

6. To offer college work to adult citizens of the community and district in accordance with their needs, interests, and desires.

7. To teach the dignity of labor and the enjoyment of rural life.

8. To further wholesome community development through interrelating between student, teacher, and citizen.

9. To offer the facilities of the school, its laboratories, and staff to the citizens of the community the college serves.

10. To coordinate the activities of the various public agencies in the development of rural community life.

11. To train young men and women for the cultural and technical demands of the future and to aid in the rehabilitation of returning servicemen and women.

At the end of the war the emphasis changed from supporting the war effort to retraining the returning veterans for useful trades or professions. In 1942 the state legislature appropriated $60,000 to the Mississippi public junior colleges for equipment for vocational and technical training, and in 1944 the legislature appropriated $120,000 for this type of training. East Mississippi continues to maintain an outstanding vocational-technical training program and has had great success in this area.

Cruce Stark became president of East Mississippi Junior College in 1945, and a tremendous building program began. An apartment building of twenty-four units was constructed. A second men's dormitory, a new administration building, a student center, an in-

dustrial arts building, a music building, a new president's home, and twenty trailers were added to the campus.

Building continued, and according to the records of the state building commission, an engineering building, an armory, an agriculture building, and an auto mechanics building were constructed in 1950. In 1955 a new field house was built, and in 1957 the science building was completed.

R. A. Harbour was selected president of East Mississippi Junior College in 1954.

The high school and the college continued to share faculty and teaching facilities until the end of the 1960–1961 school year. Although enrollment in the college was drawn from several counties, no new tax-supporting county was added until 1963, when Lowndes County elected to add its support with an initial one-half mill levy. In 1966 Clay County joined the East Mississippi Junior College District, and Oktibbeha County joined in 1967. The six counties of Lauderdale, Kemper, Noxubee, Clay, Lowndes, and Oktibbeha continue to make up the East Mississippi Junior College tax-supporting district.

During the 1963–1964 self-study, the committee on purpose found that, in the main, the purpose of the college had not changed essentially since 1943, except for its military purpose. The philosophy and purpose, the result of a slow metamorphosis, reflected the position of the college in the community. It was more and more concerned with the education of youth and their preparation for continuous college training and less and less concerned with adult training. New state programs for vocational-technical training were being studied with the view to cooperating with the state in the technical training of youth and adults for the industrial space age. Following the self-study and evaluation, East Mississippi Junior College received reaffirmation of accreditation by the Southern Association of Colleges and Schools in 1965.

The Golden Triangle Vocational-Technical Center was organized in 1968 as a division of East Mississippi Junior College. Located at Mayhew, Mississippi, in the center of the Golden Triangle Area of North Mississippi (Columbus, Starkville, and West Point), the Center provides vocational and technical education to the students of this area to prepare them for employment in business, industry, agriculture, and health occupations.

In addition to more than a dozen vocational and

technical programs, the Golden Triangle Center also operates successful adult extension and adult basic education programs. Short courses and special interest programs are offered upon request, and a full staff of counselors and instructors is maintained to assist students.

In 1968, a new cafeteria building and a library were constructed on the Scooba Campus of East Mississippi Junior College.

Earl A. Stennis became president of East Mississippi Junior College in 1970. In the fall of 1972, East Mississippi Junior College again expanded its services by opening an extension program at the Columbus Air Force Base in Columbus, Mississippi.

Construction during this period included Sullivan Hall Athletic Dormitory in 1971, physical plant complex in 1972, and the ultramodern Stennis Hall Academic Building in 1973.

In 1974 William E. Reeves was selected president of East Mississippi Junior College. A new vocational-technical center completed on the Scooba Campus would house several new programs, including the first mortuary science program to be offered by a state-supported institution in Mississippi.

The campus of East Mississippi Junior College has changed through the years. As new construction took place, as obsolete buildings were demolished, and as progress was made, one characteristic has remained on the twenty-five-acre main campus. The stately pine trees, many dating back to the founding of the school, continue to grace the campus and add to the serenity and beauty of the facility. The historic Pine Grove is one particular area that is remembered by graduates of the school. Originally called "Barbeque Hill" because of the many picnics and barbeques held under these trees, the Pine Grove is now the site of the annual Pine Grove Festival. This fine arts festival has become a tradition at East Mississippi Junior College. It serves as a teaching method to the music, art, drama, and other fine arts programs of the school, and also contributes to the cultural enrichment of area citizens. Organizations such as the East Mississippi Junior College have discovered the Pine Grove beauty and hold annual meetings there.

The purpose of East Mississippi Junior College is to offer diverse opportunities for development of the intellectual, spiritual, cultural, physical, and vocational resources of the people of this district so that they will respond creatively to life in a democratic society. In support of this program, an academic program is provided to equip students who plan to continue their education beyond junior college, and a program of terminal courses in business, technology, and the vocations is offered.

The specific objectives supporting the purposes of East Mississippi Junior College are transfer education, vocational and technical education, guidance, activities, continuing education, and community service.

Decades of dedicated faculty members who are outstanding in their particular areas of specialization, administrators who see visions of better things for the school, and students who are eager to learn have led to the achievement of these objectives at East Mississippi Junior College.

COPIAH-LINCOLN
JUNIOR COLLEGE STORY

Copiah-Lincoln Junior College in Wesson has a rich history, dating back to the agricultural high school which opened in 1915. It is a story of the emergence into a junior college in 1928, a story of the depression years and the war years, and more recently the flourishing of programs and buildings and expanding facilities to include a resident center.

Copiah-Lincoln, founded as a junior college in 1928, is now supported by the counties of Copiah, Lincoln, Simpson, Lawrence, Franklin, Jefferson, and Adams. In addition to its main campus in Wesson, the college operates a resident center in Natchez with ten fulltime and thirty parttime employees. The center began operation in September 1972, with 449 enrolled. A wide variety of academic courses is offered in a day and a night program. The resident center in Natchez is presently housed at the former Central School near Washington. Two principal buildings serve the students.

Total enrollment in all programs is expected to hit a high of nearly 3,000 students during the 1973–1974 school session. Enrollment is based on academic students, vocational-technical students in both day and night programs, and students in adult education, high school, resident center, and other programs.

On the main campus more than twenty-five principal buildings valued at more than $6,000,000 compose the physical plant. Buildings are named for early lead-

GUIDED BY THESE
PRESIDENTS

Lawrence Russell Ellzey
1928–1932

Willie H. Smith
1943–1945
(acting president)

James Malcomb Ewing
1932–1956

Francis Marion Fortenberry
1956–1968

Billy Bass Thames
1968–

162

ers of the high school and the college. A ten-year building program is now underway, which when completed will add ten million dollars in value to the present facilities.

Copiah-Lincoln Junior College is an outgrowth of Copiah-Lincoln Agricultural High School founded in 1915. The idea of establishing an agricultural high school was spurred by the Agricultural High School Law of 1912, and R. L. Landis, who became the first superintendent, led in promoting the idea. Since surrounding communities were in need of an inexpensive boarding school, a site was proposed on the Copiah and Lincoln County lines which would provide education for students from both counties.

To establish such a school the community had to provide a minimum of twenty acres of land for a site, a school building, and dormitory facilities for at least forty students. The board of supervisors then had to levy a tax not to exceed two mills.

R. E. Furr was elected president of the first board of trustees which met for the first time on December 9, 1914. Construction of two buildings for $6,806 was approved by the board on March 2, 1915, with construction to begin immediately. There were to be a classroom building and a dormitory. Russell Ellzey, later the first president of the college, was one of six elected to the first faculty of the high school.

Opening exercises for the first session of Copiah-Lincoln Agricultural High School were held on September 6, 1915. The high school department of the Wesson Public Schools had been transferred to the new campus. Forty of the 125 students enrolled boarded, with board ranging from $4.60 to $5.75 per month. As became the custom for several decades, to keep the board at a low rate the girls had to serve for a six-weeks term in the dining hall and the boys to work on the farm one day a month. Later when the junior college was established, several students worked their way through Copiah-Lincoln by being assigned various jobs on the farm.

One of the original buildings still stands today, housing the student personnel services on the second floor and the home economics department on the first floor. In the beginning it was a dormitory with girls living downstairs and the boys living upstairs. The building has been brick-veneered and remodeled three different times. The original administration building, constructed in the spring of 1916 at the cost of $11,000 by Thompson and Nelson of Meadville,

later became the academic classroom building. That building was replaced in 1968 with a three-storied structure.

Enrollment in 1918 filled both dormitories to capacity with thirty students on a waiting list. The Hotel House or Home in downtown Wesson was rented for $20 a month by Superintendent W. I. Thames for thirty male students.

The need for a new dormitory was met by the construction of a three-story brick structure to house girls. Cost was $59,615.40. First used in 1920, the building was replaced in 1971 by a more modern five-storied structure.

Not all the history is bright, however. A tornado ravaged the campus in March 1922, removing the roof of the west dormitory, damaging the roof of the east dormitory, and almost demolishing the administration building. Fire destroyed the girls' dormitory with all furnishings and belongings of more than one hundred girls and teachers on September 29, 1922. There was no loss of life and little bodily injury. People in Wesson housed and fed the 240 students and gave them clothing. Businessmen opened their stores and supplied shoes and other necessities. Tents were used for a temporary dining room and kitchen, and for housing some of the boys. The girls occupied the boys' dormitories and lived with families in town.

It was at a meeting following the fire that citizens spoke to the board about beginning to prepare for establishing a junior college. Six years later the college work was added.

Publication of a yearbook was begun in 1924–1925 with *Co-Lin* as its title. When the junior college was added, the sophomore class published the annual. The yearbook was not printed from 1931 to 1936, the depression years, nor during World War II from 1943 to 1945. When Simpson County became a supporting county of the junior college, the title was changed to the *Co-Lin Trillium*, which it remains today. The *Trillium* has won many national and state awards since 1965.

The year 1924 marked an important date in Copiah-Lincoln's history; W. S. Henley of Hazlehurst was appointed to the board of trustees. Mr. Henley continues to serve on the board, having served as its president since 1934.

As rural communities began to consolidate their schools, there was less demand for boarding facilities for high school students and a rising need for education beyond the twelfth grade. Interest in a junior college was foremost when the board of trustees met on March 6, 1923. Dr. H. M. Ivy, high school supervisor of the state department of education, outlined necessary procedures for establishing and maintaining a junior college. Russell Ellzey was authorized to secure information in regard to adding a first year of junior college work for the 1924–1925 session. However, the movement was delayed until the 1928–1929 session.

During the 1927–1928 school session Ellzey, along with the glee club, the quartet, and other students, visited every school community in the supporting counties. On June 1, 1928, an election for a $150,000 bond issue resulted in a more than ten to one decision in favor of the junior college. Money from the bond issue was to be used for a new boys' dormitory, gymnasium, dining room, and an annex to the administration building to provide classrooms, laboratories, and library space.

Enrollment was expected to be ninety for the 1928–1929 session; however, the enrollment was over 125.

Construction of several facilities added to the physical plant during the early years of the college. A new administration building with a classroom annex was constructed under the Works Projects Administration program in 1937. Additional buildings were added through the years, many having been replaced or renovated since their construction.

Since its beginning as Copiah-Lincoln Agricultural High School in 1915, eight men have led as superintendent or president. They included R. L. Landis, 1915–1918; W. I. Thames, 1918–1920; T. J. Cathy, 1920–1922; Russell Ellzey, 1922–1932, J. M. Ewing, 1932–1956; Willie H. Smith, acting president from 1943 to 1945 when Mr. Ewing was on active duty during World War II; F. M. Fortenberry, 1956–1968; and Billy B. Thames, who has served as president since January 18, 1968.

The college owns six hundred acres of land with nearly eighty-five acres on the campus property. In the early years the college operated a farm and a dairy, but after the agriculture courses were discontinued in the early 1960s the benefits from dairying declined, and the stock was sold. Pasture land, however, is rented as a source of income.

Copiah-Lincoln Junior College through the years has been accredited by the Southern Association of Colleges and Secondary Schools and the Mississippi College Council on Accreditation and Studies. Copiah-Lincoln is a member of the American Association of Junior Colleges, the Mississippi Junior College Association, and the Mississippi Association of Colleges.

Today students at Co-Lin are offered a wide variety of activities in which they may participate. The student personnel services division of the college provides for the student outside the classroom. A full-time director of student activities supervises intramural sports, including football, basketball, softball, ping pong, eight ball, golf, tobacco spitting, and pool. Cultural and other entertaining programs are given during the year. An annual arts festival attracts much interest throughout the district, bringing various performances to the campus, some of them local talent. Many activities are planned for the two weeks of the festival, including competition for high school and junior college students in the literary festival.

Other activities include the Student Government Association with the Men and Women's Resident Councils; the Student Christian Association, including representatives from religious organizations; class-related clubs such as Phi Beta Lambda, business; Distributive Education Club, Cosmetology Club, Vocational Industrial Clubs of America, Art Students' League, Modern Language Association; various clubs of interest such as Circle K, Radio Club, Future Teachers, Veterans Association, Young Republicans; Shutterbugs (photography), and the Debate Club.

The college band and Colettes perform at many functions during the school year. The Colettes are Mississippi's original dancing coeds. The groups have performed at every major event in the state, in the 1965 Macy's Thanksgiving Day Parade in New York City where they were seen on NBC and CBS, at the National Cherry Blossom Festival in Washington, D.C., in Louisville, Kentucky, in Dallas, and several times in the Cotton Carnival in Memphis.

Musical groups include the college choir, the Sojourners, a pop-folk singing group, and ensemble groups. The Co-Lin Players present several performances during the year. A chapter of Delta Psi Omega, national college honorary dramatics fraternity, is on campus. A chapter of Phi Theta Kappa, national junior college honorary society, is on campus. Co-Lin is home for Mississippi's original non-commercial radio station, WWCL-FM, and the station is run entirely by students.

In addition to the yearbook, the school newspaper, *Wolf Tales*, is published every two weeks. A literary magazine, *Microcosm*, made its debut on campus during the fall session of 1973. The *Colinian*, a publication of the student personnel services office, was printed for alumni during the 1973 session for the first time. Various other publications of the college include the general catalogue and pamphlets and brochures on different programs offered by the college.

Intercollegiate sports play a major role in the life of Co-Lin students. Football, basketball, track, baseball, golf, and tennis for men and women are offered. Long recognized for its athletic teams, Co-Lin excels in all areas. Between 1929 and 1938 the football team won seven state championships. The basketball teams were most successful during the years of 1932–1935, 1947–1948 when they won the state championship, and again in 1972–1973 when they won the state championship and were nationally ranked all season. The Wolves finished third in the final National Junior College Athletic Association poll and were the last team in the nation to be defeated, racking up eighteen straight wins. The track team won the state championship in 1967 and in 1972.

After being discontinued for several years, women's basketball is now offered.

In addition to the Colettes and the radio station, other "firsts" achieved by Co-Lin include the audio-tutorial laboratory for biology students and a simulated office for secretarial science students. Heavy equipment mechanics is the only program of its type offered in the state.

Vocational-technical education is important at Copiah-Lincoln. Full time programs are available in the areas of air conditioning, heating, and refrigeration; automotive mechanics; cosmetology; data processing; distribution and marketing; drafting and design; electronics; heavy equipment mechanics; medical laboratory technician; machine shop; practical nursing; secretarial science; and vocational welding. Night programs for adults are available in these areas, in addition to other classes.

From the humble beginnings of early vocational programs, today's programs are housed in the most modern of buildings, with the latest equipment available. In the spring of 1966 a new vocational-technical

complex was completed at the cost of $448,000 and named in honor of F. M. Fortenberry, then president of the college. A vocational technical building was completed in 1963 at a cost of $110,000. Since the complex was completed in 1966, two additional vocational-technical buildings have been completed, the Youngblood Building, housing the welding and air conditioning departments, and the Wallace Building, housing heavy equipment mechanics. The Wesson Building has been renovated to house data processing and shop courses. A health occupation building costing $500,000 is on the drawing board.

Since Billy B. Thames became president in 1968, buildings completed under his leadership in the ten-year building program include Willie H. Smith Hall, a classroom-lecture building; Ellzey Hall, a men's resident hall; Lula Stevens Hall, a five-storied structure for women students; a nine hole golf course; the Harris Transportation Center, housing all college vehicles; the Youngblood building and the Wallace building; the renovation of the college library and the J. J. Wesson building; and the Maggie Flowers Ewing Fine Arts Center and the Frank Pitts Field House, both dedicated in 1973.

Other existing buildings include the administration building, named for J. M. Ewing; the Mutton building, housing student services and home economics; the recreational center; the Graydon L. Mullen Gymnasium; bookstore building; Callender Hall, serving as a college dining hall and for recreational facilities; a speech building; Lincoln and Copiah Halls, dormitories; H. L. Stone Stadium; the old field house; Walter R. Sullivan Field for baseball; Josie Ellis Hall for teachers; and apartment buildings for married students. Several houses for faculty members are located on campus, in addition to the president's home.

Memorial building, named in memory of the more than forty former students who gave their lives during World War II, houses the Evelyn Oswalt Library. The facility contains over 24,000 volumes.

The proposed building schedule includes a greenhouse, a new loop drive, a health service education building, a new track, a $2 million student union building, additional vocational-technical facilities, married student apartments, an academic building, a library, a president's residence, additional dormitories and faculty housing, an addition of nine holes to the golf course, and additional parking, landscaping, walks, and drives.

Copiah-Lincoln's outlook is bright. With a fulltime program now offered by its center in Natchez, other programs will be added there when needed.

In response to the growing demand for shortened programs of higher education and for vocational training on the junior college level, Copiah-Lincoln's enrollment is expected to increase steadily during the coming decade. An increasing number of students are expected to enroll in vocational and vocational-technical programs, primarily in the trade and industrial occupation programs. Vocational-technical programs in the health and home economics fields will bring increases in female enrollment. By 1985, the majority of students probably will be vocational-technical. Programs will be added or expanded as needed.

Divisions of the college include vocational-technical; humanities, offering courses in English, foreign language, journalism, speech, theater, and religion; social science, with course offerings in economics, education, geography, government, history, psychology, and sociology; fine arts, including music, band, and art; business, including accounting, business, business law, commerce, office machines, shorthand, typewriting; science and mathematics with biological sciences, chemistry, engineering, home economics, mathematics, physics, and physical science; and health and physical education, including courses in health, physical education, and hygiene. Industrial arts are also offered.

Other divisions of the college include the administration, the high school which still operates on campus, and adult basic education.

A fulltime director of adult education is employed, along with a counselor. Many adults over sixteen years of age who have not completed high school enroll in adult education, which is providing them an opportunity to take the General Education Development test, an equivalent of a high school diploma.

Copiah-Lincoln also is the sponsoring agent for a Senior Aides program and is the only college in the nation to have such a program. Senior citizens over fifty-five who are unemployed or underemployed may work in the program which covers ten Southwest Mississippi counties. Forty aides are employed by public service agencies.

The story of Copiah-Lincoln Junior College is one of progress. The future years will be a challenge in meeting the needs of the citizens of its district.

EAST CENTRAL
JUNIOR COLLEGE STORY

East Central Junior College opened its doors to the first freshman class on the first Monday in September 1928. Proceedings which led to the establishment of the college were initiated on March 10, 1914, in the office of Newton County Superintendent of Education, W. W. Coursey. The county school board on that date accepted the proposal of the Decatur Public School and located the Newton County Agricultural High School in the existing public school facilities. The board also appointed two trustees for the new school at the March meeting—W. C. Mabry and D. Blackburn.

The Newton County Board of Supervisors levied one mill for support of the new agricultural high school on the first Monday in September 1914. Their previous efforts at issuing bonds for construction having been defeated, the supervisors did not provide any funds for capital improvement during the first several years of the school.

First year college work was added to the Newton County Agricultural High School in the fall of 1928 with the enrollment of eighteen beginning students. The two faculty members, Mrs. Stella Weathersby Newsome and Robert Marshall, met their classes in temporary classrooms in the basement of one of the dormitories. Only Newton County was included during that first year. The first trustees serving the college were W. C. Mabry, Jim Rivers, M. J. Scarborough, R. A. Armstrong, L. Q. C. Williams, and Dr. B. F. Hunter. R. C. Pugh was head of the institution, serving as superintendent of the agricultural high school and as president of the junior college when it was organized.

During the first year's operation Neshoba County agreed to join the district. The board of supervisors named five trustees, who, with H. C. Blount, county superintendent, represented them on the college board in 1929–1930.

In 1930, Scott County closed the Scott County Agricultural High School at Harperville and transferred the board of trustees and support to the Newton County college. Three of those six trustees from the Harperville School served East Central Junior College a combined total of ninety-four years. They will be identified for additional comment later.

The Leake County Junior College, established at

GUIDED BY THESE
PRESIDENTS

Roscoe Conklin Pugh
1928–1934

Lindsey Ogletree Todd
1934–1953

W. Arno Vincent
1953–1962

Douglas M. Montgomery
1962–1966

Charles Verdo Wright
1966–

167

the Leake County Agricultural High School in Carthage in 1927, began experiencing difficulty in its fifth year of operation. Jim Thames of Decatur, who began services on the East Central Junior College board of trustees in 1931, recalls going with a delegation from the college to talk to the Leake County Board of Supervisors, headed by E. B. Russell. Ensuing negotiations resulted in the transfer of the Leake County Junior College students to East Central Junior College at the end of the fall quarter of 1931. Bryan Barnett, who came with the Leake County group as one of their six original trustees, served on the East Central board for twenty-nine additional years (according to Jim Thames in an interview, March 25, 1973, Decatur, Mississippi).

Winston County became the fifth and last supporting county to join the East Central Junior College District in 1935. A new administration, headed by the second president, L. O. Todd, had assumed the leadership of the college in 1934. One of the first accomplishments of the new administration was to complete the enlistment of Winston County in the district. Claude Richardson was the leader of the Winston County delegation instrumental in bringing the county into the district. He served an additional fourteen years as both county supervisor and college board member.

With the five-county district complete and under the dynamic leadership of a president who was to serve for nineteen years, the college began to stabilize in the mid-thirties. As the depression continued to subside, the college expanded its physical plant, increased its faculty and students, broadened its curriculum, sought and received regional accreditation, excelled in intercollegiate sports, and took its place among Mississippi's public institutions.

A unit of the famed Thirty-First (Dixie) Division of the Mississippi National Guard was located on campus. It was made up largely of college students and was commanded by Pat Wilson, dean of men and former coach at the college. The unit was activated early in World War II, taking a full company of men from the campus. Others were drafted, leaving the college largely occupied by women—faculty and students. The college continued operation on a reduced scale from 1942 to 1945. Then following the end of World War II the veterans returned in large numbers in 1946 with the GI Bill of Rights. That year East

Central Junior College experienced its greatest period of growth in students and faculty.

From its inception in 1928 through 1945 East Central Junior College had been largely a liberal arts college, offering college parallel work in the arts and sciences, the first two years of teacher education programs, and lower division work in agriculture, home economics, and business. Now for the first time a serious effort was made to offer vocational courses in the skilled trades. In the immediate postwar period the college operated fulltime, noncredit courses in five subjects.

In 1952 the Mississippi public junior colleges began receiving capital improvement funds from the state. In 1953 East Central changed presidents for the second time. W. A. Vincent, a former student of the college then serving on the staff in mathematics, coaching, and administrative capacities, replaced Dr. Todd. One building was completed, and four other major buildings were added during Vincent's administration (nine years). It was also during this period that the state changed its basic school laws. The "minimum foundation" program was passed in 1953 restructuring the secondary districts. In 1958, East Central discontinued the high school division and thus terminated the agricultural high school of some forty-four years' duration.

Douglas Montgomery became the fourth president of the college in 1962. Technical education was begun during his tenure (four years). The state renewed emphasis on vocational education. House Bill 309 and Senate Bill 1587 were passed to provide construction funds. East Central was unable to provide the matching funds required and did not enter more extensively into vocational and technical programs. Significant building programs were completed in dormitory and food service areas, however, during this period.

The Charles V. Wright tenure as president began in 1966. In his first six years six major buildings were built with the seventh on the drawing boards. The college then had seven vocational programs with another planned for opening in the 1973 session. At present three technical programs are included in the total of thirty-one curricula.

Faculty and staff have been upgraded with the aid of federal assistance programs. East Central Junior College closed the 1972 year with the highest qualified staff (by degree and experience) ever. Regional accreditation was recently reaffirmed. Physical facilities are greatly improved with additional improvements forthcoming. Data in the office of the director of admissions in 1973 show sixty percent of all high school graduates in the five-county district who go to college anywhere matriculate first at East Central. This fact attests to public acceptance and the favorable competitive position of the college in the academic community.

The dominant personality of the trustees and county officials in the history of the college is generally conceded to be W. C. Mabry. The first man appointed to the board and the first chairman of it served thirty-five consecutive years as chairman. From 1914 to 1948 he presided over sessions leading to the establishment of the college, the addition of the outlying counties, and the growth and development of the plant. Other Newton countians who figured prominently in the development of the college included the following: Jim Rivers, a member of the board of supervisors during the early years of the agricultural high school, who served twenty years on the college board; Jim Thames, Decatur postmaster, who served twenty-five years as a trustee; C. M. Norman, the third chairman of the board (1951–1964), who served twenty-one years total; and Marshall Carson (currently serving as a committee chairman) who has served consecutively for thirty-four years. The Newton County supervisor with the longest tenure in the history of the college is J. H. Ezelle with twenty years. He was very influential in securing county funds for the building program during the mid-thirties.

In Neshoba County, F. B. Deweese and W. D. Gillis were early trustees who contributed much to the development of the institution. Judge Gillis served for twenty-four years (the longest tenure from Neshoba County) on the board and provided outstanding leadership. In more recent years, Otis Cox (nineteen years and currently serving) and Melvin Tullos have served more than three terms.

Knox Huff, A. T. Cooper, and John Wallace were original members of the board of trustees from Scott County. Huff, who served a total of twenty-three years, was the second board chairman from 1948 to 1952. He was a Forest attorney who was helpful in securing favorable junior college legislation. Wallace served twenty-eight years on the college board before leaving in 1957. Cooper retired from the board in 1972

after serving for forty-three consecutive years, which stands as the record for East Central Junior College board tenure. Mack Weems, currently a member of the board, has served for twenty-seven years, sixteen as county superintendent and eleven by appointment.

Leake County officials long active in the support of the college include Crawley Alford, supervisor for twenty-one years and trustee for twelve (still active in both capacities); Lee Fisher, supervisor for twenty-eight consecutive years; R. L. Moss, supervisor for twenty years; and trustees Bryan Barnett (twenty-nine years) and L. L. Denson (twenty-six years).

In Winston County supervisors have traditionally served as trustees. In the earlier years Claude Richardson and Earl Woodard rendered valuable service—Richardson as a member of the original Winston County group and Woodard as one of two men to serve more than twenty-five years as a county supervisor and serve concurrently as a trustee. The other was T. W. Luke, Jr., the fourth chairman of the board. He resigned as trustee in 1970 but is still serving as supervisor in Winston County in his thirtieth consecutive year. Julian Cunningham, county superintendent of education, served on the board for twenty-nine years. He had the longest tenure of any county superintendent in the history of the college.

Since becoming a junior college in 1928, the institution has had five presidents. The first, R. C. Pugh, was superintendent of the agricultural high school and remained as president from 1928 to 1934. He resigned in 1934 and later became president of Northwest Mississippi Junior College. Pugh held degrees from Millsaps (B. A.) and the University of Mississippi (M. A.), and is included in the organizing presidents.

Dr. L. O. Todd came to East Central in 1934 from Philadelphia High School where he had served for the preceding seven years as superintendent. He held a bachelor's degree from George Peabody College, a master's degree from Columbia University, and a doctorate from Peabody. Todd remained as president for nineteen years. In 1953 he became chief administrator of the Meridian Municipal School System, where he remained until his retirement in 1971. During his tenure as president at East Central, eight major buildings were added to the campus. The college and agricultural high school made significant growth and the institution gained full accreditation.

W. Arno Vincent became the third president in

1953. He is the only alumnus of the institution to have served as president. He had earned letters in football and basketball as a student at the junior college. He held a bachelor's degree from the University of Southern Mississippi, a master's degree in mathematics from the University of Mississippi, and had served as a naval officer in World War II. During the seven years before his appointment he had served on the staff in a number of capacities, including mathematics teacher, basketball coach, registrar, and director of activities. Vincent, at the time of his appointment, was the youngest man to serve as president of the college. After leaving in 1962, he served with the Mississippi Education Association and the Meridian School System before his retirement from education in 1971.

The fourth president of East Central Junior College was Douglas M. Mongtomery. He held the bachelor's degree from the University of Pennsylvania, a law degree from Harvard University, and a master's degree and the doctorate from Florida State University. Montgomery was a native of California and the only non-Mississippian to be president of the college. He was a retired military officer when he embarked on a junior college career. After leaving East Central in 1966, he held junior college presidencies in Virginia before retirement.

The fifth and current president, Charles V. Wright, Sr., came to East Central from Jones County Junior College at Ellisville, Mississippi. He had been employed there in a number of positions, the latest of which was administrative assistant to the president. Wright holds the bachelor's, master's, and doctorate degrees from the University of Southern Mississippi.

Four faculty members served for over thirty years each at East Central. Dr. Stella Weathersby Newsome, one of the two original members of the faculty in 1928, taught English and literature until 1958. Janie Huff Sullivan taught education and psychology. She began teaching in the agricultural high school in 1925 and retired from the college in 1956. Mamie Ethel Burton served as the college librarian for thirty-two years. Frank McKenzie Cross taught chemistry for thirty-seven years and is the only professor to have taught under the administrations of all five presidents in the history of the institution. Other members of the faculty having taught for more than twenty years and retiring prior to 1972 include Una Harris, English; F. E. Leatherwood, biological sciences; J. W. Bedwell,

business; and O. B. Mayo, automotive mechanics.

Two staff members in the service area remained at the college for more than twenty-five years rendering valuable service. Mrs. J. L. Jackson was dean of women for twenty-seven years, and Mr. J. A. Miller supervised the maintenance department for twenty-seven years remaining parttime for an additional four years.

SOUTHWEST MISSISSIPPI JUNIOR COLLEGE STORY

Summit, Mississippi, is a southern town where stores and repair shops almost encroach upon the sidewalks and where occasionally one hears the whistle of a locomotive, a reminder of the day when the railroad was king of transportation. East of Summit in idyllic surroundings is Southwest Mississippi Junior College.

The history of Southwest Mississippi Junior College begins with the Pike County Agricultural High School, built on the site of Godbold's Mineral Wells. Godbold's Wells was known throughout Southern Mississippi and neighboring states as a health resort. The water found here was said to have contained minerals which promoted longevity and healthfulness. Godbold's Wells, Summit's famous watering place, was chartered in 1873 as Summit Mineral Wells Company. Ted Blackmore was the organizer and promoter of these mineral waters of rare qualities.

In 1882, a two-storied structure, the Godbold's Wells Hotel, was constructed. In 1910 the first spike was driven in the railroad track for the Summit and McComb Motor Line. The line provided rail service from McComb to Summit to Godbold's Wells. The "dooley car" or "trolley line" was two open-air railroad coaches drawn by a steam engine.

In 1908 the Mississippi legislature enacted legislation permitting counties to establish agricultural high schools. On April 7, 1916, the Pike County School Board voted to establish an agricultural high school in Pike County.

On September 4, 1916, three bids were submitted to the Pike County School Board for the location of the Pike County Agricultural High School: Godbold's Wells, Jones School Community, and the Carter's Creek Community.

The promoters of the Godbold's Wells proposition offered the property of the company for $10,000 and offered to take this amount in 5% county bonds. This proposition offered 92 acres of land. The town of Summit, as a further inducement, offered $1500 cash donation and 80 acres of land lying to the west of Godbold's Wells property and opening out a way to the Good Roads.

The Jones Community offered a cash bonus of $1500 to be applied for purchasing a tract of land in the community. An option was given the Board to select one of four tracts presented.

The Carter's Creek people did not have their bid in writing.

After consideration of the presented bids and their merits, the school board decided in favor of the Godbold's Wells proposition.

On August 16, 1917, the school board presented the following resolution to the county board of supervisors:

Resolved: That the county School Board of Pike County by virtue of authority conferred by Chapter 122 of the laws of Mississippi, 1910, and amendments thereto, it is hereby determined that Pike County does hereby come under and accept the said laws of Mississippi authorizing the establishment of an Agricultural School and this Board acting in that behalf hereby establishes an Agricultural High School for the white youths of Pike County, the exact location is fixed about one and one-half miles east of the town of Summit at the Godbold's Wells.

By order of the board of supervisors of Pike County the Pike County Agricultural High School was established and located in accordance with the above resolution. The Pike County Agricultural High School began operation in September 1918. On September 3, 1918, J. M. Kenna, Superintendent, six faculty, and approximately forty pupils began an institution that would develop into Southwest Junior College.

In 1922, the Mississippi state legislature authorized the extension of course offerings in county agricultural high schools to include courses of college level, primarily to teach professional courses to future teachers. In 1928 the legislature enacted a law that provided for the creation of the Mississippi Junior College Commission. The 1928 law authorized the Junior College Commission to organize the state into junior college zones. One of the possible zones organized was for a junior college consisting of Pike, Walthall, Amite, and Wilkinson Counties. As the junior college idea began to develop in Southwest Mississippi, other counties—Marion, Franklin, and

Lawrence—were proposed for inclusion in the new junior college district.

Interest in establishing a junior college in Pike County was evidenced by meetings held throughout Southwest Mississippi in 1927 and 1928. According to an article in *The McComb Enterprise* dated September 30, 1927, a mass meeting of the parents was held on September 19, 1927.

A mass meeting of the parents and pupils of Pike County was held Monday night, September 19, at the Pike County Agricultural High School. Mr. J. M. Kenna opened the meeting with an address of welcome. The question of whether or not the Pike County Agricultural High School should dispense with the ninth and tenth grades and two years of junior college work be added, was presented to the meeting for discussion. Mr. Kenna also explained the requirements for a junior college which were: (1) All schools in Pike County must have an eight month session. (2) All teachers in the junior college must have a M. A. degree, or be working toward one. (3) The laboratories and libraries must come up to a certain standard. (4) A minimum attendance in each college class.

The following were called upon and gave very interesting talks in favor of the junior college.

Miss Nannie Gills, county Superintendent of Education, said that the incoming administration has promised to establish an eight-month term for all schools in Mississippi. This will bring up one requirement of establishing a junior college in this county, and the consolidated schools can provide for high school through the tenth grade. "Now is the time to begin thinking of a junior college in Pike county," said Miss Gillis.

Mr. W. M. Davis, member of the Board of Trustees, said, "Let's go after it now!", a remark which proves that he is very much in favor of the Junior College in Pike County.

Mr. Stubblefield, from Magnolia, gave a very interesting talk boosting the Junior College movement.

Mr. Ray McCullough, president of the Chamber of Commerce in McComb, offered his services in any movement looking to the advancement of the Agricultural High School to a Junior College.

Dr. J. W. Mayfield, pastor of the First Baptist Church of McComb, says that better work could be done here than in larger schools, that better results could be shown, and more direct information could be given, because of smaller attendance.

Mr. Cecil Cook, principal of the city school in Summit and later President of Mississippi Southern College, favors a junior college with an industrial feature. He says that the average person's idea of attending college is to learn how to make a living without working, which is a wrong idea of an education.

Mr. H. L. Whitworth, the enterprising and progressive mayor of Summit, believes we have the material and plant, and that there is no reason for not having a junior college.

Mr. R. Z. Felder, who is a charter member of the board of

GUIDED BY THESE
PRESIDENTS

James Murray Kenna, 1929–1947

Horace Dever Pickens, 1947–1948

Clyde Herman Snell, 1948–1951

Charles Clifton Moore, 1951–1952   Hubert Ted Huddleston, 1952–1972

Horace Carruth Holmes, 1972–

173

trustees, said a few words heartily boosting the idea of a junior college in Pike County.

Also reported in the September 30, 1927, edition of *The McComb Enterprise* was the following account. Pike County Agricultural High School graduated a class of thirty-eight including the summer term, and a poll was made of this class to find out how many of them would come back if they had the opportunity of doing college work, and thirty-two of them answered in the affirmative.

Further evidence is shown by an article dated October 7, 1927, in *The McComb Enterprise* by J. M. Kenna in which he discussed the standards that had to be met to establish a junior college. Also, he discussed the plan for going into college work:

For the first year discontinue the ninth grade of high school and add on the freshman year of college work, and for the second year discontinue the tenth grade and add on the sophomore college work, thereafter having eleventh and twelfth grades of high school work and freshman and sophomore college work.

Pike County is located favorably for the development of a strong junior college. The county is practically in the center of a tier of counties running from the Mississippi River on the west, to and including Marion county on the east. The county has admirable connections in every direction by means of improved roads, and is located on the trunk line of the I.C.R.R. At present there are no junior colleges nearer than Raymond on the north, and Poplarville, Perkinston and Ellisville, on the east of us. But it is pretty certain that one is going to be established in this territory south of Jackson, and it is therefore advisable that the people of this section get busy and keep some other section from preempting the field.

In line with this idea, the Board of Trustees at a recent meeting decided college work would be undertaken here promptly when the condition as to an eight months terms for all schools of the county has been met. It is possible that this condition may be met by next session.

As reported in the February 17, 1928, edition of *The Enterprise*, J. M. Kenna, superintendent of the Pike A.H.S., addressed the Exchange Club concerning the problem of converting the Pike County Agricultural High School into a junior college.

"The consolidated high schools in this county for the most part have high school departments," stated Mr. Kenna. "This has reduced the need of the agricultural high school in this field," he continued, "but a new need has arisen."

"It has been found," said the speaker, "that it is more economical for the state and the parents to send their children to a junior college close to home than to send them to a large institution afar off. Then too, there is the safety of close proximity to the home."

The speaker pointed out that the county had an investment of $175,000 in the Agricultural High School, and that this investment could be used to great advantage by assuming two years of college work. He told of the many freshmen that are weeded out of the large institutions, and said, "The weeding process is far less expensive to the state, and the parent when it is done in a junior college."

The speaker stressed the idea that he would not favor a junior college except as a junior agricultural college. He said that this was the primary idea behind the agricultural high school system, and that it should not be abandoned even in the junior colleges. He asked the hearers to consider the proposition, predicting that the problem would have to be answered some time in the future. He made no recommendation; merely put the cards on the table and requested the club members to form their own opinions. He said that the Agricultural High School was county property, the property of the taxpayers, and that the taxpayers themselves would have to answer the question as to whether the Agricultural High School would eventually be abandoned as an institution or be converted into an institution of larger service.

In an editorial dated February 17, 1928, the following statements were made:

The consolidation of our rural schools and the establishment of high school departments has impaired greatly the usefulness of the agricultural high school. But fate has not been as cruel to the agricultural high school as first thought might suggest. While being relieved of its primary field of usefulness a new need has arisen. As the development of the consolidation has encroached upon the field of the agricultural high school a new field of activity has manifested itself.

The Superintendent of the Pike County Agriculural High School has stated that it is more economical to send a student to the local institution than to the state institution. He has pointed out that the parent can save about $150 per year, which is not a small sum to the father and mother who are trying to educate their children. He has suggested that the economy of the agricultural high school training has made it advisable for some counties to convert their institutions into junior colleges and thus afford two years of college work. He has also stated that the junior college affords two years of college work close to the home of the student, and that it affords a safe moral atmosphere for younger boys and girls.

On the other hand, it must not be overlooked that the state institutions, with their extensive buildings, their modern equipment, their mass production, may afford greater education intensity. The bigger plan may be more effective, more to be desired.

With an investment of $175,000 in the Pike County Agricultural High School; with its sphere of usefulness intruded upon so to speak, by the increasing effectiveness of the consolidated school system; with the new possibility of economical training in a local junior college for the territory lying between Jackson and Hammond; with the suggestion of the superintendent of the institution that something must be done in the future; with these facts facing the people of Pike County, it is essential that thorough thought be given to the matter.

Shall we convert the Pike County Agricultural High School into a junior college?

This question was answered by a resolution adopted by the trustees of Pike County Agricultural High School in July 1929:

Resolved by the Board of Trustees of Pike County Agricultural High School, that it is the intention of this Board to institute freshman college work at Pike County Agricultural High School beginning with the session of 1929–1930, and the principal is hereby directed to begin laying plans to that end.

Transforming this small high school into a junior college required the devotion and services of a man who had vision and ability to make that vision a reality. Such a man was Mr. James Murray Kenna, founder and first president of Southwest Mississippi Junior College.

The purpose of Southwest Mississippi Junior College as found in the first catalog:

It shall be the purpose of the Southwest Mississippi Junior College to give ultimately two years of college work at the lowest possible cost to the student. It shall be the purpose of the management to make of it the poor boy or girl's school.

And it shall also be the purpose of the school to give opportunity to its students to get vocational training along several lines that will enable them to make a living after they have completed the course. It is time that many of our colleges were turning their attention more to vocational training for the professions are filled now to overflowing.

It shall be the purpose of the management of the Southwest Mississippi Junior College to conduct the dormitory and other matters that affect the cost to the student after the same plan as the Agricultural High School—that is, at cost to the student. By this means it will be possible to give the student a year's college training at no greater living expense than living at home.

To begin the junior college program in September the board of trustees, by resolution, requested that the board of supervisors provide an additional $5,000 for the agricultural high school. On August 8, 1929, the board of supervisors of Pike County adopted the following resolution:

IN THE MATTER OF FURNISHING EQUIPMENT TO THE PIKE COUNTY AGRICULTURAL HIGH SCHOOL FOR THE PURPOSE OF ESTABLISHING A JUNIOR COLLEGE THEREIN.

Whereas, the Board of Supervisors of Pike County, Mississippi, is advised by the Board of Trustees of the Pike County Agricultural High School, which is more than 20 miles distant from any of the State Colleges, did, by resolution adopted on the 3rd day of July, 1929, extend the curriculum in said Pike County Agricultural High School, so as to include therein the studies of the Freshman Year, of college work, a copy of which resolution has been received by the Board, and

Whereas, the Board of Trustees of the said Pike County Agricultural High School, has made request of this Board, for an appropriation of $5,000. in order to meet the requirements of Section 309, Chapter 283, Laws of Mississippi, 1924, in the way of equipment to establish and carry on the Junior College work contemplated for the session 1929 and 1930, at the said Agricultural High School: Therefore,

On motion duly seconded, it is ordered by the Board of Supervisors of Pike County, Mississippi, that in making the Budget of expense and expenditures of said county, as required by law, for the purpose hereinabove named, and that if necessary, it will make a special levy upon the taxable property of said County, to raise said amount.

It is further ordered that the resolution of the Board of Trustees of the Pike County Agricultural High School, providing for said College, thereby establishing said junior college, be placed upon the Minutes and records of this Board.

The faculty and administration for the first year of the junior college were: J. M. Kenna, Superintendent, J. I. Hurst, agriculture and physical education, Miss Minnie Fleming, commercial work, Miss Christine Sadler, English and history, Mrs. Edna Watkins Hewitt, Spanish, Miss Corinne Bevil, mathematics and English, and Mrs. Annie M. Felder, science. There were fifty-six students in the first freshman class. Nine college level courses were offered the first year of the college. Presently the college offers 118 college level courses, 25 technical courses and 15 terminal vocational courses.

By 1929 all the original Godbold's Wells buildings were gone. In 1921 a three-story administration-classroom building was constructed. Kenna Hall, named for J. M. Kenna, the only superintendent of the Pike County Agricultural High School and the first President of Southwest Mississippi Junior College, has served as the administration building, classrooms, dormitories, band hall and auditorium. The building was completely renovated in 1952.

In 1924 the people of the county voted a bond issue of $60,000 with which work on a boys' dormitory and an annex to the school building (Kenna Hall) for an auditorium began. In October of 1924 fire destroyed the old Godbold's Wells Hotel, which had served as a classroom-dormitory building. Using the $25,000 in insurance and an additional $25,000 bond issue, a new girls' dormitory and cafeteria were constructed. These housing facilities were to serve the college for almost half a century. A major addition to the men's dormitory was made in 1937 with funds from a Public Works Administration Grant (MISS. 1175-D). Both dormitories were renovated in 1956 with funds provided by the state of Mississippi.

In 1930, with the use of campus labor and local funds, a gymnasium was added to the physical plant of the college. The facility was renovated in 1948 and served the district for high school basketball tournaments as well as college activities until 1963. Even in retirement the building continues to serve as an intramural athletic facility. It was named in memory of R. Z. Felder—a member of the board of trustees when the junior college was founded.

To provide separate library facilities for the college, a small library was constructed in 1933. The library holdings in 1939 consisted of 3063 volumes, 169 bound magazines, sixty publications, six daily newspapers, two weekly newspapers and eight school papers. The seating capacity was sixty-six.

The library was named for pioneer trustee R. L. "Uncle Bob" Simmons. In 1961 a larger library facility was constructed. This modern air conditioned building houses the library facilities as well as a reading laboratory and two classrooms. The collection has grown to more than 20,000 volumes, 120 periodicals bound or on microfilm; tapes, filmstrips, and records. The library has special collections: the Mary Cain Collection, the Aston Collection, the Lonnie Frazier Collection, and the Madge Reeves Collection.

With the organization of the junior college in 1929, efforts were begun to enlarge the support district to include Walthall and Amite counties. In the summer of 1929 a campaign was mounted by Mr. Kenna and Superintendent of Education W. F. Bond in the high schools of Walthall and Amite counties. Continued efforts were made during the 1930s, but it was not until 1940 that Amite County voted to become a tax-supporting member of the district; Walthall County entered with tax support in 1964.

The lack of tax support from other counties led to a major problem with the state junior college commission in 1931. The junior college commission withheld state funds for Southwest. The issue was resolved by the state department of education. Funds were provided Southwest for the year in question.

In 1933, the second year of college work was added; the first edition of the college annual, *The Whispering Pines*, was published and appropriately dedicated to James Murray Kenna. The dedication page reads as follows:

An earnest scholar, an able educator, and a Christian gentleman; who because of his ceaseless efforts for a decade and a half has realized his dream of a standard junior college; who by his devotion to the college and his interest in the welfare of the student body, has won the heart of every student, thus the first volume of the "Whispering Pines" is gratefully dedicated.

The 1930s were testing years for the college. The Great Depression made higher education an "impossible dream" for most Americans. At Southwest as at other colleges, reduction in enrollment, scarcity of funds, and much frustration challenged the determination of the supporters of higher education for Southwest Mississippi. Through the tireless efforts of the board of trustees and the administration, tuition, room and board were reduced to the lowest possible rates consistent with the successful operation of the college.

The college farm under the able direction of "Dean John I. Hurst" provided many of the cafeteria food items that enabled the college to hold the cost of room and board. The board minute books contain reports of the "summer canning program." Hundreds of gallons of food grown on the college farm were preserved to be used during the next school year.

In 1934 the first junior college band was organized at Southwest under the direction of Mr. Paul Hewitt.

After several false starts, the college was able to secure federal assistance in the construction of two buildings in 1937. A science building and a demonstration home for home economics were constructed in 1937 with funds from the Works Progress Administration. The federal government provided $38,809 and Pike County provided $31,000 for these buildings. The science building was renovated in 1966 with an administrative annex added. The building was named for Mr. J. S. Brumfield, who served for twenty years as a member and secretary of the college board of trustees. The demonstration building was named for Miss Nannie Gills who served as trustee and secretary of the board from 1918 until 1938. In recent years the building has been used as a second girls' dormitory.

Other federally supported projects for the college during the 1930s were (1) a Civil Works Administration project of $1800 for the repair of the administration building and the boys' dormitory. (2) A Works Progress Administration project of $5400 for the construction of a new football field. On November 3, 1939, the first junior college football game was played on the Southwest campus—Southwest vs East Central. This field was named for D. S. Reeves, outstanding AHS athlete and junior college trustee, and was replaced in 1949 by the John I. Hurst Field. A new vocational-technical building is now located on the site of the Reeves Memorial Field. (3) A WPA project of $14,000 for the landscaping of the campus. The planting of several hundred native trees and shrubs, the construction of a rock garden, and the erection of stone columns at the entrance of the campus have made a showplace in South Mississippi.

Paved roads to the campus and paved streets for the campus were provided by the Pike County Supervisors during the 1930s with local and federal funds.

In May 1938, the National Youth Administration established a vocational training unit at Southwest for boys of school age who were not in school. These boys learned to do such things as carpentry, brick and concrete work, painting, plumbing, farm projects, and repairs to existing buildings.

In 1939 the first state championship in a major sport was won by the girls' basketball team. Compiling a 26–2 record for the season, Coach J. I. Hurst's team was the first of several state championships for the college.

The *Whispering Pines*, the student newspaper, began publication in 1935.

The 1940s were years of change for the world as well as for Southwest Mississippi Junior College. They opened with the nation trying to pull itself from the depths of the depression and with the experiments of the New Deal. World War II plunged the nation into a frenzy of activity. The coming of the war for the nation and Southwest at midterm necessitated some radical changes to meet the uncertainties with which young Americans were faced. Shortened terms, uncertain enrollments, and the demands of a full war effort caused the college to reorder its activities. College publications such as the *Pine Burr* and the *Whispering Pines*, as well as intercollegiate athletics, were discontinued. The college catalogs of the war period were often issued as supplements to previous catalogs. Aviation courses were added to the college curriculum.

With the coming of peace in 1945 and the return to what might be called normal times, the college was to experience a rapid growth in enrollment. The G. I. Bill brought hundreds of former servicemen and sometimes their wives to the Southwest campus. To meet the need for married student housing the college took advantage of surplus army buildings and a special State Building Commission grant to construct a "Veterans Apartment Building." A ten-unit trailer park was also established to provide additional housing. The apartment building constructed in 1947 now houses faculty and married students.

Following the war vocational education at Southwest was primarily for evening students—veterans—and day courses of welding and automotive mechanics taught as a supplement for industrial arts majors. In 1955 the vocational building burned. The building was rebuilt for approximately $30,000. The college was able to rebuild the facility, utilizing the insurance coverage to purchase materials and employing students, especially from the evening veteran classes. In 1967 the vocational classes were moved to the modern H. T. Huddleston Vocational Technical Complex. The old vocational building presently serves as the college maintenance facility.

In 1947 President Kenna announced his resignation effective July 1, 1947. He was succeeded by Dr. Horace D. Pickens, former head of the Department of Education at Mississippi Southern College. During his administration the college band was reactivated and a veterans' training program in Morse telegraph operators and stationmasters was begun.

In July 1948, Mr. Clyde H. Snell, former superintendent of Hinds County Schools, was elected president. During his administration the college enjoyed a continued increase in enrollment and constructed a modern 5,000 seat football stadium, under the supervision of Coach H. L. "Hook" Stone. It was later named for longtime dean, agriculturist and coach, John I. Hurst. John I. Hurst started football at the agricultural high school and coached the only Pike Agricultural High School State-Championship football team. He later coached the Southwest Junior College girls' basketball team to the state championship in 1939. The R. Z. Felder gymnasium was renovated also during the administration of Mr. C. H. Snell.

Charles C. Moore was named president on July 1, 1951. Former McComb High School athletic director, he was MHS football coach for ten years and athletic director at Sunflower Junior College at Moorhead during the 1950–1951 school year.

On July 1, 1952, Mr. Hubert Ted Huddleston became the fifth president of Southwest Mississippi Junior College. Mr. Huddleston came from the campus of Copiah-Lincoln Junior College, having served as dean of men and administrative assistant and chemistry teacher.

The Huddleston era was to span twenty years and was an era of dramatic change for the college. From the beginning of his administration, Mr. Huddleston made regional accreditation for the college his major concern. Concluding an evaluation of the college by state educators in 1955, his efforts were increased as the prospect of accreditation seemed within his grasp. The years of work culminated on December 4, 1958, at Louisville, Kentucky, when the Southern Association of Colleges and Schools granted full accreditation to the college.

Having won the state championship in girls' basketball in 1939 and tennis doubles in 1941 and 1942, the Southwest Bears found again the winning combination, when in 1955 the girls' basketball team won state championship. In 1956 Southwest won the state championship in baseball; in 1958 the Bears were undefeated state football champions, and in 1959 and 1963 the boys' basketball teams won state championships. Southwest also won state championships in tennis singles and doubles during the Huddleston era.

In 1964, Walthall County became a tax-supporting county to Southwest Junior College. The college instituted free bus transportation from Tylertown to the college. A systematic recruiting program featuring summer visitation resulted in record enrollments. From 186 in the fall of 1952, the enrollment increased to 862 in the fall of 1971.

In 1967 in the self-study the philosophy and aims of Southwest Mississippi Junior College were outlined as follows:

Believing that the basic purpose of education is to prepare one for the highest degree of self-realization, the faculty and staff are primarily concerned with the development of mental powers and the building of strong character. As an institution, Southwest Mississippi Junior College is dedicated to the idea that these purposes can be achieved through the discipline of sound learning, rooted in Christian principles. Integrity, good scholarship, democratic ideals, and rewarding interpersonal relationships are taught and exemplified by the faculty and staff. This philosophy embraces the convictions that the institution should encourage all students to think independently, to reason critically, to enhance their understanding of themselves and the world around them, to find meaningfulness and purpose in life, to deal with their fellowman fairly, and to relate to God as the Supreme Source of all true knowledge.

Students at this institution are encouraged to assume a high degree of responsibility and to gain that understanding and insight which are necessary for an intelligent and worthwhile approach to complex problems of today's society.

With the passage of Senate Bill 305 by the 1950 Mississippi legislature, the state of Mississippi finally began to provide state assistance to build facilities for the Mississippi junior colleges. The appropriation of $50,000 for each junior college in 1950 began a period of state support for capital improvements that would provide the Mississippi junior colleges with almost $30 million dollars by 1972.

The initial appropriation of $50,000 for each junior college would hardly pay for the construction of a single building. Over the years the junior colleges would husband their biennial appropriation for building, combine the appropriations, and seek to find supplemental sources to pay for the needed construction. On the Southwest campus the initial appropriation was used to fund much needed building repairs that had of necessity been delayed, due to lack of funds.

In 1952 a state appropriation of $100,000 was used to renovate Kenna Hall. In 1961 the state appropriation of $100,000 was used to help construct the new Simmons Library; in 1963, the $100,000 appropriation was used to help construct the Horace C. Holmes Gymnasium. In 1967 the H. T. Huddleston Vocational Technical facility was constructed with local, state, and federal funds. The one-million-dollar facility provides for an ever-expanding vocational-technical education program. In 1969 the W. S. Bryan Mathematics-Science Building was constructed. The modern classroom facility was named in honor of the college's longtime chemistry instructor—W. S. Bryan, Jr.

In 1971 the Student Union-Cafeteria was constructed. In keeping with the longrange plan for the college adopted by the board of trustees in 1970 new residential and student facilities were to be constructed around the college lake. The Student Union-Cafeteria overlooks the lake and is near the new dormitories. Planning was begun on the new dormitories by 1971, and President Huddleston could look towards retirement in June 1972, confident that he had given twenty years of service with devotion and courage.

On July 1, 1972, Horace C. Holmes, former dean of men, dean of instruction, basketball coach, psychology instructor and vice president, assumed the presidency of Southwest Mississippi Junior College. In keeping with the spirit of growth that had characterized the Huddleston period, President Holmes began at once to seek funding for the college building program. In the summer of 1972 he secured an additional mill of tax support from Pike, Walthall and Amite counties for buildings. With the assistance of legislative leaders and the supervisors he secured additional funding under House Bill 1402. These funds, combined with state building funds, provided the necessary funds for the construction of a men's dormitory, a women's dormitory, a fine arts auditorium building, and a new Simmons Library.

Expanded curricular offerings were also instituted; cosmetology and an Associate Degree nursing program were soon to be added to the curriculum of Southwest.

An example of the influence of Southwest Mississippi Junior College on the life of its alumni was demonstrated when, in 1971, Dr. Lula Bess Brown Ford bequeathed her estate to Southwest. This endowment will provide in excess of one-half million dollars to the college. Dr. Ford and her husband, Dr. W. C. Ford, were early graduates of the institution.

The efforts of an active alumni association have provided the college with assistance in securing local and state appropriations in support of the institution.

Each year an alumnus of the year is selected by the association. Outstanding athletes are also inducted into the college sports hall of fame.

A Southwest Junior College Development Foundation has been established to secure gifts and support of the college.

The purpose of the junior college, as stated when J. M. Kenna worked for the establishment of this institution in 1928—"The purpose of this college is to . . . give boys and girls who may be unable to go to college a chance at a college education; and to bring the benefits of higher education nearer the people"— remains the intent. The current community college ideal that permeates higher education in America today is the fruition of the dreams of the founders of Mississippi's public junior colleges. The trustees, administration and faculty of Southwest Mississippi Junior College have sought to create and nurture an atmosphere that will encourage serious study and investigation as the student acquires new skills and effective powers of reasoning and understanding.

The local board with its intimate knowledge of its constituents has provided Southwest Mississippi Junior College a firm foundation. The dedicated men and women who have served the institution have given time from their businesses and professions to provide needed direction to the college.

The success of this junior college is demonstrated by the success of its students. A roll call of alumni is not possible. However, it can be shown that Southwest Mississippi Junior College has produced thousands of successful alumni from doctors, lawyers, scientists, teachers, technicians, ministers, mechanics, welders, editors, and humorists, across the whole spectrum, to just plain happy, satisfied people who have passed a short time under the Whispering Pines.

MERIDIAN
JUNIOR COLLEGE STORY

Meridian Junior College is unique among Mississippi's public junior colleges as the only municipally governed college in the state. And while MJC's governance is unique, the legal basis for the existence of the college is found in the landmark legislation of 1928, which provided for the establishment of junior colleges in Mississippi. In addition to authorizing agricultural high schools to organize junior colleges, the law also provided that "The Trustees of a separate school district containing a population of not less than ten thousand . . . may extend the curriculum in the school or schools under their charge so as to include the studies of the Freshman or Sophomore year or both. . . ." The inclusion of this authorization and the founding of Meridian Junior College were bound together through the professional activities of Horace Macaulay Ivy.

Dr. H. M. Ivy, Superintendent of Schools in Meridian from 1923 to 1952, had previously served as high school inspector in the state department of education. Given opportunity to offer suggestions about the proposed legislation, Dr. Ivy recommended inclusion of the paragraph allowing separate school districts to extend high school offerings. In 1934, he recommended to the board of trustees of the Meridian Municipal Separate School District that the district provide a junior college as the culminating unit of the Meridian Public Schools. In 1937 following the completion of construction of a new campus, the 6-4-4 plan of school organization was initiated in Meridian.

Thus, Meridian Municipal Junior College opened the "13th grade" in 1937 with an enrollment of 132 persons. This plan of organization continued until 1964.

The 27-year period from 1937 through 1964 can be viewed as the first stage in the development of Meridian Junior College. Throughout this time emphasis was given to achieving a closely unified four-year program. The budget was an integral part of that of the Meridian Public Schools. Board decisions and policies were based on common standards. Faculty, for the most part, taught at both the high school and the junior college levels and were under the same personnel policies, including salary, as the faculty in other schools. Curricula were planned on a sequential basis from grade eleven through grade fourteen. With the establishment of an organized guidance program, counselors advised the same students throughout their school career.

This same 27-year period of development also reflected an ever-widening area of service to the total community. Initial offerings were largely for college transfer with the possible exception of a terminal secretarial curriculum. Insufficient funds precluded broader vocational offerings. However, it is significant that as early as 1935, while still involved in the original planning, both the board and representatives of the Chamber of Commerce conferred on the possibility of securing federal funds for a vocational building. A limited vocational program was initiated in 1938 with the employment of a coordinator of trade and industrial education who worked in coordination with the National Youth Administration. The Ross Collins Vocational Building, paid for by National Youth Administration funds, opened in the fall of 1942 and made possible a broader vocational program to both youth and adults of the community.

During the war years, this facility was a major training area for war production workers. More than 15,000 were trained for employment in the shipbuilding industry and in aircraft repair installations. After the war years this facility, under the G. I. Bills, served as the center for vocational training to more than 6,000 veterans of World War II and the Korean War. Courses included such areas as welding, machine shop, sheet metal work, diesel mechanics, automotive mechanics, cabinet making, electricity, air conditioning, and radio and television.

From 1945 these same trades were offered to junior college students as a terminal curriculum. An average of 258 students a year were enrolled in these curricula. While figures are not available, most of these students were probably at high school level. The same is true of the diversified occupations curriculum offered from 1940 through the early 1950s. A total of 393 students participated in this program, working at a variety of occupations for a part of the school day and attending classes for the remainder of the day. In addition various short-term courses were offered at the request of individuals, labor, and management. Another service growing out of the G. I. Bill was the beginning in 1950

GUIDED BY THESE
PRESIDENTS

Horace Macaulay Ivy, 1937–1952

Lindsey Ogletree Todd, 1952–1968

William Franklin Scaggs, 1968–

of an extensive evening academic program for the benefit of veterans who could not attend class during the day.

Meridian Junior College experienced steady but stable growth during this period. The enrollment of 849 students, both day and evening, in a broad variety of credit and noncredit courses, during the 1963–64 session—in the last year it was a four-year unit—was ample proof that Meridian Junior College was developing into a community college constantly changing to meet the needs of the community.

In 1953, Dr. L. O. Todd, who had ably served nineteen years as president of East Central Junior College, became superintendent of schools in Meridian and served until his retirement in 1971. Under Dr. Todd's leadership, the board of trustees approved a plan for reorganization of the Meridian schools. A major part of the plan was the provision of a "new" two-year college. In 1964–1965, freed from the limitations of being an integral part of a four-year unit by the board decision to change to the 6-3-3-2 organizational plan, Meridian Junior College was enabled to begin a new phase of community service as a separate unit. Until new facilities were completed on the new Highway 19 site, the student body was housed in the former Stevenson Elementary School.

Because of the rapid growth in enrollment, space has continued to be a problem. A second facility to house the division of business and specialized two-year programs was added in 1968. Construction of a student union building and a major addition to the H. M. Ivy Building were completed in 1972, and a vocational-technical complex was completed in 1974.

In 1956 the board of trustees of the Meridian Separate School District established as an upward extension of the local Negro high school the T. J. Harris Junior College. While the legal districts of Meridian Junior College and Harris Junior College were coterminous with the Meridian Municipal Separate School District, the Harris Junior College served students from across the state of Mississippi. In 1969 the Board of Trustees received a federal court order which called upon the board to "close Harris Junior College" noting that "students may attend Meridian Junior College." That fall Harris Junior College had an enrollment of 412 students, of whom 119 were residents of Lauderdale County. Today, Meridian Junior College serves about twice as many fulltime black students from Lauderdale County as were

served by both Meridian Junior College and Harris Junior College in the fall of 1969.

During its thirteen years of operation, particularly in those years prior to 1965, Harris Junior College provided opportunities for hundreds of young people who had been traditionally denied access under the "separate but equal" pattern of institutional operation in Mississippi.

Since 1965 a number of policy changes have enabled Meridian Junior College to work more effectively as a community college. Major changes include: a separate tax levy for junior college purposes, the establishment of an operating budget separate from that of the school system, the change in title and responsibilities of the chief administrator of the junior college to give him a greater degree of authority, personnel policies distinct from those of the school system with policy development and administration of policy the responsibility of the junior college. One of the most important changes was that which in effect broadened the district to include Lauderdale County when in 1967 the Lauderdale County Board of Supervisors made a tax levy for the operation of Meridian Junior College. Another very significant change occurred in 1971 as the board of trustees decided to make the president of MJC directly accountable to the board.

These changes have been accompanied by steadily growing enrollments. In 1964–1965, the total enrollment, both day and evening, credit and noncredit, numbered approximately 900 students. In 1973–1974, including continuing education activities, the college served more than 5,000 students.

The success of Meridian Junior College as a community college is directly related to the vision and wisdom of Horace Macaulay Ivy and Lindsay Ogletree Todd. Dr. Ivy conceived the idea of a public junior college in Meridian and provided the educational leadership which led to the establishment and initial development of MJC. Dr. Todd took the lead in moving the college into a period of growth and change from a municipal junior college to a community college. Yet such farsighted leadership requires community support. The many citizens who have served and now serve as trustees, the hundreds of citizens who have taken advantage of educational opportunities provided by MJC, the community leadership—both elected officials and private citizens—and the people of Meridian and Lauderdale County have repeatedly demonstrated their belief in community-based higher education. The development and growth of Meridian Junior College is an eloquent expression of this belief.

ITAWAMBA
JUNIOR COLLEGE STORY

The Itawamba Junior College was organized as an extension of the Itawamba Agricultural High School. Located in Fulton, Itawamba County, Mississippi, the high school was established in 1920 and opened its doors for operation on September 19, 1921. It was the first four-year high school in Itawamba County and was one of the three agricultural high schools established in Northeast Mississippi; the other two were located at Buena Vista in Chickasaw County and Kossuth in Alcorn County.

Itawamba Agricultural High School's first facilities consisted of an administration building, which contained classrooms on the ground floor and boys' dormitory accommodations on the top floor; and a girls' dormitory, which contained living quarters for the girls, the school dining room, kitchen, and parlor. Shortly after school opened, construction was begun on a wooden dormitory for the boys. After this building burned in 1926, a building to replace the burned one was started; and a promissory note bearing the signature of twenty people, including one of the seniors, namely, George W. Owens, was made for $20,000 to provide funds for the building of a new dormitory. The school was situated in what had been a cotton and corn field on a one hundred-acre parcel of land purchased for $4,000. Members of the board of trustees at that time were J. T. Page, H. L. Gillespie, P. O. Stovall, W. G. Crouch, and B. F. Chilcoat.

The initial enrollment of Itawamba Agricultural High School was 150 students. Curricula consisted of cooking, sewing, dairying, poultry, gardening, child care, home nursing, bookkeeping, commercial law, history, and mathematics. Practical work and many chores were a part of the training in the school's early years.

According to the 1922 *Mirror*, the graduating class consisted of nine boys and one girl. The average age of the graduates was twenty-three years. By the end of the first session, 71 of the 150 students had dropped out of school.

The cost to the student for the first year was from $8 to $12 per month for room, board, and other expenses. Strict rules of conduct required: the boys to be seated on the north side of the auditorium and the girls on the south side during assembly; boys to wear buttoned shirt collars to class; girls to refrain from wearing lipstick and to wear stockings above their knees. Courting was prohibited, but girls were permitted to go to town on Wednesdays and the boys on Saturdays. Changes during the succeeding years have brought an expanded curriculum, additional facilities, and increased enrollment. The Itawamba Agricultural High School has been one of the most distinguished high schools in Northeast Mississippi.

The official minutes of the school reveal that a meeting of its trustees, the Itawamba County Board of Education, and the Itawamba County Board of Supervisors was held in the office of the county superintendent of education on June 4, 1929. The purpose of this meeting was to consider the possibility of establishing a junior college by extending the curriculum of the agricultural high school to include freshman and sophomore college work.

In 1938 the Mississippi House of Representatives cut the agricultural high school bill, which called for $100,000 support funds, back to $80,000. This reflected a mood in the legislature to do away with the agricultural high schools by reducing the appropriation. Through the efforts of George Owens, an Itawamba Agricultural High School graduate and a member of the House of Representatives, the support fund was increased to $90,000. Mr. Owens states that he had two motives in mind: "one was to save the high schools, but another was to build a junior college in Itawamba County" (*I Was There*, Pontotoc, Miss., 1973, p. 178).

During the political campaign of 1939, one of the primary planks in Owens' platform for re-election was the extension of the curriculum of the agricultural high school to include college freshman and sophomore level courses. He was re-elected to the house of representatives and was appointed chairman of the education committee. In 1940 he introduced a bill for $50,000 to assist with the building program for the Itawamba Agricultural High School and Junior College; but because a junior college had not been organized, the bill died in committee. In 1941 Representative Owens requested the board of trustees of the Itawamba Agricultural High School to extend the curriculum to make the school a legal junior college. In an

183

ITAWAMBA JUNIOR COLLEGE

GUIDED BY THESE
PRESIDENTS

Philip Alfred Sheffield, 1948–1960

John Sherman Crubaugh, 1960–1972

Winston Odean Benjamin, 1972–

184

effort to make the other counties more interested in joining the district, Representative Owens and the board agreed to name the school Northeast Mississippi Junior College.

In 1941, interest in establishing a junior college in Northeast Mississippi was intensified. Both Booneville and Tupelo expressed interest in establishing a junior college, but neither of these towns had an agricultural high school and would qualify only for a municipal college, which neither wanted. Beginning with the May 8, 1941, issue of the *Fulton News Beacon*, appeared a series of articles written to rally public support for a junior college to be located in Itawamba County. On June 6, 1941, as recorded in Minute Book I, pages 169, 170, and 171, the Itawamba Agricultural High School Board of Trustees extended the curriculum to include college work; and instead of naming the school Northeast Junior College, it named it the Itawamba Junior College and Agricultural High School. The freshman year was to begin with the 1941–1942 session. Sophomore work was to begin the following year. The authority for the action was granted by Section 6694 of the *Mississippi Code of 1930*.

On September 23, 1941, the citizens of Itawamba County voted for a bond issue of $55,000 to establish a junior college. This money was to be used to match a WPA grant for the construction of the buildings; but because of the outbreak of World War II, the bonds were never sold and plans for establishing a junior college were set aside.

During the regular biennial session of the Mississippi legislature in 1946, House Bill 1125, Chapter 57 was passed, which appropriated $300,000 to build a Northeast Mississippi junior college. Booneville had approved the organization of an agricultural high school and junior college. It was through the efforts of Mr. Elmer McCoy of Booneville, who was chairman of the House education committee, and Mr. J. M. Bullard also of Booneville, who was a member of the appropriations committee, that the bill passed. George Owens, who was serving as assistant clerk of the House (he was defeated in the 1943 campaign for re-election as a Representative), reported, "I felt rather secure since I knew the Itawamba County Agricultural High School had established the only legal Northeast Mississippi Junior College. When the records were checked, it was found that instead of the Board of Trustees naming the Itawamba Junior College the Northeast Mississippi Junior College they had named it the Itawamba Junior College which left Booneville with the only legal Northeast Mississippi Junior College" (ibid., p. 180).

After the citizens of Itawamba County realized that they had lost the $300,000, they renewed efforts to establish a junior college. A bond issue was passed, but the greatest hurdle was to convince other counties to join the district in order to establish a tax base (assessed evaluation $20,000,000) great enough to meet the requirements for the establishment of the junior college.

In 1945, Phillip A. Sheffield was elected superintendent. He was just back from World War II and enthusiastically set about the task of convincing other counties to join the district. Monroe County was the first to commit itself to the support of the junior college. Supervisors Dr. L. W. Darracott, Dr. Fletcher Miller, Mr. Cooper H. Cantrell, Mr. R. A. Pullen, and Mr. Paul Sisk, along with numerous other leaders, promised the cooperation of the citizens of Monroe County in the establishment of the college.

In Lee County, Supervisors L. L. Bishop, C. H. Cain, J. E. Marcy, Mark Shumpert, and B. G. Coggins pledged the support of Lee County. Other Lee Countians supporting Lee County's participation were W. A. Roper, Mayor of Tupelo, Phillip Nanney, R. W. Reed, Zook Strain, Roy Black, and the superintendent of Shannon schools, Bodine Bourland.

Among Itawamba Countians working with P. A. Sheffield for the establishment of the college were Superintendent of Education Glen Loden, Truman Wilburn, and D. C. Harden. In March of 1948, after numerous visits to Jackson by Mr. P. A. Sheffield and others for conferences with officials of the state department of education, the College Accrediting Commission approved the plan for the establishment of Itawamba Junior College.

The first year of operation began in September of 1948 with the freshman class of 114 students from Itawamba, Lee, and Monroe Counties. In addition to the 114 regular students, 170 veterans were enrolled in college trade training for carpentry, brick and stone masonry, automobile mechanics, and intensive business training. An additional 200 veterans received on-the-job-training during the first year of operation.

During the first few years, because of limited funds, the president, dean, and registrar all taught classes. Funds from special programs, such as veterans trades training, were used to subsidize the operation of the institution. Veterans labor and second hand lumber from Camp McCain were used to construct many of the first buildings. A tax levy on Itawamba County provided the only building monies available for repairs and maintenance of the existing buildings and grounds. The assessed valuation of Itawamba was so low the income was sufficient neither to build new buildings nor to extensively remodel the existing buildings.

In 1953, Pontotoc County became a tax-supporting member of the district. Pontotoc Countians instrumental in gaining this support were Superintendent of Education Barney Luther, D. D. Sneed, and Supervisors J. N. Russell, Park Sneed, H. N. Purdon, John H. Beddingfield, and Wade Stegall.

Since its beginning, most of the students who have attended Itawamba Junior College have been commuting students. Buses operated by the College provide daily transportation for students from several points in the district to the campus.

During the first year of operation, two dormitories, with a capacity of forty-five, served both high school and junior college students; today five dormitories with a capacity of one hundred and eighty serve only junior college students. The enrollment has, with few exceptions, increased each year since the first year of operation.

Student fees have also steadily increased. In 1948–1949, the first year of operation, the fees for in-district nonresident students were $16.00; while the fees for an in-district boarding student were $224.50. The present fees for in-district nonresident students are $150; those for in-district boarding students are $540. During the first year of operation, however, the college trades-training enrollees paid $30 per month in fees; today fees for the vocational divisions are comparable to fees for students in the college transfer program.

When Itawamba Junior College opened, only freshman work was offered. The academic curriculum included agriculture, biology, chemistry, commerce, education, English, French, home economics, mathematics, social science, and woodworking. These were arranged in six groups and included agriculture, business, arts, engineering, home economics, and science. Each year enriched programs and expanded course offerings were added to improve the curriculum. Students now have the choice of twenty different divisions of special study as compared to the six divisions offered in the first year.

Almost all the existing buildings have been constructed since the junior college was established. The only original agricultural high school building remaining is the Agriculture Building which was constructed in 1938 by the National Youth Administration. Recent construction on the Fulton campus includes an administration building, a library, four classroom buildings containing a total of thirty classrooms, and a dormitory for women containing thirty-one rooms. In 1948, the value of the facilities on the Fulton campus was approximately $500,000; but in 1972, the improvements and additions had increased the value to approximately $4,000,000.

On April 8, 1963, representatives from the Community Development Foundation of Tupelo and the board of supervisors of Lee County met with the board of trustees and made a formal request that a vocational-technical training center be established in Tupelo as a part of Itawamba Junior College. The board of trustees voted to establish the center. Among those present from the Community Development Foundation and the Lee County Board of Supervisors were: George McLean, Harry Martin, J. C. Whitehead, Jr., Felix Black, Kyle Brown, Calvin Turner, Charlie Cain, and Harry Rutherford.

These men, along with others from the Tupelo area, provided the leadership for documenting the need for and promoting the establishment of the center in Tupelo. The Lee County Board of Supervisors agreed to levy additional taxes for the support of the center, and the Community Development Foundation provided $54,000 to be used as local matching funds for the first year's operation.

The center was established for the general purpose of providing specialized occupational education to the people of a rapidly growing area. The establishment of this center is important in that it was conceived prior to the significant national legislation of the Vocational Act of 1963.

The first classes, which started in 1964, were held in the City-County Building and in space provided by Community Warehouses, Inc. These facilities were used at little or no cost to the college until the first college-owned buildings were occupied in 1966.

Construction of permanent facilities began in June of 1965 with $200,000 provided by the Appalachian Regional Commission, $200,000 from the Mississippi

A & I Board, and $200,000 from short-term notes provided by the Lee County Board of Supervisors. The city of Tupelo donated a site consisting of ten acres from a tract of 108 acres that it had purchased for educational purposes. Some equipment was donated by local industries, and the rest was purchased by funds provided through the Division of Vocational Education of the state department of education. The facility was occupied in 1966.

A 43,500 square foot Health Occupations Building was completed in 1970. In 1971, a special vocational educational center was constructed. This building houses a coordinated program with emphasis on vocational training for mentally retarded students of high school age.

Mr. J. A. "Red" Rasberry provided the leadership for the establishment of this program. It utilizes and coordinates the services of the regular special educational program for the mentally retarded, vocational education, vocational rehabilitation, and the Regional Rehabilitation Center. It has been identified by the U. S. Office of Education as an outstanding curriculum program. The services provided by the center to business, industries, and health institutions include adult classes, seminars, start-up training, and staff upgrading programs.

In 1964 the first Mississippi Adult Basic Education Program was offered at the center. Enrollment during some years has exceeded 2000 participants. In 1967 a newspaper was printed to be used in adult literacy classes. This newspaper, *The Appalachian News*, printed with funds from a federal grant, was distributed to twenty-five states. It is still being printed weekly on a subscription basis with a circulation of more than 5000.

The establishment of Itawamba Junior College can in large measure be attributed to the leadership, vision, and dedication of a few. One of the most important of these was P. A. Sheffield, Itawamba Agricultural High School's ninth superintendent and the first president of Itawamba Junior College and Agricultural High School.

Mr. Sheffield, a native of Itawamba County, an alumnus of Itawamba Agricultural High School, and a graduate of Mississippi State University, taught in the high school from 1932 to 1938 and from September 1940 until November 1941. On December 1, 1941, he was inducted into the army and attained the rank of captain. After a tour of duty in the Pacific war zone, he

was transferred to the States where he taught special military courses at the University of Maine. After his discharge in 1945, he was elected superintendent of Itawamba Agricultural High School.

Almost immediately, he enthusiastically provided the leadership for the extension of the agricultural high school to the junior college level. Three years after his appointment as superintendent of the high school, he was selected as the first president of Itawamba Junior College. As president, he worked untiringly toward his goal of improving and expanding the college. His struggle to build a campus and to finance a quality program with limited funds continued to the day of his untimely death in September 1960.

Upon Mr. Sheffield's death, the board of trustees appointed J. S. Crubaugh to serve as the second president of the junior college. Mr. Crubaugh had been elected to serve as the first academic dean of the college when it opened in 1948 and continued to serve in that capacity until he was appointed president. Prior to 1948, he had served as teacher, coach, and principal in Lee and Chickasaw County Schools. He earned the B.S. and M.S. degrees at Mississippi State University and the M.Ed. degree at George Peabody College.

During Mr. Crubaugh's tenure as president from 1960 to 1972, most of the original agricultural high school buildings were replaced. Other notable accomplishments included curriculum enrichment and expansion, library improvements, establishment of a new campus at Tupelo to offer vocational and technical programs, the addition of an adult education program, and the expansion of community services.

On July 1, 1972, W. O. Benjamin, a native of Pontotoc County, became Itawamba Junior College's third president. He received his formal training at the University of Mississippi and had served as teacher and administrator in public schools of Mississippi for more than twenty years. Appraisals, assessments, and revaluation of educational and industrial needs are presently being made. Plans are being drawn and studies conducted to determine how the college can better serve citizens of the junior college district. The board of supervisors of Chickasaw County, at the request of the board of trustees and President Benjamin, approved a tax levy supporting the Itawamba Junior College District. Members of the Chickasaw Board of Supervisors were Mr. Robert Atkinson, Mr.

Loyd Collums, Mr. DeVan Hill, Mr. Parker Lancaster, and Mr. Calvin Lancaster.

Itawamba Junior College students have made distinct records in both the vocational and the educational department and have earned numerous awards in sports and other activities. The Itawamba Junior College fully subscribes to the philosophy that the mission of the institution is to provide educational opportunities for all. Any effort to provide these opportunities must necessarily be accomplished by a commitment to the idea of comprehensiveness. A broad spectrum of programs is necessary to meet the diverse needs of the whole community, and the junior colleges are continually seeking new ways to serve the needs of the surrounding communities. The primary purpose of the institution is to provide a program of education to meet the needs of each student at a minimum cost. More specific purposes are to provide vocational training in a number of areas, to make training available to those who desire to terminate their formal education, to offer suitable academic courses and services for those who plan to transfer credits, to offer guidance and counseling services to all students, to provide a curriculum for adult education, and to provide community services.

NORTHEAST MISSISSIPPI
JUNIOR COLLEGE STORY

In Northeast Mississippi the district, which was composed of twelve counties, did not go into the immediate organization of a junior college; but in 1936 when it was noted that so many of the young men and women from Northeast Mississippi were attending the other junior colleges, the people became interested in establishing a junior college in this area. In 1941 their interest led to the establishment of an institution in Prentiss County. Trustees were elected, and an order for an $80,000 bond issue was authorized.

Before work was started on the buildings, and even before the bonds were sold, war was declared, and all progress was stopped. However, the people of this area continued to dream of the establishment of the junior college in Booneville. In 1940 the business was resumed, and a survey of the territory made by the board of education determined that this institution should be built in Booneville, Mississippi. The district

was reorganized with Prentiss, Tippah, Alcorn, and Tishomingo Counties participating in the maintenance and support of this junior college. In the summer of 1948, Union County came into the district. The college has no record of academic service to place before the public as yet, but has the enthusiasm and the continued interest that have been manifested since 1928. We believe that the boys and girls of this area will be given that type of training which will reveal the interest that is being given in the establishment of the junior college.

From the beginning, much material assistance has been given by the various agencies and friends of the college. Thirty-nine acres of land have been purchased, by donations, at a cost of $13,000. The Fair Association has donated twenty acres of land valued at $20,000. On this fifty-nine acres the college is being built. The Peoples Water Company, in cooperation with the town officials, has built water and sewage lines at a cost of approximately $30,000. Valuable assistance has been given also in the grading and building of streets. In 1946 the state legislature appropriated $300,000 for the construction and equipping of buildings.

The Northeast Mississippi Junior College was incorporated in Prentiss County in 1941, but the construction program was delayed until the end of World War II. Upon completion of the original plant, the college was opened to students in September 1948, as an agricultural high school and junior college serving Alcorn, Prentiss, Tippah, Tishomingo, and Union Counties. The following year, the name was changed to reflect junior college status only. Since that time, the institution has expanded its offerings in curriculum and physical facilities.

In 1948, the board of trustees empowered the college to grant the degrees of associate in arts and associate of science in nursing. During subsequent years, the following certificates were authorized: intensive business education and vocational education.

In keeping with the philosophy of Northeast, a department of vocational and technical education was developed in the fall of 1965 to provide educational opportunities for persons to qualify for employment in various vocational and technical areas.

The Northeast Mississippi Junior College is located in the northeastern part of Mississippi, approximately 190 miles north of Jackson and 100 miles southeast of Memphis, Tennessee. The school has an elevation of

530 feet. The climate is moderate in both summer and winter. The college is easily accessible by automobile over U. S. Highway 45.

The Northeast Mississippi Junior College is accredited by the Southern Association of Colleges and Schools and the Mississippi State Accrediting Committee, and is a member of the State Association of Colleges and the American Association of Junior Colleges. The associate degree program in nursing is accredited by the Southern Association of Colleges and Schools and by the Board of Trustees of Institutions of Higher Learning, State of Mississippi.

The Northeast Mississippi Junior College was established to provide higher education for young men and women who qualify for admission and who can maintain the high scholastic standards which characterize an institution of higher learning.

The philosophy supporting the purposes and operations of the college may be stated in terms of the major objectives to which it constantly devotes itself: (1) transfer education; (2) vocational and technical education; (3) guidance; (4) activities; (5) continuing education; and (6) community service. The purposes of this institution are achieved through the selection and retention of a faculty with the highest principles and scholarship.

The Northeast Mississippi Junior College is cognizant of community and public needs. It accepts the challenge of assisting in these areas so far as possible within the scope of law and policy. It makes available its staff, its leadership, its facilities, and the products of its research in stimulating educational, cultural, governmental, and material growth. Education may logically be classified into two categories. First are the credit-type services, consisting primarily of evening classes scheduled on the campus. The second category includes a wide range of noncredit educational services.

The vocational-technical department of the college provides educational opportunities for persons to qualify for employment in the technical and vocational areas. These programs are designed to prepare men and women for immediate entrance into the fields of employment in which they have specialized.

The Northeast Mississippi Junior College Development Foundation, Inc., a nonprofit corporation, was established in 1969 to promote and support the educational performance of the college. The Development Foundation has qualified under the United States Internal Revenue Service regulations for tax exempt status, which makes gifts deductible for income tax purposes. Contributions, gifts, and bequests are solicited by the Foundation for the advancement of the Northeast Mississippi Junior College as an institution of excellence.

At Northeast, as on every college campus, some students are recognized as contributing much time and effort to serving their school. All of the Northeast campus events center on student participation and enjoyment. The ability to give of one's self and the value of friendly cooperation are both important factors in the preparation for each event and in the shaping of well-rounded graduates. Educational opportunities meet the student everywhere, not only in the classroom, but in the cultural programs, and committee work. Thus, he is able to develop his leadership abilities through practical experience. The combination of an ambitious student body and an interested faculty makes it possible to personalize education at Northeast. Each student receives individual guidance in planning his college career and his future. The degree of success of students at senior institutions and the success students have in employment indicate the effectiveness of instruction. Over a period of years this success has served as a criterion for evaluating the faculty.

Significant strides have been made in the academic area. These have been marked by imagination, innovation, and a sensitivity to the needs of the times. The academic program supports the concept that an educated person has a good understanding of the history of civilization, classical literature of the western world, the humanities, modern mathematics, natural sciences, and behavioral sciences. Therefore, during the freshman and sophomore years transfer students at Northeast explore a variety of subjects before concentrating on a major field of study at a senior college.

In keeping with its philosophy, Northeast strives to meet the needs of the people in its district through the transfer programs, the one- and two-year terminal programs, the vocational and technical education programs, and the adult education programs. To provide effective educational programs for this diverse group, Northeast is constantly improving its programs and facilities in the classrooms, the laboratories, and the library. No major changes have been made in the academic program in recent years.

The curriculum for each degree program includes

GUIDED BY THESE
PRESIDENTS

Roscoe Odas Stringer, 1948–1952

Ben Willis Jones, 1952–1956

William Harwood Hinton, 1956–1960

Earl Forest Hargett, 1960–1961

Edward Aubert Knight, 1961–1965

Harold Taylor White, 1965–

general education courses, courses in the major field, and electives. The courses in the major field are comparable in content to those offered in senior institutions. Thirty-five departments and/or programs of study make up the college parallel and vocational programs at Northeast.

Working tirelessly for the development of Northeast is a group of dedicated men who devote a magnanimous amount of unremunerated work to our college—the board of trustees. Making their job even more demanding is the fact that they can no longer plan ahead just by thinking on the immediate developments that they can see. They must be making plans now for what the future is expected to bring.

Progress at Northeast is traced to the influence and participation of the board of trustees. Ideas and plans formulated in monthly board meetings have grown and produced visible results. Each member is to be commended for his role in helping to bring about the developments at Northeast in 1948–1973.

One of the surest measures of a college is its alumni. Northeast is proud of its alumni who number more than 28,000 throughout the United States. The Northeast Alumni Association sponsors a full schedule of events, including homecoming, which is one of the most enjoyable programs of the year for alumni, students, and faculty alike. Many programs have been set in motion, including expansion and improvement in records and closer coordination among college alumni.

The Northeast Mississippi Junior College Alumni Association was organized in the fall of 1965. Since the assoication is relatively young, it does not have the financial support or the strength of numbers to render its potential effectiveness in service to Northeast. However, there is a general acceptance of the unique partnership that exists between the alumni and the institution.

Since the summer of 1966 Northeast, in cooperation with the state department of education, has offered an adult basic education program for those eighteen years of age or older who are in need of basic education to enable them to speak, read, and write effectively. The objectives of the program are to enable participating adults to learn to read and write English; to raise substantially the educational level of such adults with a view to making them less likely to become dependent on others; to improve their ability to benefit from some occupational training; to in-

crease their opportunity for productive and profitable employment; and to make them better able to meet their adult responsibilities.

The program of instruction includes elementary level education (grades one through eight) for adults with emphasis on the communicative skills of reading, writing, speaking, listening, and the computative skills using the content of materials that contain information on good buying, health, human relations, home and family living, and other applicable areas of interest. There is no tuition or any other charge—books and necessary materials are furnished. Based on certification from local educational agencies, a certificate is issued by the state office to those adults completing the eighth grade.

The school years 1948–1973 have been ones of steady progress for Northeast. The college has grown in size, but, more important, it has grown in strength and, we hope, in vision. These years in Northeast's history can be characterized as a period of transition. The college is not what it once was, nor is it yet what it is going to be. Change is the ever-present fact of life. This was always true. "To live is to change," wrote Newman many years ago, "and to be perfect is to have changed often." It is the tempo of change that has increased enormously. But even this quickened pace was inevitable. It must be embraced and used if it can enable the institution to perform more effectively its central mission. Indeed these years have been years of fulfillment. Services begun are bearing fruit. New construction is well along. Perspectives for further development have been brought into focus.

Many persons and groups have contributed immeasurably to this progress. The college appreciates all who have had a part in it. Especially, all who are associated with the institution are grateful to the students, the faculty, the administration, and the board of trustees who so generously helped to maintain and lift higher the already high standards of the Northeast Mississippi Junior College.

COAHOMA
JUNIOR COLLEGE STORY

The history of Coahoma Junior College predates the opening of its doors to the first college students by some twenty-five years. The foundation of the school

GUIDED BY THESE
PRESIDENTS

Benjamin Franklin McLaurin,
1949–1966

James Earl Miller, 1966–

was laid in 1924 when one of the first Negro high schools was established in Mississippi.

The first college catalog gave a short account of Coahoma Junior College's start:

The Coahoma County Agricultural High School had its beginning in 1924. The opening session of this institution was during 1924–25. For twenty-five years Coahoma County Agricultural High School has taken a lead in giving every boy and girl in and around Coahoma County an opportunity to have a high school education and training for more efficient citizenship.

In June, 1949, the Board of Trustees and Supervisors extended the curriculum to provide for two years of college work. Plans for equipment to pursue junior college work were prepared.

With the support of the Board of Trustees and Supervisors, a full freshman college curriculum will be offered for the first time during the 1949–50 term.

If any college had a humble beginning, Coahoma Junior College did. It was the extension of a high school, and in the first year the teachers were borrowed from the high school. The property was valued at $200,000 and consisted of twenty-six acres, counting the farm with thirteen buildings.

Rules for the students abounded. The students were not allowed to bring visitors into the dormitories without permission from the dormitory supervisor, were not allowed to bring visitors to the dining hall without permission of the dining hall manager, and were not allowed to leave campus without their parents' permission. Each student was required to have a Bible and a dictionary. An unclean room might have resulted in expulsion, and each boarding student gave one hour a day for duty work, while day students gave two hours a week.

The school offered courses in agriculture, biology, education, English, home economics, mathematics, social science, woodwork, auto mechanics, and interior decoration. A special school was offered for World War II veterans. For the first two years only freshman classes were offered.

B. F. McLaurin, Sr. became the fifth superintendent of Coahoma Agricultural High School in 1946. Three years later he became the first president of Coahoma Junior College.

In the twenty-fifth annual commencement exercise, the following account was given on the first faculty of the school:

B. F. McLaurin, Sr. became the first president of Coahoma Junior College, the first public junior college for

Negroes in Mississippi in 1949. Mrs. Lillian Rogers Johnson, Mrs. Mayne Higgins, and Wallace Higgins served as guidance counselors for Superintendent McLaurin. The State Supervisor of Negro Education, the late Dr. P. H. Easom, recommended Mrs. Zee Anderson Barron to help organize the college. Dr. Vernon McDaniels, consultant and Mrs. Barron formulated the philosophy and objectives of Coahoma Junior College.

Mrs. Zee Barron became the first director, teacher, registrar, personnel director, and class sponsor of the school.

Mrs. Mary G. Whiteside aided in the establishment of the junior college. She was later to become the academic dean of the college and retired only two years ago. Under Mrs. Whiteside's guidance the college changed to the quarter system and greatly expanded its academic offerings.

Funds for operating Coahoma Junior College came entirely from Coahoma County during the first year. During the 1950–1951 school year, Coahoma Junior College was included in Mississippi's system of public junior colleges and became eligible to share in funds appropriated by the state legislature for the support of junior colleges. In the late 1960s three more counties joined in the support of the junior college. These were Quitman, Sunflower, and Bolivar Counties.

The history of Coahoma Junior College is replete with names of people who founded the school and who are still serving the college. Mr. McLaurin was forced by illness to step down from the president's post in 1966, but still gives an invaluable service as vice president of the school. Mrs. Barron is head of Student Personnel Services, and Frank Gambrell, the first fulltime teacher, is the academic dean. Both were at the school in the first years of operation.

Perhaps the most noted ambassador of good will is Miss Consuella Carter, the director of the Coahoma Junior College-Agricultural High School band. Since coming to "Aggie" in 1947, Miss Carter has literally taken students who knew nothing of music and made them students in the art of learning. Her bands have travelled across the state, and of little surprise is the tremendous following the band has had at parades. Her band and its players have won numerous awards. Miss Carter, in many ways, has been responsible for bringing musical culture to the Delta farms.

The school has grown tremendously since its beginning. The last ten years in particular have seen increases in both student enrollment and physical plant. The faculty has had a corresponding increase.

In 1949, twenty-two students entered the college as freshmen. By 1969 the student enrollment increased to 879, and, in the 1974–1975 school year, 1,100 students enrolled in the college's academic, vocational, and evening courses.

During the 1968–1969 school year, thirty-eight classroom teachers were active on campus. The teacher-student ratio was 1.23. A short four years later, sixty-two instructors were teaching students at the ratio of 1.15.

Since 1965, the physical plant has also expanded. A second story was added to the main college classroom building. In the early days most of the administrative offices were housed in a one-story library. Those offices moved into a new building of their own in the early 1960s and have since been expanded. In addition, a music building has been constructed, and expansion has been made in the business college to provide facilities for the art department. The value of the campus has been put at $3.5 million.

The library is now a four-story structure which also houses the college's learning center. The newest campus building is the sprawling vocational-technical complex. The modern building is complete with classrooms, library, laboratories, workshop bays, and administrative offices.

In a short time, a $1.06 million student union will open. This building will provide recreational facilities for the students. Study rooms, a cafeteria, a bookstore, and counseling offices will also be included in the facilities.

Since 1966, the college has been headed by James Earl Miller. Mr. Miller, like most of the school's top administrators, came up through the ranks. He was an instructor and later a principal at Coahoma Agricultural High School. In 1952, he became Coahoma Junior College's first director of public relations and the second college English instructor.

Under President Miller's administration, a ten-year master plan has been worked out showing great promises for Coahoma Junior College. After completion of the union building, men's and women's dormitories will be constructed, followed by a fieldhouse coliseum, a fine arts building, a health center, and faculty housing.

The future looks bright for Coahoma Junior College as the school has made life brighter for the young men and women who attended it.

UTICA
JUNIOR COLLEGE STORY

Utica Junior College had its inception as an educational institution when Dr. William H. Holtzclaw came to the town of Utica in the fall of 1902. He was a native of Alabama and had been inspired by the famed Booker T. Washington, who was founder and president of Tuskegee Institute. Dr. Holtzclaw had failed at several attempts to establish a school before he came to the present site of the campus at Utica Junior College. The school was incorporated in 1903 as Utica Normal and Industrial Institute for the training of black young men and women (the school became widely known as Utica Institute). Because Dr. Holtzclaw was a pupil of Booker T. Washington, the school took on characteristics of Tuskegee Institute with students being instructed not only in academic subjects but also in vocational work. The campus soon became a showplace and was visited by Booker T. Washington in 1908. The history of the early years is told very vividly in a book, *The Black Man's Burden*, written by Dr. Holtzclaw in 1915.

In 1943, Dr. Holtzclaw died and was succeeded by his son, Mr. William H. Holtzclaw, Jr. It was under the leadership of the son that negotiations were begun to organize a public high school for Negroes in Hinds County. In 1946, by a special act of the state legislature, the school was made an agricultural high school. The official name of the school became Hinds County Negro Agricultural High School until October 15, 1947, when the board of trustees unanimously changed the name to Utica Institute—Hinds County Agricultural High School, Colored.

Three persons actually served as superintendent of the high school prior to the establishment of the junior college: First, Mr. William H. Holtzclaw, Jr. served immediately after his father's death; he was succeeded in July 1947 by Mr. J. W. Grantham who served until 1951; Mr. J. D. Boyd assumed the superintendency on July 1, 1951, and became the first president of the college in 1954.

The founding of the parent institution in 1902 and the junior college in 1954 makes the institution the oldest and youngest simultaneously.

At the June 8, 1954, meeting of the board of trustees of Hinds County Agricultural High School for Negroes, "Utica Institute," the junior college was established. At the January 8, 1951, meeting of the board of

GUIDED BY THESE
PRESIDENTS

John Dewey Boyd, 1954–1957

Rudolph E. Waters, 1957

Walter Washington, 1957–1969

Arthur Henry Kinnard, Jr., 1971–1973
(acting president)

Jimmie Louis Stokes, 1969—

196

trustees of Hinds County Agricultural High School for Colored, the chairman of the board, Mr. F. M. Greaves appointed Dr. Robert M. Mayo and Mr. H. H. Davis to contact key supervisors in Hinds County to arrange a conference with neighboring county superintendents and boards of supervisors. The purpose of this conference was to map out plans for establishing a junior college with joint participation by the neighboring counties of Copiah, Claiborne, and Warren. At that time, none of these counties had an interest. However, today they are supporters. The plans called for a long-range program, the conversion of present facilities, and the addition of required facilities.

The minutes of the February 5, 1952, meeting of the board of trustees cite a resolution declaring the board's intention to establish a junior college for Negroes. No further action was taken until June 8, 1954, when the board of trustees of Hinds County Agricultural High School for Negroes met at Raymond, Mississippi. At that meeting the following resolution was proposed by Mr. Stokes V. Robertson, seconded by Mr. H. H. Davis, and unanimously adopted by the board:

Whereas, the Hinds County A. H. S. for Negroes, Utica Institute, Mississippi, has operated since 1946 in a highly successful manner; and, Whereas, the enrollment of the school has increased annually; and Whereas, we believe the physical facilities to be adequate; and Whereas, a junior college is being provided for students of the white race at Raymond, Mississippi, from public funds and Section 14, House Bill No. 541, General Laws of Mississippi, 1950, makes mandatory separate junior college districts for the white and colored races:

Now, therefore, be it resolved, that this Board of Trustees does this date declare its intention with the beginning of 1954–55 school session to establish a junior college level for the first two years of college work and, further, that the first year of college work be added at the beginning of the 1954–55 school session, and further that a copy of this resolution be made available by the secretary to all necessary boards and agencies as prescribed by law.

Mr. John Dewey Boyd was superintendent of Hinds County Agricultural High School for Negroes when the college was established. He had been serving as superintendent since July 1, 1951. The members of the board of trustees of Hinds County Agricultural High School for Negroes at the time the college was established were Mr. F. M. Greaves, Mr. H. H. Davis, Mr. J. W. McKewen, Mr. Stokes V. Robertson, Mr. H. W. Lowe, and Dr. Robert M. Mayo.

The agricultural high school, under the leadership of Mr. Boyd, initiated freshman college classes during the first semester of the 1954–1955 school year. In a special session of the Mississippi State Legislature in December 1954, formal approval was granted the board to proceed with junior college work.

Initially, the curriculum of the college was limited to a broad general education program which was considered "college parallel." The following courses were outlined in the first catalog: first year; English composition, physical education, world history survey, general college mathematics, biological science survey, art, hygiene and orientation; second year; speech arts, world literature, art appreciation, health and physical education, and physical science survey. In each year afterward, changes were made in the curriculum.

In 1966, a master plan for building was completed. This master plan included a revolutionary campus plan. Up to this time, only one building on campus had been built specifically for the junior college—the first vocational-technical building completed in 1959. With the rapidly expanding student body and the demand for additional programs a new administration building was completed and occupied in the spring of 1968. This became the main junior college building. Prior to this time, the college-parallel programs had been housed in the administration building, which was completed in 1954 before college classes began.

At the beginning of the 1957–1958 school year the vocational-technical department was initiated, with carpentry the first program offered. The following year secretarial science was added, and during the 1959–1960 school year four additional programs were added. In subsequent years the enrollment of the school grew steadily, and the vocational-technical department also grew. The demands and needs of the students and community shifted; thus the college expanded into the technical field. The college added three technical programs: building construction technology, drafting and design technology, and electronics technology.

Part of the original master plan of the campus was a new vocational-technical building. This new building was planned adjacent to the administration building and was occupied during the 1968–1969 school year. The building contained modern facilities to house existing programs, and five new programs (auto body and fender repair, child care and development, cloth-

197

ing and textiles, food service and administration, machine shop and welding) were instituted. All these programs proved successful. The machine shop and welding programs have been outstanding. Students who have completed these programs are working in the district as well as all over the state of Mississippi. According to the vocational-technical director of the college, one hundred percent of all welding graduates are certified welders, and the machine shop program is the largest of its kind among junior colleges in the state.

Over the years, Utica Junior College has steadily added new programs to its curricular offerings. Since 1966 the college has operated an adult basic education program at several centers in Hinds County. This program is sponsored jointly by the federal government, the state department of education, and the local school. Noncredit adult and continuing education programs are offered as well as community service workshops and seminars.

For a number of years the college has received grants from the federal government for general and supplemental support. This support has enabled the college to provide more and better services to students and faculty. Services to the students in the areas of counseling, placement and financial aid have been noteworthy. Many innovative teaching techniques and methods have been developed by faculty members.

During the 1966–1967 school year, the institution occupied a modern campus union building, which housed all student activities, the post office, a modern cafeteria, guest living quarters, and the college bookstore operation. This was the first year the school employed a dean of students. A concerted effort was also made to organize student activities.

The college has been known for its athletic teams, having played football and basketball in the Southern Intercollegiate Conference for a number of years. Roy Hilton, a defensive end for the Baltimore Colts, played football two years at Utica. Year after year, Utica Junior College has produced winning basketball teams, having won the SIC Conference more than any other team. The basketball team has competed in the National Junior College Athletic Association, Region Seven. Plans are being made for students to participate in all sports endorsed by the Mississippi Junior College Athletic Association. Since the spring of 1972, the college has participated in baseball.

The choir and the band have made significant contributions to the state. Particularly significant, Utica Junior College is one of the founding colleges of Opera/South, an opera company founded in 1970. It has gained national and international acclaim with its opera performances at the Municipal Auditorium in Jackson, Mississippi.

The faculty at Utica Junior College has grown from six parttime teachers and three administrators in 1954 to more than fifty fulltime teachers and six top administrators. This number includes both the academic and the vocational-technical faculty and staff. The college annually receives reimbursement for a large portion of salaries of vocational-technical teachers. This aid has enabled the college to attract and maintain competent teachers in those areas.

The enrollment has grown over the years from under fifty in the initial day programs to more than nine hundred students for the 1972 fall enrollment. These figures include night programs for adult and continuing education students. The first graduating class was comprised of eleven students in 1956. The class of 1972 was composed of one hundred ninety-seven members. Students who have completed their work at the college are now gainfully employed in every walk of life throughout the United States and in several foreign countries. Their occupations range from college professors to welders and professional football and basketball players.

Currently the legal district of the college comprises Copiah, Hinds, Rankin, and Warren Counties. Most of the students who enroll are from these four counties: however, students from other counties in the state also attend and some from other states in the Union.

The physical plant, which served the high school in 1954, was then estimated to be worth less than fifty-five thousand dollars. Today the college plant is conservatively estimated to be worth more than four and one-half million dollars. For the 1972–1973 fiscal year, the operating budget was more than one million dollars (Utica Junior College Annual Budget report to the Board of Trustees of Utica Junior College, July 1, 1972).

The college is affiliated with a number of professional associations. It is accredited by the Mississippi Accrediting Commission and was officially voted into full membership of the Southern Association of Colleges and Schools in New Orleans, Louisiana, December 13, 1972, after a number of years on correspondent status. Thus, Utica Junior College became the first traditionally black junior college in the state to attain that status.

Utica Junior College presidents will take their places in the history of the development of the Utica Junior College movement. Mr. John Dewey Boyd is credited with founding the junior college. After he submitted his resignation in April 1957, Mr. Rudolph Waters served as acting president through June 30, 1957. Dr. Walter Washington assumed the presidency in July 1957, and immediately began to expand the physical plant and to separate the function of the high school from that of the college. It was under his administration that the vocational-technical programs were first instituted and three new counties added to the district. The board of trustees accepted President Washington's resignation on July 1, 1969, and named the business manager, Mr. J. Louis Stokes, as president.

President Stokes continued the building program and was able to secure additional federal funds for buildings and student aid. President Stokes was granted a leave of absence by the board of trustees, effective September 1, 1971, to work on an advanced degree. The dean of instruction, Arthur H. Kinnard, Jr., was recommended by President Stokes to serve as acting president during his absence. The board accepted President Stokes' recommendation. President Kinnard was serving in the capacity of acting president in December 1972, when Utica Junior College was accredited by the Southern Association of Colleges and Schools. He is still serving in that capacity.

Utica Junior College is unique in that it is an "institution on wheels." There are no dormitories for students except for athletes, and therefore all other students, except the few who commute by car or walk, ride buses provided by the institution. Approximately twenty-five buses bring both high school and college students to the campus daily.

The faculty members are well trained in their respective disciplines, having attained their training at the major universities in Mississippi and throughout the United States. A few of the faculty members have studied abroad.

The future of Utica Junior College looks very bright. The board of trustees has gone on record favoring the expansion of the physical plant to include a new barbering and cosmetology complex, which is already in the planning stages; a health, physical education, and recreation complex; and a fine arts center which was recommended by the Southern Association of Colleges and Schools. Other additions to the plant will be made as needed when funds become available. Already the thrust of the college has been focused on community needs. This has grown out of a series of surveys conducted by staff members of the college in connection with the State Department of Education, Vocational Division.

The board of trustees, the faculty and staff, and administration are dedicated to the principles upon which this institution was founded and are continually striving to provide education of the highest quality for everyone in the Utica Junior College District.

Junior College Presidents
1922–1972

NAME	JUNIOR COLLEGE	DATE SERVED	TOTAL YEARS
Huff, James Andrew	Pearl River	1921–1926	5
Sutherland, Robert Edward Lee	Hinds	1922–1930	8
	Pearl River	1937–1942	5 (13)
Denson, Jefferson Lee	Mississippi Gulf Coast	1925–1929	4
Morehead, Marvin Eugene	Holmes	1925–1928	3
Vandiver, Joseph Sloan	Mississippi Delta	1926–1935	9
Stringer, Simeon Lafayette	Pearl River	1926–1932	6
Berry, Porter Walker	Northwest	1926–1936	10
Bush, Millard Perry	Jones	1927–1940	13
Wallace, James David	East Mississippi	1927–1940	13
Ellzey, Lawrence Russell	Copiah-Lincoln	1928–1932	4
McDaniel, Major Cyrus	Holmes	1928–1940	12
Pugh, Roscoe Conklin	East Central	1928–1934	6
	Northwest	1936–1953	17 (23)
Darby, Cooper J.	Mississippi Gulf Coast	1929–1941	12
Kenna, James Murray	Southwest	1929–1947	18
Cain, George Judson	Hinds	1930–1938	8
Ewing, James Malcomb	Copiah-Lincoln	1932–1956	24
Stuart, Joseph Forrest	Pearl River	1932–1936	4
Todd, Lindsey Ogletree	East Central	1934–1953	19
	Meridian	1952–1968	16 (35)
West, Paul M.	Mississippi Delta	1935–1944	9
Nicholson, Arthur Benjamin	Pearl River	1936–1937	1
Ivy, Horace Macaulay	Meridian	1937–1952	15
McLendon, George Minor	Hinds	1938–1965	27
Young, James Bonnard	Jones	1940–1970	30
Branch, Ras Marshall	Holmes	1940–1949	9
May, Albert Louis	Mississippi Gulf Coast	1941–1953	12
Tubb, Jack McWhirter	East Mississippi	1940–1945	5

McLendon, Reese Dermont	Pearl River	1942–1953	11
	Northwest	1953–1972	19 (30)
Horton, William Boyd	Mississippi Delta	1944–1966	22
Stark, Cruce	East Mississippi	1945–1953	8
Pickens, Horace Dever	Southwest	1947–1948	1
Snell, Clyde Herman	Southwest	1948–1951	3
Lorance, Clarence Wilburn	Holmes	1949–1955	6
Sheffield, Philip Alfred	Itawamba	1948–1960	12
Stringer, Roscoe Odas	Northeast Mississippi	1948–1952	4
McLaurin, Benjamin Franklin	Coahoma	1949–1966	17
Moore, Charles Clifton	Southwest	1951–1952	1
Boyd, John Dewey	Utica	1954–1957	3
Jones, Ben Willis	Northeast Mississippi	1952–1956	4
Huddleston, Hubert Ted	Southwest	1952–1972	20
Hayden, Julius John, Jr.	Mississippi Gulf Coast	1953–1972	19
Johnston, Garvin Howell	Pearl River	1953–1967	14
Vincent, W. Arno	East Central	1953–1962	9
Harbour, R. Algene	East Mississippi	1953–1970	14
Branch, Frank Benjamin	Holmes	1955–1972	17
Hinton, William Harwood	Northeast Mississippi	1956–1960	4
Fortenberry, Frances Marion	Copiah-Lincoln	1956–1968	12
Washington, Walter	Utica	1957–1969	12
Waters, Rudolph E.	Utica	1957	4 months
Crubaugh, John Sherman	Itawamba	1960–1972	12
Hargett, Earl Forest	Northeast Mississippi	1960–1961	1
Knight, Edward Aubert	Northeast Mississippi	1961–1965	4
Montgomery, Douglas M.	East Central	1962–1966	4
Mayo, Robert Murrah	Hinds	1965–1972	7
White, Harold Taylor	Northeast Mississippi	1965–1972	7
Wright, Charles Verdo	East Central	1966–1972	6
Hall, James Terry	Mississippi Delta	1966–1972	6
Miller, James Earl	Coahoma	1966 1972	6
White, Marvin Ross	Pearl River	1967–1972	5
Thames, Billy Bass	Copiah-Lincoln	1968–1972	4
Stokes, Jimmie Louis	Utica	1969–1972	3
Tisdale, Thomas Terrell	Jones	1970–1972	2
Scaggs, William Franklin	Meridian	1968–1972	4
Stennis, Earl	East Mississippi	1970–1972	2
Holmes, Horace Carruth	Southwest	1972—	1
Benjamin, Winston Odean	Itawamba	1972—	1

ACTING PRESIDENTS

Deen, S. R.	Northwest Mississippi	1935–1936	1

(Served an interim following President Berry's death, October 1935 through June 1936)

Smith, Willie H.	Copiah-Lincoln	1943–1945	2

(Served an interim period while President Ewing was serving in U.S. Navy, World War II)

Kinnard, Arthur H.	Utica	1971–1972	1

(Served an interim period while President Stokes was on leave in graduate school)

The following group of men who served as presidents of a Mississippi public junior college or as state supervisors of public junior colleges in the state department of education and are now retired and living in Mississippi were requested to consider happenings, occurrences, circumstances, series of changes, events, laws or conditions that, from their experiences during their active years and observations since retirement, appear to have contributed to the growth and development of the Mississippi state system of public junior colleges during this first fifty years:

G. M. McLendon, Bolton Road, Raymond, Mississippi, served for twenty-seven years as president of a Mississippi public junior college.

H. T. Huddleston, 825 Jackson Street, McComb, Mississippi, served for twenty years as president of a Mississippi public junior college and had additional experience as teacher and administrator.

J. M. Tubb, 1839 Piedmont, Jackson, Mississippi, served as president of a Mississippi public junior college for five years and as state superintendent of education for twenty-two years with supervision of Mississippi state system of junior colleges.

R. D. McLendon, Senatobia, Mississippi, served for thirty-two years as president of two Mississippi public junior colleges.

B. L. Hill, Brandon, Mississippi, had experience as a teacher in a Mississippi public junior college and served for twenty-two years as state supervisor of junior colleges in the state department of education.

Russell M. Ellzey, 4156 Hawthorne Drive, Jackson, Mississippi, was one of the founders of a Mississippi public junior college and later served as a member of the U. S. Congress.

M. C. McDaniel, 103 Landrum, Clinton, Mississippi, was one of the founders of a Mississippi public junior college and served for twelve years as a president. He was also related to the work of organizing the first public junior college in Mississippi.

John S. Crubaugh, Shannon, Mississippi, served for twelve years as president of a Mississippi public junior college.

Kirby P. Walker, 1044 Manship Street, Jackson, Mississippi, was one of the early supervisors of Mississippi public junior colleges and agricultural high schools, state department of education and served as superintendent of the Jackson public schools.

Cooper J. Darby, 1324 Broadmoor Place, Gulfport, Mississippi, was one of the founders of a Mississippi public junior college and served for twelve years as president. He was also a member of the board of trustees as county superintendent of a supporting county.

H. M. Ivy, P. O. Box 729, Meridian, Mississippi, was one of the founders of a Mississippi public junior college and served for fifteen years as president of the only municipal public junior college in Mississippi.

G. J. Cain, 304 Dunbar, Jackson, Mississippi, served six years as dean of a Mississippi public junior college and ten years as president, and was active in the organization and establishing of the second public junior college in Mississippi. He also served for twenty years in the state department of education as director of the division of administration and finance.

John D. Boyd, Lorman, Mississippi, was one of the founders of a Mississippi public junior college for black students and served as president for three years. He was superintendent for six years of the agricultural high school that provided the upward extension of its curriculum for the establishing of a junior college.

Those of this group who have been directly or indirectly associated with the growth and development of the Mississippi state system of junior colleges through the fifty years are:

H. M. Ivy, who was associated with the state department of education at the beginning of junior colleges in Mississippi. He actively participated in the framing of the legislation that provided for the establishing of the first public junior college in the state, and later organized the first and only municipal public junior college in the state. His activities cover the entire fifty years.

Four other men on this list participated in the organization and founding of a junior college in relation to an established agricultural high school. Each of these has observed the total development of the Mississippi state system of public junior colleges. These are:

Russell M. Ellzey, M. C. McDaniel, Cooper J. Darby, and *G. J. Cain*

Two state junior college supervisors are included. The background and experience of these men give significance to their judgment as to the factors that have been of major importance in the growth and development of the public junior colleges.

In answer to a request, each past president and junior college supervisor provided a written statement identifying the following factors as important:

(1) THE VISION AND DEDICATION AND THE PROFESSIONAL INSIGHT AND INITIATIVE OF THE FOUNDERS OF THE STATE SYSTEM AS THE CORNERSTONE OF ALL OF THE STABILITY AND PERMANENCE OF THESE INSTITUTIONS.

Most of the early junior college leaders had a fairly clear understanding of the educational and economic needs and trends. They also had the foresight and the courage to undertake the difficult task of establishing a new educational institution to serve what the junior college leaders believed to be a present and growing socio-economic need. These early leaders were compelled to move rather slowly while exploring the needs for and experimenting as to the desirable contents of new terminal courses. It was also necessary to exercise caution not to move too far in advance of the needs and to win some measure of public approval of this new type of institution.

The caliber of these early junior college leaders is attested by the fact that in later years two served with distinction as presidents of senior colleges, two served as state superintendent of education, one was elected to Congress, one was elected a state senator, one became superintendent of a large city school system to which a junior college had been added, and several were successful in business undertakings.

(2) THE WISDOM OF SPECIFIC LEGISLATION IN EARLY AND LATER YEARS.

a. The passage of the public junior college law of 1928 provided rules and regulations for public junior colleges. This basic law was rewritten in 1950 and brought the statutes up to date, thereby meeting the needs of the developing junior colleges.

b. The establishing of the Junior College Commission which was expanded by a law passed at the general session in 1962.

c. The original zoning of the state was proposed and approved by the legalized Junior College Commission. Thirteen districts were approved, involving seventy-two of the eighty-two counties in the state. These districts prevented proliferation but implemented the basic philosophy of local autonomy and a corresponding responsibility for making an educational opportunity available to all. These zones provided an adequate tax base for the support of the junior college in the district. They continued through the years with minimum changes, and in 1964 an act of the legislature approved the thirteen districts and established the junior college districts as individual and separate juristic entities and bodies politic and corporate. These districts comprised each of the eighty-two counties in Mississippi.

(3) THE ACT OF THE LEGISLATURE AUTHORIZING AND PROVIDING FOR A JUNIOR COLLEGE SUPERVISOR IN THE OFFICE OF THE STATE SUPERINTENDENT OF EDUCATION.

In the early years of the junior college the office of the state superintendent of education included a supervisor of agricultural high schools and super-

visors of several other designated divisions of the state educational program. The change in the official title and duties of the state supervisor of agricultural high schools to include supervision of the junior colleges was legal recognition of the advent of a new member in the family of educational institutions of higher learning in the state.

The real significance of the early junior college supervisor is to be found in his professional training, his qualities of leadership, and his effective supervision in collecting, tabulating, publishing, and interpreting information concerning the operation and distinctive functions that the several junior colleges were performing. The junior college executives knew from practical experience the value of solidarity, careful planning, and unrelenting hard work. The junior college supervisor was the agent by and through which the public at large and members of the legislature were kept informed as to the statewide service rendered by the junior colleges.

It could be argued that the granting of authority for a state supervisor of junior colleges was a result rather than a cause or factor in developing the junior college system. Such authority was both a result and a cause in the advancement of the junior college system.

(4) THE RECOGNITION OF THE JUNIOR COLLEGES BY THE STATE LEGISLATIVE GROUP AS A NEW AND NECESSARY PHASE OF HIGHER EDUCATION IN MISSISSIPPI AND THE ACCEPTANCE OF THE IMPORTANCE OF BOTH STATE AND LOCAL SUPPORT FOR FINANCING THESE INSTITUTIONS.

Continuing support by the state legislature through appropriation commensurate with the needs of growing enrollments and the ever-increasing services of the junior colleges to the public has been one of the strongest factors in Mississippi junior college success. The legislature has been aware that the junior colleges give the public a fine bargain and that the junior college administrators have never padded a budget. In recent years the appropriation of state money for building purposes, in addition to that for general support, has made possible the construction of facilities more nearly adequate for present needs.

(5) THE ABSOLUTE COHESIVENESS OF THE JUNIOR COLLEGE PRESIDENTS IN PRESERVING AND IMPROVING THE SYSTEM.

This unity is expressed through the activities of the Mississippi Junior College Association and the Junior-Senior College Conferences through the years.

The unity of the Junior College Association as a problem-solving body is a strong supportive arm. Once a majority has determined a best course, all junior college presidents follow the course unanimously. Requests to the legislature and appeals to the education profession or to the general public carry tremendous weight when made by the Junior College Association. An extension of such cooperation is seen also in the conjoining of junior and senior college purposes through an annual Junior-Senior College Conference. The rapport therein has contributed to the mutual welfare of these two academic groups.

(6) THE NEED FOR EDUCATIONAL TRAINING BEYOND THE HIGH SCHOOL LEVEL AT LOW COST TO THE STUDENT AND A COMMITMENT FROM THE EARLY LEADERS TO MEET THIS NEED.

Also, the commitment was that the work would be college grade and equal to the training being received in the first two years at the colleges and universities in the state. Later surveys have shown the leaders kept their promise.

The general public's notion that all young people were entitled to college training was flowing at high tide concurrently with the movement to improve education at the local level. Many students were financially unable to enter a senior college. The cost of attending an agricultural high school and junior college was much less than the cost of attending a senior institution. The addition of college courses to the agricultural high school was, therefore, strongly supported for economic reasons. The great depression in the early 1930s accentuated the need for low-cost college training.

The legislative act establishing the county agricultural high schools provided that such schools should be supported at the local level by a countywide tax. The agricultural high school and junior college was the only local school supported by the wealth of the entire county and, therefore, in better financial position than other school districts to provide two years of college training. This economic factor was a prime motive for adding junior college programs.

(7) THE ACCEPTANCE OF THE RESPONSIBILITY FOR DEVELOPING A COMPREHENSIVE JUNIOR COLLEGE PROGRAM WHICH INCLUDED AN ADEQUATE CURRICULUM IN TECHNICAL AND VOCATIONAL JOB OPPORTUNITY COURSES.

The early leaders in the junior college movement were in agreement regarding the need for technical and vocational training, and the fact that adequate training in these areas could not be provided in the beginning was not due to the lack of foresight. They recognized that conditions confronting the early junior colleges dictated placing first emphasis on traditional college courses.

The monetary advantages of a college education were strongly emphasized in the early decades of this century. This emphasis, operating concurrently with improvement of the rural schools, gave rise to increased demand for a college education. Experiences with increased student enrollments and the development of educational psychology caused many leaders in education to realize that not all students were suited by native capacity and natural aptitudes to profit from the traditional four years of academic college training. The need and public desire, however, for a bread-and-butter education increased rather than decreased.

The junior college was the logical institution to supply the need for technical and vocational training that would equip the student to earn a livelihood with less than the standard four years of college training. The offering of these courses did not conflict with offering academic courses required in the first two years at a senior college.

Junior college acceptance of the enormous responsibility for developing for Mississippi an adequate vocational-technical program and the subsequent success of the program have earned the gratitude of youth and adult leaders in this state. The objective is that individual colleges meet individual needs. Practice of thrift with tax monies and innovative procedures in instruction have been notably evident in this program. The state economy benefits on an accelerating scale.

Picture Portfolio

The buildings available on the agricultural high school campuses which established a junior college for the districts between the years 1922 and 1932 followed a definite pattern. Each institution had three main buildings grouped on the campus, a girls' dormitory, a classroom and auditorium building, which also included the administrative office, and a boys' dormitory. These buildings were well constructed, and many are in use at the close of the fifty year period. Other buildings on most campuses were a large barn and a gymnasium of some type. Separate facilities which are available today in many areas did not exist on the campuses in the beginning. Expanded facilities now include buildings for libraries, fine arts, sciences, student activities, physical education, technical education, and other special areas. These are providing adequate facilities for the total program in the Mississippi public junior colleges.

The photographs to follow show examples of both the early buildings and the modern ones.

A recent construction on the campus of Pearl River Junior College at Poplarville, Mississippi, is the Administration Building. The need for separate buildings to provide space and equipment to meet the administrative needs of the junior colleges is evidence of the growth and development on each campus.

A building constructed on the campus of Pearl River Junior College, Poplarville, Mississippi, in 1922, the second year of operation of the college. Pearl River was the first to establish college work, which began in 1921. This building continues to be used at the end of the first fifty years.

This women's dormitory at Hinds Junior College, Raymond, Mississippi, one of the original buildings at the junior college which opened in 1922, continues to be used as a dormitory for women.

The library building on the campus of Hinds Junior College, Raymond, Mississippi. This facility named in honor of George M. McLendon, President Emeritus, includes areas and equipment adequate to meet the multi-purpose needs of a junior college program. It is an example of the progress made in library facilities on each public junior college campus in Mississippi.

A multi-purpose gymnasium-auditorium and student activities building, the Frank B. Branch Coliseum, named in honor of the President of the college, was constructed in 1972 on the campus of Holmes Junior College, Goodman, Mississippi. It serves as a gymnasium and an auditorium and contains classrooms for band and physical education with living quarters for visiting groups.

A vocational-technical center constructed in 1968 on the campus of the Mississippi Delta Junior College at Moorhead, Mississippi. This center exemplifies the excellent physical facilities that have been constructed on the campuses of each of the Mississippi public junior colleges for technical and vocational training.

Two original buildings of Tate County Agricultural High School, Senatobia, Mississippi, Tate Hall (left) and the Administration Building (right). These buildings have continued to serve Northwest Mississippi Junior College through the first fifty years.

McLendon Center, student union and physical education building, Northwest Mississippi Junior College, Senatobia, Mississippi, named in honor of Reese D. McLendon, President. This center, constructed in 1969, provides space for the college cafeteria and grill, the physical education department, counseling center, home economics department, and an enclosed swimming pool.

209

The M. P. Bush Fine Arts Building, named in honor of Mr. M. P. Bush, the founder and long-time president of Jones County Junior College, Ellisville, Mississippi, was constructed in 1969. It provides the most modern facilities and equipment needed to promote a complete program in art and music education. The building includes an auditorium with a seating capacity of 1500 and stage space and equipment to meet the needs of all local and professional productions.

A science building on the campus of Jones County Junior College, Ellisville, Mississippi, which was completed in 1965. The quality of instruction is greatly improved in Mississippi public junior colleges because adequate facilities and equipment such as are found in this building are provided in specific fields of instruction. It is named in honor of Thomas H. Harris of Laurel, Mississippi, who was a long-time member and chairman of the Board of Trustees.

A men's dormitory on the campus of East Mississippi Junior College, Scooba, Mississippi. This building was constructed at the time the agricultural high school was established and has continued to serve the junior college.

This dormitory was constructed for the Copiah-Lincoln Agricultural High School at Wesson, Mississippi, and provided excellent housing for the early junior college students. It continued to serve the college for a number of years.

A girl's dormitory, recently constructed on the Copiah-Lincoln campus and named in honor of Miss Lula Stevens, a long-time member of the faculty.

A men's dormitory on the campus of the Mississippi Gulf Coast Junior College, Perkinston, Mississippi. The building was constructed in 1911 at the beginning of the Harrison-Stone-Jackson Agricultural High School and is named in honor of J. A. Huff first superintendent of the school. It has been in continuous use by the college since it began in 1925.

A multi-purpose building constructed in 1967-1968 at Mississippi Gulf Coast Junior College, Perkinston, Mississippi, Dees Hall houses administrative and faculty offices, library and learning resources, and a teaching auditorium. It is named in honor of Calvin Eugene Dees, Jr., a long-time member of the Board of Trustees.

A classroom and auditorium building constructed in 1921 on the campus of Pike County Agricultural High School at Summit, Mississippi. The building is named Kenna Hall in honor of Mr. E. D. Kenna, founder of the high school and the organizer and first president of Southwest Mississippi Junior College. This facility has been used continually until the present date.

A campus view of the Academic Building and the other buildings on the campus of Meridian Junior College, Meridian, Mississippi. This is the only Mississippi public junior college in the Mississippi state system. The college was established in 1937; construction began on this new campus in 1965.

213

An administration and classroom building (above), which was constructed on the campus of East Central Agricultural High School, Decatur, Mississippi, in 1925. It is an example of the buildings constructed for the agricultural high schools which provided facilities for the beginning junior colleges on the agricultural high school campuses. The building is still in use at East Central Junior College. This Fine Arts Center (below) was constructed on the campus of East Central Junior College in 1969. Buildings of this type provide space and equipment adequate for the growth and development of students in the fine arts program.

A technical center (above) for the Itawamba Junior College district, Fulton, Mississippi. The library building (below) was constructed on the campus of Itawamba Junior College in 1969.

The Administration Building at Northeast Mississippi Junior College, Booneville, Mississippi, was constructed in 1948, the second building to be constructed on campus. It houses the administrative offices of the college and the Division of Student Affairs. The building is named in honor of the first president of the college, Mr. R. O. Stringer.

Anderson Hall, liberal arts classroom building and auditorium on the campus of the Northeast Mississippi Junior College, Booneville, Mississippi, is named in honor of Chancery Judge William H. Anderson, member of the first Board of Trustees of Northeast Mississippi Junior College.

216

This library building is located on the campus of Coahoma Junior College, Clarksdale, Mississippi. The building is named in honor of Mrs. Ethel V. Dickerson, the first librarian of the institution, and Mrs. Lillian Rogers Johnson, an early educator and supervisor of Coahoma County schools. The new library facilities, which have been constructed on the campuses of each of the public junior colleges, contribute to the continuous effort of the Mississippi public junior colleges to provide, as a first priority, a program of "academic excellence."

A school began in this building in 1903 at Utica, Mississippi. The school was first called Utica Normal and Industrial Institute. It later became Utica Institute and by legislative act an agricultural high school was established. Today, on this site, is Utica Junior College.

The new library on the campus of Utica Junior College is named in honor of William H. Holtzclaw who founded Utica Normal and Industrial Institute.

ORGANIZATIONS AND ACTIVITIES

Purposes and Objectives: From Agricultural High School to Junior College

The purposes and objectives of the agricultural high schools gave direction to the organization and development of junior colleges. Each multicounty junior college was established on the already existing campus of an agricultural high school, and each junior college in its early years shared the facilities with the high school. This pattern continued in all of the junior colleges until during the fourth decade. Four junior colleges have high school work on the campus at the present time. The agricultural high schools that did not develop a junior college program closed during the early years of the development of the junior colleges.

The following statement of purposes, copied from catalogs during the early years of development, had a strong influence on the general atmosphere that prevailed on the junior college campuses:

The purpose of the Agricultural High School and Junior College is to train boys and girls in right habits of thought, to give them preparation for the life they are to live after they leave school and to make them better men and women. While the course of study prepares them for advanced study in college, it seeks mainly to give them the training that will enable them to become law-respecting and law-abiding citizens. Every attention is given to the mental discipline of

pupils so as to train them to think accurately and to qualify them to perform the duties of citizenship. The moral and spiritual well-being of students is looked after with utmost care and thought. A major purpose is to educate as well as to instruct; to form character, as well as to give information.

Our Aims

1. To furnish the maximum advantages at the minimum cost.
2. To create equality of opportunity through an all round training of the individual.
3. To inspire that type of citizenship which will enrich country life by making the people more contented and prosperous.
4. To combine the freedom of home life with the regulated system of the school.
5. To teach courtesy in speech and action.
6. To uphold honesty in word and deed.
7. To inspire reverence toward the spiritual.
8. To encourage charity toward the less fortunate.
9. To inspire manly and womanly service in the interest of one's home, one's friends, and one's community.
10. To encourage cheerfulness of manner and a happy outlook on life.

The purpose of the agricultural high school and junior college is two-fold. First, it strives to give every boy and girl a thorough and practical high school and junior college education. Second, the school is striving in every way possible to aid the farmers of the county by various forms of extension work. The agricultural department of the school is equipped to vaccinate hogs, prune and spray orchards, terrace and tile drain land. If any farmer needs help on any such matters, we will take it as a favor if he will call on us and allow us to help him.

It is important that every student entering the high school

should realize that he must take upon himself the greater part of the responsibility for his work. Parents should co-operate and advise, and teachers should help and direct, but the student has to do the work himself.

Aims

1. To place at small cost the advantages of a standard high school and junior college within the reach of every country boy and girl.

2. To prepare not only for college, but to give training along industrial lines.

3. To co-operate with the A. & M. College, the County Farm Agent, and the County Home Economics Agent, in carrying valuable assistance to the farm and the farm home.

4. To uplift rural life, to lessen drudgery, to increase comfort, to make the home more attractive, to lead in the development of an attractive, satisfying, and enduring rural civilization.

Our Aim

Our aim is to do the greatest good to the greatest number and to see going out from this school from year to year boys and girls who by the influences thrown around them here, and by the knowledge and information received at this institution, merging into strong, stalwart characters which is the only safety and strength of any country or any people. To ac-complish this, we must have a definite, set purpose in view, and work untiringly to make that purpose a reality. We have worked energetically to select a corps of real teachers and we are proud to say that our faculty is composed of college graduates, every one of which holds one or more college degrees. We are glad to be able to say further that this is a body of high-toned Christian men and women, who are anxious to make this the very best year in the history of the school. But we want you to understand, we do not hope to do the impossible.

"Educating" as we understand it, is a drawing-out pro-cess and not a cramming-in process as some seem to think, and if it be a drawing-out process you cannot draw where there is nothing to draw from. You cannot draw water from a dry well and this is what some teachers and some schools have been trying to do, and in failing to accomplish this they have called down on themselves the severest criticisms.

The purpose of this school is to train boys and girls in right habits of thought and action; to give them a preparation for the life they are to live whether it be in the office, in the workshop, or on the farm.

While its course of study gives a preparation for college, yet it seeks mainly to give the boys and girls the training along industrial lines that will enable them to relieve the farm and home of drudgery and make the farm prosperous and the home happy. Every attention will be given to the mental discipline of pupils to train them to accurate thought and action and thus qualify them for the noble performance of the duties of life. The moral and spiritual training will be looked to with the utmost care and thought. This school endeavors to educate as well as instruct, to form character as well as give information. The morally developed heart, the skilled hand, and the trained mind are indicative of a successful life. The ideal in education is, "A sound mind in a sound body," and to this end scrupulous care will be taken to keep buildings and grounds clean and free from local cause of disease. Sanitary laws will be strictly enforced and every attention given to the preservation of health. We have a fine artesian well overflowing with good pure water, and last year we did not have a single case of serious sickness among the student body.

The program planning as well as administrative and faculty discipline followed in many areas these stated purposes. The college students during the early years remember study hours in the dormitories and during the day, scheduled times to be in at night, rising bells for the morning, as well as lights out at night, required attendance at daily chapel, and required church at-tendance on Sunday morning. The development of ideals and purposes that contributed to the building of character and qualities of good citizenship was of great importance. The administration and faculty considered these aims and purposes as an individual responsibility. The stating of these aims and purposes continued to be printed in the annual catalog and announcement with some additions and deletions until the close of the third decade.

In 1951 each public junior college participated in an evaluative program authorized by the Mississippi Junior College Association, and, as a part of this study, each junior college formulated a new statement of philosophy and purpose. A review of these written statements shows in general a unity of purpose. These included the following:

The purpose of providing a program for the de-velopment of the intellectual powers of each student was of primary importance.

A dominant purpose was character building. An effort in this development is a carefully selected fac-ulty with a personal interest contributing to character building and spiritual guidance, which included stu-dent supervision designed to instill respect for self, for others, and for authority.

To provide a program of higher education at low cost.

Emphasis on guidance, seeking to discover the tal-ents and capabilities of students and to contribute to career planning and placement.

Combining training for effective citizenship with an effort to establish a right sense of values.

Each school accepted the responsibility for a pro-gram designed to meet student needs in the areas of (1) preprofessional and general education, (2) technical and vocational job opportunity programs, (3) adult education, and (4) community services.

A determined effort to provide religious influences to meet the innate and basic need of students for spiritual and religious satisfaction.

Religious affiliations provided for students on the junior college campuses included classes in religious education and religious activities organized and guided by trained people and leaders from church groups placed on the campuses. Regular assemblies for all students with ministers, other guest speakers, and planned programs provided a religious influence. These have contributed to a program of building character and Christian leadership during the student's period of attendance at the junior college.

Social development to grasp more fully the social virtues necessary to living in a group, based on respect for other people, as well as for himself.

To promote the development of personality and leadership through wholesome social guidance and experiences through close parental cooperation with the school and through participation in various educational activities.

To develop, through student participation in various types of group activities, a desirable attitude toward all areas of human relationship.

To provide opportunities for the students to make proper adjustment to the world in which they live, and accept responsibility for service to their fellow men.

To promote the development of an aesthetic sense in students. This resulted in the addition of a number of fine arts courses to the curriculum. This purpose was of concern to the administration and faculty because of the large number of rural young people attending junior college, and during the early years in the development of the institutions the home life of the rural young person did not provide adequate opportunities for the development in the fine arts area. The present fine arts buildings, with excellent equipment, that one will find in the junior college campuses are a result of the effort from the establishment of the public junior colleges to develop the aesthetic sense in students.

Physical development for young men and young women. The physical education programs, as developed from the beginning, included class instruction, recreation, intramural and intercollegiate activities. The individual development of each student represented the real purpose of the physical develop-

ment programs. However, the intercollegiate sports contributed to real fellowship and leadership, and represented specific training for those who planned to enter coaching, physical education instruction, and other areas related to physical education.

The need for a restatement of philosophy and purpose was evident at the beginning of the fifth decade, since comprehensive programs had been developed. During the fifth decade, each junior college made a report of a self-study and evaluation for the Southern Association of Colleges and Schools. These reports included a more inclusive statement of purpose and philosophy.

A review of these statements indicates a general agreement among the junior colleges to accept the responsibility of providing opportunities for quality programs in higher education. They are dedicated to community service, and they are constantly engaged in endeavors to increase the scope and quality of their programs.

These general areas of agreement as to purpose and philosophy include the following as stated in a junior college catalogue:

To provide leadership in curricular and extracurricular activities which will promote intellectual, cultural, social, spiritual, and physical development of the student so that they will become useful, efficient members of a democratic society and will increase their own qualities of living.

To accept the challenge that education is a moral responsibility; therefore, the dominant purpose as an institution is to develop character and to develop within the student the following abilities: to search for truth, to make valid realistic decisions for himself, and to become a morally responsible person.

To provide an environment conducive to serious study in which develops logical thinking, a responsibility for leadership, and the ability to discriminate, to reason, and the power to express one's self.

To provide personal, academic, and occupational guidance which will assist individual students in discovering their abilities, aptitudes, and interests; in making adequate adjustments to college life; and in obtaining information necessary to furthering their educational or occupational careers.

To make available to students high quality education parallel to the first two years of senior college or university work in as many fields as is practical and to provide it at low cost to the student.

To provide instruction and experiences which will enable students to develop the ability to be producers of goods or services for their own economic independence and cultural enjoyment, and to use their leisure time wisely, and to serve their nation and their fellow man willingly with a firm purpose to help preserve a free society within our American system of democratic government. The institution has accepted the philosophy that it is the instructor's responsibility to guide and inspire students in the learning process, ever mindful of their individual abilities and limitations, and ever striving, through personal contact and understanding, to increase these abilities. The instructor's place, also, is to take the lead in worthwhile community projects. The purpose of the college is to provide the faculty necessary to meet the student needs. To provide technical and vocational courses designed to prepare students to achieve competence in their chosen field of work, whether in business, industry, or agriculture. To provide opportunities for adult education in academic, technical and vocational courses.

These purposes as expressed through functional areas are described in the college catalogs. The following statements are copied from catalogs on file in the office of the division of junior colleges, state department of education:

Catalog One

Transfer Education. To provide the first two years of college (in as many fields as practical) for students planning to continue their education beyond junior college.

Vocational and Technical Education. To provide occupational education in a variety of fields for those who expect to conclude their formal education in the junior college.

Guidance. To provide counseling and other guidance services which are intended to help the student find his interests, become aware of his aptitudes, abilities, and vocational opportunities.

Activities. To provide organizations and activities which will promote the intellectual, cultural, spiritual, and physical growth of the individual. This program is to enrich and supplement, not to compete with, the regular programs of study.

Continuing Education. To provide educational opportunities through admission to regular day classes, establishment of evening classes, and creation of short courses as needed, for those adults who have a desire for further knowledge, a desire to improve or develop skills, or a desire to pursue cultural or vocational interests.

Community Service. To provide, in addition to the instructional program, other services and facilities to improve the cultural, civic, economic, and spiritual growth of the college district and its neighboring areas.

Catalog Two

To make accessible to the community quality opportunities in higher education.

To provide a center for cultural development in the community.

To provide a program of student services that will assist each individual in his academic, personal, and social development.

To offer curricular patterns that will parallel those of four-year institutions.

To provide a variety of occupational programs to prepare people for immediate employment.

To provide programs for the continuing education of adults in basic, general, and specific fields.

To provide a developmental program of individualized instruction for students whose academic foundation requires strengthening.

To evaluate systematically the foregoing functions in terms of the needs of the students and the community.

Mrs. Emily Duncan Mathis, in her dissertation entitled "An Historical Study of Curricular Changes in Selected Public Junior Colleges in Mississippi," presented to the Graduate Council of the University of Tennessee in partial fulfillment of the requirement for the Degree of Doctor of Education, makes the following statements regarding the attaining of goals established by the junior colleges:

Curriculum development has played a major role in attaining these goals. As knowledge and technology advance and as new occupations emerge, it is imperative that curricular offerings increase accordingly. Therefore, the largest number of changes have occurred in vocational and technical programs and they have been largely in the form of additions. Because traditional college programs have remained somewhat stable in the four year colleges, they have also remained relatively stable in the junior colleges. Therefore, changes in the transfer programs seem to have occurred primarily within the content of individual courses, although some additions were evident. As catalog listings indicated, little attention has been given to the general education curriculum, and until some federal money is channeled in that direction, a great deal of attention is not expected. It is not difficult to see that educators concentrate on areas where money is alloted.

The junior college is now becoming more concerned with the increasing number of older adults who are returning to school on a part-time basis. The regular expansion of occupational programs reflects its efforts to serve the community in a more meaningful capacity. Greater efforts are being made to provide curricula that will accommodate business and industry of the community, as well as private citizens.

The clientele of the junior college is varied; therefore, the programs which serve them must also be varied. Because most junior colleges operate on the "open door" policy, the need for remedial programs is great. Many of those enrolled deliberately choose a type of institution which assumes, as one of its major objectives, the education of the underachiever. Others who have been out of school for several years choose to attend a junior college because they feel that the individualized approach to learning which characterizes these institutions will lessen the trauma of the re-entry process into a world of books and papers and "midnight oil." Some who plan to transfer to a four year college later, choose to attend a junior college for a year or two because it is less expensive and often more conveniently located.

Also, free transportation is provided daily for students

residing in the geographical areà which the college serves. Others attend the junior college because it provides training in vocational and technical areas which are not to be found in four year colleges. And still others attend simply to improve skills, to broaden cultural experiences, or to pursue a craft or hobby. Whatever their reasons for being there, such a varied clientele present a never-ending challenge to those who endeavor to meet the needs.

The success with which those needs are being met is, in part, a reflection of the far-sightedness of the junior college pioneers in Mississippi. Their tedious efforts to expand a new type of educational institution based on a solid foundation were not in vain, for what began as a foster child of the four-year college has now gained an identity of its own in the field of higher education, not only in Mississippi but around the world.

Its educational leadership is far-reaching. In addition to instructional duties the junior colleges assume, as a part of their responsibility to the communities they serve, the presentation of workshops, forums, plays, concerts, and lecture series. The quality of junior college personnel is constantly being upgraded, often at the expense of a particular junior college or the federal government under provisions of an educational act. Both administrators and faculty are utilized in consulting capacities by local schools, and often they are asked to speak at social, civic, or church functions. Their physical plants are also utilized often by both the local community and the school system.

The junior colleges of Mississippi also assume a leadership role in social and civic developments. Their activities are carefully planned to provide a variety of social experiences for young men and women whose backgrounds are largely rural and unsophisticated. Clubs and organizations are encouraged to promote programs of a civic nature and, thus, to be of service to the community. When desegregation in the public schools of Mississippi was ordered by the courts, the junior colleges were receptive to the change, and, despite objections of some individuals, exerted a positive influence on the community. Very few unpleasant incidents related to desegregation have been reported in Mississippi's junior colleges.

Altogether the junior colleges in Mississippi seem to be somewhat slower to change than those in some other parts of the country, the changes which have occurred have been, for the most part, sound ones, and there is good reason to believe that this will continue to be true. Unfortunately, many of the changes in curriculum which have been desirable have also been impossible until recently because of limited funds. Federal monies have altered that situation considerably in the last few years, and vast expansions have become evident. Many new buildings which are the pride of administrators, have been constructed; and much new equipment, which is the panacea of faculty, has been added, thus making possible the addition and expansion of programs. Because great changes in the vocational-technical areas began occurring in the mid-fifties when the government started putting large sums of money into the programs, it can hardly be denied that the federal government is a primary factor in curriculum change.

These purposes have contributed to the development of the junior colleges in Mississippi that are successful and are dedicated to serving every segment of society and committed to improving the quality of life for people in general.

The Mississippi Junior College Association: Planning and Guidance

The title of the organization in the beginning was The Mississippi Junior College Athletic and Literary Association. At a later date, the leaders considered that the word "literary" should be given first place in the title; therefore, the name was changed to read, The Mississippi Junior College Literary and Athletic Association. The membership of this association soon realized that their responsibilities related to a total educational program and that the title indicated limited responsibilities with designated areas. The name was officially changed, and the association was identified as The Mississippi Junior College Association, which is the present title of the organization.

The association began as an organization of the presidents of the public junior colleges in Mississippi, and the membership was open to the presidents of all junior colleges in the state. The early printed material stated, "Any junior college within the State of Mississippi, whether tax supported, denominationally supported, parochial, privately owned or corporately owned and controlled, is eligible to membership upon vote of the membership of the organization." This statement has been printed in the published handbook since the beginning. The active membership has related, to a large degree, to the presidents of the public junior colleges. The influence and action of this voluntary organization has been the dominant force in the operation of the Mississippi state system of junior colleges.

The first printed materials available provided regulations for contests among the new junior colleges. A typed copy identifying these regulations is included in the first minutes on file in the Junior College Division

Office. This original copy is not dated, but circumstances seemed to date it about 1928. The first printed and revised handbook on file is dated 1931–1932. Each year since this date a revised handbook has been published.

The association functions under the leadership of elected officers. These officers, in the beginning, included a president, vice president, secretary treasurer, and commissioner. The central junior college office in the state department of education was operated under the supervision of a person appointed by the state superintendent of education and was officially identified as the Supervisor of Agricultural High Schools and Junior Colleges. The Mississippi Junior College Athletic and Literary Association used the title of Commissioner from the beginning, and all handbooks to the present time have used this title. This title was probably accepted by the association because of the significant amount of time given to competitive activities. Also, during the early years in the operation of the association the election by the membership of a secretary-treasurer was deleted, and the commissioner was designated as the secretary-treasurer of the association.

The list of officers also included an executive committee. Three presidents were elected to serve as members of the executive committee. These were the president, vice president, and secretary-treasurer. When the commissioner was assigned the duties as secretary-treasurer, those designated to membership on the executive committee included the president, vice president, and one member elected by the association.

This association was related in its activities to the following supervisors in the state department of education:

Claude Bennett	1923–1928
Knox Broom	1928–1932
Kirby P. Walker	1932–1933
R. L. Anderson	1933–1935
J. A. Travis	1935–1936
Knox Broom	1936–1944
J. C. Windham	1944–1946
B. L. Hill	1946–1968
F. M. Fortenberry	1968–1970
George V. Moody	1970–

The junior college presidents, with the leadership of these supervisors through this organization, assumed a major role in the expansion and achievement of the junior colleges. This association continues its contribution to the Mississippi state system of junior colleges.

During the early years, the membership of the association, at the regular meetings and called meetings, gave much of their time to competitive athletics and other activities involving contests, which included band, choral, speaking, drama, literary, and student organizations. The minutes of the association, through the years, show that interest in these areas has been a part of the discussion and deliberation at each meeting.

Many other conditions and circumstances related to the needs of the institution for expansion and attainment were of great concern and required much effort and the best judgment of the college presidents.

The presidents, from the beginning, were in agreement that if the needs of the public junior colleges were met the united effort of the presidents, through the association, was necessary in interpreting these needs and presenting them in the proper places. The responsibilities of this association were not delegated, but by agreement each president accepted the responsibility for cooperating and promoting the programs and policies approved by the association. This has given great strength to the work of the association.

Attention was given to a number of things that were important to these new colleges. The interpretation of the early laws that had been passed was necessary, and the relationship of the Junior College Commission was very important to the state system. It was pleasing to the junior college presidents that the membership of the commission included three of their number elected by the association. The participation of junior college presidents as members of the commission has not changed during the fifty-year period.

Special attention was given by the members of the association during the early years in providing information to senior colleges and universities regarding the quality of the academic program. The membership of the association also recognized in the early years the importance of informing members of the legislature of the contributions and needs of the public junior colleges. This responsibility was accepted as a personal obligation of each president to support and promote the association's recommendations. They were committed to work as a unit and did not present individual requests unless approved by the association. The presidents of these institutions were aware during the first two decades that the junior colleges were not meeting fully the intent and purpose of the basic law. They were concerned about needs in the local districts supporting the college which were not being met. Many of the needs could not be met during the early years because of limited financial support from both the state and the local districts. However, the minutes show that these needs were a part of the thinking and discussions during the meetings. Topics for discussion included the philosophy of the Mississippi public junior colleges. Special emphasis talks were given by junior college presidents and other leaders regarding the expansion of the programs to meet needs. These early discussions included terminal education, which was the beginning of the comprehensive development in the technical and vocational job opportunity program and continuing programs for adults.

Conferences were planned for faculty improvement, curriculum reorganization, improvement of instruction, terminal, technical and vocational programs, the need for general education courses, and guidance. These early efforts and concerns were the beginning of the developments which resulted in the present comprehensive public junior college program in Mississippi. The activities of the Mississippi Junior College Association in developing programs to meet the needs of returning veterans was of great value, and surplus buildings and equipment brought about expansion in programs and facilities.

The maturity of the public junior colleges was evident at the beginning of the third decade, and the need for these institutions as a part of Mississippi's program of higher education was accepted on the state and local levels. Support increased rapidly, and state organizations, professional leaders, and industrial leaders gave their support to the programs being developed in the junior colleges.

The leaders of the junior colleges were involved in many areas of development during the last two decades of the first half century. These curricular changes included many additions. The much needed expansion in buildings and equipment, new branches and centers, were approved and developed in various districts.

The following statement from R. D. McLendon, retired president of Northwest Mississippi Junior College, who spent more than thirty years as the administrative head of two Mississippi public junior colleges, indicates the major role of the Mississippi Association of Junior Colleges in the development of these institutions:

The expression "Birds of a feather flock together," fittingly connotes the Mississippi public junior colleges.

In the life and development of every organization one usually is able to identify one event or contact that has wielded a major role in its development. This important event or contact in the Mississippi junior colleges was realized by the establishment of the Mississippi Junior College Association.

The junior college, born to meet the need of bringing higher education to the masses, nurtured in poverty, promoted by dedicated and able leaders, found themselves espousing a common cause—thus brought together eventually as an organization which was first called the Mississippi Junior College Athletic and Literary Association, then later changed to the Mississippi Junior College Literary and Athletic Association, and finally was called the Mississippi Association of Junior Colleges.

The infant institutions, desiring to bring their program and plight to the attention of the public, first entered into athletic competition. This outlet immediately gained favor with both the student body and the public. However, the dedicated leaders of the junior college movement realized that in order for the junior colleges to be received and accepted as higher institutions of learning, academic excellence must be established and accepted by the universities and colleges of that day. In order to realize this goal, the junior colleges exercised strong leadership in the organization of the Mississippi Junior and Senior College Association. This body, composed of both public and private junior and senior colleges and universities, dedicated themselves to the proposition of bringing a better understanding by discussing and establishing guide lines for accreditation and transfer of credits along with standards of excellence to be maintained. This organization continues to operate as a guiding force for all higher education in Mississippi.

The Junior College Association realized early that some organized body with legal status should be established. With this objective in mind the association sponsored legislation that created the Junior College Commission. This body is composed of broad representatives from both professional and lay groups and has power to establish standards, set guide lines for establishing new colleges, approve courses of study, and serve as a cohesive force to hold the public junior colleges together as a unified body.

Perhaps the greatest strength of the association has been realized through the acceptance that its strength was in unity. From 1922–1972 the association has ever been striving to gain acceptance as a part of higher education and to sell the legislature the philosophy that education of all citizens in public institutions was a responsibility of the state.

During the life of the association, every legislative program has had unanimous support of every member. No one school has ever presented an individual program, but all the junior colleges, working together, present a state-wide program. To this end unity has prevailed and today all appropriations are made by the legislature to the junior colleges for both operating and capital budgets—these assuring uniform support from the state level for every junior college.

The Mississippi Junior College Association has been the voice of the junior college in local, state, and national affairs. The leadership exercised by this body has been dominant in: establishing a state system of junior colleges, developing quality standards for education, junior college districts, developing vocational-technical education, creating a department of junior colleges within the department of education, bringing order and dignity to racial integration, improving quality of education, selling junior colleges to the legislature and public, creating the junior college commission, expanding plant and physical facilities, establishing an athletic conference, and developing a quality educational program that has brought opportunities for higher education to thousands of young people.

Today the Mississippi Junior College Association is proud to find leaders in government, education, industry, and community life whose training for leadership would never have been realized had it not been for the Mississippi junior colleges.

The development of a junior college division in the state department of education was helpful to the activities of the association. Administrative, faculty, and student organizations were developed under the leadership of the association. These organizations included coaches, registrars, deans, guidance, business officers, student associations, student publications, and faculty groups.

The united efforts of the presidents, through the Mississippi Junior College Association, have been the dominant factor in developing the Mississippi state system of public junior colleges to the level that eighty-one of the eighty-two counties are giving support to the junior college program.

The association has much satisfaction in the accomplishment of Mississippi's state system of junior colleges as reflected in each individual institution. The percentage of high school graduates who enter college and begin their college work in the junior colleges has increased through the years. The goal of the junior colleges was to reach seven out of ten of these graduates who enter college.

The development that has taken place in physical plants and equipment is a result of the united effort of the members of the association. The association, through its efforts, has maintained certain conditions and characteristics that have proven to be of great value to the Mississippi state system. These include state and local support, low cost, a comprehensive program, the local board of trustees, the determination to remain two-year programs and not seek senior college status, a deep concern for the needs of the students with the purpose to maintain a flexibility to make necessary changes to meet the need of students and to meet the needs of the district.

Junior College Commission: Direction and Control

The Commission on Junior Colleges, as created under Senate Bill 131, Laws of 1928, established its authority and control of the Mississippi state system of public junior colleges. Section 311 of this bill states:

> All junior colleges seeking to qualify under this Act shall be under the control of a state commission, known as the Commission of Junior Colleges, which shall consist of the State Superintendent of Public Education, Chairman, the heads of the University of Mississippi, the Agricultural and Mechanical College, the Mississippi State College for Women, and the heads of three junior colleges, to be selected by the heads of the junior colleges of the state.[1]

After passage of Senate Bill 131, the Commission held its first meeting on May 10, 1928, two calendar weeks after its legislative creation. This first action identified the authority of the Mississippi Commission of Junior Colleges. At a meeting of the Junior College Legalized Commission on May 10, 1928, the following action was taken:

> After some preliminary discussion, a motion was made by Dr. Walker, and seconded by Mr. Vandiver, that the present Junior College Accrediting Commission of the senior colleges be accepted as the standardizing agency as far as quality of work is concerned, and that said junior college accrediting commission make an annual report to the commission created by law, the same to be accepted as far as quality of work is concerned in disbursing state aid. Motion prevailed that the following public junior colleges be recognized for two years: Pearl River, Harrison-Stone-Jackson, Hinds, and Sunflower; and that Tate and Holmes be recognized for one year colleges.

1. Laws of 1928, Regular Session, Senate Bill 131, Chapter 303, p. 83.

Motion prevailed that at least two members of the standardizing and accrediting commission be requested to visit Jones, Kemper, Leake, and Simpson and make report to legalized commission as soon as possible. The legalized commission is further directed to advise the respective authorities in the above named institutions what shall be necessary for them to do in order to qualify as public junior colleges. It is ordered that the secretary of the legalized commission shall accompany these members of the accrediting commission.

A motion was made, and carried, requiring agricultural high schools desiring to do junior college work to make application to the junior college accrediting commission, who shall designate two members of its body and the supervisor of the agricultural high schools to visit and report to the legalized commission before any junior college work shall be undertaken.[2]

As viewed in retrospect, it appears impossible to presume that either of the seven official participants, or the designated secretary, could imagine the significance of the historical record they initiated on that tenth day of May 1928. The historical fact is that at the meeting of May 10, 1928 the Commission of Junior Colleges constituted the birth of the Mississippi State System of Public Junior Colleges, following its conception, with passage of Senate Bill 131, Laws of 1928, approved April 26, 1928.[3]

A significant action of this commission, immediately following its establishment, was to make careful study of the needs of the state and to develop districts within the state system that could support the junior colleges that have been developed. This commission prevented a mushroom growth of weak institutions. Its judgment in 1928, as to the location of the junior colleges, has proved to be sounder than that of most individuals and commissions. It took into consideration population, taxable wealth, development of elementary and secondary schools, the interest of the people in junior colleges, and transportation facilities, when it located the several schools. This commission turned over to an extralegal commission responsibility for accreditation. This latter commission set up standards that had to be met before the legal commission would recognize it as a junior college. Only three of the junior colleges that have been in operation the minimum time have failed to be accredited by the Southern Association of Colleges

and Secondary Schools. The work of all of them is recognized by the four-year colleges of the state and area.

Action was taken regarding financial support at a meeting of the Junior College Legalized Commission on June 29, 1928. On motion by S. L. Stringer, seconded by J. S. Vandiver, the commission went on record as favoring the proposition of giving all the agricultural high school-junior colleges a share of the state appropriation for the session 1927–1928.[4] After session 1927–1928 a junior college, in order to participate in state appropriation, must be accepted by the Junior College Accrediting Commission and approved by the Junior College Legalized Commission, as created by statute.

In 1928, when the first appropriation of $85,000 was made for public junior colleges, all state appropriations for education were made for the fiscal biennium beginning October 1, of the then current school session. Therefore, the allocations referred to in Stringer's and Vandiver's motion were for the session 1927–1928. The result was an "in arrears" appropriation and allocation for an academic year which began in September 1927, and was practically completed when the appropriation was made. This fiscal system of the state also resulted in the receipt of funds on a retroactive basis, beginning approximately eight months prior to the establishment of the Junior College Commission and the first appropriation.

Legislative action through the years has defined more clearly the authority and control of the Mississippi Junior College Commission. House Bill No. 541, Chapter 369, Laws of 1950, passed at the regular session, defined in greater detail the powers and duties of the Junior College Commission, as follows:

SECTION 2.

There is hereby created the Junior College Commission consisting of seven members; namely, the State Superintendent of Education, chairman, and the chancellor of the University of Mississippi, the president of Mississippi State College, Mississippi State College for Women, and of three junior colleges as defined in this act, the latter three to be selected by the presidents of the junior colleges of the state.

The Junior College Commission shall regulate the establishment and operation of junior colleges in the state and shall particularly have the following powers and duties:

(1) To make studies of the needs of the state and communities for junior college education.

(2) To divide the state into districts within which junior

2. Junior College Commission Minutes, May 10, 1928, Book One, Director's Office.

3. Junior College Commission Minutes, May 10, 1928, Book One, Director's Office.

4. Junior College Legalized Commission Minutes, June 29, 1928.

colleges may hereafter be established and fix the territorial boundaries thereof taking into consideration population, property valuation, transportation facilities, the proximity of other colleges, and other factors which contribute to a sound program of education for the state; and to designate the location of a junior college or colleges within the district.

(3) To fix standards for junior colleges to qualify for junior college appropriations, with respect to training of teachers and administrators, physical plant and equipment, administrative organization, curriculum, income per student from local tax sources, enrollment, admission requirements, general tone of the institution, and other factors that relate to the support and administration of junior colleges.

(4) To certify annually to the State Board of Educatiton or other organization, board, agency or administration designated by law to disburse appropriations for junior colleges, the names of such junior colleges which are eligible for such funds.

The Commission shall serve without compensation, but the necessary expenses of the Commission shall be paid out of junior college funds.

SECTION 3.

All junior college districts heretofore formed and presently being taxed, and junior colleges established and in operation at the time of the passage of this act under the provisions of law then in effect, are hereby confirmed and validated. Hereafter, junior colleges may be established only within the territorial boundaries of, and at locations in, districts designated by the Junior College Commission. The Commission, at the time when it shall first hereafter make certificate under sub-section (4) of Section 2 hereof, shall certify to the State Board of Education the territorial boundaries of all junior college districts hereby validated; and annually thereafter it shall so certify the territorial boundaries of any additional districts formed and additional territory added to any existing district.

SECTION 4.

Subject to the provisions of this act, junior colleges may hereafter be established by one or more counties or by one of counties and municipal separate school districts within the territorial limits of an area which has been designated by the Junior College Commission as a junior college district by proceeding as follows:

The school board of a county within a junior college district, desiring to establish a junior college therein, shall adopt a resolution to that effect, duly spread on the minutes of the board, and furnish a certified copy of same to the board of supervisors of the county. If the board of supervisors of the county shall approve the resolution of the school board to establish a junior college, such approval shall be spread on the minutes of the board of supervisors. Thereafter the county school board and the board of supervisors of the county shall jointly petition the Junior College Commission for the approval of the establishment of a junior college and to determine the location thereof. Such petititon shall be submitted on forms approved by said Commission

and shall contain such information as may be required by the Commission, including a statement of the proposed plan of operation in accordance with standards promulgated by said Commission. The Junior College Commission shall approve or disapprove the petition and shall notify the petitioners accordingly. Notification of approval shall include the designation of the location of the junior college. Upon the approval by the Junior College Commission of the petition to establish and operate a junior college, the board of supervisors of the county shall declare its intention to make a levy for the purpose of the establishing and a levy for the support of the proposed junior college, and the levy or levies shall be made upon the taxable property of the entire county, unless a majority of the qualified electors in the county vote against the proposition in an election called by the board of supervisors to determine the matter on petition therefor signed by twenty per cent of the qualified electors of such county.

In the event that two or more counties within a junior college district desire to join in the establishment of a junior college therein the school boards and the boards of supervisors of the co-operating counties shall join in the petition to the Junior College Commission, and the requirements of the preceding paragraph shall apply to each of the participating counties.

The board of trustees of a municipal separate school district within a junior college district, desiring to establish a junior college therein, shall adopt a resolution to that effect duly spread upon the minutes of the board of aldermen or commissioners of the municipality constituting or lying within the separate school district. If the mayor and board of aldermen or commissioners approve the resolution of the board of trustees to establish a junior college, such approval shall be spread on the minutes of the mayor and aldermen or commissioners. Thereafter, the board of trustees and the mayor and aldermen or commissioners shall jointly petition the Junior College Commission for the approval of the establishment of a junior college and to determine the location thereof. Such petition shall be submitted and shall be acted on in the same manner as a petition submitted by a county. Upon the approval by the Junior College Commission of the petition, the mayor and board of aldermen or commissioners of such municipality shall declare its intention to make a levy for the purpose of the establishing and a levy for the support of the proposed junior college, and the levy or levies shall be made upon the taxable property of the entire school district, including added territory, unless a majority of the qualified electors in such school district and added territory shall vote against the proposition in an election called by the mayor and aldermen or commissioners to determine the matter on petition therefor signed by twenty per cent of the qualified electors of such school district and added territory.

In any case, the petition for an election shall be filed with the board of supervisors or with the mayor and aldermen or commissioners within thirty days after publication by them one time in a newspaper published in the county or municipality, or having a general circulation therein, of the proposal to levy the taxes for the establishment and operation of the junior college.

In the event that a municipal separate school district and a county or counties should desire to join in the establishment of a junior college the procedure prescribed above shall apply to the municipal separate school district and each county concerned.[5]

Further changes in membership and powers were included in House Bill No. 428, Regular Legislative Session, 1962.

Excerpts from minutes through the years identify the control and authority of the Commission on the Mississippi state system of public junior colleges. The facts recited in the May 1 and May 16, 1931, meetings, regarding standards, as well as previous meetings dealing with standards, indicated that the Junior College Commission created as a legal commission by the 1928 legislature, was serious in setting and holding to standards.

The firm decisions of the Commission indicated emphatically that Mississippi was to have a system of junior colleges. Such firm action eliminated further requests for additional junior colleges and, with the final approval of Southwest, brought to a total of eleven the public junior colleges, until the Meridian Municipal Junior College in 1937.

The hard stand in holding the standards, thereby preventing numerous additional junior colleges, resulted in a well written article by S. L. Stringer, President of Pearl River Junior College and a member of the Commission. Mr. Stringer's article was entitled, "Junior College Birth Control in Mississippi" and received national recognition, being frequently quoted in junior college literature.

The authority and control of state aid to public junior colleges is shown by the following action of the Commission on July 14, 1931:

On Motion by J. S. Vandiver, seconded by J. N. Powers, that state aid be allowed "Pike County Junior College," provided they secure an equivalent of one-half mill tax levy from Walthall County and provided they secure an equivalent of tuition on the pro rata per capita basis from Amite County, thus making approximately $20,000,000 property valuation, carried unanimously.[6]

An illustration of action of the Commission on Junior Colleges was regarding recommendations of the Mississippi Junior College Association. This association, representing the presidents of each institu-

tion, has been a strong force in the development of the Mississippi state system of junior colleges. All recommendations of this association to the Mississippi Junior College Commission received careful consideration by the members of the Commission at the regular meeting of the Mississippi Junior College Commission on April 17, 1944. The junior college presidents, as members of the Mississippi Junior College Association, in accordance with action taken on March 17, 1944, presented a statewide plan for general shops, specific trade training, and rehabilitation training in the public junior colleges.

Meeting in the state superintendent's office on Saturday, April 17, 1948, at 10:00 A.M., members who were present were: J. M. Tubb, Chairman, Dr. Fred T. Mitchell, Dr. J. D. Williams, J. M. Ewing, Dr. L. O. Todd, and A. L. May. Minutes of the previous meeting were read and approved.

Mr. Tubb asked Dr. Todd to give a brief on the Mississippi System of Junior Colleges. (Dr. Todd had recently completed a study included in his dissertation as part of the requirement for his Ph.D. from Peabody.)

Dr. Todd stated that in his study of the Mississippi public junior colleges he had found that Mississippi had developed the best system in the United States. He included parts of the historical background of Mississippi junior colleges.

Mr. Ewing explained the set-up and functions of the Junior College Accrediting Commission and the delegation of powers to it by the Junior College Commission.

There was discussion relative to the two new junior colleges to open in September: Northeast and Itawamba.

Dr. J. D. Williams and A. L. May moved that the Bureau of Educational Research and Services, University of Mississippi, make a study of tax resources, distributions, et cetera, pertaining to junior colleges.

An illustration of control of counties within zones and establishing a municipal junior college were recorded at a meeting of the Junior College Legalized Commission on October 28, 1937, by Knox M. Broom, Secretary of the Commission and Supervisor of Junior Colleges. He stated that most favorable comments were made (regional and national) regarding laws authorizing a junior college commission for development and control of junior colleges. In Secretary Broom's investigation, Mississippi was the only

5. Laws of Mississippi, 1950, Regular Legislative Session, House Bill 541, Chapter 369, pp. 421–428.
6. Junior College Legalized Commission Minutes, July 14, 1931.

one of the thirty-four states legalizing junior colleges, making provision by law, for a state commission for control and development of public junior colleges. The Junior College Accrediting Commission aided materially in the success of Mississippi's junior colleges. When junior colleges were legalized, twenty-five or thirty communities were enthusiastically clamoring for a junior college. To avoid mistakes of other states, a definite plan for location and organization was necessary. Secretary Broom, under instructions from the Commission, was privileged to work out definite criteria for location and organization, including zoning the state. These criteria regarding zone, standards, and organization, had been submitted (by Broom) to and approved by the Commission on April 12, 1929, same being contained in Bulletin No. 58, State Department of Education.

Results of the above procedure make Mississippi's program unique in the following respects:

1. Started with a plan.
2. The plan was followed.
3. No institution so approved has been discontinued, and the enrollment has increased in ten years, from 547 in 1927–1928 to 3,102 in 1936–1937 session.

Of the twelve zones set up by the 1929 plan, eleven had been developed with a plant valuation of $2,777,535, each of the eleven approved by the Mississippi Junior College Accrediting Commission and six of the eleven accredited by the Southern Association of Colleges and Secondary Schools.

A study covering five years, comparing junior college transfers with students doing all four years in the senior colleges and the University, shows no significant difference in grades during the last two years.

During 1936–1937, thirty-one counties levied tax for general support with three additional or thirty-four for 1937–1938. Students were enrolled from eighty of the eighty-two counties in the 1936–1937 session. The average cost to the student was $147.23 per session, including room, board, and fees, with an average cost for room and board of $121.87, or $13.43 per month.

The high school enrollment in the agricultural high school-junior colleges during 1936–1937 was 1,980, making a total enrollment in the eleven junior colleges of 4,992 students. The per capita cost for general operation (less auxiliary agencies) for high school and junior college combined was $89.29 per student. The per capita investment was $547.37 per student. The average family income of Junior College National

Youth Administration students was approximately $800, whereas for senior colleges the comparable figure was $1,300.

The recorded action of the Junior College Commission during the last two decades has provided direction and leadership for each junior college in the Mississippi state system. The result is that the growth in curricula, facilities, and equipment, local and state support, and district development are providing a comprehensive program meeting the total needs of students and adults within each district by equipping them academically and technically for meeting professional, industrial, and community needs.

The Mississippi Junior College Commission has broad statutory powers and authority. However, the Commission has used these powers and authority in such a way that the growth and development of the institutions within the Mississippi state system have been permitted to grow and develop within each district and to operate with sufficient flexibility to meet the needs of each particular district.

The Commission has permitted two groups to function with sufficient freedom to enable them to contribute effectively to the total program. The above statement refers to the Mississippi Junior College Association, which operates without legal authority, and to the district board of trustees.

Since the first comprehensive junior college laws of 1928, as rewritten in 1950, the Junior College Commission had been composed of State Superintendent of Education, Chairman; Chancellor, University of Mississippi; President, Mississippi State University; President, Mississippi State College for Women; and three junior college presidents selected by the Junior College Association.

With the passage of House Bill 428, Regular Legislative Session 1962, several major changes were made:

(1) Retain the original seven members and add three, appointed by the governor, with advice and consent of Senate, one from each of the three Supreme Court Districts, for six years, with one to be named every two years.
(2) The appointees "shall be of demonstrated industrial leadership."
(3) Meeting at least once each quarter and on call by chairman or by six members; six members made a quorum.
(4) Particular emphasis on vocational and vocational-technical education.

HOUSE BILL NO 428
REGULAR LEGISLATIVE SESSION, 1962

AN ACT TO CREATE A JUNIOR COLLEGE COMMISSION;
TO PRESCRIBE ITS POWERS AND DUTIES; TO REPEAL
SECTION 6475–02 OF THE MISSISSIPPI CODE OF 1942,
RECOMPILED; AND FOR OTHER RELATED PURPOSES.

BE IT ENACTED BY THE LEGISLATURE
OF THE STATE OF MISSISSIPPI:

SECTION 1. There is hereby created a Junior College Commission, consisting of ten (10) members; namely, the State Superintendent of Education, Chairman, the Chancellor of the University of Mississippi, the President of Mississippi State University, the President of Mississippi State College for Women, and three (3) junior college presidents who shall be named by the Junior College Administration, for terms of one, two (2) and (3) years, respectively; thereafter for three year terms. Three (3) lay members shall be appointed by the governor, with the advice and consent of the senate; one member shall be appointed from each of the three (3) supreme court districts, the initial appointments to be for two (2) four (4) and six (6) years, respectively; thereafter, for six-year terms.

In case of a vacancy on the commission for any reason, the commission by majority vote shall fill the unexpired term.

The Junior College Commission, as constituted at the effective date of this act shall continue to exercise all of the functions of said commission until such time as the reconstituted Junior College Commission provided for herein shall have been appointed and organized.

SECTION 2. The members appointed to this commission shall be qualified electors residing in the district from which each is appointed and of the highest order of intelligence, character, and learning for the performance of duties of said office. These men shall be of demonstrated industrial leadership. No person shall be appointed to the Junior College Commission who is, at the time of said appointment, an employee of or a member of the board of trustees of any school or junior college of this state.

SECTION 3. Within ten (10) days after the beginning of the term of office of said members, upon call by the chairman, the commission will meet in Jackson, Mississippi, and proceed to adopt bylaws and regulations for transaction of business.

The members of said commission shall serve without salary, but shall receive a per diem allowance of fifteen dollars ($15.00) per day for time actually spent in the performance of the duties of the commission, together with actual travel and subsistence expenses incurred in attendance upon meetings of the commission and in the discharge of the duties prescribed by the commission.

The commission shall meet at least once each quarter. Special meetings may be called by the chairman, or by any six (6) members of the commission. In any case the call shall be in writing and shall be mailed to each member of the commission at least five (5) days prior to the meeting date. Any six (6) members of the commission shall constitute a quorum to transact business.

SECTION 4. The Junior College Commission shall regulate the establishment and operation of the junior colleges in the state, and shall particularly have the following powers and duties:

(1) To make studies of the needs of the state and communities for junior college education, especially in the field of vocational-technical education. In the light of these studies, the commission shall delegate vocational and vocational-technical functions to the various junior colleges of the state, based on needs as established by these studies, and recommend to the state board of education the allocation of funds to finance these programs.

(2) To divide into districts within which junior colleges may hereafter be established and fix the territorial valuation, boundaries thereof, taking into consideration population, property valuation, transportation facilities, the proximity of other colleges, and other factors which contribute to a sound program of education for the state; and to designate the location of a junior college or colleges within the district. Provided, however, that when the territorial boundaries of a district are fixed, the fixing of said boundaries shall not be construed as to deny admission to any student desiring to enroll in any junior college where the student is living or residing outside the territorial boundaries of the district of the junior college in which said student desires to enroll.

(3) To fix standards for junior colleges to qualify for junior college appropriations, with respect to training of teachers and administrators, physical plant and equipment, administrative organization, curriculum, income per student from local tax sources, enrollment, admission requirements, general tone of the institution, and other factors that relate to the support and administration of junior colleges.

(4) To certify annually to the state board of education or other organization, board, agency, or administration designated by law to disburse appropriations for junior colleges, the name of such junior colleges which are eligible for such funds.

(5) To require the junior colleges to supply such information as the commission may request and to compile, publish and make available to the legislature and other interested parties such reports based thereon as the commission may deem advisable.

SECTION 5. Specialized programs in vocational and vocational-technical education which are not available to students in their home districts, but which are offered in other districts, shall be available to such students on a non-out-of-district fee basis.

SECTION 6. The state superintendent of education shall appoint, with the approval of the state board of education, a specialist in the field of vocational and vocational-technical education in the junior college supervisor's office, to assist the junior colleges in making studies and developing course content in the vocational and vocational-technical programs of the junior colleges.

SECTION 7. Section 2, Chapter 369, laws of 1950, appearing as section 6475-02, Mississippi Code of 1942, Recompiled, and all other laws or parts of laws in conflict herewith be and the same are hereby repealed.

SECTION 8. This act shall take effect and be in force from and after its passage.

Accreditation of Junior Colleges in Mississippi

The State Association of Mississippi Colleges was established about 1920. The earliest minutes available are dated May 5, 1921. The minutes of this meeting refer to an earlier meeting at which time a State Accrediting Committee had been appointed.

The passage of legislation in 1922 at the regular session of the Mississippi legislature, and approved on March 24, 1922, authorized the extension of the curriculum in agricultural high schools and in certain municipalities to include freshman and sophomore college work.

The Association of Mississippi Colleges immediately established a Commission on Junior Colleges at its meeting in December 1922 and adopted standards. A nonlegal body approved by the Mississippi Association of Colleges has accredited junior and senior colleges in Mississippi since 1922. The following was used by the accrediting commission for biennial reports from the colleges.

STATE ASSOCIATION OF MISSISSIPPI COLLEGES

COMMISSION ON JUNIOR COLLEGES

Professor M. Latimer, Chairman, Mississippi College, Clinton, Miss.

Professor G. L. Harrell, Secretary, Millsaps College, Jackson, Miss.

Professor Lena Vaughn, Mississippi State College for Women, Columbus, Miss.

Professor F. J. Weddell, A. & M. College, Agricultural College, Miss.

Professor O. A. Shaw, University, University, Miss.

The purpose of this blank is to collect information concerning Junior Colleges for the use of the Commission, and through them for the six schools represented by the Commission. It presents, first, the standards adopted by the State Association of Mississippi Colleges in December, 1922; second, any definition that may make these standards clearer; third, questions on the matter involved.

The creation of the commission was due to the demand from the Senior Colleges for more exact information about the work being done in the other Colleges of the State to the end that the graduates of those schools may be given fair and uniform recognition when they apply for admission to the standardized institutions. This demand cannot be met without full information of the type called for in this blank.

There is no other standard for Junior Colleges recognized in the State, but if standards should be adopted by the Southern Association of Schools and Colleges that materially differ from these, then it will be necessary for this Association to conform to those standards adopted by the Southern Association.

The Commission cannot limit itself to the information asked, since one blank cannot cover all cases. It will secure additional information by inquiry, or by inspection.

This blank, when filled out, should be returned to the Chairman or Secretary of the Commission. A complete copy should be retained by the School.

Proper attention to this blank is exceedingly important, and the duty should be intrusted only to an experienced Administrator. Use separate sheets where space renders it necessary, noting the fact.

Admission to advanced standing in the Senior Colleges without examination after session 1924-25 will be limited to graduates of those schools favorably passed upon by this Commission. No advanced standing will be given to students from schools organized since 1920 unless the school has been passed favorably by this Commission. Applicants will therefore accompany their application with this blank and such other documents as are necessary.

STANDARDS AND DEFINITIONS

Below we give first, standards as adopted; second, definitions and questions. Clear and definite answers are requested.

Standard Number One. Entrance requirements. The requirement for admission shall be satisfactory completion of a four-year course of not less than fifteen units in a secondary school approved by a recognized accrediting agency. No college maintaining a Preparatory School shall be accredited by this Commission until its Preparatory School has been accredited by the State High School Accrediting Commission. Any Junior College affiliated with recognized senior colleges may be called upon at any time for a record of all students entering the freshman class, such record to contain the name of each student, his secondary school, method of admission units offered in each subject, and total units accepted.

232

MEMBERS OF COMMISSION ON JUNIOR COLLEGES-1922

M. Latimer

G. L. Harrell

Lena Vaughn

F. J. Weddell

O. A. Shaw

233

QUESTIONS: Give number of prescribed units for entrance to Freshman class: English _____, Algebra _____, Geometry _____, History _____, Foreign Language _____. How many vocational units are allowed? _____. How long have these entrance units been in force? _____
What Official administers the entrance requirements? __ How are your records of admission kept? _____
How many units of High School work does your school offer? _____. When pupils ask for advance standing in your high school, what is your method of admission? Please explain fully: _____

_____

Does the work of your Freshman class articulate with your High School? _____

_____

Standard Number Two. Requirements for graduation. The minimum requirement for graduation shall be sixty semester hours of credit.

QUESTIONS: Does your school comply fully with the requirements? Periods per week _____. Length of periods _____. Length of Session _____. How many holidays? _____.
What number of hours in literary work are required for graduation? _____. Do you count music towards graduation? _____. Are students ever graduated on lower requirements than fixed for graduation? _____
When students transfer from other schools, what is minimum residence required in your school for graduation?

Standard Number Three. Degrees. Junior Colleges shall not grant degrees.

QUESTION: What do you call your certificate of graduation?

_____

Standard Number Four. Number of College Departments. The number of separate departments maintained shall be not less than five (English, history, foreign language, mathematics and science), and the number of teachers not less than four. In order that this number of teachers may be maintained in a small school, it is recommended that the head of a Department in a Junior College shall also be head of the same department in the high school if such school is operated in connection with the Junior College. No Junior College shall be credited unless it has a registration of as many as thirty-five students.

QUESTIONS: How many College Departments do you maintain? _____. How many of these departments are presided over by Independent Heads? _____. How many heads of College departments are also heads of departments in high school? _____. Give number of college students for each year for last three years. _____

Standard Number Five. Training of Faculty. The minimum preparation of all instructors in a Junior College shall be a Bachelors Degree from a standard College with either a major or minor requirement completed in the subject taught together with two years of successful teaching in high school or college. Beginning with 1925 at least half of the faculty shall have at least nine months of graduate work.

DEFINITION: The Commission does not recognize honorary degrees as a qualification for teaching. The Commission recognizes that there are many experienced and efficient teachers without degrees and welcome any supplementary information about them.

QUESTION: Give name of all your teachers doing college or combined high school and college work, and the degrees they hold, and from what institution they were obtained. Furnish transcript.

Standard Number Six. Number of class-room hours for teachers. The average number of class-room hours per week, per instructor should not be more than eighteen. More than this number shall be regarded as endangering educational efficiency.

Standard Number Seven. Number of students in classes. The number of students in classes shall not exceed thirty (except for lectures). The number of students in a laboratory section shall not exceed the number for which desk space and equipment have been provided.

Fill In Blank Carefully

SUBJECT Name the Teacher	College Classes per wk.	H. School Classes per wk.	No. in College Classes 1st yr. 2nd yr	No. in H. S. Classes 11th 12th
English				
Math				
History				
Latin				
French				
Biol.				
Physics				
Chem.				
Agri.				
Domestic Science				
Education				
Political Science				
Athletic Coaching				

Standard Number Eight. Support. A Junior College shall have, as a minimum, an income of not less than

$12,500. The annual income should be commensurate with the number of students enrolled and the number of courses offered.

DEFINITION: The Commission construes this minimum income of $12,500 to mean that the whole shall be for support of the College Department alone. In the case of private and denominational schools, the income must be sufficient to take care of all high school work, and have this amount over and above, after having allowed proportionate amounts for upkeep of buildings, library, laboratory, etc. In case of high schools raised to the rank of Junior Colleges, appropriations must be increased by this amount over what they were before the college department was added. Making, however, reasonable adjustments in salary and upkeep expenses.

QUESTIONS: Have you an endowment? _____. What is the debt of your school? _____. What income from your endowment? _____.
From tuition and fees? _____.
From other sources? _____.
State facts about permanency of income, prospective endowment, or allotment of funds _____
_____
_____
_____

If tax supported give assessed valuation from which support comes: _____
Where head of department teaches in high school, how do you adjust his pay from two funds? _____

Standard Number Nine. Library. A working Library of not less than 2,500 volumes, exclusive of public documents, and a reading room in connection with the library shall be maintained. A definite annual income for the support of the library shall be provided.

DEFINITION: The Commission construes this standard as mandatory.
QUESTION: What number of volumes, exclusive of public documents? _____. What percentage of these do you rate as effective? _____. What is the student capacity of your reading room? _____. Size _____×_____.
How many hours per day is your library kept open? _____. Is Librarian paid for her services? _____.
How paid? _____. Annual appropriation for library _____. What number of magazines are taken? _____.
Daily paper? _____. Have you a catalog of your books? _____.

Standard Number Ten. Laboratories. The Laboratories shall be adequately equipped for individual instruction in the course offered, and an annual income for their up-keep provided. It is recommended that a school with a limited income be equipped for good work in one or two sciences and not attempt work in others, and that the amount of equipment be not less than $2000 for classes of twelve.

QUESTIONS: Give original cost of scientific apparatus in school? _____
When was the equipment purchased? _____
How many sciences are you teaching? _____
Annual expenditure for chemical? _____. Biological? _____. Physical? _____.

Standard Number Eleven. Separation of College and Preparatory Classes. Where a Junior College and a high school are maintained together, it is required that the students be taught in separate classes.

DEFINITION: The Commission considers this standard mandatory.
QUESTION: Do you allow High School students in college classes? Do you allow college students in high school classes? If you have not maintained the classes distinct, can you do so? When students are admitted from accredited High Schools, and are unable to maintain themselves, what do you do with them? Explain fully. (Number answers below): _____
_____
_____
_____
_____
_____

Standard Number Twelve. The work of the Junior College shall be organized on a college and not high school basis. This refers to the type of text books used, length of recitation periods, etc.

QUESTIONS: What percentage of your students are pursuing regular courses? _____. Is the classification of students published in the catalog? _____.
Number of students current year _____
Freshmen _____. Sophomores _____. Conditioned _____. Music _____. Art _____. Expression _____. Business _____. Other categories _____

Standard Number Thirteen. General statement concerning material equipment. The location and construction of buildings, the lighting, heating, and ventilation of rooms, the nature of the laboratories, corridors, closets, water supply, school furniture, apparatus, and methods of cleaning shall be such as to insure hygenic conditions for both students and teachers.

QUESTIONS: Number of school buildings? _____.
Number of class rooms? _____. Average student capacity of each? _____. Are hygenic conditions good? _____. Athletic facilities. Have you a gymnasium? _____. Capacity? _____. Field area? _____.

Standard Number Fourteen. General statement concerning curriculum and spirit of administration. The character of the curriculum, efficiency of instruction, and spirit of the institution shall be factors in determining its standing.

Standard Number Fifteen. Extra curricula activities. Athletics, amusements, and all other extra curricula activities shall be properly administered and shall not occupy an undue place in the life of the college.

QUESTIONS: What regulations have been adopted by the school for athletics? _____

What are the rules for eligibility? _____

How is the scholarship requirement reenforced? _____

How are the athletics controlled? _____

Are all athletics, including football, on a healthy basis?

Are you a member of any athletic association? _____

Have you a well organized literary society? _____

Does your school participate in inter-collegiate debates or other contests of a literary nature? _____.

Standard Number Sixteen. Standing of Graduates. The Junior College must be able to prepare its students so that they may sustain themselves in the Senior recognized college junior classes. In evidence statistics of the records, including high school units, of the graduates of the junior colleges in senior colleges shall be filed with the Commission on Junior Colleges on demand.

QUESTION: Do candidates from your school enter full Junior in any of the standard colleges of the state? _____

_____

Give record of your graduates in these schools over a number of years. _____

_____
_____
_____
_____
_____

Standard Number Seventeen. Inspection. No Junior College shall be accredited until it has been inspected and reported upon by an agent or agents regularly appointed by the commission. At least one member of the committee on inspection shall be qualified to pass upon proper equipment and management of a department in science. Any accredited Junior College shall be open to inspection at any time.

Standard Number Eighteen. Filing of blank. No Institution shall be placed on or retained on the approved list unless a regular information blank has been filed with the Commission. The list shall be approved from year to year by the Commission. The blank shall be filed biennially, but the Commission may, for due cause, call upon any member to file a new report in the meantime. Failure to file blank shall be sufficient cause for dropping an Institution.

The influence of state accrediting upon the development of junior colleges in Mississippi was very great. The term "academic respectability" was used many times in referring to the development of junior colleges in Mississippi. This idea of respectability and the effort to meet standards of collegiate education caused the young men and young women to feel certain that they could take the first two years of a program of higher education in the junior colleges in Mississippi, without finding themselves penalized when they transferred to senior institutions. The work of these accrediting agencies also strengthened the position of junior colleges with the state legislature. Members of the Mississippi legislature soon recognized that these junior colleges were providing a sound program of higher education and that they were worthy of the financial support of the state of Mississippi, and it was through this financial support that these junior colleges were able to expand their services to meet the needs of the young men and young women within the state.

A statement of the National Commission on Accrediting accurately describes the experiences in Mississippi:

Accrediting agencies have often been instruments for the maintenance of high educational standards; they have protected a society against inadequately prepared professional practitioners; they have aided licensing authorities and facilitated the transfer of students; they have been helpful to students and parents seeking to identify sound institutions; they have aided institutions in withstanding improper political or other noneducational pressures; and they have stimulated broad consideration of educational problems and issues of more than local concern.

THE SOUTHERN ASSOCIATION OF COLLEGES AND SCHOOLS

Accreditation of institutions of higher learning in Mississippi began when six universities of the South, including the University of Mississippi, created in 1895 an organization which is now known as the Southern Association of Colleges and Schools. Through the years this Association gained in strength and prestige as the unofficial, voluntary regional accrediting agency for the southern region. The standards which were developed for high schools and junior and senior colleges were high and constructive and were instrumental in elevating the quality of education at all levels in Mississippi and in all the South. Since the Association started with six members at a time when there were numerous normals, institutes, colleges, and universities, it was natural for a policy to be followed of looking at well-established and more prosperous institutions with a history of turning out successful graduates as being those schools to be recognized for membership in the Association and thus for accreditation. New institutions had to exist for a time and prove themselves to attain Southern Association recognition. The original policy of accepting white institutions only was continued for many years although quasirecognition was given to certain institutions through the work of a special committee of the Association beginning about 1930. It was not until 1948 that full membership came to two Mississippi colleges for the black people.

THE HIGH SCHOOL ACCREDITING COMMISSION

Because the Mississippi junior colleges grew up from the public schools, more especially the county agricultural high schools, the accreditation mechanisms for the public schools developed practices which affected the colleges.

The accreditation of Mississippi high schools began in 1898 as a result of the work of a committee of the Mississippi Teachers Association which obtained the cooperation of the University of Mississippi in visiting schools and publishing an official list. For twenty years the University continued to send professors to visit schools and to publish the official list until in 1918 a high school accrediting commission was created by the Mississippi Teachers Association. In the following year the state department of education, with a grant of funds from the general education board, assumed responsibility for high school inspection. Accreditation became a joint effort of the department and the Mississippi Education Association, the successor to the Mississippi Teachers Association.

As accreditation standards for the high schools advanced, the academic preparation of the teachers came into review. Existing colleges not members of the Southern Association of Colleges and Schools were accepted as qualified for the training of teachers if they were members of the Mississippi Association of Colleges, or if they were approved by the state department of education for the certification of teachers. In the period from 1920 to 1940, however, many of the leading educators of the state had been trained at the private normal or institute schools which flourished in Mississippi from about 1890 to

1905 but which were all nonexistent following World War I. Records and catalogs of many of these schools were available, and the high school accrediting commission, with the cooperation of the senior colleges of the state, created a committee on defunct institutions which, in 1930, began to assign a one-year or two-year college status to a number of such schools. The first list of schools so recognized included Harperville College, Iuka Normal Institute, Moffett-McLaurin Colleges, and Cooper-Huddleston Institute. Standard two-year junior college rating was extended them. From time to time thirteen other schools were added to the list. Eventually the committee was disbanded as the need for evaluating transcripts of credit from defunct schools diminished.

THE JUNIOR COLLEGE ACCREDITING ASSOCIATION

The demise of the private institute type of junior college left the people with a growing conviction of the need for publicly supported institutions of college grade with practical curriculum commitment. As the move toward the establishment of Mississippi's public junior college program became more certain of success, the existing colleges, public and private, saw an opportunity to provide guidance to the new schools. In 1920 they formed a voluntary statewide organization under the name of the Mississippi Association of Colleges. Shortly thereafter the Association created a Junior College Accrediting Association. The junior colleges in existence at this time and recognized by the Association were:

> Gulf Park College, Gulfport
> Whitworth College, Brookhaven
> Hillman College, Clinton
> All Saints College, Vicksburg
> Grenada College, Grenada
> Synodical College, Holly Springs
> Chickasaw College, Pontotoc

When the Junior College Commission was created by legal enactment in 1928 it voted to refer matters relating to the evaluation of instruction to the Junior College Accrediting Association which thereafter continued as the accrediting body for junior colleges in Mississippi until 1950. This agency was a voluntary organization limiting its services to colleges for white youth.

MISSISSIPPI ASSOCIATION OF COLLEGES

After the creation in 1950 of the Commission on College Accreditation, the Junior College Accrediting Commission was discontinued. All the official bodies as well as the several institutions felt that the independence and professional resources of a voluntary agency in this field should be maintained. Accordingly the Mississippi Association of Colleges in 1950 created a new agency to be known as the Council on Study and Accreditation of Higher Education. The scope was broadened to include all institutions of higher education in the state of Mississippi, both public and private, white and colored, junior and senior; to provide for the existing agencies the professional investigation of colleges needed; to counsel and aid institutions in meeting standards; and to revise standards as needed.

STATE DEPARTMENT OF EDUCATION

Another result of high school accreditation and the growing emphasis on teacher education was the expansion of the duties of the division of certification of the state department of education. Eventually the state department of education began publishing a list of colleges whose graduates could be certified for teaching purposes. Thus a sort of quasiaccreditation status for colleges was established even though the state department of education was not authorized by law to accredit institutions.

COMMISSION ON COLLEGE ACCREDITATION

It is important to review the above circumstances in order to realize the status of accreditation in Mississippi at the close of World War II when the great upsurge in college enrollment began and when the flow of federal funds for higher education began to reach massive proportions. For post-secondary educational institutions in Mississippi in the years prior to 1950 (1) no agency was authorized to certify institutions to federal agencies so that such institutions and their students might participate in federal grants and subsidies; (2) no agency was authorized either officially or by voluntary association to accredit black institutions; (3) no agency was equipped to assist new institutions to live through the pangs of birth by granting permits to operate so as to obtain federal funds and so as to protect student credits; (4) no agency had authority to curb creation of "diploma mills."

It is a matter of great credit to the state legislature and to Rep. James Baxter of Meridian, author of the bill, that a law was enacted which has worked well for twenty-five years and has served with considerable success to deal with the problems of accreditation of institutions of higher education for those expanding years and for the present.

As enacted by the legislature in 1950 the Commission on College Accreditation was created and was composed of the "Supervisor of Junior Colleges in the State Department of Education, the Supervisor of Negro Education in the State Department of Education, the Executive Secretary of the Board of Trustees of State Institutions of Higher Learning, and two additional members, one of whom shall be selected by the foregoing three members and who shall represent the private colleges within the state, and one member to be selected by the Mississippi Association of Colleges." When first organized the membership of the Commission was: E. R. Jobe, Chairman; Dean Purnell Wilson, Secretary; B. L. Hill; P. H. Easom; H. T. Huddleston.

The first order of business of the Commission was to adopt standards and procedures for accrediting junior and senior colleges including all races; to arrange for committees to visit and evaluate institutions; and to publish an official list of accredited postsecondary institutions for Mississippi.

No appropriation to support the work of the Commission was ever requested, and the time and effort expended by members of the Commission and of the numerous visiting evaluating committees was contributed by those officials as a part of their professional duty. Expenses of the visiting committees were paid by the college applying for recognition. A large part of the success of the Commission must be attributed to the Council on College Accreditation and Studies which continued its activity undiminished and which supplied members for the visiting committees.

After more than twenty years of existence it appears evident that the purposes for which the Commission was established have been achieved:

Permits to operate have been provided for colleges being newly organized where circumstances indicated a chance for success.

The awarding of degrees by institutions has been conducted professionally and without abuses.

Colleges have been visited by professionals who have offered stimulation and counsel.

Arrangements have been made to give needed recognition to special purpose institutions such as Bible schools or seminaries.

The usual functions of state accreditation have been extended to all institutions of collegiate grade for new and old, white and black, private and public.

The first published official list of colleges approved by the Commission on College Accreditation follows:

An example of the work of the Commission is the accreditation of Our Lady of the Snows located at Pass Christian. This senior college was established by the Oblate Fathers of the Catholic Church for the education of priests of their special order. It was an upper level institution accepting transfers only from a junior college maintained by the order for the same purpose. Members of the visiting committee repre-

Accredited Institutions of Higher Education
1956–57

The following colleges are accredited by the Southern Association of Colleges and Secondary Schools:

Institution	Control	Address	Type
1. Belhaven	Presbyterian	Jackson	Senior
2. Blue Mountain	Baptist	Blue Mountain	Senior
3. Clarke Memorial	Baptist	Newton	Junior
4. Copiah-Lincoln	Public	Wesson	Junior
5. Delta State	State	Cleveland	Senior
6. East Central	Public	Decatur	Junior
7. East Mississippi	Public	Scooba	Junior
8. Gulf Park	Private	Gulfport	Junior
9. Hinds	Public	Raymond	Junior
10. Holmes	Public	Goodman	Junior
11. Itawamba	Public	Fulton	Junior
12. Jones	Public	Ellisville	Junior
13. Meridian Municipal	Public	Meridian	Junior
14. Millsaps	Methodist	Jackson	Senior
15. Mississippi College	Baptist	Clinton	Senior
16. Mississippi Southern	State	Hattiesburg	Senior
17. Mississippi State	State	Starkville	Senior
18. M. S. C. W.	State	Columbus	Senior
19. Northeast	Public	Booneville	Junior
20. Northwest	Public	Senatobia	Junior
21. Pearl River	Public	Poplarville	Junior
22. Perkinston	Public	Perkinston	Junior
23. Sunflower	Public	Moorhead	Junior
24. University of Mississippi	State	University	Senior
25. Wood	Methodist	Mathiston	Junior

The following colleges are accredited by the Junior College Accrediting Commission and the College Accrediting Commission:

26. Southwest	Public	Summit	Junior
27. William Carey	Baptist	Hattiesburg	Senior

For Negro Students			
Accredited by Southern Association of Colleges and Secondary Schools:			
28. Alcorn A. & M.	State	Lorman	Senior
29. Jackson State	State	Jackson	Senior
30. Rust	Methodist	Holly Springs	Senior
31. Tougaloo	A. M. E.	Tougaloo	Senior
Accredited only by state agencies:			
32. Campbell	C. M. E.*	Jackson	Junior
33. Coahoma	Public	Clarksdale	Junior
34. Mississippi Industrial	C. M. E.*	Holly Springs	Junior
35. Mississippi Vocational	State	Itta Bena	Senior
36. Natchez	Baptist	Natchez	Junior
37. Okolona	Episcopal	Okolona	Junior
38. Piney Woods	Private	Piney Woods	Junior
39. Prentiss Institute	Private	Prentiss	Junior
40. Utica Institute	Public	Utica	Junior
41. Mary Holmes	Presbyterian	West Point	Junior
Applying:			
42. Saints	Church of God	Lexington	Junior
43. Harris	Public	Meridian	Junior
44. Southeastern Baptist	Baptist	Laurel	Junior

*Colored Methodist Episcopal

senting the Commission were of assistance in arranging for better library utilization, in the credit evaluation of courses, and in the recording of credits for possible transfer in the event any of the priests desired to attend a graduate school or seminary for advanced studies. The Committee judged the institution mainly in terms of the stated objectives for which it was created and the achievement observable as to the attainment of the objectives. It was fully accredited and was the first college organized at the upper level of work so recognized and the first special purpose institution in the religious field to be recognized.

As the first fifty years end it appears that a new opportunity for the Commission is presenting itself in reference to the development of branch institutions of college grade, in vocational-technical institutions which may or may not be branches of accredited colleges, and in the proliferation of proprietary postsecondary education programs.

The Mississippi Junior-Senior College Conference: The Cooperative Effort

That the goal of a state educational system is to coordinate all the different types of educational institutions and lift the level of intelligence of all the people gives direction to the work of the Junior-Senior College Conference. The words "coordinate" and "cooperate" are of great importance when one considers the total program of higher education in Mississippi, which includes the Mississippi state system of public junior colleges and other junior colleges and all other institutions of higher learning—the universities and senior colleges.

A review of the contributions made through the

work of the organization, known as the Junior-Senior College Conference, attests that the total program of higher education in Mississippi has been greatly strengthened. Since the first conference, four decades ago, many changes have taken place; and as we are beginning the last quarter of the twentieth century, we are continuing to witness changes that are profound and far reaching in our world, our nation, our state, and in the total program of higher education. These changes make it very difficult for us to understand all the implications.

The total program of higher education in Mississippi has great resources, large scale economics, much diversity and the capacity to meet a great range of eventualities. Yet, we must be aware, as we review the realities of all of the changes that have taken place, that as leaders of the programs of higher education in Mississippi we must be certain that we have a vivid sense of what we are becoming and that we must be oriented to the needs of the future.

The work of the Junior-Senior College Conference is significant for the future. The words "coordination" and "cooperation" will continue to be of great consequence. Our institutions in the future will need many times to be taken apart and then put together again. This is a task of the Junior-Senior College Conference.

A statement by J. D. Williams, Chancellor Emeritus of the University of Mississippi, written at the close of the first fifty years in the operation of the Mississippi Junior-Senior College Conference, gives assurance that the leaders of the senior and junior colleges expressed wisdom and understanding in establishing this conference.

Mississippi has been fortunate in the quality of its educational leadership especially in higher education both junior and senior colleges, public and private. In the early programs—the 1930's—most discussion was on the problem of transferring graduates from the junior colleges to the senior colleges without doing an injustice to the student. During this same early period there were many addresses by state and national educational leaders on the purpose and function of the junior college and its relation to the senior college. What is the responsibility of the state for the support and organization of higher education was a frequent question.

The 1940's was the decade in which increasing attention was given to the somewhat loosely defined subject of "general education." The curriculum became the area of interest. The 1950's provided many annual conference programs heavily weighted with the new and rapidly expanding pro-

grams of the senior colleges and the upgrading of student counseling in both the junior and senior institutions to provide accurate information and professional guidance. It was during this period that the Mississippi Junior-Senior Conference arranged for special group meetings such as presidents and public relations officers, registrars and admissions officers, academic vice-presidents, student affairs officers and business managers.

The 1960's and early 1970's emphasized "Greater Excellence." This included selection and up-grading of faculty personnel and better planning of buildings and campuses. The federal government expanded its support for higher education with the advantages and problems that continue to occupy an inordinate amount of administrators' time. The problems appear on the annual programs with regularity often in terms of "financing," of "due process," and of "equal rights." All three branches of the federal government have been about equally prominent in their impact on higher education—the executive, the legislative and the courts.

In summary, the Mississippi Junior-Senior College Conference has provided an essential forum for the discussion of mutual problems and programs by the leadership of Mississippi's institutions of higher learning—public and private and junior and senior.

The first Mississippi Junior-Senior College Conference was held on the campus of Mississippi State College at Starkville, Mississippi, in November 1934. It marked the beginning of a remarkable series of productive conferences spanning four decades.

This conference was organized during the second decade. The growth and acceptability of the public junior colleges as a distinct phase of higher education in Mississippi had created a zeal to gain "academic respectability." This emphasized the importance of working cooperatively with the universities and colleges on course offerings and transfer of credits. The leaders in the junior colleges and senior colleges were aware of the importance and necessity of good understanding and good will in solving mutual problems.

Dr. G. D. Humphrey, then president of Mississippi State College (later, President, University of Wyoming) whose interest and foresight issued the invitation to the junior college officials to attend this first meeting, contributed much toward bringing about helpful discussions among the colleges. The following statements by Dr. Humphrey indicate the desire of colleges and universities to coordinate the work of all educational institutions of higher learning in Mississippi:

The junior college of Mississippi is here to stay. There are three outstanding educational movements that are typical of

America. They are the land grant college movement, the development of the American high school, and the junior college movement. Mississippi State College realizes the place of these institutions in the educational system of the state and it shall be the purpose of State College to coordinate the work of these institutions, and to cooperate with them in the development of better educational facilities for the boys and girls of Mississippi.

The goal of a state educational system is to coordinate all of the different types of educational institutions and lift the level of intelligence of all the people. The junior college conference is one of the first moves that Mississippi State College will make to bring about the desired goal.

In compliance with an order of the Board of Trustees, the various schools at Mississippi State have set up their courses of study in lower and upper divisions, each consisting of two years of work. Graduates of junior colleges may enter the upper division, making up only those professional subjects in the lower division which are prerequisite to the upper division work. A bulletin is being prepared showing what is prerequisite in each school. Junior college students who intend to come to State will be able to arrange their courses so as to present as many of these prerequisites as possible. In some of the schools, junior college graduates can continue their work with no loss of time.

The cooperation of all institutions of higher learning, including the public universities and senior colleges, the denominational senior college, the private junior and senior colleges, is shown by the following institutions that issued invitations and served as the host college for this conference. The first three institutions to host the conference were public senior colleges:

1. Mississippi State College, Starkville
2. Mississippi State College for Women, Columbus
3. The University of Mississippi, Oxford

The next meeting was on a junior college campus, Copiah-Lincoln Junior College at Wesson. The conference then moved to Mississippi College, a denominational senior college located at Clinton, then met at Jones County Junior College at Ellisville, followed by a senior public college, then to a private junior college at Gulfpark College, Gulfport. Millsaps College in Jackson, a denominational college, was next to host the conference, then it moved again to a public senior college. The pattern set by these first few conferences, which placed meetings on the campuses of all of the varied types of institutions of higher learning in the state, has been followed through the years.

An evaluation of the contribution made in cooperation and coordination of all phases of higher education in Mississippi is expressed in letters and published statements through the years by educational leaders who have participated in the fellowship and discussions at these conferences. The following statements reflect the thinking of educators during the early years of the development of public junior colleges in Mississippi:

Dr. Herbert Drennon, Dean of the Graduate School at Mississippi State College, said:

Out of these Junior-Senior College Conferences a better understanding has developed between the public junior college and the higher institutions of learning in the state. Understanding of one another's common problems and common objectives has induced the growth of a finer spirit of cooperation and friendliness among the institutions belonging to the conference. Mississippi State College is proud of the fact that it pioneered a movement that has done much to strengthen and enrich the educational programs of the junior and senior colleges and to get rid of the spirit of conflict and competition that had existed. At the same time, not only has State College coveted this opportunity to work as neighbors with the leaders in the junior colleges but also it has rejoiced to see all of the senior colleges and the University bending their efforts to bring about a harmony of relationship among all institutions of learning that are devoted to improving the educational status of our people.

We have a common cause to serve. We must train our people vocationally and culturally. We must expend efforts and funds wisely and well in order to enrich the social, economic, political, and cultural life of our citizens. These things can best be done by those of us who are concerned with the problems of public education in Mississippi if we work together in cooperative understanding and strive for our objectives in a spirit of mutual fellowship and cordiality.

President Richard G. Cox of Gulfpark College said:

The relationship between public and private junior colleges in Mississippi is cordial and cooperative. Between the two types of institutions there is no unfriendly rivalry. The favorable national recognition that both have attained has been a source of pride and satisfaction to the executives of all junior colleges in the state.

In the whole junior college movement, variety has been encouraged in functions, curricula, methods, and fields of special emphasis. Each college, whether supported by taxation, endowment, church, or student fees, has had freedom for initiative and experimentation to meet what is conceived to be the needs of its student body. In exceptional cases in other sections of the United States the lack of a fixed pattern for all junior colleges has led to unfortunate extremes. While the curriculum of one has been restricted narrowly to the liberal arts, the offerings of another have been almost exclusively vocational.

The combined, cooperative efforts of all junior colleges, public and private, with all the variations that exist in each group, are necessary if boys and girls of America, who are capable and worthy of education beyond the high school, are to have the training to which they are entitled, and which is suited to their individual needs. This is the goal of junior colleges in Mississippi. This is the basic reason why the executives of these institutions respect each other and work harmoniously together.

Knox M. Broom, a former state supervisor of junior colleges and representative of the U. S. Office of Education stated:

Perhaps the most effective means for articulation of course offerings in the junior colleges with those of the institutions of higher learning was through the annual Junior-Senior College Conference. These conferences were held, alternating in meeting places between institutions of higher learning and junior colleges—both state and proprietary—with the executive heads, deans, and registrars of all colleges attending a two-day session. Within three years conflicts between departments and the problems of transfer credit were resolved. Thereafter, these conferences became highly professional in tone and each host school vied with the others in entertainment and program.

The following includes some statements made at the close of the first fifty years in junior college development in Mississippi. W. Alton Bryant, Vice-Chancellor Emeritus of the University of Mississippi, wrote in a letter the following information as an evaluation of the work of the Junior-Senior College Conferences:

The annual Junior-Senior College Conference brought presidents, deans, registrars, and faculty members of the institutions together for fellowship and discussion. They not only provided a forum for the exchange of ideas and a mechanism for the solution of common problems but also an informal atmosphere which produced lasting friendships and a better understanding between all the institutions. These were forums where all parties were free to speak honestly and frankly, to lay disagreements and grievances on the table for uninhibited comment, and to hammer out the fact that no one institution or group of institutions had all the answers to the problems of higher education in the state or the resources to satisfy all of its educational needs. For example, vigorous debate over a rather long period of time was required to persuade the senior institutions that the junior colleges were meeting important educational needs which the senior colleges were not equipped nor inclined to satisfy. Gradually, however, the role of the junior college with its close ties to a well-defined community, and its unique program designed to prepare some students for the last two years of college, and at the same time to provide others with a more limited academic background but with technical skills which qualified them for immediate employment came to be recognized by all the institutions as both acceptable and indispensable. At this point, terminal education at the junior college level established itself as a fact in Mississippi's system of higher education.

At practically every annual conference there was discussion, sometimes heated, of the highly structured curriculums and the differing degree requirements at the senior colleges. These topics were important to the junior colleges because the requirements varied widely from senior college to senior college and at many points affected the junior college course of study so adversely that in some areas only an unreasonable number of courses of study could satisfy the needs of students who planned to transfer for the last two years of college. This state of affairs made the catalogs of the junior colleges as difficult to read and understand as those of the senior institutions. The senior colleges were interested in discussing the curriculum and degree requirements because they wished to insure that their academic standards and quality were protected.

The problems of transfer from junior to senior college in Mississippi have been considerably reduced, but not completely eliminated. Why did it take so long? Simply because the senior colleges operated on the theory that the faculty determines the curriculum and degree requirements and because individual faculties have different ideas of what a good curriculum ought to be. There is no doubt in my mind that the junior-senior college conferences made a solid contribution to the process of persuading senior faculties to adopt more open and liberal curricula.

The conferences also brought to their participants outstanding educational authorities to discuss new trends and new techniques in education. These visitors enriched the subject matter of the meetings and stimulated discussion of how improvements could be made in the Mississippi system. It is worth noting that the conferences pre-date the impact of the nuclear age, which in direct and more subtle ways changed the teaching of science as well as most other subjects.

The story of the origin and development of the junior college system in Mississippi is a fascinating one. Its solid achievements are admirable and educationally sound, chiefly because it was blessed from its earliest days with perceptive, dedicated, and able leadership. These leaders participated actively in the annual conferences and provided leadership in the planning and the deliberations. With their colleagues in the senior colleges they made the conferences a powerful force in the effective co-ordination of higher education on the under-graduate level in Mississippi.

William D. McCain, President Emeritus of the University of Southern Mississippi, at the close of the first fifty years identifies the contributions made through the annual meeting of the conferences.

Much of the progress made in higher education in Mississippi in recent years can be attributed to a series of annual conferences referred to as the Junior-Senior College Conferences. These conferences have served as an organized effort to bring together administrators and faculty from all colleges of the state. Included as participants in the conferences have been representatives from the junior colleges, senior colleges, and universities of both the public and private sectors of higher education.

Outstanding features of the conferences have included formal presentations, informal discussions, and social functions. The informal discussion sessions have always provided for and encouraged the involvement of all participants. The topics of both the formal and informal sessions have always focused on the immediate concerns of educational leaders in the state. Specifically, the Junior-Senior College Conferences have contributed to higher education in Mississippi by:

1. Providing a means of developing acquaintances and friendships among the leaders of higher education.

2. Providing a means of better communication among the institutions and their personnel.

3. Developing a feeling of partnership in higher education among the institutions.

4. Developing a greater degree of continuity among the academic programs of the various institutions.

5. Providing for better articulation of students from the junior to the senior colleges.

6. Identifying mutual educational problems and possible solutions.

7. Contributing to an understanding of the role and scope of the various institutions.

The following testimonial reflects the thinking of President Emeritus R. A. McLemore of a private denominational senior college, Mississippi College:

The Junior-Senior College Conference developed to meet a need in the educational program of Mississippi. It was President Duke Humphrey of Mississippi State University who perceived the importance of correlating the work of the emerging junior colleges with that of the senior colleges and universities. Humphrey discussed the obvious problems with other educational statesmen and, on their recommendation, extended an invitation to each institution of higher learning to send representatives to a conference to be held at Mississippi State University.

The first Junior-Senior College Conference met in 1934. Its primary purpose was to establish a good working relationship between the junior and senior colleges. It was also expected that the conference would devote a large portion of its time to the exploration of problems common to all higher education.

The most pressing problem in the relationship of junior and senior colleges in the early period was the transfer of students. The junior colleges were interested in their graduates receiving credits that would enable them to complete the degree requirements within an additional two-year period. The senior colleges were interested in the maintenance of a quality program comparable to the one existing on their campuses. They were also concerned about the meeting of prerequisites that had been established for the different degree programs. These prerequisites frequently differed from campus to campus and made it very difficult for junior colleges to meet the requirements of all of the institutions. Over a period of years the conflicts between the institutions on the transfer of credit were gradually worked out and with mutually beneficial results.

The 40-year span following the first meeting of the Junior-Senior College Conference was a revolutionary period in higher education. There were three primary developments that affected all institutions of higher learning. Perhaps the most evident was the tremendous increase in campus population. The enrollment in institutions of higher learning increased at a phenomenal rate and brought with it a number of problems that were unknown in the earlier period. A second and closely related problem was the broadening of the curriculum. The traditional program of higher education was obviously inadequate to meet the needs of the changing student population. The necessity of making modifications, additions, and innovations was evident. The responsibility of the colleges was to find the directions in which they could go. The Junior-Senior College Conference provided the leadership in this field. The third area in which the junior-senior college was primarily interested during the middle of the twentieth century was the innovation in teaching and educational procedures. There probably has never been a period in higher education when new teaching methods were introduced on a more revolutionary scale. Very closely allied to this change was the development of physical plants and provision of laboratory facilities that made possible changes in instructional procedures.

It was the consideration of these major changes in educational philosophy that made the junior-senior college a rich resource for higher education in Mississippi. Perhaps it was through this organization more than any other that a common and acceptable program of enrichment was developed for the entire state. It is quite evident that higher education has been able to move forward with a common philosophy for the mutual benefit of the citizens as well as the enrichment of the program of the institutions of higher learning.

The junior college presidents were aware, through the years, of the great importance of this organization identified as the Junior-Senior College Conference, which provided an opportunity for the discussion of mutual problems and programs by the leadership of Mississippi's institutions of higher learning.

The time and effort required, from the beginning of junior colleges to the end of the first fifty years, for these institutions to mature on a state and national basis and to provide a comprehensive program meeting educational needs of all citizens in the junior college district has focused attention on many concerns related to the universities and colleges as well as to the junior colleges. These conferences have provided educational leaders an opportunity to reach an understanding in all phases of higher education in the state. The expressions and testimonials from college and university officials included in this chapter reflect their thinking and express an understanding which enabled the district public junior colleges to establish and develop a program designed to meet the needs of the youths and adults in each district.

It is evident that all phases of higher education in Mississippi will have many concerns during the next half century. If the total program continues to grow and serve within the framework of revolutionary changes that will be a part of the years ahead, we must say again that the words "coordination" and "cooperation" will continue to be of great consequence. The work of this organization will continue to contribute to progress.

Competitive Athletics: The Spirit Builder

The competitive spirit existed among the public junior colleges at the very outset of the system. A spirit of competition was already pervasive among the fifty-two schools known as agricultural high schools, including such activities as all high school sports, literary subjects, band, oratory, debate, piano, choral quartets, choral solos, and dramatics.

Since a large part of the early enrollment in the junior colleges was made up of graduates of agricultural high schools, quite naturally, these new junior college students brought their competitive spirit with them and easily adapted it to a similar spirit among the junior colleges. It is understandable, therefore, that state championships were awarded in the very beginning.

The eleven original junior colleges, with athletics in a number of sports, were sufficient to establish a state Junior College Conference with each school playing each of the other schools. The Mississippi public junior college teams have, with the exception of bowls, played very few out-of-state teams. The results of bowl games, which included the Junior Rose Bowl at Pasadena, California, and National Championship games under the control of the National Junior College Athletic Association, Hutchinson, Kansas, determined that the Mississippi junior college teams were able to compete equally on a national basis with teams from other states.

The junior college presidents maintain complete control of the various competitive activities. Although the presidents have approved a coaches' association, the coaches present their recommendations to the presidents for approval. All rule changes must be approved by the chief executives of the institutions.

The eligibility of participants in all competitive literary and athletic activities has, from the beginning, been the responsibility of the presidents of the institutions through the Mississippi Junior College Association. The Association publishes an official handbook each year (those from 1931 through 1971 filed with the State Division of Public Junior Colleges). The first handbook, in typed form, which circumstance dates at the 1927–28 school session, set up the organization and was entitled "Regulations Governing the Mississippi Junior College Athletic and Literary Association." The use of *athletic* in the title before *literary* indicated the importance of athletics to the beginning junior colleges. These words were reversed at a later date in the title of the organization. The first printed handbook was for the session 1931–32. Although many changes have been recorded in these handbooks through the years, the opening statement concerning eligibility has remained the same.

Each and every participant must have a clean, moral record such that the member school could trust at home and abroad. No student can participate in any event or contest unless he or she is a *bona fide* student of the institution he or she proposes to represent.

The following statements are copied from the first handbook approved by the new athletic and literary association:

ARTICLE 1—Organization.
Section 1. This organization shall be known as the Mississippi Junior College Athletic and Literary Association and shall be composed of schools of the junior college secondary grade.
Section 2. Membership. Any school within the State of Mississippi of the grade mentioned in the Section 1, whether tax supported, denominationally supported, parochial, privately owned, or corporately owned and controlled is eligible to membership upon vote of the membership of the organization.

ARTICLE 2—Officers
Section 1. The officers of the Mississippi Junior College Literary and Athletic Association shall be: president, vice-president, and secretary-treasurer, each of whom shall serve without compensation.
Section 2. Duties—President: It shall be the duty of the

president to preside at all meetings; to call meetings of the organization and to foster at all times the better interest and development of the organization.

Vice-President: It shall be the duty of the vice-president to act in the capacity of the president when the president is absent.

Secretary-Treasurer: It shall be the duty of the secretary-treasurer to keep a record of all proceedings of the organization, to have charge of all funds belonging to this organization, records of finances and make reports of same upon request of the membership and at regular meetings and to issue notices and orders of said organization.

ARTICLE 3—Purpose and Aim

Section 1. It shall be the purpose and aim of this organization to foster a better standard of scholarship among the membership of the student bodies of the various member schools, to foster clean athletics in every particular and to promote manly action and womanly action on and off the athletic field and under all circumstances and conditions.

Section 2. It shall be the purpose and aim of this organization to foster and promote the general interest of the member schools in every way possible.

ARTICLE 4—Eligibility of Participants in Literary and Athletic Contests

Section 1. Each and every participant must have a clean, moral record such that the member school could trust at home and abroad.

Section 2. Each and every participant must be making a passing grade in at least three subjects 10 consecutive days immediately prior to the contest in which he or she proposes to participate.

Section 3. No student can participate in any event or contest unless he or she is a *bona fide* student of the institution he or she proposes to represent.

Section 4. No athletic contestant shall receive remuneration for athletics.

The resident requirement for eligibility in athletic participation has been a significant factor in the operation of junior college competition on a statewide basis. The early zoning of the state on a multicounty basis for support of a junior college caused the presidents, in defining eligibility of athletes, to respect the territory assigned to each institution with limited exceptions. However, out-of-state students were considered eligible until the close of the third decade, the 1961–62 session. The handbooks indicate that from time to time certain restrictions were placed on the number of out-of-state students who could be declared eligible during each school year. Many out-of-state students were outstanding athletes in the public junior colleges in Mississippi. These students, along with many Mississippi athletes, went on to participate in the athletic programs of the nation's colleges and

universities and in the field of professional football. The names of a number of junior college athletes who played professional football were made available from the junior colleges in Mississippi. The search for names did not provide a complete list; the partial list includes the following:

Professional Football

George Hansen	Canada	Miss. Delta
Jack Manley	San Diego	East Miss.
Edward A. Khayat	Philadelphia	Gulf Coast
Charles G.		
"Dinky" Evans	Canada	Gulf Coast
Tommy Boutwell	Miami	Gulf Coast
Bucky McElroy	Chicago	Hinds
Earl Leggett	Chicago	Hinds
	Los Angeles	
	New Orleans	
Raymond Abruzzese	Boston	Hinds
	New York	
Jimmy Taylor	Green Bay	Hinds
	New Orleans	
Johnny Daher	Atlanta	Hinds
Donald Gleason	Houston	Hinds
Earl Howell	Los Angeles	Holmes
Aubrey Rozzell	Pittsburgh	Holmes
Ode Burrell	Houston	Holmes
George Gulyanics	Chicago	Jones County
Jackie Parker	Canada	Jones County
Larry Suchy	New York	Jones County
	Atlanta	
	Canada	

Eligibility of out-of-state athletes became an issue in the fourth decade. After considering the matter for a period of years, the Association voted to allow only residents of Mississippi to participate in junior college athletic competition. The regulation became effective with the 1961–1962 session and continued through the 1971–1972 session.

Some form of athletic scholarship has always been awarded to junior college athletes. During the early years, these scholarships were known as work scholarships, later changed to scholarship grants. Strict regulations pertaining to these scholarship grants were scrupulously enforced. The scholarship grants applied only to football and basketball and were limited in amount. In addition to this restriction, each particular institution had a limited number of fulltime grant-in-aid scholarships to be awarded during a school session. Despite some violations of regulations of eligibility, the program, on the whole, has been one of integrity, administered by men and women possessed of a sense of duty and purpose.

The original interschool events included football, volleyball, baseball, track, girls' and boys' basketball, and girls' and boys' tennis. Some minor changes have taken place in the athletic program during the fifty-year period. Volleyball has not received a great deal of emphasis as an interschool event, and girls' basketball, which was discontinued as an intercollegiate sport in 1955, was continued by a number of schools only as a part of the general physical education program. The Junior College Association, however, reinstated girls' basketball as a competitive sport. None of the original multicounty junior colleges has discontinued the sports which were identified in the first Association meeting, although one multicounty junior college, which was organized in 1948, discontinued football for a short period only to reinstate it at a later time. This move was encouraged by the people in this junior college district.

Although the competitive athletic program has not been financially profitable for any of the public junior colleges, it has made an important contribution to the total educational program, both as a job opportunity for many young men and women and a pivot around which junior college school spirit has been built. A survey of the coaches and physical education instructors, both men and women, in the Mississippi high schools shows that a large percentage of these have a junior college background. This has contributed to good relationships between the junior college and the high school athletic programs in the district. A number of junior college coaches have advanced to university and college coaching because of their experience and success in junior college athletics. Within each junior college district, the value of competitive athletics from a public relations standpoint has been great. Sporting events bring more persons from throughout the district to the various campuses than any other activity. A statement from a junior college coach, with many years of experience, emphasizes the importance of athletics in the junior college. He stated that sports in the junior college provide a natural rallying point for the college community and the junior college district. They provide an item of common interest to students, faculty, and alumni; they also provide a natural outlet for enthusiasms and energies of students. The leaders of the public junior colleges are worthy of commendation for their continued support of a quality athletic program in each district.

The competitive athletic program has been the foundation for a program of health and physical education, which is a vital part of the junior college curriculum. Expanded facilities are available as a result of the competitive programs, and a greater interest in intramural athletics exists at each institution. The leaders in the Mississippi public junior colleges have felt, during the years, that competitive athletics and a quality program in health and physical education, through organized classes and intramural activities, will contribute to the physical development of the individual students and will strengthen those characteristics that are essential in the lives of each individual whose future leadership and influence will bring good to his fellowmen. Because of the peripheral benefits of competitive athletics to the junior college system, the cost has been justified as an educational cost rather than as a luxury.

Considerable regional and national attention and recognition have been given to the Mississippi junior colleges because of the success of their football and basketball teams. Two schools played in the Junior Rose Bowl in Pasadena, California, and a number of junior colleges participated in events sponsored by the National Junior College Athletic Association. Two junior colleges were recognized as national champions, and a number of schools participated in regional bowl games sponsored by various organizations, in which some games were played with colleges from other states. Some of the post-season approved bowl games for Mississippi public junior colleges were:

Laurel Lions Bowl Game, Laurel, Mississippi, 1945 and played annually through 1955
Doll and Toy Bowl Game, Hattiesburg, Mississippi, 1946
Tung Bowl, Poplarville, Mississippi, 1946
Spindle Top Bowl, Beaumont, Texas, 1948
Jackson Touchdown Club Memorial Bowl Game, Jackson, Mississippi, 1949 and 1950
Gulf Bowl, Corpus Christi, Texas, 1950
Lions Bowl, Fayette, Alabama, 1950
Oleander Bowl, Galveston, Texas, 1952
Junior College Rose Bowl, Pasadena, California, 1954 Hinds Junior College, 1955 Jones County Junior College
Hospitality Bowl, Mississippi Gulf Coast, 1955 and played annually through 1963

Junior College All-American Bowl, Jackson, Mississippi, 1956 and 1957

Jackson Police Department, Jackson, Mississippi, 1962 and 1963

Shriners' Bowl Game, Shreveport, Louisiana, 1965 and played annually through 1971

Hospitality Bowl, San Angelo, Texas, 1965

National Junior College Athletic Association Championships, Savannah, Georgia, 1971

Mississippi Junior College All-State Classic, Tupelo, Mississippi, 1972

The junior college leaders have not overlooked the competition that has existed in various nonathletic activities. Marching bands have added to the competitive spirit and have been a part of the competitive athletic programs. Each band visits most of the campuses of the public junior colleges each year.

During the early years, band festivals were held on the junior college campuses. They were very competitive, and the bands were judged in various categories and rated as to their superiority. Out of the marching bands, concert groups and stage bands have developed. Each of these groups fills numerous engagements during a school year. These include various athletic and social events on and off campus. Many trips are made by these organizations within the districts and over the state, as well as on a national basis.

A number of the Mississippi public junior colleges have developed precision dance and drill units that have performed over the nation. These performances have included such events as national, civic, and patriotic conventions; major New Year's bowl games; Miss America parades; New Orleans Mardi Gras parades; parades for the U. S. Congress, and many other events.

Singing groups have been of great worth to individual students and have contributed much as performing groups. These include choirs, ensembles, quartets, and small "personality" singing groups. Their performances include on-campus and off-campus concerts, visiting high schools in the junior college districts, visits to churches, and special concerts for annual occasions such as Christmas and spring festivals. The Annual Mississippi Junior College Choral Festival has a competitive atmosphere, and at times judges have given specific ratings to each choir.

Other areas in which a spirit of competition exists include the college yearbooks and the periodic newspapers published by a student staff. Annual meetings of student groups in this work, through a state junior college press association, stimulates these activities. Literary examinations in the academic area were very competitive during the early years. These were discontinued as the institutions became more comprehensive.

All of these groups mentioned, and other groups and individuals, participate on a statewide basis and contribute to the spirit and identity of each institution. These organizations have been ambassadors of good will through the years.

Phi Theta Kappa: For Academic Performance

The leaders of the Mississippi public junior colleges were aware from the beginning that a first priority in the growth and development of these institutions was "academic excellence." A strong influence was found through Phi Theta Kappa organizations on the junior college campuses with the handbook's stated purpose, "To recognize and encourage scholarship among junior college students." A great advantage to the Mississippi programs has been that the first national office of Phi Theta Kappa was opened in Canton, Mississippi, in 1934, and has remained at this location through the years. Also, a Mississippian, Dr. Margaret Mosal, has served as the executive director since the opening of the national office. Dr. Mosal has spent a lifetime working with the leaders of the junior college movement and watching from an advantageous spot the progress that has been made.

In 1934, when the national office was established in Mississippi, there were twenty-nine chapters of Phi Theta Kappa in the nation with two chapters in Mississippi. As the second fifty years in the development of public junior colleges in Mississippi begins, there are five hundred chapters of the fraternity with eighteen in Mississippi. There are only four states without a chapter of Phi Theta Kappa.

The pioneer presidents of Mississippi junior colleges, who, through their coordinated efforts, were responsible for establishing a sound system of junior colleges, are also remembered for their leadership and support in organizing Phi Theta Kappa chapters on the junior college campuses. Recognition and appreciation are also given to today's junior college presidents who continue effective leadership and support of Phi Theta Kappa and its program.

Phi Theta Kappa offers a national competition each year with coveted awards, and chapters across the nation actively compete for the awards which also carry, along with an attractive trophy, a tuition scholarship to the Honors Institute. Many award winners in this annual competition have been Mississippi chapters, as follows:

Alpha Theta from Gulf Park College, Gulfport, Mississippi
Gamma Lambda from Hinds Junior College, Raymond, Mississippi
Gamma Nu from Perkinston Junior College, Perkinston, Mississippi (winner in all categories)
Eta Omega from Copiah-Lincoln Junior College, Wesson, Mississippi
Theta Sigma from Northwest Mississippi Junior College, Senatobia, Mississippi
Iota Zeta from Northeast Mississippi Junior College, Booneville, Mississippi
Omicron Alpha from Jeff Davis Campus of Gulf Coast Junior College, Gulfport, Mississippi
Pi Epsilon from Jackson County Campus of Gulf Coast Junior College, Gautier, Mississippi

Mississippi has supported Phi Theta Kappa over the years and has hosted national conventions, as follows:

1932 at Whitworth College, Brookhaven, Mississippi
1942 at Gulf Park College, Gulfport, Mississippi
1952 at Gulf Park College, Gulfport, Mississippi
1962 at the Buena Vista Hotel in Biloxi, Mississippi, with all chapters serving as hosts
1971 at the Buena Vista Hotel in Biloxi, Mississippi, with all junior colleges as hosts
1976 in Biloxi, Mississippi, at the Sheraton Hotel, with chapters from Mississippi and Alabama serving as hosts to the Bicentennial Convention

Phi Theta Kappa national officers in Mississippi include:

six national presidents
seven national vice-presidents
one second vice-president
four national historians
executive director since 1934

Since 1918, well over 500,000 junior college scholars have passed through the ranks of Phi Theta Kappa. Today, hundreds of them have risen to the top in their professions and are known nationwide for their achievements. Just six years ago, Phi Theta Kappa initiated the "Distinguished Alumnus of the Year Award." Mississippi is proud to claim three of the six distinguished alumni so honored:

Hal Phillips, renowned novelist who has written five "best sellers," including *The Loved and the Unloved* which became a motion picture. Hal Phillips was the winner of two Guggenheim Awards. He is a graduate of Hinds Jr. College at Raymond, Mississippi.
Howard Pollock, a graduate of Perkinston Jr. College, Perkinston, Mississippi, is a former U. S. Congressman from Alaska and first president of the Anchorage United Nations Association. He was awarded the George Washington Honor Medal.
Fred Haise, Perkinston Junior College, Perkinston, Mississippi, lunar module pilot for Apollo 13, and one of the original astronauts selected by NASA in 1966.

Mrs. Mosal, the executive director, stated that Phi Theta Kappa is proud to add an enrichment program to Mississippi junior colleges by which, each year, they are privileged to share in a fine honors program furnished by Phi Theta Kappa. State meetings are scheduled across the nation, followed by the National Convention and, finally, in June of each year, the Honors Institute. Members of Phi Theta Kappa and their advisors have the best in speakers, entertainment, and seminars as they focus on the theme chosen for the year. Started in 1968 as a one-time celebration of the Fiftieth Anniversary of Phi Theta Kappa, the idea of the Honors Institute caught fire, and, since 1968, such institutes have been scheduled all over America. Outstanding personalities on Phi Theta Kappa programs over the years include:

Justice Arthur Goldberg	Dr. Ashley Montague
Henry Cabot Lodge	Alex Haley
Eric Sevareid	Fishbait Miller
Fred Kuper	Richard Wordsworth
Mike Seeger	Rep. Shirley Chisholm
Elizabeth Spencer	Melvyn Douglas
Arthur Fiedler	Dr. Rollo May
Clive Barnes	Jean Ritchie
Edmund Muskie	The New York Harpists

Mississippi, and the state system of public junior colleges, can well be proud of the part our state has had in the growth and development of the National Honor Fraternity of the junior colleges, Phi Theta Kappa.

The Mississippi Junior College Inter-Alumni Association

PURPOSE

To promote junior college educational programs in Mississippi and to establish within the state a cooperative and concerted effort for the promotion and advancement of junior college education. It is also the purpose of this organization to assist the junior colleges of the state in every way possible.

NEED

Because of the rapid increase of students going to college, the junior colleges of the state are faced with a unique challenge—that of helping to carry the load. This organization accepts the challenge to help the junior colleges provide adequate physical facilities and instruction.

AIMS AND OBJECTIVES

This organization will attempt to aid the junior colleges of the state in four areas: Function, Facilities, Faculty and Finances.

Function: To aid the colleges as they determine the offerings so that the needs of the areas will be filled.

Facilities: To aid the colleges in filling the need for modern teaching aids, as well as adequate plants and equipment.

Faculty: The need for increased salaries for faculty is evident, and with standards being raised, the need for fully qualified faculty is evident.

Finances: Finances are the price tags of progress. Sufficient funds for the junior colleges are the key to continued success and fulfillment of community needs. This organization proposes to help to secure adequate financial support for the junior colleges of the state.

OUTLOOK

The outlook of the organization is optimistic. The need for providing higher education for high school graduates and adults of the areas is evident. The worth of the junior college is not contested.

MEETINGS

Annual meetings will be held; first in the southern portion of the state, second in the northern portion and the third in the central portion with the meetings thereafter alternating in the same order based upon invitation from a college within the area.

The organization will meet not later than July 15th of each year prior to the regular meetings of the legislature to begin work on a promotional program for the junior colleges of the state. The proposals will be developed from and limited to the proposals presented to this organization by the Mississippi Junior College Association.

That revenue for support of this organization initially be underwritten by each public junior college, with a minimum budget to be used only for printing and mailing of material and communications.

That symbols such as decals or automobile stickers be provided.

That the name of the association be The Mississippi Junior College Inter-Alumni Association.

That control of the public junior colleges of the state be maintained on a local basis and that this organization aid the local boards of trustees and administrators in every way possible as the junior colleges face the challenges presented by change and new demands.

The Mississippi Junior College Inter-Alumni Association met in regular session and A. L. Rouse offered the following resolution which was seconded by Bill Bailey, to-wit:

RESOLUTION AUTHORIZING INCORPORATION OF MISSISSIPPI JUNIOR COLLEGE INTER-ALUMNI ASSOCIATION.

WHEREAS, the general membership of the Mississippi Junior College Inter-Alumni Association is now in general session and desirous of incorporating Mississippi Junior College Inter-Alumni Association into a non profit corporation under the statutes of the State of Mississippi, and;

WHEREAS it will be for the best interest of the membership and organization to be incorporated in order to better achieve the purpose for which it is formed.

Now, therefore, be it resolved that John Monroe, Roy E. Johnson and Hammond E. Davis, be and they are hereby authorized and directed to incorporate Mississippi Junior College Inter-Alumni Association, as, MISSISSIPPI JUNIOR COLLEGE INTER-ALUMNI ASSOCIATION, Inc., under the statutes of the State of Mississippi and do any and all things necessary and requisite and required by law in order to achieve this purpose.

Resolution adopted this 15th day of July, A.D., 1965.

CERTIFICATION

I, the undersigned, Hammond E. Davis, duly elected and serving Secretary of an organization known as Mississippi Junior College Inter-Alumni Association of the State of Mississippi, hereby certify that the foregoing resolution authorizing the incorporation of Mississippi Junior College Inter-Alumni Association was adopted by said membership and that the above is a true copy of a resolution adopted by said organization and as appears in the Minutes thereof.

Witness my signature, this the   day of   A.D., 1965.

———————————————
Hammond E. Davis

Honor Alumnus Testimonials

The records of student enrollment in the Mississippi state system of public junior colleges during the first fifty years show that more than 500,000 young men and women have been enrolled. Testimonials from many of these students are available and certify to the contributions that the public junior colleges have made to them as individuals and also to the benefits received in the growth and development of the state of Mississippi because of this phase of higher education.

The Mississippi public junior colleges, through the Alumni Association, began, during the last decade of the first fifty years, to recognize certain individuals by the title Honor Alumnus. A list of these individuals and their professions and occupations shows them in various areas of leadership on both state and national levels.

A look at Mississippi's leadership indicates that many are persons who obtained part of their higher education from the state's public junior colleges. The junior college alumni are providing leadership in many fields, and their positions of prominence have been most impressive.

The year 1972 ends the first fifty years of the operation of Mississippi's public junior colleges. Billie Skelton, a staff writer for the *Clarion-Ledger*, published an article (Sunday, November 26, 1972, Section C, of the *Clarion-Ledger, Jackson Daily News*) with photographs of forty-four outstanding alumni and the names of one hundred and ten persons representing all of the sixteen Mississippi public junior colleges. The substance of much of the material included in the

statements to follow is from the article written by Billie Skelton.

A tabulation of the names of alumni as to their professions, engagements in business and industry and other occupations shows leadership in many areas. The tabulation identified the following numbers:

College presidents	9
University and college teaching	16
Political, national	7
Political, state	14
Administrative leadership in business and industry	12
Physicians	13
Space administration and astronauts	3
Armed services (two generals)	3
Attorneys and judges	5
Religion	2
Music (opera)	2
Journalism	4
Humorists	2
Secondary education	6
Novelist	1
Agriculture	1
Professional athletics	4
Hospital administration	1

However, when the accomplishments of Mississippi's junior college graduates are considered you will look at the homes and families in each county and town in Mississippi and understand how many individuals in these families will testify to the total value of their college education. Many of them will testify that, had it not been for the public junior colleges in Mississippi, they would not have received any college education.

A look at the public schools in each county shows how many junior college graduates are teaching, coaching, or in school administration. The firm commitment of the public junior colleges to accept as a dominant purpose character building and spiritual guidance is evident in a review of the leaders in the churches all over the state of Mississippi.

The contributions made by the public junior colleges in preparing Mississippi youths for excellent job opportunities is contributing to great progress in the state. An industrial leader, as president of the Mississippi Manufacturers Association, gave the following testimonial regarding job opportunity training in Mississippi public junior colleges:

A trained labor force is an indispensable ingredient for industrial growth. The well-being of industry in every area is closely allied to the educational systems which feed manpower into it.

Tremendous progress has been made in Mississippi within the last decade in both industrial growth and in the training of personnel to fill the skilled jobs so vital to industry. During these short years training centers on every junior college campus in Mississippi have been established, specially designed programs have been conducted within plants and at other locations, vocational-technical training centers have made a beginning in many secondary school districts and, in general, every effort possible has been made to keep pace with the demand.

Outstanding alumni of the Mississippi public junior colleges have been designated by the various colleges, usually at the annual homecoming celebration, as an honor alumnus of the college. Those selected are listed by colleges. A few of the testimonials received from alumni represented in this honor group are included.

Copiah-Lincoln Junior College:

Billy B. Thames, Wesson, Mississippi, President, Copiah-Lincoln Junior College

Mrs. Alma L. Smith, Wesson, Mississippi, Secretary to the president of Copiah-Lincoln

R. E. (Bob) Anderson, Wesson, Mississippi, state representative from Copiah and Lawrence Counties

Mrs. Helen Ellzey Mullen, Wesson, Mississippi, librarian at Copiah-Lincoln

E. A. (Beby) Turnage, Monticello, Mississippi, Adjutant General for the state of Mississippi

Mrs. Ruby B. Larkin, Brookhaven, Mississippi, former Lincoln County Superintendent of Education

Frank Pitts, Dallas, Texas, industrial leader and business executive

Mrs. Doris B. Green, Hazlehurst, Mississippi, music teacher

Mrs. Jean L. Ricks, Wesson, Mississippi, secretarial science instructor

Lester Furr, Wesson, Mississippi, postmaster

East Central Junior College:

Burris O. Smith, Louisville, Mississippi

Miss Lucille Wood, Decatur, Mississippi

Henry D. Horton, Louisville, Mississippi

Crowley Alford, Carthage, Mississippi

W. H. Johnson, Decatur, Mississippi, attorney

Arthur Winstead, Philadelphia, Mississippi, ex-Congressman

Leon Sims, Philadelphia, Mississippi

Dr. William Lamar Weems, Jackson, Mississippi, Chief of the Division of Urology and Professor of

Urology Surgery, University of Mississippi School of Medicine

W. Arno Vincent, Meridian, Mississippi, past president of East Central Junior College

William C. Spence, Walnut Grove, Mississippi

East Mississippi Junior College:

Fred Adams, Edwards, Mississippi, poultryman and owner of Adams Egg Farms, Inc.

Mrs. Frances Holloway, Meridian, Mississippi, teacher

Harry Lackey, Obadiah, Mississippi

Dr. Sarah Weaver, Hattiesburg, Mississippi, Chairman, Home Economics Department, University of Southern Mississippi

James W. Windham, Milwaukee, Wisconsin, President, Pabst Brewing Company

Dr. Heber Ethridge, Jackson, Mississippi, plastic surgeon

Miss Peggy Wilson, golf pro

John C. Stennis, DeKalb, Mississippi, U. S. Senator and Chairman of the Senate Armed Services Committee

Walter L. Wright, Eupora, Mississippi, retired hospital administrator and school teacher

C. Mike Watkins, Meridian, Mississippi, attorney

Dr. W. B. Sorrell, Montgomery, Alabama, pathologist

Gulf Coast Junior College:

Fred W. Haise, Jr., Seabrook, Texas, astronaut

William "Fish Bait" Miller, Washington, D. C., former Doorkeeper of U. S. House of Representatives

Howard W. Pollock, McLean, Virginia, acting administrator, National Oceanic and Atmospheric Administration

Emory O. Cunningham, Birmingham, Alabama, publisher, the Progressive Farmer Company

Dr. Otis Singletary, Lexington, Kentucky, President, University of Kentucky

Hinds Junior College:

John Bell Williams, Jackson, Mississippi, attorney and former governor of Mississippi

Dr. E. E. Thrash, Raymond, Mississippi, Executive Secretary of Board of Trustees of Institutions of Higher Learning

Clifford E. Charlesworth, Houston, Texas, flight director, Apollo 11 Moon Landing

A. F. Summer, Jackson, Mississippi, Attorney General of the state of Mississippi

Charles Griffin, Utica, Mississippi, Mississippi Congressman

Anne Hardy, Jackson, Mississippi, education

Thomas Hal Phillips, Corinth, Mississippi, movie industry and author

Tom Virden, Jackson, Mississippi, Hinds County Chancery Clerk, deceased

Jones County Junior College:

Ben A. Hilbun, Starkville, Mississippi, college administrator and former president of Mississippi State University, deceased

Carroll Gartin, Laurel, Mississippi, attorney and former Mississippi lieutenant governor, deceased

Dr. William Alton Bryant, Oxford, Mississippi, Vice-chancellor, University of Mississippi

Alonzo Houston Blackwell, Ellisville, Mississippi, former registrar, Jones County Junior College

Dr. Benjamin B. Graves, Huntsville, Alabama, President, University of Alabama at Huntsville, and former president of Millsaps College, Jackson

Dr. Wilson Lyon, Claremont, California, a Rhodes Scholar and retired president of Pomona College

Dr. W. W. Walley, Waynesboro, Mississippi, physician

Benjamin Leon Hill, Brandon, Mississippi, former State Supervisor, Public Junior Colleges, Mississippi State Department of Education, deceased

Maj. Charles Franklin Wallace, Ellisville, Mississippi, air force pilot, Vietnam War, missing in action

Dr. Eugene A. Bush, Sr., Laurel, Mississippi, physician and surgeon

Dr. Byrd (Mrs. J. R. Dumas) Burton, Tempe, Arizona, Chairman, Home Economics Department, Arizona State University

F. Sneed McInvale, Laurel, Mississippi, Director of Public Affairs, Masonite Corporation

Stanton Augustus Hall, Hattiesburg, Mississippi, attorney and circuit judge

Leslie C. DeVall, Ed. D., Lake Charles, Louisiana, football coach and athletic director, McNeese State College

Meridian Junior College:

Mrs. Bertha Lee White, Bailey, Mississippi, businesswoman and past state legislator

Mrs. Vivian Valentine, Meridian, Mississippi, administrative assistant, Meridian Industrial Foundation

Tony Sansone, Meridian, Mississippi, television advertising executive

Northwest Mississippi Junior College:

Mrs. William F. Winter, Jackson, Mississippi, wife of a lieutenant governor of Mississippi

Dr. G. Daniel Copeland, Memphis, Tennessee, cardiologist

Pearl River Junior College:

Dr. Garvin H. Johnston, Jackson, Mississippi, State Superintendent of Education

Frank A. Fortenberry, Columbia, Mississippi, head of chemistry department, Pearl River Junior College

Southwest Mississippi Junior College:

Dr. W. C. Ford and Dr. Lula Bess Ford, Houston, Texas, founders and owners of Psychological Testing Services, Inc., deceased

Howard J. (Jerry) Clower, Yazoo City, Mississippi, humorist

Mary Dawson Cain, Summit, Mississippi, newspaper editor

Bobby Gerald Wilson, Hammond, Louisiana, Baptist minister, and counselor, Vocational Rehabilitation, Louisiana Department of Education

Utica Junior College:

Bennie Thompson, Bolton, Mississippi, mayor of city of Bolton

TESTIMONIALS

Dr. Benjamin B. Graves, a university president, states, "In reflecting back on my junior college education, I suppose the most honest thing to say would be that accessibility to a college was a critical factor at that time, inasmuch as my family, along with most others in Mississippi, were still trying to dig themselves out of the disastrous depression of the 30's. I was thoroughly determined to go to college from a very early age, and I am sure I would have gotten through in some form or fashion had not the junior college been accessible. Nevertheless, access was important. On top of this coincidental factor, however, I would say that the quality of the academic instruction at the junior college I attended, along with the marvelous opportunities in the extra curricular area, were really the major contributions. I encountered some instructors at both the high school and junior college level equal in talent to some I encountered all the way to the doctoral level. In terms of inspiration, I think they even exceeded some of those later professors.

"On the matter of the worth of the Mississippi Junior College Program to the educational needs of Mississippi, I can say without qualifications that though that state has lagged behind in many areas, its pioneering effort in the area of junior colleges has added a dimension to education in that state that I am sure has had much to do with changing Mississippi's course in history. Again, the matter of relative access to students from all over the state was probably the critical factor."

Mrs. William Winter, wife of Mississippi's former Lt. Gov. William Winter and president of the Inter-Alumni Association of the Junior Colleges of Mississippi, made the following statement regarding her appreciation for the junior college program of the state: "On the basis of my own personal experience, plus my associations with many others who have been associated with junior colleges, I have come to the conclusion that our system of junior colleges in Mississippi has been and remains one of the most vital parts of our total education structure. Without the junior college system and its ability to make available to virtually every young man and woman in our state the opportunity to get a quality college education at a minimum cost, we would have denied to thousands of boys and girls a chance for a meaningful life." She further stated that she would always be grateful to those in the junior college program who have provided the vision and the leadership that have moved it steadily upward in its ability to serve the people of Mississippi.

Former Gov. John Bell Williams of Mississippi states, "I was a Junior College student in the days of the great depression of the 1930's, at a time when all students were struggling to defray the expenses of their education. Because of this common bond, or for whatever reason, the friendships gained in Junior College have been the warmest, most genuine and lasting of any made throughout my youth. I have always reflected on my days in Junior College as the best and most exciting period of my entire educational career. There was a unique closeness of personal relation-

ships between students and faculty members that I did not find in my later years of higher education.

"I can give personal testimony to hundreds of cases of highly successful College and University trained men and women—covering virtually every field of endeavor—whose formal education would have terminated with High School had not our Junior Colleges been available to them.

"With this in mind, I am firmly convinced that the Mississippi system of Junior Colleges, more than anything else, is responsible for elevating the average level of educational achievement in our state over the last four decades."

Mr. Jerry Clower, business executive and nationally known humorist, states, "I joined the United States Navy the day after I finished high school, with only eight in my class, at East Fork Consolidated School, Liberty, Mississippi. After the war I returned home. Had I not had Southwest Junior College to attend, I would never have risked the big senior college. I would just have been scared to make that big a jump.

"I sincerely believe that there is more education handed out per dollar invested by the Mississippi junior colleges than by any other form of education today."

Mississippi's Attorney General, A. F. Summer of Jackson, Mississippi, states, "I think I received a better education by going to a junior college for two years than I would have had if I had started at a four-year institution." He cited excellent teachers, terrific discipline and a lack of distracting extra- or noncurricular activities as three important elements. "As a consequence," he added, "I learned that if you prepare yourself well enough, you can take on anybody, anywhere, anytime.

"There were other factors that contributed to me as an individual student. I felt that I benefitted from the smaller student body at the junior college and the fact that students could compete more against their peers. I feel that the junior college offered a greater sense of camaraderie and more opportunity for the development of individualism, and that it offered a better educational transition for a student from a small town or rural area. Also, the low cost provided extra motivation for students to go to college.

"All in all, my two years of junior college was

educationally the best thing that ever happened to me."

Dr. W. W. Walley, a practicing physician in Waynesboro, Mississippi, states, "The junior college system in Mississippi really meant everything to me. Without it I would never have had the opportunity for higher education. I entered junior college from a C.C.C. camp with nothing except ambition, and was given the opportunity to earn all of my expenses during the two years I attended junior college. At times I was in debt to the school, but they did not give up on me and allowed me to continue.

"The transition from the junior college to 'Ole Miss' as a medical student was smooth. I had no trouble scholastically and received credit for all work completed at the junior college.

"Another plus that I received from my junior college experience was the emphasis placed on church attendance and the encouragement I received, both by word of mouth and by example. I developed a habit that sustained me through five years of army life and through my professional years.

"I am sure that the junior college system is here to stay, as well it should be because it is meeting a need that could not be met in any other way."

Mr. Thomas Hal Phillips, novelist, screen writer and former Public Service Commissioner, says, "It seems to me a college or university has two major assets: Faculty and Library. The faculty would include the entire teaching and administrative force; the library would include laboratories and all apparatus for conducting the business of teaching.

"In my own case, for the first two years of college I was more dependent on the faculty than on the library or the laboratory. As a junior college student I received marvelous personal attention from a faculty which, it seems to me, could not have been better. When we are young and our dreams and ambitions are so fragile we need all the special and personal attention possible.

"Naturally, the university or the senior college is equipped to do things which the junior college can not do. But it is also true that the junior college is equipped to do certain things which the university either can not do, or can not do quite so well. Particularly in our own state of Mississippi the junior college system is indispensable. Proximity is a factor; cost is a factor; but in the complex business of education there is no substitute for the student-faculty relationship. Almost every man or woman I know who has achieved distinction in some field is more than willing to give great credit to a teacher or, more than likely, to teachers.

"The most significant contribution the junior college made to me was the personal relationship, that personal interest, that personal touch from faculty members who not only made me aware of unlimited possibilities but made me believe I could achieve at least one of them."

Mr. Frank Pitts, an industrial leader and business executive, stated, "The public junior college I attended gave me an opportunity to attend college without very much money and to get two years of education beyond the high school very close to home. This was all of the formal college training that I had and I feel that without the junior college I would not have had any part of a college education. Therefore, the junior college program is very close to my heart.

"I feel that the public junior colleges in Mississippi have pioneered a dual approach to education, vocational and liberal arts. I believe that the junior colleges are trying to help students discover talents and abilities in order for them to choose realistic educational goals and make wise vocational choices. I am convinced that the junior colleges are contributing materially to industrial development and to the present and future employment of young people."

Dr. W. Lamar Weems of the University of Mississippi Medical Center states, "The primary reason for my choosing a junior college was the financial savings for my parents. Other benefits accrued, however, which I had not anticipated. The atmosphere of a small campus and the personal relationships which developed in that environment proved to be of lasting value. The opportunity to participate in campus activities in a way which is denied the average student on a large campus provides an opportunity for the development of self identity and confidence. I can truthfully say that I was not deprived academically by attendance of a junior college if the test of academic achievement is quality of preparation for higher education and responsiblity. I pay tribute to many individuals who made a positive contribution to my education. They were the finest and most dedicated classroom teachers whom I encountered in my academic travels to the M.D. degree. In my opinion, the public junior colleges have played a vital role in the educational effort in Mississippi and that role should not be neglected in the plans for higher education in the future."

Dr. Thomas G. Ross, a physician in Jackson, Mississippi, writes, "I graduated from a small high school in 1932. This was right in the bottom of the depression. My mind was set on medicine. I was unable to afford a four-year school, and I was told about our junior colleges.

"I made a visit to Copiah-Lincoln Junior College and saw that this was the school of my choice. It was truly a great institution. I worked the greatest part of my school years to pay my expenses. My second year, I was the lab assistant in chemistry and this gave me perhaps the greatest start to my medical career.

"It was a good school with lots of personal supervision and really genuine teachers. I feel that today they play an even greater role in our state with emphasis not only in furthering education but in vocational-technical education as well.

"I am pleased to recommend junior colleges to students, and I hope that they will continue to play a very important role in our state."

Mrs. Mary Dawson Cain, editor and publisher of *The Summit Sun* since 1936, states that the perseverance and determination of the founders of the Mississippi public junior colleges to provide an educational institution within financial reach of young people in the area, and to provide a transition period from high school to college, opened the door for many to secure a college education. She further states she felt that only the junior college could adequately prepare many students for the larger college.

Mrs. Cain says the junior college she attended had, from its inception, been a deeply religious institution, and students there have learned spiritual truths and values which have prepared them for institutions where religion was often the butt of ridicule. This spiritual atmosphere of the college was influenced and strengthened by the Christian leadership of the administration and faculty.

Mrs. Cain expressed appreciation for being chosen as one of the honor alumni of the junior college which she attended. Her words are, "I could think of nothing except the words of the song Ed Ames made famous—'My Cup Runneth Over.' "

Some general statements from alumni:

"The accessibility to professors on junior college campuses was a big help to students."

"Many students from a rural area might be lost on a large university or senior college campus."

"The necessity of working while in junior college to help pay expenses and the hours of study added to the job hours conditioned students to habits of application and self-discipline that is a part of the makeup of people who excell."

"I consider my two years in junior college to be the highlight of my entire period of education."

"I graduated from high school in the bottom of the depression. My mind was set on studying medicine and a junior college gave me a job to pay the greater part of my expenses. The personal supervision given to me and the really genuine teachers gave me the start to my medical career."

These statements and testimonials by alumni who are serving in various positions of leadership are reminders that each public junior college, as a part of the Mississippi state system, has established itself as a vital part of the total program of higher education in Mississippi, and is committed to the purpose that all young men and young women who desire a college education will not be denied the opportunity to get two years in a public junior college.

LOCAL LEADERSHIP

A/Statistics

Fiscal Information
PLANT VALUE

Name of College	First Year	Year 1972	Acres
Coahoma	$ 75,000.00	$ 3,400,000.00	43
Copiah-Lincoln*	225,000.00	4,506,073.00	600
East Central*	90,000.00	5,165,284.00	200
East Mississippi*	100,000.00	2,500,000.00	300
Gulf Coast (Perkinston)*	145,000.00	8,974,688.00	900
Hinds*	300,000.00	11,500,000.00	1000
Holmes*	75,000.00	7,400,000.00	300
Itawamba	232,600.00	4,825,000.00	283
Jones*	250,000.00	6,750,000.00	360
Meridian	225,000.00	3,500,000.00	55
Mississippi Delta*	172,900.00	5,170,924.00	357
Northeast Mississippi	365,692.00	8,938,970.00	82
Northwest Mississippi*	100,000.00	9,831,629.00	488
Pearl River*	150,000.00	4,204,730.00	384
Southwest*	225,000.00	3,520,000.00	570
Utica	55,000.00	4,806,439.00	736
TOTAL	$2,786,192.00	$94,988,737.00	6658

*These were the eleven institutions established during the beginning as the upward extension of an operating agricultural high school (symbol used throughout fiscal reports).

Fiscal Information
LABORATORY AND INSTRUCTIONAL
EQUIPMENT

Name of College	Value in first year of operation	Value in 1972 (Including audio-visual)
Coahoma	$ 300.00	$ 330,000.00
Copiah-Lincoln*	5,000.00	1,600,000.00
East Central*	1,200.00	257,738.00
East Mississippi*	1,200.00	280,256.00
Gulf Coast*	1,500.00	600,000.00
Hinds*	1,000.00	1,318,100.00
Holmes*	1,500.00	197,171.00
Itawamba	9,000.00	1,327,150.00
Jones*	4,000.00	855,196.00
Meridian	3,500.00	512,000.00
Mississippi Delta*	8,597.00	937,527.00
Northeast Mississippi	18,581.00	709,495.00
Northwest Mississippi*	1,000.00	1,111,457.00
Pearl River*	2,500.00	375,000.00
Southwest*	2,500.00	698,000.00
Utica	3,500.00	700,000.00
TOTAL	$64,878.00	$11,809,090.00

257

Fiscal Information
VALUE OF LIBRARY BOOKS AND NUMBER OF VOLUMES

Name of College	First Year	1972	Vols. begin	Vols. 1972
Coahoma	$ 1,600.00	$ 136,449.00	600	15,161
Copiah-Lincoln*	1,500.00	204,732.00	900	22,700
East Central*	1,000.00	200,000.00	800	20,000
East Mississippi*	2,500.00	102,851.00	1,000	16,837
Gulf Coast*	7,140.00	101,674.00	2,500	22,500
Hinds*	2,500.00	217,326.00	500	39,201
Holmes*	2,300.00	140,000.00	1,301	28,000
Itawamba	11,790.00	213,000.00	3,650	30,500
Jones*	3,500.00	241,665.00	1,575	32,937
Meridian	12,000.00	144,000.00	4,272	18,000
Mississippi Delta*	5,000.00	101,674.00	2,500	22,500
Northeast Mississippi	10,000.00	149,000.00	3,000	23,000
Northwest Mississippi*	600.00	149,464.00	300	18,700
Pearl River*	5,000.00	52,299.00	350	26,700
Southwest*	3,000.00	175,000.00	500	18,000
Utica	2,000.00	114,380.00	500	13,000
TOTAL	$71,430.00	$2,443,714.00	24,248	367,736

Fiscal Information
TECHNICAL AND VOCATIONAL EQUIPMENT 1972

Name of College	Value
Coahoma	$ 305,200.00
Copiah-Lincoln*	668,000.00
East Central*	500,000.00
East Mississippi*	668,733.00
Gulf Coast*	240,000.00
Hinds*	781,281.00
Holmes*	580,851.00
Itawamba	495,000.00
Jones*	754,689.58
Meridian	424,639.00
Mississippi Delta*	473,094.00
Northeast Mississippi	637,454.00
Northwest Mississippi*	718,930.00
Pearl River*	250,000.00
Southwest*	350,000.00
Utica	318,467.00
TOTAL	$8,166,338.58

Fiscal Information
AUDIO-VISUAL EQUIPMENT 1972

Name of College	Value
Coahoma	$ 30,000.00
Copiah-Lincoln*	100,000.00
East Central*	30,000.00
East Mississippi*	48,682.00
Gulf Coast*	200,000.00
Hinds*	235,283.00
Holmes*	61,934.00
Itawamba	92,150.00
Jones*	37,545,00
Meridian	62,000.00
Mississippi Delta*	114,373.00
Northeast Mississippi	136,356.00
Northwest Mississippi*	48,693.00
Pearl River*	25,000.00
Southwest*	48,000.00
Utica	150,000.00
TOTAL	$1,420,016.00

Number of Counties Supporting Junior College Program in Mississippi During Decades Shown

Name of College	1922–1932	1932–1942	1942–1952	1952–1962	1962–1972
Coahoma†			1	1	4
Copiah-Lincoln*	2	3	4	4	7
East Central*	4	5	5	5	5
East Mississippi*	2	3	3	3	6
Gulf Coast*	3	4	4	4	4
Hinds*	1	1	2	3	4
Holmes*	2	2	2	7	9
Itawamba			4	5	5
Jones*	3	7	8	8	8
Meridian†		1	1	1	1
Mississippi Delta*	3	3	3	4	8
Northeast Mississippi			5	5	5
Northwest Mississippi*	2	7	9	10	11
Pearl River*	2	5	5	5	6
Southwest*	1	2	2	2	3
Utica†				2	4
Total	25	42	56	65	81

†(Since some counties within a legal district support two junior colleges, the figure totals in the columns may differ from the totals given for counties.)

MISSISSIPPI STATE DEPARTMENT OF EDUCATION
P.O. Box 771
Jackson, Mississippi 39205

INFORMATION RE: Establishment of Community or Junior Colleges

The following information is requested by the Mississippi State Superintendent of Education for historical purposes. A summary will be returned to those who request same.

(All questions or statements refer to PUBLIC community or junior colleges)

1. Date ORIGINAL law was passed permitting the operation or establishment 19____.
2. Date first such college was operated in 19____.
3. The ORIGINAL law provided for: (check one)
   (1) Local support only _____
   (2) State support only _____
   (3) Combination of local and state support _____
4. The PRESENT law provides for: (check one)
   (1) Local support only _____
   (2) State support only _____
   (3) Combination of local and state support _____
5. If there has been a change in numbers 3 and 4, above, i.e., the ORIGINAL and the PRESENT laws for support, date such change was made 19_____.
6. Do you have a legally established STATE SYSTEM of public community or junior colleges _____.
7. If *yes* to number 6, when was the STATE SYSTEM ESTABLISHED 19_____.
8. Per cent of public community or junior colleges in the state accredited by your Regional Accrediting Agency _____%.
9. A summary of this information is requested: Yes _____; No _____
This form completed by _____
This information verified by _____
Date _____, 1973.
A self-addressed and pre-posted envelope is enclosed for your convenience and early reply.

	1	2	3(1) A	3(2) B	3(3) C	4(1) A	4(2) B	4(3) C	5	6	7	8	9
Alabama	1963	1964	X				X		—	yes	1964	94.44	yes
Alaska	1962	1962			X		X		—	yes	1962	100	no
Arizona	1927	1920			X		X		1960	yes	1960	100	yes
Arkansas	1965	1966			X		X		1973	yes	1965	100	yes
California	1910	1910			X		X		—	yes	1968	100	yes
Colorado	1937	1925			X		X		1967	yes	1967	42	yes
Connecticut	1965	1965	X				X		1967 1969	yes	1965	33⅓	yes
Delaware	1966	1967			X		X		—	yes	1966	66	yes
Florida	1947	1933			X	X			1971	yes	1957	100	yes
Georgia	1958	—			X			X	1964	yes	1931	100	yes
Hawaii	1964	1965	X				X		—	yes	1964	71	no

State										
Idaho	1939	1939	X			X	1963	yes	1963	100	yes
Illinois	—	1901	X			X	1965	yes	1965	100	yes
Indiana	1801	1801	See report on Fed. Land Grant		X		no		100	yes
Iowa	1927	1918	X			X	1949	no	—	87	yes
Kansas	1917	1920	X			X	1965	yes	1965	47	yes
Kentucky	1962	1962		X	X		—	(By Univ. of Ken.) yes	1962	100	
Louisiana	Did not complete questionnaire. See Letter							no			
Maine	No designated public junior colleges							no			
Maryland	1961	1927 1946		X		X		no		87	yes
Massachusetts	1948	1946	X			X	1958	yes	1958	90	yes
Michigan	1963	1964		X		X	—	no		85	yes
Minnesota	1925	1914	X			X	1957 1963	yes	1963	55	yes
Mississippi	1922	1921	X	X		X	1928	yes	1928	94.93	yes
Missouri	—	1914	X			X	1965 1972	no		60	yes
Montana	1939	1939	X			X	1971	no		100	yes
Nebraska	1931	1926	X			X	1967 1971	yes	1971	30	yes
Nevada	1969	1967		X	X			yes	1969	all candidates	yes
New Hampshire	No established system of publicly supported junior college in the state										
New Jersey	1962	1966		X		X		yes	1967	75	yes
New Mexico	1956	1950	X			X	1969	no		100	yes
New York	1953	1953		X		X		no		82	no
North Carolina	1963	1963		X		X		yes	1963	57	yes
North Dakota	1931	1939	X			X	1959	no		100	yes
Ohio	1962	1962		X		X		no		100	yes
Oklahoma	1901	1901		X	X		1967	no		85	no
Oregon	1961	1961		X		X		yes	1961	92.3	yes
Pennsylvania	1955	1955		X		X	—	yes	1963	100	no
Rhode Island	1960	1964			X		Statement: Authorized by legislative act creating Rhode Island Junior College				
South Carolina	1972	1973		X		X		yes	1972	100	yes
South Dakota	Forms not completed No public junior colleges No law authorizing the establishment										
Tennessee	1965	1967		X	X			yes	1972	66.6	yes
Texas	1929	1922	X			X	1941	no		100	yes
Utah	1888 1911 1937			X	X			yes	1969	100	no

										One College	
Vermont	1962	1971	X		X			yes	1962	0	yes
Virginia	1964	1965		X		X		yes	1966	47	yes
Washington	1941	1925		X		X	1967	yes	1967	100	yes
West Virginia			X		X			yes	1969	100	yes
Wisconsin	Letter states that there is no junior college system in Wisconsin; however, a large number of public junior colleges are operating in the state.										
Wyoming	1945	1945	X			X	1957	no	Jr. Col. Comm. 1951	43	yes

B/Trustees

The following is a listing of members of boards of trustees serving each junior college district during the first fifty-year period, 1922–1972.

These represent eighty-one of Mississippi's eighty-two counties. The county not included is Wilkinson County, which is a part of the Southwest Junior College District.

The names included in these lists were secured from the administration of each junior college and from official records. Unfortunately, these records may be incomplete or inaccurate.

Board of Trustees
Pearl River Junior College

PEARL RIVER COUNTY

Name of Trustee	Term of Service	Total Years
J. L. Megehee	1920–1930	10
C. E. Bass	1920–1924	4
I. S. Kirkland	1920–1935	15
J. A. Bilbo	1921–1932	11
D. F. Smith	1921–1932	11
J. N. Stewart	1924–1928 1936–1947	15
Mrs. H. L. Arledge	1924–1932	8
A. B. Nicholson	1928–1930	2
C. McDonald	1930–1931	1
J. O. Williams	1932–1935	3
T. G. Gipson	1932–1935	3
Grayson Keaton	1932–1935	3
T. D. Whitfield	1932–1933	1
J. W. Greene	1934–1935	1
L. A. Hurst	1934–1935	1
Ray Fornea	1936–1938	2
C. H. Hyde	1936–1937	1
Sollie Burge	1936–1938	2
D. F. Smith	1936–1938	2
H. W. Fornea	1936–1938	2
J. J. Holcomb	1940–1944	4
P. M. Hall	1940–1947	7

Charlie Blackwell	1940–1944	4
H. K. Rouse	1939–1947	8
A. S. Davis	1941–1959	18
A. O. Amacker	1944–1952 1956–1960	12
Johnnie B. Davis	1945–1947	2
Osborne Moody	1948–1972	24
Enoch Seal, Sr.	1948–1952	4
Monroe Smith	1948–1952	4
Johnnie Grice	1948–1952	4
A. H. Knight	1953–1962	9
Harry Sones	1953–1956 1960–1964	7
D. L. Wesley	1952–1959	7
Edmond Mitchell	1953–1956	3
I. C. Rawls, Jr.	1959–1967	8
Aubrey Lowe	1960–1970	10
J. E. Mitchell	1956–1972	16
W. D. Russ	1962–1966	4
T. P. Fornea	1964–1968	4
Leo Z. Seal	1966–1972	6
Russell Sinquefield, Sr.	1967–1972	5
Paul Monroe	1968–1972	4
Grady Brown	1970–1972	2
J. P. Buckley	1972	
Tercy Smith	1972	
Spence Lumpkin, Jr.	1972	

MARION COUNTY

Name of Trustee	Term of Service	Total Years
Mrs. J. B. Summer	1930–1931	1
E. I. Watts	1930–1931	1
J. W. Hitt	1930–1931	1
J. C. Broom	1930–1938	8
T. C. Fortenberry	1930–1932	2
Isaac Singley	1932–1933	1
M. C. Connerly	1932–1933	1
Kelly Hammond	1932–1943	11
F. S. Hammond	1932–1935	3
N. L. Watts	1939–1950	11
J. Bond	1944–1945	1
H. F. Dunaway	1944–1951	7
W. E. Simmons	1951–1952	1
Frank Fortenberry	1952–1972	20
N. L. Watts	1940–1943 1945–1955	13
Garvin Allen	1956–1964	8
Carl Loftin	1964–1972	8
Frank Rayburn	1972	1

LAMAR COUNTY

Name of Trustee	Term of Service	Total Years
Z. A. Foshee	1938–1943	5
J. R. Saucier	1938–1943	5
A. A. Pigford	1939–1940	1
J. T. Johnson	1944–1948	4
Dr. D. B. Stevenson	1944–1946	2
Dr. R. R. McNease	1947–1948	1
C. D. Jackson	1948–1954	6
D. C. Bilbo	1948–1956	8
Quitman Lott	1954–1956	2
Everette Eaton	1956–1972	16
Jason Lee	1956–1960	4
M. D. Anderson	1960–1966	6
Billy Ray Hatten	1966–1972	6

JEFFERSON DAVIS COUNTY

Name of Trustee	Term of Service	Total Years
F. A. Parker	1938–1945	7
D. F. Price	1938–1943	5
John Bynum	1944–1960	16
R. G. Lavingstone	1945–1952	7
Dennis Fortenberry	1952–1972	20
Hugh Cole	1960–1964	4
Charles Speed	1964–1972	8

HANCOCK COUNTY

Name of Trustee	Term of Service	Total Years
Albert S. McQueen	1934–1935	1
S. L. Toguett	1934–1935	1
K. G. McCarty	1936–1944 1960–1964 1972	13
Walter Gex, Jr.	1936–1937	1
S. L. Farve	1944–1948	4
Ed E. Breland	1948–1960	12
Rev. S. P. Powell	1948–1966	18
Robert Ladner	1964–1968	4
Omer Haas	1966–1972	6
Eugene Ladner	1968–1972	4

FORREST COUNTY

Name of Trustee	Term of Service	Total Years
Milton Evans	1970–1972	2
George C. Curry	1970–1972	2
Ellis Flynt	1972	

Board of Trustees
Hinds Junior College

HINDS COUNTY

Name of Trustee	Term of Service	Total Years
H. V. Watkins	1922–1944	22
C. S. Spann	1922–1923	1
F. M. Coleman	1922–1936	14
D. C. Simmons	1922–1936	14
D. W. Graham	1922–1933	11
C. A. Williams	1923–1940	17
F. M. Greaves	1933–1968	35
T. H. Naylor	1936–1946	10
M. Ney Williams	1936–1941	5
R. E. Addkison	1936–1946	10
H. H. Davis	1940–1972	32
F. K. Hawkins	1940–1944	4
W. D. Lowe	1944–1965	21
Stokes V. Robertson	1944–1959	15
J. W. McKewen	1946–1965	19
C. H. Snell	1946–1955	9
Robert M. Mayo	1947–1955	8
J. E. Aldridge	1955–1969	14
G. W. Morgan	1959–1968	9
R. A. Callaway	1965–1969	4
R. E. Woolley	1965–1972	7
Walter R. Bivins	1968–1972	4
Ted Kendall, III	1968–1972	4
Dr. Jack B. Fowler	1968–1972	4
Dr. Clyde Muse	1969–1971	2
W. H. Cochran	1971–1972	1

262

M. Cumbest	1932–1952	20
A. W. Ezelle	1927–1929	2
E. E. Flurry	1925–1946	21
Norman V. Flurry	1946–1972	26
R. A. Friar	1930–1931	1
N. P. Gautier	1960–1965	5
Donald Gibson	1960–1961	1
G. M. Hamilton	1953–1972	19
H. P. Heidelberg	1930–1952	22
Lester Mack	1953–1963	10
M. H. Mallette	1941–1972	32
O. H. Martin	1934–1936	2
A. F. Megehee	1932–1952	20
Carl Megehee	1952–1960	8
M. M. Morgan	1953–1956	3
Miss Mary O'Keefe	1932–1942	10
Warner Peterson	1961–1972	11
G. L. Puhle	1961–1972	11
R. A. Roberts	1963–1972	9
R. H. Slaughter, Jr.	1962–1972	10
Frank Spann	1947–1952	5
E. V. Suthoff	1937–1948	11
L. B. Watson	1925–1928	3

STONE COUNTY

Name of Trustee	Term of Service	Total Years
C. O. Batson	1925–1931	6
P. A. Batson	1943–1948	5
L. A. Blackwell	1952–1960	8
A. F. Bond	1925–1929	4
Gordon Bond	1962–1972	10
H. H. Bond	1930–1931	1
W. H. Bond	1927–1929	2
B. L. Breland	1960–1968	8
G. A. Breland	1925–1931	6
G. W. Breland	1924–1925 1936–1937	2
J. H. Breland	1939–1943	4
Buren Broadus	1925–1926	1
J. W. Broadus	1933–1936	3
Webb Broadus	1927–1933 1934–1935	7
W. M. Callahan	1936–1938	2
Ellis Caraway	1936–1938	2
J. A. Cherry	1937–1943	6
Hiriam J. Davis	1964–1972	8
J. N. Dedeaux	1936–1941	5
C. E. Dees	1933–1936	3
C. E. Dees, Jr.	1942–1948 1952–1965	19
John C. Dees	1941–1943	2
B. A. Evans	1952–1956	4

B. A. Lott	1943–1962	19
T. W. Lott	1932–1943	11
W. S. Mauldin	1965–1972	7
E. J. Miller	1969–1972	4
Robert Newton	1933–1936	3
Attis O'Neal	1947–1966	19
D. D. O'Neal	1939–1952	13
Ford O'Neal	1937–1939	2
Clayton Patton	1966–1971	5
Mrs. Rosa Reabold	1943–1944	1
J. E. Roberson	1932–1939	7
D. E. Smith	1932–1964	32
C. C. Swetman	1925–1935	10
W. W. Taylor	1947–1972	25

Board of Trustees
Holmes Junior College

HOLMES COUNTY

Name of Trustee	Term of Service	Total Years
T. G. Stephenson	1925–1928	3
W. J. Nelson, Sr.	1925–1928	3
G. H. Love	1925–1928	3
Dr. A. M. Phillips	1925–1934	9
E. L. Hines	1925–1928 1936–1951	18
W. R. Ellis	1928–1938	10
E. S. Steigler	1928–1932	4
Martin Smith	1928–1932	4
P. H. Williams	1928–1936	8
J. T. Skelton	1932–1950	18
C. G. Campbell	1932–1939	7
B. W. Humphrey	1935–1957	22
Miss Dorothy McBee	1938–1948	10
G. H. McMorrough	1938–1972	34
B. M. Jones	1939–1942	3
Frank Eakin	1942–1972	30
L. R. Thompson	1948–1968	20
Ras M. Branch	1950–1956	6
Ralph L. Ray	1951–1967	16
George F. Mitchell	1956–1964	8
T. O. Buford	1957–1971	14
Paul Hand	1964–1965	1
Marion Ousley	1964–1972	8
Egbert J. Hines, Jr.	1967–1972	5
H. A. Grisham	1968–1970	2
N. C. Hathorn	1970–1972	2
James Burrell	1971–1972	1
Dr. Paul B. Brumby	1972	1
S. F. Allen	1971–1972	2
Henry B. McClellan, Jr.	1972	1

LEFLORE COUNTY

Name of Trustee	Term of Service	Total Years
L. S. Rogers	1931–1961	30
W. G. Poindexter	1931–1957	26
Otis W. Allen	1958–1972	14
Stanny Sanders	1961–1972	11

WASHINGTON COUNTY

Name of Trustee	Term of Service	Total Years
O. W. Holmes	1961–1964	3
Mrs. Norma C. O'Bannon	1961–1969	8
John Darnell	1963–1972	9
W. D. Gardner	1964–1969	5
Jeff Bogue	1969–1972	3
Hugh G. Paine	1969–1972	3

SHARKEY COUNTY

Name of Trustee	Term of Service	Total Years
H. D. Bishop	1963–1972	9
H. T. Greer	1963–1972	9

ISSAQUENA COUNTY

Name of Trustee	Term of Service	Total Years
Dunbar W. Lee	1963–1972	9
Pat Waren	1964–1968	4

COAHOMA COUNTY

Name of Trustee	Term of Service	Total Years
Malcolm Commer	1963–1972	9
Paul Hunter	1963–1972	9

BOLIVAR COUNTY

Name of Trustee	Term of Service	Total Years
Moody Helms	1963–1972	9
L. I. Mayers	1963–1972	9

Board of Trustees
Northwest Mississippi Junior College

TATE COUNTY

Name of Trustee	Term of Service	Total Years
W. W. May	1927–1936	9
Mrs. Winnie Clayton Smith	1927–1940	13
M. A. Burford	1927–1940	13
R. P. White	1927–1933	6
A. D. Elder	1927–1933	6

	Term of Service	Total Years
T. M. Gregory	1927–1940	13
O. B. Wooten	1934–1951	17
R. E. Floyd	1934–1936	2
M. H. Bowden	1936–1944	8
H. L. Murphy	1936–1940	4
Jeva Winter	1940–1948	8
C. O. Pate	1940–1943	3
W. L. Wallace	1940–1966	26
V. H. Spier	1940–1972	32
Clyde Ashe	1944–1955	11
W. M. Tindall	1944–1957	13
C. B. Walker	1948–1972	24
James H. Wilborn	1951–1959	8
Max Billingsley	1955–1972	17
Ben G. Wynne	1957–1972	15
F. O. Givens, Sr.	1959–1972	13
H. M. Wallace	1966–1972	6

QUITMAN COUNTY

Name of Trustee	Term of Service	Total Years
Mrs. Lula O. Prater Jones	1928–1942	24
Mrs. P. H. Lowrey	1928–1937	9
Mrs. William S. Taylor	1928–1972	44
I. B. Boland	1928–1937 1946–1952	15
W. T. Covington	1928–1932	4
J. B. Ross	1937–1950	13
Mrs. Virginia Lamb	1937–1945	8
L. D. Bishop	1937–1939	2
Mrs. R. E. Chapman	1937–1945	8
John C. Rich	1946–1969	23
J. M. Stamper	1946–1949	3
C. H. Caffey	1952–1972	20
Mrs. J. L. Campbell	1952–1972	20
L. V. Craig	1952–1968	16
Wilson Edmondson	1952–1972	20
Cecil O. Sharp	1968–1972	4
William A. Gee	1969–1972	3

TALLAHATCHIE COUNTY

Name of Trustee	Term of Service	Total Years
Robert Harrison	1934–1939	5
Webster Buchanan	1939–1944	5
W. W. Gunn	1944–1948	4
Wade Kellum	1944–1965	21
Al Thomas	1948–1952	4
J. G. Thomason	1952–1960	8
W. L. Brewer	1960–1972	12
W. J. Shackleford	1967–1972	5
Joe L. Tennyson	1972	

B. G. Patty	1930–1966	36
Whiteway Patty	1966–1972	6
Henry R. Sparkman	1936–1943	7
L. T. Anderson	1941–1955	14
Frank Hurst	1943–1960	17
Wade Little	1944–1958	14
John Barrett	1951–1956 1963–1969	11
Paul Daniels	1953–1963	10
Eva Sue Melvin	1960–1963	3
Verle Heath	1960–1968	8
W. E. Skinner, Jr.	1960–1963	3
W. S. Lavender	1963–1972	9
Thomas B. Summerford	1963–1972	9
A. R. Koon	1969–1972	3
L. T. Anderson, Jr.	1956–1972	16
Dewey Owings	1970–1972	2

LOWNDES COUNTY

Name of Trustee	Term of Service	Total Years
A. D. Hatcher	1965–1972	7
Cline Gilliam	1965–1972	7
T. B. Guinn	1965–1969	4
Clayton Junkin	1965–1970	5
H. J. Pearson	1965–1972	7
A. W. Eaves	1965–1970	5
Billy R. Swedenburg	1970–1972	2
Randolph Brown	1970–1972	2
Benton L. Landrum	1971–1972	1
David C. Shelton	1972	
George Gerhart	1972	

CLAY COUNTY

Name of Trustee	Term of Service	Total Years
W. G. McQuiston	1967–1972	5
Thomas E. Douglas	1967–1970	3
Paul Vickers	1967–1972	5
W. C. Loden	1967–1971	4
U. V. Dill	1967–1972	5
John H. Bryan, Jr.	1967–1971	4
Lyle J. Smith	1970–1972	2
David Waide	1971–1972	1
Clark Young	1971–1972	1

OKTIBBEHA COUNTY

Name of Trustee	Term of Service	Total Years
Thad E. Easterwood	1967–1968	1
M. T. Griffin	1967–1972	5
M. S. Camp	1967–1972	5
W. O. Shivers	1967–1972	5
Travis Palmer	1967–1972	5

P. L. Douglas	1967–1972	5
John R. Ware	1968–1972	4

Board of Trustees
Copiah-Lincoln Junior College

COPIAH COUNTY

Name of Trustee	Term of Service	Total Years
J. S. Youngblood	1928–1940	12
R. E. Rea	1928–1962	34
A. S. Thomas	1928–1940	12
W. S. Henley	1928–1972	44
Jack Sullivan	1928–1935	7
J. S. Decell	1928–1929	1
M. Bart Starnes	1931–1932	1
H. T. Funchess	1932–1939	7
S. M. Furlow	1934–1936	2
Frank Oswalt	1936–1947	11
R. C. Bufkin	1939–1943	4
Dr. Otho Messer	1939–1972	33
J. C. Reynolds	1939–1943	4
E. R. Izard	1944–1966	22
T. V. Rush	1943–1953	10
Spence Templeton	1945–1946	1
B. W. Cagle	1946–1953	7
Gordon Sullivan	1943–1944	1
R. E. Middleton	1948–1952	4
E. F. Anderson	1952–1959	7
John J. King	1953–1956	3
Earl Donahoe	1954–1955	1
Fred W. Anderson	1955–1960	5
Sturge Dodds	1957–1972	15
Lester R. Furr	1960–1972	12
C. C. Graves, Jr.	1960–1972	12
George Myers	1967–1972	5
Dale Sullivan	1972	
P. D. Armstrong	1972	

LINCOLN COUNTY

Name of Trustee	Term of Service	Total Years
Prentiss Furr	1928–1940	12
L. H. Baggett	1928–1936	8
Dr. David Magee	1928–1939	11
Andy Greer	1928–1932	4
George Moak	1928–1929	1
L. P. May	1928–1932	4
Edgar King	1929–1933	4
Thomas Price	1933–1937	4
Eddie Young	1933–1941	8
C. J. Holloway	1934–1948	14
Clyde E. Day	1936–1940	4
J. H. Reeves	1937–1940	3

Bryan Barnett	1932–1960	29
Mrs. C. K. Waggoner	1932–1936	4
C. O. Brooks	1936–1940	4
Dr. T. V. Horne	1937–1940	4
L. B. Townsend	1939–1943	5
L. A. Faulkner	1939–1943	5
Forrest Munday	1940–1944 1968–1972	8
E. C. Edwards	1941–1950	10
Henry C. Ashcraft	1944–1947	4
J. W. Salers	1944–1950	7
Howard Leach	1944–1948	4
L. L. Denson	1944–1969	26
Burton McMillan	1948–1951	4
J. Leon Smith	1951	1
L. B. Barnes	1951–1952	2
Leonard Crowe	1952–1956	5
J. D. Wiggins	1952–1956	4
J. H. Hamilton	1952–1953	2
A. D. Richardson	1953–1963	11
T. T. Foster	1954–1958	5
Guy Richardson	1956–1960	4
Malcolm Spence	1957–1961	5
P. B. Dickens	1959–1972	13
Coleman Oliver	1960–1964	4
D. C. Alford	1961–1972	12
Jerry Moore	1962–1972	10
J. T. Logan	1963–1968	5
Olin Nicholson	1963–1971	9
Kenneth Horn	1967–1968	1
P. T. Young	1970–1972	3
E. L. Williams	1971–1972	2
Fred Ray Blocker	1972	
H. M. Price	1972	

NESHOBA COUNTY

Name of Trustee	Term of Service	Total Years
W. A. Burt	1929–1934	6
H. A. Moore	1929–1934	6
H. C. Blount	1929–1931	3
F. B. Deweese	1929–1938	10
Genie Ethridge	1929–1934	6
T. T. Cooper	1929–1934	6
L. B. Walton	1932–1940	9
J. W. Crawford	1935–1940	6
W. R. Ray	1935–1940	6
Olin Lee	1935–1940	6
W. D. Gillis	1935–1958	24
W. A. Winstead	1936–1942	7
Albert Underwood	1941–1942	2
J. A. McDonald	1941–1953	13
G. L. Sansing	1941–1954	14
O. L. Wood	1941–1942	2

B. G. Salter	1943–1951	9
J. C. Salter	1943–1951	9
B. J. Milling	1943–1948	5
Lamar Whinnery	1948–1952	4
M. L. Hayes	1952–1956	5
Ples Barrett	1952–1961	10
I. M. Latimer	1952–1956	4
Odis Cox	1954–1972	19
H. L. Thomas	1955–1964	10
Jack Cheatham	1956–1960	4
O. J. Evans	1957–1960	4
Herman Alford	1959–1970	12
A. D. Bassett	1960–1964	5
C. G. Barrett	1961–1970	10
Melvin Tullos	1962–1972	11
T. C. Ward	1964–1967	4
Albert Elliott	1965–1972	8
Prentiss Copeland	1968–1972	5
W. T. Blackwell	1968–1972	5
Jim Mason	1971–1972	2

SCOTT COUNTY

Name of Trustee	Term of Service	Total Years
A. T. Cooper	1930–1972	43
J. Knox Huff	1930–1952	23
W. H. Jones	1930–1940	11
Robert S. Weems	1930–1932	2
H. C. Anderson	1932–1936	4
Dr. W. F. Johnson	1930–1943	14
Walter Breeland	1936–1944	8
John Wallace	1930–1957	28
L. C. Jones	1941–1945	5
Mack Weems	1940–1956 1962–1972	27
Macon Patrick	1944–1951	8
Homer Fikes	1946–1950	5
Armstead Street	1950–1964	15
Marx Huff	1952–1961	10
L. R. Anthony	1952–1961	10
Jack Waggoner	1956–1961	5
Arter Harrison	1956–1960	4
W. E. Elliott	1960–1964	4
Leo Lee	1962–1972	11
W. W. McCann	1962–1972	11
J. A. Lee	1965–1972	8
Maurice Harrison	1964–1968	4
A. F. Hollingsworth	1968–1972	5

WINSTON COUNTY

Name of Trustee	Term of Service	Total Years
T. T. Griffin	1935–1936	2
Claude Richardson	1935–1948	14
O. H. Craig	1935–1942	8

I. W. Horton	1935–1942	8
R. B. Yarbrough	1935–1942	8
S. J. Hopkins	1935–1939	5
Earl Woodward	1939–1960	22
Roger Allen	1936–1940	4
B. M. McCully	1943–1944	2
E. H. Boswell	1943–1944	2
Dr. E. H. Anderson	1943–1944	2
S. Frank Roberts	1943–1948	3
Houston C. Carr	1945–1963	19
T. W. Luke, Jr.	1945–1970	26
Julian Cunningham	1940–1970	30
B. G. Hull	1948–1972	25
Olyn Sanders	1948–1963	16
Alvin Massey	1961–1972	12
M. D. Boydston	1964–1970	6
C. C. Huntley, Jr.	1964–1968	4
H. B. Hudspeth	1971–1972	2
Guy Richardson	1968–1972	5
Garner Hatcher	1971–1972	2

Board of Trustees
Southwest Junior College

PIKE COUNTY

Name of Trustee	Term of Service	Total Years
W. M. Davis	1929–1949	20
L. S. Felder	1929–1938	9
Mrs. Nannie Gillis	1929–1939	10
Burton Godbold	1929–1948	19
J. T. Hutchinson	1929–1949	20
R. L. Simmons, Sr.	1929–1930	1
D. S. Reeves	1928–1938	10
C. A. Reeves	1938–1962	24
C. M. Rhodus	1938–1949	11
Mrs. Mildred Ellzey Stiers	1939–1947	8
W. C. Price	1940–1941	1
A. B. Williams	1940–1947	7
George Wingo	1941–1948	7
Karey Andrews	1947–1960	13
J. S. Brumfield	1948–1967	19
D. W. Conerly	1949–1964	15
Robert Girling	1949–1955	6
Gent Hutchinson	1949–1956	7
Hugh Norman	1949–1951	2
O. W. Phillips	1949–1956	7
H. H. Huffman	1956–1972	6
Hilton Mixon	1956–1968	12
H. L. Stone	1956–1968	12
W. L. Dickerson	1960–1966	6
Hollis Alford	1962–1972	10
J. J. Varnado	1964–1967	3
N. B. Gillis, Jr.	1967–1971	4

Joe Pigott	1967–1972	5
Homer Addison	1968–1972	4
Dr. Warren A. Hiatt	1968–1972	4
Harold A. Young	1968–1972	4
E. G. Covington, Jr.	1971–1972	1
Jewel Rushing	1972	

WALTHALL COUNTY

Name of Trustee	Term of Service	Total Years
Jerry Conerly	1964–1972	8
L. A. Johnson	1964–1971	7
J. D. Herring	1972	

AMITE COUNTY

Name of Trustee	Term of Service	Total Years
W. V. Caulfield	1940–1947	7
Jack Ewing	1940–1943	3
J. A. Robertson	1940 1947	7
Kenneth Stewart	1940–1944	4
W. E. Trask	1940–1941	1
R. L. Wilson	1940–1950	10
H. L. Lewis	1941–1972	31
Jack Causey	1944–1953	9
J. M. Williams	1945–1948	3
J. H. Poole	1947–1957	10
Mrs. Annie Andrews	1948–1972	24
Dempsey Newman	1949–1952	3
Britte Hughey	1950–1972	22
M. L. Causey	1952–1956	4
Percy Hazelwood	1953–1972	19
E. H. Hurst	1956–1972	16
Sidney Hughes	1957–1960	3
Troy Travis	1960–1972	12

Board of Trustees
Meridian Junior College

LAUDERDALE COUNTY

Name of Trustee	Term of Service	Total Years
C. A. Ray, Sr.	1923–1938	15
B. J. Carter, Jr.	1929–1942	13
J. B. Melton, Sr.	1930–1945	15
M. V. B. Miller	1934–1943	9
Mrs. I. A. Rosenbaum, Sr.	1935–1944	9
T. G. Cleveland	1939–1952	13
J. C. Wilbourn	1944–1945	1
Clarke Pearce	1944–1954	10
J. A. Covington, Jr.	1944–1952	8
C. A. Ray, Jr.	1945–1955	10
Mrs. Betsy Graham	1946–1956	10

Walter R. Bivins	1968–1972	4
C. G. Muse	1969–1971	2
Jack B. Fowler	1968–1972	4
W. H. Cochran	1971–1972	2
T. H. Kendall, III	1968–1972	4

RANKIN COUNTY

Name of Trustee	Term of Service	Total Years
Robert L. Compere	1956–1960	4
L. L. Autry	1960–1968	8
Max Alman	1964–1972	8
C. W. Jones	1967–1972	5
E. L. Perritt	1972	

COPIAH COUNTY

Name of Trustee	Term of Service	Total Years
Clyde C. Graves	1960–1972	12
E. Ray Izard	1954–1956	12
George Myers	1968–1972	4
Dale Sullivan	1972	
Louis Burghard	1972	

WARREN COUNTY

Name of Trustee	Term of Service	Total Years
Sharp W. Banks	1962–1972	10
J. E. Blackburn	1964–1968	4
Clyde R. Donnell	1968–1972	4

C/Supervisors

The following is a listing of members of boards of supervisors serving each junior college district during the first fifty-year period, 1922–1972.

These represent eighty-one of Mississippi's eighty-two counties. The county not included is Wilkinson County, which is a part of the Southwest Mississippi Junior College District.

The names included in these lists were secured from the administration of each junior college and from official records. Unfortunately, the records may be incomplete and inaccurate.

Supervisors
Pearl River Junior College

PEARL RIVER COUNTY

Name of Supervisor	Term of Service	Total Years
J. Sol Moody	1920–1936	16
Hamp S. Stewart	1920–1932	12
George W. Amaker	1920–1924 1928–1932	8
W. H. Burke	1920–1924	4
D. R. Johnson	1920–1924 1932–1936	8
Monroe Tate	1924–1932	8
Carl Bass	1924–1928 1932–1936	8
Pete Lumpkin	1924–1932 1936–1948	20
Nolas Ladner	1932–1944	12
W. C. Bass	1932–1936	4
E. H. Stevens	1932–1944	12
Ellis Mitchell	1936–1944	8
W. J. Fronea	1936–1940	4
J. Benton Seals	1940–1948	8
C. A. Baughman	1944–1948	4
Sollie H. Burge	1944–1956 1968–1972	16
Ralph Stockstill	1944–1952	8
Paul Watts	1948–1972	24
Laurence (Red) Holden	1948–1968	20
Joe R. Lee	1948–1960	12
W. E. (Bill) Moody	1952–1964	12
Clifford N. Ladner	1956–1968	12
C. L. Thompson	1960–1964	4
A. W. Stockstill	1964–1972	8
Hollis C. Stockstill	1964–1972	8
L. K. Sones, Jr.,	1968–1972	4
G. W. Moody	1972	
E. M. Clark	1972	
Tommie J. Whitfield	1972	

LAMAR COUNTY

Name of Supervisor	Term of Service	Total Years
T. F. Thurman	1936–1940	4
W. D. Evans	1936–1940	4
Roy Ledbetter	1936–1940	4
W. W. Dearman	1936–1940	4
W. A. Cole	1936–1940	4
J. R. Saucier	1936–1944	8
F. K. Phillips	1940–1960	20
A. G. Beall	1940–1956	16
Talmage Saucier	1940–1948	8
R. B. Parker	1940–1944	4
S. W. Howell	1944–1948	4
John Graham	1944–1948	4
Ben Sones	1948–1972	24
R. S. Lott	1948–1960	12
Lemuel R. Boyer	1948–1968 1972	21
Emmett Byrd	1956–1972	16
Albert Entrekin	1960–1968	8
Joe Traylor	1960–1972	12
Homer Elliott	1968–1972	4
W. M. Patterson	1968–1972	4
John W. Anderson	1972	
Selvyn Rayborn	1972	

JEFFERSON DAVIS COUNTY

Name of Supervisor	Term of Service	Total Years
R. E. (Robert) Tyrone	1936–1940 1944–1952 1960–1972	24
N. F. Manton	1936–1940	4
L. W. King	1936–1948	12
W. D. Griffith	1936–1940	4
Tom B. Slater	1936–1952	16
Austin Stamps	1940–1944	4
Walter C. Williamson	1940–1956	16
W. B. Parish	1940–1944	4
J. P. Parish	1944–1960	16
Daniel R. Deen	1948–1956	8
John C. Burrow	1952–1960	8
Robert L. Daughdrill	1952–1964	12
J. L. Robbins	1956–1972	16
Willie Fortenberry	1956–1972	16
Reggie C. Lee	1960–1972	12
Ezra Garner	1964–1972	8
Robert Glynn Rogers	1972	
Oris Stephens	1972	
Cleatus P. McNease	1972	

MARION COUNTY

Name of Supervisor	Term of Service	Total Years
John T. Hutson	1932–1936	4
L. A. Newsom	1932–1952	20
R. W. Hammond	1932–1936	4
J. E. Forbes	1932–1948	16
J. J. Beacham	1932–1948	16
J. Ira Rayburn	1936–1948	12
J. J. Sumrall	1936–1940	4
W. N. Forbes	1940–1948	8
H. Oscar Morris	1948–1972	24
C. E. Thornhill	1948–1964	16
Leon McKenzie	1948–1960 1964–1968	16
A. Buford Smith	1948–1956	8
Sheldon Fortenberry	1952–1960	8
Wm. M. Patterson	1956–1972	16
Mrs. S. L. Fortenberry	1960–1964	4
E. F. (Jack) Stringer	1960–1964 1968–1972	8
Frank Fortenberry	1964–1972	8
Laverne S. Pittman	1964–1972	8
W. R. Morris	1972	
Billy Ray McKenzie	1972	

HANCOCK COUNTY

Name of Supervisor	Term of Service	Total Years
Charles B. Murphy	1936–1948	12
John B. Wheat	1936–1948	12
Calvin Shaw	1936–1944	8
Jack Lott	1936–1940 1948–1960	16
T. E. Kellar	1936–1940	4
Ladner Necaise	1940–1948	8
Ed P. Ortte	1940–1952	12
J. S. Shaw	1944–1960	16
Joe C. Jones	1948–1956	8
Frank Keller	1948–1956	8
R. J. Hubbard, Jr.,	1952–1968	16
Charles A. Russ, Jr.	1956–1'64	8
Mrs. Frank Keller	1956–1960	4
Ike M. Frierson	1960–1968	8
Charles Lavinghouse	1960–1968	8
James A. Necaise	1960–1968	8
Harlan G. Dean	1964–1968	4
Charles A. Russ, III	1968–1972	4
Dolph Dellar	1968–1972	4
Joseph A. Cuevas	1968–1972	4
J. C. Mauffray	1968–1972	4
Russell J. Elliott	1968–1972	4
Jerry L. Ladner	1972	
Oscar Peterson	1972	
H. (Bully) Zengarling	1972	
James Travirca	1972	

FORREST COUNTY

Name of Supervisor	Term of Service	Total Years
W. U. Sigler	1968–1972	4
Albert S. Woods, Jr.	1968–1972	4
J. H. Grayson	1968–1972	4
J. A. P. Carter, Jr.	1968–1972	4
Hix Anderson, Jr.	1968–1972	4

Supervisors
Hinds Junior College

HINDS COUNTY

Name of Supervisor	Term of Service	Total Years
J. D. Gordon	1920–1924	4
E. C. Fletcher	1920–1928	8
E. M. Broome	1920–1932	12
Lamar Puryear	1920–1928	8
Lewis J. Jones	1920–1924	4
Lewis B. Williams	1924–1928 1936–1940	8
W. Lynn Jones	1924–1928	4
H. A. Cannada	1928–1944	16
L. M. Gordon	1928–1940	12
E. D. Graves	1928–1936	8
George P. Luckett	1928–1932	4
S. C. Heard	1932–1936	4
James B. Lusk	1932–1936	4
Tom L. Gordon	1936–1948	12
E. B. Flewellyn	1936–1944	8
J. C. Hall	1940–1948	8
Perry Luckett	1940–1948	8
E. F. Ragan	1944–1964	20
S. M. Hubbard	1944–1968	24
Walter Ferguson	1948–1952	4
Hunter Moorehead	1948–1952	4
Floyd Hawkins	1948–1952	4
H. Power Hearn	1952–1956	4
W. L. Fairchild	1952–1956	4
Mrs. Floyd Hawkins	1952–1960	8
Ross P. Dodds	1956–1960	4
Dan Ferguson	1956–1964	8
Tom Virden	1960–1968	8
L. J. Beasley	1960–1972	12
Malcolm Warren	1964–1972	8
Mrs. Dan Ferguson	1964–1965	1
Johnnie Taylor	1964–1972	8
J. L. (Pete) McGee	1968–1972	4
Dr. Noel K. McKey	1968–1972	4
Pal R. Jones	1972	

RANKIN COUNTY

Name of Supervisor	Term of Service	Total Years
J. M. May	1948–1956	8
E. J. McRae	1948–1952 1956–1960	8
R. L. Cross	1948–1972	24
B. F. Coats	1948–1960	12
Tom Ponder	1948–1952 1960–1964	8
Cecil Marbury	1952–1956	4
Carr Burnham	1952–1960	8
Milton Singletary	1956–1972	16
Rom H. Rives	1960–1972	12
Gay Gill	1960–1968	8
Woodrow W. Swilley	1964–1968	4
Hilton Richardson	1968–1972	4
Steen Patrick	1968–1972	4
Kenneth Bridges	1972	
Ralph Moore	1972	

WARREN COUNTY

Name of Supervisor	Term of Service	Total Years
Tom B. Harris	1952–1956	4
A. E. Tucker	1952–1964	12
George S. Kelley	1952–1964	12
O. J. Bori	1952–1960	8
P. T. Hullum	1952–1956 1964–1972	12
A. H. Hall	1956–1968	12
J. L. McCaskill	1956–1972	16
Paul A. Pride	1960–1972	12
Robert Dowe	1964–1972	8
Herbert Boler	1968–1972	4
Thomas F. Akers	1972	
James R. Andrews	1972	
Clyde Donnell	1972	

CLAIBORNE COUNTY

Name of Supervisor	Term of Service	Total Years
A. H. Eaton	1964–1968	4
T. H. Trevilion	1964–1968	4
F. G. Peyton	1964–1968	4
J. J. Millsaps	1964–1968	4
Davis N. Starnes	1964–1972	8
William Matt Ross	1968–1972	4
Mott R. Headley, II	1968–1972	4
Kenneth P. Vaughan	1968–1972	4
H. Cannon Ainsworth	1968–1972	4

Supervisors
Mississippi Gulf Coast Junior College

STONE COUNTY

Name of Supervisor	Term of Service	Total Years
G. J. Alexander	1924–1928	4
W. E. Batson	1924–1928	4
Eugene H. Bond	1928–1932	4
A. W. Davis	1928–1930	2
W. A. Smith	1928–1930	2
E. R. Davis	1930–1932	2
J. T. Walton	1924–1932	8
Vernon E. Brown	1932–1936	4
R. A. Switzer	1924–1932 1940–1944	12
W. W. Lott	1924–1944	20
G. A. Breland	1932–1940	8
W. A. Miller	1936–1948	12
John B. Brown	1936–1944	8
P. G. Hickman	1936–1940	4
Otis Bond	1940–1960	20
R. L. Robinson	1941–1942	1
O. B. Brown	1944–1972	28
Mrs. R. A. Switzer	1944–1948	4
C. E. Dees, Sr.	1944–1948	4
Emmett R. Bond	1944–1956	12
E. R. Smith	1932–1936 1948–1952	8
Billie Parker	1948–1964	16
John C. Dees	1952–1972	20
Percy C. O'Neal	1956–1968	8
Leland Bond	1960–1968	8
Lee Overstreet	1964–1972	8
Johnnie C. West	1968–1972	4
W. M. (Bill) Hancock	1964–1971	7
Mrs. Bill Hancock	1971–1972	1

HARRISON COUNTY

Name of Supervisor	Term of Service	Total Years
A. W. Ladner	1924–1928	4
E. J. Adams, Sr.	1924–1932	8
C. S. Pigford	1932–1936	4
Paul Evans	1924–1932	8
Walter Nixon	1924–1932	8
Loren O'Neal	1924–1927	3
H. B. Hopper	1928–1936	8
Edward Fairley	1928–1940	12
Oscar O'Neal	1936–1940	4
J. Loren Saucier	1936–1940	4
Dewey Lawrence	1940–1964	24
O. F. Cassibry	1940–1956	16
Hugh Fitzpatrick	1940–1948	8
W. M. Ladner	1940–1956	16
W. Luther Blackledge	1940–1956	16
Julius J. Hayden	1948–1960	12
Roy Edward Dedeaux	1956–1964	8
Gatha Ladner	1956–1968	12
G. Dennis Broadus	1956–1968	12
Nick French	1960–1968	8
Laz Quave	1964–1972	8
R. C. Simpson	1964–1972	8
Francis J. Hursey	1968–1972	4
Wendell C. Lewis	1968–1972	4
Arlan Robinson	1968–1972	4

JACKSON COUNTY

Name of Supervisor	Term of Service	Total Years
W. L. Nelson	1924–1928	4
William F. Martin	1924–1926	2
E. A. Denson	1924–1932	8
Hermes F. Gautier	1926–1928 1932–1948	18
J. K. Lemon	1924–1929	5
Robert McLeod	1928–1932	4
Fred Taylor	1924–1932	8
B. W. Wilson	1928–1932	4
H. W. Cochran	1932–1944	12
K. W. Burnham	1924–1948	24
A. P. (Fred) Moran	1928–1968	40
R. L. Vaughan	1932–1944	12
Roy O. (Lum) Cumbest	1944–1972	28
George A. Cruthirds	1944–1952	8
Edward A. Khayat	1948–1972	24
Joe V. Krebs	1948–1952	4
George B. Hague	1952–1960	8
Olin H. Davis	1952–1972	20
Maness M. Bartlett	1960–1968	8
J. C. May	1968–1972	4
William T. Roberts	1968–1972	4

GEORGE COUNTY

Name of Supervisor	Term of Service	Total Years
E. B. Ward	1944–1948	4
Florian Maples	1940–1944	4
Wiley J. Parker	1940–1948	8
Carl T. Havard	1940–1944 1964–1968	8
J. H. Davis	1940–1944	4
W. T. Moody	1940–1960	20
N. G. Fairley	1944–1948	4
J. H. Whittington	1944–1952	8
E. G. Yonge	1945–1948	3

Henry A. Read	1948–1960	12
Clemon Wall	1948–1956	8
W. E. (Pat) Howell	1948–1956	8
R. J. Green	1952–1972	20
Otis Bufkin	1956–1964	8
Woodrow Cochran	1956–1964	8
Lloyd M. Eubanks	1960–1964 1968–1972	8
Robert L. Rouse	1960–1968	8
Sam H. Loftin, Jr.	1964–1972	8
Clemon Howell	1964–1972	8
Joe L. Cochran	1968–1972	4

Supervisors
Holmes Junior College

HOLMES COUNTY

Name of Supervisor	Term of Service	Total Years
V. Rheinhardt	1925–1942	17
Marvin Stanley	1925–1928	3
J. W. Stroud	1925–1928	3
T. J. Brown	1925–1936	11
Martin L. Smith	1925–1928 1932–1948	19
Jesse H. Walton	1928–1940	12
J. R. Brown	1928–1936	8
J. H. Rogers	1928–1932	4
Marion Rogers	1936–1960	24
Kirk Thomas	1936–1956	20
Earl H. Fowler	1940–1948	8
George W. Ellison	1944–1948	4
C. G. Campbell	1948–1959	11
Joe Moore	1948–1951	3
Mrs. Joe Moore	1951–1952	1
Lonnie Boatwright	1952–1956	4
Claude Keirn	1952–1956	4
Roy Brown	1956–1960	4
W. W. Salley	1956–1964	8
W. Leslie Smith	1956–1966	10
Mrs. C. G. Campbell	1959–1960	1
Ray Campbell	1960–1968	8
Estell Scott	1960–1968	8
L. C. Johnson	1960–1968	8
Charles H. Smith	1964–1968	4
Oscar Rogers	1966–1972	6
Grady Ellis	1968–1972	4
B. T. Taylor	1968–1972	4
D. C. Conn	1968–1972	4
Leslie I. Farmer	1968–1972	4

CARROLL COUNTY

Name of Supervisor	Term of Service	Total Years
A. E. Lott	1928–1936	8
J. H. Williford	1928–1936	8
J. B. Bruce	1928–1936	8
E. L. Chambley	1928–1932	4
James Somerville	1928–1936	8
Harry P. Mullen	1932–1944	12
J. G. Lott	1936–1940	4
J. B. Williams	1936–1940	4
C. R. Elliott	1936–1940 1944–1948 1952–1958	14
Marion Ely	1936–1948	12
H. E. Ashmore	1940–1952	12
S. B. Taylor	1940–1948	8
J. W. Moses	1940–1944	4
Ralph Taylor	1944–1948	4
B. O. Clark	1948–1952	4
Lonnie E. Galey	1948–1952	4
Kermit G. Johnson	1948–1952	4
Weldon Baskin, Jr.	1948–1952	4
E. E. Alderman	1952–1960	8
D. C. Lott	1952–1964	12
B. L. Mann	1952–1960	8
Willie C. Welch	1956–1972	16
George W. Galey	1958–1972	14
Cecil L. Herbert, Sr.	1960–1972	12
Claude R. Lott	1960–1972	12
Percy D. Corder	1964–1972	8
Vernon Welch	1972	

ATTALA COUNTY

Name of Supervisor	Term of Service	Total Years
E. Watson Frazier	1956–1972	16
A. G. Noah	1956–1960	4
C. D. Oakes	1956–1968	12
W. B. Smith	1956–1964	8
Lee Johnson	1956–1972	16
Horace Hutchinson	1960–1972	12
Alvin McCrory	1964–1972	8
Robert Ellard	1968–1972	4

MONTGOMERY COUNTY

Name of Supervisor	Term of Service	Total Years
Joe Russell	1958–1960	2
Dewitt Mitchell	1958–1960	2
Claude Patridge	1958–1960	2
Marvin Abel	1958–1972	14

J. W. Braswell	1958–1972	14
Marion Williams	1960–1968	8
Albert Hayward	1960–1972	12
Clarence Oliver	1960–1972	12
Grady Ellis	1968–1972	4
John L. Baskin	1972	
Henry H. Woods	1972	
Wesley Weed	1972	

GRENADA COUNTY

Name of Supervisor	Term of Service	Total Years
Ben Sanders	1959–1964	5
George R. Williams	1959–1972	13
Robert Burke, Jr.	1959–1972	13
Lewis A. Williams, Jr.	1959–1972	13
Noel Staten	1959–1972	13
Frank Gibbs	1964–1972	8

CHOCTAW COUNTY

Name of Supervisor	Term of Service	Total Years
Hollis H. Bagwell	1959–1972	13
Clyde Morgan	1959–1967	8
J. L. Thompson	1959–1960	1
Edgar Reel	1959–1967	8
Hudson Orr	1959–1960	1
J. E. Ray	1960–1972	12
G. W. Stephenson	1960–1968	8
James Stark	1968–1972	4
Olen McPherson	1968–1972	4
Q. L. Ray	1968–1972	4

YAZOO COUNTY

Name of Supervisor	Term of Service	Total Years
A. Norwood Nichols	1964–1972	8
Grady Davis	1964–1972	8
A. S. King	1964–1972	8
L. N. Phillips	1964–1972	8
W. S. Hancock	1964–1972	8
Sam Fisher	1972	
A. B. Hogue	1972	

MADISON COUNTY

Name of Supervisor	Term of Service	Total Years
A. B. Mansell, Jr.	1961–1972	11
L. D. Chapman	1961–1964	3

C. E. Rice	1961–1964	3
E. D. Mansell	1961–1972	11
L. D. Wallace	1961–1963	2
J. S. Harris	1963–1972	9
A. E. Crawford	1964–1972	8
P. H. Luckett, Jr.	1964–1972	8

WEBSTER COUNTY

Name of Supervisor	Term of Service	Total Years
Pascal Hodges	1963–1968	5
Herman Clanton	1963–1972	9
James B. Dean	1963–1972	9
J. Mack Peacock	1963–1972	9
Wayne Johnson	1963–1972	9
A. D. Hall, Jr.	1968–1972	4
A. J. Knight	1972	
J. M. Crowley	1972	

Supervisors
Mississippi Delta Junior College
SUNFLOWER COUNTY

Name of Supervisor	Term of Service	Total Years
W. H. Phipps	1928–1932	4
W. D. Parker	1928–1936	8
W. R. French	1928–1960	32
D. O. Ringold	1928–1932	4
W. D. Marlow	1928–1932	4
C. S. Simmons	1932–1940	8
R. D. McLean	1932–1948	16
G. T. Blackwood	1932–1948	16
C. M. Davis	1936–1952	16
Fred Jones	1940–1944 1952–1964	16
Dr. W. L. Ervin	1944–1952	8
Mrs. W. L. Ervin	1952 only	1
C. L. Kirk	1948–1952	4
G. W. Manning, Jr.	1948–1972	24
H. A. Carpenter	1952–1964	12
George W. Cockrell	1952–1968	16
Noel K. Toler	1960–1972	12
J. W. Corder	1960–1972	12
W. L. (Bubber) Jackson, Jr.	1964–1972	8
Charles Hughes	1964–1972	8

HUMPHREYS COUNTY

Name of Supervisor	Term of Service	Total Years
John A. Bridges	1932–1940 1948–1952	12

Dr. W. S. Taylor	1932–1936	4
T. M. Macbeth	1932–1936	4
W. R. Carson	1932–1936	4
B. A. Holaday	1932–1948	16
R. P. Hamaker	1936–1944	8
B. S. Reed	1936–1968	32
Webb McRaney	1936–1944	8
J. A. Mortimer	1940–1948	8
Clyde Scruggs	1944–1952	8
Alfred Abel	1944–1956	15
	1964–1967	
B. W. Smith	1948–1952	4
C. B. Aycock	1952–1972	20
W. E. Hamaker	1952–1960	8
R. B. Harris	1952–1972	20
J. T. Wood	1956–1964	8
R. D. Bearden	1960–1972	12
Mrs. J. Alfred Abel	1968 only	1
Ronny Buchanan	1968–1972	4
James Long	1968–1972	4

LEFLORE COUNTY

Name of Supervisor	Term of Service	Total Years
Pamplin Smith	1932–1944	12
Mims S. Wilson	1932–1936	4
G. Latham Ray	1932–1936	4
William T. Rich	1932–1940	8
D. C. Hill	1932–1936	4
C. A. Foreman	1936–1944	8
W. S. Vardaman	1936–1952	16
Walter Moore	1936–1948	12
Lee W. Ely	1940–1960	20
J. J. Frasier	1944–1952	8
W. J. Lipscomb	1944–1972	28
Douglas Smith	1948–1956	8
Rufus Freeman	1952–1964	12
B. T. Terry	1952–1960	8
Louis S. Poindexter	1956–1964	8
Robert H. Swanzy	1960–1968	8
James D. Green	1960–1972	12
Ulysses A. Smith	1964–1968	4
James M. Hooper, Jr.	1964–1972	8
O. B. Landrum	1968–1972	4
William L. Kellum	1968–1972	4

BOLIVAR COUNTY

Name of Supervisor	Term of Service	Total Years
O. J. Scott, Sr.	1960–1968	8
W. A. Welshans	1960–1972	12
A. S. Weissinger	1960–1964	4
C. Milton Smith	1960–1972	12
C. L. Beckham	1960–1964	4

Max L. Dilworth	1964–1968	4
Elmer L. Prewitt	1964–1968	4
J. E. Bobo	1968–1972	4
Kermit Stanton	1968–1972	4
Elmer L. Prewitt	1968–1972	4

COAHOMA COUNTY

Name of Supervisor	Term of Service	Total Years
J. Van Wilson	1960–1968	8
W. L. McKee, Jr.	1960–1964	4
W. A. (Bill) Hughes	1960–1972	12
J. E. Merritt	1960–1964	4
W. E. Young	1960–1968	8
Lawrence B. Craig	1964–1968	4
W. Wert Cooper	1964–1968	4
T. L. (Red) Brunt	1968–1972	4
John B. McKee, Jr.	1968–1972	4
Curtis E. Presley	1968–1972	4
Graham Bramlett	1968–1972	4

ISSAQUENA COUNTY

Name of Supervisor	Term of Service	Total Years
Dr. G. L. Johnson	1960–1968	8
Frank White	1960–1968	8
Archie I. Irwin	1960–1972	12
A. E. Scott	1960–1968	8
John A. Darnell	1960–1964	4
Ed Holcomb, Jr.	1964–1968	4
Mrs. Jeryl T. Johnson	1968–1972	4
Mrs. Alma White	1968–1972	4
B. B. Scott	1968–1972	4

SHARKEY COUNTY

Name of Supervisor	Term of Service	Total Years
Joe Carson	1960–1972	12
Spencer B. Powers	1960–1972	12
S. B. Glassco	1960–1968	8
H. T. Greer	1960–1972	12
P. H. Hodges	1960–1964	4
Jimmie King	1964–1968	4
Brevik Schimmel	1968–1972	4
W. E. Patterson, Jr.	1968–1972	4

WASHINGTON COUNTY

Name of Supervisor	Term of Service	Total Years
M. H. Rich	1960–1968	8
Jeff Davis	1960–1972	12
Herman Caillouet	1960–1968	8
Fred Neal	1960–1972	12
W. P. Powers	1960–1968	8

Paul C. Love	1968–1972	4
Roy L. Fulton	1968–1972	4
Virgil L. Sandifer	1968–1972	4

Supervisors
Northwest Mississippi Junior College

TATE COUNTY

Name of Supervisor	Term of Service	Total Years
Sam Sneed	1926–1940	14
M. B. Brown	1926–1928	2
F. F. Pack	1926–1932	6
J. P. Roberts	1926–1928	2
S. A. Jones	1926–1928	2
H. S. Metcalf	1928–1936	8
J. B. Kerr	1928–1932	4
Joe C. Graham	1928–1932	4
E. C. Durley	1932–1936	4
J. T. Williams	1932–1936	4
R. P. White	1932–1940	8
Lester Samuels	1936–1940	4
Theber Williams	1936–1940	4
M. B. Brown	1936–1940	4
R. E. Floyd	1940–1960	20
T. E. Smith	1940–1960	20
E. Perkins	1940–1944	4
J. B. Kerr	1940–1944	4
W. C. Hancock	1940–1952	12
R. C. Ferguson	1944–1948	4
P. B. Pounders	1944–1948	4
R. E. Hudson	1948–1956	8
T. J. Newton	1948–1960	2
Leroy Crockett	1952–1972	20
W. D. Todd, Jr.	1956–1968	12
Delma Baker	1960–1972	12
E. F. Hale, Jr.	1960–1972	12
James Rhodes	1960–1968	8
Jamie L. Beard	1968–1972	4
Charles Gaines	1968–1972	4
T. B. McIver	1972	

QUITMAN COUNTY

Name of Supervisor	Term of Service	Total Years
E. W. Taylor	1928–1936	8
S. W. Jones	1928–1932	4
J. H. Manning	1928–1936	8
G. T. Reed	1928–1932	4
R. P. Sorrels	1928–1932	4
F. L. Lyons	1932–1936	4
J. M. Turner	1932–1936	4

C. W. McCullar	1932–1936	4
L. B. Lollar	1936–1944	8
Clausen Peden	1936–1940	4
A. Jamison	1936–1948	12
J. V. Bingham	1936–1940	4
C. G. Rotenberry	1936–1944	8
R. W. Davis	1940–1952	12
I. B. Boland	1940–1952	12
F. E. Stewart	1944–1952	8
W. D. Brians	1944–1964	20
Clint Mitchell	1948–1964	16
J. D. Pettit	1952–1969	17
C. G. Chrestman	1952–1972	20
W. B. Moore	1952–1972	20
W. A. Turner	1964–1968	4
Fletcher S. Haynes	1964–1972	8
James H. Reed	1968–1972	8
Mrs. J. D. Pettit	1969–1970	1
T. C. Simpson	1970–1972	2

TALLAHATCHIE COUNTY

Name of Supervisor	Term of Service	Total Years
Guy W. Burkhalter	1939–1946	7
Tom O. Adams	1939–1948	9
J. H. Shackelford	1939–1948	9
J. D. Ray	1939–1952	13
Roy Tatum	1939–1944	5
Homer Luckett	1944–1948	4
E. H. Wheat	1946–1948	2
J. C. McCachren	1948–1972	24
Tom Harris	1948–1960	12
A. L. Pressgrove	1948–1962	14
Doak M. Worley	1948–1952	4
Lee Russel Allison	1952–1964	12
F. A. Jackson	1952–1964	12
Julius M. Roberson	1960–1972	12
Guy Wolfe	1962–1972	10
Mrs. L. R. Allison	1964–1965	1
Jim Pennington	1964–1972	8
A. A. Mabus	1965–1968	3
Jack Flautt	1968–1972	4
Walter Guy Burkhalter	1972	
Brooks Bloodworth	1972	

PANOLA COUNTY

Name of Supervisor	Term of Service	Total Years
W. J. Hays	1939–1944	5
H. D. Crenshaw	1939–1944	5
G. W. Randolph	1939–1944	5
S. L. Dees	1939–1940	1

W. P. Lemaster	1939–1952	13
H. N. Finnie	1940–1948	8
J. Howard Cash	1944–1954	10
B. B. Breterick	1944–1957	13
G. W. Randolph	1944–1948	4
W. L. Benson	1948–1956	8
Earl G. Hubbard	1948–1964	16
Thatcher Bishop	1952–1960	8
Frank Barnett	1954–1960	6
W. N. Aldridge	1956–1972	16
Bill F. Knox	1957–1972	15
C. U. Smart	1960–1968	8
Shuford Jones	1961–1970	9
D. Bowen Wilson	1964–1972	8
Horace Matthews	1968–1972	4
James Travis	1970–1972	2
J. B. Anderson	1972	

YALOBUSHA COUNTY

Name of Supervisor	Term of Service	Total Years
J. D. Floyd	1938–1940	2
R. S. Oakley	1938–1948	10
W. B. Williamson	1938–1944	6
J. A. Massey	1938–1944	6
Mrs. Annie Criss	1938–1940	2
Dr. R. J. Criss	1940–1952	12
W. A. Lacook	1940–1952	12
O. E. Rowsey	1944–1952	8
T. R. Kuykendall	1944–1948	4
A. T. Moorman	1948–1960	12
W. Vernon Craig	1948–1968	20
Carl A. Parker	1952–1962	10
"Doc" Bell	1952–1960	8
W. L. Harrison	1952–1964	12
Thomas Swearengen	1960–1972	12
E. Doke French	1960–1972	12
Ira Pittman	1962–1964	2
Frank Pate	1964–1972	8
Ben T. Simpson	1964–1972	8
Richard Ross	1968–1972	4
Fred Earl Moorman	1972	
Dariel Koonce	1972	

DESOTO COUNTY

Name of Supervisor	Term of Service	Total Years
W. H. McCargo	1940–1944	4
R. W. Latimer	1940–1944	4
Britt Hughey	1940–1948	8
T. L. Earnhart	1940–1944	4
H. L. Lauderdale	1940–1948	8
Jack Earnheart	1944–1960	16
John M. Forte	1944–1948	4

Tom Flynn	1944–1948	4
W. M. Maxwell	1948–1968	20
W. H. Austin	1948–1964	16
Malcolm S. Baxter	1948–1960	12
J. T. Flinn	1948–1960	12
R. E. Darby	1960–1972	12
Harvey Hamilton	1960–1968	8
Harry S. Wheeler	1960–1968	8
L. A. Scott	1964–1972	8
W. Howard Allen	1968–1972	4
G. T. Garner	1968–1972	4
Walton A. Scott	1968–1972	4
Johnny Wallace	1972	
Will Renfro	1972	

TIPPAH COUNTY

Name of Supervisor	Term of Service	Total Years
T. M. Jamieson	1940–1949	9
Sam Deen	1940–1948	8
G. O. Stanford	1940–1948	8
Hugh Smith	1940–1944	4
A. Dees	1940–1944	4
Earl Gaillard	1944–1949	5
C. Lyman Rowell	1944–1949	5
A. L. Hall	1948–1949	1
Frank Bennett	1948–1949	1

BENTON COUNTY

Name of Supervisor	Term of Service	Total Years
Bryant C. Hines	1948–1968	20
J. W. Hardaway	1948–1952	4
W. L. Jordan	1948–1956	8
J. K. McGaughy	1948–1972	24
G. O. Taylor	1948–1964	16
M. H. Curtis	1952–1956	4
J. H. Carpenter	1956–1964	8
George M. Davis	1956–1972	16
Wyatt Thomas	1964–1972	8
Earl Childers	1964–1972	8
Bobby N. James	1968–1972	8
Johnny Wilkerson	1972	

TUNICA COUNTY

Name of Supervisor	Term of Service	Total Years
B. F. Harbert	1952–1960	8
R. T. Abby	1952–1960	8
E. R. (Jack) Evans	1952–1956	4
S. C. Wilson	1952–1972	20
S. E. Watson	1952–1956	4

L. A. Gidden	1956–1964	8
W. D. Garrett, Jr.	1956–1968	12
W. A. Leatherman	1960–1972	12
J. M. Watson	1960–1964	4
Marvin Watson	1964–1966	2
Paul Battle, Jr.	1964–1972	8
T. O. Earnheart	1966–1972	6
Charles Austin	1968–1972	4

LAFAYETTE COUNTY

Name of Supervisor	Term of Service	Total Years
W. W. Grimes	1954–1956	2
E. E. Murray	1954–1956	2
J. P. Jones	1954–1960	6
J. S. Roy	1954–1956	2
C. B. Shipp	1954–1966	12
Kenneth Knight	1956–1964	8
E. H. Windham	1956–1957	1
B. R. Gunter	1956–1964	8
Charles W. McGonagill	1957–1960 1968–1972	7
Walter Houston	1960–1968	8
Franklin Parks	1960–1972	12
Frank T. Ramage	1964–1972	8
Mrs. C. B. Shipp	1966–1967	1
Jim Q. Tatum	1967–1968	1
J. C. Tatum	1968–1972	4
Thomas Ray Gunter	1964–1972	8

MARSHALL COUNTY

Name of Supervisor	Term of Service	Total Years
Edgar Lee Bolden	1960–1972	12
P. T. McAlexander	1960–1964	4
C. R. Pipkin	1960–1972	12
Odell Wilson	1960–1972	12
J. P. Woods	1960–1972	12
J. C. Totten	1964–1972	8
T. P. St.John	1972	
Joe Cooper	1972	

CALHOUN COUNTY

Name of Supervisor	Term of Service	Total Years
Stanley Williams	1965–1972	7
E. W. Overby	1965–1972	7
John Warner	1965–1972	7
Wilson (Bill) Blue	1965–1972	7
Lon Pryor	1965–1972	7
Bill McGuire	1972	

Supervisors
Jones County Junior College

JONES COUNTY

Name of Supervisor	Term of Service	Total Years
J. W. DeVall	1924–1928	4
George Jefcoats	1924–1932	8
Arnold Pearson	1924–1936	12
Allen Boutwell	1924–1932 1936–1940	12
Walter Grayson	1924–1932 1936–1944	16
J. C. Austin	1928–1932	4
C. J. McCormick	1932–1936	4
Dan Shows	1932–1936	4
J. R. Garrick	1932–1936	4
E. P. Orso	1936–1956	20
Longino Reddoch	1936–1948	12
Bunk Jordan	1936–1956	20
Floyd Walters	1940–1952	12
Archie Jordan	1944–1952	8
H. L. Graves	1948–1956	8
Berry Entrekin	1952–1960	8
Hubert Bryant	1952–1972	20
J. E. Crosby	1956–1964	8
George Maxey	1956–1964	8
J. L. Lightsey	1956–1964	8
George Harrison	1960–1972	12
Hubert Hosey	1964–1972	8
J. P. Parker	1964–1972	8
James L. Rasberry	1964–1972	8

CLARKE COUNTY

Name of Supervisor	Term of Service	Total Years
W. E. Moore	1932–1936 1940–1948	12
W. L. Bounds	1932–1948	16
R. E. Williams	1932–1936	4
Rev. C. E. Griffin	1932–1936	4
Roy Smith	1932–1940	8
Harvey Norris	1936–1940	4
A. B. Irby	1936–1940	4
D. A. Irby	1936–1940	4
Ira B. Moore	1940–1968	28
O. E. Griffin	1940–1944	4
J. E. Phillips	1940–1950	10
Harvey Dearman	1944–1956	12
W. C. Taylor	1948–1972	24
U. C. Wells	1948–1972	24
E. A. Collins	1950–1952	2
Jodie C. Jacobs	1952–1960	8
Joe Evans	1956–1960	4

Marvin Pickard	1960–1972	12
Floyd Turner	1960–1972	12
Paul Gavin	1968–1972	4

COVINGTON COUNTY

Name of Supervisor	Term of Service	Total Years
A. E. Aultman	1928–1932	4
J. W. Goudy	1928–1932	4
J. M. B. Carter	1928–1932	4
W. D. McRaney	1928–1932	4
W. H. Sanford	1932–1936	4
Ben F. Aultman	1932–1936	4
Carr V. Dees	1932–1936	4
J. Dixon Rogers	1928–1936	8
Frank Moore	1936–1948	12
O. T. Graham	1936–1948	12
W. H. Herrin	1936–1944 1948–1956	16
Willie Campbell	1936–1944	8
W. W. Speed	1936–1944	8
Howard Jordan	1944–1948	4
Lawrence L. Little	1944–1948	4
Rozzie McQueen	1944–1956	12
Sam Napier	1948–1956	8
M. E. Napier	1948–1952	4
Wiley D. Graham	1952–1956	4
Howard Odum	1956–1968	12
Dewitt Clark	1956–1972	16
Howard F. Williamson	1956–1964	8
Leeman Mayfield	1956–1968	12
Ramsey McQueen	1964–1972	8
Guycell Hughes	1968–1972	4
J. L. Warren	1968–1972	4
Howard Flynt	1968–1972	4

GREENE COUNTY

Name of Supervisor	Term of Service	Total Years
D. E. Breland	1932–1936	4
T. T. Platt	1932–1936	4
Gaines West	1932–1936	4
W. T. McLeod	1932–1940 1944–1948	12
S. S. Backston	1932–1936	4
H. E. McInnis	1936–1940	4
W. L. Robertson	1936–1940	4
C. H. Wade, Jr.	1936–1940	4
W. S. Turner	1936–1940	4
Mrs. Dan Hyatt	1940–1944	4
C. L. Avera	1940–1948	8

S. S. Henderson	1940–1944	4
R. L. McInnis	1940–1944	4
W. E. File	1940–1944	4
V. E. Cooper	1944–1948	4
Luke James	1944–1948	4
L. M. Daughdrill	1944–1948	4
I. S. Turner	1948–1952	4
L. N. Kittrell	1948–1960	12
Sam K. Freeman	1948–1960	12
Quitman Davis	1948–1952 1956–1960	8
J. L. Hillman	1948–1960	12
W. E. Douglas	1952–1956	4
Ford James	1952–1956 1960–1972	16
Emmitt E. Smith	1956–1964	8
J. C. Bristow	1960–1972	12
C. E. (Ed) Brewer	1960–1968	8
E. T. White	1960–1972	12
Billy G. Cooper	1964–1972	8
S. J. Henderson	1968–1972	4

JASPER COUNTY

Name of Supervisor	Term of Service	Total Years
J. C. Smith	1928–1932	4
W. H. Gibson	1928–1932	4
J. C. Bassett	1928–1932	4
M. B. Stringer	1928–1932	4
G. W. Kelly	1928–1932	4
W. L. Green	1932–1936	4
J. W. Chatham	1932–1936	4
C. H. Wall	1932–1936	4
J. J. Ishee	1932–1936	4
M. G. Travis	1932–1936	4
J. C. Smith	1936–1940	4
W. H. Gibson	1936–1940	4
S. A. Hickman	1936–1948	12
D. G. Brown	1936–1964	28
T. G. (Tom) Thornton	1936–1940	4
R. A. Smith	1940–1944	4
J. H. Buckley	1940–1960	20
C. C. Lightsey	1940–1948	8
S. C. Sims	1944–1968	24
J. C. Bassett	1948–1956	8
C. S. Thomas	1948–1964	16
Roscoe A. Perry	1956–1964	8
J. I. Fowler	1960–1968	8
Warren Tally	1964–1972	8
Risher Holder	1964–1972	8
Weldon McClellan	1964–1972	8
C. V. Pugh	1968–1972	4
J. W. Davis	1968–1972	4

Supervisors

PERRY COUNTY

Name of Supervisor	Term of Service	Total Years
G. F. Mixon	1932–1936 1944–1948	8
H. C. Shoemake ·	1932–1940 1948–1956	16
C. M. Edwards	1932–1936	4
F. E. Davis	1932–1936 1940–1952	16
Lonzo Rayburn	1932–1936	4
J. A. Fillingame	1936–1944 1952–1964	20
Pettis Walley	1936–1940	4
Tim Hinton	1936–1940	4
R. W. Shattles	1936–1948	12
Lee Travis	1940–1948	8
S. B. Carey	1940–1948	8
Roy McKenzie	1948–1968	20
W. J. (Bill) Carey	1948–1952	4
Fred A. Breland	1948–1952	4
H. L. Jones	1952–1968	16
Forrest Kittrell	1952–1960	8
Bura Conway	1956–1972	16
Elbert Deakles	1960–1968	8
I. A. Garraway	1964–1968	4
George F. Mixon, Jr.	1968–1972	4
W. F. (Bill) Bowen	1968–1972	4
Paul D. Johnston	1968–1972	4
Alvin Howard	1968–1972	4

SMITH COUNTY

Name of Supervisor	Term of Service	Total Years
W. S. Corley	1932–1936	4
L. K. Eaton	1932–1936 1940–1944	8
N. A. Sullivan	1932–1940	8
George W. Earles	1932–1940	8
Bondy Bruce	1932–1936	4
J. H. Garner	1936–1940	4
C. E. Boykin	1936–1940 1944–1948	8
O. D. Daniel	1936–1944	8
Homer Thompson	1940–1956 1964–1968	20
W. L. Walker	1940–1944 1948–1956	12
W. W. Martin	1940–1972	32
J. Ance Little	1944–1948	4
J. L. Craft	1944–1952	8
Joe D. Stringer	1948–1952	4
Anse Blakeney	1952–1956	4
Aaron Roberts	1952–1972	20
A. E. Bounds	1956–1964	8

Edgar Shanks	1956–1968	12
Searcy Howell	19 6–1972	16
Kendall L. Hancock	1968–1972	4
Tom Mayfield	1968–1972	4

WAYNE COUNTY

Name of Supervisor	Term of Service	Total Years
John L. Sullivan	1932–1948	16
R. W. Fagan	1932–1936	4
C. C. Weaver	1932–1944	12
G. S. Stanley	1932–1936	4
J. O. Bunch	1932–1936 1940–1948	12
Sam B. Mauldin	1936–1940 1960–1968	12
John W. Dykes	1936–1944	8
G. N. Jones	1936–1940	4
J. W. Cran	1940–1960	20
T. M. Fleming	1944–1952	8
Oscar Barnett	1944–1952	8
Mack L. Dunn	1948–1968	20
W. E. (Shorty) Hutto	1948–1968	20
Paul Chapman	1952–1960	8
Ulmer Pryor	1952–1972	20
Pete Duvall	1960–1972	12
E. C. Douglas	1968–1972	4
Edward Jones	1968–1972	4
Roland Dean	1968–1972	4

Supervisors
East Mississippi Junior College
LAUDERDALE COUNTY

Name of Supervisor	Term of Service	Total Years
R. H. Seymour	1932–1936	4
T. L. Johnson	1932–1948	16
Dr. S. McDonald	1932–1940	8
L. D. Walker	1932–1966	34
D. W. Carr	1932–1944	12
Ross R. Bounds	1936–1948	12
O. L. King	1940–1960	20
E. C. Gunn	1940–1952	12
William S. Wright	1948–1968	20
Brad Rhaley	1948–1956	8
Roy P. Griffin	1952–1968	16
R. N. McElroy	1956–1972	16
J. P. White	1956–1960	4
James F. Spears	1960–1972	12
Mrs. L. D. Walker	1966–1968	4
Mrs. William S. Wright	1968–1972	4
Lamar Taylor	1968–1972	4
S. L. Wilson	1968–1972	4

287

KEMPER COUNTY

Name of Supervisor	Term of Service	Total Years
E. L. Gilbert	1932–1948	16
L. J. Hudnall	1932–1948	16
S. E. Bounds	1932–1940	8
J. I. Luke	1932–1936 1940–1944	8
J. L. Harbour	1932–1936	4
Henry Davis	1936–1940	4
L. L. Shumate	1936–1940	4
Martin McKee	1940–1948	8
S. J. Creekmore	1940–1948	8
A. E. Hicks	1944–1948	4
John Persons	1948–1968	20
T. W. Puckett	1948–1952	4
Jack W. Harbour	1948–1960	12
Lavelle Luke	1948–1952	4
Ernest P. Bateman	1948–1968	20
N. G. Briggs	1952–1956	4
Russell Shepard	1952–1960	8
Louie Briggs	1956–1968	12
Fred Chisolm	1960–1972	12
Vanzee Luke	1960–1972	12
Eddie Sparkman	1968–1972	4
Clyde Edwards	1968–1972	4
George P. Spinks	1968–1972	4

NOXUBEE COUNTY

Name of Supervisor	Term of Service	Total Years
Nelson Stevens	1932–1944	12
J. R. Sparkman	1932–1936	4
R. T. McDavid	1932–1936	4
W. L. Thomas	1932–1936 1940–1948	12
T. W. Madison	1932–1936	4
J. E. Robbins	1936–1948	12
J. W. Eiland	1936–1940 1944–1956	16
T. L. Thompson	1936–1940 1948–1960	16
J. O. Cook	1936–1940	4
Eugene Jackson	1940–1944	4
C. S. Jackson	1940–1944	4
W. L. Thomas	1940–1948	8
Dan S. Norwood	1940–1964	24
D. H. Britton	1944–1948	4
B. S. Marler	1948–1972	24
Lucian Minor	1948–1952	4
William S. Mullins	1952–1972	20
Herbert C. Hunter	1960–1972	12
H. H. (Hub) Butler	1960–1972	12
G. E. Redus	1964–1972	8

CLAY COUNTY

Name of Supervisor	Term of Service	Total Years
J. L. Blankenship	1964–1972	8
Herman M. Shirley	1964–1972	8
Walter R. Hurst	1964–1968	4
J. Shelton Brand	1964–1968	4
W. F. Walker	1964–1968	4
Johnnie L. Poss	1968–1972	4
Howard Crosswhite	1968–1972	4

LOWNDES COUNTY

Name of Supervisor	Term of Service	Total Years
F. B. (Bill) Blalock	1964–1972	8
S. A. (Bill) Smith	1964–1968	4
B. R. Shepherd	1964–1972	8
Alton E. Bounds	1964–1968	4
A. B. Gillam	1964–1972	8
Mayo (Chubby) Ellis, Jr.	1964–1972	8
W. G. (Bit) Thompson	1968–1972	4

OKTIBBEHA COUNTY

Name of Supervisor	Term of Service	Total Years
Guy Critz	1964–1972	8
Preston B. Fulgham	1964–1972	8
C. T. Turner	1964–1972	8
Hugh Fancher Shaw	1964–1972	8
T. C. Gray, Sr.	1964–1968	4
Curtis Buckner	1968–1972	4

Supervisors
Copiah–Lincoln Junior College

COPIAH COUNTY

Name of Supervisor	Term of Service	Total Years
W. M. Wilson	1928–1932	4
M. E. Furr	1928–1940	12
Joe W. Smith	1928–1940	12
R. E. Dear	1928–1932	4
F. M. Brewer	1928–1940	12
John C. Lowe	1933–1940	7
J. L. King	1933–1936	3
M. B. Starnes	1933–1936	3
Spence Templeton	1933–1944	11
W. W. Erwin	1933–1936	3
L. E. Hood	1936–1940	4
George Marx	1940–1972	28
A. B. Barlow	1940–1964	14

M. F. Hennington	1940–1952	12
Walter Barlow	1940–1951	11
W. W. Bishop	1944–1949	5
P. D. Armstrong	1952–1972	20
Paul Edwards	1952–1960	12
Troy Templeton	1952–1954	2
Mrs. Troy Templeton	1954–1956	2
W. E. Hood	1955–1972	17
Virgil Smith	1960–1972	12
Lamar Smith	1964–1972	8
Tommy Heard	1972	
B. B. Berry	1972	

LINCOLN COUNTY

Name of Supervisor	Term of Service	Total Years
W. M. Turnbough	1928–1930	2
J. Loyd Pitts	1928–1930	2
W. L. McGraw	1928–1932	4
G. W. Lewis	1928–1936	8
Louis Calcote	1928–1936	8
Jim Boone	1929–1932	3
Willie Furr	1929–1936	7
J. Wiley Pevey	1932–1936	4
W. F. Turnbo	1932–1940	8
Quin Rutland	1936–1942	6
J. Q. Brister	1936–1940	4
Sam Wactor	1936–1940	4
Louis Entrican	1936–1944	8
Mrs. Rosa Turnbough	1937–1940	3
Martin Holmes	1940–1951	11
Leroy Leggett	1940–1968	28
Jim Coker	1944–1964	20
Clint C. Brister	1944–1956	12
J. Hugh James	1944–1955	11
Nelson Case	1956–1968	12
Kinzie Reeves	1956–1965	9
Mrs. Kinzie Reeves	1965–1968	3
Grady Tarver	1965–1968	3
W. A. Rogers	1968–1972	4
R. L. Adams	1968–1972	4
Oddee Smith	1968–1972	4
Ben Laird	1968–1972	4
Claude Diamond	1968–1972	4

LAWRENCE COUNTY

Name of Supervisor	Term of Service	Total Years
Talmadge Brister	1966–1972	6
Ras Case	1966–1971	5
J. W. Daniels	1966–1972	6
Roy May	1966–1972	6
H. E. Reed	1966–1972	6
Joe Givins	1968–1972	4

FRANKLIN COUNTY

Name of Supervisor	Term of Service	Total Years
Newman Scott	1949–1956	7
E. M. McLemore	1949–1952	3
Ernest Zumbro	1949–1960	11
P. L. Lofton	1949–1972	23
Cicero Nettles	1949–1956	7
Harvey Prather	1952–1956	4
Frank Allen	1952–1972	20
Lee Hester	1956–1972	16
John Ducker	1956–1967	11
William Arnold	1960–1966	6
Hilton M. Zumbro	1964–1972	8
Carl Ray Lehman	1967–1972	5

SIMPSON COUNTY

Name of Supervisor	Term of Service	Total Years
G. P. Brown	1935–1936	1
M. Q. Holbrook	1935–1936	1
J. E. Boggan	1935–1936	1
J. E. Smith	1935–1936	1
Luther Barlow	1935–1936	1
J. T. Pruitt	1936–1940	4
H. S. Tullos	1936–1944	8
C. W. Chappell	1936–1944	8
M. W. Buckley	1936–1942	6
G. D. Neely	1936–1944	8
T. E. Berry	1940–1947	7
C. L. Steen	1942–1947	5
J. A. Ashley	1944–1955	11
H. B. Smith	1944–1953	9
C. P. Mahaffey	1944–1951	7
Garfield May	1952–1972	20
W. P. Harris	1952–1972	20
Fordie Walker	1953–1965	12
C. G. Baldwin	1964–1972	8
L. B. Thompson	1964–1968	4
Leslie Little	1964–1972	8
R. E. Lee	1968–1972	4

ADAMS COUNTY

Name of Supervisor	Term of Service	Total Years
Robert E. Bee	1968–1972	4
A. Bond Sojourner	1968–1972	4
James H. Carter	1968–1972	4
Ike Foster	1968–1972	4
E. A. Redd	1968–1972	4

Supervisors
East Central Junior College

NEWTON COUNTY

Name of Supervisor	Term of Service	Total Years
A. S. Smith	1928–1931	4
W. C. Milling	1928–1931	4
Lee Smith	1928–1931	4
G. S. Monroe	1928–1931	4
Clarence Chapman	1928–1936	8
T. E. Jones	1932–1939	8
J. H. Henry	1932–1935	4
J. W. Williams	1932–1935	4
E. E. Woodham	1932–1943	12
J. H. Ezelle	1936–1943 1952–1963	20
H. M. James	1936–1939	4
W. H. Davis	1936–1947	12
Marshall Stamper	1940–1951	12
T. T. Thames	1940–1947	8
F. L. Hunter	1944–1951	12
H. D. Foreman	1948–1959	12
W. M. Prince	1948–1963	16
Clyde Kilpatrick	1948–1963	16
W. W. Harris	1952–1959	8
Jodie Bradford	1960–1972	12
G. A. Smith	1960–1972	12
Olen Richardson	1964–1967	4
Blucher Simmons	1964–1972	8
Hulon Harrison	1968–1972	4
Hoye Pace	1968–1972	4
Harmon Jones	1972	

LEAKE COUNTY

Name of Supervisor	Term of Service	Total Years
E. B. Russell	1932–1935	4
B. I. Faucett	1932–1935	4
Ben Herring	1932–1935	4
Lesley Burnett	1932–1935	4
Frank Gilmore	1932–1935 1944–1951	12
T. J. Kemp	1936–1939	4
H. H. Brooks	1936–1943	8
H. O. Haley	1936–1945	10
H. S. Arthur	1936–1939 1948–1951	8
H. C. Chipley	1936–1939 1952–1955	8
Kelly Roberts	1940–1947	8

Herman Murphy	1940–1951	12
J. B. Langston	1940–1947	8
Lee Fisher	1945–1972	28
G. C. Williams	1948–1951	4
Lafayette Smith	1952–1959	8
R. L. Moss	1952–1972	20
Crawley Alford	1952–1972	20
W. J. Johnston	1956–1967	12
Newton Burkes	1960–1971	12
D. F. Dickens	1968–1972	4
William Wooten	1972	
Benny Truesdale	1972	
Leon Watkins	1972	

NESHOBA COUNTY

Name of Supervisor	Term of Service	Total Years
A. C. Shepherd	1929–1931	3
C. H. Harbour	1929–1931	11
L. C. Long	1929–1931	3
W. W. McBeath	1929–1931	7
Newt Ingram	1929–1931	3
A. E. Harbour	1932–1935	4
M. E. Bates	1932–1935	4
W. D. Reynolds	1932–1935	4
J. A. Howell	1932–1935	4
T. J. Gamblin	1932–1935	4
I. N. Ingram	1936–1939	4
Albert Shepard	1936–1939	4
J. B. Fulton	1936–1939	4
W. T. Cole	1939–1947	9
A. E. Dees	1940–1947	8
Uhl Walton	1940–1947 1953–1959	15
R. J. Breazeale	1940–1943	4
E. E. Lowry	1944–1947	4
Rev. Ethel Beall	1944–1959	16
G. L. Sansing	1948–1951	4
H. T. Barnes	1948–1959	12
H. H. Hayes	1948–1951	4
Earl Cumberland	1948–1959	12
Charlie Chisolm	1952–1959	8
Clady Wilson, Sr.	1952–1953	2
Carl Deweese	1960–1971	12
J. P. Stokes	1960–1971	12
T. C. Chisolm	1960–1965	6
Irby Goldman	1960–1967	8
H. L. Breazeale	1960–1972	12
J. L. McCraw	1965–1972	8
Ed Dickerson	1968–1972	4
A. J. Chaney	1972	
Duane Gray	1972	

WINSTON COUNTY

Name of Supervisor	Term of Service	Total Years
O. H. Craig	1935–1936	2
J. E. Wilkes	1935–1936	2
Claude Richardson	1935–1947	13
Rev. J. D. Fulton	1935–1936	2
Woodward Horton	1935–1936	2
Ben M. McCully	1936–1943	8
Earnest H. Boswell	1936–1943	8
S. Oscar Clay	1936–1939	4
W. E. Woodward	1936–1960	25
W. O. Kirk	1940–1943	4
E. H. Anderson, Jr.	1943–1944	1
S. Frank Roberts	1944–1947	4
T. W. Luke, Jr.	1944–1972	28
Houston C. Carr	1944–1963	20
Olyn Sanders	1948–1963	16
B. G. Hull	1948–1972	24
Alvin Massey	1960–1972	12
C. C. Huntley, Jr.	1964–1972	8
M. D. Boydston	1964–1972	8

SCOTT COUNTY

Name of Supervisor	Term of Service	Total Years
W. R. Hunt	1930–1935	6
E. M. Davis	1930–1931 1936–1947	14
A. A. Singleton	1930–1931 1936–1939	6
L. T. Sessums	1930–1931 1936–1939	6
D. E. Putnam	1930–1931	2
O. O. Massey	1932–1935	4
R. A. McEwen	1932–1935	4
W. A. Latham	1932–1935	4
M. L. Anthony	1932–1935	4
M. A. Davis	1935	1
J. J. Fountain	1936–1943 1952–1955	12
W. J. Sanders	1936–1939 1944–1951	12
Harvey Jones	1940–1943	4
N. B. Rushing	1940–1943	4
L. J. Lang	1940–1943	4
Hobson Harvey	1944–1971	28
Joe C. Hamilton	1944–1951	8
R. O. Armstrong	1944–1955	12
William Cooper	1948–1971	24
L. L. Anthony	1952–1962	10
R. E. Bustin	1956–1963	8
C. C. Munday	1956–1963	8

J. S. Riser	1963–1967	5
Waldo Pryor	1964–1972	8
W. J. Measells, Jr.	1964–1972	8
W. D. McDill	1968–1972	4
Louis Eure	1972	
Jack Miles	1972	

Supervisors
Southwest Mississippi Junior College
PIKE COUNTY

Name of Supervisor	Term of Service	Total Years
Joe Brent	1928–1932	4
V. J. Brumfield	1928–1932	4
Robert M. Frith	1928–1936	8
J. W. Gatlin	1928–1932	4
I. A. Varnado	1928–1932	4
A. B. Barclay	1932–1941	9
Luther Gatlin	1932–1936	4
H. E. Reeves	1932–1936	4
Hugh L. Simmons	1932–1960	28
H. E. Barnett	1936–1940	4
A. P. Brent	1936–1944	8
H. F. Webb	1936–1944	8
S. L. Stewart	1940–1952	12
A. G. Flippen	1941–1948	7
J. J. Boyd	1944–1948	4
E. F. O'Quin	1944–1948	4
Donald P. Dunn	1948–1952	4
Dolph Ellzey	1948–1968	20
H. C. Rebold	1948–1960	12
A. B. Regan	1952–1968	16
H. B. Wood	1952–1961	9
Homer W. Addison	1960–1964	4
Jesse Hall	1960–1972	12
Sam N. Alford	1961–1972	11
Jean Wood	1961–1962	1
Prentiss P. Ball	1964–1968	4
Edward Brumfield	1968–1972	4
Doyle Forman	1968–1972	4
C. R. McCalip	1968–1972	4

AMITE COUNTY

Name of Supervisor	Term of Service	Total Years
James Blount	1940–1948	8
Edgar Brady	1940–1948	8
R. W. Clark	1940–1956	16
C. N. Gallant	1940–1948	8
Earl Moore	1940–1948	8

E. E. Lawson	1948–1972	24
Homer L. Smith	1948–1964	16
Earl Wells	1948–1956	8
Talmage Wooley	1948–1972	24
H. K. Barron	1956–1972	16
Edgar Tynes	1956–1972	16
L. L. Williams	1964–1972	8
Eugene McClendon	1972	
Tommy Talbert	1972	

WALTHALL COUNTY

Name of Supervisor	Term of Service	Total Years
D. F. Boyd	1964–1968	4
L. W. Brock	1964–1968	4
J. L. Conerly	1964–1972	8
Nolan Martin	1964–1968	4
Johnnie Stringer	1964–1972	8
Travis Alford	1968–1972	4
Buford Boyd	1968–1972	4
Preston P. Dillon	1968–1972	4
Clifton Hinson	1972	

Supervisors
Meridian Junior College

LAUDERDALE COUNTY

Name of Supervisor	Term of Service	Total Years
William S. Wright	1964–1968	4
Ransom N. McElroy	1964–1972	8
J. F. Spears	1964–1972	8
L. D. Walker	1964 (9 mos.)	
Mrs. L. D. Walker	1964 (3 mos.)	
Lamar Taylor	1965–1972	7
Roy P. Griffin	1964–1968	4
Mrs. William S. Wright	1968–1972	4
S. L. Wilson	1968–1972	4

Supervisors
Itawamba Junior College

ITAWAMBA COUNTY

Name of Supervisor	Term of Service	Total Years
J. E. Montgomery	1948–1960	12
H. G. Franks	1960–1972	12

T. C. Wilburn	1948–1964	16
Willie McFerrin	1964–1972	8
Curtis Franks	1972	
J. H. Watson	1948–1959	11
I. J. Walton	1959–1960	1
Randall Spradling	1960–1972	12
Owen Spearman	1948–1964	16
J. K. Lockridge	1964–1968	4
Cecil Cody	1968–1972	4
L. B. Davis	1948–1956	8
L. L. Robinson	1956–1968	12
Hoyt Senter	1968–1972	4
Charlie Johnson	1972	

LEE COUNTY

Name of Supervisor	Term of Service	Total Years
L. L. Bishop	1948–1960	12
Hurley Malone	1960–1968	8
H. L. Bishop	1968–1972	4
Jim Barnett	1972	
C. H. Turner	1948–1972	24
James L. Long	1972	
J. E. Marcy	1948–1952	4
Ernest Evans	1952–1960	8
Kyle Brown	1960–1968	8
Quenton Jenkins	1968–1972	4
Mark Shumpert	1948–1956	8
Clifford Pettigrew	1965–1966	1
Mrs. Ruby Nell Carr	3 mos. in 1966	
J. K. Lipford	1966–1972	6
B. G. Coggin	1948–1952	4
C. H. Cain	1952–1972	20

MONROE COUNTY

Name of Supervisor	Term of Service	Total Years
R. F. Miller	1948–1960	12
Relda C. Morgan	1960–1972	12
Cooper H. Cantrell	1948–1951	3
Frank Durett, Sr.	2 mos. in 1951	
Troy L. Thomas	1951–1970	19
Jimmie W. Kirkpatrick	1970–1972	2
J. W. Cockerham	1944–1948	4
Mrs. Lizzie Cockerham	2 mos. in 1948	
L. W. Darracott	1948–1952 1956–1960	8
James Allen Cockerham	1971–1972	1
R. A. Pullen	1948–1956	8
Joe T. Morgan	1956–1960	4

Ben Lilley	1960–1970	10
L. M. Halbert	1970–1972	2
Paul Sisk	1948–1970	22
Delma R. Francis	1970–1972	2

PONTOTOC COUNTY

Name of Supervisor	Term of Service	Total Years
J. Neely Russell	1953–1956	3
L. D. Caldwell	1956–1972	16
Grady O. Baker	1972	
Parks Sneed	1953–1960	7
Alvin C. Hale	1960–1968	8
Lester H. Sneed	1968–1972	4
H. Hilton Purdon	1952–1964	12
Frank Collums	1964–1968	4
Colan E. Barefield	1968–1972	4
George W. Washington	1972	1
John H. Beddingfield	1952–1956	4
Louis Y. Ball	1956–1964	8
Charles R. Gray	1964–1972	8
Wade Stegall	1953–1964	11
Charlie Roye	1964–1972	7
Mrs. Charlie Roye	2 mos. in 1971	
Robert Henderson	1971–1972	1

CHICKASAW COUNTY

Name of Supervisor	Term of Service	Total Years
J. C. Alford	1932–1940	8
J. J. Byars	1932–1936	4
E. A. Anderson	1932–1940	8
W. R. Doss	1932–1940	8
J. S. Gordin	1932–1936	4
S. E. Chestman	1936–1940	4
J. E. Dendy	1936–1948	12
L. E. Wooldridge	1940–1944	4
Earl Aaron	1940–1944	4
O. E. Shell	1940–1948	8
Frank D. Doss	1940–1960	20
S. A. Farr	1944–1956	12
W. A. White	1944–1952	8
DeVan Hill	1948–1972	24
Calvin Lancaster	1948–1972	24
Mrs. W. A. White	1952–1956	4
Robert F. Atkinson	1956–1972	16
D. E. Lester	1956–1964	8
O. A. Kimbrough	1960–1968	8
Lloyd H. Collums	1964–1972	8
Parker Lancaster	1968–1972	4

Supervisors
Northeast Mississippi Junior College

ALCORN COUNTY

Name of Supervisor	Term of Service	Total Years
J. P. Briggs	1948–1952	4
J. G. Driver	1948–1964	16
C. W. Edge	1948–1968	20
L. W. Coleman	1948–1960	12
H. D. Mathis	1948–1954	6
Mark Dillingham	1952–1964	12
Jeff Briggs	1954–1960	6
H. L. Denton	1960–1972	12
Sully Ayers	1960–1972	12
T. A. Little	1964–1972	8
D. C. Mathis	1964–1972	8
Scott Honnoll	1968–1970	2
Mrs. Scott Honnoll	1970–1972	2
Curtis Brawner	1972	
Willard Crum	1972	

PRENTISS COUNTY

Name of Supervisor	Term of Service	Total Years
Jim E. Scott	1948–1952	4
J. V. Windham	1948–1964	16
Sam Kesler	1948–1956	8
John W. Williams	1948–1960	12
J. L. Sims, Jr.	1948–1968	20
James L. West	1952–1968	16
Charles M. Gordon	1956–1972	16
Joseph Johnson	1960–1964	4
Sam Jumper	1964–1972	8
Ross Pharr	1964–1972	8
Bobby Tidwell	1968–1971	3
W. V. Horn	1968–1972	4
George Lauderdale	1971–1972	2

TISHOMINGO COUNTY

Name of Supervisor	Term of Service	Total Years
W. H. Gardner	1948–1956	8
Russell Bonds	1948–1972	24
O. L. Wade	1948–1964	16
W. L. Storment	1948–1968	20
Sixty Yarber	1948–1952	4
Walton Montgomery	1952–1956	4
Herbert Biggs	1956–1968	12
Steve South	1956–1968	12
A. C. Ryan	1964–1972	8
Carl Hendrix	1968–1972	4
M. R. Whitehead	1968–1972	4
Leon Cook	1968–1972	4
Gerald Parsons	1972	1

UNION COUNTY

Name of Supervisor	Term of Service	Total Years
R. M. Perry	1948–1956	8
Dorman Smith	1948–1960	12
Cliff Smith	1948–1951	3
Buster Hines	1948–1972	24
Naaman Branyan	1948–1960	12
Cliff Davis	1951–1952	1
Joel R. Clayton	1952–1956	4
S. M. Moody	1956–1972	16
H. R. Bennett	1956–1964	8
R. N. Butts	1960–1964	4
George Wages	1960–1972	12
R. H. Dye	1964–1970	6
Sam Barkley	1964–1972	8
Jerry T. Haynes	1970–1972	2
James Robertson	1972	1
A. L. Gillespie	1971–1972	2

TIPPAH COUNTY

Name of Supervisor	Term of Service	Total Years
T. M. Jamieson	1948–1952	4
A. L. Hall	1948–1952	4
Frank Bennett	1948–1972	24
Earl Gailard	1948–1964	16
C. L. Rowell	1948–1956	8
W. C. Horton	1952–1956	4
Preston Smith	1952–1960	8
W. O. Burton	1954–1956	2
Bennett Harrison	1956–1968	12
C. C. Childs	1956–1972	16
B. M. Harold	1960–1972	12
Millikin Chapman	1964–1972	8
Roy James	1968–1972	4
C. C. Bennett	1972	
M. S. Rooker, Jr.	1972	

W. L. McKee, Jr.	1956–1964	8
W. A. (Bill) Hughes	1960–1972	12
Lawrence B. Craig	1964–1968	4
W. Wert Cooper	1964–1968	4
T. L. Brunt	1968–1972	4
John B. McKee, Jr.	1968–1972	4
Curtis E. Presley	1968–1972	4
Graham Bramlett	1968–1972	4

SUNFLOWER COUNTY

Name of Supervisor	Term of Service	Total Years
Noel K. Toler, Sr.	1964–1972	8
W. L. Jackson, Jr.	1964–1972	8
James W. Corder	1964–1972	8
George W. Cockrell	1964–1968	4
G. W. Manning, Jr.	1964–1972	8
Charles Hughes	1968–1972	4

QUITMAN COUNTY

Name of Supervisor	Term of Service	Total Years
J. D. Pettit	1964–1968	4
Harold M. Chrestman	1964–1972	8
Clint Mitchell	1964–1968	4
W. B. Moore	1964–1972	8
Fletcher Haynes	1964–1972	8
T. C. Simpson	1968–1972	4
James Reed	1968–1972	4

BOLIVAR COUNTY

Name of Supervisor	Term of Service	Total Years
O. J. Scott, Sr.	1964–1968	4
W. A. Welshans	1964–1972	8
Max L. Dilworth	1964–1968	4
Milton Smith	1964–1972	8
Elmer L. Prewitt	1964–1972	8
J. E. Bobo	1968–1972	4
Kermit Stanton	1968–1972	4

Supervisors
Coahoma Junior College

COAHOMA COUNTY

Name of Supervisor	Term of Service	Total Years
J. B. Hopkins	1948–1952	4
Harry J. Landry	1948–1956	8
Dave L. Salomon	1948–1960	12
J. E. Merritt	1948–1964	16
W. E. Young	1948–1968	20
J. Van Wilson	1952–1968	16

Supervisors
Utica Junior College

HINDS COUNTY

Name of Supervisor	Term of Service	Total Years
H. Power Hearn	1954–1956	2
E. F. Ragan	1954–1962	8
S. M. Hubbard	1954–1968	14
W. L. Fairchild	1954–1956	2

				RANKIN COUNTY		
Mrs. Floyd Hawkins	1954–1960	6		*Name of Supervisor*	*Term of Service*	*Total Years*
Ross P. Dodds	1956–1960	4		Milton Singletary	1965–1972	7
Dan Ferguson	1956–1964	8		Woodrow W. Swilley	1965–1968	3
Tom Virden	1960–1968	8		R. L. Cross	1965–1972	7
L. J. Beasley	1960–1972	12		Tom H. Rives	1965–1972	7
Mrs. Anna Ragan	1963–1964	1		Gay Gill	1965–1968	3
Malcolm Warren	1964–1972	8		Hilton Richardson	1968–1972	4
Johnnie S. Taylor	1964–1972	8		Steen Patrick	1968–1972	4
J. L. "Pete" McGee	1968–1972	4		Kenneth Bridges	1972	
Noel K. McKey	1968–1972	4		Ralph Moore	1972	
Pal R. Jones	1972					

WARREN COUNTY

Name of Supervisor	Term of Service	Total Years
Alvin H. Hall	1964–1968	4
Robert Dowe	1964–1972	8
P. T. Hullum	1964–1972	8
Paul Pride	1964–1972	8
J. L. McCaskill	1964–1972	8
Thomas F. Akers	1972	
James R. Andrews	1972	
Clyde Donnell	1972	
Herbert Boler	1968–1972	4

COPIAH COUNTY

Name of Supervisor	Term of Service	Total Years
George Marx	1960–1972	12
A. B. Barlow	1960–1964	4
P. D. Armstrong	1960–1972	12
W. E. Hood	1960–1972	12
Virgil Smith	1960–1972	12
Lamar Smith	1964–1972	8
Tommy Heard	1972	
B. B. Berry	1972	

D/Laws

This section contains the four basic laws establishing public junior colleges in Mississippi.

CHAPTER 204
Senate Bill No. 251.

By
Dr. Julius Christian Zeller, Senator
from Yazoo County, 19th District[1]

AN ACT permitting the addition of work of junior college grade to the program of studies of a municipal separate district high school or of an agricultural high school and specifying the conditions on which same may be done.

Junior college grade—trustees may extend curriculum in certain schools.

SECTION 1. Be it enacted by the Legislature of the State of Mississippi, That the trustees of a separate school district containing a municipality with a population of not less than ten thousand according to the most recent federal census or of an agricultural high school that is not less than twenty miles distant from any of the state colleges with the exception of the Alcorn Agricultural and Mechanical College may extend the curriculum in the school or schools under their charge and include the studies of the freshman or sophomore year, or both, of college work, when they deem such additional work necessary to properly provide for the educational needs of such school district, county or counties.

Expense to be met out of regular funds.

SECTION 2. No appropriation shall be made out of the state treasury for the support of such college work. The additional expense that is incurred shall be met out of the usual funds of such districts, county or counties; provided that no part of such funds shall be so expended except under the following conditions:

1. The minimum scholastic requirements of all teachers or instructors in the junior college shall be graduates either from the University of Mississippi, Agricultural and Mechanical College, Mississippi State College for Women or any college of equal grade, provided that teachers giving instruction in subjects for which sophomore credit is given shall have had in addition to said graduation, post graduate work in a university or college of recognized standing amounting to at least one year.

2. Every student registering in a junior college shall have successfully completed at least fifteen units of high school work as defined by the state accrediting commission.

3. The work of the junior college must be organized on a collegiate and not on a high school basis.

4. No school shall have the rating and classification of a junior college unless it has a registration of at least twenty students who have had accepted not less than fifteen units for entrance if the said institution offers freshman work only; and thirty-five students who have had accepted not less than fifteen units for entrance if said institution offers freshman and sophomore work.

5. The library in a junior college attempting to do freshman work shall have not less than one thousand well selected volumes, not including pamphlets or government publications, and if attempting both freshman and sophomore work it shall have not less than one thousand five hundred volumes.

6. The laboratory equipment shall have an aggregate value of not less than two thousand dollars ($2,000.00).

7. No school shall attempt junior or college work unless the high school department is approved as a full four-year high school by the state department of education.

Diplomas may be issued under certain conditions.

SECTION 3. When a student has successfully completed the course prescribed for the freshman and sophomore years any junior college that has been properly accredited under this act may issue a diploma to such student. Provided, however, that if the junior college is organized as part of a high school in a separate school district it may deliver a diploma bearing the title of an associate of arts, and if the junior college is organized as part of an agricultural high school it may deliver a diploma bearing the title of an associate of agriculture to men, and an associate of arts to women as a testimonial of the completion of two years of college work.

Board of education to enforce this act.

SECTION 4. The state board of education shall be responsible for the enforcement of the provisions of this act.

SECTION 5. This act shall take effect from and after its passage. Approved March 24, 1922.

The permissive legislation passed in 1922 set up reasonably high academic standards (for that day) by requiring: (1) fifteen high school units (the number then required for high school graduates); (2) one year beyond the baccalaureate degree for teaching sophomores; (3) a minimum number of students; (4) library standards well beyond those required for accredited high schools for that day; and (5) a small, but minimum standard for laboratory equipment.

The early intent of the legislature was an emphasis on the vocational slant by prescribing an "Associate of Agriculture" to men. This vocational aspect under the permissive legislation of 1922 was to be almost completely stimied for some two decades for many reasons, among which were: (1) the pressure for "academic respectability"; (2) lack of funds to finance the always expensive vocational subjects; and (3) the idea of most students, parents, and the general public that all good students should look toward the earning of a bachelor's degree.

[1] Dr. Zeller went to State Superintendent W. F. Bond for assistance in preparing Senate Bill No. 251. Superintendent Bond referred him to H. M. Ivy, High School Inspector, of the State Department of Education. Dr. Ivy had some knowledge of junior colleges in other states and assisted Dr. Zeller in preparing the bill. (This information is from a conference with H. M. Ivy at Meridian Junior College on February 1, 1973, in the presence of Dr. William Scaggs, President of Meridian Junior College, Dr. L. O. Todd, J. B. Young and J. M. Ewing.)

Junior College Law
State of Mississippi 1924
House Bill Number—98

Chapter 283

Junior Colleges—Chapter 40

AN ACT to enact certain school laws and to re-enact certain school laws and to repeal certain others, for the purpose of clarifying and harmonizing the statutory school laws of the state and codifying them.

SECTION 308. The trustees of a separate school district containing a municipality with a population of not less than ten thousand according to the most recent federal census or of an agricultural high school that is not less than twenty miles distant from any of the state colleges with the exception of the Alcorn Agricultural and Mechanical College may extend the curriculum in the school or schools under their charge and include in the studies of the freshman or sophomore year, or both, of college work, when they deem such additional work necessary to properly provide for the educational needs of such school district, county or counties.

SECTION 309. NO APPROPRIATION SHALL BE MADE OUT OF THE STATE TREASURY FOR THE SUPPORT OF SUCH COLLEGE WORK.—The additional expense that is incurred shall be met out of the usual funds of such districts, county or counties provided that no part of such funds shall be so expended except under the following conditions:

1. The minimum scholastic requirements of all teachers or instructors in the junior college shall be graduation either from the University of Mississippi, Agricultural and Mechanical College, Mississippi State College for Women or any college of equal grade, provided that teachers giving instruction in subjects for which sophomore credit is given shall have had in addition to said graduation, post graduate work in a university or college of recognized standing amounting to at least one year.

2. Every student registering in a junior college shall have successfully completed at least fifteen units of high school work as defined by the state accrediting commission.

3. The work of the junior college must be organized on a collegiate and not a high school basis.

4. No school shall have the rating and classification of a junior college unless it has a registration of at least twenty students who have had accepted not less than fifteen units for entrance if the said institution offers freshman work only; and thirty-five students who have had accepted not less than fifteen units for entrance if said institution offers freshman and sophomore work.

5. The library in a junior college attempting to do freshman work shall have not less than one thousand well selected volumes, not including pamphlets or government publications, and if attempting both freshman and sophomore work it shall have not less than one thousand five hundred volumes.

6. The laboratory equipment shall have an aggregate value of not less than two thousand dollars ($2000.00).

7. No school shall attempt junior college work unless the high school department is approved as a full four year high school by the state department of education.

SECTION 310. When a student has successfully completed the course prescribed for the freshman and sophomore years any junior college that has been properly accredited under this act may issue a diploma to such student. Provided, however, that if the junior college is organized as part of a high school in a separate school district it may deliver a diploma bearing the title of an associate of arts, and if the junior college is organized as part of an agricultural high school it may deliver a diploma bearing the title of an associate of agriculture to men, and an associate of arts to women as a testimonial of the completion of two years of college work.

SECTION 311. The state board of education shall be responsible for the enforcement of the provisions of this act.

SECTION 312. That officers and trustees elected, appointed or put in office by virtue of any laws repealed or impliedly amended by this act, shall continue in office for the unexpired terms for the purpose of discharging their duties according to the terms of this act, and all organizations now existing under the school laws of the state shall continue for the purposes of this act, and all contracts valid under any laws hereby repealed or impliedly amended, shall continue in force for the purposes of this act.

SECTION 313. That the purposes of this act are to clarify and harmonize the statutory school laws of the state, and this act shall be construed and interpreted in the light of this purpose.

SECTION 314. That this act shall not be construed or interpreted to repeal any of the laws of the state of Mississippi which are not related to or do not pertain to schools.

. . . .

SECTION 316. If for any reason any section, paragraph, provision, clause or part of this act shall be held unconstitutional or invalid that fact shall not affect or destroy any other section, paragraph, provision, clause, or part of the act not in and of itself invalid, but the remaining portion shall be in force without regard to that so invalidated. And if any section of this act shall fail any section which would have been repealed if this had not failed, shall remain in full force and effect.

SECTION 317. That this act take effect and be in force from and after the first day of July, 1924.

Approved, April 11th, 1924.

Junior College Law
State of Mississippi 1928
Senate Bill No. 131

Chapter No. 303

Originated in the Senate
H. E. KING, Secretary of the Senate

AN ACT amending sections 308, 309, 310, and 311 of chapter 283 of the laws of the state of Mississippi, 1924, providing for the organization and operation of junior colleges.

SECTION 1. BE IT ENACTED BY THE LEGISLATURE OF THE STATE OF MISSISSIPPI. That Sections 308, 309, 310, and 311 of Chapter 283, of the Laws of the State of Mississippi for 1924 be amended to read as follows:

Section 308. That Junior Colleges consisting of the work of the Freshman and Sophomore years shall be organized for the purpose of providing such courses as will make the studies of the Agricultural High Schools and the Junior Colleges a connected and correlated whole or complete unit of educational work. These courses shall consist of agriculture, including horticulture, dairying, animal husbandry and commercial gardening; domestic science and the household arts; commercial branches, including banking, accountancy and transportation; and the mechanical arts, such as carpentry, masonry, painting, shop work in iron and wood and repairing and constructing of motor vehicles. Wherever it is practicable, instruction shall also be given in teacher training, music and

public speaking. Insofar as possible the Junior Colleges shall offer a complete course of instruction so that their graduates may immediately thereafter enter professional schools if they so elect.

The trustees of a separate school district containing a municipality with a population of not less than ten thousand according to the most recent Federal census or of an Agricultural High School that is not less than twenty miles distant from any of the State Colleges, with the exception of Alcorn Agricultural and Mechanical College, may extend the curriculum in the school or schools under their charge so as to include the studies of the Freshmen or Sophomore year or both, of college work when they deem such additional work necessary to properly provide for the educational needs of such school district, county or counties. Provided further, that separate school districts and county Agricultural High Schools may unite with other separate school districts or with other counties in the establishment of a Junior College. In the event of municipalities desiring to unite with other separate school districts or with a county in the establishment of a Junior College, such a desire shall be made a matter of record by the majority vote of the school trustees of the municipality and upon a petition of ten percent of the qualified electors an election shall be called. If the majority of those voting shall favor the establishment of such school the Mayor and Board of Aldermen shall make a levy for the support of said Junior College. Counties desiring to unite in the establishment and support of a Junior College either with municipal separate school disricts or with other counties, shall make such a desire a matter of record by majority vote of the county school board and upon a petition of ten per cent of the qualified electors an election shall be called. If the majority of those voting shall favor the establishment of such a school the Board of Supervisors shall make a levy for the support of said Junior College. It is necessary that each separate school district and each county joining in the establishment of a Junior College shall have a record of a majority vote by the proper and respective school authorities and a majority vote of the qualified electors participating in the election. The County School Board and the Board of Supervisors of a county desiring to co-operate in the maintenance and support of a Junior College located in another county, may authorize the County Superintendent of Education to issue a certificate against the county school fund, the County Agricultural High School fund, or the Special Junior College fund, for an amount sufficient to cover the cost of instruction in the said Junior College of all students in attendance from the county desiring to co-operate with said Junior College, same to be based on actual attendance for the previous scholastic year. All monies going to the support of Junior Colleges authorized by this Act shall be paid out on the certificate of the County Superintendent of Education in the county from which such support is derived. All funds collected for the support of a Junior College from whatever separate districts or counties they may be derived, shall be paid to the County Superintendent of Education of the county in which the Junior College is located and shall be turned over by him to the Board of Trustees of the Junior College, who shall use such fund for the purpose of maintaining the Junior College and for such purposes only.

Counties co-operating in the maintenance of a Junior College by making a tax shall have equal representation on the Board of Trustees and the Trustees shall be elected as provided for by the laws governing such election. Counties co-operating by direct appropriation based on attendance shall be represented on the Board of Trustees by the County Superintendent of Education who shall be an ex-officio member of said Board.

Section 309. (1) The minimum scholastic requirement of all teachers or instructors in the Junior College shall be graduation, either from the University of Mississippi, the Agricultural and Mechanical College, the Mississippi State College for Women or any college of equal grade, provided the teachers giving instruction in subjects for which Sophomore credit is given shall have had in addition to said graduation, post graduate work in a University or College of recognized standing amounting to at least one year.

Provided, however, that in Junior Colleges now established the above requirements shall apply to at least one-third of the teachers and instructors in the scholastic year of 1928–29, two-thirds in 1929–30 and to all such teachers and instructors for the scholastic year of 1930–31.

(2) Every student registering in a Junior College shall have successfully completed at least fifteen units of high school work as defined by the State Accrediting Commission.

(3) The work of the Junior College must be organized on a collegiate and not a high school basis.

(4) No school shall have the rating and classification of a Junior College unless it has a registration of at least twenty students who have had accepted not less than fifteen units for entrance if the said institution offers Freshman and Sophomore work. In the event that an institution endeavoring to become a Junior College offers the work of the Freshmen year and fails to offer the work of the Sophomore year within two years after the organization of the work of the Freshman year, then such an institution shall be deemed as having failed to qualify under this act and its work cannot be accepted in lieu of the work of a Junior College; but in the case of institutions offering one year of college work at the time of the passage of this Act such institution shall have two years in which to put on the Sophomore year.

(5) The Library in a Junior College attempting to do Freshman work shall have not less than one thousand well selected volumes, not including pamphlets or government publications, and if attempting both

Freshman and Sophomore work it shall have not less than one thousand and five hundred volumes.

(6) The laboratory equipment shall have an aggregate value of not less than two thousand dollars.

(7) No school shall attempt Junior College work unless the high school department is approved a full four year high school by the State Department of Education.

Section 310. When a student has successfully completed the course prescribed for the Freshman and Sophomore years any Junior College that has been properly accredited under this Act may issue a diploma to each student. Provided, however, that if the Junior College is organized as part of a high school in a separate school district it may deliver a diploma bearing the title of AN ASSOCIATE OF ARTS, and if the Junior College is organized as part of an Agricultural High School it may deliver a diploma bearing the title AN ASSOCIATE OF AGRICULTURE (to men), and AN ASSOCIATE OF ARTS (to women) as a testimonial of the completion of two years of college work.

Section 311. All Junior Colleges seeking to qualify under this Act shall be under the control of a State Commission, known as the Commission of Junior Colleges, which shall consist of the State Superintendent of Public Education, Chairman, the Heads of the University of Mississippi, the Agricultural and Mechanical College, the Mississippi State College for Women, and the heads of the three Junior Colleges, to be selected by the heads of the Junior Colleges of the State.

The said Commission is to serve without compensation and the actual necessary expenses of the said commission shall be paid out of the general school fund.

SECTION 2. That this Act take effect and be in force from and after its passage.

PASSED THE SENATE MARCH 6, 1928.
BIDWELL ADAMS,
PRESIDENT OF THE STATE.
PASSED THE HOUSE OF REPRESENTATIVES, APRIL 16, 1928.
THOS. L. BAILEY,
SPEAKER OF THE HOUSE OF REPRESENTATIVES.

APPROVED BY THE GOVERNOR, THE 26 DAY OF APRIL, 1928.
THEO. G. BILBO, GOVERNOR

Junior College Law
State of Mississippi 1950
House Bill No. 541

Chapter 369

AN ACT to establish junior colleges in the state of Mississippi, and to declare their purpose and function; and to provide for the personnel of the junior college commission, and to define their powers and duties; and to authorize the levy of taxes for the support and enlargement of junior colleges, and to provide for the distribution of revenue thereby derived; and to validate existing junior college districts; and to provide for the operation, management, maintenance, enlargement and improvement of junior colleges; and for other purposes.

BE IT ENACTED BY THE LEGISLATURE OF THE STATE OF MISSISSIPPI:

SECTION 1. The creation, establishment, maintenance and operation of junior colleges are hereby authorized. They shall offer to students who have completed not less than 15 high school units, courses correlated to those of senior colleges or professional schools; and education and training preparatory for occupations such as agriculture, industry, business, homemaking, and other occupations on the semi-professional and vocational-technical level. They may offer courses and services to students regardless of their previous educational attainment or further academic plans.

In addition to the foregoing the junior colleges shall provide, through courses or other acceptable educational measures, the general education necessary to individuals and groups which will tend to make them capable of living satisfactory lives consistent with the ideals of a democratic society.

SECTION 2. There is hereby created the Junior College Commission consisting of seven members; namely, the State Superintendent of Education, chairman, and the chancellor of the University of Mississippi, the president of Mississippi State College, Mississippi State College for Women, and of three junior colleges as defined in this act, the latter three to be selected by the presidents of the junior colleges of the state.

The Junior College Commission shall regulate the establishment and operation of junior colleges in the state and shall particularly have the following powers and duties:

> (1) To make studies of the needs of the state and communities for junior college education.
> (2) To divide the state into districts within which junior colleges may hereafter be established and fix the territorial boundaries thereof taking into consideration population, property valuation, transportation facilities, the proximity of other colleges, and other factors which contribute to a sound program of education for the state; and to designate the location of a junior college or colleges within the district.
> (3) To fix standards for junior colleges to qualify for junior college appropriations, with respect to training of teachers and administrators, physical plant and equipment, administrative organization, curriculum, income per student from local tax sources, enrollment, admission requirements, general tone of the institution, and other factors that relate to the support and administration of junior colleges.
> (4) To certify annually to the State Board of Education or other organization, board, agency or administration designated by law to disburse appropriations for junior colleges, the names of such junior colleges which are eligible for such funds.
> The Commission shall serve without compensation, but the necessary expenses of the Commission shall be paid out of junior college funds.

SECTION 3. All junior college districts heretofore formed and presently being taxed, and junior colleges established and in operation at the time of the passage of this act under the provisions of law then in effect, are hereby confirmed and validated. Hereafter, junior colleges may be established only within the territorial boundaries of, and at locations in, districts designated by the Junior College Commission. The Commission, at the time when it shall first hereafter make certificate under sub-section (4) of Section 2 hereof, shall certify to the State Board of Education the territorial boundaries of all junior college districts hereby validated; and annually thereafter it shall so certify the territorial boundaries of any additional districts formed and additional territory added to any existing district.

SECTION 4. Subject to the provisions of this act, junior colleges may hereafter be established by one or more counties or by one or more counties and municipal separate school districts within the territorial limits of an area which has been designated by the Junior College Commission as a junior college district by proceeding as follows:

The school board of a county within a junior college district, desiring to establish a junior college therein, shall adopt a resolution to that effect, duly spread on the minutes of the board, and furnish a certified copy of same to the board of supervisors of the county. If the board of supervisors of the county shall approve the resolution of the school board to establish a junior college, such approval shall be spread on the minutes of the board of supervisors. Thereafter the county school board and the board of supervisors of the county shall jointly petition the Junior College Commission for the approval of the establishment of a junior college and to determine the location thereof. Such petition shall be submitted on forms approved by said Commission and shall contain such information as may be required by the Commission, including a statement of the proposed plan of operation in accordance with standards promulgated by said Commission. The Junior College Commission shall approve or disapprove the petition and shall notify the petitioners accordingly. Notification of approval shall include the designation of the location of the junior college. Upon the approval by the Junior College Commission of the petition to establish and operate a junior college the board of supervisors of the county shall declare its intention to make a levy for the purpose of the establishing and a levy for the support of the proposed junior college, and the levy or levies shall be made upon the taxable property of the entire county, unless a majority of the qualified electors in the county vote against the proposition in an election called by the board of supervisors to determine the matter on petition therefor signed by twenty per cent of the qualified electors of such county.

In the event that two or more counties within a junior college district desire to join in the establishment of a junior college therein the school boards and the boards of supervisors of the cooperating counties shall join in the petition to the Junior College Commission, and the requirements of the preceding paragraph shall apply to each of the participating counties.

The board of trustees of a municipal separate school district within a junior college district, desiring to establish a junior college therein, shall adopt a resolution to that effect duly spread upon the minutes of the board, and furnish a certified copy of same to the mayor and board of aldermen or commissioners of the municipality constituting or lying within the separate school district. If the mayor and board of aldermen or commissioners approve the resolution of the board of trustees to establish a junior college, such approval shall be spread on the minutes of the mayor and aldermen or commissioners. Thereafter, the board of trustees and the mayor and aldermen or commissioners shall jointly petition the Junior College Commission for the approval of the establishment of a junior college and to determine the location thereof. Such petition shall be submitted and shall be acted on in the same manner as a petition submitted by a county. Upon the approval by the Junior College Commission of the petition, the mayor and board of aldermen or commissioners of such municipality shall declare its intention to make a levy for the purpose of the establishing and a levy for the support of the proposed junior college, and the levy or levies shall be made upon the taxable property of the entire school district, including added territory, unless a majority of the qualified electors in such school district and added territory shall vote against the proposition in an election called by the mayor and aldermen or commissioners to determine the matter on petition therefor signed by twenty percent of the qualified electors of such school district and added territory.

In any case, the petition for an election shall be filed with the board of supervisors or with the mayor and aldermen or commissioners within thirty days after publication by them one time in a newspaper published in the county or municipality, or having a general circulation therein, of the proposal to levy the taxes for the establishment and operation of the junior college.

In the event that a municipal separate school district and a county or counties should desire to join in the establishment of a junior college, the procedure prescribed above shall apply to the municipal separate school district and each county concerned.

SECTION 5. Except as provided in this section and in Section 12 of this act, there shall be six trustees from each county of the junior college district which originally entered into and gave financial aid in establishing the junior college. The county superintendent of education shall be a member, and there shall be one member from each supervisor's district. Counties which subsequent to the establishment of the junior college joined the district shall have only two trustees, one of whom shall be the county superintendent of education. But the board of trustees so constituted, by appropriate resolution, may enlarge its number to six trustees from each county, in which case one shall be the superintendent of education and there shall be one chosen from each supervisor's district. In any case in which there is an equal number of trustees the board of trustees may appoint another person to membership.

The trustees of junior colleges validated in this act shall hold office to the end of their present terms. Hereafter, the terms of office shall be five years, but upon selection of trustees first hereafter in each county, one shall be elected for a term of five years, one for a term of four years, one for a term of three years, one for a term of two years, and one for a term of one year, so as to prevent the retirement of more than one member in any one county in any one year. At the expiration of terms of trustees or upon election of trustees for junior colleges hereafter established, the board of supervisors, by and with the advice and consent of the members of the county school board, shall elect the requisite number of discreet persons of good moral character, sufficient education and experience, and of proven interest in public education, who are qualified electors of the county, as trustees of the junior college; and annually thereafter the board of supervisors in like manner shall fill vacancies. All trustees so appointed shall be listed in the minutes of the board of supervisors and their appointment shall be certified by the chancery clerk to the president of the junior college. This section shall not apply to trustees of a junior college established solely by a municipal separate school district, but the trustees of the municipal separate school district shall be the trustees of such junior college.

Each junior college trustee may be paid, out of junior college funds, expenses not to exceed five ($5) per meeting, for not more than twelve meetings per year.

SECTION 6. The duties of the trustees shall be the

general government of the junior college and directive of the administration thereof. Subject to the provisions of this act, they shall have full power to do all things necessary to the successful operation of the junior college. However, the executive head of the junior college shall be the president of the college who shall be selected by the board of trustees for a term not to exceed four years.

SECTION 7. The president of the junior college shall have power to recommend to the board of trustees all teachers who shall be employed and he shall have authority to remove or suspend any member of the faculty subject to the approval of the trustees; and he shall be general manager of the fiscal and administrative affairs of the junior college with full authority to select, direct and discharge any and all employees who are not teachers.

The president shall have authority, subject to the provisions of this act and to the approval of the trustees, to arrange and specify courses of study, fix schedules, to establish and enforce rules and discipline for the government of teachers and students; and he shall be general custodian of the property of the institution.

SECTION 8. Title to lands may be acquired and buildings and other improvements may be erected thereon for the use and benefit of junior colleges; and title to all such property hereafter acquired shall be vested in the trustees and their successors in office.

Any board of supervisors or board of trustees of any municipal separate school district which presently holds title to the lands, buildings, and improvements of a junior college may convey title to same to the board of trustees and their successors in office of such junior college pursuant to a resolution of such board of supervisors or board of trustees of a municipal separate school district, duly adopted and spread on the minutes of said board of supervisors.

SECTION 9. When a student has successfully completed the course prescribed for the freshman and sophomore years, any junior college which has been properly accredited under this act may issue a diploma to such student, bearing the title of AN AS-SOCIATE OF ARTS, AN ASSOCIATE OF AGRICULTURE, or any other appropriate title as testimonial of the completion of two years of college work.

SECTION 10. Nothing in this act shall be construed to repeal any statute relating to county agricultural high schools; and it is expressly provided that such schools may be operated in conjunction with junior colleges. But when so operated they shall be under control of the president and trustees of the junior colleges.

When a junior college through the agricultural high school provides high school facilities of any school district, then the pupils from that district may be enumerated as other pupils in the common schools and the school district or county superintendent may pay to the junior college tuition such as determined by the State Department of Education for any other schools, and no agricultural high school funds shall be disbursed for pupils for whom such tuition is paid.

SECTION 11. Taxes for the support, enlargement and improvement of junior colleges shall be levied annually against all of the property of each county and of each municipal separate school district, including added territory, which has established or may hereafter establish, or which has joined or may hereafter join, in the establishment or support of a junior college; but in no case shall such levy exceed three mills for support and three mills for enlargement and improvement for each junior college within the district of which the county or municipal separate school district may be a component.

The levy for support for any year in any given county or separate school district is that presently prevailing therein unless a change is recommended to the tax levying authorities by the board of trustees or by a vote of the people ascertained in an election called for that purpose by the tax levying authorities subsequent to the petition herefor signed by twenty per cent (20%) of the qualified electors.

All funds derived from such taxes shall be paid into the county depository of the county in which the junior college is located, upon receive warrants of the chancery clerk of said county. Such funds shall be paid out of the depository in the manner prescribed by order of the board of trustees of the junior college for purposes provided by statute.

In case a junior college is supported by a municipal separate district, such funds shall be paid to the clerk of the municipal separate school district upon receive warrants of said clerk and shall be paid out on order of the board of trustees of the municipal separate district.

SECTION 12. Junior colleges established heretofore, or hereafter established under the provisions of this act, solely by a municipal separate school district shall be subject to the provisions of this act, provided that the government and administration of such junior colleges shall be vested in the trustees of the municipal separate school district.

SECTION 13. Trustees of a junior college may borrow money in anticipation of taxes for the purpose of paying all expenses authorized by law for operating the junior college. The loan shall be evidenced by a note or notes bearing the signatures of the president and secretary of the board of trustees and seal of the college and shall mature not later than the first day of April next after issuance. Interest of not exceeding 4 per cent per annum may be paid for such loan, to be fixed by the resolution or order of the trustees authorizing such loans.

SECTION 14. There shall be separate junior college districts for the white and colored races.

SECTION 15. The board of trustees of a junior college, in its sound discretion, may transport students who reside in the district and in convenient commuting distance from the college. But no additional allocation

of any appropriation shall be made for such transportation; and the board of trustees shall promulgate uniform rules to prevent discrimination in all matters of transportation.

SECTION 16. A junior college, in the discretion of its trustees, may charge fees and tuition.

SECTION 17. Each junior college shall have an official seal to be impressed upon all instruments of the junior college requiring seal, which may be in the form of a circle and which shall imprint the name and location of the college and the words "Official Seal."

SECTION 18. Sections 6475, 6476, 6477, 6478, 6480, and 6481 of the Mississippi Code of 1942 and all other laws in conflict with this act are hereby repealed. But nothing herein shall be construed as affecting the statutes relating to agricultural high schools, or their relations with junior colleges except as herein specifically provided.

SECTION 19. This act shall take effect and be in force from and after its passage.

Approved March 31, 1950.

Junior College Law
State of Mississippi
Laws of 1964
House Bill No. 215

Chapter 398

AN ACT to establish junior college districts as individual and separate juristic entities and bodies politic and corporate; to more clearly define the role of junior colleges and the financial support thereof in this state; to repeal sections 6475–04, 6475–07 and 6476–01, Mississippi code of 1942; and for related purposes.

BE IT ENACTED BY THE LEGISLATURE OF THE STATE OF MISSISSIPPI:

SECTION 1. There are hereby created the following junior college districts comprising the entire counties therein named and having boundaries thereof, each of which shall be separate juristic entities and bodies politic and corporate:

(a) Copiah-Lincoln Junior College District shall be comprised of the counties of Adams, Copiah, Frank-

lin, Jefferson, Lawrence, Lincoln, and Simpson.

(b) East Central Junior College District shall be comprised of the counties of Leake, Neshoba, Newton, Scott, and Winston.

(c) East Mississippi Junior College District shall be comprised of the counties of Clay, Kemper, Lauderdale, Lowndes, Noxubee, and Oktibbeha.

(d) Hinds Junior College District shall be comprised of the counties of Hinds, Rankin, Warren, and Claiborne.

(e) Holmes Junior College District shall be comprised of the counties of Attala, Carroll, Choctaw, Grenada, Holmes, Madison, Montgomery, Webster, and Yazoo.

(f) Itawamba Junior College District shall be comprised of the counties of Chickasaw, Itawamba, Lee, Monroe, and Pontotoc.

(g) Jones County Junior College District shall be comprised of the counties of Clarke, Covington, Greene, Jasper, Jones, Perry, Smith, and Wayne.

(h) Mississippi Delta Junior College District shall be comprised of the counties of Bolivar, Coahoma, Humphreys, Issaquena, Leflore, Sharkey, Sunflower, and Washington.

(i) Northeast Junior College District shall be comprised of the counties of Alcorn, Prentiss, Tippah, Tishomingo, and Union.

(j) Northwest Junior College District shall be comprised of the counties of Benton, Calhoun, DeSoto, Lafayette, Marshall, Panola, Quitman, Tallahatchie, Tate, Tunica, and Yalobusha.

(k) Pearl River Junior College District shall be comprised of the counties of Forrest, Hancock, Jefferson Davis, Lamar, Marion, and Pearl River.

(1) Southwest Junior College District shall be comprised of the counties of Amite, Pike, Walthall, and Wilkinson.

SECTION 2. Except as otherwise provided in this act, all of the property belonging to the board of trustees of any existing junior college and all of the property belonging to either or all of the counties heretofore and at the passage of this act cooperating in the existing junior colleges or the agricultural high schools and junior colleges located at the existing campuses and utilized or held for the present or future use and benefit of such junior colleges and/or agricultural high schools and junior colleges shall be and the same is hereby transferred to and vested in the boards of trustees of the said above-enumerated junior college districts created in Section 1 of this act.

SECTION 3. The board of trustees of any junior college district shall have the powers to do all things necessary to the successful operation of the said district and the college or colleges or attendance centers located therein to insure educational advantages and oppor-

tunities of all the enrollees within the district, and one or more boards of trustees may cooperate in establishing, operating, and maintaining attendance centers. The board of trustees shall annually prepare a budget which shall contain a detailed estimate of the revenues and expenses anticipated for the ensuing year for general operation and maintenance and shall set forth the reasonable requirements for anticipated needs for capital outlays for land, buildings, initial equipment for new buildings and major repairs, a reasonable accumulation for such purposes being hereby expressly authorized.

SECTION 4. Any junior college district is hereby authorized and empowered to operate junior college attendance centers at existing sites of junior college plants and facilities and at such other places within the district, subject to the approval of the State Junior College Commission, as the board of trustees shall determine to be in the best interest of the district. The said district shall be governed by the board of trustees, and each district shall be under the executive direction of a president elected by the board.

SECTION 5. The president of any junior college shall have the power to recommend to the trustees all teachers to be employed in the district, and he may remove or suspend any member of the faculty subject to the approval of the trustees, and he shall be the general manager of all fiscal and administrative affairs of the district with full authority to select, direct, employ and discharge any and all employees other than teachers.

The board may make provisions and establish policies for leave for faculty members and other key personnel.

The president shall have the authority, subject to the provisions of this act and the approval of the trustees, to arrange and survey courses of study, fix schedules, establish and enforce rules and discipline for the governing of teachers and students and shall be the general custodian of the property of the district.

SECTION 6. Any junior college district is charged with the responsibility for providing preprofessional courses, liberal arts, technical, vocational, and adult education courses and shall undertake to provide the same as conveniently as is possible to the residents of the district, and to this end, the board of trustees is authorized and empowered to transport such enrollees as, in its discretion, should be transported in the best interest of the district.

SECTION 7. In addition to other authority granted by this act or existing statutes, the trustees may borrow money in anticipation of taxes, not to exceed fifty per cent of the previous year's ad valorem tax receipts, for the purpose of paying any expenses authorized by law for the operation, maintenance and support of the college. The loan shall be evidenced by note bearing the signatures of the chairman of the board and of the secretary of the board of trustees, and the seal of the college shall be thereon impressed, and said notes shall mature not later than the thirtieth day of June next thereafter, nor shall same bear interest in excess of four and one-half per cent per annum.

In event that bonds shall have been authorized for projects determined by the board of trustees and such bonds validated, the board of trustees is authorized to utilize any available funds for the immediate commencement of such project and to reimburse the funds from which any such expenditures are made from the proceeds of the bonds when the same are received.

SECTION 8. The district, in the discretion of the board of trustees, may charge fees and tuitions.

SECTION 9. The trustees are authorized to execute oil, gas, and mineral leases of any of the property owned by the board of trustees of the district, but such leases shall not extend for a term beyond five (5) years unless oil, gas, or other minerals shall be in production under said leases at the expiration of said period. The terms and conditions of said lease, within the limitations above set out, shall be for the determination and within the discretion of the board of trustees.

SECTION 10. When any land or other property owned by the district shall cease to be used or needed by the district, the same may be sold by the board of trustees upon sealed bids after three (3) weeks advertisement in a newspaper in the county where the said property is located. Personal property having a value determined by the board of less than Five Hundred Dollars (500.00) may be sold without such advertisement, but in such event, notice shall be posted in at least three (3) public places in the county where such property is situated or where it is to be sold, giving notice of the time and place of such sale, and such property shall be sold to the highest and best bidder for cash. Such notice shall be posted for ten (10) days before the sale.

SECTION 11. The delineation and enumeration of the powers and purposes hereinbefore set out shall be deemed to be supplemental and additional and shall not be construed to restrict the powers of the governing authorities of the district or of any college located therein so as to deny to the said district and the college or colleges therein the rights, privileges, and powers previously authorized by statute.

SECTION 12. Any board of trustees may, in its discretion, by the concurrence of two-thirds (⅔) of its authorized members present and voting and for good cause shown therefor, to be spread upon its minutes by way of its resolution or order, which shall contain a proposal as to the anticipated income from which the funds are to be repaid, authorize the junior college district to borrow money from time to time for periods not to exceed five (5) years under such terms and conditions as the board deems necessary and requisite, but not to exceed the rate of four and one-half per cent per annum, and upon its issuing its promissory note or notes or other negotiable instruments bearing the signature of both the chairman and secretary of the board of trustees and the official seal of the college affixed thereon, and to repay such loans from its general fund, whether the same shall have been derived from ad valorem tax receipts or otherwise. Before executing the notes or other evidences of indebtedness authorized by this subsection, the district shall first secure in writing sealed bids from not less than two (2) Mississippi banking institutions chartered to do business in this State, wherein each bank shall indicate the terms and conditions, including interest rates, under which it is willing to make a loan or loans to said district.

SECTION 13. On or before the thirtieth day of each month, the board of supervisors of each county belonging to a junior college district and levying taxes for the support and maintenance thereof shall transmit or have the chancery clerk to transmit its warrant or warrants constituting all of the revenues received from taxation for the prior month for said purposes to the chief executive officer or president of its respective junior college district, and all such county warrants evidencing a county's annual income from its authorized tax levy shall be forthwith deposited in one or more banking institutions and public depositories previously selected by the board of trustees, and spread upon its official minutes. The board of trustees shall, by appropriate orders spread upon its minutes, authorize its chief executive officer or president to expend such funds for lawful purposes only and in accordance with its annual budget previously adopted. The board of trustees may require its designated employees, including its president, and fiscal agents to enter into and file with the president of the college a surety bond to insure the faithful performance of the public duties of each officer or agent who is authorized to receive and expend the funds of the district, and such bond may be of such denomination and conditions as the board of trustees may deem necessary and requisite, and the premium thereon shall be paid from the funds of the district.

SECTION 14. In the event any county shall have outstanding bonds, or other indebtedness, which were sold or levied for the support and maintenance of a public junior college which is in operation on the date this act becomes law and such county shall become a part of a legally constituted junior college district as provided in Section 1 of this act, the board of supervisors of such county or the governing authorities of the municipality, as the case may be, shall continue to levy taxes upon such county or municipality until such bonds or other indebtedness shall be fully paid according to the terms thereof.

SECTION 15. Notwithstanding the provisions of this act, junior college districts heretofore established and approved by the Junior College Commission to serve the territory comprising a municipal separate school district and in operation on the passage of this act are hereby confirmed. Their government shall be vested in the municipal separate school district board of trustees, which board or boards shall have powers over the municipal separate school district junior college, as it has over other schools in the district, and the powers granted to the junior college districts named in this act.

SECTION 16. (a) Notwithstanding the provisions of this act to the contrary, any existing publicly operated junior college, lying in and operated by a county bordering on the Mississippi River, may, in the discretion of the board of supervisors of such county, continue to operate said college under such terms and conditions as said board may deem necessary and requisite in the premises. The governing authorities of other counties and municipalities are authorized and empowered, in the discretion of said governing bodies, to appropriate funds for the support of said junior college.

(b) The provisions of the preceding subsection shall not impair nor abrogate the aforesaid county's obligations, duties, powers, and rights as a member county of the junior college district to which it is made a part by Section 1 of this act.

SECTION 17. The board of trustees is expressly authorized and empowered to make a thorough study and evaluation of the costs of operation of the junior college district, and said board shall recommend a fair and acceptable tax rate for district general support and maintenance from each of the member counties.

The board of trustees of any junior college district as constituted at the time of the passage of this act shall have the authority to recommend the tax levy necessary for a newly contributing county to have representation on the board of trustees of said junior college.

In lieu of taxation, the board of trustees may fix the amount of enrollee tuition in an amount commensurate with the per capita cost of operating the district. Provided, however, that no county shall levy a smaller tax millage for capital improvements and general support than was levied for the previous year, unless requested to make such reduction by the board of trustees of the district. Provided further, that when a county has a general reassessment of property to increase the county ad valorem tax assessments, such counties may reduce the millage for general support and capital improvements, provided their aggregate budget for junior college purposes is not lower than was paid the previous year.

Provided further, however, that any agricultural high school which is not located on or adjacent to an existing junior college shall continue to be operated as heretofore and shall in no way be affected by the provisions of this act.

SECTION 18. It is expressly provided that nothing in this act shall be construed as affecting a junior college district heretofore established under authority of Chapter 381, Laws of 1962.

SECTION 19. Sections 6475–04, 6475–07, and 6476–01, Mississippi Code of 1942, be and they are hereby repealed.

SECTION 20. This act shall take effect and be in force from and after July 1, 1964.

E/Standards

The following standards were approved in the beginning by the State Association of Mississippi Colleges and later authorized and approved by the Mississippi Junior College Accrediting Commission.

State Association of Mississippi Colleges

Commission on Junior Colleges

STANDARDS Adopted by the State Association of Mississippi Colleges, December, 1922

STANDARD NUMBER ONE. (Entrance Requirements) The requirement for admission shall be satisfactory completion of a four-year course of not less than fifteen units in a secondary school approved by a recognized accrediting agency. No college maintaining a Preparatory School shall be accredited by this Commission until its Preparatory School has been accredited by the State High School Accrediting Commission. Any Junior College affiliated with recognized senior colleges may be called upon at any time for a record of all students entering the freshman class, such record to contain the name of each student, his secondary school, method of admission, units offered in each subject, and total units accepted.

STANDARD NUMBER TWO. (Requirements for Graduation) The minimum requirement for graduation shall be sixty semester hours of credit.

STANDARD NUMBER THREE. (Degrees) Junior Colleges shall not grant degrees.

STANDARD NUMBER FOUR. (Number of College Departments) The number of separate departments maintained shall be not less than five (English, history, foreign language, mathematics and science), and the number of teachers not less than four. In order that this number of teachers may be maintained in a small school, it is recommended that the head of a Department in a Junior College shall also be head of the same department in the high school if such school is operated in connection with the Junior College. No Junior College shall be credited unless it has a registration of as many as thirty-five students.

STANDARD NUMBER FIVE. (Training of Faculty) The minimum preparation of all instructors in a Junior College shall be a Bachelor's Degree from a standard college with either a major or minor requirement completed in the subject taught together with two years of successful teaching in high school or college. Beginning with 1925 at least half of the faculty shall have at least nine months of graduate work.

STANDARD NUMBER SIX. (Teaching Load) The average number of class-room hours per week, per instructor should not be more than eighteen. More than this number shall be regarded as endangering educational efficiency.

STANDARD NUMBER SEVEN. (Number of Students in Classes) The number of students in classes shall not exceed thirty (except for lectures). The number of students in a laboratory section shall not exceed the number for which desk space and equipment have been provided.

STANDARD NUMBER EIGHT. (Financial Support) A Junior College shall have, as a minimum, an income of not less than $12,500. The annual income should be commensurate with the number of students enrolled and the number of courses offered.

STANDARD NUMBER NINE. (Library) A working Library of not less than 2,500 volumes, exclusive of public documents, and a reading room in connection with the library shall be maintained. A definite annual income for the support of the library shall be provided.

STANDARD NUMBER TEN. (Laboratories) The Laboratories shall be adequately equipped for individual instruction in the course offered, and an annual income for their up-keep provided. It is recommended that a school with a limited income be equipped for good work in one or two sciences and not attempt work in others, and that the amount of equipment be not less than $2000 for classes of twelve.

STANDARD NUMBER ELEVEN. (Separation of College and Preparatory Classes) Where a Junior College and a high school are maintained together, it is required that the students be taught in separate classes.

STANDARD NUMBER TWELVE. (Organization) The work of the Junior College shall be organized on a college and not high school basis. This refers to the type of text books used, length of recitation periods, etc.

STANDARD NUMBER THIRTEEN. (General Statement Concerning Material Equipment) The location and construction of buildings, the lighting, heating, and ventilation of rooms, the nature of the laboratories, corridors, closets, water supply, school furniture, apparatus, and methods of cleaning shall be such as to insure hygenic conditions for both students and teachers.

STANDARD NUMBER FOURTEEN. (General Statement Concerning Curriculum and Spirit of Administration) The character of the curriculum, efficiency of instruction, and spirit of the institution shall be factors in determining its standing.

STANDARD NUMBER FIFTEEN. (Extra Curricula Activities) Athletics, amusements, and all other extra curricula activities shall be properly administered and shall not occupy an undue place in the life of the college.

STANDARD NUMBER SIXTEEN. (Standing of Graduates) The Junior College must be able to prepare its students so that they may sustain themselves in the Senior recognized college junior classes. In evidence statistics of the records, including high school units, of the graduates of the junior colleges in senior colleges shall be filed with the Commission on Junior Colleges on demand.

STANDARD NUMBER SEVENTEEN. (Inspection) No Junior College shall be accredited until it has been inspected and reported upon by an agent or agents regularly appointed by the commission. At least one member of the committee on inspection shall be qualified to pass upon proper equipment and management of a department in science. Any accredited Junior College shall be open to Inspection at any time.

STANDARD NUMBER EIGHTEEN. (Filing of Blank) No Institution shall be placed on or retained on the approved list unless a regular information blank has been filed with the Commission. The list shall be approved from year to year by the Commission. The blank shall be filed biennially, but the Commission, may, for due cause, call upon any member to file a new report in the meantime. Failure to file blank shall be sufficient cause for dropping an Institution.

(This list of standards only is extracted from the accreditation form appearing in full in Section III.)

Standards of the Mississippi Public Junior Colleges

Approved By The Mississippi Junior College Accrediting Commission

1. *Statement of Principles.* A flexible rather than a rigid system should be the guiding principle in formulating standards for educational institutions in a democracy. Schools and colleges should be encouraged to be different rather than be pressed into set molds to make them all alike. Junior colleges should carefully define their aims and objectives and be judged by the means employed and the success obtained in reaching those aims and objectives. The junior college should be judged as a whole, in terms of what it *is* and *does*, giving special attention to the quality as well as to the quantity of work done. To be accredited, a junior college must be legally authorized or chartered as an educational institution.

2. *Organization.* The junior college is an institution offering two years of instruction above high school and suited to the needs of its particular constituency. Two types are recognized: first, a two-year institution embracing two years of collegiate study based on the successful completion of an accredited high school course; second, an institution embracing two years of standard collegiate study integrated with two or more years of accredited high school study, administered as a single unit. In any case, the last two years are to be equivalent in prerequisites and thoroughness to the work offered in standard two-year junior colleges. The program of the last two years may be so organized as to be preparatory to the last two years of senior liberal arts, professional, or fine arts colleges; or it may be general, semi-professional, or terminal. The commission recognizes the rating of the high school accrediting commission on such grades as are maintained in the high school department.

3. *Entrance requirements.* The junior college shall require for admission graduation from an approved secondary school, with a minimum of 15 acceptable units, or the equivalent of this requirement as shown by examination. Certificates for admission should show the quality of work accomplished and give information as to the personality, character, general ability, and health of the student. Psychological tests are advised. All possible information about a student should be obtained before registration is completed. A program of guidance or orientation should be provided by each institution as a part of its entrance procedure.

4. *Graduation.* Junior colleges shall not grant degrees. For the diploma of graduation, or the title of associate arts, the student, in addition to meeting the entrance requirement for the particular type of curriculum he is pursuing, must complete at least 60 semester hours of academic credit, or the equivalent, with such qualitative requirements as each institution may require. A minimum of two hours of laboratory work shall count as the equivalent of one hour of lecture, recitation, or test.

5. *Faculty.* The training and experience of the members of the faculty are important items in evaluating a junior college. The junior college teacher of academic subjects shall have a master's degree or at least one year of graduate work. The courses taught by any teacher should be in the field of specialization. Teachers may teach on either the high school level, or the college level, or both when prepared as stated above. In the last two years of the college, there should be not more than 20 students for each teacher. The faculty members should belong to learned societies appropriate for their special work, and should be familiar with the publications of their societies. The faculty meetings should be stimulating and helpful. The salary scale shall be such as to secure and retain teachers of thorough training; the salary of department heads should be, in general, not less than $150. per month exclusive of board and living expenses; the salary of other teachers should be in proportion.

6. *Instruction.* The junior college should be known as an institution in which effective teaching is accomplished. Data of instructional efficiency should include information concerning classroom methods, tests, examinations, grading systems, faculty and student interest in the subjects taught, faculty and instructional self-analysis of instructional results; including the compilation and distribution on a comparative basis of grades by departments and by individual teachers.

7. *Teaching load.* A schedule of 18 credit hours a week should be the maximum as should class enrollment of 40 students. The teaching of a high school class meeting five hours a week will be considered the equivalent of three credit hours in a teacher's load. Two hours laboratory work shall be counted as one credit hour. Faculty committee assignments, sponsorship of extra-curricular activities, and other non-teaching duties shall be given consideration in the teaching load. As far as possible, every teacher should have some responsibility for contact with students in their extra-curricular activities.

8. *Financial support.* Each junior college shall show conclusive evidence that it is adequately able to finance the program defined by its stated objectives. Whether this financial support be derived from endowment, state or public sources, church donations, or student fees, it must be clearly demonstrated that this support has been regularly received over a period of at least three years, and there is reasonable assurance that it will continue. This support shall be adequate to secure and retain well-prepared teachers

with successful experience, and be sufficient to sustain every educational activity undertaken by the institution.

An important item of financial support is the expenditure per student for instructional purposes as explained in Standard No. 9. The extent to which the institution depends upon student fees, the regularity of income endowment, church and other stable sources, the avoidance of debt, and the accounting procedures of the institution are all items of importance. In any case, the minimum and annual income from sources other than student fees should be $10,000.

9. *Instructional expenditures.* The percentage of income spent for instructional purposes is an important factor in measuring a college program. To arrive at the figure desired, there should be added the following items: (1) The total salaries of the teaching staff, omitting those of administrative officers; (2) The expenditures for salaries for librarians, the purchasing of books and periodicals, and binding; and (3) The expenditure for classroom and laboratory supplies, but not permanent equipment; the total sum thus derived should be divided by the average number of students attending the institution during the regular session of nine months, and the result should show an expenditure of not less than $75. per student annually.

10. *Library.* The collection of books and periodicals should be compared frequently with the Mohrhardt's list or other standard guides. The library building should be well lighted, and have reading room space for at least 20 per cent of the student enrollment, be fireproof, if possible, and have adequate quarters for the working staff. For a small junior college, there should be a collection of books, adequately cataloged, carefully selected with reference to the subjects taught, and professionally administered, of not fewer than 3,000 volumes, exclusive of public documents. At least 40 magazines and periodicals should be taken each session. Attention shall be given to the possession of standard works of general and special reference, their number and recency.

The librarian should be a full-time library employee, have a degree in library science, and have faculty rank.

There should be an annual expenditure of an average of at least $2.50 per student for books, periodicals,

and binding. All students should receive at least elementary training in the use of the library. A careful record shall be kept of the use of the library by faculty and students.

11. *Laboratories.* The laboratories shall be equipped for individual instruction for each laboratory course offered in science, as well as for all vocational, semi-professional courses. If the fine arts, including drawing, painting, commercial art, and music, are offered, the equipment in these departments shall be considered in accrediting a junior college.

12. *Physical plant.* The material equipment, including the building, grounds, laboratories, apparatus, lighting, heating, ventilation, the nature and condition of its lavatories, corridors, classrooms, closets, water supply, furniture, and methods of cleaning and general sanitary conditions, shall all be considered in accrediting a junior college.

13. *Student personnel work.* A program of guidance should be provided. Scholastic and personal data, including records of all physical examinations and of vocational and placement advice, should be kept for each student.

A system of permanent records, showing clearly both the secondary and the college credits for each student, shall be accurately administered.

14. *Extra-curricular activities.* There should be provision for extra-curricular activities and ample opportunity for development of leadership and initiative. These activities, including athletics, amusements, sports, fraternities, and sororities, should all be under general faculty supervision and should not occupy an undue place in the life of the junior college. If the junior college engages in inter-collegiate athletics, it should hold membership in some athletic conference or association of approved standing.

In evaluating the program of a junior college, account shall be taken of all student activities, such as student government, student publications, literary societies, debating and speech activities, science, music, art, and foreign language clubs, religious and social service organizations.

15. *General tone of the institution.* The general atmosphere and spirit of its administration, the nature of its publicity, the truthfulness of its publications, and on the part of those who solicit, its code of ethics, and its standing in the estimation of senior colleges,

universities, and other educational agencies shall all be carefully considered in determining the rating of a junior college.

16. *Record of transfer students.* The records of transfer students transferred to higher institutions over a period of years should be carefully considered in accrediting a junior college.

17. *Inspection and report.* No junior college shall be recommended for membership until it has been checked by a committee authorized by the association and the report of this committee, through the executive secretary, shall be submitted to the commission for final action. Inspection fee for applying institutions shall be $25., and there shall be a $5.00 annual fee for inspection for each member institution. Any member junior college of the association shall be open to inspection at any time by the executive secretary, or authorized committee, and shall report to the commission annually unless a member of the Southern Association, in which case a report shall be made every three years and special reports at any time required by the association through the executive secretary.

Standards Approved by the Mississippi Junior College Commission

In compliance with Chapter 369, Laws of Mississippi, 1950, the Junior College Commission recognizes its responsibility to "Regulate the establishment and operation of junior colleges in the state."

STANDARD ONE:
STATEMENT OF POLICY

A. The Junior College Commission considers that its task is to offer leadership and supervision to the end that a quality program of junior college education will be available to all of the people in every section of Mississippi.

B. The Commission affirms the principle of local initiative and local control in the administration of junior colleges as far as this is possible consistent with the provisions of Chapter 369, Laws of Mississippi, 1950.

C. The junior college is an educational institution that is dedicated particularly to the service of the community and state that support it. It may include in its program certain years of high school work along with other services and courses that are prescribed to be offered in Section 1, Chapter 369, Laws of Mississippi, 1950.

D. Before any institution can qualify for junior college appropriations, it shall meet the standards of the Mississippi Junior College Commission.

E. The Junior College Commission affirms the proposition that no district shall be described nor a junior college established by one or more counties or by one or more separate school districts or by any combination of counties and municipal separate school district until there is sufficient evidence:

(1) That the enrollment will be sufficient for an effective junior college program within a cost that will not be excessive. Experience has shown that for a minimum program there should be not less than 200 regular full-time college students, and if a program is to be diversified, there should be at least a minimum of 400 students. Particular attention should be given to long-term population trends in the district before it shall be established.

(2) That the valuation of the assessed property is sufficient to guarantee an adequate program of education including buildings and maintenance costs. Trends in valuation and population will be considered.

(3) That the people of the district are willing to support the junior college by attendance, by the levying of sufficient taxes, and by the maintenance of sound professional administration.

F. Studies will be made under the authority and supervision of the Commission whenever one or more of the following conditions prevail:

(1) A local district, i.e., a county or counties, a municipal separate school district or districts, or a combination of counties and separate school districts requests a study for the purpose of organizing a junior college.

(2) The State Board of Education requests a study of a given area or areas.

(3) The majority of the approved public junior colleges of the state requests a study.

(4) Competent authority, as recognized by the Commission, requests a study.

(5) The Commission deems a study necessary.

G. The standards of the Mississippi Junior College Commission apply to public junior colleges only.

STANDARD TWO:
NEW DISTRICTS AND NEW SCHOOLS

Minimum standards for the creation of a district within which a junior college may be established hereafter shall be:

A. In a district of one or more counties, there shall

be a minimum average of at least six hundred high school graduates during the five years next preceding the establishment of a new junior college. (Exception: if in the judgment of the Commission the population is large enough to insure a minimum junior college enrollment of two hundred and a potential enrollment of four hundred based on a potential total of six hundred high school graduates within a five year period after the determination of this fact, the Commission may approve the creation of a new district and the establishment of a new junior college.) In case the proposed district is in and for a municipal separate school district, the minimum number of high school graduates shall be four hundred. The purpose of this standard is to make more likely an enrollment of four hundred college students.

B. The valuation of the district shall be such that a two mill levy on the assessed valuation will meet the minimum standards of local support for maintenance purposes.

C. There shall be a minimum plant valuation of $2,000.00 per capita of probable enrollment before a college can be approved for establishment.

D. No junior college may be located in a county where there is already located a public senior college or university for the same race, or within twenty miles of such senior college.

The Boards designated in Section 4 of Chapter 369, Laws of Mississippi, 1950, and in the petition to the Commission shall set out in detail the plan of operation of the proposed institution as may be required by the Junior College Commission.

STANDARD THREE

Before the Junior College Commission may certify annually to the State Board of Education or other organization, board, agency, or administration designated by law to disburse appropriations for junior colleges, the names of such junior colleges which are eligible for such funds, the junior colleges shall file reports as required by the Junior College Commission and shall meet the standards hereinafter enumerated.

STANDARD FOUR

A. *Legal Status.* Junior Colleges of Mississippi which seek to qualify under standards of the Junior College Commission shall be organized under the provisions set forth under Chapter 369, Laws of Mississippi, 1950.

B. *Administrative Organization.*

(1) *Board of Trustees.* Junior Colleges seeking to qualify under standards of the Junior College Commission shall give evidence that the local control and administration operates in conformity with Chapter 369, Laws of Mississippi, 1950. The Board of Trustees shall give evidence of the fact that it assumes full responsibility for the government of the junior college; and it shall fix responsibility and delegate authority as prescribed in Section 7 of Chapter 369, Laws of Mississippi, 1950.

(2) *President.* The president shall be responsible to the Board of Trustees for a functional organization, with such administrative officers as deans, registrar, business manager, etc., as shall be necessary for sound and efficient administration of the affairs of the college. In junior colleges of the size of Mississippi institutions, the administrative organization need not be elaborate nor expensive but should require capable individuals. The president shall be responsible to the Board of Trustees for such matters as are delegated to him, particularly those named in Section 7 of Chapter 369, Laws of Mississippi, 1950.

C. *Academic Organization.* Junior colleges shall be organized to perform an educational function. Curricula shall meet the standards set up by this Commission and shall meet the mandate of Section 1 of Chapter 369, Laws of Mississippi, 1950. Teachers shall be chosen for their ability to teach, and they should be given the encouragement and security that is necessary for them to perform adequately their function.

D. *General Administration.* The general administration of the college shall be such as will reflect itself in the successful operation of the institution, with particular regard to:

(1) Financial stability;
(2) Ability to secure and hold high caliber teachers;
(3) Proper maintenance, care, and cleanliness of buildings and grounds;
(4) Percentage of entering students who graduate;
(5) Success of transfer and terminal students;
(6) Educational needs and otherwise providing leadership in the community;
(7) Evidence of no political interference.

STANDARD FIVE: CURRICULUM

The curricula offerings of the junior college shall be such as to carry out the mandate of Chapter 369, Laws of Mississippi, 1950, and such as to carry out the purposes and objectives of the institution. Each junior college should publish its objectives and list its special objectives, if any. Each junior college should in general serve its community or area.

It is expected that each junior college will offer curricula and courses as follows:

A. *College and University Parallel Curricula.* Each junior college shall offer at least one college or university parallel curriculum of not less than sixty semester or ninety quarter hours of academic work. The courses shall be correlated with those of senior colleges and professional schools.

B. *Vocational-Technical and Semi-Professional Curriculum.* Subject to the fulfilment of its stated purpose and objectives and to the law, junior colleges shall offer curricula of a vocational-technical, and semi-professional type, on the collegiate level. Upon completion of such curricula, graduates should be so trained as to be able to secure and hold employment in the field of their training. (NOTE: No specific courses are listed, indicating that any junior college may offer any course desired. It might be that the Commission would want to consider the idea of listing certain courses which might be given by any or all junior colleges, and limiting other courses on a definite "allocation of function" basis.)

C. *Vocational or Trade-Training Curriculum.* Courses of a strictly vocational or trade-training type should be offered subject to the needs of the community. High school graduation should not be a prerequisite for this type of curriculum. This type of program should include such fields as: (a) automobile mechanics, (b) barbering, (c) body and fender work, (d) cabinet making, (e) electricity, (f) radio, (g) refrigeration and air conditioning, etc.

D. *Short Term Curricula.* Where the needs of the community justify such training, there should be special courses of training for specific jobs. These courses may vary in length according to the requirements of the courses. They should be offered to groups who desire and will profit by them without regard to previous educational training or future academic plans. These courses should carry no college credit and should not be set up on a collegiate academic basis.

E. *Adult Education.* The needs of the adult population of the community should be met with adequate educational courses insofar as possible. Such courses may be offered in conformity to "A ," "B," "C," or "D" of this standard. In any case, it should be clearly stated that the course is a "college credit" or a "noncredit" course. If it is a college credit course, it shall meet all standards for other college courses.

F. *Diploma and Certificate.* When a student has successfully completed any curriculum that requires a minimum of sixty semester or ninety quarter hours, the colleges that meet the standards of this Commission may issue a diploma and confer a title, or degree, to such student; and the title, or degree, may be an Associate of Arts, an Associate of Agriculture, or any other appropriate title, or Associate degree. Junior Colleges may issue a diploma or certificate testimonial of completion of other curricula in the college.

STANDARD SIX:
TRAINING OF TEACHERS
AND ADMINISTRATORS

The training and experience of the members of the faculty are important items in evaluating a junior college.

(1) Faculty members should have the background and knowledge of the junior college afforded by graduate courses, workshops, and seminars in the special field of the junior college, its history, basic philosophy, special problems and methods. Members of the faculty should be encouraged by the institution to participate in such in-service programs. In selecting new staff members, this item should be considered.

(2) The college should have a program of in-service training for its faculty members. Included in this training should be a study of the nature, history, and basic philosophy of the junior college.

(3) The junior college instructor of academic subjects shall have the Master's Degree or its equivalent and the courses taught by the instructor shall be in fields of specialization.

(4) Each instructor in vocation-technical or in vocational trades-training curricula shall possess satisfactory vocational training, vocational experience, and personal qualifications for his specific work.

(5) Faculty members should belong to learned societies appropriate to their special work and should be familiar with the publications of the societies.

(6) Faculty meetings should be democratic, stimulating and helpful.

(7) The ratio of faculty members to students should, in general, not exceed twenty students to one instructor on a full-time teaching basis.

(8) The salary should be sufficient as to secure and retain instructors of thorough preparation. The salary of a beginning junior college instructor should be a minimum of $2,400.00 for nine months' work. There should be appropriate increments for additional training, experience, and responsibility.

(9) The standard teaching load in semester hours or their equivalent is recognized to be sixteen. The maximum teaching load is eighteen semester hours, and only a

small percentage of the faculty may be permitted to carry this maximum. The teaching schedule should be arranged so that the total teaching load per week of each instructor will ordinarily not exceed 450 student credit hours. Two hours of laboratory work shall be counted as one credit hour. In three-year or four-year junior colleges, the teaching of a high school class meeting five hours a week will be considered the equivalent of three credit hours in an instructor's load.

(10) The president of the junior college shall be a person of proven ability as a teacher or an administrator and have at least a Master's Degree. Section one of Standard Six shall apply to the president as well as to classroom teachers. If the president does not have special preparation for junior college administration, it is expected that he will take training specifically designed to prepare him for junior college administration.

STANDARD SEVEN: INSTRUCTION

The junior college should be an institution in which effective teaching is accomplished. The primary interest of the faculty should be sound, thorough, and inspirational teaching rather than research. Data on instructional efficiency should include information concerning classroom methods, tests, examinations, grading systems, analysis of instructional results, including the compilation and distribution of grades by departments and instructors, the development and use of syllabi and their continuous revision and adjustment.

STANDARD EIGHT: PHYSICAL PLANT AND EQUIPMENT

The physical plant and equipment, including the buildings, grounds, laboratories, apparatus, lighting, heating, ventilation, sanitation, water supply, furniture, as well as the general maintenance should be of the quality which may be expected of an institution desiring accreditation. Completeness, appearance, maintenance, and general management, as well as type, quality, and avoidance of obsolescence are important factors.

STANDARD NINE: THE LIBRARY

The library should be well lighted and have reading room space for at least twenty percent of the student enrollment. It should be fire-resistant, if possible, and have adequate facilities for housing, maintaining, and using the library as an important instructional department of the college.

The junior college should have a collection of at least six thousand volumes exclusive of public documents, carefully selected, adequately cataloged, and readily available for use. At least fifty magazines and periodicals should be available each session, especially selected to serve in the instructional program. Standard works of general and special reference sufficient to meet the needs of the student body should be available. Circulation statistics and other data concerning the use made of the library should be kept, in addition to the accession book.

Beginning institutions must have not fewer than three thousand usable books the first year of operation and meet the six thousand volume standard prescribed above in not less than three years.

There should be an annual expenditure of at least $3.00 per student for books, periodicals, and binding.

The library shall be professionally administered by a librarian who is a full-time employee and who has a major in library science. The librarian shall have faculty rank. All students should receive at least elementary training in the use of the library from the librarian or under the librarian's direction.

There shall be such assistants as the necessity of administrative efficiency requires. The size of the institution, the adequacy of its physical equipment, and the number of hours which the library is kept open daily will determine the number of staff members needed and will constitute a rough measure of the effectiveness of the library service. The collection of books and periodicals should be compared frequently with nationally recognized library lists.

STANDARD TEN: LABORATORIES

The science laboratories and laboratories for vocational-technical and semi-professional courses should be equipped for individual instruction in each laboratory course offered. If the fine arts, including drawing, dramatics, painting, and music are offered, the equipment in these departments shall be considered in accrediting the junior college. Each laboratory and vocational shop shall be judged upon its own merits with regard to its adequacy:

(1) The room shall be large enough to properly house the equipment and provide safe, comfortable working space for the students.
(2) The shop or laboratory shall be provided with proper equipment with regard to quality, quantity, and recency of design. Shops shall provide adequate work experience in the vocational-technical field of training

to correspond with work experience after finishing the course.

(3) The number of work stations provided in a shop must be adequate to provide efficient training for students enrolled in a shop section.

STANDARD ELEVEN:
ADMISSION REQUIREMENTS

The two-year junior college shall require for admission to its standard academic and general curricula a minimum of fifteen acceptable units or the equivalent, as shown by examination, from an approved high school.

Certificates of admission shall be on standard forms and should show the quality of work accomplished and give information concerning the personality, character, general ability, and health. Psychological and achievement test information should also be secured by the college prior to or at the time of entrance.

In general, terminal curricula, including vocational-technical courses, shall have the same entrance requirements as those listed above. However, students not meeting the requirements for admission to standard academic and general curricula may be admitted to terminal curricula on individual approval if they are at least eighteen years of age.

STANDARD TWELVE: ENROLLMENT

The minimum enrollment should be 200 full-time students, exclusive of students enrolled from another junior college district.

STANDARD THIRTEEN:
FINANCIAL REPORT

A. Junior colleges shall not be organized nor will they be approved by the Commission to secure state funds unless and until there is evidence that the local districts will support adequately the college from local tax sources. The Commission recognizes two measures of local effort:

(1) The Commission considers an average levy of two mills for maintenance purposes on the total assessed property of the district as a desirable minimum. The statutory limit of three mills for maintenance purposes should be levied if necessary to maintain a diversified program of high quality. In terms of the purchasing power of the 1950 dollar, there should be available from all sources $350.00 per student for operating expenses exclusive of auxiliary agencies and capital outlay.

(2) In no event shall the per capita income for college students from local maintenance tax sources be less than $125.00 per college student, unless a statutory limit of three mills over the entire district fails to bring in this amount.

In calculating the above, the number of students shall be the number used in disbursing per capita funds from state appropriations.

It is the responsibility of the college administration to maintain financial records that will make it possible for the Commission to distinguish between the cost of operating the several units of the college: academic college, adult education, vocational-technical education, high school, and similar units.

B. The percentage of income spent for direct instructional purposes is an important factor in measuring the college program. To arrive at the direct instructional cost, the following items shall be considered:

(1) The total salaries of the teaching staff, omitting the administrative officers. The salaries of laboratory assistants and any others who are directly concerned with the instructional activities should be included.

(2) The expenditure for the salaries of librarians, library assistants, library supplies, the purchase of books and periodicals, the cost of binding, repair and maintenance of library materials.

(3) The expenditure for classroom, laboratory, and any other supplies used directly for instructional activities, but not permanent equipment.

(4) The total sum thus derived should not be less than 65 percent of the operating cost of the college and shall not be less than 60 percent of the total operating cost.

STANDARD FOURTEEN:
STUDENT ACTIVITIES AND STUDENT PERSONNEL

The junior college should encourage democratic student life and activities. Student activities should be student managed and directed with faculty cooperation. A well balanced program of extra-curricular activities should be established which will promote participation by students, but not to excess.

The college should provide a program of pre-registration, orientation, and guidance with proper emphasis upon acquainting the students with scholastic work and the activities and life of the college. To this end student personnel service should include a program of educational, vocational, personal, and social guidance and counseling.

A standardized testing program should be provided, making use of at least a minimum number of the best known and most reliable instruments. Placement and follow-up service should be provided and if students are admitted who work part-time, the college should assume some responsibility for their guidance and assistance.

Boarding and rooming facilities, if provided, should be under the supervision of the institution with provision made for frequent and regular inspection and proper supervision in order to maintain high standards of conduct and sanitation.

The athletic program of the college shall be under faculty supervision and control.

STANDARD FIFTEEN: RECORDS

The academic, personnel, health, activity, and other records of students shall be systematically kept and protected from fire, loss, and damage.

The registrar shall keep files of admission, matriculation, attendance, and scholarship records, transcripts received, and other essential data.

Individual records shall be kept for each faculty member showing the period of service, advancements, evidence of professional growth, advanced study, research and publications, noteworthy achievements, and instructional experience.

The records of the business office shall provide ample safeguard for funds and be easily audited. They shall be based upon an officially adopted budget.

STANDARD SIXTEEN: SELF SURVEY OR EVALUATION

Each junior college shall once in five years have a self-survey or evaluation in conformity with instructions of the Junior College Commission.

STANDARD SEVENTEEN: QUALITY OF WORK

A very important factor is *quality of work* required of students. The following are recognized as minimum requirements:

A. *Qualitative Requirements*
   (1) The quality of work will be of such caliber and quality as is commonly expected to be done on a college level.
   (2) The quality of work may and should be greatly enhanced by reasonably small classes and personalized instruction.
   (3) An indication of the quality of work will be measured by the ability of graduates to succeed (a) in advanced college courses, and (b) in jobs for which they have been trained.

B. *Quantitative Requirements*
   (1) A school year of nine four-week months is recognized as a regular full year of work.
   (2) A class period is not less than fifty minutes, exclusive of time between classes, for lecture, and not less than one hundred minutes, exclusive of time between classes, for laboratory periods.
   (3) A semester hour is defined as 18 class periods or 900 minutes for lecture, and 1800 minutes for laboratory; a quarter hour is 12 class periods or 600 minutes for lecture, and 1200 minutes for laboratory. (This does not include time for passing between classes).
   (4) A normal load is 15 academic hours for regular full-time students; the minimum load for a full-time student is 12 academic hours, and in no case shall be more than 19 academic hours. A student carrying as much as 18 hours should have at least a B average.
   (5) Summer school work will be of the same type and caliber as regular session work and credits based on the same number of minutes of class time. The maximum credit earnable in five weeks is six semester hours and in the same ratio for any other length of summer session.
   (6) Evening classes for college credit will be of the same type and caliber as regular day school work and credits based on the same number of minutes of class time.

C. *Vocational Requirements*
   (1) Vocational or trades-training courses should be such as will actually prepare a student to secure and hold a job in his field of preparation.
   (2) If credit is to be given in these courses, the time requirement should be a minimum of two hours of shop work for one hour of credit.
   (3) No course should be offered in this field without sufficient shop space and equipment to provide superior training.
   (4) Evening classes in this program should meet the same standards as the regular day program.

D. *Non-Credit Evening Class Requirements*
   (1) There should be evening classes organized to meet the needs of the community—this implies classes for non-college credit.
   (2) The standards of work in non-credit courses should meet the needs of the individual without regard to collegiate academic standards.

STANDARD EIGHTEEN: GENERAL TONE AND STABILITY OF THE INSTITUTION

The general atmosphere and spirit of its administration, the nature of its publicity, the truthfulness of its publications and on the part of those who solicit students, its code of ethics, and its standing in the estimation of senior colleges, universities, other junior colleges, and other educational agencies shall be the final and a most important standard considered in determining the evaluation of a junior college.

Mississippi Public Junior College Standards
As Approved by the Junior College Commission
1962

The establishing and maintenance of junior colleges in the State of Mississippi is a joint responsibility of local and state governments. Chapter 352, Laws of Mississippi, 1962, states that the Junior College Commission shall have the following powers and duties:

(1) To make studies of the needs of the state and communities for junior college education, especially in the field of vocational and vocational-technical education. In the light of these studies, the commission shall delegate vocational and vocational-technical functions to the various junior colleges of the state, based on needs as established by these studies, and recommend to the state board of education the allocation of funds to finance these programs.

(2) To fix standards for junior colleges to qualify for junior college appropriations, with respect to training of teachers and administrators, physical plant and equipment, administrative organization, curriculum, income per student from local tax sources, enrollment, admission requirements, general tone of the institution, and other factors that relate to the support and administration of junior colleges.

(3) To certify annually to the state board of education or other organization, board, agency, or administration designated by law to disburse appropriations for junior colleges, the name of such junior colleges which are eligible for such funds.

(4) To require the junior colleges to supply such information as the commission may request and to compile, publish, and make available to the legislature and other interested parties such reports based thereon as the commission may deem advisable.

STANDARD I:
ORGANIZATION AND ADMINISTRATION

The junior college shall be an educational institution that is dedicated to the service of its district and state that support it. It may include in its program certain years of high school work along with other services as prescribed by Section 1, Chapter 369, Laws of Mississippi, 1950.

The counties comprising the districts of each junior college shall be in keeping with Chapter 381, Laws of Mississippi, 1962, and Chapter 398, Laws of Mississippi, 1964, and shall have a governing board as provided for in Chapter 381, Laws of Mississippi, 1962, and Chapter 402, Laws of Mississippi, 1964, and shall exercise the powers as listed in Chapter 398, Laws of Mississippi, 1964.

Each junior college shall have a president as its executive head who will be selected under the provisions of Section 6, Chapter 369, Laws of Mississippi, 1950, and Section 4, Chapter 398, Laws of Mississippi, 1964. In addition to the president, there shall be such administrative officers as administrative assistants, deans, registrars, business managers, etc., as shall be necessary for sound and efficient administration of the affairs of the college.

The general administration of the college shall be such as will reflect itself in the successful operation of the institution, with particular regard to:

(1) Fulfilling its stated purposes and objectives.
(2) Educational needs and otherwise providing leadership in the community.
(3) Ability to secure and hold high-caliber teachers.
(4) Proper maintenance, care, and cleanliness of buildings and grounds.
(5) Success of transfer and terminal students.
(6) Percentage of entering students who graduate.
(7) Financial stability.
(8) Evidence of no political interference.

The organization of branch campuses or attendance centers shall be approved by the Junior College Commission. Criteria to be considered shall include:

(1) Student population to be served.
(2) Financial stability of the junior college district.
(3) Existing educational institutions and their offerings.
(4) Educational programs to be offered by newly established branch campuses.

Institutions applying for permission to establish a branch campus shall justify in detail its request based on the above criteria.

STANDARD II: EDUCATIONAL PROGRAM

The educational program of the junior college shall be such as to carry out the mandate of Chapter 369,

Laws of Mississippi, 1950, and Chapter 398, Laws of Mississippi, 1964, and such as to carry out the purposes and objectives of the institution. Each junior college shall publish its purposes and objectives in its official publications.

The junior college should be an institution in which effective teaching is accomplished. The primary interest of the faculty should be sound, thorough, and inspirational teaching rather than research. Data on institutional efficiency should include information concerning classroom methods, tests, examinations, grading systems, analysis of instructional results, including the compilation and distribution of grades by departments and instructors, the development and use of syllabi and their continuous revision and adjustment.

It is expected that each junior college will offer curricula and courses as follows:

A. *College and University Parallel Curricula.* Each junior college shall offer curricula that are correlated with the curricula offered by the lower division of senior colleges or universities.

B. *Technical and Semi-Professional Curricula.* Subject to the fulfillment of its stated purpose and objectives and to the law, junior colleges shall offer curricula of a technical and semi-professional type on the collegiate level.

C. *Vocational Curricula.* Courses of a vocational or trade-training type should be offered, subject to the needs of the community. High school graduation should not be a prerequisite for these curricula.

D. *Short-Term Curricula.* Where the needs of the community justify such training, there should be special courses of training for specific jobs. These courses may vary in length according to the requirements of the courses. They should be offered to groups who desire and will profit by them without regard to previous educational training or future academic plans. These courses should carry no college credit and should not be set up on a collegiate academic basis.

E. *Adult Education.* The needs of the adult population of the community should be met with adequate educational courses insofar as possible. Such courses may be offered in conformity as to "A," "B," "C," or "D" of this standard. In any case, it should be clearly stated that the course is a "college credit" or a "non-credit" course. If it is a college credit course, it shall meet all standards for other college courses.

F. *Diploma and Certificate.* When a student has successfully completed any curriculum that requires a minimum of sixty semester or ninety quarter hours of academic work, the colleges that meet the standards of this commission may issue a diploma and confer a title, or degree, to such student; and the title, or degree may be an Associate of Arts, an Associate of Science, or any other appropriate title as associate degree. Junior Colleges may issue a diploma or certificate testimonial of completion of other curricula in the college.

All vocational and technical courses shall receive prior approval of the Junior College Commission before becoming a part of the vocational-technical curricula of the junior colleges.

Admission requirements. The junior college shall require for admission to its academic and technical curricula a minimum of fifteen acceptable units from an approved high school or by successful completion of the G.E.D. Test.

Students may be admitted to the vocational programs on an individual basis if they are eighteen years of age or older.

Enrollment. The minimum enrollment should be sufficient for the institution to carry out its stated purpose and objectives.

STANDARD III: FINANCIAL RESOURCES

The financial resources of each junior college shall be such as to maintain a quality educational program, faculty, library and physical plant that would enable the institution to achieve its desired purpose and objectives.

An average levy of two mills for maintenance purposes on the total assessed property of the district is a desirable minimum. However, the statutory limit of three mills should be levied if necessary to maintain a diversified program of high quality.

Operating income from all sources should not be less than $550.00 per student. This amount is exclusive of auxiliary agencies and capital outlay.

In no event shall the student per capita income from local tax sources for maintenance and operation be less than $250.00 unless the statutory limit of three mills over the entire district fails to yield this amount.

The Commission looks with favor upon a levy that would produce a minimum of $100.00 per student for capital improvement.

In calculating the above expenditures, the number

of students used shall be the same as the number used in disbursing per capita funds from state appropriation.

Each junior college will follow the system of accounting as recommended by the Mississippi State Department of Audit. The procedures set forth by this department have an effective date of July 1, 1969. This system provides for the identification of the various categories of expenditures.

The percentage of income spent for direct instructional purposes is an important factor in measuring the college program. To arrive at the direct instructional cost, the following items shall be considered:

(1) The total salaries of the teaching staff, prorating the administrative officers who teach (the salaries of laboratory assistants and any others who are directly concerned with the instructional activities should be included).

(2) The expenditure for classroom, laboratory, and any other supplies used directly for instructional activities, but not fixed equipment.

It is recommended that not less than 65 percent of the operational budget be expended for instructional purposes. In no case shall the expenditure for this purpose be less than 60 percent.

The records of the business office shall be properly protected from fire and theft. Personnel charged with the responsibility of handling monies shall be properly bonded in keeping with state law.

A record of the income and expenditures should be based upon an officially adopted budget on file with the Executive Secretary of the Junior College Commission.

The Junior College Commission looks with favor upon and recommends adjustments of out-of-state tuition in keeping with the increasing costs of the instructional program. It further recommends periodic re-evaluation of student fees.

STANDARD IV: LIBRARY

The library should be well lighted and have reading room space for at least 25 percent of the student enrollment. It should be fire-resistant, if possible, and have adequate facilities for housing, maintaining, and using the library as an important instructional department of the college.

The junior college should have a collection of at least ten thousand volumes, exclusive of public documents, carefully selected, adequately cataloged, and readily available for use. Adequate magazines and periodicals should be available each session, especially selected to serve in the instructional program. Standard works of general and special reference sufficient to meet the needs of the student body should be available. Circulation statistics and other data concerning the use made of the library should be kept, in addition to the accession of books.

Branch campuses must have not fewer than five thousand usable books the first year of operation and meet the ten thousand volume standard prescribed above in not less than three years.

Centers must furnish adequate library service in keeping with the courses offered at the center.

The annual expenditure for the library should be at least 3 to 5 percent of the operating budget. The expenditures for books, bindings, periodicals, and supplies shall not be less than $8.00 per student.

The library shall be administered by a professional library staff who shall have faculty rank. There shall be a sufficient number of assistants to assure adequate library services. The size of the institution, the adequacy of its physical equipment, and the number of hours which the library is kept open daily will determine the number of staff members needed and will constitute a rough measure of the effectiveness of the library service. The collection of books and periodicals should be compared frequently with nationally recognized library holdings.

STANDARD V: FACULTY

The selection, development, and retention of a competent faculty for all levels of instruction is of major importance to each institution. The relationship between faculty objectives and institutional purposes determines in large measure the effectiveness of the total educational program.

The academic preparation and experience of the faculty are significant factors in determining the quality of the institution's educational program. The continuous professional growth of all faculty members should be encouraged, and the institutions should assist members of their faculty to further their professional development.

If faculty members are to be effective teachers, they must have reasonable security. Therefore, each institution should provide adequate salaries, a program of well-planned benefits, provision for tenure, and assurance of freedom to teach.

Selection of faculty. Specific assignments of responsibility should exist for identifying, appraising, negotiating with and selecting new faculty members. Criteria for prospective faculty members should be established which are in keeping with the purposes and philosophy of the institution.

After the necessary interviews, consultations with departmental chairman and/or dean, the president will recommend to the board of trustees his choice of faculty members.

Faculty organization. The faculty of all institutions should be so organized that their business may be properly conducted. Faculty membership should be clearly defined.

In small institutions, the faculty should be organized as a whole. In larger institutions, it may be organized by divisions. The jurisdiction of the faculty in academic affairs should be clearly defined and should provide adequate scope for the exercise of faculty responsibility. The faculty should be concerned primarily with fundamental academic policies. Provision for open and regular channels of communication between faculties and administration should be clearly defined and followed.

The rules and regulations relating to faculty organization, by-laws, and responsibilities should be recorded and accessible to all concerned.

Academic preparation of faculty. All junior college teaching faculty members should hold advanced degrees (at least a master's degree specialization in the field in which they teach). Any exception must be justified by special competence in the field of knowledge.

The Commission strongly encourages every institution to comply with the standards of the regional accreditation agency in meeting faculty requirements.

Faculty members should belong to learned societies and professional organizations, appropriate to their special work, and should be familiar with their publications.

The ratio of faculty members to students should not exceed twenty students to one instructor on a full-time teaching basis.

The standard teaching load in semester hours or their equivalent is recognized to be sixteen. The maximum teaching load is eighteen semester hours, and only a small percentage of the faculty may be permitted to carry this maximum. The teaching schedule should be so arranged that the total teaching load per week of each instructor will ordinarily not exceed 450 student credit hours. Two hours of laboratory work shall be counted as one credit hour.

The president of the junior college shall be a person of proven ability as a teacher and administrator and have at least a master's degree. If the president does not have special preparation for junior college administration, it is expected that he will take training specifically designed to prepare him for junior college administration.

STANDARD VI: STUDENT PERSONNEL

The junior college should encourage democratic student life and activities. A well-balanced program of student activities should be developed. This program should be student managed with faculty and administrative direction.

The college should provide a program of orientation and guidance with proper emphasis on acquainting students with scholastic work and the activities and life of the college. To this end, a student personnel service should include a program of educational, vocational, personal, and social guidance and counseling.

A well-developed testing program should be provided, making use of an adequate number of the best-known and most reliable instruments. The college should also assume some degree of responsibility in placement and follow-up service, offering the greatest degree of assistance possible.

Institutions providing boarding and rooming facilities should maintain supervision over these. They should also make provision for frequent and regular inspection of these in order to maintain high standards of conduct and sanitation.

The programs of intramural and intercollegiate athletics shall be supervised and controlled by persons having faculty status.

Records. The academic, personnel, health, activity, and other records of students shall be systematically kept and protected from fire, loss, and damage.

The registrar shall keep files of admission, attendance, and scholarship records, transcripts received, and other essential data.

Individual records shall be kept for each faculty member showing the period of service, advancements, evidence of professional growth, advanced study, research and publications, noteworthy achievements, and instructional experience.

STANDARD VII:
GENERAL REQUIREMENTS

A very important factor is *quality of work* required of students. The following are recognized as minimum requirements:

A. *Qualitative requirements:*
1. The quality of work will be of such caliber and quality as is commonly expected to be done on a college level.
2. The quality of work may and should be greatly enhanced by reasonably small classes and personalized instruction.
3. An indication of the quality of work will be measured by the ability of graduates to succeed (1) in advanced college courses and (b) in jobs for which they have been trained.

B. *Quantitative requirements:*
1. A school year of nine four-week months is recognized as a regular full year of work.
2. A class period is not less than 50 minutes, exclusive of time between classes, for lecture and not less than 100 minutes, exclusive of time between classes, for laboratory periods.
3. A semester hour is defined as eighteen class periods or 900 minutes for lecture and 1800 minutes for laboratory; a quarter hour is twelve class periods or 600 minutes for lecture and 1200 minutes for laboratory. (This does not include time for passing between classes).
4. The normal student load is considered to be fifteen academic hours; the minimum load for a full-time student is twelve academic hours.
5. Summer school work will be of the same type and caliber as regular session work and credits based on the same number of minutes of classtime. The maximum credit earnable in five weeks is six semester hours and in the same ratio for any other length of summer session.
6. Evening classes for college credit will be of the same type and caliber as regular day school work and credits based on the same number of minutes of classtime.

C. *Vocational requirements.*
1. Vocational or trades-training courses should be such as will actually prepare a student to secure and hold a job in his field of preparation.
2. The load for full-time vocational students shall be a minimum of 25 clock hours per week.
3. No courses should be offered in this field without sufficient shop space and equipment to provide superior training.
4. Evening classes in this program should meet the same standards as the regular day program.

D. *Technical requirements.*
1. Technical courses shall be two years in length and shall merit an associate level degree.
2. Student load in the technical area should be in keeping with the requirements of the academic area.
3. Careful consideration should be given to the proper balance of academic subjects and manipulative skills in each technical curriculum.

E. *Non-credit evening classes.*
1. Non-credit evening classes should be organized to meet the needs of the community.
2. The standards of work in non-credit courses should meet the needs of the individual without regard to collegiate academic standards.

STANDARD VIII: BRANCH CAMPUSES

No branch campus or attendance center will be established without prior approval of the Junior College Commission.

It shall be the responsibility of the institution in its application to the Commission to submit proper justification, needs, ability to support, and other evidence as may be requested by the Commission.

STANDARD IX:
SELF-SURVEYS AND EVALUATION

Junior colleges that are members of the regional accrediting association shall file with the Executive Secretary of the Junior College Commission a copy of their periodic self-study report, a copy of the visiting committee's report, and the five-year interim report required by the regional accrediting agency.

Junior colleges that are not members of the regional accrediting association shall file with the Executive Secretary of the Junior College Commission a copy of the annual report made to the Council on Studies and Accreditation of the Mississippi Association of Colleges.

STANDARD X: PHYSICAL PLANT

The physical facilities, including buildings, equipment, and campus, should be designed and maintained to serve the needs of the institution in relation to its stated purposes. There should be sufficient campus area to provide adequately for buildings and such activities as are related to the educational program of the institution. The physical facilities should be used as efficiently as possible in keeping with the educational program of the institution and the students it serves. The architectural design and appearance of the physical plant should be in harmony as far as practicable and should be aesthetically compatible to the educational mission of the institution. A master plan for campus development should be maintained.

The Junior College Commission Standards
Authorized by Chapter 352
Laws of Mississippi, 1962
As Revised and Approved 1972

STANDARD I:
ORGANIZATION AND ADMINISTRATION

The junior college shall be an educational institution that is dedicated to the service of its district and state that support it. It may include in its program certain years of high school work along with other services as prescribed by Section 37-29-1, Mississippi Code of 1972.

The counties comprising the districts of each junior college shall be in keeping with Sections 37-29-21, 35, 37, and 39, Mississippi Code of 1972. The districts shall have a governing board as provided for in Sections 37-29-65 and 37-29-409, Mississippi Code of 1972, and shall exercise the powers as listed in Sections 37-29-67 and 37-29-411, Mississippi Code of 1972.

Each junior college shall have a president as its executive head who will be selected under the provisions of Sections 37-29-61 and 37-29-405, Mississippi Code of 1972, and shall have the powers and responsibilities so delegated in Sections 37-29-63 and 37-29-407, Mississippi Code of 1972. The president of the junior college shall be a person of proven ability as a teacher and administrator and have a Master's Degree. If the president does not have special preparation for junior college administration, it is expected that he will take training specifically designed to prepare him for junior college administration.

In addition to the president, there shall be such administrative officers as administrative assistants, deans, registrars, business managers, etc., as shall be necessary for sound and efficient administration of the affairs of the college.

The general administration of the college shall be such as will reflect itself in the successful operation of the institution with particular regard to:

(1) Financial stability
(2) Ability to secure and hold high caliber teachers
(3) Proper maintenance, care, and cleanliness of buildings and grounds
(4) Success of transfer and terminal students
(5) Percentage of entering students who graduate
(6) Educational needs and otherwise providing leadership in the community
(7) Evidence of freedom from political interference

The organization of branch campuses or attendance centers shall be approved by the Junior College Commission. Criteria to be considered shall include:

(1) Student population to be served
(2) Financial stability of the junior college district
(3) Existing educational institutions and their offerings
(4) Educational programs to be offered by newly established branch campus

Institutions applying for permission to establish a branch campus shall justify in detail its request based on the above criteria.

STANDARD II:
EDUCATIONAL PROGRAM

The purpose of the junior college should be clearly defined and this definition should be incorporated into a statement which is a pronouncement of the institution's role in the educational world. The purpose of the junior college shall be in keeping with Section 37-29-01, Mississippi Code of 1972.

The educational program of the junior college shall be such as to carry out the purposes and objectives of the institution. Each junior college shall publish its purposes and objectives in its official publications.

The junior college should be an institution in which effective teaching is accomplished. The primary interest of the faculty should be sound, thorough, and inspirational teaching rather than research. Data on institutional efficiency should include information concerning classroom methods, tests, examinations, grading systems, analysis of instructional results, including the compilation and distribution of grades by departments and instructors, the development and use of syllabi and their continuous revision and adjustment.

It is expected that each junior college will offer curricula and courses as follows:

A. College and University Parallel Curricula

Each junior college shall offer curricula that is correlated with the curricula offered by the lower division of senior college or university. The institution must demonstrate that an effective relationship exists between corresponding programs in the colleges and universities served by the junior college.

B. Technical and Semi-Professional Curricula

Subject to the fulfillment of its stated purpose and objectives and to the law, junior colleges shall offer curricula of a technical, and semi-professional type on the collegiate level.

C. Vocational Curriculum

Courses of a vocational or trade-training type should be offered, subject to the needs of the community. High school graduation should not be a prerequisite for this type curriculum. For technical and vocational programs, the institution must demonstrate that an effective relation exists between curriculum content and current practices in business and industry.

D. Short-Term Curricula (See Standard VIII: Special Activities)

Where the needs of the community justify such training, there should be special courses of training for specific jobs. These courses may vary in length according to the requirements of the courses. They should be offered to groups who desire and will profit by them without regard to previous educational training or future academic plans. These courses should carry continuing education unit (c.e.u.) credit and should not be set up on a collegiate academic basis.

E. Adult Education

The needs of the adult population of the community should be met with adequate educational courses insofar as possible. Such courses may be offered in conformity as to "A," "B," "C" or "D" of this standard. In any case it should be clearly stated that the course is a "college credit" or a "c.e.u." course. If it is a college credit course, it shall meet all standards for other college courses.

F. Diploma and Certificate

When a student has successfully completed any curriculum that requires a minimum of sixty semester or ninety quarter hours of academic work, the colleges that meet the standards of this Commission may issue a diploma and confer a title, or degree may be an Associate of Arts, an Associate of Science, or any other appropriate title, as Associate Degree. Junior colleges may issue a diploma or certificate testimonial

of completion of other curricula in the college. It is recommended that the Associate of Applied Science degree be issued to those completing technical programs.

All vocational and technical courses shall receive prior approval of the Junior College Commission before becoming a part of the vocational-technical curricula of the junior colleges.

It is expected that each junior college will offer curricula and courses as follows:

A. *College and University Parallel Curricula*

Each junior college shall offer curricula that is correlated with the curricula offered by the lower division of senior college or university. The institution must demonstrate that an effective relationship exists between corresponding programs in the colleges and universities served by the junior college.

B. *Technical and Semi-Professional Curricula*

Subject to the fulfillment of its stated purpose and objectives and to the law, junior colleges shall offer curricula of a technical, and semi-professional type on the collegiate level.

C. *Vocational Curriculum*

Courses of a vocational or trade-training type should be offered, subject to the needs of the community. High school graduation should not be a prerequisite for this type curriculum. For technical and vocational programs, the institution must demonstrate that an effective relation exists between curriculum content and current practices in business and industry.

D. *Short-Term Curricula (See Standard VIII: Special Activities)*

Where the needs of the community justify such training, there should be special courses of training for specific jobs. These courses may vary in length according to the requirements of the courses. They should be offered to groups who desire and will profit by them without regard to previous educational training or future academic plans. These courses should carry continuing education unit (c.e.u.) credit and should not be set up on a collegiate academic basis.

E. *Adult Education*

The needs of the adult population of the community should be met with adequate educational courses insofar as possible. Such courses may be offered in conformity as to "A," "B," "C" or "D" of this standard. In any case it should be clearly stated that the course is a "college credit" or a "c.e.u." course. If it is a college credit course, it shall meet all standards for other college courses.

F. *Diploma and Certificate*

When a student has successfully completed any curriculum that requires a minimum of sixty semester or ninety quarter hours of academic work, the colleges that meet the standards of this Commission may issue a diploma and confer a title, or degree may be an Associate of Arts, an Associate of Science, or any other appropriate title, as Associate Degree. Junior colleges may issue a diploma or certificate testimonial of completion of other curricula in the college. It is recommended that the Associate of Applied Science degree be issued to those completing technical programs.

All vocational and technical courses shall receive prior approval of the Junior College Commission before becoming a part of the vocational-technical curricula of the junior colleges.

Admission Requirements. There should be a definite and clearly defined policy regarding admissions, and such policy should be published and available to the public. The junior college shall require for admission to its academic and technical curricula a minimum of fifteen acceptable units from an approved high school, successful completion of the G.E.D. Test, or demonstrated competency in accordance with published admission policies.

Students may be admitted to the vocational programs on an individual basis.

Enrollment. The minimum enrollment should be sufficient for the institution to carry out its stated purpose and objectives. Sufficient enrollment should be maintained in each technical and vocational education program to justify its existence.

A permanent file of course descriptions, both credit and non-credit should be maintained. At least one-fourth of total credit required for an associate degree shall be general education, including courses designed to develop skill in oral and written communication. Learning experiences for which credit is awarded must be under the full control and supervision of the educational institution. Behavioral or performance objectives should be established reflecting levels of competencies to be attained by course and program.

STANDARD III: FINANCIAL RESOURCES

The financial resources of each junior college shall be such as to maintain a quality educational program, faculty, library, and physical plant that would enable the institution to achieve its desired purpose and objectives. Educational and general expenditures shall be used to evaluate the adequacy of financial operations. These will include:

(1) General Administration
(2) Student Services
(3) General Institutional Expenses
(4) Staff Benefits
(5) Instructional Expenses
(6) Learning Resources
(7) Physical Plant Operation

An average levy of two mills for maintenance purposes on the assessed property of the district is a desirable minimum. However, the statutory limit of three mills should be levied if necessary to maintain a diversified program of high quality.

Operating income from all sources should not be less than $800 per student. This amount is exclusive of auxiliary agencies and capital outlay.

In no event shall the student per capita income from local maintenance tax sources be less than $200 unless the statutory limit of three mills over the entire district fails to yield this amount.

In calculating the above expenditures, the number of students used shall be the same as the number of academic and vocational students used in disbursing per capita funds from state appropriation.

Each junior college will follow the *Accounting Manual for Public Mississippi Junior Colleges, 1969,* prescribed by the Mississippi State Department of Audit.

The percentage of income spent for direct instructional purposes is an important factor in measuring the college program. To arrive at the direct instructional cost, the following items shall be considered:

(1) The total salaries of the teaching staff, prorating the administrative officers who teach. The salaries of laboratory assistants and any others who are directly concerned with the instructional activities should be included.
(1a) Staff benefits of (1) above
(2) The expenditure for classroom, laboratory, and any other supplies used directly for instructional activities, but not fixed equipment.
(3) It is recommended that not less than 65 percent of the operational budget be expended for instructional purposes. In no case shall the expenditure for this purpose be less than 60 percent.

The annual expenditure for library should be at least three to five percent of the operating budget. The expenditures for books, bindings, periodicals, and supplies shall not be less than $8 per student.

The records of the business office shall be properly protected from fire and theft. Personnel charged with the responsibility of handling monies shall be properly bonded in keeping with state law.

A record of the income and expenditures should be based upon an officially adopted budget on file with the Executive Secretary of the Junior College Commission.

The Junior College Commission looks with favor upon and recommends adjustments of out-of-state tuition in keeping with the increasing costs of the instructional program. It further recommends periodic re-evaluation of student fees.

Once funds have been allocated for an institution, budget making, establishing priorities, and control of expenditures should be entirely within the institution under the jurisdiction of the governing board subject to the general policy provisions of the statutes and to the commitments represented through budgetary requests by the institution.

STANDARD IV: LIBRARY

The library should have reading room space for at least twenty-five percent of the largest number of students on campus at any one period of the day. It should be well-lighted, fire-resistant, if possible, and have adequate facilities for housing, maintaining, and using the library as an important instructional department of the college. The library should remain open for service a minimum of sixty hours per week.

The junior college should have a collection of at least twenty thousand volumes exclusive of public documents, carefully selected, adequately cataloged, and readily available for use. Adequate magazines and periodicals should be available each session, especially selected to serve in the instructional program. Standard works of general and special reference sufficient to meet the needs of the student body should be available. Circulation statistics and other data concerning the use made of the library should be kept in addition to the accession of books.

Operationally separate units (branch comprehensive campuses) must have not fewer than five thousand usable books the first year of operation and ten thousand volumes in not less than three years.

Centers must furnish adequate library service in keeping with the courses at the center.

The library shall be administered by a professional library staff who shall have faculty rank. There shall be a sufficient number of assistants to assure adequate library services. The size of the institution, the adequacy of its physical equipment, and the number of hours which the library is kept open daily will determine the number of staff members needed and will constitute a rough measure of the effectiveness of the library service. The collection of books and periodicals should be compared frequently with nationally recognized library holdings.

Library Statistics of Colleges and Universities, Institutional Data (U. S. Department of Health, Education, and Welfare, Library Services Branch) should be used as reference with regard to this standard.

STANDARD V: FACULTY

The selection, development and retention of a competent faculty for all levels of instruction is of major importance to each institution. The relationship between faculty objectives and institutional purposes determines in large measure the effectiveness of the total educational program.

The academic preparation and experience of the faculty are significant factors in determining the quality of the institution's educational program. The continuous professional growth of all faculty members should be encouraged, and the institutions should assist members of their faculty to further their professional development.

If faculty members are to be effective teachers, they must have reasonable security. Therefore, each institution should provide adequate salaries, a program of well-planned benefits, provision for tenure, and assurance of freedom to teach.

Selection of Faculty. Specific assignments of responsibility should exist for identifying, appraising, negotiating with and selecting new faculty members. Criteria for prospective faculty members should be established which are in keeping with the purposes and philosophy of the institution.

After the necessary interviews, consultations with departmental chairman, and/or dean, the president will recommend to the board of trustees his choice of faculty members. Policies and procedures for the termination of appointments should be stated in writing and should be in accord with commonly accepted practices.

Faculty Organization. The faculty of all institutions

should be so organized that their business may be properly conducted. Faculty membership should be clearly defined.

In small institutions, the faculty should be organized as a whole. In larger institutions, it may be organized by divisions. The jurisdiction of the faculty in academic affairs should be clearly defined and should provide adequate scope for the exercise of faculty responsibility. The faculty should be concerned primarily with fundamental academic policies. Provision for open and regular channels of communication between faculties and administration should be clearly defined and followed.

The rules and regulations relating to faculty organization, bylaws, and responsibilities should be recorded and accessible to all concerned.

Academic Preparation of Faculty. All junior college teaching members should hold advanced degrees. (Master's degree specialization in the field in which they teach.) Any exception must be justified by special competence in the field of knowledge.

The Commission strongly encourages every institution to comply with the standards of the regional accreditation agency in meeting faculty requirements which include the following: at least forty percent of the teaching faculty in humanities, social studies, and natural sciences must possess educational preparation equivalent to one year of advanced study beyond the master's degree, and some faculty members should possess educational preparation equivalent to two years of advanced study beyond the master's degree or have an earned doctoral degree.

Faculty members should belong to learned societies and professional organizations, appropriate to their special work and should be familiar with their publications. Rapid technological advances and constantly changing employment practices demand that faculty keep abreast of current developments in specialized, technical and vocational fields.

Individual records shall be kept for each faculty member showing the period of service, advancements, evidence of professional growth, advanced study, research and publications, noteworthy achievements, and instructional experience.

The standard teaching load in semester hours or their equivalent is recognized to be sixteen. The maximum teaching load is eighteen semester hours, and only a small percentage of the faculty may be permitted to carry this maximum. The teaching schedule should be arranged so that the total teaching load per week of each instructor will ordinarily not exceed 450 student credit hours. Two hours of laboratory work shall be counted as one credit. It is recommended that all instructors have an on-campus schedule of at least 35 hours/week.

STANDARD VI: STUDENT PERSONNEL

The junior college should encourage democratic student life and activities. A well balanced program of student activities should be developed. This program should be student managed with faculty and administrative direction.

The college should provide a program of orientation and guidance with proper emphasis on acquainting students with scholastic work and the activities and life of the college. To this end, student personnel service should include a program of educational, vocational, personal, and social guidance and counseling. Career information, communication with potential employers, counseling, testing services, placement, and follow-up activities are desirable components of an effective process of career planning.

Institutions providing housing and food facilities should maintain supervision over these. They should also make provision for frequent and regular inspection of these in order to maintain high standards of conduct and sanitation.

The programs of intramural and intercollegiate athletics shall be supervised and controlled by persons having faculty status.

The jurisdiction of judicial bodies, disciplinary responsibilities of institutional officials, and all disciplinary procedures should be clearly defined in written form, widely publicized and freely available.

The academic, personnel, health, activity, and other records of students shall be systematically kept and protected from fire, loss, and damage.

The registrar shall keep files of admission, attendance, and scholarship records, transcripts received, and other essential data. Each institution should have adequate and accurate student records for both credit and non-credit courses.

STANDARD VII: GENERAL REQUIREMENTS

A very important factor is quality of work required

of students. The following are recognized as minimum requirements:

A. *Qualitative Requirements*
1. The quality of work will be of such caliber and quality as is commonly expected to be done on a college level.
2. The quality of work may and should be greatly enhanced by reasonably small classes and personalized instruction.
3. An indication of the quality of work will be measured by the ability of graduates to succeed (a) in advanced college courses, and (b) in jobs for which they have been trained.

B. *Quantitative Requirements*
1. A class period should be not less than fifty minutes exclusive of time between classes, for lecture, and not less than one hundred minutes, exclusive of time between classes, for laboratory periods.
2. A semester hour is defined as a minimum student-teacher contact of 750 minutes for lecture, and 1500 minutes for laboratory; a quarter hour is 500 minutes for lecture, and 1000 minutes for laboratory. (This does not include time for passing between classes, registration, or final examinations.)
3. The normal student load is considered to be 15 academic hours per semester. The minimum load for a full-time student is 12 academic hours per semester.
4. Summer school and evening class work will be of the same type and caliber as regular session work and credits based on the same number of minutes of class time.

C. *Vocational Requirements*
1. Vocational or trades training courses should be such as will actually prepare a student to secure and hold a job in his field of preparation.
2. The load for full-time vocational student shall be a minimum of 25 clock hours per week.
3. No course should be offered in this field without sufficient shop space and equipment to provide superior training.
4. Evening classes in this program should meet the same standards as the regular day program.

D. *Technical Requirements*
1. Technical courses shall be the equivalent of four semesters in length and shall merit an associate level degree.
2. Student load in the technical area should be in keeping with the requirements of the academic area.
3. Careful consideration should be given to the proper balance of academic subjects and manipulative skills in each technical curriculum.

E. *Continuing Education*
1. Continuing education classes should be organized to meet the needs of the community.
2. The standards of work in continuing education courses should meet the needs of the individual without regard to collegiate academic standards.
3. C.E.U.-defined in Standard VIII-Special Activities

STANDARD VIII: SPECIAL ACTIVITIES
(Branches, Off-Campus Classes,
Continuing Education, Etc.)

Special activities include operationally separate units, off-campus classes and units, conferences, institutes, short courses and workshops.

A. *Operationally Separate Units*
An operationally separate unit is a degree-granting division or unit of an institution, located in a geographical setting separated from the parent institution or central administration and authorized for a stated purpose in relation to the parent institution and the area served. A degree-granting unit shall have such administrative organization, programs, financial resources, library, and physical facilities that it can be evaluated as an autonomous institution in terms of the standards of the Mississippi Junior College Commission. Furthermore, it must follow regular procedures for membership in the Southern Association of Colleges and Schools.

B. *Off-Campus Classes and Units*
Courses taught in an off-campus setting should maintain the academic integrity of the institution. Special attention should be given to insure the appropriateness of the courses to the students. Courses requiring laboratories, extended library study, or other special materials should not be offered unless arrangements are made to provide the necessary resources.

When an off-campus program in a particular locality grows to the extent that the institution is offering a comprehensive academic program to a specific student body, then the institution should consider the establishment of a special off-campus unit such as a center or regional campus.

C. *Conferences, Institutes, Etc.*
Standard definitions of Southern Association of Colleges and Schools for Conference, Institute, Short Course, Workshop Seminar, and Special Training Program may be used for other special activities both on-campus and off-campus.

No branch campus or attendance center will be established without prior approval of the Junior College Commission.

It shall be the responsibility of the institution in its application to submit proper justification, needs, ability to support, and other evidence as may be requested by the Commission.

The amount of credit for each course or program should be determined in advance through the regular channels of administrative procedures. Non-credit programs should be appropriately identified and recorded by means of the continuing education unit (c.e.u.). A c.e.u. is defined as ten (10) contact hours of participation in an organized continuing education (Adult or Extension) experience under responsible sponsorship, capable direction, and qualified instruction. The c.e.u. records will serve as a part of the full-time equivalent student account for the institution.

Bibliography

I. Books, Pamphlets, Periodicals and Catalogs

BOOKS

Broom, Knox. *History of Mississippi Public Junior Colleges, 1928–1953.* (Mississippi Junior College Association). Raymond, Mississippi: Published by Keith Press, 1953.

Jaggars, Richard L. *A Unified Program of Teacher Education and Certification in the Southern States.* Sewanee, Tennessee: University Press, 1941.

Koos, Leonard V. *The Junior College Movement.* Boston: The Atheneum Press, 1925.

PAMPHLETS

Membership Directory, American Association of Junior and Community Colleges, 1972.

PERIODICALS

The Junior College Journal, October, 1930, I, no. 1, pp. 12–14. Published by Stanford University Press.

Mississippi Educational Advance, April 1947, 38, no. 7.

Southern Association Quarterly, 1932.

CATALOGS

Mississippi Junior College Catalogs. (On file in Mississippi State Department of Education, Director of Junior Colleges.)

II. Articles

Bogue, Jesse P. "The Mississippi State System of Junior Colleges." *The Mississippi Educational Advance* (April 1947) 38, no. 7, p. 27.

Broom, Knox M. "Mississippi Public Junior Colleges." *The Mississippi Educational Advance* (April 1947) 38, no. 7, p. 26.

Broom, Knox M. "Co-operating With Veterans." *The Mississippi Educational Advance* (April 1947) 38, no. 7, pp. 30–31.

Humphrey, G. D. "Coordination of All Educational Institutions Much Desired Goal." *Mississippi State Alumnus* (January 1935) 10, no. 1, p. 1.

III. Personal Communications: Interviews, Letters, and Telephone Conversations

INTERVIEWS

The following persons were interviewed when the junior colleges were visited regarding the writing of the story:

Coahoma—Clarksdale, Mississippi
   Miller, James, President
   Barron, Mrs. Zee A., student personnel
   Gorman, Lee Roy, Business Manager
   McLaurin, B. F., past president and now Vice President
   Reid, Charles, Director of Public Relations and Institutional Development

Copiah-Lincoln—Wesson, Mississippi
   Thames, Billy B., President
   Felder, Miss Virginia, former teacher, now retired from University of Southern Mississippi
   Hunter, B. F., Dean
   Smith, Mrs. Grover, secretary to the President
   Strickland, Mrs. Carol, business education instructor, now at Jones County Junior College
   Youngblood, W. D., wholesale grocer

East Central—Decatur, Mississippi
   Wright, Charles V., President
   Bracken, Denver, Dean of Students
   Griffin, B. L., Business Manager, now retired
   Rives, Frank, Registrar
   Roberts, R. C., former teacher
   Thames, Jim, former member board of trustees
   Tucker, Brad, Dean of Academics

Bibliography

East Mississippi—Scooba, Mississippi
Stennis, Earl, President
Currie, Keys, Business Manager
Mitchell, W. D., Superintendent of Kemper County
Salter, Larry, Director of Public Relations
Thomas, Mrs. C. H., former secretary to President J. D. Wallace

Gulf Coast—Perkinston, Mississippi
Hayden, J. J., Jr., President
Davis, Jim, member of 1918 high school class
Davis, Rev. W. N., local minister
Dees, Calvin, member board of supervisors, representative and senator
Evans, Ed., member of administrative staff
McDaniel, Hershel, first college graduate in 1927
Moffett, Guy D., retired physics teacher
Scarbrough, Mrs. Wyvona B., Executive Secretary, Alumni Association
Swetman, C. C., former secretary of board of trustees
Wyatt, Tom, mail carrier during early days of the school

Hinds—Raymond, Mississippi
Mayo, Robert M., President
Cain, G. J., former president (1928–1938)
Herrin, Miss Mildred, Registrar
Sheffield, Grady L., Business Manager
Stewart, Miss Lurline, head of mathematics department

Holmes—Goodman, Mississippi
Branch, Frank B., President
Allen, Stanley F., Business Manager
Branch, Mrs. Frank, Registrar
McLelland, Henry, Assistant Business Manager
Ousley, Marion A., postmaster

Itawamba—Fulton, Mississippi
Benjamin, W. O., President
Abel, Cecil W., Academic Dean
Caples, Billy Q., Assistant Dean of Students
Crubaugh, John H., Registrar
Loden, Glenn C., Superintendent of Education
Smith, G. W., head of business education department
Spencer, Charles, Director of Admissions, Tupelo Campus
Wilson, Argie, biology instructor

Jones—Ellisville, Mississippi
Tisdale, T. Terrell, President
Blackwell, Houston, registrar, retired
Hill, Troy P., faculty member and first guidance director, retired
Moody, W. J., member of first faculty and registrar, retired
Ogletree, B. F., vice president and dean, retired

Meridian—Meridian, Mississippi
Scaggs, William, President and former dean
Ivy, H. M., former president (1937–1952)
Reed, W. A., Jr., Director, T. H. Harris Campus, Meridian Junior College

Smedley, Roger T., Jr., Registrar at Harris Campus
Todd, L. O., former president (1952–1968)

Mississippi Delta—Moorhead, Mississippi
Hall, J. T., President
Hall, Mrs. J. T., secretary to the president
Teague, Earl, resident of Moorhead, Mississippi
Tharp, Melvin E., vocational agriculture instructor
Thigpen, H. A., former dean, head of science department
Wooten, Miss Laney, Director of Publications and Journalism

Northeast—Booneville, Mississippi
White, Harold T., President
Chase, Mrs. Sarah C., retired instructor
Daws, H. H., instructor
Rhodes, James L., administrative assistant
Stone, Jerry Clay, community services and continuing education
Woods, Miss Earline, Fiscal Officer

Northwest—Senatobia, Mississippi
McLendon, R. D., President
Bobo, Mrs. Estelle, dean of women, retired
Burford, Senator Cecil, Alumni President, member of first college student body
Burke, Mrs. Sue, teacher and registrar, retired
Gully, Miss Josephine, teacher and librarian, retired
Moore, Herbert K., student of agricultural high school
Quinn, Mrs. J. R., retired high school teacher
Taylor, Mrs. William S., member of first board of trustees
Welch, A. G., Business Manager

Pearl River—Poplarville, Mississippi
White, Marvin R., President
Jenkins, Ike, former student
Seal, Enoch, Academic Dean
Thomas, "Brownie," teacher, retired
Thomas, Emmett, teacher, retired

Southwest—Summit, Mississippi
Holmes, Horace C., President
Breeland, Charles R., Registrar
Craig, Mrs. Mildred, instructor
Huddleston, H. T., retired president
Hurst, John I., retired dean
Miller, Norman, Dean of Instruction

Utica—Utica, Mississippi
Stokes, J. Louis, President
Barnes, George E., Dean of Instruction
Hackett, Obra V., Dean of Students
Kinnard, Arthur H., Jr., former acting president, dean
Lewis, Rev. B. E., teacher
Lewis, Mrs. B. E., teacher

OTHER PERSONAL INTERVIEWS

Ellzey, Russell M., retired president and organizer of Copiah-Lincoln Junior College, Wesson, Mississippi

Supervisors, Lincoln County

Tucker, Annie M., Associate Director of Nursing Education, Board of Institutions of Higher Learning

TAPED INTERVIEWS WITH INDIVIDUALS

Brooks, C. O., Carthage, Mississippi, former teacher in Leake County

Caughman, Royce, Mendenhall, Mississippi, editor of *Simpson County News*

Cobb, Smith, Jackson, Mississippi, Agricultural and Industrial Board

Davis, Jim, Perkinston, Mississippi, early student at Perkinston Junior College

Evans, Ed, Perkinston, Mississippi, early student and football player at Perkinston Junior College

Griffith, R. W., Jackson, Mississippi, former assistant state superintendent of education

Hale, Coach "Goat" Jackson, Mississippi, first junior college coach at Pearl River Junior College

Herrin, Miss Mildred, Raymond, Mississippi, registrar, Hinds Junior College

Hill, B. L., Brandon, Mississippi, former state supervisor of junior colleges

Hill, Troy P., Ellisville, Mississippi, first full-time guidance director in a Mississippi public junior college at Jones County Junior College

Hurst, John I., Summit, Mississippi, former teacher and coach, Southwest Junior College

Ivy, H. M., Meridian, Mississippi, former President of Meridian Junior College

Jenkins, Ike, Perkinston, Mississippi, early student at Perkinston Junior College

Johnston, Garvin, Jackson, Mississippi, State Superintendent of Education

Lewis, Mrs. B. E., Utica, Mississippi, teacher during early years at Utica Junior College

Lewis, Rev. B. E., Utica, Mississippi, minister and teacher during early years at Utica Junior College

Lipscomb, J. N., Macon, Mississippi, former dean of School of Agriculture, A. & M. College

Majure, Troy, Jackson, Mississippi, State Director, Vocational Education Division, Mississippi State Department of Education

Mathis, Mrs. Emily Duncan, teacher at Christian Brothers College, Memphis, Tennessee, dissertation for terminal degree on "Curricular Changes in Mississippi Public Junior Colleges"

McDaniels, Hershel, Perkinston, Mississippi, member of first freshman class in 1927 at Perkinston Junior College

McElreath, Pete, Oxford, Mississippi, former mayor of Oxford, Mississippi, teacher and coach, graduate of Jones County Junior College

Moffett, Guy D., Perkinston, Mississippi, retired physics teacher at Perkinston Junior College (now Gulf Coast Junior College) and a student during the early years.

Munn, Mrs. Effie, Mendenhall, Mississippi, former student at Simpson County Junior College

Pitts, Frank, Dallas, Texas, industrial executive, alumnus of Copiah-Lincoln Junior College

Reeves, Frank, Decatur, Mississippi, registrar at East Central Junior College

Smith, A. P., Monticello, Mississippi, former superintendent of Simpson County Agricultural High School

Stewart, Miss Lurline, Raymond, Mississippi, head of mathematics department, Hinds Junior College

Strickland, H. L., Ellisville, Mississippi, teacher and coach for more than thirty years, Jones County Junior College

Taylor, Mrs. William S., Como, Mississippi, member of board of trustees, Northwest Junior College, Quitman County, for more than forty-four years

Thomas, "Brownie," Poplarville, Mississippi, former student and football player at Pearl River Junior College

Thomas, Oren, Poplarville, Mississippi, former student and football player at Pearl River Junior College

Todd, L. O., Meridian, Mississippi, former president of Meridian Junior College

Tubb, Jack M., Jackson, Mississippi, former state superintendent of education for twenty-two years

Tucker, Brad, Decatur, Mississippi, dean at East Central Junior College

Young, Mrs. Katie, Ellisville, Mississippi, former mathematics teacher and first college basketball coach for girls, Jones County Junior College

Zeller, Mrs. R. B., Hazlehurst, Mississippi, wife of Dr. R. B. Zeller and daughter-in-law of Sen. Julius C. Zeller of Yazoo County

LETTERS

Baker, Mrs. J. B., Baldwin, Mississippi, daughter of R. E. L. Sutherland, founder of Hinds Junior College

Barnes, George E., Dean of Instruction, Utica Junior College, Utica, Mississippi

Benjamin, W. O., President, Itawamba Junior College, Fulton, Mississippi

Blair, Miss Laura, Jackson, Mississippi, Nursing Education, State Department of Education

Boyd, John D., former president and founder, Utica Junior College, Utica, Mississippi

Branch, Frank B., President, Holmes Junior College, Goodman, Mississippi

Bryant, W. Alton, Vice President, University of Mississippi, Oxford, Mississippi

Cain, George J., President (retired), and early builder of Hinds Junior College, Raymond, Mississippi

Callaway, Mrs. Doris, Jackson, Mississippi, relative of S. L. Stringer, early president and builder at Pearl River Junior College

Carlson, William D., Laramie, Wyoming, President, University of Wyoming

Clower, Jerry, humorist, Yazoo City, Mississippi

Coffenbarger, Jack O., public relations, Hinds Junior College, Raymond, Mississippi

Colvert, C. C., Professor Emeritus and Consultant, University of Texas, Austin, Texas

Crubaugh, John S., President (retired), of Itawamba Junior College, Fulton, Mississippi

Darby, Cooper J., early president and builder at Perkinston Junior College, Perkinston, Mississippi

Daws, H. H., faculty member, Northeast Mississippi Junior College, Booneville, Mississippi

Denson, William C., Denson Education Tours, Houston, Texas, former junior college teacher and coach

Eakes, Mrs. John W., Jackson, Mississippi, sister of R. C. Pugh, founder of East Central Junior College, Decatur, Mississippi

Ellzey, Russell M., President (retired) and organizer of a Mississippi public junior college

Felder, Miss Virginia, Hattiesburg, Mississippi, former junior college teacher

Flautt, Mrs. Mary W., Tutwiler, Mississippi, daughter of J. C. Windham, former supervisor of agricultural high schools and junior colleges

Frazier, Mrs. Frances B., Librarian, Copiah-Lincoln Junior College, Wesson, Mississippi

Graves, Ben W., President, University of Alabama, Huntsville, Alabama

Griffith, R. W., Jackson, Mississippi, former assistant state superintendent of education

Hall, J. T., President, Mississippi Delta Junior College, Morehead, Mississippi

Hayden, J. J., Jr., President, Gulf Coast Junior College, Perkinston, Mississippi

Hill, B. L., retired supervisor, Mississippi State System of Public Junior Colleges

Hogarth, Charles V., President, Mississippi Women's University, Columbus, Mississippi

Holmes, Horace C., President, Southwest Mississippi Junior College, Summit, Mississippi

Huddleston, H. T., President (retired), Southwest Mississippi Junior College, Summit, Mississippi

Huff, Grace C., Pascagoula, Mississippi, relative of James Huff, founder of Pearl River Junior College, Poplarville, Mississippi

Huff, Lester, Forest, Mississippi, relative of James Huff, founder of Pearl River Junior College, Poplarville, Mississippi

Huff, T. Marx, Forest, Mississippi, attorney and relative of James Huff, founder of Pearl River Junior College, Poplarville, Mississippi

Ivy, Horace M., President (retired), and founder of Meridian Junior College, Meridian, Mississippi

Jones, James Vanoy, Ellisville, Mississippi, alumnus, Jones County Junior College

Kinnard, Arthur H., Jr., former acting president of Utica Junior College, Utica, Mississippi

Koon, Henry B., President, Northwest Mississippi Junior College, Senatobia, Mississippi

Loftin, T. D., relative of R. E. L. Sutherland, founder of Hinds Junior College, Raymond, Mississippi

Lovitt, Norman, Hattiesburg, Mississippi, alumnus, Jones County Junior College

Lumpkin, Marshall, Woodville, Mississippi, Superintendent, Woodville High School

McCain, W. D., Hattiesburg, Mississippi, President Emeritus, University of Southern Mississippi

McDaniel, Major C., President (retired) and early builder of a Mississippi public junior college

McLaurin, B. F., President (retired) and founder of Coahoma Junior College, Clarksdale, Mississippi

McLendon, George M., President (retired), Southwest Mississippi Junior College, Summit, Mississippi

McLendon, R. D., President (retired), Northwest Junior College, Senatobia, Mississippi

Martin, T. K., Vice President, Mississippi State University, Starkville, Mississippi

Mayo, Robert M., President, Hinds Junior College, Raymond, Mississippi

Miller, James E., President, Coahoma Junior College, Clarksdale, Mississippi

Monroe, John, Lucedale, Mississippi, former president Inter-Alumni Association of Public Junior Colleges

Noonkester, Ralph, President, William Carey College, Hattiesburg, Mississippi

Ogletree, B. F., Nashville, Tennessee, former dean and vice president of Jones County Junior College, Ellisville, Mississippi

Pitts, Frank L., alumnus of Copiah-Lincoln Junior College, industrialist, Dallas, Texas, Pitts Oil Company

Reed, W. A., former director, Harris Campus, Meridian Junior College, Meridian, Mississippi

Reeves, William, President, East Mississippi Junior College, Scooba, Mississippi

Rhodes, James L., administrative assistant, Northeast Mississippi Junior College, Booneville, Mississippi

Roberts, R. C., former teacher, East Central Junior College, and in the State Department of Education, Jackson, Mississippi

Ross, Thomas G., physician, Jackson, Mississippi

Salter, Larry K., Director of Public Relations, East Mississippi Junior College, Scooba, Mississippi

Scaggs, William, President, Meridian Junior College, Meridian, Mississippi

Shannon, William G., Associate Executive Director, American Association of Community and Junior Colleges, Washington, D.C.

Sheffield, Mrs. Phillip, Fulton, Mississippi, wife of former president of Itawamba Junior College, Fulton, Mississippi

Shoemake, Ellis, Brooklyn, Mississippi, Superintendent, Forrest County Agricultural High School

Sorrell, W. B., pathologist, Montgomery, Alabama

Spencer, Charles, Veteran's Affairs Office, Itawamba Junior College, Tupelo Campus, Tupelo, Mississippi

Stennis, Earl, former president, East Mississippi Junior College, Scooba, Mississippi

Stokes, J. Louis, President, Utica Junior College, Utica, Mississippi

Stone, Jerry Clay, Continuing Education, Northeast Mississippi Junior College, Booneville, Mississippi

Stringer, Oliver W., Chillicothe, Ohio, brother of S. L.

Stringer, early president and builder at Pearl River Junior College, Poplarville, Mississippi

Stringer, Mrs. R. O., Hattiesburg, Mississippi, wife of former president of Northeast Mississippi Junior College, Booneville, Mississippi

Stutts, Ralph McGee, graduate of Northeast Mississippi Agricultural High School, Booneville, Mississippi

Thames, Billy B., President, Copiah-Lincoln Junior College, Wesson, Mississippi

Thomas, Mrs. C. H., former secretary to President J. D. Wallace, founder of East Mississippi Junior College, Scooba, Mississippi

Tisdale, T. Terrell, President, Jones County Junior College, Ellisville, Mississippi

Todd, Mrs. L. O., Meridian, Mississippi, wife of former president of Meridian Junior College, Meridian, Mississippi

Tubb, Jack M., retired state superintendent of education and former junior college president

Tucker, Miss Annie, Jackson, Mississippi, Nursing Education, Institutions of Higher Learning

Vandiver, Joseph S., University of Florida, Gainesville, Florida, son of J. S. Vandiver, founder of Mississippi Delta Junior College, Moorhead, Mississippi

Walker, Kirby P., supervisor in the beginning years of Mississippi state system of public junior colleges, and retired superintendent of Jackson City Schools

Walley, W. W., physician, Waynesboro, Mississippi

Weems, W. Lamar, physician, University of Mississippi Medical Center, Jackson, Mississippi

White, Harold T., President, Northwest Mississippi Junior College, Booneville, Mississippi

White, Marvin R., President, Pearl River Junior College, Poplarville, Mississippi

Wooten, Miss Laney, instructor in journalism, Mississippi Delta Junior College, Moorhead, Mississippi

Williams, John Bell, former governor of Mississippi, Jackson, Mississippi

Williams, J. D., Oxford, Mississippi, Chancellor Emeritus, University of Mississippi

Wright, Charles V., President, East Central Junior College, Decatur, Mississippi

Young, Fred W., Southwide Educational Enterprises, Inc., former high school superintendent, Yazoo City, Mississippi

Youngblood, D. V., Southern Wholesale Company, Brookhaven, Mississippi

TELEPHONE CONVERSATIONS AND PERSONAL VISITS

Abney, James W., Montrose, Mississippi

Abney, Mrs. Mary Etta, Montrose, Mississippi

Anderson, Mrs. R. L., wife of former supervisor of junior colleges

Austin, Miss Luna, Ellisville, Mississippi, former member of faculty, Mississippi State College for women

Baker, Mrs. J. B., daughter of R. E. L. Sutherland

Benjamin, W. O., President, Itawamba Junior College, Fulton, Mississippi

Blackledge, Mrs. Theresa, Librarian, Jones County Junior College

Blair, Mrs. Laura, State Vocational Division, State Department of Education

Bond, Miss Ethel, secretary, Gulf Coast Junior College District

Branch, Frank B., President, Holmes Junior College, Goodman, Mississippi

Bryant, W. Alton, former vice president, University of Mississippi

Callaway, Mrs. Doris, Jackson, Mississippi

Cooley, Mrs. Pat, assistant librarian, Jones County Junior college

Darby, C. J., early president, Perkinston Junior College (now Gulf Coast)

Denson, W. C., former coach and teacher, Jones County Junior College

Eakes, Mrs. J. W., sister-in-law of R. C. Pugh

Eaton, Miss Dorrence, former English teacher, Jones County Junior College

Egger, Mrs. James, Columbus, Mississippi

Ellzey, Russell, organizer of Copiah-Lincoln Junior College

Ewing, Mrs. James M., wife of James M. Ewing, President Emeritus, Delta State College, and co-author of the *Mississippi Public Junior College Story*

Ewing, James, North Georgia College, Dahlonega, Georgia, son of James M. Ewing, President Emeritus, Delta State College, and co-author of the *Mississippi Public Junior College Story*

Flautt, Mrs. Mary, Tutwiler, Mississippi

Fortenberry, F. M., Supervisor of Junior Colleges

Foxworth, Mrs. Ann, Poplarville, Mississippi

Griffith, R. W., former assistant state superintendent of education

Hall, J. T., President, Mississippi Delta Junior College, Moorhead, Mississippi

Hayden, J. J., Jr., President, Gulf Coast Junior College, Perkinston, Mississippi

Hill, B. L., former state supervisor of junior colleges

Hill, Troy P., first fulltime guidance director in a Mississippi public junior college

Hogue, Larry, State Department of Education

Holmes, Horace C., President, Southwest Mississippi Junior College, Summit, Mississippi

Huddleston, H. T., former president, Southwest Junior College

Huff, Lester, Forest, Mississippi

Hurt, Harvey, *Wayne County News*, Waynesboro, Mississippi

Ivy, H. M., organizer of Meridian Municipal Junior College

Jobe, E. R., Executive Director, Board of Institutions of Higher Learning, retired

Kinnard, A. H., former acting president, Utica Junior College, Utica, Mississippi

Koon, Henry B., President, Northwest Mississippi Junior College, Senatobia, Mississippi

Long, Miss Bettye, State Representative, Lauderdale County

Lovitt, Norman, Hattiesburg, Mississippi, former teacher at Jones County Junior College

Lumpkin, Mrs. John, Poplarville, Mississippi

McCain, W. D., President Emeritus, University of Southern Mississippi

McDaniels, M. C., retired president, Holmes Junior College

McKee, Barney, Director, University Press of Mississippi

McLemore, R. A., first dean of Jones County Junior College, President Emeritus, Mississippi College

McLendon, G. M., retired president, Hinds Junior College

McLendon, R. D., former president, Northwest Mississippi Junior College

Majure, Troy, Director Vocational Education, State Department of Education

Mayo, Robert M., President, Hinds Junior College, Raymond, Mississippi

Miller, James E., President, Coahoma Junior College, Clarksdale, Mississippi

Monroe, John, former state alumni president

Montage, Mildred L., Nursing Education

Moody, W. J. member of original faculty of Jones County Junior College

Moore, Miss Elise, Jackson, Mississippi

Morehead, Miss Mildred, daughter of founder of Holmes Junior College

Morehead, Virgil P., son of founder of Holmes Junior College

Mosal, Mrs. Margaret, Executive Director, National Office of Phi Theta Kappa

Naylor, T. H., State Department of Education

Neal, Miss Aline, Brandon, Mississippi

Ogletree, B. F., former junior college vice-president and dean

Ogletree, Powell, alumni office, University of Southern Mississippi

Reed, W. A., Jr., Director of Harris Campus, Meridian Junior College

Reeves, William, President, East Mississippi Junior College, Scooba, Mississippi

Reppert, Mrs. Nancy, city hall, Liberty, Missouri

Scaggs, William, President, Meridian Junior College, Meridian, Mississippi

Schneider, Earl E., Laurel, Mississippi

Scott, Jake, Board of Institutions of Higher Learning

Scott, Miss Julia, Columbus, Mississippi

Shannon, William G., Associate Executive Director, American Association of Community and Junior Colleges, Washington, D.C.

Shoemake, Ellis, Superintendent, Forrest County Agricultural High School

Stark, Cruce, former president, East Mississippi Junior College

Stokes, J. Louis, President, Utica Junior College

Stringer, Judge W. M., Moberly, Missouri

Thames, Billy B., President, Copiah-Lincoln Junior College, Wesson, Mississippi

Tisdale, T. Terrell, President, Jones County Junior College, Ellisville, Mississippi

Todd, L. O., former president, East Central Junior College

Todd, Mrs. L. O., Meridian, Mississippi, wife of former president of East Central Junior College

Travis, Jack, attorney and son of former state supervisor of public education

Tubb, Jack M., former president, East Mississippi Junior College and former state superintendent of education

Tucker, Miss Annie, Board of Institutions of Higher Learning, Nursing Education

Vandiver, J. S., Jr., son of former state superintendent of education

Walker, Kirby P., former state supervisor of public junior colleges and former superintendent of Jackson City Schools

Webb, R. P., forty years a teacher at Jones County Junior College

West, Herman, Mississippi Women's University

White, Harold T., President, Northeast Mississippi Junior College, Booneville, Mississippi

White, Marvin R., President, Pearl River Junior College, Poplarville, Mississippi

Wilkins, Mrs. Gertrude, Jackson, Mississippi

Williams, J. D., Chancellor Emeritus, University of Mississippi

Wilson, Mrs. Dorothy, Ellisville, Mississippi

Wooten, Lancy, publications, Mississippi Delta Junior College, Moorhead, Mississippi

Wright, Charles V., President, East Central Junior College, Decatur, Mississippi

IV. Legal Documents, Bulletins, and Reports

LEGAL DOCUMENTS

The Constitution of the State of Mississippi, 1890. Mississippi Code 1930, Volume 1.

Eighty-eighth Congress of the United States, December 18, 1963. Public Law 88–210, H. R. 4955, Voc. Ed. Act 1963.

Ninetieth Congress of the United States, October 16, 1968, Public Law 90–576, H. R. 18366, Voc. Ed. Amendment 1968.

General Laws of Mississippi, 1908. Senate Bill 302, pp. 19–79. (Chapter 102)

General Laws of Mississippi, 1910. Senate Bill 4 (Chapter 122), p. 10.

General Laws of Mississippi, 1922. Senate Bill 251, pp. 270–272.

General Laws of Mississippi, 1924. House Bill 98, Chapter 283, Sub-Chapter 40, Section 308–311, p. 509.

General Laws of Mississippi, 1928. Senate Bill 131, pp. 81, 398–401 (Chapter 303), House Bill 263, pp. 173, 231.

General Laws of Mississippi, Extraordinary Session, 1928.

House Bill 122, Chapter 42, p. 65.

General Laws of Mississippi, Extraordinary Session, 1929. House Bill 42, Chapter 14, p. 11, House Bill 43, Chapter 13, pp. 10–11.

General Laws of Mississippi, 1930. House Bill 754, Chapter 65, p. 113, House Bill 636, Chapter 78, p. 135, House Bill 682, Chapter 205, p. 408.

General Laws of Mississippi, 1932, House Bill 467, Chapter 30, House Bill 870, Chapter 166, p. 465.

General Laws of Mississippi, Extraordinary Session, 1935. House Bill 67, Chapter 48, p. 182.

General Laws of Mississippi, 1942. House Bill 622, Chapter 18, p. 28

General Laws of Mississippi, 1946. House Bill 1094, Chapter 6, p. 14.

General Laws of Mississippi, 1948. House Bill 1090, Chapter 31, p. 33.

General Laws of Mississippi, 1950. House Bill 541, Chapter 369, pp. 421–428.

General Laws of Mississippi, Extraordinary Session 1953. Senate Bill 1205, Chapter 14, p. 45.

General Laws of Mississippi, 1954. House Bill 295, Chapter 268, p. 305.

General Laws of Mississippi, 1960. Senate Concurrent Resolution.

General Laws of Mississippi, 1962. House Bill 597, Chapter 381, pp. 657–665. Senate Concurrent Resolution 163, Chapter 705, p. 1204.

General Laws of Mississippi, 1964. House Bill 215, Chapter 398, Section 17, pp. 577–583. House Bill 308, Chapter 276, pp. 370–374. Senate Bill 1587, Chapter 401, pp. 584–587. Senate Bill 1846, Chapter 402, p. 587.

General Laws of Mississippi, 1966. Senate Bill 1967, Chapter 416, pp. 766–767.

General Laws of Mississippi, 1968. Senate Bill 1832, Chapter 388, pp. 603–607. House Bill 509, Chapter 390, p. 607.

General Laws of Mississippi, 1973.

BULLETINS

Mississippi State Department of Education Bulletin No. 58, By Knox M. Broom, Issued by W. F. Bond, State Superintendent of Education.

REPORTS

United States Census Report of 1920.

United States Census Report of 1930.

"Biennial Report to the Legislature, 1923–1924 and 1924–1925." By W. F. Bond.

"Information Forms," 1972. Supplied by Mississippi Junior College Presidents.

V. Records

American Association of Junior Colleges Records.

Mississippi State Board of Education, Disbursement Records, July 26, 1928.

Mississippi State Department of Education, Division of Junior Colleges

Enrollment Records, 1943–1944.

Mississippi Public Junior Colleges Data, 1972.

Fiscal Records, 1922–1972.

Enrollment Records, 1972.

County Tax Information in Junior College Districts, 1972.

Mississippi Board of Institutions of Higher Learning, Report on Negro Education, 1961.

Holmes Junior College, Disbursement Forms.

Jones County Junior College, Registrar's Records.

VI. Recorded Minutes

Mississippi Junior College Association

Minutes, July 1, 1932

Minutes, July 15, 1936

Minutes, June 15, 1942

Minutes, February 8, 1955

Minutes, December 13, 1962

Minutes, August 24, 1964

Mississippi Junior College Commission

Minutes, May 10, 1928

Minutes, October 20, 1928

Minutes, February 7, 1929

Minutes, April 11, 1929

Mississippi Junior College Inter-Alumni Association

Minutes, July 14, 1965

Mississippi State Department of Education, Division of Junior Colleges

Minutes, May 10, 1962

Minutes, June 29, 1964

Southern Association of Junior Colleges

Minutes of Meeting in Atlanta, Georgia, April 9, 1940

Minutes of Meeting in Atlanta, Georgia, December 2, 1968

Minutes of Meeting in New Orleans, Louisiana, December 11, 1972

VII. Newspapers

Jackson *Daily Clarion-Ledger* (1888—   ).

Waynesboro *Wayne County News* (1921—   ).

VIII. Dissertations

Jobe, E. R. "Curriculum Development in Mississippi Public White High Schools." PhD. dissertation, George Peabody College for Teachers, 1950.

Lucas, Aubrey Keith. "The Mississippi Legislature and Mississippi Higher Education, 1890–1960." PhD. dissertation, Florida State University, 1966.

Mathis, Emily Duncan. "An Historical Study of Curricular Changes in Selected Public Junior Colleges in Mississippi." EdD dissertation, University of Tennessee, 1971.

Stark, Cruce. "A Study of the Mississippi System of Public Junior Colleges." EdD dissertation, University of Houston, 1952.

Todd, Lindsay Ogletree. "Meeting the Needs of Junior College Students." PhD dissertation, George Peabody College for Teachers, 1943.

Tucker, Bradford Jolly. "An Analysis of Expenditures in Mississippi Public Junior Colleges, 1969–1970." EdD dissertation, Mississippi State College, 1972.

Wright, Charles V. "A Follow-Up Study of Mississippi Junior College Graduates." EdD dissertation, University of Southern Mississippi, 1963.

Index

341